International Copyright Law: U.S. and E.U. Perspectives

International Copyright Law: U.S. and E.U. Perspectives

TEXT AND CASES

Jane C. Ginsburg

Morton L. Janklow Professor of Literary and Artistic Property Law, Columbia University School of Law, New York, USA

Edouard Treppoz

Professor, University Jean Moulin Lyon 3, France

Edward Elgar
PUBLISHING

Cheltenham, UK • Northampton, MA, USA

Published by
Edward Elgar Publishing Limited
The Lypiatts
15 Lansdown Road
Cheltenham
Glos GL50 2JA
UK

Edward Elgar Publishing, Inc.
William Pratt House
9 Dewey Court
Northampton
Massachusetts 01060
USA

A catalogue record for this book
is available from the British Library

Library of Congress Control Number: 2014957087

MIX
Paper from
responsible sources
FSC® C013056

ISBN 978 1 78347 797 5 (cased)
ISBN 978 1 78347 799 9 (paperback)
ISBN 978 1 78347 798 2 (eBook)

Typeset by Servis Filmsetting Ltd, Stockport, Cheshire
Printed and bound in Great Britain by T.J. International Ltd, Padstow

Contents in brief

Full contents

PART II   APPLICATION OF INTERNATIONAL COPYRIGHT AND NEIGHBORING RIGHTS CONVENTIONS

Acknowledgements

Many thanks to our colleagues Susy Frankel, Daniel Gervais, Anthea Roberts and Bart Szewczyk for extensive comments on the manuscript. We are especially grateful to our exceptionally helpful and diligent research assistants, Taylor Jones, Columbia Law School JD class of 2014 and David Rüther, Columbia Law School LLM class of 2014. We also would like to thank the students enrolled in the Columbia Law School international copyright law course in Spring 2014 (Abigail Everdell, Cheryl Foong, Carla Framil-Ferran, Aleksander Latinov, Jieun Paik, Olena Ripnick-O'Farrell, David Rüther, and Kristy Tholanikunnel), who gave us extraordinary feedback on the beta version of this Casebook.

We are grateful to the World Intellectual Property Organization (WIPO) for authorization to reproduce the text of the copyright treaties that it administers, as well as to excerpt from the 1978 and 2003 WIPO Guides. Thanks as well to the American Law Institute for permission to excerpt from *Intellectual Property—Principles Governing Jurisdiction, Choice of Law and Judgments in Transnational Disputes* (ALI 2008).

Table of cases

France

Spain

United Kingdom

United States of America

WTO Dispute Resolution

Table of legislation

Model Laws, Restatements and Principles

1

History, structure and context of international copyright law

1.1 Introduction

Overview. This casebook introduces students to the complex and evolving landscape of international copyright law. It focuses primarily on the conventions administered by the World Intellectual Property Organization (WIPO). The first and most fundamental of these is the Berne Convention, originally promulgated in 1886, and now claiming 168 member states. The contours of the Berne Convention have deeply shaped the international copyright landscape. The structure of the Berne Convention (requirement of internationality, rule of national treatment and substantive minima) forms a template adopted by the subsequent copyright and neighboring rights conventions, all of which build on or refer to the Berne Convention (see Figure 1.2 below). Chief among the neighboring rights treaties is the 1961 Rome Convention, in interlocking structure with the later WIPO Performances and Phonograms Treaty (1996) and the Beijing Treaty on Audiovisual Performances (2012). The WIPO Copyright Treaty (1996) and the Marrakesh Treaty (2013) extend the copyright rights and exceptions set out in the Berne Convention. Like the planets that orbit the sun, and the moons that revolve around a planet, the various copyright and neighboring rights treaties are interrelated and interdependent, and primordially influenced by the Berne Convention. The casebook mirrors this importance, studying each text but delving most deeply into the Berne Convention.

Nevertheless, this presentation would be incomplete were it limited to the WIPO treaties. International copyright law has expanded beyond the WIPO galaxy. With the 1994 TRIPS Accord, intellectual property and copyright law entered the ambit of the World Trade Organization. While the TRIPS' integration of the Berne Convention purports to alter neither that treaty's norms nor its structure, the superimposition of the international trade framework makes two significant differences, both respecting the practical implementation of the treaty's obligations. First, TRIPS encompasses a section on enforcement of intellectual property rights, an issue largely untouched by the WIPO conventions. Second, where a contracting party might once have ignored with impunity its international obligations under WIPO treaties, a member state's non-compliance with TRIPS may now incur sanctions at the WTO level. Equally, and in the long run perhaps even more importantly, the WTO Panels that resolve disputes arising out of allegations of member state failure to respect TRIPS-incorporated Berne Convention norms form a unique (in the true sense of the word) source of supranational interpretation of international copyright law. Otherwise, construction of international obligations falls to the member states, whose conclusions bind only those persons and institutions within their separate jurisdictions. The emerging WTO caselaw (albeit not binding on member state courts) enhances international harmonization by adding a supranational gloss to the copyright and neighboring norms set out in supranational texts. As a result, in order to convey a fuller understanding of international copyright and neighboring rights, this casebook integrates relevant excerpts from WTO Panel decisions.

Synthetic rather than analytic. Since all these texts create a generally coherent set of rules, the casebook is organized by issue rather than treaty by treaty. Presenting the material by substantive question not only illuminates each treaty in light of the others, but also allows students to perceive the influence of the Berne Convention on subsequent treaties, including neighboring rights conventions. Presentation by issue also highlights the differences between the various texts, and poses the often vexing question of the interaction between these texts.

Law of treaties as a prerequisite. We believe that the study of international copyright cannot commence immediately with the texts of the various conventions. Such an approach would in effect begin *in medias res* because the treaties must first be understood within the broader framework of public international law. Hence, following an historical overview and a brief introduction to WIPO and WTO and to the legal institutions of the U.S. and the E.U., the casebook devotes its first Part to general principles of treaty interpretation, and to the interaction between national and international norms. We also explore the process of international texts implemented by national courts, those of the U.S. and the E.U. (collectively or via its member states), in the absence of a supranational harmonizing authority. Those sources show that if compliance is sought locally, international copyright treaties will never prevail over the highest local norm.

This preference for local law reminds us of the potential significance of the WTO and perhaps other alternative fora as a source of superior and enforceable international norms.

International norms in local perspective. Because copyright and neighboring rights treaty interpretation nonetheless remains essentially a matter of local interpretation, we focus systematically on the two local perspectives of our respective expertise: U.S. and E.U. The approach remains synthetic, and albeit comparative, fundamentally international. In other words, this is not a casebook on comparative copyright law, recounting the copyright systems of the U.S. and E.U. as integral entities and exposing their similarities and differences. Rather, we examine how the U.S. and the E.U. law have understood and implemented their international obligations in the fields of copyright and neighboring rights. In that endeavor, the casebook inevitably provides students with a comparative law grounding and enables them to draw a comparative assessment. But the book's objective is different, and we believe unique in the persistence of its focus on the international norms. The U.S. and E.U. sources serve to illuminate the meaning of the international standards. Thus, for example, the decisions of the Court of Justice for the European Union (CJEU) excerpted in this book are featured not for their construction of E.U. copyright and neighboring rights law as such, but for their (usually) express interpretation of E.U. norms as implementations of international norms. Where no WTO Panel decision offers a supranational solution, these local decisions interpreting international treaties could moreover exercise an influence far beyond E.U. boundaries. The local sources also invite discussion of the extent to which the member states are (or may not be) complying with their international obligations. The latter inquiry is particularly pertinent for the U.S. caselaw, which rarely refers directly to international norms, but which nonetheless requires analysis in the light of, and for consistency with, those norms.

Hence, for each issue arising under the treaties—from whether the treaty is applicable in the first place, to the implementation of particular substantive minimum standards of rights and limitations—the casebook first presents the international norm and (where available) its supranational interpretation, followed by its legislative and judicial implementation in the U.S. and the E.U. A concluding chapter in Part II of the casebook identifies the lacunae in the treaties. Questions throughout each section not only test the student's close reading of the primary sources, but, more importantly, explore the implications of the sources for the construction of the international norms. Frequently, these questions pinpoint ambiguities in the texts and, because there is no "right answer" in local or international positive law, challenge students (and instructors) to think through what the solution *should* be, in light of the competing objectives.

Conflict of laws in the absence of a harmonized norm. Having begun with the law of treaties, this casebook ends with conflict of laws. In theory, international norms supplant any role for conflict of laws. But that outcome would be true only if harmonization were so comprehensive as to preclude any local variations. In fact, the scope of harmonization of copyright and neighboring rights rules is far from complete, as the chapter on the treaties' lacunae illustrates. Moreover, the substantive standards the treaties impose are minima: member states may exceed the required level of protection. Finally, as our table of membership (Table 1.1 below) shows, international obligations vary with treaty membership. Countries that are members of all copyright and neighboring rights treaties have more obligations than countries that have joined only the Berne Convention or the WTO. The ensuing differences in the degree of protection, as well as the national discrepancies that may attend the absence of any governing supranational standard, shift the inquiry to local law. As a result, the determination of the applicable local law is essential. In the absence of supranational substantive or private international law rules, the concluding Part of the casebook necessarily adopts a comparative presentation. This Part explores not only the positive private international law of copyright in the U.S. and the E.U. but also two comprehensive proposals for private international law rules for copyright and neighboring rights. These proposals, elaborated against the backdrop of electronic commerce, and therefore sensitive to the augmented likelihood that international copyright controversies may simultaneously implicate the laws of many countries, should prove a useful adjunct to the study of international copyright and neighboring rights law.

1.2 Historical note on international protection until the Berne Convention

1.2.1 Before there were international copyright conventions

Almost as soon as there were printing presses there came printing privileges. Ruling authorities perceived two problems that privileges might resolve. Publishing would further the Renaissance revival of the classical authors as well as enhance the communication of contemporary Latin and vernacular literature and scholarship. But, along with making desirable works more available, uncontrolled publishing could also disseminate undesirable ideas. Second, uncontrolled publishing could discourage the financial undertaking required to print books: second-comers could undercut the profits of the first to invest in the labor and materials of printing. Limiting the number of printers would serve both the Crown by controlling ideas, and the publisher by controlling competition.

In the sixteenth century, as indeed today, the monopoly in works of authorship that privileges conferred was territorial. Each sovereign's grant of a privilege produced effects only within the borders that the sovereign controlled. Sovereigns did, however, grant foreign authors' or printers' petitions for local privileges. But one sovereign, the Pope, conferred privileges that purported to be multiterritorial. Because the Pope exercised both secular power over the Papal States (in central Italy) and spiritual authority over all Catholic lands, papal printing privileges present the first attempt to confer supranational protection over reproduction and distribution of copies of works. Papal privileges generally conferred the sole right to print, sell and import the work. Over the course of the sixteenth century, the scope of papal privileges expanded to cover translations, first from Latin to Italian (and vice versa) and subsequently to all vernaculars, and to cover reproductions in whole or in part, with deletions, augmentations, or other alterations. Petitioners from within and without the Papal States requested coverage for all of Italy and all lands directly or indirectly subject to the Holy Roman Church.

Along with fines and confiscation of the books, the principal sanction for violation of an extraterritorial papal privilege was the supraterritorial remedy of automatic excommunication, a penalty that petitioners must have considered sufficiently efficacious to warrant the effort and expense of obtaining papal privileges. Nonetheless, claimants who anticipated that their works would be bestsellers frequently sought, in addition to papal privileges, multiple privileges from a variety of secular sovereigns, most often Venice, France, the Holy Roman Empire, and several Italian principalities, notably Florence. One particularly vigilant grantee, Francesco Priscianese, author of an Italian-language Latin grammar book, received privileges from several sovereigns. He published the full text of the papal and Imperial privileges in the initial pages of the book, followed by this statement: "We have also for the said time the fullest privileges from the Most Christian King of France, from the Most Illustrious Venetian Senate, and from Florence, and from Ferrara, and from other Rulers of Italy, which we do not copy out in order not to create a Volume of Privileges."[1]

---

1 "Habbiamo anchora per il detto tempo privilegi amplissimi dal Christianissimo Re di Francia, dallo Illustrissimo Senato Venetiano, & di Fiorenza, & di Ferrara, & d'altri Signori d'Italia, i quali non copiamo qui per no[n] fare un Volume di Privilegi." FRANCESCO PRISCIANESE, DE PRIMI PRINCIPII DELLA LINGUA ROMANA (Venice 1540), BAV at Stamp.Cappon.IV.373(int.2); Stamp.Cappon.IV.374(int.1). Priscianese's

Priscianese and other sixteenth century authors or printers who sought multiple national privileges herald the attempts of their nineteenth century counterparts to obtain copyright protection in several national markets. But if an international trade in works of authorship persisted, and doubtless grew, throughout the intervening centuries, the barriers to protection seem to have increased, as national copyright laws, particularly in Britain and the U.S. explicitly barred protection for foreign-published works. The 1710 British Statute of Anne, the first copyright act, provided in section 7:

> Provided that nothing in this Act contained do Extend or shall be construed to extend to prohibit the importation vending or selling of any Books in Greek Latin or any other foreign language printed beyond the seas any thing in this Act contained to the contrary notwithstanding.

And the U.S., taking a leaf from the book of its former colonial master, provided in section 5 of the first Federal copyright act, 1790:

> [N]othing in this act shall be construed to extend to prohibit the importation or vending, reprinting or publishing within the United States, of any map, chart, book or books, written, printed, or published by any person, not a citizen of the United States, in foreign parts or places without the jurisdiction of the United States.

Similarly, section 1 of the first U.S. copyright act explicitly limited federal copyright to citizens and residents of the U.S. Perhaps these measures sought to favor local authors over foreigners, but in practice they had the opposite effect, because foreign works, being freely copiable, undersold local, royalty-generating works. As a result, nineteenth century American authors such as Mark Twain, Washington Irving and James Fenimore Cooper joined with British authors in urging the U.S. Congress to pass international copyright legislation.[2] But it would take 100 years from the first copyright act for Congress to pass an international copyright bill.

---

privilege can be found at ARM XLI v 14 F339 (Aug. 27, 1539). *See also* ANGELA NUOVO, COMMERCIO LIBRARIO NELL'ITALIA DEL RINASCIMENTO 225–7 (1998) (describing the practice of the publishing house of the Tramezzino brothers to obtain privileges from multiple sovereigns inside and outside Italy). Regarding the Papal printing privilege regime, see Jane C. Ginsburg, *Proto-property in Literary and Artistic Works: Sixteenth-Century Papal Printing Privileges*, 36 COLUM. J. L. & THE ARTS 345 (2013).

2 See generally, Catherine Seville, THE INTERNATIONALISATION OF COPYRIGHT LAW: BOOKS, BUCCANEERS AND THE BLACK FLAG IN THE NINETEENTH CENTURY (2006).

In the interim, and in the absence of treaties binding other countries as well, authors attempted to manipulate the nationality of their works in order to obtain protection outside their home countries. These endeavors did not always succeed, as a pair of nineteenth century British cases involving operas written by foreign authors illustrates. *D'Almaine* v. *Boosey* [1835] 160 E. R. 117, involved melodies from the 1834 opera *Lestocq*, by Daniel François Auber, recomposed as dance music by Philippe Musard and published by Boosey without the authorization of the British publisher (D'Almaine) to whom Auber had assigned his rights for Britain. But, did Auber, as a French composer resident in France, have any rights to assign for Britain? The British publisher argued that the work was first published in Britain by a British resident before any French publication (though the parties disputed this), and therefore should not fall under the statute's exclusion of foreign-published works. The court agreed that first publication in Britain was all the statute required:

> The point whether the copyright of a foreigner is protected at all in this country does not arise in the present case, because the plaintiff [publisher] D'Almaine is not a foreigner. He could acquire the copyright of a publication as well from a foreigner as an Englishman. If he is the owner of the work it makes no difference whether he composed it himself or bought it from a foreigner.

160 Eng. Rep. p. 122. The court thus effectively ratified the practice of bringing non-resident foreign-authored works within the ambit of the British law by arranging for first publication in Britain. Manipulation of the place of first publication so as to achieve some degree of international copyright protection proved an essential tactic not only for composers, but also for book authors, particularly American authors, who otherwise were prey to piracy in a major English-language market—as were British authors in the U.S. (as Dickens and other British authors frequently lamented). But the House of Lords nullified the effect of the practice in *Jeffreys* v. *Boosey* (1854) 4 HLC 815, involving yet another operatic aria, "Come per me sereno," from Bellini's *La Sonambula*. Bellini had assigned his rights to the Italian music publisher Ricordi, who in turn assigned U.K. publication rights to Boosey. The opera was first published in London in 1831, before its publication anywhere else. In 1844 Boosey renewed the copyright in the registry of the Stationers Company. Under *d'Almaine*, Boosey would have taken all the steps needed to secure and maintain the rights for the U.K. (and its colonies). The defendant publisher Jeffreys, however, successfully contended that Ricordi had no rights to assign for the U.K. because the only way to acquire a copyright for Great Britain was to be a British subject or resident. Under *d'Almaine* it sufficed that

the publisher be British, but *Jeffreys* v. *Boosey* looked to the nationality (or residence) of the creator of the work. If Bellini, as a non-resident composer, could not hold a British copyright, then neither could his Italian or British assignees. On the other hand, if British residence as well as first publication were required to obtain protection in Britain and its colonies, authors and publishers could manipulate both the place of first publication and of the author's residence, thanks to a generous notion of residence established by the House of Lords in 1868 in *Routledge* v. *Low*, LR 3 HL 100. In that case an American author's novel was first published in England and registered with the Stationers Company, and the author, the New Yorker, Maria Cummings, was spending a few days in Canada at the time of first publication. Canada being a British colony, and a few days' visit sufficing to establish Canadian residence, which in turn was deemed British residence, and Ms Cummings having transferred her rights to the British publisher, all the pieces were in place to qualify for a British copyright.

In France, after the abolition of *Ancien Régime* privileges, foreign authors were entitled to French copyright protection under the general rules of the Civil Code (1804). Civil Code article 11 announced a condition of reciprocity: "an alien enjoys in France the same civil rights as those that are or will be granted to French persons by the treaties of the nation to which that alien belongs". Thus, a foreign author would be the beneficiary of French copyright law only if the foreigner's home country accorded copyright protection to French authors. Things slowly changed. First, in 1810, a Décret recognized for the first time the assimilation of a foreigner to a national author, provided that the work of authorship was first published in France. Initially limited to the right of reproduction, this assimilation was extended to the right of public performance by a 1844 law. This liberal conception of French copyright law reached its apex in 1852, when a Décret abandoned the condition of reciprocity, and instead applied French copyright law to all works of authorship independently of any condition of first publication in France. Such a universalist move might be related to the conceptualization of French copyright law as a natural right offered to all. Nevertheless, this liberal legislative view was limited by the courts, which adopted a restrictive interpretation of the Décret. In a case involving the opera composer Giuseppe Verdi (Cass. Req., 14 Dec. 1857: DP 1858, 1, p. 161), the highest French civil law court (Cour de cassation) had to determine the application of the Décret to three operas created by Verdi (il Trovatore, la Traviata and Rigoletto) publicly performed in France without the authorization of the author. The court acknowledged that the scope of the Décret encompassed the reproduction of foreign works, but excluded the public performance of those works not first published in France. The restrictive result of the highest French civil law court contrasted with its purely theoretical characterization of copyright as a natural right in an earlier portion of the same decision. The court justified its restrictive ruling in order to conform French law to bilateral treaties recently signed at that time, especially the treaty signed the 22 August 1852 with Belgium. These treaties covered both reproduction and public performance rights, nevertheless, only the reproduction right was judicially enforced. Were the Décret to be interpreted to accord foreign authors the protection of both rights, the Décret would (arguably) have provided stronger protection than the treaties. Thus, in order to assure independent significance to the treaties, the Décret would be interpreted more narrowly. A second case revealed a similarly restrictive approach to the Décret of 1852, again invoking international treaties to reinforce such an interpretation. The case concerned two operas of Gaetano Donizetti (*Lucia di Lammermoor* and *Lucrezia Borgia*) and the distribution in France of their scores without the consent of the author (Cass. Req., 25 July 1887: DP 1888, 1, p. 5). The *Verdi* decision's restriction of the scope of the Décret did not apply, because the plaintiff did not allege an unauthorized public performance. The court nevertheless refused to grant the foreign author the benefit of the French copyright law, ruling that the Décret's protection extended only to a work still protected in its country of origin. Applying the Italian law, France's highest civil law court determined that the works at issue no longer enjoyed exclusive rights because Donizetti had died, and Italy's 40-year post-mortem copyright term in fact constituted a "domaine public payant" which entitled anyone to reproduce the works, subject to payment to the rightholder (see Italian copyright law of 1865, art. 9 para. 2) during the 40 years following the author's death. Thus, the French law was not applicable due to the lack of equivalent protection in Italy. This restrictive interpretation of the Décret was here also reinforced by the French and Italian bilateral Treaty of 1862, which also applied a criterion of reciprocity.

The cases just reviewed all concerned published works, with publication supplying a potential means of associating a foreign-authored work with another territory for which the author (or his publisher) sought protection. In some countries, particularly the U.S., while foreign-published works were not protected until the U.S. passed its first international copyright statute in 1891, *un*published works were protected against unauthorized publication or public performance, regardless of the author's nationality. Protection derived from the common law of the separate states, for reasons strongly evocative of natural rights, as an 1872 New York decision illustrates:

> The right to literary property is as sacred as that to any other species of property. The courts of the State are open to an alien friend pursuing his property, and seeking to recover it from a wrong-doer, and there is

nothing in any positive law, or in the policy of the government, which would close the door against the same alien friend seeking protection for the fruits of his mental labor, by restraining its publication against his wishes. The protection afforded by the common law to literary labor is very slight at best, but such as it is, it is accorded to alien friend and citizen alike, and both are regarded with equal favor.

Palmer v. De Witt, 47 NY 532, 539 (1872). The principle of protection of all foreign authors' unpublished works has now been incorporated into the U.S. federal copyright statute, 17 U.S.C. sec 104(b). As the New York court emphasized, this *jus naturale* (natural rights) approach to unpublished works derives from principles of the common law, rather than from statutory copyright, which, we have seen, excluded foreign *published* works. (U.S. statutory copyright law today, however, now covers unpublished works, but continues to provide protection to all unpublished works, even if their authors are citizens or residents of States with whom the U.S. lacks treaty relations.) Other countries have also long considered some aspects of copyright to come within the ambit of natural rights, and have accordingly extended protection to foreign authors regardless of the absence of copyright relations between the country where protection is sought and the country of origin of the work. Thus, the French Copyright Act distinguishes between economic and moral rights. While, in the absence of an international convention, protection of economic rights requires a showing of reciprocity (that the country of origin protects works of French authors), France will in any event protect the foreign author's moral rights.

Article L111-4 (French IP Code)

Subject to the international conventions to which France is party, in the event that it is ascertained, after consultation with the Minister for Foreign Affairs, that a State does not afford to works disclosed for the first time in France, in any form whatsoever, protection that is adequate and effective, works disclosed for the first time on the territory of such State shall not enjoy the copyright protection afforded by French legislation.

However, neither the integrity nor the authorship of such works may be impaired.

1.2.2 Bilateral treaties

Sam Ricketson and Jane C. Ginsburg, International Copyright and Neighbouring Rights: The Berne Convention and Beyond (Oxford 2006) (paras. 1.29–1.41; footnotes omitted)*

The early agreements
The first bilateral agreements were entered into by Prussia with the other German states between the years 1827 and 1829. . . . The main actors in [other] early agreements were the U.K. and France. Apart from its convention with Prussia in 1846, the U.K. entered into important conventions with Hanover, France, Belgium, Spain, and Sardinia-Italy. However, with respect to the country whose publishers were inflicting the greatest degree of injury on British authors—the United States—the U.K. failed to reach any agreement, although there were movements in favour of such a treaty on both sides of the Atlantic. France also sought to limit the effect of international piracy on its authors by entering conventions with the countries that were centres of such activities. . . . After 1852, copyright conventions were also made by a number of other important European states, notably Belgium, Spain, and Italy. Many of these were made as part of, or in conjunction with, broader trading and commerce treaties entered into by these countries . . . The net result was that, by 1886 [when the Berne Convention was promulgated], there was an intricate network of conventions, declarations, and arrangements in place between the majority of European states, as well as between several Latin American states.

By and large, the format of each convention was fairly standard: their basis was national treatment, supplemented by specific obligations undertaken by each state to accord a particular level of treatment to authors of works from the other state in relation to such matters as translation and performance rights, restrictions on rights, subject matter protected, and so on. By 1886, a number of the older conventions had been revised or replaced, either to take account of such geopolitical changes as the unifications of Germany and Italy, or to refine or enlarge the level of protection granted (or both). A summary of the bilateral conventions in force in 1886 is given at the end of this [excerpt, see Figure 1.1]. . . . The major country that stood out completely from any international copyright arrangements was the U.S.A. Throughout the nineteenth century, this country was a major centre for book piracy, particularly for books from the U.K. Although it had a vigorous literary and artistic life, the vested interests of publishers and printers, on the one hand, and the strong public pressure for plentiful supplies of cheap books, on the other, militated against any moves for the United States to enter into international copyright relations.

---

* By permission of Oxford University Press.

Contents of bilateral agreements
There were great variations in the contents of these pre-1886 conventions; nevertheless, particular provisions tended to recur.

Persons protected: Various approaches were evident here. Some conventions, for example, limited protection to authors who were nationals of the contracting states; others gave protection, on the basis of territoriality, to authors of works published in the respective territory of each contracting state, regardless of nationality. Several conventions, while adopting the criterion of nationality, also protected the publishers of works published in the territory of either contracting state where the authors of these works were nationals of other states. Finally, there were a number of conventions which adopted neither the criterion of nationality nor territoriality, but simply required each state to accord protection to authors to the extent to which they were protected in the other state. . . .

Works protected: There were a number of differences in the terminology used here. Many of the early conventions required protection to be given to authors of 'works of the intellect and of art', to which dramatic and musical works were often added. Later conventions spoke more commonly of "literary and artistic works", to which the adjective "scientific" was sometimes added. This was usually followed by an extensive definition, such as that in the Franco-German and Franco-Italian Conventions of 1883 and 1884:

> The expression 'literary or artistic works' includes books, pamphlets or other writings; dramatic works, musical compositions, dramatico-musical works; drawings, paintings, sculptures, engravings; lithographs, illustrations, maps; plans, sketches and plastic works relating to geography, topography, architecture or natural science, and, in general, to any other production in the literary, scientific or artistic domain.

These enumerations often differed from convention to convention; some also omitted or expressly excluded particular categories of works, while others protected unpublished as well as published works. In addition, they merely set the limits or boundaries of the protection potentially available under the convention. This did not necessarily mean that such works were to be accorded protection in each country, as the principle of national treatment meant only that each country was required to give the same level of protection as that accorded nationals under its own law. . . .

The principle of national treatment: This was the general rule adopted in the conventions, and meant that authors from country A were entitled to receive, in country B, the same rights and remedies accorded to its own authors by country B. This requirement was differently expressed, but to the same effect, in the various conventions, but was usually subject to the limitation, either expressly or impliedly made, that protection claimed under a convention should not exceed the level of protection accorded to the author in his own country. The basic rights in respect of which national treatment was accorded were those of reproduction and public performance (in the case of dramatic and musical works). Translation rights, however, were generally subject to special limitations, and were dealt with in separate provisions. There were, almost invariably, a number of restrictions that were placed on the reproduction right, for example, in relation to newspaper articles and use for teaching purpose, and sometimes restrictions were placed on the exercise of public performing rights. Most conventions also contained provisions which expressly prohibited (in addition to their reproduction) the importation, exportation, sale, and circulation in each country of infringing copies of works, wherever those copies originated.

Translation rights: Although these were the most important rights for authors seeking protection for their works in foreign countries, the majority of conventions placed significant restrictions on the way in which such rights were to be exercised. This may have been due to a lingering distrust, on the part of various governments, of the willingness or capacity of authors to supply translations of their works in different languages, or to do so within reasonable periods of time. Allied to this may have been the fear that, unless there was some means by which this gap could be closed by the making of other translations, their respective publics would suffer. Again, there may have been a residual desire to continue the protection of vested interests that had profited, for a long time, from the making of unauthorized translations of foreign works. But whatever the reason, by 1886 there were still only a few conventions that protected translation rights unreservedly, assimilating them wholly to reproduction rights. The other conventions generally contained some kind of limitation on the exercise of translation rights, requiring the translation to be made within a particular time of first publication of the original work, and then only according rights for a relatively short period, such as between five and ten years. A number of conventions, notably those made by the U.K., required registration of the work within a given time after publication in its country of origin, and also that the author reserve his translation rights at the time of original publication. Several older conventions still in force in 1886 had no provisions concerning translation rights, with the result that these rights were not protected at all under those conventions.

Restrictions on reproduction rights: As a consequence of the general adoption in these conventions of the principle of national treatment, authors claiming protection for their reproduction rights in another country by virtue of a convention were accorded the same level of protection as were national authors or works first published in that country. Such national treatment was also subject to the limitations on those rights that were imposed by the law of that country. In addition, there were restrictions to be found in most conventions. The most frequent were those dealing with the copying of works for inclusion in chrestomathies or anthologies, or of parts of works for educational or scientific purposes. Such copying was usually allowed, but subject to various conditions. More liberal were the provisions dealing with the making of reproductions of newspaper and periodical articles. Such borrowings were also usually permitted, but some conventions had restrictions in relation to particular categories of articles, and most forbade reproduction (except in the case of articles of political discussion) where the author had expressly reserved his rights in advance. Both kinds of provision raised difficult issues concerning the appropriate balance to be struck between the rights of authors and those of the public, . . .

Duration of protection: Since the provisions of the various national copyright laws revealed little uniformity on this question, uniformity at an international level was hardly to be expected. The general approach taken was a further gloss on the principle of national treatment: protection was only accorded under the conventions to authors as long as their rights in their country of origin subsisted, and, in any event, the duration of their protection in the other country was not to exceed that accorded to nationals by the law of the country in which protection was claimed. There were exceptions to this general rule: in a number of conventions, the period of protection was determined by the law of the country in which protection was claimed, while some others actually fixed the period of copyright protection for authors claiming under them. As with the provisions of national laws, however, it is difficult to discern any uniform approach in these last-mentioned conventions to the question of duration.

. . .

Formalities: The conventional requirements as to these differed markedly, and were the cause of much cost and confusion to authors seeking protection for their works abroad. Only a few conventions dispensed entirely with the need to comply with formalities such as registration or deposit in order to gain protection under them. For example, several conventions made by Germany required only that the author's name be indicated at the beginning of the work, and the Franco-Spanish Convention of 1880 required no formalities as long as the author could prove his "right of property" under the law of the country of origin. A number of other conventions were satisfied if proof of compliance with the formalities of the country of origin was shown.

BILATERAL CONVENTIONS IN FORCE IN 1886
(The numeral after each country is the total number of conventions to which that country is party.)

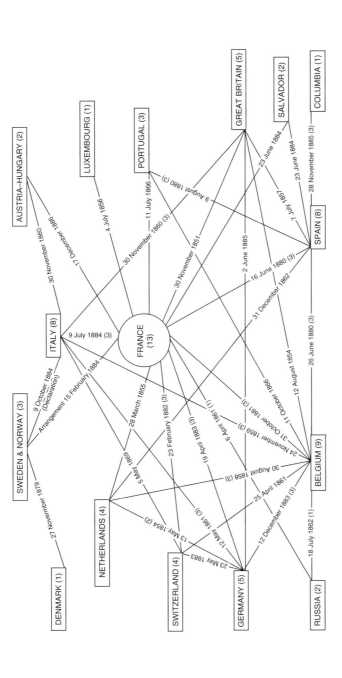

(1) Both denounced by Russia in 1885 to have effect from 14 July 1887 re France & 14 January 1887 re Belgium.
(2) Not ratified by Netherlands.
(3) Treaties with most favoured nation clauses.

Source: From Sam Ricketson and Jane C. Ginsburg, *International Copyright and Neighbouring Rights: The Berne Convention and Beyond* (Oxford 2006), page 40. By permission of Oxford University Press.

Figure 1.1 Summary of the bilateral conventions in force in 1886

On the other hand, there were a significant number of conventions, most notably those made by the UK, under which registration and deposit in the country where protection was claimed was necessary, at least in relation to some categories of works.

. . .

QUESTIONS

1. Consider (in due course) the structure and substantive rules of the bilateral agreements in light of contemporaneous or subsequent multilateral treaties. What underlying policies inform them?
2. What does the position of the U.S. during the nineteenth century tell us today about copyright and developing countries?
3. What is the advantage of the rule of national treatment?

1.2.3 The first multilateral treaty (between the Empire of Austria and the Kingdom of Sardinia, 1840)*

The first multilateral international convention was promulgated in 1840 between the Empire of Austria and the Kingdom of Sardinia. The agreement, negotiated in pre-unification Italy, was from the start intended to be ratified by other Italian states (article 27 "invites" the adherence of other Italian governments). It succeeded in obtaining the adherence of all Italian pre-unification states except for Naples. The Austro-Sardinian Convention consists of fully enunciated substantive rules concerning copyright subject matter, scope, duration, infringement and remedies. Accordingly, it was understood to apply directly in the ratifying states and to augment or even replace prior provisions of domestic law. Several of the Austro-Sardinian Convention's provisions anticipate the Berne Convention, although, as we shall see, the Berne Convention imposes fewer substantive norms, instead leaving most issues to the national laws of member states bound by the Convention's rule of national treatment to grant foreign authors the same protection as national authors. The following excerpts from the Convention are particularly noteworthy:**

---

* Many thanks to Professor Laura Moscati, whose ground-breaking article *Il caso Pomba-Tasso e l'applicazione della prima convenzione internazionale sulla proprietà intellettuale*, in MÉLANGES EN L'HONNEUR D'ANNE LEFEBVRE-TEILLARD, Paris, Ed. Panthéon-Assas, LGDJ, 2009, pp. 747–64, revealed the significance of the Austro-Sardinian Treaty of 1840 to the evolution of international copyright. See also Luigi Carlo Ubertazzi, *I Savoia e gli autori*, QUADERNI DI AIDA No. 3, pp. 37–66 (2000). An English translation of the full text of the treaty (together with the German and Italian language originals) is available at http://copy.law.cam.ac.uk/cam/tools/request/showRepresentation?id=representation_d_1840. (The translation in the casebook text above, however, was prepared by the Editors.)

** For more detailed analysis, emphasizing the novelty of these provisions, see Moscati, *supra*, at 751–7.

1. Works or productions of the intellect or of art, published in the respective states, constitute a property which belongs to those who are their authors, in order to enjoy or to dispose of them throughout all their lives; only they or their rightholders have the right to authorize their publication.

    . . .

3. Translations made in one of the respective states from manuscripts or published works in foreign languages, beyond the territories of the said states are also considered as original productions, within the coverage of article 1. Translations made in one of the respective states from works published in another [member] state are equally covered by article 1.

    An exception is made in the case in which the author, who is a subject of one of the [member states], having published his work, announces therein his intent himself to publish a translation in the said states, and to do so within six months; in that case, the author will conserve all of his rights even for the translation.

4. Notwithstanding the provisions of article 1, articles published in newspapers or other periodicals may be freely reproduced in other newspapers or periodicals, so long as they do not exceed three printed pages in the initial publication, and so long as the source is indicated.

    . . .

7. Infringement is the action by which one reproduces through mechanical means a work in whole or in part without the consent of the author or of his rightholders.

8. There is infringement in the sense of the preceding article not only when there is a perfect resemblance between the original work and the copied work, but also when, under the same title, or under a different title, there is an identity of object between the two works, and there is the same order of ideas and the same distribution of parts. The later work in such a case is considered an infringement even if that work has been considerably shortened or augmented.

9. When reductions for different instruments, extracts and other adaptations of musical compositions can be considered as works of the intellect, they will not be deemed infringements.

10. With respect to infringement, every article of an encyclopedia or periodical which exceeds three printed pages is considered a work in its own right.

11. The author of a literary or scientific work has the right to prevent the usurpation of the title that he has chosen, when such action can mislead the public concerning the apparent identity of the work; but

in this case there is no infringement, and the author is entitled only to a simple indemnity in proportion to the harm suffered. Moreover, general titles, such as Dictionary, Vocabulary, Treatise, Commentary, and the organization of a work in alphabetical order, do not entitle the authors who have used these titles to prohibit other authors from treating the same subjects under the same title and with the same method of organization.

. . .

QUESTIONS

1. Article 1 declares works of authorship published in states party to the treaty to be "a property that belongs to their authors." What of works published in states not members of the treaty? What of unpublished works?
2. Consider article 3's elaborate treatment of translations. What policies do you infer underlie this provision?
3. Consider article 9's treatment of musical arrangements. What policies do you infer underlie this provision?
4. Consider the treatment of works of information in articles 4, 10 and 11. What policies do you infer underlie these provisions? Compare (in due course) Berne Convention article 10*bis*(1).
5. To what extent does the Convention protect the selection and arrangement of the contents of a work? Compare (in due course) Berne Convention article 2(5).
6. Under what circumstances are titles of works protected? Under what justification?

1.2.4   The Berne Framework

Jane C. Ginsburg, International Copyright: From a "Bundle" of National Copyright Laws to a Supranational Code?, 47 J. COPYRIGHT SOC'Y U.S.A. 265 (2000) (excerpts; footnotes omitted)

1. The genesis of the Berne Convention: roots of the debate between supranational norms and national treatment

From the outset of the movement for international copyright protection, two distinct principles have vied for primacy. On the one hand, the non-discrimination principle of national treatment preserves the integrity of domestic legislation, but ensures that foreign authors will be assimilated to local authors. On the other hand, supranational norms guarantee international uniformity and predictability, and thus enhance the international dissemination of works of authorship. A compromise approach institutes national treatment, but avoids local underprotection by imposing minimum substantive standards that member countries must adopt. The development of the Berne Convention illustrates all three of these approaches.

In 1858, the first international Congress of Authors and Artists met in Brussels. The resolutions the Congress passed laid the groundwork for the writing and drafting of the Berne Convention. The Congress' resolutions urged elimination of formalities, national treatment, and uniform national legislation. Thus, from the outset, national norms were to work in tandem with international norms, but the latter were to be implemented through uniform domestic legislation.

At the first intergovernmental meeting in 1883 to form the Berne Union, however, the emphasis initially shifted away from the non-discrimination principle of national treatment, and toward international uniformity. The German delegation, in a diplomatic questionnaire, asked whether it might be better to abandon the national treatment principle in favor of a treaty that would codify the international law of copyright and establish a uniform law among all contracting states. Although most participating countries viewed the proposition as a desirable one, they voted against it because it would have required great modifications of their domestic laws, which many countries could not implement all at once. Thus, rejecting a treaty that would institute a uniform law of international copyright, the 14 participating nations chose to retain the national treatment approach.

The German proposition was nevertheless critical in that it revealed the differing copyright philosophies of the participants: while one group favored a codified and uniform law of international copyright, another preferred as little unification and as much national independence as possible. These differing philosophical positions became manifest in the ensuing discussions of the substantive provisions of the Berne Convention. For example, countries that favored a universal law argued that the Convention should protect all authors who published in a Union state regardless of nationality.

When the 1884 Conference began, an 18-article draft awaited the participants. The draft contained all of the basic principles adopted at the 1883 conference: national treatment, abolition of formalities as a prerequisite for copyright protection, recognition during the entire term of the copyright of the author's exclusive right to authorize translations of her work, and the establishment of an International Bureau of the Union. However, in light of the differing philosophies of international copyright protection, the 1884 draft was changed to protect only authors who were nationals of Union countries and publishers of works published in the Union. In general, in comparison to the universalist draft adopted at the 1883 Conference, the final draft of 1884 moved away from the idea of a comprehensive uniform international law of copyright.

The draft introduced by the 1885 Conference was even less protective and less universal in scope than the 1884 version. The participants declined to adopt universally binding legislation, and instead left to the individual countries decisions as to the nature and the scope of copyright protection for foreign authors. The underlying rationale was that a flexible international treaty would permit more countries to accede to the Union, thus increasing membership. The adoption of a comprehensive and universal copyright law was thus sacrificed for a narrower body of rules accepted by a wide array of countries.

In order to further this goal of greater adherence, a number of provisions were amended and replaced by references to national law for provisions that previously constituted the beginning of a uniform codification of international copyright law. This draft was then ratified and signed at the 1886 Conference. Although the Convention did not achieve every goal outlined at the first Congress of 1858, it represented a major step towards international copyright protection. More significantly, despite the diverging philosophies of the participating countries, the 1886 Berne text laid the groundwork for later evolution toward the more universalist ideal expressed in earlier drafts.

2. The 1886 Berne Convention and its successors: the growth of supranational norms

The basic structure of the Berne Convention has remained relatively unchanged throughout each of its revisions. It contains substantive minimum standards of protection [including the prohibition of formalities], as well as a general directive to accord Unionist authors national treatment. Each subsequent revision of the Berne Convention, from 1896 through 1971, as well as the 1994 Agreement on Trade Related Aspects of Intellectual Property [TRIPS], and the 1996 WIPO Copyright Treaty [WCT], however, have adopted more substantive minimum standards to which Union members must adhere, while retaining a key "pragmatic" feature: the Berne minima apply to a Union member's protection of works from *other* Berne members; no Berne member is obliged to accord its *own* authors treaty-level protection. Thus domestic norms may continue to apply to purely domestic copyright controversies, although, as a practical matter, local legislators may have difficulty justifying better treatment of foreign than domestic authors.

The original Berne Convention provided an explicit, but not exclusive, list of works to be protected. The Berne Convention also defined the conditions for protection, known as points of attachment, and also specified rules governing the term of protection. Subsequent conferences have amended each of these provisions in order to increase the scope of authors' rights. Among the minimum standards that all member countries were required to recognize, the original Berne Convention first established the translation right; more exclusive rights, as well as some optional exceptions, were added over the course of subsequent revisions.

1.3 Basic principles of international copyright law and international neighboring rights

Among international copyright law and neighboring rights conventions, the Berne Convention has served as a template for other conventions, which generally follow its structure. By contrast, a shift in structure and expression occurs when copyright and other intellectual property rights enter the world of international trade and its specific rules (thus moving from the auspices of WIPO to the WTO).

The comparison between the Berne Convention and the Austro-Sardinian Convention shows that the goals achieved by those conventions account for their different structures. A Convention seeking to impose uniform content for national laws possesses a simple structure, equivalent to a domestic text enacting substantive rules. On the other hand, the different goal sought by the Berne Convention underlies its more elaborate structure. The goal is not primarily to harmonize, but to prohibit discrimination against foreign authors. As explained in Part II, such a goal was achieved by different tools, the main one being the rule of national treatment. But the Berne Convention also sets a baseline of protection for foreign authors that supplements its non-discrimination principle. Hence the prohibition of formalities and the provision of broadly worded substantive minima. Those tools structure the Berne Convention.

One consequence flowing from the Convention's purpose is the distinction between domestic issues not governed by the Convention and international issues potentially governed by the Convention. The Convention's non-interference in member states' treatment of their own authors explains the existence of specific rules related to the applicability of the Convention. The framework of the Berne Convention is therefore the following: rules govern-ing whether the Convention applies at all to the controversy at hand; national treatment; substantive minima; and standard final clauses for Conventions related to the signature and entry in force of the convention. (In addition there are dispositions related to the establishment of a Union.)

Subsequently enacted copyright and neighboring rights Conventions dupli-cate this framework, adding only one provision addressing the relationship between the Berne Convention and the new conventions, in order to avoid any conflict of conventions. As to copyright law, the WIPO Copyright Treaty (WCT) is clearly seen as the continuation of the Berne Convention. Articles 1 and 3 express that continuity by specifying in article 1 that the treaty is a special agreement of the Berne Convention; and in article 3 by incorporating the standards of the Berne Convention on applicability, national treatment and the prohibition of formalities. The other articles of the WCT strengthen and modernize Berne's substantive minima.

With respect to neighboring rights, the Conventions retain the Berne struc-ture, as the Rome Convention reveals. With one exception, designed to recon-cile any conflicts between authors' rights (copyright proper) and performers' rights (neighboring rights). Thus, the first article of the Rome Convention is dedicated to the safeguarding of copyright proper, to ensure that perform-ers' rights do not derogate from authors' rights. The articles of the Rome Convention adopt the framework of the Berne Convention, addressing the applicability of the Convention, national treatment, the question of formalities, the substantive minima and the final articles. The WIPO Performances and Phonograms Treaty supplements the Rome Convention (without, however, obliging member states to apply the Rome Convention), again following a common structure, with the exception of the one article addressing the rela-tionship of authors' rights and performers' rights conventions. Finally, the recent Beijing Treaty on Audiovisual Performances shares the same structure.

By contrast, the 2013 Marrakesh Treaty to Facilitate Access to Published Works by Visually Impaired Persons and Persons with Print Disabilities (not to be confused with the 1994 Marrakesh Agreement Establishing the World Trade Organization), departs from this structure. But the "VIP" treaty's scope is much narrower, concerning only the harmonization of laws concern-ing the specific issue of access to published works by the visually-impaired.

Turning from WIPO to UNESCO and the WTO, the goals of the trea-ties administered by these organizations change and as a result the struc-ture of the conventions changes as well. The UNESCO Convention on the

Protection and Promotion of the Diversity of Cultural Expressions clearly encourages member countries to enact those principles in their domestic law. With the WTO, copyright law enters a new world, the one of international trade. Protection of intellectual property is no longer the goal in itself but becomes a means for regulating trade. Nevertheless, the choice was made to use the international *acquis* (the ensemble of norms derived from the all the treaties, taken together), strengthening it by the specific tools of international trade. To a significant extent, therefore, the TRIPS Accord shares a similar structure based on applicability rules, national treatment and substantive minima. The WTO-specific touch comes from the "most favored nation" rules—unknown in copyright conventions, and from the Dispute Resolution mechanism.

This last innovation is of great importance. Under article 33 of the Berne Convention and article 30 of the Rome Convention, the International Court of Justice (ICJ) has jurisdiction in disputes between the member states. Nevertheless, member states never resorted to this mechanism for dispute resolution. On the contrary, the WTO Dispute Resolution mechanism can be enforced, hence its efficiency. As declared on the WTO website:

> Dispute settlement is the central pillar of the multilateral trading system, and the WTO's unique contribution to the stability of the global economy. Without a means of settling disputes, the rules-based system would be less effective because the rules could not be enforced. The WTO's procedure underscores the rule of law, and it makes the trading system more secure and predictable. The system is based on clearly defined rules, with timetables for completing a case. First rulings are made by a panel and endorsed (or rejected) by the WTO's full membership. Appeals based on points of law are possible (https://www.wto.org/english/thewto_e/whatis_e/tif_e/disp1_e.htm).

Furthermore, if the country still does not respect its international obligations and does not comply with the panel's decision, the complaining state may ask the Dispute Settlement Body for permission to impose limited trade sanctions ("suspend concessions or obligations") against the other side. Those trade sanctions are indeed the added value of the WTO Dispute settlement mechanism. Where the ICJ was never seized for a breach of the Berne Convention or the Rome Convention, the WTO Dispute Resolution mechanism has already been seized 34 times in relation to the TRIPS and ten times for copyright issues,* since the entry into force of the TRIPS

---

* For the substance of these disputes see the WTO website: http://www.wto.org/english/tratop_e/dispu_e/dispu_subjects_index_e.htm#selected_subject

Agreement. Among those ten disputes, eight were settled by parties reaching mutually satisfactory solutions; there have only been two panel resolutions: DS160 United States — Section 110(5) of US Copyright Act (Complainant: European Communities) 26 January 1999; DS362 China — Measures Affecting the Protection and Enforcement of Intellectual Property Rights (Complainant: United States) 10 April 2007.

QUESTIONS

1. What might be the consequences of bringing copyright within the ambit of the WTO?
2. How do you explain the primacy of the Berne Convention among the international norms?
3. Consider the peculiarities of the Marrakesh Treaty relative to other WIPO Treaties or to the TRIPS Agreement. What explains them? What may that treaty suggest for the future of international copyright and neighboring rights accords?
4. Do you think that the move from WIPO, an organization dedicated to IP, to WTO, an organization not dedicated to IP, could have any consequence as to the level of protection?
5. Why does the WTO Dispute Resolution mechanism enhance the respect of international obligations between member states of the Berne Convention?

1.4 Structure and context of international copyright law

1.4.1 Treaties and organizations dealing with international copyright and related rights law*

WIPO

The World Intellectual Property Organization is an intergovernmental organization and a self-funded, specialized agency of the United Nations. WIPO was formed by the 1967 Stockholm Convention, and its mission is "to lead the development of a balanced and effective international

---

* Many thanks to Taylor Jones, Columbia Law School class of 2014, for assistance in the preparation of these introductory notes.

   Editors' note: The following section does not include the Geneva Convention for the Protection of Producers of Phonograms against Unauthorized Duplication of their Phonograms (1971) or the Brussels Convention Relating to the Distribution of Program-Carrying Signals Transmitted by Satellite (1974) because neither treaty is addressed in the subsequent sections of the casebook

intellectual property (IP) system that enables innovation and creativity for the benefit of all." World Intellectual Property Organization, *Inside WIPO*, WIPO, http://www.wipo.int/about-wipo/en/index.html (last visited November 23, 2013). Membership is open to any state that is a party to "the Paris Union, the Special Unions and Agreements established in relation with that Union, the Berne Union, [or] any other international agreement designed to promote the protection of intellectual property whose administration is assumed by [WIPO]." *See* Convention Establishing the Intellectual Property Organization arts. 5, 2(vii) July 14, 1967, 21 U.S.T. 1770, 828 U.N.T.S. 3. Membership is also open to U.N. member states, or by invitation from the Organization. *Ibid.* at art. 5(2).

Copyright

Berne Convention for the Protection of Literary and Artistic Works (1886); Current version, Paris Revision of 1971

The Berne Convention is the most significant multilateral copyright convention today, with 168 member states as of December 2014. It gives effect to three fundamental principles—(1) national treatment; (2) lack of formalities, or "automatic" protection; and (3) independence of protection—and provides minimum standards of protection. The minimum standards specify which works must be protected, which rights are protected and the duration of protection. Protected rights include the author's "moral" rights to be recognized as the creator of her work and to protect the integrity of her work. Economic rights that the Convention obliges member states to protect include the rights of reproduction, adaptation and communication to the public. For most works, the term of protection must be at least 50 years after the death of the author. Finally, the convention establishes special provisions for developing countries. *See* Treaties and Contracting Parties: Berne Convention, www.wipo.int (last visited Dec. 18, 2014).

WIPO Copyright Treaty (WCT) (1996)

WIPO, *Treaties and Contracting Parties: WIPO Copyright Treaty (WCT)*, http://www.wipo.int/treaties/en/ip/wct/summary_wct.html (last visited June. 25, 2014):

> The WCT is a special agreement under the Berne Convention. Any Contracting Party (even if it is not bound by the Berne Convention)

must comply with the substantive provisions of the 1971 (Paris) Act of the Berne Convention for the Protection of Literary and Artistic Works (1886). Furthermore, the Treaty mentions two subject matters to be protected by copyright: (i) computer programs, whatever may be the mode or form of their expression, and (ii) compilations of data or other material ("databases"), in any form, which by reason of the selection or arrangement of their contents constitute intellectual creations. (Where a database does not constitute such a creation, it is outside the scope of this Treaty.) As to the rights of authors, the Treaty deals with three: (i) the right of distribution, (ii) the right of rental, and (iii) the right of communication and making available to the public. Finally, the Treaty requires remedies for the circumvention of technological protection measures and removal or alteration of electronic rights management information.

Marrakesh Treaty to Facilitate Access to Published Works for Persons who are Blind, Visually Impaired, or otherwise Print Disabled (2013)

Press Release, *Historic Treaty Adopted, Boosts Access to Books for Visually Impaired Persons Worldwide*, http://www.wipo.int/pressroom/en/briefs/ limitations.html (last visited June 25, 2014):

> The treaty . . . addresses the "book famine" by requiring its contracting parties to adopt national law provisions that permit the reproduction, distribution and making available of published works in accessible formats through limitations and exceptions to the rights of copyright rightholders.
>
> It also provides for the exchange of these accessible format works across borders by organizations that serve the people who are blind, visually impaired, and print disabled. It will harmonize limitations and exceptions so that these organizations can operate across borders. This sharing of works in accessible formats should increase the overall number of works available because it will eliminate duplication and increase efficiency. Instead of five countries producing accessible versions of the same work, the five countries will each be able to produce an accessible version of a different work, which can then be shared with each of the other countries.

Neighboring rights

> *Rome Convention for the Protection of Performers, Producers of Phonograms and Broadcasting Organizations (1961)*

WIPO, *Treaties and Contracting Parties: Rome Convention,* http://www.wipo.int/treaties/en/ip/rome/summary_rome.html (last visited June 25, 2014):

> The [Rome] Convention secures protection in performances of performers, phonograms of producers of phonograms and broadcasts of broadcasting organizations.
>
> (1) Performers (actors, singers, musicians, dancers and those who perform literary or artistic works) are protected against certain acts to which they have not consented, such as the broadcasting and communication to the public of a live performance; the fixation of the live performance; the reproduction of the fixation if the original fixation was made without the performer's consent or if the reproduction was made for purposes different from those for which consent was given.
>
> (2) Producers of phonograms have the right to authorize or prohibit the direct or indirect reproduction of their phonograms. In the Rome Convention, "phonograms" means any exclusively aural fixation of sounds of a performance or of other sounds. Where a phonogram published for commercial purposes gives rise to secondary uses (such as broadcasting or communication to the public in any form), a single equitable remuneration must be paid by the user to the performers, to the producers of the phonograms, or to both. Contracting States are free, however, not to apply this rule or to limit its application.
>
> (3) Broadcasting organizations have the right to authorize or prohibit certain acts, namely the rebroadcasting of their broadcasts; the fixation of their broadcasts; the reproduction of such fixations; the communication to the public of their television broadcasts if such communication is made in places accessible to the public against payment of an entrance fee.
>
> The Convention allows exceptions in national laws to [those] rights as regards private use, use of short excerpts in connection with the reporting of current events, ephemeral fixation by a broadcasting organization by means of its own facilities and for its own broadcasts, use solely for the purpose of teaching or scientific research and in any other cases—except for compulsory licenses that would be incompatible with the Berne Convention—where the national law provides exceptions to copyright in literary and artistic works. Furthermore, once a performer has consented to the incorporation of his performance in a visual or audiovisual fixation, the provisions on performers' rights have no further application. As to duration, protection must last at least until the end of a 20-year period.

WIPO Performances and Phonograms Treaty (WPPT) (1996)

The WPPT protects the rights of performers and producers of phonograms. With respect to performances fixed in phonograms, performers are granted exclusive rights of reproduction, distribution, rental and making available, subject to certain limitations and exceptions. With respect to unfixed, or live, performances, the WPPT grants performers the rights of broadcasting, fixation and communication to the public. Like performers, producers of phonograms gain exclusive rights of reproduction, distribution, rental and making available, subject to certain limitations and exceptions. The treaty obliges each party to grant national treatment to foreign performers and producers of phonograms. The term of protection must be at least 50 years from fixation. Finally like the WCT, the Treaty requires remedies for the circumvention of technological protection measures and removal or alteration of electronic rights management information.

Beijing Treaty on Audiovisual Performances (2012)

The Beijing Treaty was adopted in June of 2012 but will not enter force until 30 signing parties deposit instruments of ratification or accession. *See* Beijing Treaty art. 26, June 26, 2012, *available at* http://www.wipo.int/treaties/en/text.jsp?file_id=295837. It grants performers rights in fixed audiovisual performances, which receive little or no protection under the Rome Convention, TRIPS, and the WPPT. *See* Silke von Lewinski, *The Beijing Treaty on Audiovisual Performances* 1 (Max Planck Institute for Intellectual Property and Competition Law Research Paper No. 13-08), *available at* http://papers.ssrn.com/sol3/papers.cfm?abstract_id=2239109. The Treaty grants independent moral rights of attribution and integrity that remain with the performer despite the transfer of economic rights. *See* art. 5(1). It also protects the rights of broadcast and communication to the public, reproduction, distribution, rental, and making available to the public on demand. *Ibid.* at arts 6–10. Article 11 gives contracting parties an option to provide equitable remuneration rather than exclusive rights of broadcast and communication to the public or to decline to provide these rights altogether. *Ibid.* at art. 11(2)–(3). Contracting parties have great freedom with respect to the transfer of rights. *Ibid.* at art. 12. Finally, the Treaty requires remedies for the circumvention of technological protection measures and removal or alteration of electronic rights management information. *Ibid.* at arts 15–16.

WIPO Treaties and International Enforcement

Despite the broad coverage of the WIPO-administered treaties, many parties were dissatisfied with their lack of effective enforcement procedures. Article 33 of the Berne Convention places infringement complaints before the United Nations (U.N.) International Court of Justice but allows any party to opt out of the Article. Furthermore, enforcement of ICJ decisions requires either voluntary cooperation or referral to the U.N. Security Council. *See* Doris E. Long, *Copyright and the Uruguay Round Agreements: A New Era of Protection or an Illusory Promise?*, 22 AIPLA Q.J. 531, 546 n.49 (1994). A majority of parties have indeed opted out, and the procedure was not used a single time from 1967 to 1990. *See* Frank Emmert, *Intellectual Property in the Uruguay Round – Negotiating Strategies of the Western Industrialized Countries*, 11 Mich. J. Int'l L. 1317, 1343 (1990); *see also* Edward Lee, *Measuring TRIPS Compliance and Defiance: The WTO Compliance Scorecard*, 18 J. Intell. Prop. L. 401, 406 n.14 (2011) ("No country ever brought a Berne Convention dispute before the ICJ."). Another source of dissatisfaction with the ICJ was its lack of intellectual property expertise. *See* Emmert, *supra* at 1343.

Given these shortcomings, countries sought to develop new mechanisms of enforcement through amendments to the General Agreement on Tariffs and Trade (GATT). The resulting agreement is the subject of the next section. For more on dispute resolution, see Chapter 1.3, *supra*, pp. 23–24, on basic principles of international copyright law and international neighbouring rights.

WTO [TRIPS]

World Trade Organization, The World Trade Organization in Brief http://www.wto.org/english/thewto_e/whatis_e/inbrief_e/inbr01_e.htm

The World Trade Organization came into being in 1995. One of the youngest of the international organizations, the WTO is the successor to the General Agreement on Tariffs and Trade (GATT) established in the wake of the Second World War.

. . .

GATT and the WTO have helped to create a strong and prosperous trading system contributing to unprecedented growth.

The system was developed through a series of trade negotiations, or rounds, held under GATT. The first rounds dealt mainly with tariff reductions but later negotiations included other areas such as anti-dumping and non-tariff measures. The last round—the 1986–94 Uruguay Round – led to the WTO's creation.

. . .

The WTO's rules—the agreements—are the result of negotiations between the members. The current set were the outcome of the 1986–94 Uruguay Round negotiations which included a major revision of the original [GATT].

GATT is now the WTO's principal rule book for trade in goods. The Uruguay Round also created new rules for dealing with trade in services, relevant aspects of intellectual property, dispute settlement, and trade policy reviews. The complete set runs to some 30,000 pages consisting of about 30 agreements and separate commitments (called schedules) made by individual members in specific areas such as lower customs duty rates and services market-opening.

. . .

The WTO's procedure for resolving trade quarrels under the Dispute Settlement Understanding is vital for enforcing the rules and there-fore for ensuring that trade flows smoothly. Countries bring disputes to the WTO if they think their rights under the agreements are being infringed. Judgments by specially appointed independent experts are based on interpretations of the agreements and individual countries' commitments.

The system encourages countries to settle their differences through con-sultation. Failing that, they can follow a carefully mapped out, stage-by-stage procedure that includes the possibility of a ruling by a panel of experts, and the chance to appeal the ruling on legal grounds. Confidence in the system is borne out by the number of cases brought to the WTO— more than 300 cases in ten years compared to the 300 disputes dealt with during the entire life of GATT (1947–94).

Trade-Related Aspects of Intellectual Property Rights (TRIPS) (1994)

The TRIPS Agreement was adopted in April 1994. The level of protection it provides corresponds to the Berne and Rome Conventions, and the substantive provisions of the Berne Convention, with the exception of moral rights, have been incorporated by reference into the TRIPS Agreement. TRIPS expands substantive protection by providing rental rights, by clarifying that computer software and databases are copyrightable works, and by extending protection for performers and producers of phonograms from the 20 years provided by the Rome Convention to a term of 50 years. It also provides standards for the enforcement of intellectual property rights and extends the WTO dispute settlement system to intellectual property rights. *See* Mihaly Ficsor and WIPO, Guide to Copyright and Related Rights Treaties Administered by WIPO and Glossary of Copyright and Related Rights Terms ¶¶ 27–28 (2003).

Aside from its robust dispute resolution provisions, the TRIPS Agreement most notably expanded upon previous multilateral intellectual property agreements by importing most-favored-nation (MFN) treatment from the international trade context. As Professor Daniel Gervais, then a GATT (TRIPS Division) Legal Officer during the Uruguay Round, explains, the MFN clause promotes uniformity in international protection:

> Article 4 introduced a new element in the international intellectual property framework, namely most-favoured nation treatment. Under this system, well known in the multilateral trade arena, any advantage, favour, privilege or immunity granted (usually bilaterally) to nationals of any (not just of another WTO Member) other country must be accorded to nationals of all WTO Members. The rule['s] . . . purpose is to ensure greater uniformity of the multilateral trade environment. Its principal relevance in this framework would be where an advantage, favour (e.g. as regards registration, deposit or fees) has been granted bilaterally and is not subject to the national treatment clause (either because it falls under an exception or because it does not apply to nationals of the country concerned).

Daniel Gervais, The TRIPS Agreement: Drafting History and Analysis ¶ 2.73 (4th ed. 2012).

Article 4 provides exceptions to MFN where the favoured treatment is: (a) based on agreements on "judicial assistance or law enforcement" and not confined to intellectual property; (b) pursuant to specified provisions of the Berne Convention or Rome Convention; (c) "in respect of the rights of performers, producers of phonograms and broadcasting organizations not provided under [the TRIPS] Agreement;" or (d) pursuant to certain pre-TRIPS intellectual property agreements.

See ibid. at ¶ 2.63; *see also* CARLOS M. CORREA, TRADE RELATED ASPECTS OF INTELLECTUAL PROPERTY RIGHTS: A COMMENTARY ON THE TRIPS AGREEMENT 67–72 (2007) (describing application of the exceptions).

United Nations Educational, Scientific and Cultural Organization (UNESCO)

The Universal Copyright Convention (1952)

Mihaly Ficsor and WIPO, Guide to Copyright and Related Rights Treaties Administered by WIPO and Glossary of Copyright and Related Rights Terms ¶ 13 (2003):

> The Universal Copyright Convention was worked out and adopted under the aegis of UNESCO in 1951. This took place mainly on the initiative of the United States of America, which, due to certain specific features of its legislation (such as the existence of formalities as conditions of protection and a complex regulation concerning the term of protection of copyright not fulfilling the requirements of the Berne Convention) was not able to accede to the Berne Convention. . . . The UCC only contained some quite general obligations concerning the rights to be granted, and it allowed the application of formalities (but simplified their fulfillment for other countries party to the UCC by providing that the indication of a simple standardized copyright notice was sufficient).

Once the U.S. joined the Berne Convention, followed by Russia and China, the UCC's importance significantly dwindled because the principal role of the UCC had been to offer multilateral protection to the U.S. and later the U.S.S.R., on terms less stringent than Berne imposed. Once all the major political and economic powers had come into the Berne Union, these states had little further need for the UCC, since there remained very few countries who were members of the UCC but not of Berne.

Table 1.1* below lists WIPO-administered treaties relevant to copyright and neighboring rights and covered in this casebook, as well as the UCC and the TRIPS Agreement, and national membership in each treaty, organized alphabetically by country within continents.

---

* Many thanks to Taylor Jones, Columbia Law School class of 2014, for the preparation of the table.

Table 1.1 "Membership in International Copyright Treaties"

STATE	TREATIES	WIPO						WTO	UNESCO
KEY: italics: non UN member small caps: UN observer		Berne Convention[1]	Rome Convention	WIPO Copyright Treaty	WIPO Performances & Phonograms Treaty	Beijing Treaty[2]	Marrakesh Treaty	TRIPS	Universal Copyright Convention[3]
PARTIES		168	92	91	92	0	0	159	65
AFRICA									
Algeria	5	4/19/1998	4/22/2007	1/31/2014	1/31/2014				5/18/1973
Angola	1							11/23/1996	
Benin	4	8/1/1960		4/16/2006	4/16/2006			2/22/1996	
Botswana	4	4/15/1998		1/27/2005	1/27/2005	—		5/31/1995	
Burkina Faso	5	8/19/1963	1/14/1988	3/6/2002	5/20/2002	—		6/3/1995	
Burundi	1					—	—	7/23/1995	
Cameroon	2	1/1/1960				—	—	12/13/1995	2/1/1973
Cape Verde	3	7/7/1997	7/3/1997					7/23/2008	
Central African Republic	2	9/3/1977				—	—	5/31/1995	
Chad	2	11/25/1971				—	—	10/19/1996	
Comoros	1	4/17/2005				—	—		
Congo, Democratic Rep.	2	6/30/1960						1/1/1997	
Congo, Rep. of the	3	8/15/1960	5/18/1964			—	—	4/30/1995	
Cote d'Ivoire	2	1/1/1962				—	—	1/1/1995	

Table 1.1 (continued)

Country	#									
Morocco	5	6/16/1917		7/20/2011	7/20/2011	–	–	–	1/1/1995	10/28/1975
Mozambique	2	11/22/2013				–	–	–	8/26/1995	
Namibia	2	3/21/1990		–	–	–	–	–	1/1/1995	
Niger	4	8/3/1960	5/18/1964	–	–				12/13/1996	2/15/1989
Nigeria	3	9/14/1993	10/29/1993	–		–			1/1/1995	
Rwanda	3	3/1/1984					–		5/22/1996	8/10/1989
Sahrawi Arab Democratic Republic	0					–	–	–		
Sao Tome and Principe	0					–	–	–		
Senegal	5	8/25/1962		5/18/2002	5/20/2002	–	–	–	1/1/1995	4/9/1974
Seychelles	0						–			
Sierra Leone	1						–		7/23/1995	
Somalia	0									
Somaliland, Rep. of	0									
South Africa	2	10/3/1928		–			–		1/1/1995	
South Sudan	0									
Sudan	1	12/28/2000				–				
Swaziland	2	12/14/1998				–			1/1/1995	
Tanzania, United Rep. of	2	7/25/1994				–			1/1/1995	
Togo	6	4/30/1975	6/10/2003	5/21/2003	5/21/2003	–	–	–	5/31/1995	2/28/2003
Tunisia	3	12/5/1887				–			3/29/1995	3/10/1975
Uganda	1					–			1/1/1995	
Zambia	2	1/2/1992				–			1/1/1995	
Zimbabwe	2	4/18/1980				–			3/5/1995	

STATE	TREATIES	WIPO Berne Convention	Rome Convention	WIPO Copyright Treaty	WIPO Performances & Phonograms Treaty	Beijing Treaty	Marrakesh Treaty	WTO TRIPS	UNESCO Universal Copyright Convention
KEY: italics: non UN member small caps: UN observer									
ASIA									
Abkhazia, Republic of	0								
Afghanistan	0						—		
Armenia	5	10/19/2000	1/31/2003	3/6/2005	3/6/2005			2/5/2003	
Azerbaijan	4	6/4/1999	10/5/2005	4/11/2006	4/11/2006				
Bahrain	5	3/2/1997	1/18/2006	12/15/2005	12/15/2005			1/1/1995	
Bangladesh	3	5/4/1999						1/1/1995	5/5/1975
Bhutan	1	11/25/2004							
Brunei Darussalam	2	8/30/2006						1/1/1995	
Cambodia	1		—					10/13/2004	
China	5	10/15/1992		6/9/2007	6/9/2007	—	—	12/11/2001	7/30/1992
Georgia	5	5/16/1995	8/14/2004	3/6/2002	5/20/2002			6/14/2000	
Hong Kong	1							1/1/1995	
India	3	4/1/1928	—			—		1/1/1995	1/7/1988
Indonesia	4	9/5/1997		3/6/2002	2/15/2005	—		1/1/1995	
Iran	0								
Iraq	0								
Israel	3	3/24/1950	12/30/2002	—	—			4/21/1995	
Japan	6	7/15/1899	10/26/1989	3/6/2002	10/9/2002	—		1/1/1995	7/21/1977
Jordan	4	7/28/1999		4/27/2004	5/24/2004	—		4/11/2000	
Kazakhstan	4	4/12/1999	6/30/2012	11/12/2004	11/12/2004				
Korea, North (Dem. P. Rep.)	1	4/28/2003				—			
Korea, South (Rep. of)	6	8/21/1996	3/18/2009	6/24/2004	3/18/2009	—		1/1/1995	7/1/1987

Country								
Kuwait	2	12/2/2014						1/1/1995
Kyrgyzstan (Kyrgyz Republic)	5	7/8/1999	8/13/2003	3/6/2002	8/15/2002			12/20/1998
Laos	2	3/14/2012						2/2/2013
Lebanon	2	9/30/1947	8/12/1997			—		
Macao, China	1							1/1/1995
Malaysia	4	10/1/1990		12/27/2012	12/27/2012			1/1/1995
Maldives	1							5/31/1995
Mongolia	4	3/12/1998		10/25/2002	10/25/2002	—		1/29/1997
Myanmar	1							1/1/1995
Nagorno-Karabakh	0							
Nepal	2	1/11/2006				—		4/23/2004
Northern Cyprus	0							
Oman	4	7/14/1999		9/20/2005	9/20/2005			11/9/2000
Pakistan	2	7/5/1948						1/1/1995
PALESTINE	0							
Philippines	5	8/1/1951	9/25/1984	10/4/2002	10/4/2002			1/1/1995
Qatar	4	7/5/2000		10/28/2005	10/28/2005	—		1/13/1996
Saudi Arabia	3	3/11/2004					4/13/1994	12/11/2005
Singapore	4	12/21/1998		4/17/2005	4/17/2005			1/1/1995
South Ossetia, Rep. of	0							
Sri Lanka	3	2/4/1948					10/25/1983	1/1/1995
Syrian Arab Republic	2	6/11/2004	5/13/2006			—		
Taipei, Chinese	1							1/1/2002
Taiwan	0							
Tajikistan	5	3/9/2000	5/19/2008	4/5/2009	8/24/2011			3/2/2013
Thailand	2	7/17/1931						1/1/1995
Timor-Leste	0							
Turkey	5	1/1/1952	4/8/2004	11/28/2008	11/28/2008	—		3/26/1995
Turkmenistan	0							
United Arab Emirates	5	7/14/2004	1/14/2005	7/14/2004	6/9/2005			4/10/1996
Uzbekistan	1	4/19/2005						
Vietnam	3	10/26/2004	3/1/2007					1/11/2007
Yemen	1	7/14/2008						

Table 1.1 (continued)

STATE KEY: italics: non UN member small caps: UN observer * E.U. member	TREATIES	WIPO Berne Convention	Rome Convention	WIPO Copyright Treaty	WIPO Performances & Phonograms Treaty	Beijing Treaty	Marrakesh Treaty	WTO TRIPS	UNESCO Universal Copyright Convention
EUROPE									
Albania	6	3/6/1994	9/1/2000	8/6/2005	5/20/2002			9/8/2000	11/4/2003
Andorra	2	6/2/2004	5/25/2004						
Austria*	6	10/1/1920	6/9/1973	3/14/2010	3/14/2010	—		1/1/1995	5/14/1982
Belarus	4	12/12/1997	5/27/2003	3/6/2002	5/20/2002				
Belgium*	5	9/5/1887	10/2/1999	8/30/2006	8/30/2006	—		1/1/1995	
Bosnia and Herzegovina	5	3/1/1992	5/19/2009	11/25/2009	11/25/2009				7/12/1993
Bulgaria*	6	12/5/1921	8/31/1995	3/6/2002	5/20/2002	—		12/1/1996	3/7/1975
Croatia*	6	10/8/1991	4/20/2000	3/6/2002	5/20/2002			11/30/2000	7/6/1992
Cyprus*	6	8/16/1960	6/17/2009	11/4/2003	12/2/2005	—		7/30/1995	9/19/1990
Czech Republic*	6	1/1/1993	1/1/1993	3/6/2002	5/20/2002	—		1/1/1995	3/26/1993
Denmark*	6	7/1/1903	9/23/1965	3/14/2010	3/14/2010	—		1/1/1995	4/11/1979
Estonia*	5	10/26/1994	4/28/2000	3/14/2010	3/14/2010	—		11/13/1999	
EUROPEAN UNION	3			3/14/2010	3/14/2010	—		1/1/1995	
Finland*	6	4/1/1928	10/21/1983	3/14/2010	3/14/2010	—		1/1/1995	8/1/1986
France*	6	12/5/1887	7/3/1987	3/14/2010	3/14/2010	—		1/1/1995	9/11/1972
Germany*	6	12/5/1887	10/21/1966	3/14/2010	3/14/2010	—		1/1/1995	10/18/1973
Greece*	5	11/9/1920	1/6/1993	3/14/2010	3/14/2010	—		1/1/1995	
Hungary*	6	2/14/1922	2/10/1995	3/6/2002	5/20/2002	—		1/1/1995	9/15/1972
Iceland	3	9/7/1947	6/15/1994					1/1/1995	
Ireland*	5	10/5/1927	9/19/1979	3/14/2010	3/14/2010	—		1/1/1995	
Italy*	6	12/5/1887	4/8/1975	3/14/2010	3/14/2010	—		1/1/1995	10/25/1979
Kosovo, Rep. of	0								

Latvia*	5	8/11/1995	8/20/1999	3/6/2002	5/20/2002		2/10/1999	8/11/1999
Liechtenstein	6	7/30/1931	10/12/1999	4/30/2007	4/30/2007		9/1/1995	
Lithuania*	5	12/14/1994	7/22/1999	3/6/2002	5/20/2002		5/31/2001	
Luxembourg*	5	6/20/1888	2/25/1976	3/14/2010	3/14/2010	–	1/1/1995	
Macedonia, The Former Yugoslav Rep.	6	9/8/1991	3/2/1998	2/4/2004	1/2/1904	–	1/2/1904	4/30/1997
Malta*	4	9/21/1964		3/14/2002	3/14/2010		1/1/1995	
Moldova (Rep. of)	5	11/2/1995	12/5/1995	3/6/2002	5/20/2002	–	7/26/2001	
Monaco	3	5/30/1889	12/6/1985	–	–			9/13/1974
Montenegro	6	6/3/2006	6/3/2006	6/3/2006	6/3/2006	–	4/29/2012	4/26/2007
Netherlands*	6	11/1/1912	10/7/1993	3/14/2010	3/14/2010	–	1/1/1995	8/30/1985
Norway	4	4/13/1896	7/10/1978				1/1/1995	5/7/1974
Poland*	6	1/28/1920	6/13/1997	3/23/2004	10/21/2003	–	7/1/1995	12/9/1976
Portugal*	6	3/29/1911	7/17/2002	3/14/2010	3/14/2010		1/1/1995	4/30/1981
Romania*	5	1/1/1927	10/22/1998	3/6/2002	5/20/2002	–	1/1/1995	
Russian Federation	6	3/13/1995	5/26/2003	2/5/2009	2/5/2009		8/22/2012	12/9/1994
San Marino	0							
Serbia	5	4/27/1992	6/10/2003	6/13/2003	6/13/2003			9/11/2001
Slovakia*	6	1/1/1993	1/1/1993	3/6/2002	5/20/2002	–	1/1/1995	3/31/1993
Slovenia*	6	6/25/1991	10/9/1996	3/6/2002	5/20/2002	–	7/30/1995	11/5/1992
Spain*	6	12/5/1887	11/14/1991	3/14/2010	3/14/2010	–	1/1/1995	4/10/1974
Sweden*	6	8/1/1904	5/18/1964	3/14/2010	3/14/2010	–	1/1/1995	6/27/1973
Switzerland	6	12/5/1887	9/24/1993	7/1/2008	7/1/2008	–	7/1/1995	6/21/1993
Ukraine	5	10/25/1995	6/12/2002	3/6/2002	5/20/2002		5/16/2008	
United Kingdom*	6	12/5/1887	5/18/1964	3/14/2010	3/14/2010	–	1/1/1995	5/19/1972
VATICAN CITY (HOLY SEE)	2	9/12/1935	–	3/14/2010	3/14/2010	–		2/6/1980

Table 1.1 (continued)

STATE	TREATIES	WIPO Berne Convention	Rome Convention	WIPO Copyright Treaty	WIPO Performances & Phonograms Treaty	Beijing Treaty	Marrakesh Treaty	WTO TRIPS	UNESCO Universal Copyright Convention
NORTH AMERICA									
Antigua and Barbuda	2	3/17/2000						1/1/1995	
Bahamas, The	2	7/10/1973							9/27/1976
Barbados	4	3/16/1983	9/18/1983					1/1/1995	3/18/1983
Belize	2	6/17/2000						1/1/1995	
Canada	3	4/10/1928	6/4/1998	—	—			1/1/1995	
Costa Rica	6	6/10/1978	9/9/1971	3/6/2002	5/20/2002	—	—	1/1/1995	12/7/1979
Cuba	2	2/20/1997						4/20/1995	
Dominica	3	8/7/1999	11/9/1999					1/1/1995	
Dominican Republic	6	12/24/1997	1/27/1987	1/10/2006	1/10/2006			3/9/1995	2/8/1983
El Salvador	6	2/19/1994	6/29/1979	3/6/2002	5/20/2002	—	—	5/7/1995	12/29/1978
Grenada	2	9/22/1998						2/22/1996	
Guatemala	5	7/28/1997	1/14/1977	2/4/2003	1/8/2003	—		7/21/1995	
Haiti	2	1/11/1996				—		1/30/1996	
Honduras	5	1/25/1990	2/16/1990	5/20/2002	5/20/2002	—		1/1/1995	
Jamaica	5	1/1/1994	1/27/1994	6/12/2002	6/12/2002	—		3/9/1995	
Mexico	6	6/11/1967	5/18/1964	3/6/2002	5/20/2002	—		1/1/1995	7/31/1975
Nicaragua	5	8/23/2000	8/10/2000	3/6/2003	3/6/2003			9/3/1995	
Panama	6	6/8/1996	9/2/1983	3/6/2002	5/20/2002	—		9/6/1997	6/3/1980
Saint Kitts and Nevis	2	4/9/1995						2/21/1996	
Saint Lucia	5	8/24/1993	8/17/1996	3/6/2002	5/20/2002			1/1/1995	
St Vincent & the Grenadines	4	8/29/1995		2/12/2011	2/12/2011			1/1/1995	1/22/1985

KEY:
italics: non UN member
small caps: UN observer

Trinidad and Tobago	5	8/16/1988		11/28/2008	11/28/2008	–		3/1/1995	5/19/1988
United States of America	5	3/1/1989		3/6/2002	5/20/2002	–	–	1/1/1995	9/18/1972

OCEANIA

Australia	6	4/14/1928	9/30/1992	7/26/2007	7/26/2007			1/1/1995	11/29/1977
Cook Islands	0								
Fiji	3	*10/10/1970*	*4/11/1972*					1/14/1996	
Kiribati	0								
Marshall Islands	0								
Micronesia	1	10/7/2003							
Nauru	0								
New Zealand	2	4/24/1928						1/1/1995	
Niue	0								
Palau	0								
Papua New Guinea	1					6/9/1996			
Samoa	2	7/21/1996				5/10/2012			
Solomon Islands	1					7/26/1996			
Tonga	2	6/14/2001				7/27/2007			
Tuvalu	0								
Vanuatu	2	12/27/2012						8/24/2012	

SOUTH AMERICA

Argentina	5	6/10/1967	3/2/1992	3/6/2002	5/20/2002			1/1/1995	
Bolivia	4	11/4/1993	11/24/1993	–	–			9/12/1995	12/22/1989
Brazil	4	2/9/1922	9/29/1965			–	–	1/1/1995	9/11/1975
Chile	5	6/5/1970	9/5/1974	3/6/2002	5/20/2002			1/1/1995	

Table 1.1 (continued)

STATE	TREATIES	WIPO						WTO	UNESCO
KEY: italics: non UN member small caps: UN observer		Berne Convention	Rome Convention	WIPO Copyright Treaty	WIPO Performances & Phonograms Treaty	Beijing Treaty	Marrakesh Treaty	TRIPS	Universal Copyright Convention
SOUTH AMERICA									
Colombia	6	3/7/1988	9/17/1976	3/6/2002	5/20/2002	–	–	4/30/1995	3/18/1976
Ecuador	6	10/9/1991	5/18/1964	3/6/2002	5/20/2002			1/21/1996	6/6/1991
Guyana	2	10/25/1994						1/1/1995	
Paraguay	5	1/2/1992	2/26/1970	3/6/2002	5/20/2002		–	1/1/1995	
Peru	6	8/20/1988	8/7/1985	3/6/2002	7/18/2002	–	–	1/1/1995	4/22/1985
Suriname	2	2/23/1977						1/1/1995	
Uruguay	6	7/10/1967	7/4/1977	6/5/2009	8/28/2008		–	1/1/1995	1/12/1993
Venezuela	4	12/30/1982	1/30/1996	–	–			1/1/1995	1/11/1996

Note:
1 Dates appear in the following format: m(m)/d(d)/yyyy. The date signifies entry into force except where noted. A date in italic typeface indicates that the country has not acceded to the Paris Act. All other countries have acceded to at least the Paris Act, and, in some cases, other Acts as well.
2 A dash indicates a signature but no entry into force. The Beijing Treaty will enter into force when 30 eligible countries have deposited instruments of ratification or accession. See Beijing Treaty art. 26. No country other than the Syrian Arab Republic has deposited an instrument as of November 24, 2013. The Marrakesh Treaty, for which this chart also lists only signatories, will enter into force when 20 eligible parties have deposited the requisite instrument. See Marrakesh Treaty art. 18.
3 Dates in UCC column indicate deposit of an instrument. The Convention enters into force for each country three months after deposit of that country's instrument. An exception applies where a signing party has deposited an instrument of succession. In such cases entry into force occurs when the country assumes sovereign independence. See http://www.unesco.org/eri/la/convention.asp?KO=15241&language=E&order=alpha.

Figure 1.2 on the following two pages explains the relationship of the most important treaties on copyright and neighboring rights.*

1.4.2 U.S. and E.U. bilateral treaties

In the mid-1980s, bilateral agreements again became an important means of achieving international protection. In particular, the U.S. and the E.U. used bilateral agreements to gain protection in countries that were not party to existing conventions or to increase the level of protection in countries that were. For a more detailed discussion of these issues discussed in the following note,** *see* Silke von Lewinski, INTERNATIONAL COPYRIGHT LAW AND POLICY 349–83 (2008).

U.S.

i. Factors leading to the revival of bilateral treaties

The U.S. began including intellectual property in bilateral trade agreements as part of a larger effort to reduce the unprecedented global trade deficit and strengthen the national economy, which had been weakening since the 1960s.[1] Lost revenues due to intellectual property piracy were a significant factor motivating trade policy adjustments.[2] The U.S. had not yet joined the Berne Convention despite increasing pressure, and faith in the UCC had waned since the U.S. withdrew from UNESCO.[3] The Reagan administration announced three policy initiatives to increase international copyright protection: strengthening domestic copyright law; pursuing multilateral agreements with enforcement capacity; and entering bilateral agreements with major trade partners.[4]

The Omnibus Trade and Competitiveness Act of 1988 implemented the new policy approach by refining the Trade Act of 1974. The U.S. Trade Representative (USTR) was required under section 301 of the 1988 Act

---

* Many thanks to David Rüther, Columbia Law School LLM 2014, for preparing this chart.

** Many thanks to Taylor Jones, Columbia Law School class of 2014, for drafting the following note.

1 Jonathan C. Carlson, *The United States Commitment to International Trade Law: The Role of a Declining Hegemon*, 1 TRANSNAT'L L. & CONTEMP. PROBS. 81, 106 (1991); SILKE VON LEWINSKI, INTERNATIONAL COPYRIGHT LAW AND POLICY ¶ 12.04 (2008).

2 Emery Simon, *Office of the United States Trade Representative, U.S. Trade Policy and Intellectual Property Rights*, 50 ALB. L. REV. 501, 502 (1985).

3 *See* 1 SAM RICKETSON & JANE C. GINSBURG, INTERNATIONAL COPYRIGHT AND NEIGHBOURING RIGHTS: THE BERNE CONVENTION AND BEYOND ¶ 4.46 (2d. ed. 2006). The lack of enforcement mechanisms severely limited the effectiveness of the UCC.

4 *See* Simon, *supra* note 2.

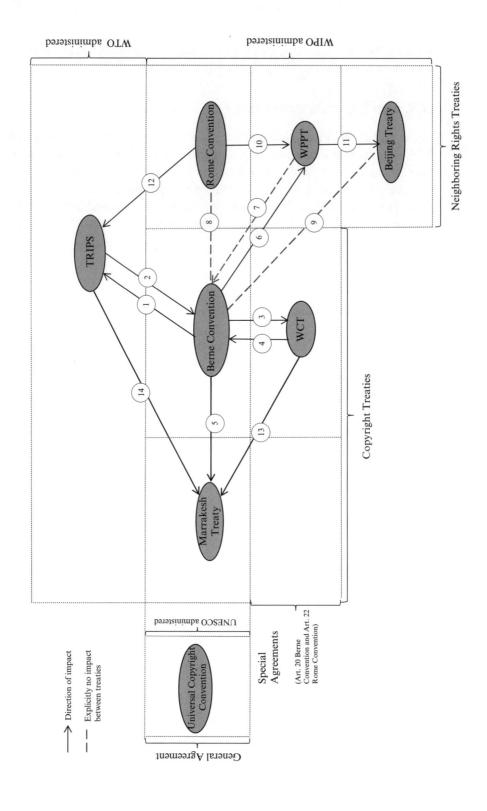

WTO administered

WIPO administered

Neighboring Rights Treaties

Rome Convention

WPPT

Beijing Treaty

TRIPS

Berne Convention

WCT

Marrakesh Treaty

Copyright Treaties

UNESCO administered

Universal Copyright Convention

General Agreement

Special Agreements

(Art. 20 Berne Convention and Art. 22 Rome Convention)

→ Direction of impact

--- Explicitly no impact between treaties

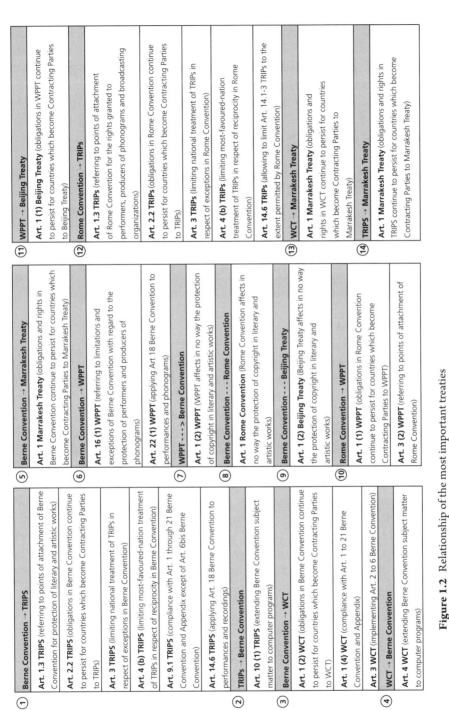

① Berne Convention → TRIPS

Art. 1.3 TRIPS (referring to points of attachment of Berne Convention for protection of literary and artistic works)

Art. 2.2 TRIPS (obligations in Berne Convention continue to persist for countries which become Contracting Parties to TRIPs)

Art. 3 TRIPS (limiting national treatment of TRIPs in respect of exceptions in Berne Convention)

Art. 4 (b) TRIPS (limiting most-favoured-nation treatment of TRIPs in respect of reciprocity in Berne Convention)

Art. 9.1 TRIPS (compliance with Art. 1 through 21 Berne Convention and Appendix except of Art. 6bis Berne Convention)

Art. 14.6 TRIPS (applying Art. 18 Berne Convention to performances and recordings)

② TRIPs → Berne Convention

Art. 10 (1) TRIPS (extending Berne Convention subject matter to computer programs)

③ Berne Convention → WCT

Art. 1 (2) WCT (obligations in Berne Convention continue to persist for countries which become Contracting Parties to WCT)

Art. 1 (4) WCT (compliance with Art. 1 to 21 Berne Convention and Appendix)

Art. 3 WCT (implementing Art. 2 to 6 Berne Convention)

④ WCT → Berne Convention

Art. 4 WCT (extending Berne Convention subject matter to computer programs)

⑤ Berne Convention → Marrakesh Treaty

Art. 1 Marrakesh Treaty (obligations and rights in Berne Convention continue to persist for countries which become Contracting Parties to Marrakesh Treaty)

⑥ Berne Convention → WPPT

Art. 16 (1) WPPT (referring to limitations and exceptions of Berne Convention with regard to the protection of performers and producers of phonograms)

Art. 22 (1) WPPT (applying Art 18 Berne Convention to performances and phonograms)

⑦ WPPT - - -> Berne Convention

Art. 1 (2) WPPT (WPPT affects in no way the protection of copyright in literary and artistic works)

⑧ Berne Convention - - - Rome Convention

Art. 1 Rome Convention (Rome Convention affects in no way the protection of copyright in literary and artistic works)

⑨ Berne Convention - - - Beijing Treaty

Art. 1 (2) Beijing Treaty (Beijing Treaty affects in no way the protection of copyright in literary and artistic works)

⑩ Rome Convention → WPPT

Art. 1 (1) WPPT (obligations in Rome Convention continue to persist for countries which become Contracting Parties to WPPT)

Art. 3 (2) WPPT (referring to points of attachment of Rome Convention)

⑪ WPPT → Beijing Treaty

Art. 1 (1) Beijing Treaty (obligations in WPPT continue to persist for countries which become Contracting Parties to Beijing Treaty)

⑫ Rome Convention → TRIPS

Art. 1.3 TRIPS (referring to points of attachment of Rome Convention for the rights granted to performers, producers of phonograms and broadcasting organizations)

Art. 2.2 TRIPS (obligations in Rome Convention continue to persist for countries which become Contracting Parties to TRIPs)

Art. 3 TRIPS (limiting national treatment of TRIPs in respect of exceptions in Rome Convention)

Art. 4 (b) TRIPS (limiting most-favoured-nation treatment of TRIPs in respect of reciprocity in Rome Convention)

Art. 14.6 TRIPS (allowing to limit Art. 14.1-3 TRIPs to the extent permitted by Rome Convention)

⑬ WCT → Marrakesh Treaty

Art. 1 Marrakesh Treaty (obligations and rights in WCT continue to persist for countries which become Contracting Parties to Marrakesh Treaty)

⑭ TRIPS → Marrakesh Treaty

Art. 1 Marrakesh Treaty (obligations and rights in TRIPS continue to persist for countries which become Contracting Parties to Marrakesh Treaty)

Figure 1.2 Relationship of the most important treaties

to respond to violations of existing trade agreements and any other "act, policy, or practice [that] is unjustifiable and burdens or restricts United States commerce."[5] The USTR also had the discretion to respond to "an act, policy, or practice" that was "unreasonable or discriminatory and burdens or restricts United States commerce."[6] Authorized responses included suspending U.S. trade agreements with the offending country, imposing duties or import restrictions, and "enter[ing] into binding agreements" with the offending country.[7]

Section 182 of the 1988 Act requires the USTR to publish an annual "Special 301" report identifying "those countries that deny adequate and effective protection for IPR [intellectual property rights] or deny fair and equitable market access for persons that rely on IPR protection." The Report includes a "Watch List," and placement on the list "indicates that particular problems exist in that country with respect to IPR protection, enforcement, or market access for persons relying on IPR. Countries placed on the 'Priority Watch List' are the focus of increased bilateral attention concerning the problem areas."[8]

As intellectual property protection became a priority, the USTR increasingly initiated Section 301 proceedings without a petition from private parties.[9] The U.S. therefore used the threat of retaliation to motivate trade partners toward negotiated bilateral agreements. In the early days of renewed enthusiasm over bilateral agreements, Section 301 action produced bilateral trade agreements with Korea, Brazil, and eventually Japan.[10]

Aside from enhancements to the Section 301 process, the Trade Act of 1988 also set out four specific negotiating objectives for intellectual property. First, the Act called generally for adequate protection and enforcement by foreign countries. Second, it required the pursuit of three priorities in ongoing GATT negotiations: substantive standards providing "adequate" international protection, effective enforcement mechanisms, and effective dispute resolution procedures that would improve on existing GATT procedures. Finally, the Act also called for stronger standards of protection and enforcement in existing international conventions administered by other organizations.

---

5 19 U.S.C.A. § 2411(a)(1)(B).

6 19 U.S.C.A. § 2411(b). One definition provides that an act or policy is "unreasonable" if it "denies fair and equitable provision of adequate and effective protection of intellectual property rights." 19 U.S.C.A. § 2411(d).

7 19 U.S.C.A. § 2411(c).

8 DEMETRIOS MARANTIS, OFFICE OF THE UNITED STATES TRADE REPRESENTATIVE, 2013 SPECIAL 301 REPORT 58 (2013).

9 *See* Carlson, *supra* note 1.

10 Id. at 107–8.

The bilateral trade agreements of the U.S. can be divided into first-generation trade agreements, which came before the conclusion of TRIPS, and second-generation trade agreements, which came after TRIPS, the WPPT, and WCT. These second-generation trade agreements are still being formed.[11]

ii. First-generation agreements

The first generation of bilateral agreements had many features in common, typically containing substantive provisions similar to TRIPS and NAFTA.[12] Agreements often called for adherence to the substantive standards of existing international conventions, especially the Rome and Berne Conventions but also the Geneva, Brussels, and Paris Conventions. Works protected covered literary and artistic works (including computer programs), as well as data collections, phonograms, and others. Substantive rights included rights of rental (for computer programs), importation, initial public distribution, and public communication. Other provisions allowed for the assignment or transfer of these rights to individuals or corporations.

iii. Second-generation agreements

By the late 1990s, several developments had considerably altered the international copyright landscape. The TRIPS Agreement was concluded in 1994, and the WIPO Copyright Treaty and Performances and Phonograms Treaty were signed in 1996. Furthermore, the U.S. had emerged from the collapse of the Soviet Union as the sole world superpower. The U.S. used its position of power to pursue heightened levels of protection with individual countries, sometimes to the detriment of state sovereignty interests.[13] On the other hand, article 4 of the TRIPS Agreements would extend to other WTO members any extra protection given to the U.S. through bilateral agreements.[14] As one of the authors has indicated, "the move toward bilateralism must have implications

---

11 LEWINSKI, *supra* note 1 at ¶ 12.17–12.20.

12 Id. at ¶ 12.15. The North American Free Trade Agreement (NAFTA) between Mexico, the US, and Canada entered into force in 1994. *See* INTERNATIONAL TRADE ADMINISTRATION, U.S. DEPARTMENT OF COMMERCE, TOP U.S. EXPORT MARKETS: FREE TRADE AGREEMENT AND COUNTRY FACT SHEETS 26 (2008). The intellectual property provisions, contained in NAFTA Chapter 17, took a preliminary draft of TRIPS as their starting point. *See* Martin D.H. Woodward, *TRIPS and NAFTA's Chapter 17: How Will Trade-Related Multilateral Agreements Affect International Copyright?*, 31 TEX. INT'L L.J. 269, 273 (1996). The two agreements are therefore "analogous in substance and character" with respect to intellectual property rights. *Id.*

13 LEWINSKI, *supra* note 1, at 12.08; RICKETSON & GINSBURG, *supra* note 3, at ¶ 4.55.

14 RICKETSON & GINSBURG, *supra* note 3, at ¶ 4.55.

for the multilateral system as the bilateral agreements come to contain stipulations that reflect the domestic standards of the hyperpower."[15]

Second-generation agreements fall into three categories:

a. Trade and Investment Framework Agreements (TIFAs)

United States Trade Representative, Trade & Investment Framework Agreements   http://www.ustr.gov/trade-agreements/trade-investment-framework-agreements:

> Trade and Investment Framework Agreements . . . provide strategic frameworks and principles for dialogue on trade and investment issues between the United States and the other parties to the TIFA.

> Although the names of Framework Agreements may vary, e.g., the Trade, Investment, and Development Agreement (TIDCA) with the South African Customs Union, or the United States-Icelandic Forum, these agreements all serve as a forum for the United States and other governments to meet and discuss issues of mutual interest with the objective of improving cooperation and enhancing opportunities for trade and investment. . . . Topics for consultation and possible further cooperation include market access issues, labor, the environment, protection and enforcement of intellectual property rights, and, in appropriate cases, capacity building.

The terms of a TIFA are usually quite general. The U.S.-Oman TIFA simply recognizes "the importance of providing adequate and effective protection and enforcement of intellectual property rights and of membership in and adherence to intellectual property rights conventions."[16] The agreement goes to recognize mutual trade objectives of the parties and establish a joint Council on Trade and Investment, to meet once a year to discuss relevant trade issues.[17]

b. Bilateral Investment Treaties (BITs)

Media Note, United States Concludes Review of Model Bilateral Investment Treaty, www.state.gov (Apr. 20, 2012), http://www.state.gov/r/pa/prs/ps/2012/04/188198.htm (announcing the completion of the 2012 Model BIT):

---

15 Id.
16 Concerning the Development of Trade and Investment Relations rec. 12, U.S.-Oman, July 7, 2004, available at www.ustr.gov/sites/default/files/US-Oman%20TIFA.pdf.
17 Id. at art. 2.

A BIT is an international agreement that provides binding legal rules regarding one country's treatment of investors from another country. The United States negotiates BITs on the basis of a high-standard "model" text that provides investors with improved market access; protection from discriminatory, expropriatory, or otherwise harmful government treatment; and a mechanism to pursue binding international arbitration for breaches of the treaty. High-standard BITs, such as those based on the US model, improve investment climates, promote market-based economic reform, and strengthen the rule of law. The United States has more than 40 BITs in force with countries around the world, and the investment chapters of US free trade agreements (FTAs) contain substantially similar rules and protections. USTR and the Department of State co-lead the US BIT program.

The Model treaty defines "investment" to include intellectual property rights and aims to achieve national or most-favored-nation treatment.[18] As the use of a 42-page model agreement might suggest, some see BITs as a way for the U.S. unduly to impose its interests on other countries.[19]

c. Post 1995 Free Trade Agreements (FTAs)

Free Trade Agreements often contain the most detailed intellectual property rights provisions. According to the Council on Foreign Relations, "[f]ree trade agreements, many of which are bilateral, are arrangements in which countries give each other preferential treatment in trade, [perhaps by] eliminating tariffs and other barriers on goods."[20] The U.S. uses FTAs to pursue levels of protection that exceed existing multilateral agreements like WCT, WPPT, and TRIPS[21] Often they require accession to the Brussels Convention, the WCT, and the WPPT. Other common features include "non-derogation in respect of any or specified international legal obligations between the parties; application in time ... ; transparency obligations in respect of the implementing [instruments] ... that have to be in writing and published; and general national treatment clauses."[22]

Beyond requiring adherence to specific multilateral agreements, FTAs often contain specific provisions covering copyright in language similar to these

---

18 LEWINSKI, *supra* note 1, ¶ 12.18.

19 Id. at ¶ 12.19.

20 Robert McMahon, *The Rise in Bilateral Free Trade Agreements*, COUNCIL ON FOREIGN RELATIONS (June 13, 2006), http://www.cfr.org/trade/rise-bilateral-free-trade-agreements/p10890.

21 LEWINSKI, *supra* note 1, ¶ 12.26.

22 Id. at ¶ 12.28.

agreements or to U.S. law. The example of the U.S. FTA with Australia, a seasoned Berne member, is striking. As one editor has elsewhere noted: "the provisions with respect to copyright and neighboring rights were extraordinarily detailed, and sought to reflect in Australian law the detailed requirements of U.S. law, notable with respect to the term of protection, circumvention measures, copyright management information, temporary reproductions, and safe harbors for internet service providers."[23] The U.S. often transplants its own copyright standards by way of bilateral agreements, achieving a level of protection that was unattainable through TRIPS negotiations.[24]

E.U.

At around the same time the U.S. was initiating bilateral agreements covering intellectual property, the E.U. was doing the same. A 1988 E.U. Green Paper emphasized the "absence of adequate substantive standards protecting intellectual property, [and] the lack of effective enforcement where such standards exist."[25] The subsequent collapse of the Soviet Union also had implications for the E.U., as it sought to establish bilateral relations with potential candidates for accession in Eastern and Central Europe.

The E.U. negotiates three general types of agreements with non-E.U. countries: (1) association agreements aimed toward E.U. accession; (2) free trade associations; and (3) development associations. Each of these typically includes "rules on free trade, rules of origin, free movement of persons, and even rules prohibiting discrimination of nationals of the other party in certain situations."[26]

Like the U.S. FTAs, the E.U. concluded bilateral agreements aimed toward E.U. accession in two successive generations. The first generation, concluded between 1989 and 1991, focused on newly independent countries of Central and Eastern Europe.[27] The parties tailored the intellectual property provisions of these agreements according to the economic and political needs of the transitioning countries.[28] As such, their provisions simply established minimal protection and expressed a commitment to future cooperation.

---

23 RICKETSON & GINSBURG, *supra* note 3, ¶ 4.54.
24 See LEWINSKI, supra note 1, ¶ 12.34–12.35.
25 Id. at ¶ 12.43.
26 Id. at 12.45–12.47.
27 Id. at 12.44.
28 Id. at 12.48.

The E.U. concluded the second generation of bilateral agreements after 1992. They served as a preliminary step to accession agreements, or "Europe Agreements," and included more demanding intellectual property provisions than first-generation agreements.[29]

Europe Agreements "were considered the last step before accession to the E.U."[30] They covered a wide range of trade topics, and required intellectual property protection commensurate with E.U. standards, both in recognition and enforcement. The agreements also required adherence to certain international conventions within a specified time frame.

The E.U. also concluded stabilization and association agreements (SAAs) to promote "political stabilization, economic prosperity, and peace for the entire region."[31] SAAs may include intellectual property provisions, including an obligation to ensure "adequate and effective protection and enforcement," most-favored-nation treatment, and a level of protection "similar to that existing in the Community" within five years of entry into force of the agreement.[32] Finally, the agreements may require adherence to specific multilateral conventions, including Berne, Geneva, WCT, WPPT, Rome, and others, within the same five-year period.[33]

The E.U. is currently negotiating FTAs with several countries, including the U.S., Japan, Canada, seven other countries and two regional partnerships (including the Transatlantic Trade and Investment Partnership).[34] In these negotiations, the E.U. "aim[s] to include comprehensive IPR chapters. The IPR chapters should as far as possible offer similar levels of IPR protection to that existing in the E.U., the E.U. also aims to take into account the level of development of the countries concerned."[35]

---

29 Id. at 12.49–12.50.

30 Id.

31 Id. at 12.52.

32 Stabilization Association Agreement, E.U.-Montenegro, May 1, 2010, available at http://eur-lex.europa.eu/LexUriServ/LexUriServ.do?uri=OJ:L:2010:108:0001:0354:EN:PDF.

33 Id.

34 European Commission, Memo, The E.U.'s bilateral trade and investment agreements – where are we? (Aug. 2013).

35 European Commission, *Intellectual Property*, ec.europa.eu (last visited Nov. 8, 2013) http://ec.europa.eu/trade/policy/accessing-markets/intellectual-property/.

Other countries

Other countries have brought intellectual property rights within the purview of bilateral agreements as well. Some of these agreements are formed by single countries seeking to enhance trade relations with common partners, while others are formed by regional associations with third-party states. Like the FTAs of the E.U. and the U.S., these agreements appeared in growing numbers in the mid 1990s.[36]

The European Free Trade Association has 25 FTAs with 35 countries.[37] These agreements often include intellectual property provisions, calling for national treatment and most-favored-nation status. Several Latin American countries also maintain bilateral agreements covering intellectual property. Similar to the U.S. BITs, these agreements include intellectual property among other investment provisions. Intellectual property protection guarantees national treatment, most-favored-nation treatment, and "adequate and effective protection and enforcement of intellectual property rights."[38] Other provisions might be based on the NAFTA intellectual property obligations.[39]

The Trans-Pacific Strategic Economic Partnership Agreement between Singapore, New Zealand, Brunei and Chile includes intellectual property protection, but its copyright provisions cover rights of reproduction and distribution only by reference to the WCT and WPPT and rights of performers by reference to TRIPS.[40] That agreement may be most significant as a starting point for the current multilateral negotiations toward a "Trans-Pacific Partnership" that will encompass many more countries, including Australia, Canada, and the U.S. Australia and New Zealand have concluded bilateral agreements covering intellectual property. Finally, Japan has concluded several bilateral agreements that cover intellectual property rights among other investment issues. The copyright and related rights provisions include a making available right, modeled on Article 8 of the WCT, as well as technological anti-circumvention measures and ISP safe-harbors modeled on the WCT and WPPT. Enforcement provisions are similar to TRIPS but less detailed.[41]

---

36 LEWINSKI, *supra* note 1, at ¶ 12.61.
37 Free Trade Agreements, WWW.EFTA.INT (last visited June 26, 2014) http://www.efta.int/free-trade/free-trade-agreements. The EFTA now has only four member states.
38 LEWINSKI, *supra* note 1, at 12.63–12.64.
39 Id.
40 Id. at 12.67.
41 Id.

Conclusion

As von Lewinski indicates, U.S. FTAs are more detailed and demanding than non-U.S. FTAs, and they generally seek protection that mirrors U.S. copyright standards.[42] Non-U.S. parties establish more flexible FTAs, especially when the parties include developing countries.[43] Bilateral agreements generally incorporate established standards of protection by reference to existing multilateral agreements. In the most general and least contentious terms, bilateral trade agreements have again found a place in the universe of international copyright protection because they allow parties to tailor the level of protection according to their needs and capabilities, an advantage usually not afforded in the multilateral context. Put more tendentiously, bilateral trade agreements allow the stronger trading partner to impose a higher level of protection than the multilateral treaties require, and therefore offer the stronger parties a more appealing, if perhaps one-sided, route to international coverage.[44]

1.5 Basic legal institutions and copyright principles in the U.S. and E.U.

1.5.1 U.S.

Legal institutions

The U.S. has a federal system of government. The U.S. Constitution delegates specific powers, including over copyright and intellectual property, to the national government. The federal government consists of the Congress (Senate and House of Representatives), President, Supreme Court, lower federal courts, and administrative agencies. Powers not delegated to the national government remain with the states, each of which has its own state constitution, legislature, judiciary, and executive branch.

---

42 *See* 19 U.S.C.A. 3802(b)(4)(A)(i)(II) ("The principal negotiating objectives of the United States regarding trade-related intellectual property are— . . . (II) ensuring that the provisions of any multilateral or bilateral trade agreement governing intellectual property rights that is entered into by the United States reflect a standard of protection similar to that found in United States law.")

43 LEWINSKI, *supra* note 1, at 12.77.

44 *See* RICKETSON & GINSBURG, *supra* note 3, at 4.53–4.55:

> Inevitably, Australian copyright law will come to mirror that of US copyright law—an excellent result, no doubt, for US copyright owners, but possibly to the impoverishment of Australian domestic lawmaking and policy. More generally, the move towards bilateralism must have implications for the multilateral system as the bilateral agreements come to contain stipulations that reflect the domestic standards of the hyperpower.

Federal courts have subject-matter jurisdiction over three main types of cases: interpretation of federal law, including copyright law (so-called federal question jurisdiction; with respect to copyright law, the federal courts have exclusive jurisdiction); disputes between states or citizens of different states, including foreign governments (so-called diversity jurisdiction); and disputes involving the U.S. as a party. In the first instance, disputes within federal jurisdiction are adjudicated by U.S. district courts. There are 94 federal district courts throughout the U.S. At least one district court is located in each state. Each case is assigned to one judge, who issues a final decision.

Under the U.S. Constitution, parties have a right to trial by jury in all criminal and most civil cases. Juries typically consist of panels of 12 citizens, who determine facts based on the evidence presented at trial and apply the law as determined by the judge to reach a decision. Actual trials, however, are relatively rare, as most legal disputes are resolved by the judge based on the written pleadings (such as motions to dismiss or motions for summary judgment) or settled by the parties themselves.

Final judgments of district courts can be appealed as a matter of right to the U.S. court of appeals of the particular circuit in which the district court sits. There are 13 such circuits. For instance, the U.S. Courts of Appeals for the Second Circuit hears cases from district courts located in New York, Connecticut, and Vermont. One court of appeals, for the Federal Circuit, has jurisdiction based wholly on the subject matter rather than geography, including over patent and trademark (but not copyright) disputes. Each case on appeal is initially assigned to a panel of three judges, who issue a final decision. Under unusual circumstances, such as a split among panels or when a legal question is particularly important, cases may then be heard by the full court of appeals in an *en banc* procedure.

Final judgments of appellate courts can be petitioned for review to the Supreme Court, which has discretion whether to accept a case. The Court receives approximately 10,000 such petitions for a writ of certiorari and hears approximately 100 cases per year.

As of 2007, Congress had authorized 678 district court judgeships and 179 court of appeals judgeships. There are also nine Justices on the Supreme Court. Federal judges and justices are nominated by the President and confirmed by the Senate, and generally serve life terms. Although judges and justices technically may be removed from office through impeachment proceedings (involving an indictment by the House of Representatives and conviction by the Senate), in practice only a few judges have been impeached and those removed were found to have committed high crimes and misdemeanors. This tradition lasting over 200 years ensures that federal judges can exercise independent judgment without external control or interference.

Legislation and regulation

Under Article 1, Section 1 of the U.S. Constitution, "all legislative Powers herein granted shall be vested in a Congress of the United States." Congressional power includes legislation over matters such as national security, foreign and interstate commerce, and taxation. In particular, it includes power "[t]o promote the Progress of Science and useful Arts, by securing for limited Times to Authors and Inventors the exclusive Right to their respective Writings and Discoveries." It also includes the broadly worded grant to "make all Laws which shall be necessary and proper for carrying into Execution the foregoing Powers." All legislative bills must be passed by majority vote both in the House and Senate, and be signed by the President, in order to become law.

Under Article VI, the U.S. Constitution, federal legislation, and U.S. treaties are made supreme over state constitutions and legislation:

> This Constitution, and the laws of the United States which shall be made in pursuance thereof; and all treaties made, or which shall be made, under the authority of the United States, shall be the supreme law of the land; and the judges in every state shall be bound thereby, anything in the Constitution or laws of any State to the contrary notwithstanding.

U.S. treaties can be enforced directly in U.S. courts if they are self-executing and do not require implementing legislation. However, most U.S. treaties have been interpreted by U.S. courts to be non-self-executing and require further Congressional action before they can be enforced judicially. Treaties are signed by the President and ratified by a two-thirds majority of the Senate. Congressional-executive agreements, signed by the President and ratified by a majority of each Congressional chamber, are interchangeable with treaties as a matter of U.S. and international law and are equivalent to federal statutes as a matter of U.S. law.

In addition to legislation, a significant amount of rule-making in the U.S. is provided through regulation by administrative agencies. Established by federal statute, agencies are staffed with technical experts to address specific regulatory problems, such as anti-competitive trade practices, environmental issues, or financial securities. Administrative agencies promulgate more detailed rule-making for policy problems that are too complex or variable to be addressed by Congressional legislation. They will also often have adjudicatory proceedings that are substantially indistinct from court proceedings from the perspective of the involved parties. The rule-making and adjudication process is governed by the Administrative Procedure Act and can be challenged in federal court.

Overview of U.S. copyright law

The U.S. Constitution establishes Congress's power to enact copyright laws. Article I, Section 8, clause 8 provides: "The Congress shall have power . . . To promote the progress of science and useful arts, by securing for limited times to authors and inventors the exclusive right to their respective writings and discoveries." This provision is both a source of and a limitation on Congress's power to enact copyright and patent statutes. It recognizes both the general public interest in fostering creativity, and the individual rights of creators—for limited times—over the fruits of their intellectual labors. The Framers perceived, as James Madison urged in Federalist 43, that:

> The utility of this power will scarcely be questioned. The copyright of authors has been solemnly adjudged, in Great Britain, to be a right of common law. The right to useful inventions seems with equal reason to belong to the inventors. The public good fully coincides in both cases with the claims of individuals. The States cannot separately make effectual provision for either of the cases, and most of them have anticipated the decision of this point, by laws passed at the instance of Congress.

From the outset, the founders of the U.S. recognized that works of authorship were destined to traverse the boundaries of the several states, and thus required uniform regulation throughout the Republic.

Further examination of the copyright clause yields themes that recur throughout U.S. copyright law. Every component of the clause raises fundamental questions. For example, does the preambular phrase "to promote the progress of science" state a general aspiration for a copyright system, or does it constrain Congress' power by authorizing only laws which result in the advancement of learning? How would a court judge what kinds of legislative measures are consistent with that objective? Must Congress' measures provide incentives to create new works? To disseminate works, new or old? If the aim to progress does not generally cabin the content of copyright laws, is that goal relevant to the determination whether any particular author, work or category of work may enjoy a copyright? (Are assessments whether copyright afforded an incentive to creation, or whether a work promotes knowledge any less elusive when applied to individual authors or works rather than to the copyright system as a whole?) Does the promotion of progress play a role in the evaluation of defenses to copyright infringement? Does the promotion of progress furnish the sole rationale for copyright protection in the U.S.? If not the only justification, is it the dominant one?

Pursuing the inquiry past the preamble, what does "limited times" mean? The phrase appears to envision a public domain free of proprietary claims, but how "limited" in time is the period of proprietorship, and how immutable is the public domain? The clause empowers Congress to "secur[e]" authors' exclusive rights; does the term imply the reinforcement of a pre-existing right? Did the Framers thus assume the existence of an author's natural property right in the fruits of his intellectual labor? And who is an "author?" The work's human creator? The person or entity who hired the human creator? The person or entity who purchased or operated the machine or device that generated the work? The rights Congress has power to secure are "exclusive;" does Congress therefore lack power to substitute in whole or in part a system of remuneration which would compensate authors but deny them the control over their works that exclusive rights afford? Finally, what is a "writing?" Does the term imply that the work must exist in some material form before a federal copyright law may cover it? Does the term exclude certain kinds of works from the subject matter of copyright? Does the term, standing alone or in conjunction with "authors," imply any threshold of creativity, quality or purpose to the work?

Robert A. Gorman, Jane C. Ginsburg and R. Anthony Reese, Copyright: Cases and Materials (8th Ed. Foundation Press 2011) (pages 38-49)*

1. NATURE OF COPYRIGHT

A copyright is essentially a set of exclusive rights in literary, musical, choreographic, dramatic and artistic works. The rights under copyright pertain to the reproduction, adaptation, public distribution, and public display or performance of the work. The copyright owner's exclusive rights, however, are limited in several important respects. There are three basic limitations:

(a)   Because a copyright protects only against copying (or paraphrasing or "colorable alterations" of) the copyrighted work, a copyright does not

---

* Reprinted with permission of West Academic.

prohibit another author from independently producing the same or a similar work. (Thus, to use a familiar simian example, if one hundred monkeys sat down at one hundred typewriters, and one of them eventually produced Hamlet, this remarkable result could not be copyright infringement.)

(b) Anyone may copy the ideas from a copyrighted work; copyright protects only the particular expression of ideas. Frequently, however, this "idea/expression dichotomy" is easier to state than to apply. . . . For the moment, an example may suffice to illustrate the difference. The idea that remorse may overwhelm the subconscious is not protectible; Lady Macbeth's sleepwalking scene is a particular expression of that idea, and would be subject to protection, were Shakespeare's works not already in the public domain (i.e., any copyrights in such works have expired).

(c) A copyright extends neither to systems explained in a work, nor to discrete facts contained within a work. Like the idea/expression dichotomy, the distinction between facts and their expression can be elusive. By way of example, consider the copyrightability of this Overview. The overall presentation of the topic and the specific words chosen would be protectible, but the facts the reader learns are not. Thus there is no copyright protection for the fact that the Copyright Act covers choreographic works, even though the reader may have ascertained this only by perusing this discussion.

2.   SUBJECT MATTER OF COPYRIGHT

Copyright is available for "original works of authorship fixed in any tangible medium of expression, now known or later developed from which they can be perceived, reproduced or otherwise communicated, either directly or with the aid of a machine or device." 17 U.S.C.A. § 102(a). This formulation includes several ingredients. First, in accordance with the provision in art. I, sec. 8, cl. 8 of the Constitution, which grants authors the exclusive right to their "writings," fixation in a tangible medium is a prerequisite. For example, an extemporaneous speech or a completely improvised dramatic or musical work would not be within the subject matter of copyright. It should be noted, however, that, under its Commerce Clause authority, Congress has granted performing artists the right to control the fixation, live transmission and distribution of their live musical performances. See 17 U.S.C.A. § 1101. Moreover, such creations might be protected under other legal theories, such as "common-law copyright," "unfair competition," or "right of publicity."

In addition to being "fixed," a protected work must reflect "originality" and "authorship." These requirements also follow the constitutional provision for protection for the "writings" of "authors." The legislative history of the 1976 Copyright Act makes clear that the standards for satisfying these requirements are intended to be pretty much what they have been throughout the years. These standards have not been high. An author need not have made an objective contribution to society. (Such a contribution would be required of an inventor in order to earn a patent.) Similarly, an author need not produce a work of recognized intellectual or artistic merit. It suffices if the author refrains from copying from prior works and contributes at least more than a minimal amount of creativity. Courts have often stated that neither judges nor administrators may appropriately act as the arbiters of merit. Rather, a system of protection will promote knowledge even if particular works do not.

Although works copied from other works do not qualify for protection, many works are consciously based on earlier works. They may incorporate part of the earlier work but significantly add to it. Examples would be translations, revisions, or adaptations. These are called "derivative works." They can be protected, but only to the extent of the new material that is added. The same principle applies to a "compilation," which is defined as "a work formed by the collection and assembling of preexisting materials or of data that are selected, coordinated, or arranged in such a way that the resulting work as a whole constitutes an original work of authorship." Thus a compilation ranges from a collection of unadorned facts, such as the names and addresses in a college alumni directory, to subjective listings, such as a food critic's choice of the ten best restaurants in New York City, to highly elaborated works, such as an anthology of poetry with accompanying critical essays. It would also include, in this electronic era, computerized databases. Copyright protection for the compilation extends only to the material newly contributed by the compiler, particularly the selection and arrangement of the component elements; it will not, for example in the last illustration, affect the copyright status—or the public-domain status—of the poetry incorporated in the compilation.

3. DURATION, OWNERSHIP, AND FORMALITIES

a. DURATION OF COPYRIGHT

When copyright protection begins and ends depends on when the work was created. As to works created today or in the future, copyright attaches automatically as soon as the work is put down on paper, tape, computer memory, digital disk, or some other tangible medium. 17 U.S.C.A. § 102(a). Its duration depends on whether its author was one individual; more than one individual;

or someone creating the work in the employ of or at the direction of some other person or organization. The last situation may result in a so-called "work made for hire." To take, at this time, only the example of a literary, musical or artistic work created by an individual after January 1, 1978, copyright lasts for a period of 70 years from the death of the author. This contrasts with the two-term format that has characterized our copyright law since its beginnings and that was in place under the 1909 Act—an initial term of 28 years, starting typically with the work's publication with copyright notice, followed by a 28-year renewal term if timely application were made to the Copyright Office.

The period of copyright protection for a work that was created before the present law became effective on January 1, 1978, depends on a number of factors: whether it was "published" (a term of art that was elaborated under the prior statutes) and whether it was on January 1, 1978 protected in its initial or renewal term of copyright under the 1909 Act. . . . Unpublished works (e.g., manuscripts and personal letters) are protected until 70 years after the author's death. For any unpublished work whose term under the 1976 Act would have expired before the end of 2002, Congress provided a grace period to encourage these works' publication: if the work was published before the end of 2002, it would be protected through the end of 2047. Any such work not published before 2003 is now in the public domain. Works published before 1923 are in the public domain. A further complication pertains to sound recordings fixed before February 15, 1972 (the effective date of the amendment bringing sound recordings within the scope of federal copyright). These continue to be protected by state law until February 15, 2067. Whether a given pre-1972 sound recording is in fact protected today will depend on the particular state's common law or statute. See, e.g., *Capitol Records v. Naxos of America*, 4 N.Y.3d 540 (2005) (holding published sound recording whose term expired in its country of origin—the U.K.—to be protected in New York until federal cutoff date of 2067).

b.   OWNERSHIP

The Copyright Act gives initial copyright ownership to the author (or authors who jointly create a work). 17 U.S.C.A. § 201(a). In the case of "works made for hire"—a work prepared by an employee within the scope of his employment and certain works commissioned from independent contractors—the employer is considered the author. As "intangible property," a copyright can be transferred from the author to another, inter vivos or by will or by intestate succession, in whole or in part. To be an effective transfer, a grant of "exclusive" rights must be in writing and signed by the grantor; a "non-exclusive" grant may be valid even though oral. The grant may cover the entire scope of copyright, or be limited to a particular time period or territory (e.g., a one-year license to perform a copyrighted play in New York City) or medium of expression (e.g., only the right to print a novel but not the right to serialize it in a magazine or prepare a screenplay based on it). A grant need not be recorded in the U.S. Copyright Office, but there are significant advantages in doing so.

In addition to the considerable flexibility afforded the copyright owner to subdivide his or her copyright and otherwise exploit it, the 1976 Act confers a special protective privilege on author-transferors and their families. Because of the highly speculative value of literary, artistic and musical works—at least shortly after they are created—an author who grants an interest in a copyright, after January 1, 1978, may terminate that grant, upon complying with certain procedures, effective 35 years after the grant was made. (There is also a termination right with respect to a certain narrow category of copyright transfers made prior to January 1, 1978.) This termination option cannot be contracted away or waived in advance.

Finally, one should note the distinction between ownership of a copyright, or of any of the exclusive rights under a copyright, and ownership of "any material object in which the work is embodied." Suppose an artist paints a work, and sells the finished canvas. Unless the artist has made specific provision otherwise, he or she retains all exploitation rights in the work. Thus the artist would have the sole right to create postcards—a derivative work—based on the painting. But the artist cannot prevent the buyer from selling, renting, or making certain public displays (for example, in an art gallery) of the physical object—the canvas—which the buyer now owns. See 17 U.S.C.A. §§ 109, 202.

c.   NOTICE AND REGISTRATION OF COPYRIGHT

The role of the copyright notice has been sharply reduced since U.S. adherence to the Berne Convention, which, with respect to foreign works, forbids conditioning the enjoyment of copyright upon compliance with formalities. Nonetheless, because adherence does not affect the status of works published before the effective date of the ratification, familiarity with pre-Berne notice requirements remains important. These requirements, in turn, differ depending on whether the work is governed by the 1976 Act or by its predecessor the 1909 Act.

Before January 1, 1978, in order to enjoy a copyright, published works had to bear a copyright notice, which would follow a prescribed form. If the notice was not properly affixed upon publication, the work went into the public domain. These rules remain important even after 1978 if a pre–1978 U.S. work is at issue.

The 1976 Act liberalized the notice rules for works published on or after January 1, 1978. As originally written, the 1976 Act continued to prescribe the use of a copyright notice on all copies and phonorecords publicly distributed (anywhere in the world) under authority of the copyright owner. The notice consisted of the three familiar elements—a copyright word or symbol, the name of the copyright owner, and the year of first publication. But the formal requirements were made more flexible, both with respect to location of the notice and the consequences of error in, or total lack of, notice.

Subsequently, after 200 years of requiring some form of notice as a condition of a valid copyright, our law was changed effective March 1, 1989. Notice is no longer necessary on copies and phonorecords publicly distributed after that date. Nonetheless, copyright notice continues to be routinely used; there are modest statutory incentives to do so, and in any event the notice is an effective and inexpensive way for the copyright owner to call its claim to the attention of potential users.

A common misunderstanding is that registration with the Copyright Office is a condition to a valid copyright. In fact, registration of claims to copyright is optional. But the advantages of registration are very significant. Among other things, it is generally a prerequisite to an action for infringement; and it provides a number of advantages in proving a case and securing remedies. See 17 U.S.C.A. §§ 408–12. Accordingly, it is most advisable to register promptly in the case of any work of significance. The registration procedure is relatively simple. A short application form states the required information regarding authorship, year in which the work was created, and the like—and is to be accompanied by deposit of one or two copies of the work (as prescribed by regulation) and a $45 fee. The Copyright Office examines the application and deposit copies to see that they are generally in proper form. The Office does not compare the deposit copies to earlier material or judge their worth.

4. SCOPE OF EXCLUSIVE RIGHTS UNDER COPYRIGHT

a. EXCLUSIVE RIGHTS

Among the exclusive rights comprised within a copyright, the reproduction right, or right to produce copies, is the most basic of all. The right protects against copying in any medium, including within the temporary memory of a computer. The right also protects against paraphrasing. But the right prohibits only actual use of the copyright owner's work as a model, either directly or indirectly; it does not cover coincidental similarities in a work created independently and without reference to the first. Moreover, the second author must have copied protected material. As explained earlier, a second author may freely copy a copyrighted work's ideas and discrete facts, so long as he or she does not also copy the expression or particular manner in which the first author set forth these ideas and facts. In addition, to violate the exclusive right of reproduction, the second author's copying must be "substantial." No set rule or formula can determine when the defendant's copying has been substantial; even a small extract from a larger work may be found to infringe, depending on the nature of the copyrighted work and of the portion copied.

The adaptation right, or right to make derivative works, overlaps somewhat with the reproduction right. Thus, a poster containing a photograph of a copyrighted painting is in a sense a "copy." But, whether or not a translation or a motion picture version of a copyrighted novel is comfortably thought of as a "copy," they too will infringe if unauthorized—for they are "derivative works." A derivative work "is a work based upon one or more pre-existing works," and includes "any . . . form in which a work may be recast, transformed, or adapted."

The copyright owner also has the exclusive right to distribute the work to the public "by sale or other transfer of ownership, or by rental, lease, or lending." The distribution right covers both traditional hard copies and digital copies, including those disseminated over digital networks, such as the Internet. The right clearly prohibits sales of unlawfully produced copies of a work. Whether the right also protects the copyright owner against sale of licensed copies at a time or place or under circumstances that the copyright owner did not authorize depends principally on whether the accused act was the first or a subsequent distribution of the copy involved. The copyright owner has the right to control only the first public distribution of a particular copy of the work, whether by rental or sale. After first distribution, it is not infringement (although it may be breach of contract) for the owner of particular copies within the U.S. to rent or sell them without authority of the copyright owner. An important exception to this so-called "first sale doctrine" is the unauthorized rental for profit of phonograph records or computer programs—even though those records or programs were lawfully manufactured and lawfully purchased by the commercial renter; the purpose of course is to inhibit those who would make a profit inducing retail patrons to engage in home copying.

The rights of public performance and display are of great importance to dramatic, musical, and audiovisual works. This last category includes both conventional works such as motion pictures, and works in newer media such as computer videogames. The display right also covers pictorial, graphic, and sculptural works, although the copyright proprietor may not, absent an appropriate contractual provision, prevent the owner of a particular copy (including the original) from displaying it in a museum, art gallery, or other public place.

The statute defines a public performance or display as one presented at a place open to the public or where a substantial number of persons outside of a normal circle of a family or its social acquaintances is gathered, or presented by a transmission, such as a radio or television broadcast. Thus, absent the consent of the copyright owner, reading a copyrighted lecture or poem aloud in a public auditorium, or showing a painting or sculpture on a television program (or a website computer network), will constitute respectively an infringing public performance and public display.

How can the copyright owner of, say, a popular song monitor all of the possible infringements of his or her musical work through public perform-ances in nightclubs, concert halls, and radio and television broadcasts, and Internet streaming? That is the task of the so-called performing rights societies, most notably the American Society of Composers, Authors and Publishers (ASCAP) and Broadcast Music Incorporated (BMI). These societies license the performance rights in nondramatic musical composi-tions, pursue unlicensed users, and distribute royalties to their composer, lyricist, and publisher members. Performing rights societies are the most well-established examples of collective licensing entities in the U.S.—and are serving as a model for licensing arrangements for the photocopying of books and periodicals. By representing the interests of large numbers of copyright holders, the performing rights societies are able to secure better enforcement and compensation than could individual claimants. The collective nature of the licensing also benefits users: rather than seek out individual authors, a party wishing to perform quantities of copy-righted music may obtain all the requisite authorizations from one or two sources.

Amendments introduced in 1995 and 1998 extend the public performance right to the copyright owners of sound recordings, but only with respect to digital transmissions. Thus, when a sound recording is played in a discotheque or over traditional broadcast radio, the composers of the underlying music are entitled to performance right royalties, but the performing artists and record producer are not. By contrast, if the performance derives from a digital transmission, the performance rights in the sound recording apply.

b. COPYRIGHT LITIGATION

28 U.S.C.A. § 1338(a) vests the federal courts with exclusive jurisdiction over claims that arise under the copyright (and patent) statutes. The Supreme Court of Indiana has held that in a contract action brought by a publisher against an author, in which the author files a counterclaim against the publisher for copyright infringement, a state court may hear and decide the copyright counterclaim. The court examined 28 U.S.C.A. § 1338(a), which gives exclusive jurisdiction to federal courts over copyright actions, and concluded that the case—the claim and counterclaim together—was not a "civil action arising under any Act of Congress relating to . . . copyrights." See *Green v. Hendrickson Pubs., Inc.*, 770 N.E.2d 784, 63 U.S.P.Q.2d 1852 (Ind. 2002).

A party seeking to prove the infringement of exclusive rights under copyright, and particularly of the reproduction and derivative works rights, must make out the following elements of a claim: (1) Ownership of a valid copyright (or of an exclusive right under copyright). If registration occurs within five years of first publication of the work, the certificate of registration serves as prima facie evidence of the validity of the copyright. (2) Copying of plaintiff's work by the defendant. Because copyright protects against reproduction, but not against independent generation of the same or similar work, there can be no copyright infringement unless defendant came into contact with and in fact copied plaintiff's work. Copying is ordinarily proved through circumstantial evidence: did the defendant have access to the plaintiff's work and are there similarities of expression (i.e., the sequence of words or notes) that are probative of copying rather than independent origination. The copying need not have been intentional: subconscious or unconscious copying of a work can constitute infringing copying. The kind of similarity that permits an inference of copying is called probative similarity. (3) As a result of the copying, defendant's work is substantially similar to plaintiff's. Substantial similarity may be determined with respect to either the quantity or the quality of the copying. Copying a small, but central, portion of plaintiff's original work can constitute substantial and infringing copying.

If plaintiff succeeds in the above demonstration, it has made out a prima facie case of copyright infringement. The burden now shifts to the defendant to justify its conduct, if it can, by application of a relevant statutory exception to copyright infringement (discussed immediately below).

If the copyright owner prevails, the available remedies include preliminary and permanent injunctions against further infringements, impoundment and destruction of infringing articles, and damages. Damages can either be actual, as determined by the plaintiff's actual damages and the defendant's profits, or can take the form of what is known as "statutory damages;" the latter measure, with a largely deterrent objective, is to be determined by the jury under the circumstances of the case, and typically fits within a minimum of $750 and a maximum of $30,000 for each work infringed (with a possible assessment as high as $150,000 per work where the infringement is willful). The court also has discretion to award the prevailing party its attorney's fees.

5. LIMITATIONS ON THE EXCLUSIVE RIGHTS UNDER COPYRIGHT

a. EXEMPTIONS AND COMPULSORY LICENSES

The exclusive rights of copyright proprietors to reproduce, adapt, distribute, and publicly perform and display their works encounter manifold and complicated statutory limitations. For example, the Copyright Act permits many classroom, religious, and charitable performances and displays of copyrighted works. The statute exempts most live classroom uses, including the performance of copyrighted dramatic works. Songs may be sung, and other musical compositions played, in most school settings—and also in a number of other noncommercial settings. Instructional broadcasts, including in the form of "digital distance education" over the Internet, are also exempted from copyright liability if they meet statutory requirements. The Act also provides that a public performance or display of a work through a transmission on a "home-type receiving apparatus" is not an infringement, if there is no direct charge to see or hear the transmission, and if there is no further public transmission. Essentially, this provision concerns the use by small commercial establishments of a radio to provide background music. Radio and television transmissions of music by larger establishments, using more sophisticated equipment, were exempted by Congress in a controversial 1998 amendment.

In other instances, the Act removes certain reproductions, performances, and displays from the copyright owner's exclusive control and substitutes a "compulsory licensing" scheme. These compromise provisions permit certain uses of the copyrighted work without the copyright owner's consent, but require the user to adhere to statutory formalities, and to pay specified fees to the copyright owner. The most important and longstanding example of the compulsory license—incorporated in our law since the 1909 Act—relates to making recordings of nondramatic musical works. The current statute provides that once the copyright owner of a nondramatic musical composition has authorized distribution to the public in the United States of a "phonorecord" embodying the composition, another producer may make and distribute phonorecords of the composition to the public. The compulsory licensee may not, without authorization, simply duplicate a preexisting recording; it must produce an independent sound recording with its own musical performers and arrangement. Therefore, the statute permits the compulsory licensee some leeway to arrange the music (technically, the making of a derivative work). The arranger will not, however, enjoy a copyright in her resulting derivative musical composition unless she reaches a negotiated agreement with the copyright owner of the underlying musical work.

The 1976 Act, as originally written, extended the compulsory-license format to other situations as well: performances of music in jukeboxes, certain retransmissions of television programs by cable services, and certain uses of music and art by public broadcasting stations. The jukebox compulsory license has since been displaced by negotiated arrangements between jukebox operators and performing rights societies, so as to comply with the pertinent provisions of the Berne Convention.

b.   FAIR USE

Perhaps the best known, most important, and most elusive exception to the exclusive rights of the copyright owner is embodied in the doctrine known as fair use. The doctrine, a feature of our copyright law since the middle of the nineteenth century through judicial creation and elaboration, was developed in order to allow unauthorized uses that the courts thought were reasonable and that did not unduly deprive the plaintiff's work of a market. Fair use was expressly incorporated in the statute for the first time in the 1976 Act, in Section 107.

That section lists several kinds of illustrative uses subject to the defense, including criticism, comment, news reporting, teaching, scholarship, and research. Nonetheless, a defendant who has reproduced, adapted, or publicly distributed, performed, or displayed a copyrighted work without authorization must do more than invoke one of the above socially beneficent purposes. The statute also enumerates four factors to be reviewed in the disposition of the defense. These factors are: the nature of the defendant's use; the nature of the copyrighted work; the amount and substantiality of the portions taken from the copyrighted work; and the effect of the taking upon the potential market for the copyrighted work. These four factors are not exhaustive.

Because the fair-use doctrine is still "an equitable rule of reason," courts are free to consider other factors, or to give greater weight to some factors than to others, depending on the given case. A defendant invoking the fair-use defense must establish that the balance of the statutory and any additional judicial criteria weighs in his or her favor.

Fair use has been characteristically invoked as a defense in cases involving historical and biographical works that have quoted from or paraphrased earlier such works or original source materials still in copyright. It has also been invoked by parodists who have borrowed from an earlier work, "conjuring it up" in order to poke fun at it. Among the most perplexing applications of the fair use doctrine has been to the succession of new copying technologies, such as audiotaping, videotaping, and photocopying, and digital duplication over the Internet. The Supreme Court has held, for example, that home videotaping of copyrighted television programs shown on free broadcast television, to facilitate later viewing, is a fair use. Lower courts continue to wrestle with the question of photocopying for a variety of purposes, both commercial and nonprofit. A factor that some courts have considered in assessing the fairness of certain photocopying practices is the existence of the Copyright Clearance Center, an international consortium of publishers of general and also scientific and technical books and journals, which undertakes collective licensing efforts, much as ASCAP and BMI do for authors and publishers of musical compositions copyright holders. Fair use questions are arising with increasing frequency in connection with the duplication and use of copyrighted material in digital form, such as computer programs and more conventional literary, musical and audiovisual works transmitted over the Internet. Courts have so far assumed or held unauthorized file-sharing on the Internet, typically of copyrighted music recordings, is not a fair use.

. . .

Several commentators have contended that the First Amendment affords a privilege, separate from statutory exemptions or limitations, to make otherwise infringing reproductions, adaptations, performances, or displays of a copyrighted work. While some courts recognize a potential tension in theory between copyright and the First Amendment, the courts have generally found that copyright accommodates First Amendment concerns, and have declined to recognize a First Amendment-copyright conflict on the facts of the cases so far. The Supreme Court, in fact, has held that two features inherent in copyright law secure protection of free speech interests. First, copyright does not prevent the free dissemination of the author's facts and ideas. Second, even "expression" may be copied, by virtue of the fair use doctrine, in many instances in which there is a compelling societal justification for doing so.

1.5.2 Introduction to the European Union and the construction of European copyright law*

a. European institutions

"The E.U. is a unique economic and political partnership between— as of today—28 countries that together cover much of the European continent."[1] The E.U. consists of and is administered by various institutions, bodies and agencies. The five main institutions and its tasks will be briefly explained.

i. European Parliament

The European Parliament is the first institution named in article 13 TEU. Its competences and composition are further defined in article 14 TEU and articles 223–234 TFEU. The E.U. citizens directly elect for five years the members of the European Parliament (MEP) (art. 14 TEU). Each member state gets a predefined number of seats in the European Parliament, which is degressively proportionate to the member state's population. All member states elect their representatives for the seats in the European Parliament separately. The European Parliament exercises, jointly with the Council, legislative and budgetary functions, it exercises functions of political control and consultation, and elects the President of the Commission (art. 14(1) TEU).

ii. European Council

The European Council "consists of the Heads of State or Government of the Member States, together with its President and the President of the Commission" (art. 15(2) TEU). The European Council is not involved in law-making. Its main function is to determine the general political directions and priorities of the European Union (art. 15(1) TEU). A few other competences of the European Council are mentioned in the TEU and TFEU: they include competencies in the composition of the European Parliament (art. 14(2) subparagraph 2 TEU) and Council (art. 236

---

* The Editors thank David Rüther, Columbia LLM 2014, for assistance in the preparation of this note.

1 http://europa.eu/about-eu/index_en.htm (last visited June 19, 2014).

TFEU), amending internal policies of the European Union (art. 46(6) TEU) and changing the legislative procedure for a given area or case (art. 46(7) TEU). "The European Council shall meet twice every six months" (art. 15(3) TEU).

iii. The Council

The Council, also known as Council of the European Union, is the second legislative body in the bicameral system, besides the European Parliament (art. 16(1) TEU). It "consist[s] of a representative of each Member State at ministerial level" (art. 16(2) TEU). The composition of the Council varies. The national governments send different ministers depending on the subject matter discussed in the Council meetings. Besides its shared law-making power and E.U. budget approval, the Council coordinates the economic policies, foreign and defense policies and the access to justice between the member states. It also signs agreements between the E.U. and other countries.

The Council should not be confused with the Council of Europe, which is not an E.U. body.

iv. European Commission

The European Commission is one of the main institutions of the E.U. with numerous responsibilities and rights. The division of powers applies only to a certain extent to the Commission. Its main focus is the executive authority. The Commission's tasks include:

> promo[ting] the general interest of the Union[,] [...] ensur[ing] the application of the Treaties, and of measures adopted by the institutions pursuant to them[,] [...] oversee[ing] the application of Union law under the control of the Court of Justice of the European Union[,] [...] execut[ing] the budget and manag[ing] programmes [and] [...] exercis[ing] coordinating, executive and management functions, as laid down in the Treaties. With the exception of the common foreign and security policy, and other cases provided for in the Treaties, [the Commission] shall ensure the Union's external representation. (art. 17(1) TEU.)

However, the Commission is also involved in legislative acts. "Union legislative acts may only be adopted on the basis of a Commission proposal, except where the Treaties provide otherwise." (art. 17(2) TEU).

The Commission is composed of 28 Commissioners, one from each member state, for the term of five years (art. 17(3) TEU). The President of the Commission assigns each Commissioner a specific policy area. Due to the accession to the E.U. of various countries the number of Commissioners increased. To return to an acceptable number of Commissioners the E.U. will reduce the commissioner positions. "As from 1 November 2014, the Commission shall consist of a number of members, including its President and the High Representative of the Union for Foreign Affairs and Security Policy, corresponding to two thirds of the number of Member States, unless the European Council, acting unanimously, decides to alter this number." (art. 17(5) TEU).

The European Council nominates the President and appoints the other Commissioners in agreement with the nominated President. The appointment of all Commissioners, including the President, is subject to the approval of the European Parliament (art. 17(7) TEU). In office, the Commissioners remain accountable to the Parliament, which has the power to dismiss the Commission (art. 17(8) TEU).

v. The Court of Justice of the European Union

The Court of Justice of the European Union rules both on primary and secondary E.U. law. It "rule[s] on actions brought by a Member State, an institution or a natural or legal person; give[s] preliminary rulings, at the request of courts or tribunals of the Member States, on the interpretation of Union law or the validity of acts adopted by the institutions; rules in other cases provided for in the Treaties." (art. 19(3) TEU).

The CJEU is divided into the Court of Justice (often referred to as European Court of Justice or ECJ), the General Court (previously: Court of First Instance) and specialized courts (art. 19(1) TEU). The ECJ and the General Court are both comprised of 28 judges, one judge per member state (art. 19(2) TEU). The judges decide in panels of three, five, or 13 judges. In exceptional cases the ECJ sits in full court. Additionally, the ECJ is helped by nine Advocates-General (art. 252 TFEU). Their "duty [is to] act with complete impartiality and independence, to make, in open court, reasoned submissions on cases" (art. 252 TFEU). The General Court has no such Advocates-General, but judges can take the position of Advocates-General in certain situations. Each judge and Advocate-General is appointed for a renewable six-year term.

The jurisdiction of the ECJ and the General Court is determined by article 256(1) TFEU and article 51 Statute of the Court of Justice of the European

Union. The General Court has, for all proceedings but treaty infringement proceedings, actions of annulments brought by a member state, proceedings for failure to act brought by a member state or an institution against another institution and preliminary rulings initial jurisdiction. However, the rulings made by the General Court may, within two months, be subject to an appeal, limited to points of law, to the ECJ.

The E.U. Civil Service Tribunal is currently the only specialized court. It rules on disputes between the European Union and its staff.

Types of cases

The five most important types of proceedings in front of the CJEU are:

- Treaty infringement proceedings (arts 258, 259 TFEU): member states can be sued if they do not abide by the obligations in the TEU, TFEU, Euratom Treaty and secondary E.U. law. However, the CJEU or the Commission cannot enforce the obligation if the court finds that a member state has not respected its treaty obligations. The Commission is entitled to set a monetary penalty against the member state.
- Action for annulment (art. 263 TFEU): a party in an action for annulment can be a member state, an E.U. institution and even individuals or organizations if they are affected by E.U. actions. In an action for annulment, "[t]he Court of Justice of the European Union [. . .] review[s] the legality of legislative acts, of acts of the Council, of the Commission and of the European Central Bank, other than recommendations and opinions, and of acts of the European Parliament and of the European Council" (art. 263 TFEU).
- Action for Failure to Act (art. 265 TFEU): member states and other institutions of the Union may bring an action before the CJEU if any institution, body, or agency of the E.U., in infringement of the Treaties, fails to act, for example if a member state fails to implement a directive by the deadline set for implementation. Even natural and legal persons can be a party under certain prerequisites (art. 265(3) TFEU).
- Reference for a Preliminary Ruling (art. 267 TFEU): preliminary rulings are by far the most rendered decisions of the CJEU. In preliminary rulings the Court interprets primary and secondary E.U. law, as well as (in-)validates and interprets acts of E.U. institutions, bodies, offices and agencies. Courts and tribunals of a member state can request a preliminary ruling on any question regarding E.U. law, as long as the

interpretation has potential to affect the case before the national court. A member state's court or tribunal must reference the Court of Justice for a preliminary ruling if there is no judicial remedy under national law against the decision of the court or tribunal. If the Court of Justice already answered the question in another preliminary ruling the national court or tribunal should not refer it to the Court of Justice. The same applies to obvious questions that leave no scope for any reasonable doubt (*acte-clair* doctrine).

- Action for Damages (art. 268 TFEU): in cases of non-contractual liability compensation for damages caused by E.U. institutions and its servants the Court of Justice of the European Union decides.

As to European copyright law, preliminary rulings are of high importance. As we will see in the readings, they are a powerful tool to harmonize European copyright law beyond the explicit terms of the directives.

b. E.U. Legislation

The main goal of the E.U. is the progressive integration of member states' economic and political systems and the establishment of a single market based on the free movement of goods, people, money and services. To this end, its member states cede part of their sovereignty through the TFEU and TEU which empower the E.U. institutions to adopt laws. These secondary laws (regulations, directives and decisions) take precedence over national law and are binding on national authorities. The E.U. also issues non-binding instruments, such as recommendations and opinions.

i. Treaties of the E.U.

What is now known as the E.U. has its origin in the European Coal and Steel Community (ECSC), which was created in the aftermath of the Second World War. The *Treaty of Paris* establishing the European Coal and Steel Community, signed on April 18, 1951 and entering into force on July 23, 1952, created an interdependence in coal and steel production aiming to make it impossible for a country to increase and mobilize its military without others knowing.

With the *Treaties of Rome*, signed on March 25, 1957 and entered into force on January 1, 1958, the two other predecessors of the E.U., the European Economic Community (EEC) and the European Atomic Energy Community (EURATOM), were established in order to foster economic cooperation among the six original signatories by creating a common market: "the idea being that countries who trade with one another become economically interdependent and more likely avoid conflicts among each other."[1] The six original signatories of the ECSC, EEC and EURATOM were France, Germany, Italy, Belgium, the Netherlands and Luxembourg.

The *Brussels Treaty*, signed on April 8, 1965 and entered into force on July 1, 1967, streamlined the European institutions by merging the legislative and executive bodies of the three communities.

On February 17, 1986 the *Single European Act* was signed and entered into force on July 1, 1987. The treaty introduced political and institutional changes in order to speed up decision-making in preparation for a single market and to reform the institutions in preparation for the membership of Portugal and Spain.

The *Maastricht Treaty on European Union*, signed on February 7, 1992 and entered into force on November 1, 1993, was a milestone in creating the E.U. as it exists today. The Maastricht Treaty created the European Union with a three pillar structure: the European Communities, consisting of EC (European Community, formerly known as EEC before it was renamed in the Maastricht Treaty), ECSC and EURATOM; Common Foreign and Security Policy; and the third pillar concerning police and judicial cooperation in criminal matters. By the implementation of the three-pillar structure the E.U. shifted its original objective of being an economic union to an economic and political union. However, the subjects of the second and third pillar required intergovernmental cooperation and were not delegated to one of the EC institutions. Another impetus for the shift to a political union was the creation of a European citizenship by the Maastricht Treaty. Furthermore, that treaty established the economic and monetary union leading to the single currency Euro in 2002.

In preparation for the arrival of future member countries to the E.U. the *Treaty of Amsterdam*, signed on October 2, 1997 and entered into force on May 1, 1999, and the *Treaty of Nice*, signed on February 26, 2001 and entered into force on February 1, 2003, solved some institutional problems. These treaties addressed the make-up of the Commission, changed the weight of votes in the E.U. Council, and enhanced cooperation between member countries. Besides this, the Treaty of Amsterdam transferred some of the third pillar's intergovernmental cooperation to the EC.

---

1 Ibid.

The most recent treaty is the *Lisbon Treaty*, which was signed on December 13, 2007 and entered into force on December 1, 2009. This treaty amended the existing E.U. treaties extensively. Some of the most relevant changes are as follows. The treaty again adjusted the institutional structure of the E.U. because of the increased number of member states. The Lisbon Treaty reformed the decision-making process in the council, and adjusted the composition of the European Parliament and Commission. It created the positions of the President of the European Council and the High Council for Foreign Affairs and Security Policy. Both positions have mainly an administrative and representative function. The *Lisbon Treaty* replaced the three-pillar structure, which was introduced by the Maastricht Treaty, with an elaborate division of competences between the E.U. and its member states. Furthermore, the E.U. obtained the status of a legal personality and obtained additional powers from the member states. In addition, the Lisbon Treaty gave binding effect to the *Charter of Fundamental Rights* in the E.U.

Since the E.U. is based on the rule of law, every action taken by it must be founded on the previously explained treaties, which have been approved voluntarily and democratically by all E.U. member countries. The two most important, current primary treaties that lay out the entire structure, competences and policies of the E.U. are the Treaty on European Union (TEU)[2] and Treaty on the Functioning of the European Union (TFEU).[3] Both are consolidated versions of the above-mentioned treaties. This primary E.U. law is the law on which the E.U. is built in contrast to secondary E.U. law, which refers to legislative acts of the E.U. (regulations, directives, decisions).

Even though the E.U. was founded on multilateral treaties between sovereign countries it is not an international organization or confederation. The direct election of a European Parliament by the European citizens and a limited law-making power of E.U. institutions are only two characteristics that do not coincide with an international organization or confederation. Neither is the E.U. a federation nor a confederation. All member states retain their sovereignty after accession. Instead, the E.U. is a supranational union. It has competences to the extent that member states have delegated their national competences to the E.U. The E.U. can exercise these competences exclusively or in conjunction with the member states—depending whether it is a shared

---

2 The TEU is based on the Maastricht Treaty on European Union amended by the Treaty of Amsterdam, Treaty of Nice, Treaty of Lisbon and the accession treaties.

3 The TFEU is based on the Treaty establishing the European Economic Community (Treaties of Rome) amended by the Treaty of Lisbon.

or exclusive competence—as long as the E.U. complies with the principle of conferred powers and subsidiarity. "Under the principle of conferral, the [EU] shall act only within the limits of the competences conferred upon it by the Member States in the Treaties to attain the objectives set out therein. Competences not conferred upon the [EU] in the Treaties remain with the Member States." (Art. 5 II TEU). "Under the principle of subsidiarity, in areas which do not fall within its exclusive competence, the Union shall act only if and in so far as the objectives of the proposed action cannot be sufficiently achieved by the Member States, either at central level or at regional and local level, but can rather, by reason of the scale or effects of the proposed action, be better achieved at Union level." (Art. 5 III TEU).

The prior Treaties did not contain any explicit powers for legislation in intellectual property law. Nevertheless, the provisions empowering the Communities to adopt measures for the coordination and approximation of legal provisions in order to achieve the free movement of services and for the purpose of the establishment and functioning of the Internal Market were considered sufficiently broad to encompass Communities action in the IP field. As currently stated by copyright directives, the differences in copyright protection offered by the laws of the member states have direct and negative effects on the functioning of the common market.

The recitals of Directive 2001/84/EC of the European Parliament and of the Council of 27 September 2001 on the resale right for the benefit of the author of an original work of art offer an example of appeal to the internal market as the legal basis for the Directive:

> (9) The resale right is currently provided for by the domestic legislation of a majority of Member States. Such laws, where they exist, display certain differences, notably as regards the works covered, those entitled to receive royalties, the rate applied, the transactions subject to payment of a royalty, and the basis on which these are calculated. The application or non-application of such a right has a significant impact on the competitive environment within the internal market, since the existence or absence of an obligation to pay on the basis of the resale right is an element which must be taken into account by each individual wishing to sell a work of art. This right is therefore a factor which contributes to the creation of distortions of competition as well as displacement of sales within the Community.

> (10) Such disparities with regard to the existence of the resale right and its application by the Member States have a direct negative impact on the

proper functioning of the internal market in works of art as provided for by Article 14 of the Treaty. In such a situation Article 95 of the Treaty constitutes the appropriate legal basis.

The Lisbon Treaty does not change the analysis when it comes to harmonization. There is still no independent legislative competence for harmonization in this field. As shown by the latest directives, the functioning of the internal market without distortions of competition based on differences concerning copyright protection is still the key for the E.U. approximation by directives. The relevant texts are the following:

Article 26 TFEU

1. The Union shall adopt measures with the aim of establishing or ensuring the functioning of the internal market, in accordance with the relevant provisions of the Treaties.

2. The internal market shall comprise an area without internal frontiers in which the free movement of goods, persons, services and capital is ensured in accordance with the provisions of the Treaties.

3. The Council, on a proposal from the Commission, shall determine the guidelines and conditions necessary to ensure balanced progress in all the sectors concerned.

Article 53 (1) TFEU

In order to make it easier for persons to take up and pursue activities as self-employed persons, the European Parliament and the Council shall, acting in accordance with the ordinary legislative procedure, issue directives for the mutual recognition of diplomas, certificates and other evidence of formal qualifications and for the coordination of the provisions laid down by law, regulation or administrative action in Member States concerning the taking-up and pursuit of activities as self-employed persons.

Article 56 TFEU

Within the framework of the provisions set out below, restrictions on freedom to provide services within the Union shall be prohibited in respect of nationals of Member States who are established in a Member State other than that of the person for whom the services are intended.

Article 62 TFEU

The provisions of Articles 51 to 54 shall apply to the matters covered by this Chapter (Art. 56–62 TFEU).

Article 114(1) TFEU

Save where otherwise provided in the Treaties, the following provisions shall apply for the achievement of the objectives set out in Article 26. The European Parliament and the Council shall, acting in accordance with the ordinary legislative procedure and after consulting the Economic and Social Committee, adopt the measures for the approximation of the provisions laid down by law, regulation or administrative action in Member States which have as their object the establishment and functioning of the internal market.

As to intellectual property, the innovation of the Lisbon Treaty was to provide a basis for "the creation of European intellectual property rights to provide uniform intellectual property through the Union." While the scope of protection given by any domestic law is usually national, for European intellectual property rights the scope becomes European. These European intellectual property rights already exist for industrial property but not yet for copyright.

Article 118 TFEU

In the context of the establishment and functioning of the internal market, the European Parliament and the Council, acting in accordance with the ordinary legislative procedure, shall establish measures for the creation of European intellectual property rights to provide uniform protection of intellectual property rights throughout the Union and for the setting up of centralised Union-wide authorisation, coordination and supervision arrangements.

ii. Regulations

Regulations are the most direct form of E.U. law. They are on the same level as national legislation, "binding in its entirety and directly applicable in all Member States" (art. 288 TFEU). National governments do not have to take action themselves to implement E.U. regulations. While there are as yet no regulations respecting copyright law, the three regulations concerning private international law are relevant to a course in international copyright law, and will be more fully addressed in Part III of this Casebook:

Regulation (EC) No 593/2008 of the European Parliament and of the Council of 17 June 2008 on the law applicable to contractual obligations (Rome I)

Regulation (EC) No 864/2007 of the European Parliament and of the Council of 11 July 2007 on the law applicable to non-contractual obligations (Rome II)

Regulation (EU) No 1215/2012 of the European Parliament and of the Council of 12 December 2012 on jurisdiction and the recognition and enforcement of judgments in civil and commercial matters (Brussels Regulation, recast)

iii. Directives

E.U. Directives lay down certain end results that must be met by the member states. But they "leave to the national authorities the choice of form and methods" (art. 288 TFEU). Directives concern the member states to which they are addressed. It could be one, more or all of the member states. Each directive gives the national authorities a deadline—necessary to take account of differing national situations—by which it must be implemented into national law. Directives are used to harmonize different national laws with each other, and are particularly common in matters affecting the operation of the single market.

As we have seen previously, the goal of directives in intellectual property and especially in copyright is to approximate member states law in order to reduce any differences concerning the protection given. In the related field of industrial property, such as trademark or design protection, the approximation was totally achieved by one directive including the main issues of trademark or design protection. When it came to copyright, the process of harmonization was much disputed and hardly achieved. Instead of one directive covering the main issues, several directives have harmonized the field, even if not yet completely. The main reason concerns the classical opposition among member states between those, such as France, favoring a civil law approach and those, such as U.K., favoring a common law approach. This is why, before the Information Society Directive, directives were dedicated to specific issues commonly accepted by both traditions. As a result, moral rights are still not harmonized by E.U. law.

The copyright Directives are:

a. **In general:**

Directive 2001/29/EC Copyright in the Information Society [Info Soc Diretive][4]

> The objectives of the Directive on the harmonisation of certain aspects of copyright and related rights in the information society (2001/29/EC) are to adapt legislation on copyright and related rights to reflect technological developments and to transpose into Community law the main international obligations arising from the two treaties on copyright and related rights adopted within the framework of the World Intellectual Property Organisation (WIPO) in December 1996. It is an essential building block for the Information Society. The final text is a result of over three years of thorough discussion and an example of co-decision making where the European Parliament, the Council and the Commission have all had a decisive input.

b. **Directives concerning subject matter**

Directives on Protection of Computer Programs[5]

> Directive 91/250/EEC has been repealed and replaced by Directive 2009/24/EC, without prejudice to the obligations of the Member States relating to the time-limits for transposition into national law of the Directives. The Directive on the legal protection of computer programs (91/250/EEC) was a real European "first" for copyright law, the first copyright measure to be adopted following the publication of the White Paper on completing the Single Market by 1992. The objective of the Directive is to harmonize Member States' legislation regarding the protection of computer programs in order to create a legal environment which will afford a degree of security against unauthorized reproduction of such programs.

Directive 96/9 Protection of Databases[6]

> The Directive on the legal protection of Databases was adopted in February 1996. The Directive created a new exclusive "sui generis" right

---

4 http://ec.europa.eu/internal_market/copyright/copyright-infso/index_en.htm (last visited June 19, 2014).
5 http://ec.europa.eu/internal_market/copyright/prot-comp-progs/index_en.htm (last visited June 19, 2014).
6 http://ec.europa.eu/internal_market/copyright/prot-databases/index_en.htm (last visited June 19, 2014).

for database producers, valid for 15 years, to protect their investment of time, money and effort, irrespective of whether the database is in itself innovative ("non-original" databases). The Directive also harmonized copyright law applicable to the structure and arrangement of the contents of databases ("original" databases). The Directive's provisions apply to both analogue and digital databases.

c. Directives concerning copyright term[7]

Council Directive 93/98/EEC of 29 October 1993 harmonizing the term of protection of copyright and certain related rights

Directive 93/98/EEC has been repealed and replaced by Directive 2006/116/EC, without prejudice to the obligations of the Member States relating to the time-limits for transposition into national law of the Directives, and their application.

Directive 2006/116/EC of the European Parliament and of the Council of 12 December 2006 on the term of protection of copyright and certain related rights (codified version)

Directive 2006/116/EC harmonizes the terms of protection of copyright and neighboring rights. The Directive establishes a total harmonization of the period of protection for each type of work and each related right in the Member States – e.g. 70 years after the death of the author for works and 50 years after the event setting the time running for neighboring rights. Furthermore, it deals with other issues, such as the protection of previously unpublished works, of critical and scientific publications and of photographic works.

Directive 2011/77/EU of the European Parliament and of the Council of 27 September 2011 amending Directive 2006/116/EC on the term of protection of copyright and certain related rights

The directive to extend the term of protection for performers and sound recordings to 70 years was adopted on 12 September 2011. The aim of the directive is to bring performers' protection more in line with that already given to authors – 70 years after their death. The extended term will enable performers to earn money for a longer period of time and in

---

7 http://ec.europa.eu/internal_market/copyright/term-protection/index_en.htm (last visited June 19, 2014).

any event throughout their lifetime. The income from copyright remuneration is important for performers, as they often do not have other regular salaried income. The extended term will also benefit record producers who will generate additional revenue from the sale of records in shops and on the Internet. This should allow producers to adapt to the rapidly changing business environment and help them maintain their investment levels in new talent.

The directive also contains accompanying measures which aim specifically to help performers. The "use it or lose it" clauses which will now have to be included in the contracts linking performers to their record companies will allow performers to get their rights back if the record producer does not market the sound recording during the extended period. In this way the performer will be able to either find another record producer willing to sell his music or do it himself, something that is possible easily via the Internet. Finally, record companies will have to set up a fund into which they will have to pay 20 percent of their revenues earned during the extended period. The money from this fund compensates session musicians.

d. Directives concerning rights

Directives on Rental and Lending Rights[8]

Directive 92/100/EEC has been repealed and replaced by Directive 2006/115/EC, without prejudice to the obligations of the Member States relating to the time-limits for transposition into national law of the Directives. Directive 92/100/EEC harmonizes the provisions relating to rental and lending rights as well as on certain rights related to copyright. It provides for exclusive rights to authorize or prohibit the rental and lending of both works subject to copyright and other objects subject to neighboring rights. Furthermore, it provides for a harmonization of certain neighboring rights including the right of fixation, reproduction, broadcasting and communication to the public and distribution. Beneficiaries of rights related to copyright are performers, phonogram producers, film producers and broadcasters. The Directive (art. 4) addresses collective management as a model for the management of the equitable remuneration right, but does not make collective management a requirement. As regards the exclusive public lending right, Member

---

8 http://ec.europa.eu/internal_market/copyright/rental-right/index_en.htm (last visited June 19, 2014).

States can derogate from it, provided that at least authors obtain remuneration for such lending. The distribution right (art. 9) is limited by the principle of Community exhaustion; as a result, Member States are prevented from applying international exhaustion. Finally, the principal director of a cinematography work is to be considered as an author of such work.

Directive 93/83 Satellite and Cable[9]

The Directive 93/83/EEC aims at facilitating the cross border transmission of audiovisual programmes such as, particularly broadcasting via satellite and retransmission by cable. In view of that objective, mechanisms are set up in order to ensure that creators and producers of programmes obtain a fair remuneration, on grounds of intellectual property rights, for the use of their creations.

Directive 2001/84/EC Resale Right[10]

The objective of the Directive on the resale right for the benefit of the author of an original work of art (2001/84/EC) is to provide creators with an adequate and standard level of protection and eliminate the distortion in the conditions for competition currently existing within the single market for contemporary art. The Directive will give artists the benefit of this right, regardless of where in the Union their works are sold. In addition, it will give the Commission a basis on which to promote the international recognition of resale rights.

Directive 2012/28/EU Orphan Works[11]

The Directive 2012/28/EU sets out common rules on the digitization and online display of so-called orphan works. Orphan works are works like books, newspaper and magazine articles and films that are still protected by copyright but whose authors or other rightholders are, notwithstanding a diligent search, either unknown or unlocatable, and therefore cannot be contacted to obtain copyright permissions. The Directive limits the use of orphan works to certain institutions: European libraries and public broadcasters.

---

9 http://ec.europa.eu/internal_market/copyright/satellite-cable/index_en.htm (last visited June 19, 2014).

10 http://ec.europa.eu/internal_market/copyright/resale-right/index_en.htm (last visited June 19, 2014).

11 http://ec.europa.eu/internal_market/copyright/orphan_works/index_en.htm (last visited June 19, 2014).

Directive 2014/26/EU on collective management of copyright[12]

The European Union has adopted a Directive 2014/26/EU on collective rights management and multi-territorial licensing of rights in musical works for online uses. The Directive aims at ensuring that rightholders have a say in the management of their rights and envisages a better functioning of collective management organisations as a result of E.U-wide standards. The new rules will also ease the multi-territorial licensing by collective management organisations of authors' rights in musical works for online use. The Commission will work closely with the Member States to achieve a correct transposition of the provisions of the Directive into national law by the transposition date of 10 April 2016.

e. Enforcement:

Directive 2004/48 on the Enforcement of Intellectual Property Rights[13]

The Directive on the enforcement of intellectual property rights such as copyright and related rights, trademarks, designs or patents was adopted in April 2004. The Directive requires all Member States to apply effective, dissuasive and proportionate remedies and penalties against those engaged in counterfeiting and piracy and so creates a level playing field for right holders in the E.U. It means that all Member States will have a similar set of measures, procedures and remedies available for rightholders to defend their intellectual property rights (be they copyright or related rights, trademarks, patents, designs, etc,) if they are infringed.

iv. Decisions

"Decisions are E.U. determinations relating to specific cases. They can come from the Council (sometimes jointly with the European Parliament) or the Commission. They can require authorities and individuals in Member States either to do something or stop doing something, and can also confer rights on them."[14] "[Decisions] [are] binding in its entirety. A decision which specifies those to whom it is addressed shall be binding only on them." (art. 288 TFEU). For example:

---

12 http://ec.europa.eu/internal_market/copyright/management/index_en.htm
13 http://ec.europa.eu/internal_market/iprenforcement/directive/index_en.htm (last visited June 19, 2014).
14 http://ec.europa.eu/eu_law/introduction/what_decision_en.htm (last visited June 19, 2014).

Council Decision (of 22 December 1994) concerning the conclusion on behalf of the European Community, as regards matters within its competence, of the agreements reached in the Uruguay Round multilateral negotiations (1986–1994) (94/800/EC);

Council Decision of 16 March 2000, on the approval on behalf of the European Community of the WIPO Copyright Treaty and the WIPO Performances and Phonograms Treaty.

Part I

Applicability of international copyright and neighboring rights conventions

2

From international conventions to national laws (or relations between international and national norms)

2.1   Interpretation of an international convention

The interpretation of an international convention poses special difficulties because it calls for uniform international interpretation in order to foster the convention's goal of international harmonization, yet in most cases the bodies undertaking that task will be national judiciaries, legislatures or administrations The same-named concepts may have different meanings in domestic law and international norms. To promote international uniformity of interpretation in approach to international treaties, the Vienna Convention on the Law of Treaties offers rules of interpretation. Although the Berne predates the Vienna Convention, the incorporation of this treaty into the TRIPS Agreement in effect brings the Vienna Convention to bear because article 3.2 of the World Trade Organization Dispute Settlement Understanding makes the TRIPS subject to "customary rules of interpretation of public international law."[1] Similarly, although, many Berne countries, including the United States, are not parties to the Vienna Convention, the Vienna Convention may be said to reflect custom, including in the United States;[2] its rules of interpretation may therefore be helpful even as to non-members.

---

1 Art. 3.2 provides:

> The dispute settlement system of the WTO is a central element in providing security and predictability to the multilateral trading system. The Members recognize that it serves to preserve the rights and obligations of Members under the covered agreements, and to clarify the existing provisions of those agreements in accordance with customary rules of interpretation of public international law. Recommendations and rulings of the DSB cannot add to or diminish the rights and obligations provided in the covered agreements.

2 See Restatement (Third) of the Foreign Relations Law of the United States § 145 (1986). Article 4

The Vienna Convention requires that the interpreter focus not only on the text but also on the object and purpose of the international instrument. It tells us *how* to interpret an international norm.[3] But it does not tell us *who* interprets the norm. In the absence of a supranational tribunal with the power to bind all treaty members to its interpretation (see discussion *infra*), national or regional courts elaborate the meaning of the international text. Conflict of laws may therefore arise from divergent national interpretations of an international convention.

2.1.1 General considerations: Vienna Convention on the Law of Treaties (1969)

Article 31 – General rule of interpretation

1. A treaty shall be interpreted in good faith in accordance with the ordinary meaning to be given to the terms of the treaty in their context and in the light of its object and purpose.

2. The context for the purpose of the interpretation of a treaty shall comprise, in addition to the text, including its preamble and annexes:

(*a*) any agreement relating to the treaty which was made between all the parties in connection with the conclusion of the treaty;
(*b*) any instrument which was made by one or more parties in connection with the conclusion of the treaty and accepted by the other parties as an instrument related to the treaty.

3. There shall be taken into account, together with the context:

(*a*) any subsequent agreement between the parties regarding the interpretation of the treaty or the application of its provisions;
(*b*) any subsequent practice in the application of the treaty which establishes the agreement of the parties regarding its interpretation;
(*c*) any relevant rules of international law applicable in the relations between the parties.

---

of the Vienna Convention provides for non-retroactivity, meaning the Berne and Rome Conventions are indeed excluded. The US is a signatory of the Vienna Convention but has not ratified it. *See* https://treaties.un.org/Pages/ViewDetailsIII.aspx?&src=TREATY&mtdsg_no=XXIII~1&chapter=23&Temp=mtdsg3&lang=en.

3 See, e.g., Susy Frankel, *The WTO's Application of 'the Customary Rules of Interpretation of Public International Law' to Intellectual Property* (2006) 46 VIRG. J.OF INTN'L L. 365–431.

Object and Purpose of Copyright Treaties

Berne Convention (1971 Paris Revision) (Preamble)

The countries of the Union, being equally animated by the desire to protect, in as effective and uniform a manner as possible, the rights of authors in their literary and artistic works, . . .

TRIPS Agreement (1994)

Preamble

Members,

Desiring to reduce distortions and impediments to international trade, and taking into account the need to promote effective and adequate protection of intellectual property rights, and to ensure that measures and procedures to enforce intellectual property rights do not themselves become barriers to legitimate trade; . . .

Article 7 Objectives

The protection and enforcement of intellectual property rights should contribute to the promotion of technological innovation and to the transfer and dissemination of technology, to the mutual advantage of producers and users of technological knowledge and in a manner conducive to social and economic welfare, and to a balance of rights and obligations.

Article 8 Principles

1. Members may, in formulating or amending their laws and regulations, adopt measures necessary to protect public health and nutrition, and to promote the public interest in sectors of vital importance to their socio-economic and technological development, provided that such measures are consistent with the provisions of this Agreement.

2. Appropriate measures, provided that they are consistent with the provisions of this Agreement, may be needed to prevent the abuse of intellectual property rights by right holders or the resort to practices which unreasonably restrain trade or adversely affect the international transfer of technology.

QUESTIONS

1. Taking these provisions into account, what are the object and the purpose of the TRIPS Agreement? How could they influence the interpretation of the substantive provisions of the Agreement?
2. To what extent might the object and purpose of the Berne Convention be different? To the extent they differ, could the TRIPS's object and purpose influence the interpretation of the Berne Convention, for example when a WTO Panel interprets the Berne Convention?

Who interprets?
When it comes to the Berne and Rome Conventions, both treaties refer disputes concerning the interpretation and application of the treaties to the International Court of Justice (ICJ), the principal judicial organ of the United Nations. The conventions thus grant interpreting authority to an impartial international organization.

But the referral of interpreting authority to the ICJ in article 33 Berne Convention[4] and article 30 Rome Convention[5] encounters several deficiencies. First, only states can initiate ICJ proceedings, individuals have no standing. Therefore, if individuals seek to have their issue adjudicated at the ICJ, they have to find a state willing to sue the non-complying Berne or Rome member country. A second disadvantage is that the Berne Convention allows for reservations as to the jurisdiction of the ICJ.[6] The

---

4 Article 33

Disputes:

1. Jurisdiction of the International Court of Justice; 2. Reservation as to such jurisdiction; 3. Withdrawal of reservation

(1) Any dispute between two or more countries of the Union concerning the interpretation or application of this Convention, not settled by negotiation, may, by any one of the countries concerned, be brought before the International Court of Justice by application in conformity with the Statute of the Court, unless the countries concerned agree on some other method of settlement. The country bringing the dispute before the Court shall inform the International Bureau; the International Bureau shall bring the matter to the attention of the other countries of the Union.

(2) Each country may, at the time it signs this Act or deposits its instrument of ratification or accession, declare that it does not consider itself bound by the provisions of paragraph (1). With regard to any dispute between such country and any other country of the Union, the provisions of paragraph (1) shall not apply.

(3) Any country having made a declaration in accordance with the provisions of paragraph (2) may, at any time, withdraw its declaration by notification addressed to the Director General.

5 Article 30

Settlement of disputes

Any dispute which may arise between two or more Contracting States concerning the interpretation or application of this Convention and which is not settled by negotiation shall, at the request of any one of the parties to the dispute, be referred to the International Court of Justice for decision, unless they agree to another mode of settlement.

6 The following countries have taken advantage of the opportunity to refrain from ICJ jurisdiction regarding

Stockholm Revision of the Berne Convention in 1967 introduced the reservation option because some countries were dissatisfied with an obligatory jurisdiction of the ICJ. Another drawback of the ICJ's interpreting authority is the scope of a rendered judgment. The judgments and any interpretations therein bind only the parties to the proceeding. Any country that was not party to the dispute or did not enter the dispute later is not bound by the findings and interpretations of the ICJ. If the Berne or Rome member countries seek a binding interpretation, they must enter into an interpreting agreement accepted by every single member country. But the most debilitating disadvantage for the interpreting authority of the ICJ is the unenforceability of its judgments and the weak sanctioning options of the UN.[7] For this reason, no dispute has so far been referred to the ICJ based on the Berne or Rome Conventions.

Dispute resolution for TRIPS violations has proven to be more efficient and has already been used among the WTO member states. Article 64 TRIPS refers disputes regarding interpretation and application of TRIPS norms, including Berne Convention articles 1 to 21 (excluding art. 6*bis*), to a WTO Panel for resolution. The WTO Panel makes a recommendation to the WTO dispute settlement body (DSB) which adopts the report. The prevailing states may then bring proceedings under the rules of the Understanding on Rules and Procedures Governing the Settlement of Disputes, Annex 2 to the WTO Agreement, (DSU) for compliance, including imposition of sanctions. The sanctions of the WTO are significantly more effective than sanctions by the UN. The states that prevail before the WTO Panel may be authorized to retaliate in the same or analogous fields; if those measures are not appropriate, the prevailing states may cross-retaliate against the TRIPS violator in fields of trade involving IP laws other than the one at issue in the proceeding, or in non IP-related fields of trade.[8] However, if the sanctions do not prove to be successful there is nothing else the WTO or the contracting parties can do (See infra United States – Section 110(5) of the US Copyright Act (WT/DS160) (*US – Section 110(5) Copyright Act*)), since the judgments of the WTO Panel are not binding on national courts.

Berne subject matter: Algeria, the Bahamas, Cuba, Democratic People's Republic of Korea, Egypt, Guatemala, India, Indonesia, Israel, Jordan, Lesotho Liberia, Libya, Lithuania, Malta, Mauritius, Mongolia, Nepal, Oman, Saint Lucia, South Africa, Tanzania, Thailand, Tunisia, Turkey, Venezuela, Vietnam.

7 Article 94 UN Charter mentions means for sanctioning non-compliance with ICJ judgments.

8 To date, while cross-retaliation has occasionally been authorized under the TRIPS, member states have not yet in fact adopted retaliation measures. See Susy Frankel, *The TRIPS Agreement and Cross-Retaliation* in Trade Agreements at the Crossroads (Susy Frankel and Meredith Kolsky Lewis (eds), Routledge, 2014), 208–25.

Hyundai Electronics Co v. United States, 53 F. Supp 2d 1334 (Ct. Int'l Trade 1999)

As an initial matter, the WTO report itself has no binding effect on the court. . . . Congress made this clear when it . . . provided that the response to an adverse WTO panel report is the province of the executive branch and, more particularly, the Office of the U.S. Trade Representative. See URAA § 129 (codified as 19 U.S.C. § 3538). Thus, the WTO panel report does not constitute binding precedential authority for the court. Of course, this is not to imply that a panel report serves no purpose in litigation before the court. To the contrary, a panel's reasoning, if sound, may be used to inform the court's decision.

C-245/02 Anheuser-Bush Inc. v. Budějovický Budvar, národní podnik ECLI: EU:C:2004:717

67   Article 16 of the TRIPS Agreement confers on the proprietor of a registered trade mark a minimum standard of exclusive rights agreed at international level which all the members of the WTO must guarantee in their domestic legislation. Those exclusive rights protect the proprietor against any infringements of the registered trade mark that may be committed by non-authorised third parties (see also the Report of the WTO Appellate Body, issued on 2 January 2002, United States – Section 211 of the Omnibus Appropriations Act (AB-2001-7) WT/DS/176/AB/R, paragraph 186).

. . .

70   It follows from those factors that the interpretation of the relevant provisions of the national trade-mark law so far as possible in the light of the wording and purpose of the relevant provisions of Community law, in the present case those of Directive 89/104, is not prejudiced by an interpretation in keeping with the wording and purpose of the relevant provisions of the TRIPS Agreement [citations omitted].

QUESTIONS

1. Why do WTO Panel and Appellate Body decisions not constitute binding precedential authority for U.S. courts? (See *infra* under subsequent practice). To what extent might the WTO Panel's analysis inform a U.S. court's decision?
2. When the ECJ states that an interpretation of national law in keeping with the wording and purpose of the TRIPS Agreement does not "prejudice"

interpretation of national law in light of Community law, does that suggest that if a TRIPs-consistent interpretation of national law were in tension with Community law, then the TRIPs-consistent interpretation should not be applied?

3. Does/should the interpretations of WTO Panels control the interpretations of the ECJ with respect to European norms derived from the Berne Convention and the TRIPS Agreement? See *infra*, Part II Chapter 5.5 Exceptions and limitations and 5.5.3 Generalization of the "Three-Step Test".

2.1.2 Context: Agreed statements

Vienna Convention Article 31 – General rule of interpretation

. . .

2. The context for the purpose of the interpretation of a treaty shall comprise, in addition to the text, including its preamble and annexes:

(*a*) any agreement relating to the treaty which was made between all the parties in connection with the conclusion of the treaty;. . . .

Examples of agreed statements concerning the WIPO Copyright Treaty, adopted by the Diplomatic Conference on December 20, 1996

Article 1
Relation to the Berne Convention

(1) This Treaty is a special agreement within the meaning of Article 20 of the Berne Convention for the Protection of Literary and Artistic Works, as regards Contracting Parties that are countries of the Union established by that Convention. This Treaty shall not have any connection with treaties other than the Berne Convention, nor shall it prejudice any rights and obligations under any other treaties.

(2) Nothing in this Treaty shall derogate from existing obligations that Contracting Parties have to each other under the Berne Convention for the Protection of Literary and Artistic Works.

(3) Hereinafter, "Berne Convention" shall refer to the Paris Act of July 24, 1971 of the Berne Convention for the Protection of Literary and Artistic Works.

(4) Contracting Parties shall comply with Articles 1 to 21 and the Appendix of the Berne Convention.

Agreed statement Concerning Article 1(4):

The reproduction right, as set out in Article 9 of the Berne Convention, and the exceptions permitted thereunder, fully apply in the digital environment, in particular to the use of works in digital form. It is understood that the storage of a protected work in digital form in an electronic medium constitutes a reproduction within the meaning of Article 9 of the Berne Convention.

Article 3
Application of Articles 2 to 6 of the Berne Convention

Contracting Parties shall apply mutatis mutandis the provisions of Articles 2 to 6 of the Berne Convention in respect of the protection provided for in this Treaty.

Agreed statement concerning Article 3:

It is understood that in applying Article 3 of this Treaty, the expression "country of the Union" in Articles 2 to 6 of the Berne Convention will be read as if it were a reference to a Contracting Party to this Treaty, in the application of those Berne Articles in respect of protection provided for in this Treaty. It is also understood that the expression "country outside the Union" in those Articles in the Berne Convention will, in the same circumstances, be read as if it were a reference to a country that is not a Contracting Party to this Treaty, and that "this Convention" in Articles 2(8), 2bis(2), 3, 4 and 5 of the Berne Convention will be read as if it were a reference to the Berne Convention and this Treaty. Finally, it is understood that a reference in Articles 3 to 6 of the Berne Convention to a "national of one of the countries of the Union" will, when these Articles are applied to this Treaty, mean, in regard to an intergovernmental organization that is a Contracting Party to this Treaty, a national of one of the countries that is member of that organization.

QUESTION

What is the binding authority of these agreed statements? Does it make a difference if the interpretation applies to an expression not mentioned in the WIPO Copyright Treaty but in the Berne Convention whose norms are incorporated in the Treaty?

C-306/05 Sociedad General de Autores y Editores de España (SGAE) v. Rafael Hoteles SA ECLI:EU:C:2006:764 [2006]

[The following case concerns the interpretation of the expression "communication to the public." It addresses whether the use of television sets and the playing of ambient music within hotel guestrooms could be characterized as an act of communication to the public by the hotel under article 3 of the Directive 2001/29 (on the harmonisation of certain aspects of copyright and related rights in the information society)].

Legal context

Applicable international law

3   The Agreement on Trade-Related Aspects of Intellectual Property Rights ('the TRIPS Agreement'), as set out in Annex 1C to the Marrakesh Agreement establishing the World Trade Organization, was approved on behalf of the European Community by Council Decision 94/800/EC of 22 December 1994 concerning the conclusion on behalf of the European Community, as regards matters within its competence, of the agreements reached in the Uruguay Round multilateral negotiations (1986–1994) (OJ 1994 L 336, p. 1).

4   Article 9(1) of the TRIPS Agreement provides:

'Members shall comply with Articles 1 through 21 of the Berne Convention (1971) and the Appendix thereto. However, Members shall not have rights or obligations under this Agreement in respect of the rights conferred under Article 6*bis* of that Convention or of the rights derived therefrom.'

5   Article 11 of the Berne Convention for the Protection of Literary and Artistic Works (Paris Act of 24 July 1971), as amended on 28 September 1979 ("the Berne Convention") provides:

'1.   Authors of dramatic, dramatico-musical and musical works shall enjoy the exclusive right of authorising:

(i) the public performance of their works, including such public performance by any means or process;
(ii) any communication to the public of the performance of their works.

2.   Authors of dramatic or dramatico-musical works shall enjoy, during the full term of their rights in the original works, the same rights with respect to translations thereof.'

6   Article 11*bis*(1) of the Berne Convention provides:

'Authors of literary and artistic works shall enjoy the exclusive right of authorising:

(i) the broadcasting of their works or the communication thereof to the public by any other means of wireless diffusion of signs, sounds or images;

(ii) any communication to the public by wire or by rebroadcasting of the broadcast of the work, when this communication is made by an organization other than the original one;

(iii) the public communication by loudspeaker or any other analogous instrument transmitting, by signs, sounds or images, the broadcast of the work.'

7   The World Intellectual Property Organisation (WIPO) adopted in Geneva, on 20 December 1996, the WIPO Performances and Phonograms Treaty and the WIPO Copyright Treaty. Those two treaties were approved on behalf of the Community by Council Decision 2000/278/EC of 16 March 2000 (OJ 2000 L 89, p. 6).

8   Article 8 of the WIPO Copyright Treaty provides:

'Without prejudice to the provisions of Articles 11(1)(ii), 11*bis*(1)(i) and (ii), 11ter(1)(ii), 14(1)(ii) and 14*bis*(1) of the Berne Convention, authors of literary and artistic works shall enjoy the exclusive right of authorising any communication to the public of their works, by wire or wireless means, including the making available to the public of their works in such a way that members of the public may access these works from a place and at a time individually chosen by them.'

9   Joint declarations concerning the WIPO Copyright Treaty were adopted by the Diplomatic Conference on 20 December 1996.

10   The joint declaration concerning Article 8 of that Treaty provides:

"It is understood that the mere provision of physical facilities for enabling or making a communication does not in itself amount to communication within the meaning of this Treaty or the Berne Convention. It is further understood that nothing in Article 8 precludes a Contracting Party from applying Article 11*bis*(2)."

. . .

45   With reference to the question whether the installation of television sets in hotel rooms constitutes, in itself, a communication to the public within the meaning of Article 3(1) of Directive 2001/29, it should be pointed out that the 27th recital in the preamble to that directive states, in accordance with Article 8 of the WIPO Copyright Treaty, that "[t]he mere provision of physical facilities for enabling or making a communication does not in itself amount to communication within the meaning of [that] Directive."

QUESTION

Does the European Court of Justice (ECJ) make any distinction between the treaty text and the agreed statement? Is that consistent with the Vienna Convention? Or with the drafting of the text that the court interpreted?

Example of footnote in the TRIPS Agreement

> **Article 3**
> **National Treatment**
>
> 1. Each Member shall accord to the nationals of other Members treatment no less favourable than that it accords to its own nationals with regard to the protection[3] of intellectual property, subject to the exceptions already provided in, respectively, the Paris Convention (1967), the Berne Convention (1971), the Rome Convention or the Treaty on Intellectual Property in Respect of Integrated Circuits. In respect of performers, producers of phonograms and broadcasting organizations, this obligation only applies in respect of the rights provided under this Agreement. Any Member availing itself of the possibilities provided in Article 6 of the Berne Convention (1971) or paragraph 1(b) of Article 16 of the Rome Convention shall make a notification as foreseen in those provisions to the Council for TRIPS.
>
> 2. Members may avail themselves of the exceptions permitted under paragraph 1 in relation to judicial and administrative procedures, including the designation of an address for service or the appointment of an agent within the jurisdiction of a Member, only where such exceptions are necessary

to secure compliance with laws and regulations which are not inconsistent with the provisions of this Agreement and where such practices are not applied in a manner which would constitute a disguised restriction on trade.

3. For the purposes of Articles 3 and 4, "protection" shall include matters affecting the availability, acquisition, scope, maintenance and enforcement of intellectual property rights as well as those matters affecting the use of intellectual property rights specifically addressed in this Agreement.

QUESTION

Is a footnote to the TRIPS Agreement equivalent under the Vienna Convention to an agreed statement under the WIPO Treaties?

2.1.3 Subsequent agreements and practices

Underlying agreement: Berne Convention (1971 Paris text)

Article 2
Protected Works:

1. "Literary and artistic works" . . .

(1) The expression "literary and artistic works" shall include every production in the literary, scientific and artistic domain, whatever may be the mode or form of its expression . . .

Subsequent agreements

Clarification (expansion) of subject matter

TRIPs Agreement (1994)

Article 2
Intellectual Property Conventions

. . .

2. Nothing in Parts I to IV of this Agreement shall derogate from existing obligations that Members may have to each other under the . . . Berne Convention, the Rome Convention . . .

Article 10
Computer Programs and Compilations of Data

1. Computer programs, whether in source or object code, shall be protected as literary works under the Berne Convention (1971).

WIPO Copyright Treaty (1996)

Article 4
Computer Programs

Computer programs are protected as literary works within the meaning of Article 2 of the Berne Convention. Such protection applies to computer programs, whatever may be the mode or form of their expression.

Agreed statements concerning Article 4: The scope of protection for computer programs under Article 4 of this Treaty, read with Article 2, is consistent with Article 2 of the Berne Convention and on a par with the relevant provisions of the TRIPS Agreement.

WTO Panel, WT/DS160/R 15 June 2000 United States – Section 110(5) of the U.S. Copyright Act, Report of the Panel

[For a general presentation of the case see Part II Chapter 5.5 (Exceptions)]

6.70 We discussed the need to interpret the Berne Convention and the TRIPS Agreement in a way that reconciles the texts of these two treaties and avoids a conflict between them, given that they form the overall framework for multilateral copyright protection. The same principle should also apply to the relationship between the TRIPS Agreement and the WCT. The WCT is designed to be compatible with this framework, incorporating or using much of the language of the Berne Convention and the TRIPS Agreement [citations omitted]. The WCT was unanimously concluded at a diplomatic conference organized under the auspices of WIPO in December 1996, one year after the WTO Agreement entered into force, in which 127 countries participated. Most of these countries were also participants in the TRIPS negotiations and are Members of the WTO [citations omitted]. For these reasons, it is relevant to seek contextual guidance also in the WCT when developing interpretations that avoid conflicts within this overall framework, except where these treaties explicitly contain different obligations.

QUESTIONS

1. In the above case, the Panel regarded the WCT as providing relevant contextual guidance. But, as Professor Susy Frankel has noted, at the time of the dispute over section 110(5) of the U.S. Copyright Act, neither the U.S. nor the complaining states had ratified the WIPO Copyright Treaty, nor had it even come into effect (see S. Frankel, *WTO Application of 'the Customary Rules of Interpretation of Public International Law' to Intellectual Property*, 2006 VIRGINIA JOURNAL OF INTERNATIONAL LAW, Vol. 46:2, p. 413). Was the panel wrong to have treated the WCT as a subsequent agreement whose text may inform interpretation of a preceding agreement?

2. To what extent do these subsequent agreements clarify the meaning of the Berne Convention? Is the effect of the subsequent agreements limited to states which are members of those agreements? Could Lebanon, which is a member neither of the TRIPS nor of the WCT, refuse to protect computer programs as literary and artistic works?

Clarification (limitation) of subject matter

Rome Convention for the Protection of Performers, Producers of Phonograms and Broadcasting Organizations (1961)

Article 1
Safeguard of Copyright Proper

Protection granted under this Convention shall leave intact and shall in no way affect the protection of copyright in literary and artistic works. Consequently, no provision of this Convention may be interpreted as prejudicing such protection.

Article 3
Definitions: . . . (b) Phonogram . . .

For the purposes of this Convention:

. . .

(b) "phonogram" means any exclusively aural fixation of sounds of a performance or of other sounds

QUESTIONS

1. How does the Rome Convention clarify the scope of Berne Convention subject matter?
2. Could the U.S., which includes sound recordings within the subject matter of copyright, decline to protect foreign sound recordings on the ground that they do not come within the ambit of the Berne Convention (for purposes of this question do not take into account any other treaties to which the U.S. is a party)?

Subsequent state practice

Vienna Convention Article 31(3)

. . .

3. There shall be taken into account, together with the context:

(*a*) any subsequent agreement between the parties regarding the interpretation of the treaty or the application of its provisions;
(*b*) any subsequent practice in the application of the treaty which establishes the agreement of the parties regarding its interpretation;

In 1980, the U.S. Congress amended the U.S. Copyright Act in order to confirm the protection of computer programs by copyright:

17 U.S.C. § 101 § Definitions

A "computer program" is a set of statements or instructions to be used directly or indirectly in a computer in order to bring about a certain result.

In 1991, an E.U. Directive followed the same approach:

Council Directive 91/250/EEC of 14 May 1991 on the legal protection of computer programs

Article 1 – Object of protection

1. In accordance with the provisions of this Directive, Member States shall protect computer programs, by copyright, as literary works within the meaning of the Berne Convention for the Protection of Literary and

Artistic Works. For the purposes of this Directive, the term 'computer programs' shall include their preparatory design material.

QUESTIONS

1. If the U.S. and the E.U. had already, prior to the TRIPS and the WCT, provided in domestic law for copyright protection of computer programs, can that be considered a subsequent state practice, requiring interpretation of the Berne Convention to include computer programs?
2. See ECJ decision in *Infopaq* (case C-5/08) *infra*, pp. 281 et seq. The ECJ there interpreted the Berne Convention to incorporate a condition of originality. To what extent can the ECJ's interpretation of article 2 of the Berne Convention in the *Infopaq* case be characterized as a subsequent state practice?

WTO Panel, WT/DS160/R 15 June 2000 United States – Section 110(5) of the U.S. Copyright Act, Report of the Panel

[For a general presentation of the case see Part II Chapter 5.5 (Exceptions) at pp. 452 et seq.]

(iii)   The minor exceptions doctrine

6.42   As we noted above, the US view is that Article 13 of the TRIPS Agreement clarifies and articulates the scope of the minor exceptions doctrine, which is applicable under the TRIPS Agreement. Before considering the applicability of Article 13 to Articles 11*bis*(1)(iii) and 11(1)(ii) of the Berne Convention (1971) as incorporated into the TRIPS Agreement, we will first examine whether the minor exceptions doctrine applies under the TRIPS Agreement. This examination involves a two-step analysis. As the first step, we analyse to what extent this doctrine forms part of the Berne Convention *acquis*; in doing so, we will also consider the different views of the parties as to the scope of the doctrine. The second step is to analyse whether that doctrine, if we were to find that it applies under certain Articles of the Berne Convention (1971), has been incorporated into the TRIPS Agreement, by virtue of Article 9.1 of that Agreement, together with Articles 1–21 of the Berne Convention (1971).

General rules of interpretation

6.43   As frequently referred to by WTO Panels and the Appellate Body, the fundamental rules of treaty interpretation are Article 31 [citations omitted]. "General rule of interpretation" and Article 32 "Supplementary means of interpretation"* of the Vienna Convention. We note that, pursuant to Article 31(1) of the Vienna Convention, we have to interpret in good faith the provisions within our terms of reference in accordance with the ordinary meaning to be given to the terms of the treaty in their context and in the light of its object and purpose. We have already addressed the terms of these Articles. But our task does not end with that. The ordinary meaning has to be given to the terms of a treaty in their context and in the light of its object and purpose [citations omitted].

6.44   In that respect, we note that Article 31(2) of the Vienna Convention provides that:

> "The context for the purpose of the interpretation of a treaty shall comprise, in addition to the text, including its preamble and annexes: (a) any agreement relating to the treaty which was made between all the parties in connexion with the conclusion of the treaty; . . ."[citations omitted].

6.45   The International Law Commission explains in its commentary on the final set of draft articles on the law of treaties that this provision is based on the principle that a unilateral document cannot be regarded as forming part of the context unless not only was it made in connection with the conclusion of the treaty, but its relation to the treaty was accepted by the other parties [citations omitted]. "On the other hand, the fact that these two classes of documents are recognized in paragraph 2 as forming part of the 'context' does not mean that they are necessarily to be considered as an integral part of the treaty. Whether they are an actual part of the treaty depends on the intention of the parties in each case" [citations omitted]. It is essential that the agreement or instrument should be related to the treaty. It must be concerned with the substance of the treaty and clarify certain concepts in the treaty or limit its field of application [citations omitted]. It must equally be drawn up on the occasion of the conclusion of the treaty [citations omitted]. Any agreement or instrument fulfilling these criteria will form part of the "context" of the treaty and will thus not be treated as part of the preparatory works but rather as an element in the general rule of interpretation [citations omitted].

---

* Editors' note:

Vienna Convention Article 32

Supplementary means of interpretation

Recourse may be had to supplementary means of interpretation, including the preparatory work of the treaty and the circumstances of its conclusion, in order to confirm the meaning resulting from the application of article 31, or to determine the meaning when the interpretation according to article 31:

(a) leaves the meaning ambiguous or obscure; or

(b) leads to a result which is manifestly absurd or unreasonable.

6.46   Also uncontested interpretations given at a conference, e.g., by a chairman of a drafting committee, may constitute an "agreement" forming part of the "context" [citations omitted]. However, interpretative or explanatory statements by members of a drafting committee in their personal capacity should be considered, if at all, simply as part of the preparatory works. We recall in this respect that, according to Article 32 of the Vienna Convention, preparatory works of a treaty are relevant as supplementary means of interpretation, together with the circumstances of its conclusion, inter alia, in order to confirm the meaning resulting from the application of Article 31 of that Convention.

The legal status of the minor exceptions doctrine under the Berne Convention

6.47   We will now apply these fundamental rules of interpretation to the provisions of the Berne Convention (1971) within our terms of reference, with a view to ascertaining the legal status of the minor exceptions doctrine in relation to Articles 11*bis*(1) and 11(1) of that Convention.

6.48   We note that, in addition to the explicit provisions on permissible limitations and exceptions to the exclusive rights embodied in the text of the Berne Convention (1971), the reports of successive revision conferences of that Convention refer to "implied exceptions" allowing member countries to provide limitations and exceptions to certain rights. The so-called "minor reservations" or "minor exceptions" doctrine is being referred to in respect of the right of public performance and certain other exclusive rights. [citations omitted] Under that doctrine, Berne Union members may provide minor exceptions to the rights provided, inter alia, under Articles 11*bis* and 11 of the Berne Convention (1971) [citations omitted].

. . .

6.50   With respect to public performance of works, until 1948 only a national treatment obligation was provided for under the Berne Convention. Subparagraphs (i) and (ii) of Article 11 of that Convention originated in the Brussels Act of 1948. Their wording remained essentially unchanged in the Stockholm Act of 1967 and the Paris Act of 1971. No specific exception clause applicable to this right was added to the text of the Convention. However, when the general right of public performance was embodied for the first time in Article 11 of the Brussels Act, a statement was included in the General Report of the Brussels Conference referring to the minor exceptions doctrine.

6.51   The provisions currently contained in Article 11*bis*(1)(i) and 11*bis*(2) were first introduced into the Berne Convention at the Rome

Conference of 1928, but subsequently modified. Subparagraphs (ii) and (iii) of Article 11*bis*(1) were added to the Convention at the Brussels Conference of 1948. In discussing subparagraphs (ii) and (iii) of Article 11*bis*(1), the General Report of the Brussels Conference states that the minor exceptions doctrine applies also to the exclusive rights under Article 11*bis*.

6.52   More specifically, it was proposed at the Brussels Conference of 1948 that a general provision be inserted into the Berne Convention under which it would be permissible for States parties to the Convention to retain various minor exceptions that already existed in their national laws. However, the proposal was not adopted by the Conference due to a concern that such a general provision could encourage the widening of existing minor exceptions or the introduction of additional minor exceptions in national laws. But the Conference did not question the very existence and maintenance of minor exceptions in national laws as such. In the context of the discussions on Article 11, it was agreed that rather than dealing with this matter in the text of the Convention itself, a statement concerning the possibility to provide minor exceptions in national law would be included into the General Report [citation omitted].

6.53   When ascertaining the legal status of the minor exceptions doctrine, it is important to note that the General Report states that the Rapporteur-General had been "entrusted with making an express mention of the possibility available to national legislation to make what is commonly called minor reservations" [citations omitted]. We believe that the choice of these words reflects an agreement within the meaning of Article 31(2)(a) of the Vienna Convention between the Berne Union members at the Brussels Conference to retain the possibility of providing minor exceptions in national law. We arrive at this conclusion for the following reasons. First, the introduction of Articles 11*bis*(1)(iii) and 11(1)(ii) occurred simultaneously with the adoption of the General Report expressly mentioning the minor exceptions doctrine. Second, this doctrine is closely related to the substance of the amendment of the Berne Convention in that it limits the scope of the exclusive rights introduced by Articles 11*bis*(1)(iii) and 11(1)(ii) of the Berne Convention. Third, an "agreement" between all the parties exists because, on the one hand, the Rapporteur-General is being "entrusted to expressly mention" minor exceptions and, on the other hand, the General Report of the Brussels Conference reflecting this express mentioning was formally adopted by the Berne Union members. We therefore conclude that an agreement within the meaning of Article 31(2)(a) of the Vienna Convention between all the parties on the possibility to provide minor exceptions was made in connection with the conclusion of a revision of the Convention introducing additional exclusive rights, including those contained in Articles 11*bis*(1)(iii) and 11(1)(ii), to which these limitations were to apply, and that this agreement is relevant as context for interpreting these Articles [citations omitted].

6.54   As pointed out above, the wording of Articles 11*bis* and 11 remained essentially the same at the Diplomatic Conferences in Stockholm (1967) and Paris (1971) where the General Reports were also formally adopted by the Berne Union members. The reports of the Stockholm Conference reconfirm our conclusion concerning the existence of an agreement on minor exceptions. The report of the Main Committee I [citations omitted] refers to the existence of an agreement between the Berne Union members that minor exceptions are permitted, inter alia, in respect of Articles 11 and 11*bis* of the Berne Convention [citations omitted].

6.55   Furthermore, we recall that Article 31(3) of the Vienna Convention provides that together with the context (a) any subsequent agreement, (b) subsequent practice [citations omitted], or (c) any relevant rules of international law applicable between the parties, shall be taken into account for the purposes of interpretation. We note that the parties and third parties have brought to our attention several examples from various countries of limitations in national laws based on the minor exceptions doctrine [citations omitted]. In our view, state practice as reflected in the national copyright laws of Berne Union members before and after 1948, 1967 and 1971, as well as of WTO Members before and after the date that the TRIPS Agreement became applicable to them, confirms our conclusion about the minor exceptions doctrine [citations omitted].

QUESTIONS

1. What are the criteria for inclusion of "minor exceptions" within the scope of the Berne Convention? How does the Panel draw the line between an agreement which forms part of the context of a treaty, and a supplementary means of interpretation? Why are minor exceptions recognized under the Berne Convention? What are the differences between general agreement and subsequent practice? To what extent did subsequent state practice contribute to the Panel's interpretation?

2. Under Article IX:2 of the Marrakesh Agreement Establishing the World Trade Organization, "(a) "The Ministerial Conference and the General Council shall have the exclusive authority to adopt interpretations of this Agreement and of the Multilateral Trade Agreements." Does this rule preclude Panel decisions adopted by the contracting parties from

having binding effect on subsequent Panels? Can any Panel's finding be characterized as a subsequent practice within the meaning of the Vienna Convention and therefore binding on the courts of member states?

Japan - Taxes on Alcoholic Beverages - AB-1996-2 - Report of the Appellate Body, WT/DS8/AB/R; WT/DS10/AB/R; WT/DS11/AB/R (October 4, 1996)

We do not believe that the CONTRACTING PARTIES, in deciding to adopt a panel report, intended that their decision would constitute a definitive interpretation of the relevant provisions of GATT 1947. Nor do we believe that this is contemplated under GATT 1994. There is specific cause for this conclusion in the *WTO Agreement*. Article IX:2 of the *WTO Agreement* provides: "The Ministerial Conference and the General Council shall have the exclusive authority to adopt interpretations of this Agreement and of the Multilateral Trade Agreements". Article IX:2 provides further that such decisions "shall be taken by a three-fourths majority of the Members". The fact that such an "exclusive authority" in interpreting the treaty has been established so specifically in the *WTO Agreement* is reason enough to conclude that such authority does not exist by implication or by inadvertence elsewhere.

2.1.4   Prevailing language

General considerations: Vienna Convention

Article 33 – Interpretation of treaties authenticated in two or more languages

1. When a treaty has been authenticated in two or more languages, the text is equally authoritative in each language, unless the treaty provides or the parties agree that, in case of divergence, a particular text shall prevail.

2. A version of the treaty in a language other than one of those in which the text was authenticated shall be considered an authentic text only if the treaty so provides or the parties so agree.

3. The terms of the treaty are presumed to have the same meaning in each authentic text.

4. Except where a particular text prevails in accordance with paragraph 1, when a comparison of the authentic texts discloses a difference of meaning which the application of articles 31 and 32 does not remove,

the meaning which best reconciles the texts, having regard to the object and purpose of the treaty, shall be adopted. Specific considerations in international copyright and neighbouring rights Conventions.

Application to copyright treaties

Berne Convention Article 37
Final Clauses (The language clause)

(1) (a) This Act shall be signed in a single copy in the French and English languages and, subject to paragraph (2), shall be deposited with the Director General.

(b) Official texts shall be established by the Director General, after consultation with the interested Governments, in the Arabic, German, Italian, Portuguese and Spanish languages, and such other languages as the Assembly may designate.

(c) In case of differences of opinion on the interpretation of the various texts, the French text shall prevail.

C-145/10 Eva-Maria Painer v. Standard VerlagsGmbH and Others ECLI:EU:C:2013:138 [2011]

[Ms Painer is a professional photographer. In the course of her work, she took a photo portraying Natascha K. Sometime after the portrait was taken Natascha K. was kidnapped, but escaped almost ten years later. Following Natascha K.'s escape and prior to her first public appearance, the defendants published the portrait in newspapers, magazines and websites without indicating the name of Ms Painer, or instead indicating a name other than Ms Painer's as the photographer. Several of those publications also published a portrait, created by computer from the original portraits, which, in the absence of any recent photographs of Natascha K. preceding her first public appearance, represented the supposed image of an older Natascha K. Ms Painer's infringement claim required interpretation of the scope of copyright protection of a photograph in light of an exception from the reproduction right contained in article 5(3)(d) of the Directive 2001/29 (on the harmonisation of certain aspects of copyright and related rights in the information society). The exception authorizes "quotations for purposes such as criticism or review, provided that they relate to a work or other subject-matter which has already been lawfully made available to the public, that, unless this turns out to be impossible, the source, including the author's name, is indicated, and that their use is in accordance with fair practice, and to the extent required by the specific purpose." The pertinent portion of the Court's analysis of the condition that the quoted work have "already been lawfully made available to the public" follows:]

118   As a preliminary point, it should be noted that in order to answer question 2(a) and (b) the Court must interpret the same provision of E.U. law, namely Article 5(3)(d) of Directive 2001/29.

119   Under that provision, Member States may provide for an exception to the author's exclusive right of reproduction of his work in respect of quotations for purposes such as criticism or review, provided that (i) they relate to a work or other subject-matter which has already been lawfully made available to the public; (ii) unless this turns out to be impossible, the source, including the author's name, is indicated; and (iii) their use is in accordance with fair practice, and to the extent required by the specific purpose.

120   That provision is intended thus to preclude the exclusive right of reproduction conferred on authors from preventing the publication, by means of quotation accompanied by comments or criticism, of extracts from a work already available to the public.

121   It is common ground that the work relied upon in the main proceedings is a portrait photograph of Natascha K.

122   It is appropriate to observe that the referring court starts from the assumption that a photographic work comes within the scope of Article 5(3)(d) of Directive 2001/29. Moreover, that assumption is not disputed by any of the parties to the main proceedings, by any of the Member States which have lodged observations or by the European Commission.

123   It is from that point of view that question 2(a) and (b) must be answered, without ruling on the correctness of the assumption or on the question of whether the contested photographs were in fact used for the purpose of quotation.

124   In that preliminary respect, it is also appropriate to define the meaning of the expression "mis[e] à la disposition du public" (made available to the public) in the French version of Article 5(3)(d) of Directive 2001/29.

125   In that regard, it is important to point out that neither Article 5(3)(d) of Directive 2001/29 nor any general provision of that directive defines

what is meant by the French expression "mis[e] à la disposition du public". Moreover, that expression is used in several contexts with different wording, as is illustrated, in particular, by Article 3(2) of that directive.

126   In those circumstances, according to settled case-law, Article 5(3) (d) of Directive 2001/29 must be interpreted, in so far as possible, in the light of the applicable rules of international law, and in particular those set forth in the Berne Convention [citations omitted], it being understood that, under Article 37 thereof, its French version is to prevail if there are differences of opinion on the interpretation of the various language versions.

127   It is clear from the French text of Article 10(1) of the Berne Convention, the material scope of which is comparable to that of Article 5(3) (d) of Directive 2001/29, that the only quotations permissible, under certain conditions, are quotations from a work which has already been lawfully made available to the public.

WCT Article 24 (same article in WPPT article 32)
Languages of the Treaty

(1) This Treaty is signed in a single original in English, Arabic, Chinese, French, Russian and Spanish languages, the versions in all these languages being equally authentic.

(2) An official text in any language other than those referred to in paragraph (1) shall be established by the Director General of WIPO on the request of an interested party, after consultation with all the interested parties. For the purposes of this paragraph, "interested party" means any Member State of WIPO whose official language, or one of whose official languages, is involved and the European Community, and any other intergovernmental organization that may become party to this Treaty, if one of its official languages is involved.

Rome Convention Article 33
Languages

1. The present Convention is drawn up in English, French and Spanish, the three texts being equally authentic.

2. In addition, official texts of the present Convention shall be drawn up in German, Italian and Portuguese.

TRIPS Agreement Article 9
Relation to the Berne Convention

1. Members shall comply with Articles 1 through 21 of the Berne Convention (1971) and the Appendix thereto. . . .

WTO Panel, WT/DS160/R 15 June 2000 United States – Section 110(5) of the U.S. Copyright Act Report of the Panel

[For a general presentation of the case see Part II Chapter 5.5 (Exceptions) at pp. 452 et seq.]

6.229   The crucial question is which degree or level of "prejudice" may be considered as "unreasonable",[204]

[204] The term used in the French version of the Berne Convention is "injustifié". According to Article 37(1)(c) of the Berne Convention, both the English and the French text of the Convention are equally authentic, but "in case of differences of opinion on the interpretation of the various texts, the French text shall prevail". However, Article 37 of the Berne Convention has not been incorporated into the TRIPS Agreement. To the extent that Articles 1–21 of the Berne Convention have been incorporated into the TRIPS Agreement by virtue of its Article 9.1, the general rule of Article XVI of the Agreement Establishing the WTO applies, i.e., that the English, French and Spanish versions of the covered agreements are equally authentic. Article 33 of the Vienna Convention on the Law of Treaties stipulates that treaties which are authentic in several languages should be interpreted harmoniously, i.e., presuming that expressions in the treaty have the same meaning in all authentic languages.

QUESTIONS

1. When a national (or regional) court interprets a provision of the Berne Convention and the parties offer divergent interpretations based on the local national language, and the French text, which interpretation prevails? Does the answer change when the interpreter is a WTO Panel?
2. When a national court interprets a provision of the WCT or WPPT and the parties offer divergent interpretations based on the national language or the French text, which interpretation prevails?
3. When a national court interprets a provision of the WCT or WPPT and the parties offer divergent interpretations based on the English and French texts, which interpretation prevails?

4. When a TRIPS panel interprets a provision of the Berne Convention and the contending governments offer divergent interpretations based on the English and Italian texts, which interpretation prevails?

WTO Panel, 26 January 2009 WT/DS 362/R – China – Measures Affecting the Protection and the Enforcement of Intellectual Property Rights

[The following case concerned a complaint by the United States against China. One matter on which the United States requested consultation concerned article 59 (one of the provisions on enforcement measures) and especially the definition of "destruction."]

7.249 The "authority" required by Article 59 concerns two types of remedies, namely "destruction or disposal". The meaning of "destruction" is not controversial. As for "disposal", the Panel notes that the English text of Article 59 does not qualify this word so that it could, in accordance with its ordinary meaning, refer both to disposal outside the channels of commerce as well as to release into the channels of commerce. However, read in context, the word "disposal" could be a reference to an order that goods be "disposed of" outside the channels of commerce as set out in Article 46. This ambiguity is resolved by reference to the French and Spanish texts, which are equally authentic [citations omitted]. The French text of Article 59 refers to authority to order "la mise hors circuit" which is a reference to the authority to order that infringing goods be "écartées des circuits commerciaux" in Article 46. The Spanish text of Article 59 refers to authority to order "eliminación" which, read in its context as an alternative to "destrucción", is evidently a reference to the authority to order that infringing goods be "apartadas de los circuitos comerciales" in Article 46. Accordingly, the correct interpretation of the term "disposal" in the first sentence of Article 59 is disposal "outside the channels of commerce".

QUESTIONS

Do the French and the Spanish version prevail over the English version? Could other language versions be used? Why?

NOTES

The French and English texts of the Berne Convention differ at several points. For example:
Article 2.8 (French version) "faits divers qui ont le seul caractère de simples informations de presse;" (English version) "miscellaneous facts having the

character of mere items of press information." "Miscellaneous facts" may be broader than the French original: a "fait divers" implies a news item of lurid interest, usually involving a crime.

Article 9.2 (French version) "ne cause un préjudice injustifié" (English version) "does not unreasonably prejudice." A more precise translation of the French would be "does not cause an unjustified prejudice."

Article 10(1) (French version) "revues de presse" (English version) "press summaries." "Revues de presse" requires a thematic selection and comparison, which is not necessary true for "press summaries;" moreover, "summaries" implies some rewriting of the source material, where a "revue de presse" may consist of actual quotations.

Article 14ter (french version) "législation nationale de l'auteur" (English version) "country to which the author belongs". A more precise translation would be "the author's national law".

What difference might these disparities of meaning make to interpretation of the treaty?

2.1.5 Supplementary means of interpretation

Vienna Convention Article 32 – Supplementary means of interpretation

Recourse may be had to supplementary means of interpretation, including the preparatory work of the treaty and the circumstances of its conclusion, in order to confirm the meaning resulting from the application of article 31, or to determine the meaning when the interpretation according to article 31:

(a) leaves the meaning ambiguous or obscure; or
(b) leads to a result which is manifestly absurd or unreasonable.

QUESTIONS

Are "supplementary means of interpretation" limited to documents produced before the adoption of the final version of the text? What about subsequently produced documents? Does it matter who produced them?

Titles of treaty articles

Berne Convention (WIPO publication)

Footnote 2 Each Article and the Appendix have been given titles to facilitate their identification. There are no titles in the signed (English) text.

Rome Convention (WIPO publication)

Footnote 2 Articles have been given titles to facilitate their identification. There are no titles in the signed text.

QUESTION

Under the Berne Convention and the Rome Convention, the titles of the various articles were not part of the text as enacted, but were added by WIPO later on. By contrast, under the WPPT, the WCT and the TRIPS Agreement, titles are part of the Conventions' original text. What difference does it make regarding the role of the titles as aides to interpretation of the treaties?

WIPO Guides

The following cases both concerned the interpretation of the expression "communication to the public." The first case has already been presented. The second case inquires whether the broadcasting of phonograms in a private dental clinic could be characterized as an act of communication to the public under the Information Society Directive and under Directive 92/100 (on the rental right and lending right and on certain rights related to copyright in the field of intellectual property)

C-306/05 Sociedad General de Autores y Editores de España (SGAE) v. Rafael Hoteles SA ECLI:EU:C:2006:764 [2006]

[This case has already been described, see *supra*, page 97]

40   It should also be pointed out that a communication made in circumstances such as those in the main proceedings constitutes, according to Article 11*bis*(1)(ii) of the Berne Convention, a communication made by a broadcasting organisation other than the original one. Thus, such a transmission is made to a public different from the public at which the original act of communication of the work is directed, that is, to a new public.

41   As is explained in the Guide to the Berne Convention, an interpretative document drawn up by the WIPO which, without being legally binding, nevertheless assists in interpreting that Convention, when the author authorises the broadcast of his work, he considers only direct users, that is, the owners of reception equipment who, either personally or within their own private or family circles, receive the programme. According to the Guide, if reception is for a larger audience, possibly for profit, a new

section of the receiving public hears or sees the work and the communication of the programme via a loudspeaker or analogous instrument no longer constitutes simple reception of the programme itself but is an independent act through which the broadcast work is communicated to a new public. As the Guide makes clear, such public reception falls within the scope of the author's exclusive authorisation right.

C-135/10 Società Consortile Fonografici (SCF) v. Marco Del Corso ECLI:EU:C:2012:140 [2012]

85   As regards, to begin with, the "indeterminate" nature of the public, the Court has observed that, according to the definition of the concept of "communication to the public" given by the WIPO glossary, which, while not legally binding, none the less sheds light on the interpretation of the concept of public, it means "making a work . . . perceptible in any appropriate manner to persons in general, that is, not restricted to specific individuals belonging to a private group".

QUESTIONS

The WIPO Guides are produced by the staff of the World Intellectual Property Organization, the entity charged with administering the Berne and Rome Conventions and other intellectual property accords. What is the status of the WIPO Glossary or the Guide to the Berne Convention? Could they be characterized as supplementary means of interpretation? If not, what, if any, use is the WIPO Guide to interpreting the treaties? See *infra*, [cross-reference], discussion of divergences between different editions of the WIPO Guides with respect to the scope of the Rome Convention obligation of national treatment. What about scholarly treatises and articles?

WTO Panel, 26 January 2009 WT/DS 362/R – China – Measures Affecting the Protection and the Enforcement of Intellectual Property Rights, Report of the Panel

[The following case concerned a complaint by the United States against China. One matter on which the U.S. requested consultation was the threshold above which a member state is required to bring criminal proceedings. For the U.S., the threshold fixed by Chinese law did not respect article 61 of the TRIPS Agreement requiring criminal proceedings against persons committing copyright piracy "on a commercial scale". The U.S. and China did not agree as to the definition of commercial scale.]

(vii)   Supplementary means of interpretation

7.582 China initially submitted that the draft Model Provisions contained a definition which formed the basis for discussion of the term in the negotiation of the TRIPS Agreement [citations omitted].

7.583   The United States responded that the status of this document under the Vienna Convention is unclear. If the document could be used as a supplementary means of interpretation, it would confirm that a variety of factors would need to be taken into account to determine whether an act is on a commercial scale [citations omitted].

7.584   Canada and Japan refer to the explanatory observation on "commercial scale" that accompanied the draft Model Provisions, noting that it referred to quantitative as well as nonquantitative factors. The European Communities sees limited interest in recourse to supplementary means of interpretation but notes the same point [citations omitted].

7.585   ... It appears that the explanatory observation did not represent the common intentions of the WIPO Committee of Experts on Measures Against Counterfeiting and Piracy, much less the common intentions of the participants in the negotiation of the TRIPS Agreement.

7.586   The draft Model Provisions were mentioned in the records of the TRIPS negotiations, in May 1988 [citations omitted] and August 1988 [citations omitted], in the context of a discussion of the scope of a framework on trade in counterfeit goods (that was never concluded). Documents of the WIPO Committee of Experts, including the draft Model Provisions, were communicated to the TRIPS negotiating group and made available in the GATT Secretariat for consultation by interested delegations, but not circulated, in June 1988. The Panel considers that this evidence indicates that the negotiators of the TRIPS Agreement were aware of the explanatory observation by the International Bureau of WIPO addressing "commercial scale", but it does not indicate that the content of that explanatory observation represented their common intentions.

7.587   There is a certain temporal correlation between the work of the WIPO Committee of Experts and the use of the term "commercial scale" in the drafting of Article 61 of the TRIPS Agreement. The European Communities' proposal for the negotiations on the enforcement of trade-related intellectual property rights in May 1989 ("EC proposal") [citations omitted] contained a draft provision on criminal procedures and sanctions that bears a strong similarity to the first, second and fourth sentences of Article 61 in the final text of the TRIPS Agreement. It was also the first proposal to use the words "on a commercial scale". In response to a question from the Panel, the European Communities informed the Panel that: "In spite of intense research, the European Communities has not been able to find any trace that the phrase 'on a commercial scale' in the EC proposal of 30 May 1989 was sourced from another instrument" [citations omitted].

7.588 In any event, there are differences between the draft Model Provisions of the WIPO Committee of Experts, the EC proposal on criminal procedures and sanctions to the TRIPS negotiating group, and the terms of Article 61 of the TRIPS Agreement. In particular, the draft Model Provisions incorporated the phrase "on a commercial scale" within the concepts of "counterfeiting" and "piracy" whilst Article 61 uses the phrase "on a commercial scale" to qualify the concepts of "wilful trademark counterfeiting or copyright piracy". Further, the explanatory observation that accompanied the draft Model Provisions was limited to the act of manufacturing whilst Article 61 encompasses the range of acts of counterfeiting and piracy.

7.589 The records of the TRIPS negotiations do not disclose any discussion of the meaning of the phrase "on a commercial scale".

7.590 Therefore, the Panel does not consider that the explanatory observation that accompanied the draft Model Provisions sheds any further light beyond that noted at paragraph 7.562 above on the intentions of the TRIPS negotiators when they used the term "commercial scale".

QUESTIONS

Why is the draft Model Provisions of the WIPO Committee of Experts not recognized as a supplementary means of interpretation? Would it have been possible to have a WIPO document recognized as a supplementary means of interpretation for the TRIPS Agreement?

2.1.6 Special meaning

Vienna Convention Article 31 – General rule of interpretation

. . .

4. A special meaning shall be given to a term if it is established that the parties so intended.

WTO Panel, WT/DS 362/R – China – Measures Affecting the Protection and the Enforcement of Intellectual Property Rights

[This case has been previously described, see *supra*, page 117]

7.558 The Panel observes that the general rule of treaty interpretation in Article 31 of the Vienna Convention refers in paragraph 1 to the ordinary meaning of the terms of the treaty, read in context. Where the terms are a single term, or ordinarily used together, then the treaty interpreter should refer to the ordinary meaning of that single term, or of each term in the particular context of each other. This is a distinct exercise from that in paragraph 4 of Article 31 of the Vienna Convention which requires a "special meaning" to be given to a term if it is established that the parties so intended. No party to this dispute considers that a "special meaning" should be given to the phrase "on a commercial scale", and nor does the Panel.

QUESTIONS

How does a judge choose between interpreting a notion using the ordinary meaning or the special meaning? Does the Panel help resolve this question?

2.2 Self-executing nature of an international convention?

Berne Convention Article 36
Application of the Convention

(1) Any country party to this Convention undertakes to adopt, in accordance with its constitution, the measures necessary to ensure the application of this Convention.

(2) It is understood that, at the time a country becomes bound by this Convention, it will be in a position under its domestic law to give effect to the provisions of this Convention.

WPPT Article 23
Provisions on Enforcement of Rights

(1) Contracting Parties undertake to adopt, in accordance with their legal systems, the measures necessary to ensure the application of this Treaty.

QUESTION

Do the Berne Convention or the WPPT specify how member states are to give effect to the provisions of the Convention?

2.2.1   U.S.

Section 111, Restatement (Third) of the Foreign Relations Law of the United States

(3) Courts in the United States are bound to give effect to international law and to international agreements of the United States, except that a "non-self-executing" agreement will not be given effect as law in the absence of necessary implementation.

(4) An international agreement of the United States is "non-self-executing"

a) If the agreement manifests an intention that it shall not become effective as domestic law without the enactment of implementing legislation,
b) If the Senate in giving consent to a treaty, or Congress by resolution, requires implementing legislation, or
c) If implementing legislation is constitutionally required.

17 U.S.C. Section 104(c)

(c) Effect of Berne Convention—No right or interest in a work eligible for protection under this title may be claimed by virtue of, or in reliance upon, the provisions of the Berne Convention, or the adherence of the United States thereto. Any rights in a work eligible for protection under this title that derive from this title, other Federal or State statutes, or the common law, shall not be expanded or reduced by virtue of, or in reliance upon, the provisions of the Berne Convention, or the adherence of the United States thereto.

An Act to approve and implement the trade agreements concluded in the Uruguay Round of multilateral trade negotiations URAA ("Uruguay Round Amendments Act")

SEC. 102. RELATIONSHIP OF THE AGREEMENTS TO UNITED STATES LAW AND STATE LAW.

(a) RELATIONSHIP OF AGREEMENTS TO UNITED STATES LAW.—

(1) UNITED STATES LAW TO PREVAIL IN CONFLICT.—No provision of any of the Uruguay Round Agreements [TRIPS], nor the application of any such provision to any person or circumstance, that is inconsistent with any law of the United States shall have effect.

QUESTIONS

1. Do the above texts comply with article 36 of the Berne Convention?
2. Suppose U.S. copyright law does not in some respects conform to international obligations. What recourse does an injured party have? See *infra*, sections 2.3 and 2.4.

2.2.2 E.U.

Council Decision (of 22 December 1994) concerning the conclusion on behalf of the European Community, as regards matters within its competence, of the agreements reached in the Uruguay Round multilateral negotiations (1986–1994) (94/800/EC)

THE COUNCIL OF THE EUROPEAN UNION,

Whereas, by its nature, the Agreement establishing the World Trade Organization, including the Annexes thereto, is not susceptible to being directly invoked in Community or Member State courts, . . .

C-135/10 Società Consortile Fonografici (SCF) v. Marco Del Corso ECLI:EU:C:2012:140 [2012]

[The case concerned the characterization of the transmission of protected phonograms in a private dental practice by way of background music. If the transmission constituted "communication to the public" within the meaning of international neighboring rights law and European Union law, it would give rise to an obligation to pay equitable remuneration to the rightholders. The Italian Court referred the following question to the ECJ:]

35 . . .Are the [Rome Convention], the [Agreement] and the [WPPT] directly applicable within the Community legal order?]

43   As regards, second, the question whether individuals are entitled to rely directly on the provisions of the TRIPS Agreement and the WPPT, it must be observed that, according to the case-law of the Court of Justice, it is not sufficient that they are part of the legal order of the Union. Those provisions must also appear, as regards their content, to be unconditional and sufficiently precise and their nature and broad logic must not preclude their being so relied on [citations omitted].

44   The first condition is met where the provisions relied on contain clear and precise obligations which are not subject, in their implementation or effects, to the adoption of any subsequent measure. . ..

45   As regards the TRIPS Agreement, it must be recalled that, according to the last recital in the preamble to Decision 94/800,* the Agreement establishing the World Trade Organization, including its Annexes is not susceptible to being directly invoked in European Union or Member State courts.

46   Moreover, the Court has already held that, having regard to their nature and structure, the provisions of the TRIPS Agreement do not have direct effect. Those provisions are not, in principle, among the rules in the light of which the Court is to review the legality of measures of the Community institutions under the first paragraph of Article 230 EC [now Article 263 TFEU] and are not such as to create rights upon which individuals may rely directly before the courts by virtue of European Union law [citations omitted].

47   Article 23(1) of the WPPT provides that the Contracting Parties undertake to adopt, in accordance with their legal systems, the measures necessary to ensure the application of that Treaty.

48   It follows that the application of the provisions of the WPPT, in their implementation or effects, is subject to the adoption of subsequent measures. Therefore, such provisions have no direct effect in the law of the European Union and are not such as to create rights for individuals which they may rely on before the courts by virtue of that law.

---

* Editors' Note: Decision 94/800 Council Decision (of 22 December 1994) concerning the conclusion on behalf of the European Community, as regards matters within its competence, of the agreements reached in the Uruguay Round multilateral negotiations (1986–1994); this recital states: "Whereas, by its nature, the Agreement establishing the World Trade Organization, including the Annexes thereto, is not susceptible to being directly invoked in Community or Member State courts".

QUESTIONS

Why did the Court refuse to give direct effect to the WPPT? To what extent does article 23(1) of the WPPT influence the solution? What is the relevance of the nature and the structure of the TRIPS Agreement to identifying any direct effect of the WPPT? Are there differences with the WPPT?

2.3 Interpretation of domestic law in light of international norms

2.3.1 U.S.

Section 114 Restatement (Third) of the Law, the Foreign Relations of the U.S.

> Where fairly possible, a U.S. statute is to be construed so as not to conflict with international law or with an international agreement of the U.S.

Restatement section 114 announces a rule known as the "*Charming Betsy* doctrine," named after *Murray v. The Charming Betsy*, 6 U.S. 64 (1804), a decision of Chief Justice Marshall, concerning forfeiture of a vessel. The statute governing forfeitures applied to American citizens, but the vessel owner, albeit born an American citizen, had acquired Danish nationality and was domiciled in the (then-)Danish territory of St. Thomas. Chief Justice Marshall declared that:

> an act of Congress ought never to be construed to violate the law of nations if any other possible construction remains, and consequently can never be construed to violate neutral rights or to affect neutral commerce further than is warranted by the law of nations as understood in this country.

Accordingly, since the statute was not clearly directed to non-U.S. domiciliaries, the Court held the ship had been unlawfully seized. From "the law of nations" the *Charming Betsy* rule has come to be applied to interpretation of statutes in light of U.S. treaty obligations. But in the absence of self-executing norms or specific implementing legislation, U.S. courts may be reluctant to interpret statutes to give effect to the treaty norm, as the following excerpt indicates.

The following is one of the few decisions to address the application of the *Charming Betsy* canon to copyright law:

Capitol Records v. Thomas, 579 F.Supp.2d 1210 (D. Minn. 2008) [The court rejected the contention that the U.S. ratification of the WIPO Copyright Treaty and WPPT, requiring member states to implement the right of "making available," obliged U.S. courts to interpret the statutory distribution right consistently with the treaty. The conventional "making available right" covers offering access to protected works, as well as actual transmission or delivery of the content of the works. At issue in *Capitol Records* was whether the distribution right set out in § 106(3) of the U.S. Copyright Act extends only to actual distributions or also covers offers to distribute.]

I. Implications of International Law

1. U.S. Treaty Obligations Regarding the Making-Available Right

The United States is party to the World Intellectual Property Organization ("WIPO") Copyright Treaty ("WCT") and the WIPO Performances and Phonograms Treaty ("WPPT"). S. Rep. No. 105–190, 5, 9 (1998). It is undisputed that the WCT and the WPPT recognize a making-available right that is not dependent on proof that copies were actually transferred to particular individuals. WCT art. 6(1), art. 8; WPPT art. 12(1), art. 14. Additionally, by ratifying and adopting the treaties, the legislative and executive branches indicated that U.S. law complied with the treaties by protecting that making-available right.

Amici also note that the United States has entered various Free Trade Agreements ("FTA") that require the United States to provide a making-available right. See, e.g., U.S.-Australia Free Trade Agreement, art. 17.5, May 18, 2004.

2. *Charming-Betsy* Doctrine

c. Application of the Doctrine in This Case

The Court acknowledges that past Presidents, Congresses, and the Register of Copyrights have indicated their belief that the Copyright Act implements WIPO's make-available right. The Court also acknowledges that, given multiple reasonable constructions of U.S. law, the *Charming-Betsy* doctrine directs the Court to adopt the reasonable construction that is consistent with the United States' international obligations. However, after reviewing the Copyright Act itself, legislative history, binding Supreme Court and Eighth Circuit precedent, and an extensive body of case law examining the Copyright Act, the Court concludes that Plaintiffs' interpretation of the distribution right is simply not reasonable. The *Charming-Betsy* doctrine is a helpful tool for statutory construction, but it is not a substantive law. It is always the case that "clear congressional action trumps customary international law and previously enacted treaties." *Guaylupo-Moya*, 423 F.3d at 136 (holding that it is improper to apply the *Charming-Betsy* canon when "the relevant provisions [of domestic law] are unambiguous"). Here, concern for U.S. compliance with the WIPO treaties and the FTAs cannot override the clear congressional intent in § 106(3).

QUESTION

For a view that the congressional intent underlying the § 106(3) distribution right is clear—but clearly contrary to the interpretation adopted by the *Capitol Records* district court, see Peter Menell, *In Search of Copyright's Lost Ark*, 59 J. COPYRIGHT SOC'Y U.S.A. 1 (2011) (contending that the distribution right extends to offers to distribute as well as to actual distributions; this interpretation would conform the U.S. distribution right to the scope of the Conventions' "making available" right).—When different authorities are equally convinced of the opposite conclusions regarding statutory scope, what role should the *Charming Betsy* doctrine play?

2.3.2   E.U.

Interpretation in light of international conventions

C-306/05 Sociedad General de Autores y Editores de España (SGAE) v. Rafael Hoteles SA ECLI:EU:C:2006:764 [2006]

[This case has already been described, see *supra*, page 97]

35   Moreover, Community legislation must, so far as possible, be interpreted in a manner that is consistent with international law, in particular where its provisions are intended specifically to give effect to an international agreement concluded by the Community [citation omitted].

QUESTIONS

What does "so far as possible" mean? Could an interpretation contrary to international law be permissible under European or U.S. Law? Could a national text be contrary to an international text, when the national text is clear and does not require any interpretation?

The extension of the legal order of the European Union to conventions to which the Union is not a member

The E.U. is member of the following treaties: WPPT, WCT and TRIPS.

C-135/10 Società Consortile Fonografici (SCF) v. Marco Del Corso ECLI:EU:C:2012:140 [2012]

[Already presented, see page 122, this case raised the following questions to the ECJ:]

35. As it considered that there was some doubt over the question whether the broadcasting of phonograms in private professional practices such as dental practices, was included in the definition of 'communication to the public' for the purposes of international law and European Union law, the Corte d'appello decided to stay the proceedings and to refer the following questions to the Court of Justice for a preliminary ruling:

'1. Are the [Rome Convention], the [TRIPs Agreement] and the [WPPT] directly applicable within the Community legal order?

2. Are the abovementioned sources of uniform international law also directly effective within the context of private-law relationships?

3. Do the concepts of 'communication to the public' contained in the above mentioned treaty-law texts mirror the Community concepts contained in Directives 92/100 [rental right] and 2001/29 [Info Soc] and, if not, which source should take precedence?'

36 By its first to third questions, which should be examined together, the referring court asks, essentially, first, whether the Rome Convention, the TRIPS Agreement and the WPPT are directly applicable in the legal order of the European Union and whether individuals may rely on them directly. Next, it wishes to know whether the definition of "communication to the public" in those international conventions is the same as that in Directives 92/100 [Rental Right] and 2001/29 [Info Soc] and, finally, in the event that the last question is answered in the negative, which source of law should prevail.

37 First, as regards the question whether the Rome Convention, the TRIPS Agreement and the WPPT are directly applicable in the legal order of the European Union, it must be recalled at the outset that, under Article 216(2) of the TFEU (Treaty on the Functioning of the European Union),

'[a]greements concluded by the Union are binding upon the institutions of the Union and on its Member States'.

38   The TRIPS Agreement and the WPPT were signed by the European Union and approved by Decisions 94/800 and 2000/278 respectively. Consequently, that agreement and treaty bind the institutions of the European Union and the Member States.

39   Moreover, according to the settled case-law of the Court, the provisions of agreements concluded by the Union form an integral part of the Union legal order [citations omitted] and are therefore applicable in the Union.

40   The TRIPS Agreement and the WPPT are such agreements.

41   As regards the Rome Convention, it must be pointed out, first, that the European Union is not a contracting party to that convention and, second, that it cannot be regarded as having taken the place of its Member States as regards its application, if only because not all of those States are parties to that convention.

. . .

42   Consequently, the provisions of the Rome Convention do not form part of the legal order of the European Union.

49   As regards the Rome Convention, it must be recalled that, under Article 1(1) of the WPPT, nothing in that treaty is to derogate from existing obligations that Contracting Parties have to each other under the Rome Convention.

50   Accordingly, although the European Union is not a contracting party to the Rome Convention, it is none the less required, under Article 1(1) of the WPPT, not to stand in the way of the obligations of the Member States under that convention. Accordingly, that convention has indirect effects within the European Union.

51   Third, as regards the question of the relationship between the concept of 'communication to the public' in the TRIPS Agreement, the WPPT and the Rome Convention and that in Directives 92/100 and 2001/29, it must be recalled that, according to settled case-law, European Union legislation must, so far as possible, be interpreted in a manner that is consistent with international law, in particular where its provisions are intended specifically to give effect to an international agreement concluded by the European

Union (see, inter alia, ... Case C-306/05 *SGAE* [2006] ECR I-11519, paragraph 35).

52   In that regard, it is common ground that, as recital 15 in the preamble to Directive 2001/29 makes clear, that directive is intended to implement a number of the Union's new obligations under the WCT and the WPPT, which are considered, according to the same recital, to update the international protection for copyright and related rights significantly. In those circumstances, the concepts contained in that directive must be interpreted, as far as is possible, in the light of those two Treaties (see, to that effect, Case C-456/06 *Peek & Cloppenburg* [2008] ECR I-2731, paragraph 31).

53   Moreover, it follows from recital 10 of Directive 92/100 that the legislation of the Member States should be approximated in such a way as not to conflict with the international conventions on which many Member States' laws on copyright and related rights are based.

54   As that directive is intended to harmonise certain aspects of the law on copyright and related rights in the field of intellectual property in compliance with the relevant international agreements such as, inter alia, the Rome Convention, the TRIPS Agreement and the WPPT, it is supposed to establish a set of rules compatible with those contained in those agreements.

55   It follows from all those considerations that the concepts appearing in Directives 92/100 and 2001/29, such as 'communication to the public' must be interpreted in the light of the equivalent concepts contained in those international agreements and in such a way that they are compatible with those agreements, taking account of the context in which those concepts are found and the purpose of the relevant provisions of the agreements as regards intellectual property.

56   Having regard to the foregoing considerations, the answer to the first to third questions is:

- the provisions of the TRIPS Agreement and the WPPT are applicable in the legal order of the European Union,
- as the Rome Convention does not form part of the legal order of the European Union it is not applicable there; however, it has indirect effects within the European Union
- individuals may not rely directly either on that convention or on the TRIPS Agreement or the WPPT;
- the concept of 'communication to the public' must be interpreted

in the light of the equivalent concepts contained in the Rome Convention, the TRIPS Agreement and the WPPT and in such a way that it is compatible with those agreements, taking account of the context in which those concepts are found and the purpose of the relevant provisions of the agreements as regards intellectual property.

C-277/10 Martin Luksan v. Petrus Van der Let ECLI:EU:C:2012:65 [2012]

[The case concerned a dispute between the principal director of a documentary and his producer. The dispute arose because the producer made the movie available on the Internet without the authorization of the director. The producer considered that, as producer and under Austrian law applicable to the contract, all exclusive exploitation rights in the film vest in him. The director challenged the compliance of the Austrian law with European law, under which he claimed the right should vest in him. The case concerns the interpretation of four Directives (Directive 92/100 Rental Right, Directive 93/83 Satellite broadcasting and cable retransmission, Directive 93/98 Term of Protection and Directive 2001/29 Information Society) in order to determine who is the owner of rights protecting a cinematographic work. The question raised was the conformity of the Austrian law to those European Directives. The Austrian Government relied in its observations upon paragraph 2(b), in conjunction with paragraph 3, of article 14bis of the Berne Convention, an article which relates to cinematographic works and which, in the Austrian Government's submission, authorizes it to grant those rights exclusively to the producer of the work. (We will consider the interpretation of art. 14bis in Part II, Chapter 6, pp. 539–45.)]

59 It should also be observed that the European Union, which is not a party to the Berne Convention, is nevertheless obliged, under Article 1(4) of the WIPO Copyright Treaty, to which it is a party, which forms part of its legal order and which Directive 2001/29 is intended to implement, to comply with Articles 1 to 21 of the Berne Convention (see, to this effect, *Football Association Premier League and Others*, paragraph 189 and the case-law cited). Consequently, the European Union is required to comply inter alia with Article 14*bis* of the Berne Convention.

QUESTIONS

1. How and why does the ECJ take into account treaties to which the E.U. is not a contracting party?
2. Article 1 of the WIPO Treaty requires that Contracting Parties comply with articles 1 to 21 and the Appendix of the Berne Convention, whereas

article 1 of the WPPT Treaty requires that member states not derogate from the Rome Convention. Does the contrast between "shall comply with" the Berne Convention and "[not] derogate from" the Rome Convention imply any difference in the way treaty obligations bear on member states? Does the ECJ treat the obligations differently?

3. To what extent does seeking to interpret a national or regional norm in the light of international norms mean that the court is seeking to render the local norm compatible with international norms? What difference, if any, is there between striving for compatibility with international norms and recognizing the direct effect of those norms? How does the E.U. position compare to the U.S.?

2.4 Hierarchy of norms and international conventions under U.S. and E.U. law

The proliferation of legal norms at different levels (domestic, federal, European and international) requires a method for combining and/or articulating them in order to solve apparent conflicts. The goal of the "hierarchy of norms" is to organize the chaos by identifying which law should prevail in case of conflict. Due to the hierarchy, the higher norm will prevail on the lesser norm. At a national level, the hierarchy is established by the national constitution, considered the supreme norm above any other norms. This is true under American and French laws for example. International treaties complicate the picture. A well-established solution is to locate those international treaties above acts of the legislature. A state may not elude its international obligations simply by changing its legislation. Nevertheless, it seems hardly imaginable to place those international treaties above the national constitution. Thus, the hierarchy of norms locates international conventions between acts of the legislature and the constitution.

While this hierarchy operates on a national level, it raises problems on an international level. At an international level, states should respect their international obligations, regardless of the substance of their constitutions. A state's invocation of its constitution before an international court would not justify its failure to respect an international treaty. This is especially true in IP with the WTO and its mechanism of dispute resolution. Each member state should respect the TRIPS Agreement, regardless of the substance of its constitution. Thus, the hierarchy is relative and may change depending on whether the conflict has to be solved at a national level or an international level. From a national level, the constitution is always at the top. From an international level, the international conventions are always at the top. Furthermore, the European construction complicates the situation.

From a French perspective, the hierarchy is still crowned by the national constitution. From a European perspective and before the European Court of Justice, the hierarchy is crowned by the European primary law. Adopting a constitutional analysis, the European judge places its supreme norm at the top. Under the E.U. hierarchy, then, international copyright treaties are not above European primary law. Nevertheless, at the WTO level, this European hierarchy would have to yield to the international norm, just as would the American hierarchy. As a result, there is not one uniform substantive hierarchy, but several, depending on the court seized (at least three for a European member state: the hierarchy established in the member state, the hierarchy established in Brussels and eventually the hierarchy established in Geneva at the WTO).

2.4.1 U.S.

U.S. Constitution Art VI § 2 (the "Supremacy Clause")

This Constitution, and the laws of the United States which shall be made in pursuance thereof; and all treaties made, or which shall be made, under the authority of the United States, shall be the supreme law of the land; and the judges in every state shall be bound thereby, anything in the Constitution or laws of any State to the contrary notwithstanding.

Reid v. Covert, 354 U.S. 1 (1957)

[The case concerned the constitutionality of military tribunals for offenses committed abroad. U.S. soldiers committed murders in Japan and in Great Britain. One question raised was about the ranking of the international agreements signed with those countries in the hierarchy of norms, especially vis-à-vis the Constitution.]

There is nothing in this language which intimates that treaties and laws enacted pursuant to them do not have to comply with the provisions of the Constitution. Nor is there anything in the debates which accompanied the drafting and ratification of the Constitution which even suggests such a result. These debates as well as the history that surrounds the adoption of the treaty provision in Article VI make it clear that the reason treaties were not limited to those made in "pursuance" of the Constitution was so that agreements made by the United States under the Articles of Confederation, including the important peace treaties which concluded the Revolutionary War, would remain in effect. It would be manifestly contrary to the objectives of those who created the Constitution, as well as those who were responsible for the Bill of Rights—let alone alien to our entire constitutional history and tradition—to construe Article VI as permitting the United States to exercise power under an international agreement without observing constitutional prohibitions. In effect, such construction would permit amendment of that document in a manner not sanctioned by Article V. The prohibitions of the Constitution were designed to apply to all branches of the National Government and they cannot be nullified by the Executive or by the Executive and the Senate combined.

There is nothing new or unique about what we say here. This Court has regularly and uniformly recognized the supremacy of the Constitution over a treaty.

Restatement (Third) of the Foreign Relations Law of the United States

Section 115 Inconsistency Between International Law or Agreement and Domestic Law: Law of the United States

1 An act of Congress supersedes an earlier rule of international law or a provision of an international law or a provision of an international agreement as law of the United States if the purpose of the act to supersede the earlier rule of provision is clear or if the act and the earlier rule or provision cannot be fairly reconciled. . . .
2 A provision of a treaty of the United States that becomes effective as law of the United States supersedes as domestic law any inconsistent preexisting provision of a law or treaty of the United States.

QUESTIONS

What is the relevance of Restatement section 115 to copyright and neighboring rights? Suppose the U.S. were to enact a statute reintroducing mandatory copyright formalities in violation of article 5(2) of the Berne Convention (see *infra*, pp. 261 et seq.)? Or suppose the U.S. were to ratify a treaty requiring that authors receive name credit if their works are quoted in the press or for educational purposes (as mandated by article 10 of the Berne Convention, see *infra*, page 438), even though neither domestic legislation nor caselaw have imposed such a condition on quotation rights? Before what, if any, institutions may the injured party seek redress in case of non-compliance with international norms?

Golan v. Holder, 565 U.S. ___, 132 S. Ct. 873 (2012)

▪ Justice Ginsburg delivered the opinion of the Court.

The Berne Convention for the Protection of Literary and Artistic Works (Berne Convention or Berne), which took effect in 1886, is the principal accord governing international copyright relations. Latecomer to the international copyright regime launched by Berne, the United States joined the Convention in 1989. To perfect U.S. implementation of Berne, and as part of our response to the Uruguay Round of multilateral trade negotiations, Congress, in 1994, gave works enjoying copyright protection abroad the same full term of protection available to U.S. works. Congress did so in § 514 of the Uruguay Round Agreements Act (URAA), which grants copyright protection to preexisting works of Berne member countries, protected in their country of origin, but lacking protection in the United States for any of three reasons: The United States did not protect works from the country of origin at the time of publication; the United States did not protect sound recordings fixed before 1972; or the author had failed to comply with U.S. statutory formalities (formalities Congress no longer requires as prerequisites to copyright protection).

Members of the Berne Union agree to treat authors from other member countries as well as they treat their own. Berne Convention, Sept. 9, 1886, as revised at Stockholm on July 14, 1967, Art. 1, 5(1), 828 U.N.T.S. 221, 225, 231–233. Nationals of a member country, as well as any author who publishes in one of Berne's 164 member states,* thus enjoy copyright protection in nations across the globe. Each country, moreover, must afford at least the minimum level of protection specified by Berne. The copyright term must span the author's lifetime, plus at least 50 additional years, whether or not the author has complied with a member state's legal formalities. And, as relevant here, a work must be protected abroad unless its copyright term has expired in either the country where protection is claimed or the country of origin. Art. 18(1)–(2).

A different system of transnational copyright protection long prevailed in this country. Until 1891, foreign works were categorically excluded from Copyright Act protection. Throughout most of the twentieth century, the only eligible foreign authors were those whose countries granted reciprocal rights to U.S. authors and whose works were printed in the United States. See Act of Mar. 3, 1891, § 3, 13, 26 Stat. 1107, 1110; Patry, The United States

---

* Editors' note: at the time of the *Golan* decision the Berne Convention counted 164 members; as of December 2014 there were 168 members.

and International Copyright Law, 40 Houston L. Rev. 749, 750 (2003). For domestic and foreign authors alike, protection hinged on compliance with notice, registration, and renewal formalities.

The United States became party to Berne's multilateral, formality-free copyright regime in 1989. Initially, Congress adopted a "minimalist approach" to compliance with the Convention. H. R. Rep. No. 100–609, p. 7 (1988) (hereinafter BCIA House Report). The Berne Convention Implementation Act of 1988 (BCIA), 102 Stat. 2853, made "only those changes to American copyright law that [were] clearly required under the treaty's provisions," BCIA House Report, at 7. Despite Berne's instruction that member countries—including "new accessions to the Union"—protect foreign works under copyright in the country of origin, Art. 18(1) and (4), the BCIA accorded no protection for "any work that is in the public domain in the United States," § 12, 102 Stat. 2860. Protection of future foreign works, the BCIA indicated, satisfied Article 18. See § 2(3), 102 Stat. 2853 ("The amendments made by this Act, together with the law as it exists on the date of the enactment of this Act, satisfy the obligations of the United States in adhering to the Berne Convention . . . ."). Congress indicated, however, that it had not definitively rejected "retroactive" protection for preexisting foreign works; instead it had punted on this issue of Berne's implementation, deferring consideration until "a more thorough examination of Constitutional, commercial, and consumer considerations is possible." BCIA House Report, at 51, 52.

The minimalist approach essayed by the United States did not sit well with other Berne members. While negotiations were ongoing over the North American Free Trade Agreement (NAFTA), Mexican authorities complained about the United States' refusal to grant protection, in accord with article 18, to Mexican works that remained under copyright domestically. The Register of Copyrights also reported "questions" from Turkey, Egypt, and Austria. Thailand and Russia balked at protecting U.S. works, copyrighted here but in those countries' public domains, until the United States reciprocated with respect to their authors' works.

Berne, however, did not provide a potent enforcement mechanism. The Convention contemplates dispute resolution before the International Court of Justice. But it specifies no sanctions for noncompliance and allows parties, at any time, to declare themselves "not . . . bound" by the Convention's dispute resolution provision. Unsurprisingly, no enforcement actions were launched before 1994. Although "several Berne Union Members disagreed with [our] interpretation of Article 18," the USTR told Congress, the Berne Convention did "not provide a meaningful dispute resolution process." [General Agreement

on Tariffs and Trade (GATT): Intellectual Property Provisions, Joint Hearing before the Subcommittee on Intellectual Property and Judicial Administration of the House Committee on the Judiciary and the Subcommittee on Patents, Copyrights and Trademarks of the Senate Committee on the Judiciary, 103d Cong., 2d Sess., p. 137 (1994) (URAA Joint Hearing)] (statement of [Ira S. Shapiro, General Counsel, Office of the U. S. Trade Representative (USTR)]). This shortcoming left Congress "free to adopt a minimalist approach and evade Article 18." Karp, Final Report, Berne Article 18 Study on Retroactive United States Copyright Protection for Berne and other Works, 20 COLUM.–VLA J. L. & ARTS 157, 172 (1996).

The landscape changed in 1994. The Uruguay round of multilateral trade negotiations produced the World Trade Organization (WTO) and the Agreement on Trade-Related Aspects of Intellectual Property Rights (TRIPS). The United States joined both. TRIPS mandates, on pain of WTO enforcement, implementation of Berne's first 21 articles. TRIPS, Art. 9.1, 33 I. L. M. 1197, 1201 (requiring adherence to all but the "moral rights" provisions of article 6bis). The WTO gave teeth to the Convention's requirements: Noncompliance with a WTO ruling could subject member countries to tariffs or cross-sector retaliation. The specter of WTO enforcement proceedings bolstered the credibility of our trading partners' threats to challenge the United States for inadequate compliance with article 18. See URAA Joint Hearing 137 (statement of Shapiro, USTR) ("It is likely that other WTO members would challenge the current U.S. implementation of Berne Article 18 under [WTO] procedures.").[8]

Congress' response to the Uruguay agreements put to rest any questions concerning U.S. compliance with article 18. Section 514 of the URAA, 108 Stat. 4976 (codified at 17 U.S.C. § 104A), extended copyright to works that garnered protection in their countries of origin, but had no right to exclusivity in the United States for any of three reasons: lack of copyright relations between the country of origin and the United States at the time of publication; lack of subject-matter protection for sound recordings fixed before 1972; and failure to comply with U.S. statutory formalities (e.g., failure to provide notice of copyright status, or to register and renew a copyright). See § 104A(h)(6)(B)–(C).

---

8 Proponents of prompt congressional action urged that avoiding a trade enforcement proceeding—potentially the WTO's first—would be instrumental in preserving the U.S.' "reputation as a world leader in the copyright field." URAA Joint Hearing 241 (statement of Eric Smith, International Intellectual Property Alliance (IIPA)). In this regard, U.S. negotiators reported that widespread perception of U.S. noncompliance was undermining its leverage in copyright negotiations. Unimpeachable adherence to Berne, Congress was told, would help ensure enhanced foreign protection, and hence profitable dissemination, for existing and future U.S. works.

QUESTIONS

1. Is the court suggesting that the U.S. compliance with international norms turns on the international enforceability of those norms? What might that imply for international norms promulgated subsequent to, and outside the scope of the TRIPS Agreement? See *infra*, page 350 [questions following "umbrella solution"].

2. In United States – Section 110(5) of the US Copyright Act (WT/ DS160) *(US – Section 110(5) Copyright Act*, (excerpted *infra* pp. 452 et seq.) the Panel found the U.S. in violation of the TRIPs Agreement. It recommended that the DSB request the U.S. to bring Section 110(5)(B) into conformity with the TRIPS Agreement. The U.S. did not implement the report's recommendation.

> The Arbitrators made their award in November 2001, determining that the level of benefits to the European Communities nullified or impaired as a result of Section 110(5)(B) was €1,219,900 per annum. In January 2002 the European Communities requested authorization to retaliate by levying a special fee from US nationals in connection with border measures concerning copyright goods which would not exceed the arbitral award. The United States objected to the level of retaliation proposed and the principles on which it was based. The DSB agreed to refer the matter to arbitration under Article 22.6, but work was suspended almost immediately by mutual request of the parties. The United States has been making regular status reports on its implementation since December 2001 up to the present time, which is a requirement under Article 21.6 of the DSU.

Matthew Kennedy and Hannu Wager, *WTO Dispute Settlement and Copyright: The First Seven Years*, PROCEEDINGS OF THE 2002 ALAI CONGRESS, NEUCHATEL 236–37 (2003) [citations omitted]. The U.S. still has not amended its law to conform to the TRIPS Agreement. Do the teeth the WTO gives to the Berne Convention really bite?

2.4.2 E.U.

Article 216 TFEU

1. The Union may conclude an agreement with one or more third countries or international organisations where the Treaties so provide or where the conclusion of an agreement is necessary in order to achieve, within the framework of the Union's policies, one of the objectives referred to in the Treaties, or is provided for in a legally binding Union act or is likely to affect common rules or alter their scope.

2. Agreements concluded by the Union are binding upon the institutions of the Union and on its Member States.

Article 218 TFEU

. . .

11. A Member State, the European Parliament, the Council or the Commission may obtain the opinion of the Court of Justice as to whether an agreement envisaged is compatible with the Treaties. Where the opinion of the Court is adverse, the agreement envisaged may not enter into force unless it is amended or the Treaties are revised.

QUESTION

Where should an international treaty be placed in the hierarchy of norms, pursuant to the TFEU?

T-201/04 Microsoft Corp. v Commission of the European Communities ECLI:EU:T:2007:289 [2007]

The following case concerns the difficult interaction of IP law and competition law at the European level, and more precisely a refusal by Microsoft to license to its competitors the communication protocol specifications of its software. From an IP perspective, such a refusal is consistent with the grant of exclusive rights. Nevertheless, from a competition point of view such a refusal may prohibit the creation of a new product. The General Court (previously known as Tribunal of First Instance) was seized in order to set a balance between IP and Competition. The owner of the IP rights invoked the TRIPS Agreement, contending that it prevailed over European competition law.

777   Microsoft claims that, by requiring it to license to its competitors the communication protocol specifications which it owns, the contested decision infringes Article 13 of the TRIPS Agreement [which limits the circumstances under which member states may impose compulsory licenses]. It submits that the cumulative conditions laid down in that agreement are not met in the present case.

. . .

798   The Court holds that the principle of consistent interpretation thus invoked by the Court of Justice applies only where the international agreement at issue prevails over the provision of Community law concerned. Since

an international agreement, such as the TRIPS Agreement, does not prevail over primary Community law, that principle does not apply where, as here, the provision which falls to be interpreted is Article 82 EC.*

QUESTIONS

Would the hiererchy of authorities be the same under a WTO Panel? Does it matter?

C-277/10 Martin Luksan v. Petrus Van der Let ECLI:EU:C:2012:65 [2012]

[This case has already been described, see *supra*, page 130]

37   By its first question, the national court asks, in essence, whether Articles 1 and 2 of Directive 93/83 [Cable and Satellite Directive], and Articles 2 and 3 of Directive 2001/29 [Information Society Directive] in conjunction with Articles 2 and 3 of Directive 2006/115 and with Article 2 of Directive 2006/116 [Rental Right Directive], must be interpreted as meaning that rights to exploit a cinematographic work such as those at issue in the main proceedings (satellite broadcasting right, reproduction right and any other right of communication to the public through the making available to the public) vest by operation of law, directly and originally, in the principal director, in his capacity as author of that work. It asks whether, consequently, the abovementioned provisions preclude national legislation which allocates the rights in question by operation of law exclusively to the producer of the work.

38   It should be noted at the outset that the various rights to exploit a cinematographic or audiovisual work have been dealt with in a number of directives. First, Chapter II of Directive 93/83 regulates the satellite broadcasting right. Next, the reproduction right and the right of communication to the public through the making available to the public are governed respectively by Articles 2 and 3 of Directive 2001/29. Finally, rental right and lending right are covered by Articles 2 and 3 of Directive 2006/115.

---

*   Editors' note: Article 82 EEC Treaty [now Article 102 TFEU]

Any abuse by one or more undertakings of a dominant position within the common market or in a substantial part of it shall be prohibited as incompatible with the common market in so far as it may affect trade between Member States.

Such abuse may, in particular, consist in:

(a) directly or indirectly imposing unfair purchase or selling prices or other unfair trading conditions;

(b) limiting production, markets or technical development to the prejudice of consumers;

(c) applying dissimilar conditions to equivalent transactions with other trading parties, thereby placing them at a competitive disadvantage;

(d) making the conclusion of contracts subject to acceptance by the other parties of supplementary obligations which, by their nature or according to commercial usage, have no connection with the subject of such contracts.

. . .

53   Thus, the provisions referred to in the previous three paragraphs allot, by way of original grant, to the principal director in his capacity as author the rights to exploit a cinematographic work that are at issue in the main proceedings.

54   However, notwithstanding these provisions of secondary legislation, the Austrian Government relies in its observations submitted to the Court upon paragraph 2(b), in conjunction with paragraph 3, of Article 14*bis* of the Berne Convention, an article which relates to cinematographic works and which, in its submission, authorises it to grant those rights to the producer of the work alone.

55   It is apparent from those provisions of the Berne Convention, read together, that, by way of derogation, it is permitted for national legislation to deny the principal director certain rights to exploit a cinematographic work, such as, in particular, the reproduction right and the right of communication to the public.

56   In this connection, it should be noted first of all that all the Member States of the European Union have acceded to the Berne Convention, some before 1 January 1958 and others before the date of their accession to the European Union.

57   As regards, more specifically, Article 14*bis* of the Berne Convention, relating to cinematographic works, it is to be observed that this article was inserted following the revisions to the convention adopted in Brussels in 1948, then in Stockholm in 1967.

58   Thus, the Berne Convention displays the characteristics of an international agreement for the purposes of Article 351 TFEU,* which provides

---

*   Editors' note: Article 351 (ex Article 307 TEC)

The rights and obligations arising from agreements concluded before 1 January 1958 or, for acceding States, before the date of their accession, between one or more Member States on the one hand, and one or more third countries on the other, shall not be affected by the provisions of the Treaties.

To the extent that such agreements are not compatible with the Treaties, the Member State or States concerned shall take all appropriate steps to eliminate the incompatibilities established. Member States shall, where necessary, assist each other to this end and shall, where appropriate, adopt a common attitude.

In applying the agreements referred to in the first paragraph, Member States shall take into account the fact that the advantages accorded under the Treaties by each Member State form an integral part of the establishment of the Union and are thereby inseparably linked with the creation of common institutions, the conferring of powers upon them and the granting of the same advantages by all the other Member States.

inter alia that the rights and obligations arising from agreements concluded before 1 January 1958, or, for acceding States, before the date of their accession, between one or more Member States, on the one hand, and one or more third countries, on the other, are not to be affected by the provisions of the Treaties.

59   It should also be observed that the European Union, which is not a party to the Berne Convention, is nevertheless obliged, under Article 1(4) of the WIPO Copyright Treaty, to which it is a party, which forms part of its legal order and which Directive 2001/29 is intended to implement, to comply with Articles 1 to 21 of the Berne Convention (see, to this effect, *Football Association Premier League and Others*, paragraph 189 and the case-law cited). Consequently, the European Union is required to comply inter alia with Article 14*bis* of the Berne Convention.

60   Accordingly, the question arises whether the provisions of Directives 93/83 and 2001/29 referred to in paragraphs 50 to 52 of the present judgment must be interpreted, in the light of Article 1(4) of the WIPO Copyright Treaty, as meaning that a Member State may in its national legislation, on the basis of Article 14*bis* of the Berne Convention and in reliance upon the power which that convention article is said to accord to it, deny the principal director the rights to exploit a cinematographic work that are at issue in the main proceedings.

61   In this regard, it should be recalled first of all that the purpose of the first paragraph of Article 351 TFEU is to make clear, in accordance with the principles of international law, that application of the Treaty does not affect the commitment of the Member State concerned to respect the rights of third countries under an agreement preceding its accession and to comply with its corresponding obligations [citations omitted].

62   However, when such an agreement allows, but does not require, a Member State to adopt a measure which appears to be contrary to European Union law, the Member State must refrain from adopting such a measure [citations omitted].

63   That case-law must also be applicable *mutatis mutandis* when, because of a development in European Union law, a legislative measure adopted by a Member State in accordance with the power offered by an earlier international agreement appears contrary to European Union law. In such a situation, the Member State concerned cannot rely on that agreement in order to exempt itself from the obligations that have arisen subsequently from European Union law.

64   In providing that the principal director of a cinematographic work is to be considered its author or one of its authors, the European Union legislature exercised the competence of the European Union in the field of intellectual property. In those circumstances, the Member States are no longer competent to adopt provisions compromising that European Union legislation. Accordingly, they can no longer rely on the power granted by Article 14*bis* of the Berne Convention.

C-510/10 DR and TV2 Danmark A/S v. NCB — Nordisk Copyright Bureau ECLI:EU:C:2012:244 [2012]

[This case concerned the interpretation of InfoSoc Directive article 5 on exceptions and more particularly section (2) (d) on ephemeral reproduction. In this case, the ephemeral reproductions were not made by the broadcasting organization but by an independent company commissioned by the latter. The issue was whether the exception encompassed third-party reproductions.]

25   By its first question, the national court asks, in essence, whether the term 'by means of their own facilities' in Article 5(2)(d) of Directive 2001/29,* as clarified by recital 41 in the preamble to that directive, ** is to be interpreted with reference to national law or to European Union law.

26   It must be recalled, first, that, under Article 2 of Directive 2001/29, Member States are, in principle, to grant to authors the exclusive right to authorise or prohibit direct or indirect, temporary or permanent, reproduction by any means and in any form, in whole or in part, of their works.

27   Under Article 5(2)(d) of that directive, however, Member States may provide for an exception or limitation to the author's exclusive reproduction right in his work in respect of ephemeral recordings of works made by broadcasting organisations "by means of their own facilities" and for their own broadcasts.

---

* Editors' note: Directive 2001/29 article 5 (2).

Member States may provide for exceptions or limitations to the reproduction right provided for in Article 2 in the following cases: . . .

(d) in respect of ephemeral recordings of works made by broadcasting organisations by means of their own facilities and for their own broadcasts; the preservation of these recordings in official archives may, on the grounds of their exceptional documentary character, be permitted. . .

** Editors' note: (41) When applying the exception or limitation in respect of ephemeral recordings made by broadcasting organisations it is understood that a broadcaster's own facilities include those of a person acting on behalf of and under the responsibility of the broadcasting organisation.

28   It must be stated at the outset that the wording of that latter provision is directly inspired by that of Article 11*bis*(3) of the Berne Convention.

29   With regard to the Berne Convention, the European Union, although not a party to it, is nevertheless obliged, under Article 1(4) of the WIPO Copyright Treaty, to which it is a party, which forms part of its legal order and which Directive 2001/29 is intended to implement, to comply with Articles 1 to 21 of the Berne Convention (see, to that effect, Joined Cases C-403/08 and C-429/08 *Football Association Premier League and Others* [2011] ECR I-0000, paragraph 189 and the case-law cited). Consequently, the European Union is obliged to comply with, inter alia, Article 11*bis* of the Berne Convention (see, by analogy, Case C-277/10 *Luksan* [2012] ECR I-0000, paragraph 59).

30   Article 11*bis*(3) of that Convention expressly states that it is a matter for legislation in the countries of the Berne Union to determine the regulations for ephemeral recordings made by a broadcasting organisation by means of its own facilities and used for its own broadcasts.

31   That being so, by adopting Directive 2001/29/EC on the harmonisation of certain aspects of copyright and related rights in the information society, the European Union legislature is deemed to have exercised the competence previously devolved on the Member States in the field of intellectual property. Within the scope of that directive, the European Union must be regarded as having taken the place of the Member States, which are no longer competent to implement the relevant stipulations of the Berne Convention (see, to that effect, *Luksan*, paragraph 64).

32   It is on that basis that the European Union legislature granted the Member States the option of introducing into their national laws the exception in respect of ephemeral recordings, as set out in Article 5(2)(d) of Directive 2001/29, and clarified the scope of that exception by stating, in recital 41 in the preamble to that directive, that a broadcaster's own facilities include those of a person acting "on behalf of [and/or] under the responsibility of the broadcasting organisation".

33   Secondly, it must be borne in mind that, according to settled case-law, the need for a uniform application of European Union law and the principle of equality require that the terms of a provision of European Union law which makes no express reference to the law of the Member States for the purpose of determining its meaning and scope must normally be given an independent and uniform interpretation throughout the European Union [citations omitted].

34   The wording of Directive 2001/29 does not make any reference to national laws as regards the meaning of the expression "by means of its own facilities" in Article 5(2)(d) of that directive. It follows that that expression must be regarded, for the purposes of applying that directive, as covering an autonomous concept of European Union law, which must be interpreted in a uniform manner throughout the territory of the European Union.

35   This conclusion is supported by the subject-matter and purpose of Directive 2001/29. The objective of Directive 2001/29, which is based, in particular, on Article 95* EC and is intended to harmonise certain aspects of the law on copyright and related rights in the information society and to ensure that competition in the internal market is not distorted as a result of differences in the legislation of Member States [citation omitted], requires the elaboration of autonomous concepts of European Union law. The European Union legislature's aim of achieving a uniform interpretation of the concepts contained in Directive 2001/29 is apparent in particular from recital 32 in the preamble thereto, which calls on the Member States to arrive at a coherent application of the exceptions to and limitations on reproduction rights, with a view to ensuring a functioning internal market.

36   Consequently, although it is open to the Member States, as has been pointed out in paragraph 32 of this judgment, to introduce an exception in respect of ephemeral recordings into their domestic law, an interpretation according to which Member States which, exercising that option afforded to them by European Union law, have introduced an exception of that kind, are free to determine, in an un-harmonised manner, the limits thereof, inter alia as regards the facilities used to make those ephemeral recordings, would be contrary to the objective of that directive as set out in the preceding paragraph, inasmuch as the limits of that exception could vary from one Member State to another and would therefore give rise to potential inconsistencies [citations omitted].

37   In the light of the foregoing considerations, the answer to the first question is that the expression 'by means of their own facilities' in Article 5(2)(d) of Directive 2001/29 must be given an independent and uniform interpretation within the framework of European Union law.

. . .

---

* Editors' note: Article 95 was the legal basis for the approximation of laws created by the Directive. The equivalent under the TFEU is article 115. Approximation is a means provided for in art 95 of the Treaty of Rome to achieve progressive harmonization of the national laws of the member states according to standards set by EC law. Directives are the preferred legislative method for achieving approximation or harmonization of member state laws.

58   In the light of the foregoing, the answer to the second question is that Article 5(2)(d) of Directive 2001/29, read in the light of recital 41 in the preamble to that directive, must be interpreted as meaning that a broadcasting organisation's own facilities include the facilities of any third party acting on behalf of or under the responsibility of that organisation.

QUESTIONS

1. Does it make a difference to the analysis if the Berne Convention permits, but does not require, member states to adopt particular rules (for example, regarding ownership of rights in cinematographic works)? Do you think that the exercise of the option is similar under *Luksan* and *TV2 Danmark*?

2. What should be the authentic interpretation of an ephemeral recording exception under the Berne Convention? Is it relevant that the *travaux* of the 1971 Paris Revision of the Berne Convention indicate that the drafters rejected an amendment that would have authorized the making of ephemeral recordings by third parties? See SAM RICKETSON & JANE C. GINSBURG, INTERNATIONAL COPYRIGHT AND NEIGHBOURING RIGHTS: THE BERNE CONVENTION AND BEYOND (2d. ed. 2006), para 13.76: "At the Stockholm Conference, the Monegasque delegation sought to modify paragraph (3) so as to permit the making 'by or for a broadcasting organization' but this amendment was withdrawn in the course of discussion in Main Committee I (Documents 1949 (1951, 903 (Documents S/77: ibid, 691)." Do you think that the interpretation of article 5(2)(d) of Directive 2001/29 made by the ECJ in the *TV2 Danmark* complies with the Berne Convention? If not, before what, if any, institutions may the injured party seek redress?

2.5   Institutional limits and international conventions

As we have seen, international copyright conventions focus on international situations, seeking to avoid any discrimination against foreign authors or performers. The goal is not primarily to harmonize substantive copyright law on a domestic level. Nevertheless, an indirect harmonization may occur, by virtue of amendment of national laws to meet substantive conventional minima of protection. The institutional proceedings being different for a law or for a treaty (for example, in the U.S., a law must be passed by a majority of both houses and signed by the President, while a treaty needs to be ratified by a two-thirds majority of the Senate and signed by the President), the risk exists that treaty member states might circumvent domestic lawmaking by promulgating international treaties. Even in states where treaties are not self-executing, the possibility of overriding prior limits on the state's power to enact copyright laws remains, for the newly-incurred treaty obligation may seem a *fait accompli* requiring national implementing legislation to conform to the international norm.* The situation is compounded when a treaty is used to overcome a constitutional limit. Suppose a treaty norm were inconsistent with national law; would ratification of the treaty allow the member state to circumvent a domestic limitation on its power to enact copyright or neighboring rights laws?

2.5.1   U.S.

U.S. Constitution art. II, § 2, cl. 2

[The President] shall have power, by and with the advice and consent of the Senate, to make treaties, provided two thirds of the Senators present concur . . .

Missouri v. Holland, 252 U.S. 416 (1920)

Mr Justice Holmes delivered the opinion of the court.

This is a bill in equity brought by the State of Missouri to prevent a game warden of the United States from attempting to enforce the Migratory Bird Treaty Act of 1918 [citations omitted], and the regulations made by the Secretary of Agriculture in pursuance of the same. The ground of the bill is that the statute is an unconstitutional interference with the rights reserved to the States by the Tenth Amendment, and that the acts of the defendant done and threatened under that authority invade the sovereign right of the State and contravene its will manifested in statutes.

. . . It is unnecessary to go into any details, because, as we have said, the question raised is the general one whether the treaty and statute are void as an interference with the rights reserved to the States.

To answer this question it is not enough to refer to the Tenth Amendment, reserving the powers not delegated to the United States, because by Article

---

* *See, e.g.*, Pamela Samuelson, *The U.S. Digital Agenda at Wipo*, 37 Va. J. Intl. L. 369, 373–4 (1997):

> The digital agenda that Clinton administration officials pursued in Geneva was almost identical to the digital agenda they had put before the U.S. Congress during roughly the same time period. . . . Had this effort succeeded in Geneva, Clinton administration officials would almost certainly have then argued to Congress that ratification of the treaties was necessary to confirm U.S. leadership in the world intellectual property community and to promote the interests of U.S. copyright industries in the world market for information products and services.

II, § 2, the power to make treaties is delegated expressly, and by Article VI treaties made under the authority of the United States, along with the Constitution and laws of the United States made in pursuance thereof, are declared the supreme law of the land. If the treaty is valid there can be no dispute about the validity of the statute under Article I, § 8, as a necessary and proper means to execute the powers of the Government. The language of the Constitution as to the supremacy of treaties being general, the question before us is narrowed to an inquiry into the ground upon which the present supposed exception is placed.

It is said that a treaty cannot be valid if it infringes the Constitution, that there are limits, therefore, to the treaty-making power, and that one such limit is that what an Act of Congress could not do unaided, in derogation of the powers reserved to the States, a treaty can not do. . . Acts of Congress are the supreme law of the land only when made in pursuance of the Constitution, while treaties are declared to be so when made under the authority of the United States. It is open to question whether the authority of the United States means more than the formal acts prescribed to make the convention. We do not mean to imply that there are no qualifications to the treaty-making power; but they must be ascertained in a different way. It is obvious that there may be matters of the sharpest exigency for the national well being that an act of Congress could not deal with but that a treaty followed by such an act could, and it is not lightly to be assumed that, in matters requiring national action, "a power which must belong to and somewhere reside in every civilized government" is not to be found.

Reid v. Covert, 354 U.S. 1 (1957)

This Court has also repeatedly taken the position that an Act of Congress, which must comply with the Constitution, is on a full parity with a treaty, and that when a statute which is subsequent in time is inconsistent with a treaty, the statute to the extent of conflict renders the treaty null [citations omitted]. It would be completely anomalous to say that a treaty need not comply with the Constitution when such an agreement can be overridden by a statute that must conform to that instrument.

There is nothing in *Missouri v. Holland*, 252 U.S. 416, which is contrary to the position taken here. There the Court carefully noted that the treaty involved was not inconsistent with any specific provision of the Constitution. The Court was concerned with the Tenth Amendment which reserves to the States or the people all power not delegated to the National Government. To the extent that the United States can validly make treaties, the people and the

States have delegated their power to the National Government and the Tenth Amendment is no barrier [citations omitted].

Bond v. United States, 134 S. Ct. 2077 (2014)

In our federal system, the National Government possesses only limited powers; the States and the people retain the remainder. The States have broad authority to enact legislation for the public good—what we have often called a "police power." *United States v. Lopez*, 514 U. S. 549, 567 (1995). The Federal Government, by contrast, has no such authority and "can exercise only the powers granted to it," *McCulloch v. Maryland*, 4 Wheat. 316, 405 (1819), including the power to make "all Laws which shall be necessary and proper for carrying into Execution" the enumerated powers, U. S. Const., Art. I, §8, cl. 18. For nearly two centuries it has been "clear" that, lacking a police power, "Congress cannot punish felonies generally." *Cohens v. Virginia*, 6 Wheat. 264, 428 (1821). A criminal act committed wholly within a State "cannot be made an offence against the United States, unless it have some relation to the execution of a power of Congress, or to some matter within the jurisdiction of the United States." *United States v. Fox*, 95 U. S. 670, 672 (1878).

The Government frequently defends federal criminal legislation on the ground that the legislation is authorized pursuant to Congress's power to regulate interstate commerce. In this case, however, the Court of Appeals held that the Government had explicitly disavowed that argument before the District Court. 681 F. 3d, at 151, n. 1. As a result, in this Court the parties have devoted significant effort to arguing whether section 229, as applied to Bond's offense, is a necessary and proper means of executing the National Government's power to make treaties. U. S. Const., Art. II, §2, cl. 2. Bond argues that the lower court's reading of *Missouri v. Holland* would remove all limits on federal authority, so long as the Federal Government ratifies a treaty first. She insists that to effectively afford the Government a police power whenever it implements a treaty would be contrary to the Framers' careful decision to divide power between the States and the National Government as a means of preserving liberty. To the extent that *Holland* authorizes such usurpation of traditional state authority, Bond says, it must be either limited or overruled.

The Government replies that this Court has never held that a statute implementing a valid treaty exceeds Congress's enumerated powers. To do so here, the Government says, would contravene another deliberate choice of the Framers: to avoid placing subject matter limitations on the National Government's power to make treaties. And it might also undermine confidence in the United States as an international treaty partner. Notwithstanding this debate, it is "a well-established principle governing the prudent exercise of this Court's jurisdiction that normally the Court will not decide a constitutional question if there is some other ground upon which to dispose of the case." *Escambia County v. McMillan*, 466 U. S. 48, 51 (1984) (per curiam); *see also Ashwander v. TVA*, 297 U. S. 288, 347 (1936) (Brandeis, J., concurring).

[The Court held that, under the plain meaning of the text, the criminal statute in question did not apply to the defendant's conduct. Thus, the Court did not reach the question of the status of *Missouri v. Holland.*]

Kiss Catalog Ltd. v. Passport International Productions, Inc., 405 F. Supp. 2d 1169 (C.D. Cal. 2005)

[The following decision addressed a challenge to legislation passed as part of the U.S.' obligations under the TRIPS agreement. Article 14(1) of the TRIPS provides:

> In respect of a fixation of their performance on a phonogram, performers shall have the possibility of preventing the following acts when undertaken without their authorization: the fixation of their unfixed performance and the reproduction of such fixation. Performers shall also have the possibility of preventing the following acts when undertaken without their authorization: the broadcasting by wireless means and the communication to the public of their live performance.

[The corresponding legislation, 17 U.S.C. § 1101 provides in relevant part:

(a) Unauthorized Acts.—Anyone who, without the consent of the performer or performers involved —
  (1) fixes the sounds or sounds and images of a live musical performance in a copy or phonorecord, or reproduces copies or phonorecords of such a performance from an unauthorized fixation,
  (2) transmits or otherwise communicates to the public the sounds or sounds and images of a live musical performance, or
  (3) distributes or offers to distribute, sells or offers to sell, rents or offers to rent, or traffics in any copy or phonorecord fixed as described in paragraph (1), regardless of whether the fixations occurred in the United States, shall be subject to the remedies provided in sections 502 through 505, to the same extent as an infringer of copyright.
(b) Definition. — As used in this section, the term "traffic in" means

transport, transfer, or otherwise dispose of, to another, as consideration for anything of value, or make or obtain control of with intent to transport, transfer, or dispose of.

(c) Applicability. — This section shall apply to any act or acts that occur on or after the date of the enactment of the Uruguay Round Agreements Act.

[The defendant allegedly violated the anti-trafficking provision of section 1101 by selling phonorecords consisting of unauthorized fixations of live musical performances by the rock band "Kiss."—Defendant challenged the constitutionality of section 1101 on the ground that the statute did not specify a time limit to performers' rights to bring "anti-bootlegging" claims, and therefore violated the "limited times" restriction of the Constitutional copyright clause. Another issue concerned Congress' power to enact legislation protecting unfixed works; were the copyright clause's reference to the "writings" of authors understood to require that the work must already have been fixed before Congress may protect it, then legislation covering unfixed performances would exceed Congress' power under the copyright clause.]

Dale S. Fischer, United States District Judge.

INTRODUCTION AND PROCEDURAL BACKGROUND

On December 21, 2004, the Honorable William J. Rea, to whom this case was originally assigned, granted Defendants' motion to dismiss the Seventh Claim for Relief for violation of 17 U.S.C. § 1101, the anti-bootlegging statute, finding that § 1101(a)(3) violated the "for limited Times" requirement of the Copyright Clause and was therefore unconstitutional. *KISS Catalog, Ltd. v. Passport Int'l Prods.*, 350 F. Supp. 2d 823, 837 (C.D. Cal. 2004) ("Order").

The United States learned of this finding only after the Order was entered, and sought leave to intervene in the action. On June 7, 2005, Judge Rea granted that request. On August 5, 2005, due to Judge Rea's death, the action was transferred to this Court for all further proceedings. This matter is now before the Court on the motion of the United States to reconsider the finding that § 1101(a)(3) ("Statute") is unconstitutional. Plaintiffs have joined in the motion; Defendants have opposed it.

DISCUSSION

. . .

II. SECTION 1101(a)(3) IS A CONSTITUTIONAL EXERCISE OF CONGRESS' COMMERCE CLAUSE POWER

. . .

Until Judge Rea's Order, no published decision had yet addressed the constitutionality of 17 U.S.C. § 1101(a)(3). Only two, *United States v. Moghadam*, 175 F.3d 1269 (11th Cir. 1999), cert. denied, 529 U.S. 1036, 120 S. Ct. 1529, 146 L. Ed. 2d 344 (2000), and *United States v. Martignon*, 346 F. Supp. 2d 413 (S.D.N.Y. 2004), discuss a related criminal statute, 18 U.S.C. § 2319A. *Moghadam* and *Martignon*, after a careful consideration of whether the anti-bootlegging legislation is a constitutional exercise of congressional power under the Copyright Clause or the Commerce Clause, reached opposite conclusions.

This analysis of the constitutionality of the Statute addresses two separate considerations: (a) did Congress have the power to enact the legislation? and (b) if so, is the legislation "fundamentally inconsistent" with the Copyright Clause?

This Court agrees with the analysis of *Moghadam*: the Statute is constitutional.

A. The Commerce Clause Empowers Congress to Enact the Statute

Because Congress may exercise only those powers granted to it by the Constitution, e.g., *United States v. Lopez*, 514 U.S. 549, 552, 115 S. Ct. 1624, 131 L. Ed. 2d 626 (1995), the Court must determine whether Congress had the power to enact the Statute in the first instance. The Copyright Clause, U.S. Const. art. I, § 8, cl. 8, the Commerce Clause, id. cl. 3, and the Necessary and Proper Clause, id. cl. 18, are the generally suggested sources of such power.

Congress may have believed that it was acting pursuant to the Copyright Clause, which provides that Congress has the power to "promote the Progress of Science and useful Arts, by securing for limited Times to Authors and Inventors the exclusive Right to their respective Writings and Discoveries." See *Moghadam*, 175 F.3d at 1272 ("[W]hat little legislative history exists tends to suggest that Congress viewed the anti-bootlegging provisions as enacted pursuant to its Copyright Clause authority," citing 140 Cong. Rec. H11441, H11457 (daily ed. Nov. 29, 1994) (statement of Rep. Hughes)); *Martignon*, 346 F. Supp. 2d at 419. But see 3 Melville B. Nimmer & David Nimmer, Nimmer on Copyright § 8E.05[A] (2005) ("In the context of Chapter 11 [of Title 17], the question arises how

Congress viewed its enactment authority. There is no answer."). The Statute was placed within Title 17, and incorporates the statutory remedies for copyright infringement.[10] 17 U.S.C. § 1101(a).

It appears unlikely, however, that Congress could have derived the power to enact the Statute from the Copyright Clause. See, e.g., *Moghadam*, 175 F.3d at 1274 ("[A]lthough in the modern era the term Writings' allows Congress to extend copyright protection to a great many things, those things have always involved some fixed, tangible and durable form."); *KISS Catalog, Ltd.*, 350 F. Supp. 2d at 831 ("[I]t would seem that a live performance protected by § 1101 is not a fixed work. . . . Thus, one would be inclined to think that . . . live performances could not be regulated via the Copyright Clause."); *Martignon*, 346 F. Supp. 2d at 424 ("[B]y virtue of the fact that it regulates unfixed live performances, the anti-bootlegging statute is not within the purview of Congress' Copyright Clause power."); 1 Nimmer, Nimmer on Copyright, supra, § 1.08[C][2] ("If the word 'writings' is to be given any meaning whatsoever, it must, at the very least, denote some material form, capable of identification and having a more or less permanent endurance" [citation omitted]); Susan M. Deas, *Jazzing Up the Copyright Act? Resolving the Uncertainties of the United States Anti-Bootlegging Law*, 20 HASTINGS COMM. & ENT. L.J. 567, 578 (1998); David Nimmer, *The End of Copyright*, 48 VAND. L. REV. 1385, 1409 (1995) ("[N]o respectable interpretation of the word Writings' embraces an untaped performance of someone singing at Carnegie Hall.").

This does not end the analysis, however, as Congress' intent is not dispositive. See *Woods v. Cloyd W. Miller Co.*, 333 U.S. 138, 144, 68 S. Ct. 421, 92 L. Ed. 596 (1948) ("The question of the constitutionality of action taken by Congress does not depend on the recitals of the power which it undertakes to exercise."). Moreover, "[d]ue respect for the decisions of a coordinate branch of Government demands that [courts] invalidate a congressional enactment only upon a plain showing that Congress has exceeded its constitutional bounds." *United States v. Morrison*, 529 U.S. 598, 607, 120 S. Ct. 1740, 146 L. Ed. 2d 658 (2000). There is a "presumption of constitutionality." Id. Therefore, it is the Court's obligation to look elsewhere for a source of congressional power to enact the Statute.

---

10 Judge Rea held that the Statute did not incorporate 17 U.S.C. § 302, which limits the duration of copyright protection. KISS Catalog, Ltd., 350 F. Supp. 2d at 832. At least one author has touted incorporating that durational limit into the Statute as an approach to preserving constitutionality. Angela T. Howe, *United States v. Martignon and Kiss Catalog v. Passport International Products: The Anti-Bootlegging Statute and the Collision of International Intellectual Property Law and the United States Constitution*, 20 BERKELEY TECH. L.J. 829, 851 (2005). The U.S. had not addressed this issue and the Court requested further briefing. Because the U.S. agreed that the durational limitation of 17 U.S.C. § 302 cannot be incorporated into the Statute, the Court assumes, without deciding, that it is not incorporated.

The United States argues that the Commerce Clause grants such authority. This Court agrees with the United States and with the Eleventh Circuit's analysis in *Moghadam*, 175 F.3d at 1274–77. Indeed, Judge Rea believed the Statute could be enacted under the Commerce Clause if not for the conflict with the Copyright Clause. KISS Catalog, Ltd., 350 F. Supp. 2d at 833–34 and n.7. ("[T]hat copyright-like protection for live performances touches on commerce is a proposition that should be without serious dispute.")

Though *Martignon* criticized *Moghadam*'s "swift conclusion" that the legislation is authorized under the Commerce Clause (potential Copyright Clause limitations aside), this Court agrees that the Statute is well within Congress' Commerce Clause powers as broadly defined by, *inter alia*, *Gonzales v. Raich*, 125 S. Ct. 2195, 162 L. Ed. 2d 1 (2005), and *Lopez*. As the United States Supreme Court most recently made clear in these cases, Congress' authority to enact legislation pursuant to the Commerce Clause has been interpreted broadly in the modern era. Indeed, Supreme Court "case law firmly establishes Congress' power to regulate [even] purely local activities that are part of an economic class of activities that have a substantial effect on interstate commerce." *Raich*, 125 S. Ct. at 2205 [citations omitted]. This is true even where the affected market is an illegal one. 125 S. Ct. at 2206 (acknowledging an illegal market for marijuana).

Moghadam assumed, without deciding, that the anti-bootlegging legislation could not stand under the Copyright Clause. 175 F.3d at 1274. It simply turned to an alternate source, the Commerce Clause, noting that the test of constitutionality under that clause is "whether a rational basis existed for concluding that a regulated activity sufficiently affected interstate commerce." Id. at 1275 (quoting *Lopez*, 514 U.S. at 557). Even in the absence of legislative findings of an interstate commerce nexus, the court easily concluded: "The link between bootleg compact discs and interstate commerce and commerce with foreign nations is self-evident." Id. at 1276. "Bootleggers depress the legitimate markets because demand is satisfied through unauthorized channels." Id. In addition, that § 1101 was enacted in connection with an international treaty called for by the World Trade Organization establishes its connection with—if not its reliance on—interstate and international commerce. Id.; accord Howe, supra, at 846 (citing, *inter alia*, Office of United States Trade Representative, at http://www.ustr.gov. (last visited March 19, 2005)).

This Court finds that the Commerce Clause grants Congress the power to enact the Statute.[11]

---

11 Because the Court finds § 1101(a)(3) valid under the Commerce Clause, the Court need not consider

QUESTIONS

Suppose, emulating the UK Copyright, Patents and Designs Act (see *infra* pp. 291–92), Congress defined "fixation" to include fixations made without authorization. Would the statutory scope of fixation exceed the boundaries of a "Writing" in the Constitutional sense? Does the answer to that question influence your response to the question whether Congress may protect unfixed performances, under any of the clauses evoked in *Kiss Catalog*?

Feist v. Rural Telephone, 499 U.S. 340 (1991)

[The Supreme Court held that a white pages telephone book lacked sufficient creativity to qualify for statutory copyright. The Court further emphasized that the Constitution requires a minimum of creativity, and that the listings of telephone subscriber names and phone numbers failed to meet that standard.]

Originality is a constitutional requirement. The source of Congress' power to enact copyright laws is Article I, '8, cl. 8, of the Constitution, which authorizes Congress to "secure for limited Times to Authors . . . the exclusive Right to their respective Writings." In two decisions from the late nineteenth century—*The Trade-Mark Cases*, 100 U.S. 82 (1879); and *Burrow-Giles Lithographic Co. v. Sarony*, 111 U.S. 53 (1884) - this Court defined the crucial terms "authors" and "writings." In so doing, the Court made it unmistakably clear that these terms presuppose a degree of originality. . . Leading scholars agree on this point. As one pair of commentators succinctly puts it: "The originality requirement is *constitutionally mandated* for all works." Patterson & Joyce, *Monopolizing the Law: The Scope of Copyright Protection for Law Reports and Statutory Compilations*, 36 UCLA L. Rev. 719, 763, n. 155 (1989) (emphasis in original) (hereinafter Patterson & Joyce). *Accord id.*, at 759–760, and n. 140; Nimmer '1.06[A] ("originality is a statutory as well as a constitutional requirement"); *id.*, '1.08[C][1] ("a modicum of intellectual labor . . . clearly constitutes an essential constitutional element").

. . .

The selection, coordination, and arrangement of Rural's white pages do not satisfy the minimum constitutional standards for copyright protection. As mentioned at the outset, Rural's white pages are entirely typical. Persons

---

whether it might alternatively be authorized under the Necessary and Proper Clause. There has been some suggestion that the Necessary and Proper Clause would even more clearly provide a constitutional source for the Statute . . . .

desiring telephone service in Rural's service area fill out an application and Rural issues them a telephone number. In preparing its white pages, Rural simply takes the data provided by its subscribers and lists it alphabetically by surname. The end product is a garden-variety white pages directory, devoid of even the slightest trace of creativity.

Rural's selection of listings could not be more obvious: it publishes the most basic information—name, town, and telephone number—about each person who applies to it for telephone service. This is "selection" of a sort, but it lacks the modicum of creativity necessary to transform mere selection into copyrightable expression. Rural expended sufficient effort to make the white pages directory useful, but insufficient creativity to make it original.

We note in passing that the selection featured in Rural's white pages may also fail the originality requirement for another reason. Feist points out that Rural did not truly "select" to publish the names and telephone numbers of its subscribers; rather, it was required to do so by the Kansas Corporation Commission as part of its monopoly franchise. *See* 737 F. Supp., at 612. Accordingly, one could plausibly conclude that this selection was dictated by state law, not by Rural.

Nor can Rural claim originality in its coordination and arrangement of facts. The white pages do nothing more than list Rural's subscribers in alphabetical order. This arrangement may, technically speaking, owe its origin to Rural; no one disputes that Rural undertook the task of alphabetizing the names itself. But there is nothing remotely creative about arranging names alphabetically in a white pages directory. It is an age-old practice, firmly rooted in tradition and so commonplace that it has come to be expected as a matter of course. . . It is not only unoriginal, it is practically inevitable. This time-honored tradition does not possess the minimal creative spark required by the Copyright Act and the Constitution.

We conclude that the names, towns, and telephone numbers copied by Feist were not original to Rural and therefore were not protected by the copyright in Rural's combined white and yellow pages directory. As a constitutional matter, copyright protects only those constituent elements of a work that possess more than a *de minimis* quantum of creativity.

QUESTIONS

1. In light of *Feist*, could the U.S. ratify and implement an international treaty extending copyright protection to unoriginal databases? An international

treaty obliging its signatories to grant some kind of protection (including *sui generis* protection) against copying and communicating the unoriginal contents of databases?

2. Under current U.S. copyright law, most fashion design is not protectable because the items of clothing are "useful articles" whose decorative elements are not "separable" from their function. Could the U.S., consistent with the Constitution, ratify and enact legislation implementing an international treaty to protect fashion design?

2.5.2   E.U.

Treaty on the Functioning of the European Union
Article 2

1. When the Treaties confer on the Union exclusive competence in a specific area, only the Union may legislate and adopt legally binding acts, the Member States being able to do so themselves only if so empowered by the Union or for the implementation of Union acts.

2. When the Treaties confer on the Union a competence shared with the Member States in a specific area, the Union and the Member States may legislate and adopt legally binding acts in that area. The Member States shall exercise their competence to the extent that the Union has not exercised its competence. The Member States shall again exercise their competence to the extent that the Union has decided to cease exercising its competence.

Article 3

1. The Union shall have exclusive competence in the following areas:

. . .

(e) common commercial policy.

2. The Union shall also have exclusive competence for the conclusion of an international agreement when its conclusion is provided for in a legislative act of the Union or is necessary to enable the Union to exercise its internal competence, or in so far as its conclusion may affect common rules or alter their scope.

Article 207 (ex Article 133 TEC)

1. The common commercial policy shall be based on uniform principles, particularly with regard to changes in tariff rates, the conclusion of tariff and trade agreements relating to trade in goods and services, and the commercial aspects of intellectual property, foreign direct investment, the achievement of uniformity in measures of liberalisation, export policy and measures to protect trade such as those to be taken in the event of dumping or subsidies. The common commercial policy shall be conducted in the context of the principles and objectives of the Union's external action.

2. The European Parliament and the Council, acting by means of regulations in accordance with the ordinary legislative procedure, shall adopt the measures defining the framework for implementing the common commercial policy.

3. Where agreements with one or more third countries or international organisations need to be negotiated and concluded, Article 218 shall apply, subject to the special provisions of this Article.

The Commission shall make recommendations to the Council, which shall authorise it to open the necessary negotiations. The Council and the Commission shall be responsible for ensuring that the agreements negotiated are compatible with internal Union policies and rules.

The Commission shall conduct these negotiations in consultation with a special committee appointed by the Council to assist the Commission in this task and within the framework of such directives as the Council may issue to it. The Commission shall report regularly to the special committee and to the European Parliament on the progress of negotiations.

4. For the negotiation and conclusion of the agreements referred to in paragraph 3, the Council shall act by a qualified majority.

For the negotiation and conclusion of agreements in the fields of trade in services and the commercial aspects of intellectual property, as well as foreign direct investment, the Council shall act unanimously where such agreements include provisions for which unanimity is required for the adoption of internal rules.

The Council shall also act unanimously for the negotiation and conclusion of agreements:

(a) in the field of trade in cultural and audiovisual services, where these agreements risk prejudicing the Union's cultural and linguistic diversity.

Article 218

1. Without prejudice to the specific provisions laid down in Article 207, agreements between the Union and third countries or international organisations shall be negotiated and concluded in accordance with the following procedure.

2. The Council shall authorise the opening of negotiations, adopt negotiating directives, authorise the signing of agreements and conclude them.

3. The Commission, or the High Representative of the Union for Foreign Affairs and Security Policy where the agreement envisaged relates exclusively or principally to the common foreign and security policy, shall submit recommendations to the Council, which shall adopt a decision authorising the opening of negotiations and, depending on the subject of the agreement envisaged, nominating the Union negotiator or the head of the Union's negotiating team.

4. The Council may address directives to the negotiator and designate a special committee in consultation with which the negotiations must be conducted.

5. The Council, on a proposal by the negotiator, shall adopt a decision authorising the signing of the agreement and, if necessary, its provisional application before entry into force.

6. The Council, on a proposal by the negotiator, shall adopt a decision concluding the agreement.

Except where agreements relate exclusively to the common foreign and security policy, the Council shall adopt the decision concluding the agreement:

(a) after obtaining the consent of the European Parliament in the following cases:

. . .

The European Parliament and the Council may, in an urgent situation, agree upon a time-limit for consent.

. . .

7. When concluding an agreement, the Council may, by way of derogation from paragraphs 5, 6 . . ., authorise the negotiator to approve on the Union's behalf modifications to the agreement where it provides for them to be adopted by a simplified procedure or by a body set up by the agreement. The Council may attach specific conditions to such authorisation.

8. The Council shall act by a qualified majority throughout the procedure.

. . .

10. The European Parliament shall be immediately and fully informed at all stages of the procedure.

11. A Member State, the European Parliament, the Council or the Commission may obtain the opinion of the Court of Justice as to whether an agreement envisaged is compatible with the Treaties. Where the opinion of the Court is adverse, the agreement envisaged may not enter into force unless it is amended or the Treaties are revised.

C-114/12 European Commission v. Council of the The European Union ECLI:EU:C:2014:2151

[The case concerned the legal basis for ratification and negotiation of international conventions. If the text comes within the scope of article 3(2) of the TFEU, the Union has an exclusive competence. The case addressed the negotiations for a Convention of the Council of Europe* on the protection of the rights of broadcasting organisations; the Convention's goal was to enhance the protection of neighbouring rights of broadcasting organisations. The Council of the European Union and the Representatives of the Governments of the Member States meeting in the Council adopted the following decision concerning the legal basis for ratification and negotiation of this future convention:

'The Council [of the European Union]. . . and the Representatives of the Governments of the Member States . . . meeting within the Council,

---

* The Council of Europe is not an E.U. institution. It includes 47 member states, which have all ratified the European Convention on Human Rights.

Having regard to the [TFEU], and in particular Article 218(3) and (4) thereof,

Having regard to the recommendation from the . . . Commission,

Whereas:

(1)   The Commission should be authorised to participate, on behalf of the Union, in the negotiations for a Convention of the Council of Europe on the protection of the rights of broadcasting organisations as regards matters falling within the Union's competence and in respect of which the Union has adopted rules.

(2)   The Member States should participate on their own behalf in those negotiations only in so far as matters that arise in the course of the negotiations fall within their competence. With a view to ensuring the unity of the external representation of the Union, the Member States and the Commission should cooperate closely during the negotiation process,

have adopted this decision:

Article 1

1. The Commission is hereby authorised to participate in the negotiations for a Convention of the Council of Europe on the protection of the rights of broadcasting organisations and to conduct these negotiations on behalf of the Union as regards matters falling within the Union's competence and in respect of which the Union has adopted rules, in consultation with the Intellectual Property Working Party (Copyright) (the "special committee").

2. The Commission shall conduct the negotiations in question in accordance with the negotiating directives set out in the Annex to this Decision and/or agreed positions of the Union established specifically for the purposes of these negotiations within the special committee.

3. Where the subject-matter of the negotiations falls within Member States' competence, the Presidency [of the Council of the European Union] shall fully participate in the negotiations and shall conduct them on behalf of the Member States on the basis of a prior agreed common position. Where an agreed common position cannot be reached, the Member States shall be entitled to speak and vote on the matter in question independently, . . .

The Commission, throughout the procedure leading to the Convention's adoption, had maintained that the E.U. has exclusive competence in the matter and therefore opposed the adoption of a 'hybrid act' by the Council of the European Union and the Representatives of the Governments of the Member States. The Commission sought an annulment of the decision of the Council and the Representatives of the Governments of the Member States]

64   The first plea is based, in essence, on an infringement of Article 3(2) TFEU.

65   As a preliminary point, it should be noted that, among the various cases of exclusive external competence of the E.U. envisaged by that provision, only that which is referred to in the last clause of the provision, namely the situation in which the conclusion of an international agreement 'may affect common rules or alter their scope', is relevant in the present case.

66   In that regard, it must be stated that the words used in that last clause correspond to those by which the Court (citations omitted) defined the nature of the international commitments which Member States cannot enter into outside the framework of the E.U. institutions, where common E.U. rules have been promulgated for the attainment of the objectives of the Treaty.

. . .

68   According to the Court's case-law, there is a risk that common E.U. rules might be adversely affected by international commitments, or that the scope of those rules might be altered, which is such as to justify an exclusive external competence of the European Union, where those commitments fall within the scope of those rules (citations omitted).

69   A finding that there is such a risk does not presuppose that the areas covered by the international commitments and those covered by the E.U. rules coincide fully (citations omitted).

70   As the Court has consistently held, the scope of common E.U. rules may be affected or altered by such commitments also where those commitments fall within an area which is already largely covered by such rules (citations omitted).

71   In addition, Member States may not enter into such commitments outside the framework of the E.U. institutions, even if there is no possible contradiction between those commitments and the common E.U. rules (citations omitted).

. . .

74   That said, it is important to note that, since the European Union has only conferred powers, any competence, especially where it is exclusive, must have its basis in conclusions drawn from a specific analysis of the relationship between the envisaged international agreement and the E.U. law in force, from which it is clear that such an agreement is capable of affecting the common E.U. rules or of altering their scope (citations omitted).

. . .

76   In the present case, it must be observed at the outset that the contested decision gives no detail as to the content of the negotiations for the future Convention of the Council of Europe on the protection of the rights of broadcasting organisations. Nor does the contested decision identify the elements of those negotiations which, in the words of Article 1(1) thereof, fall within the Union's competence and those which, in the words of Article 1(3) thereof, fall within Member States' competence.

77   In those circumstances, as regards the content of the envisaged negotiations, it is appropriate to take into account, for the purposes of the present analysis, the 2002 Recommendation [Recommendation Rec(2002)7 on enhancing the protection of neighbouring rights of broadcasting organisations], the 2008 Memorandum [memorandum on a possible Convention of the Council of Europe on protection of neighbouring rights of broadcasting organisations] and the 2010 Report, which were placed on the file by the Commission in support of its first plea and in respect of which none of the parties has disputed that they provided the most recent relevant information in that regard.

78   As for the area concerned in the present case, those documents of the Council of Europe indicate that the negotiations in question are aimed at the adoption of a Convention relating to the protection of neighbouring rights of broadcasting organisations.

79   As is clear from Directives 93/83 [Satellite and Cable], 2001/29 [Info Soc], 2004/48 [Enforcement], 2006/115 [Rental and Lending Rights] and 2006/116 [Term of protection], those rights are the subject, in E.U. law, of a harmonised legal framework which seeks, in particular, to ensure the proper functioning of the internal market and which, having integrated a number of developments linked to technological challenges, the new digital environment and the development of the information society, established a regime

with high and homogeneous protection for broadcasting organisations in connection with their broadcasts.

80   It follows that the protection of those organisations' neighbouring rights — the subject-matter of the Council of Europe negotiations — must be understood as the relevant area for the purposes of the present analysis.

81   The fact that that harmonised legal framework has been established by various legal instruments which also govern other intellectual property rights is not such as to call into question the correctness of that approach.

82   The assessment of the existence of a risk that common E.U. rules will be adversely affected, or that their scope will be altered, by international commitments cannot be dependent on an artificial distinction based on the presence or absence of such rules in one and the same instrument of E.U. law.

. . .

84   Having thus defined the area concerned, the Court notes that, . . . the Convention of the Council of Europe in question should be based on the E.U. *acquis*, which broadly covers the substantive law on intellectual property, particularly that relating to broadcasting organisations.

86   As regards, first, the elements identified in Section I of that list, the Republic of Poland indeed states that the term 'broadcasting organisation' might, for the purposes of the future convention in question, be defined in a broad sense so as to extend to web or 'simulcasting' broadcasters.

87   However, regardless of whether, in the context of new digital technologies, the reference to broadcasts transmitted by wire or over the air, contained in Articles 2 and 3(2)(d) of Directive 2001/29, Articles 7(2) and 9(1)(d) of Directive 2006/115 and Article 3(4) of Directive 2006/116, permits the inclusion of such broadcasters in the scope of the common E.U. rules in the area concerned, it is, on any view, undeniable, as the Commission submits, that a negotiation which seeks, in one way or another, to include those broadcasters in the scope of the future Convention of the Council of Europe, in particular by means of the adoption, for the purposes of that convention, of a definition of 'broadcasting organisation' in 'technologically neutral' terms, as suggested in paragraph 13 of the 2010 Report, would have a horizontal effect on the scope of the body of common E.U. rules relating to the protection of neighbouring rights of such organisations.

88   As regards, secondly, the elements identified in Section II of the list set out in the Appendix to the 2008 Memorandum, the parties agree that the elements relating to the right of fixation, the right of reproduction, the right of making available to the public, the right of distribution, the limitations and exceptions to those rights, the term of protection of those rights, the obligations concerning technical measures and those concerning rights management information are covered by common E.U. rules and that the negotiations on those elements are capable of affecting or altering the scope of those common rules.

89   On the other hand, there is disagreement between the parties regarding four elements mentioned in that Section II, namely the right of retransmission, the right of communication to the public, the protection of pre-broadcast signals and the enforcement of neighbouring rights of broadcasting organisations.

90   So far as concerns, first, the right of retransmission, the Republic of Poland and the United Kingdom state that E.U. law has carried out only a minimum harmonisation inasmuch as it refers only, in the words of Article 8(3) of Directive 2006/115, to rebroadcasting by wireless means. However, the negotiations in question might also result in establishing for broadcasting organisations an exclusive right of retransmission by wire, in particular through the internet.

. . .

92   As the Commission maintains, Council of Europe negotiations which, as suggested in paragraph 54 of the 2008 Memorandum, seek to extend that right to retransmission by wire or through the internet would therefore be capable of altering the scope of the common E.U. rules on the right of retransmission.

93   Moreover, as the Commission also states, the right of broadcasting organisations concerning retransmission by wire is already partially covered, as such, by common E.U. rules owing to the interaction between the various intellectual property rights of those organisations which are governed by E.U. law. As the Court held in the judgment in *ITV Broadcasting and Others* (C-607/11, EU:C:2013:147), the exclusive right of communication to the public enjoyed, pursuant to Article 3(1) of Directive 2001/29, by terrestrial television broadcasting organisations over their broadcasts protected by copyright includes the exclusive right to authorise or prohibit the rebroadcasting of such works by another organisation by means of the internet.

94   So far as concerns, secondly, the right of communication to the public, the Council and several Member States intervening in its support state that the negotiations in question might go beyond the E.U. *acquis* by extending, contrary to Article 8(3) of Directive 2006/115, the scope of that right so as to include places accessible to the public without payment of an entrance fee.

95   In that regard, it must, however, be observed, as the Commission has stated, that neither the 2008 Memorandum nor the 2010 Report contain any indication to that effect and that the Council and the intervening Member States have not provided any evidence in support of their claims.

96   On the contrary, as set out in the 2002 Recommendation and, in particular, in point (f) of the section 'Rights to be granted' contained in the Appendix to that recommendation, and paragraph 24 of the Explanatory Memorandum of that recommendation, the scope of the right of communication to the public would be modelled on the right provided for in Article 13(d) of the Rome Convention, which restricts it to places accessible to the public against payment of an entrance fee.

97   So far as concerns, thirdly, the protection of pre-broadcast signals, the Council and several Member States intervening in its support rightly observe that broadcasting organisations do not enjoy, under existing E.U. law, protection for those signals as such, although, as set out in paragraphs 41 to 43 and 54 of the 2008 Memorandum and in paragraph 14 of the 2010 Report, the negotiations in question might result in the introduction of such a protection because of the vulnerability of those signals with regard to unauthorised acts of appropriation or exploitation.

98   However, one of the approaches, noted by the Commission, which according to paragraph 43 of the 2008 Memorandum is worthy of consideration, namely the extension of the term 'broadcasts' to pre-broadcast signals in such a way as to include those signals in the scope of protection of the various rights conferred on broadcasting organisations, would undeniably be capable of altering, in a horizontal manner, the scope of the common E.U. rules in the area concerned.

. . .

100   So far as concerns, fourthly, the enforcement of neighbouring rights of broadcasting organisations, the Council and several Member States intervening in its support, without disputing that the sanctions and legal remedies in the event of an infringement of those rights are governed, in E.U.

law, by Article 8 of Directive 2001/29 and by a body of common rules contained in Directive 2004/48, state, however, that the negotiations in question might result in the introduction, contrary to E.U. rules, of the obligation for contracting parties to adopt criminal sanctions in the event of such infringements.

101   However, it must be stated, as the Commission has observed, that neither the 2008 Memorandum nor the 2010 Report contains any indication to that effect and that the claims set out in the previous paragraph have not been substantiated by any evidence relating to the forthcoming negotiations within the Council of Europe.

102   It is apparent from the above analysis that the content of the negotiations for a Convention of the Council of Europe on the protection of neighbouring rights of broadcasting organisations, as is defined by the 2002 Recommendation, the 2008 Memorandum and the 2010 Report, falls within an area covered to a large extent by common E.U. rules and that those negotiations may affect common E.U. rules or alter their scope. Therefore, those negotiations fall within the exclusive competence of the European Union.

103   It follows that the contested decision was adopted in breach of Article 3(2) TFEU.

QUESTIONS

1. What would have been the consequence if the Memorandum had covered criminal sanctions in the event of infringement? Why? What would be the consequence if the final text of the convention covered criminal sanctions?
2. Do you think that an international treaty enhancing the enforcement of moral rights falls within article 3(2) of the TFEU?
3. What would be the consequence of this decision for the negotiation of any future agreement adding to the TRIPS obligations?

3

Points of attachment of international protection

As Table 1.1 *supra* pp. 33–42 shows, adherence to international copyright and neighboring rights treaties around the world and even within continents is neither universal nor uniform. It is therefore highly important to ascertain whether and which treaties are applicable. In order to address this first question, one has to determine the relevant point(s) of attachment required by each Convention and check if that point of attachment connects to a member state. In addition, as these Conventions deal with international situations, one also must distinguish between domestic and international situations. The definition of an international situation might vary from one text to another. For the Berne Convention, the requisite internationality results only when the country for which the protection is sought is not the same as the country of origin. By contrast, for neighboring rights conventions, the condition is satisfied as soon one of the points of attachment retained is located in a different country than the country where protection is sought. Finally, in order to ascertain whether the work or the performance qualifies for protection, one must address the temporal application of a given treaty.

3.1 Various points of attachment

3.1.1 The Berne Convention

Authorship

> **Article 3**
> **Criteria of Eligibility for Protection**
> *1. Nationality of author; place of publication of work; 2. Residence of author;...*
>
> (1) The protection of this Convention shall apply to:
>
> (a) authors who are nationals of one of the countries of the Union, for their works, whether published or not;

. . .

(2) Authors who are not nationals of one of the countries of the Union but who have their habitual residence in one of them shall, for the purposes of this Convention, be assimilated to nationals of that country.

QUESTIONS

1. An Angolan songwriter lives in Paris where he composes music. While visiting a Berlin discothèque, he recognized his musical composition being played without his authorization. Are Berne's points of attachment fulfilled?
2. A Few years later, our composer acquires French nationality by marriage to a French citizen; he and his wife then move to Angola for a while. While in Angola, he learns that a French record producer has reused some of his same arrangements for the new song of a famous French pop singer. Are Berne's points of attachment fulfilled?

Subsidiary attachment for cinematographic and architectural works

Article 4

Criteria of Eligibility for Protection of Cinematographic Works, Works of Architecture and Certain Artistic Works

The protection of this Convention shall apply, even if the conditions of Article 3 are not fulfilled, to:

(a) authors of cinematographic works the maker of which has his headquarters or habitual residence in one of the countries of the Union;
(b) authors of works of architecture erected in a country of the Union or of other artistic works incorporated in a building or other structure located in a country of the Union.

QUESTIONS

1. An Afghan architect living in the Seychelles builds his house there and a museum in Mauritius. These buildings were reproduced in a French newspaper without any mention of his name. Are Berne's points of attachment fulfilled?
2. A famous Ethiopian muralist is commissioned to create frescos for a palazzo in Rome. Without the artist's authorization, a local photographer takes pictures of the frescos and sells postcards at newsstands in Rome. Does the Berne Convention apply?

3. One of his compatriots, a composer, has created the sound track of a French movie shot in Ethiopia. The movie was produced by a French producer. Later, the Ethiopian composer realizes that his name was not credited at the end of the movie. Are Berne's points of attachment fulfilled?

Publication

> **Article 3**
> **Criteria of Eligibility for Protection:**
> *3. "Published" works; 4. "Simultaneously published" works*
>
> (1) The protection of this Convention shall apply to:
>
> . . .
>
> (b) authors who are not nationals of one of the countries of the Union, for their works first published in one of those countries, or simultaneously in a country outside the Union and in a country of the Union.
>
> . . .
>
> (3) The expression "published works" means works published with the consent of their authors, whatever may be the means of manufacture of the copies, provided that the availability of such copies has been such as to satisfy the reasonable requirements of the public, having regard to the nature of the work. The performance of a dramatic, dramatico-musical, cinematographic or musical work, the public recitation of a literary work, the communication by wire or the broadcasting of literary or artistic works, the exhibition of a work of art and the construction of a work of architecture shall not constitute publication.
>
> (4) A work shall be considered as having been published simultaneously in several countries if it has been published in two or more countries within thirty days of its first publication.

QUESTIONS

1. An Iraqi writer living in Baghdad wrote a graphic novel about the situation in his country. An American publisher offers to distribute in the U.S. the graphic novel translated in English. The writer accepts the deal, provided that the graphic novel will be also distributed in Iraq in Arabic

at the same time. The writer discovers that some unauthorized copies of that Arabic-language version of his graphic book are distributed in Lebanon. Are Berne's points of attachment fulfilled? For which work of authorship?

2. An Iranian singer-songwriter living in Iran wrote songs and publicly performed them all over the world. For his new album, he decided to perform the songs in Iran, France, Germany and Russia in advance of publication of the album. Distribution of copies of the album is scheduled for the end of the year, but the Iranian composer has learned that the songs were earlier performed in France by another singer without his authorization. Are Berne's points of attachment fulfilled?

3. How do you understand the definition of "publication" in the Berne Convention? What does "copies" mean in this text? How are "copies" distinct from performance, recitation, communication by wire or wireless means, or exhibition? Reconsider this question in the context of the initial dissemination of works in digital format, *infra* section 3.3.2 pp. 189 et seq.

Same points of attachment under **WIPO Copyright Treaty (article 3)**

WCT Article 3
Application of Articles 2 to 6 of the Berne Convention

Contracting Parties shall apply mutatis mutandis the provisions of Articles 2 to 6 of the Berne Convention in respect of the protection provided for in this Treaty.

Agreed statements concerning Article 3: It is understood that in applying Article 3 of this Treaty, the expression "country of the Union" in Articles 2 to 6 of the Berne Convention will be read as if it were a reference to a Contracting Party to this Treaty, in the application of those Berne Articles in respect of protection provided for in this Treaty. It is also understood that the expression "country outside the Union" in those Articles in the Berne Convention will, in the same circumstances, be read as if it were a reference to a country that is not a Contracting Party to this Treaty, and that "this Convention" in Articles 2(8), 2bis(2), 3, 4 and 5 of the Berne Convention will be read as if it were a reference to the Berne Convention and this Treaty. Finally, it is understood that a reference in Articles 3 to 6 of the Berne Convention to a "national of one of the countries of the Union" will, when these Articles are applied to this Treaty, mean, in regard to an intergovernmental organization that is a Contracting Party to this Treaty, a national of one of the countries that is member of that organization.

3.1.2 Rome Convention

Article 4
Performances Protected. Points of Attachment for Performers

Each Contracting State shall grant national treatment to performers if any of the following conditions is met:

(a) the performance takes place in another Contracting State;
(b) the performance is incorporated in a phonogram which is protected under Article 5 of this Convention;
(c) the performance, not being fixed on a phonogram, is carried by a broadcast which is protected by Article 6 of this Convention.

Article 5
Protected Phonograms:
1. Points of Attachment for Producers of Phonograms; 2. Simultaneous Publication; 3. Power to exclude certain Criteria

1. Each Contracting State shall grant national treatment to producers of phonograms if any of the following conditions is met:

(a) the producer of the phonogram is a national of another Contracting State (criterion of nationality);
(b) the first fixation of the sound was made in another Contracting State (criterion of fixation);
(c) the phonogram was first published in another Contracting State (criterion of publication).

2. If a phonogram was first published in a non–contracting State but if it was also published, within 30 days of its first publication, in a Contracting State (simultaneous publication), it shall be considered as first published in the Contracting State.

3. By means of a notification deposited with the Secretary–General of the United Nations, any Contracting State may declare that it will not apply the criterion of publication or, alternatively, the criterion of fixation. Such notification may be deposited at the time of ratification, acceptance or accession, or at any time thereafter; in the last case, it shall become effective six months after it has been deposited.

QUESTION

What is the place of first publication of a phonogram that exists only in digital form and is available only from a website? *Cf.* Questions 1–2 following *Kernal Records OY* v. *Moseley*, 694 F.3d 1294 (11th Cir. 2012) and *Moberg* v. *33T LLC*, 666 F. Supp. 2d 415 (D. Del. 2009) (concerning the country of first publication when a work is first publicly disclosed over the Internet), *infra* 3.3.2 pp. 192 et seq.

Article 6
Protected Broadcasts:
1. Points of Attachment for Broadcasting Organizations; 2. Power to Reserve

1. Each Contracting State shall grant national treatment to broadcasting organisations if either of the following conditions is met:

(a) the headquarters of the broadcasting organisation is situated in another Contracting State;
(b) the broadcast was transmitted from a transmitter situated in another Contracting State.

2. By means of a notification deposited with the Secretary-General of the United Nations, any Contracting State may declare that it will protect broadcasts only if the headquarters of the broadcasting organisation is situated in another Contracting State and the broadcast was transmitted from a transmitter situated in the same Contracting State. Such notification may be deposited at the time of ratification, acceptance or accession, or at any time thereafter; in the last case, it shall become effective six months after it has been deposited.

QUESTIONS

1. An American performer is singing in a nightclub in Berlin, where his performance is recorded, without his authorization. Which, if any, might be relevant points of attachment for neighboring rights treaties?
2. A French performer is singing in a nightclub in New York. The performance is fixed by an American producer in New York, the phonogram is first published in France. Which, if any, might be relevant points of attachment for neighboring rights treaties?

Declarations, reservations, etc.

The instruments of ratification or accession, or subsequent notifications, deposited with the Secretary-General of the United Nations by the following states contain declarations made under the articles mentioned hereafter (with reference to publication in the following WIPO publications: *Le Droit d'auteur* (Copyright) for the years 1962 to 1964, in *Copyright* for the years 1965 to 1994, in *Industrial Property and Copyright* until May 1998 and, in *Intellectual Property Laws and Treaties* from June 1998 until December 2001):

For examples of reservations noticed under the Rome Convention, see, e.g., France, articles 5(3) (concerning article 5(1)(c)) and 16(1)(a)(iii) and (iv) [1987, p. 184]. [http://www.wipo.int/treaties/en/remarks.jsp?cnty_id=1112C]; Canada, article 5(3) (concerning articles 5(1) (b) and (c)), 6(2) (concerning article 6(1)) and 16(1)(a)(iv) [1998, p. 42]; Germany, Articles 5(3) (concerning Article 5(1)(b)) and 16(1) (a)(iv) [1966, p. 237]. [http://www.wipo.int/treaties/en/remarks.jsp?cnty_id=1096C]

Same points of attachment under **WPPT Treaty (article 3)**

WPPT Treaty Article 3
Beneficiaries of Protection under this Treaty

(1) Contracting Parties shall accord the protection provided under this Treaty to the performers and producers of phonograms who are nationals of other Contracting Parties.

(2) The nationals of other Contracting Parties shall be understood to be those performers or producers of phonograms who would meet the criteria for eligibility for protection provided under the Rome Convention, were all the Contracting Parties to this Treaty Contracting States of that Convention. In respect of these criteria of eligibility, Contracting Parties shall apply the relevant definitions in Article 2 of this Treaty.

(3) Any Contracting Party availing itself of the possibilities provided in Article 5(3) of the Rome Convention or, for the purposes of Article 5 of the same Convention, Article 17 thereof shall make a notification as foreseen in those provisions to the Director General of the World Intellectual Property Organization (WIPO).

Agreed statement concerning Article 3(2): For the application of Article 3(2), it is understood that fixation means the finalization of the master tape ("bande-mère").

Agreed statement concerning Article 3: It is understood that the reference in Articles 5(a) and 16(a)(iv) of the Rome Convention to "national of another Contracting State" will, when applied to this Treaty, mean, in regard to an intergovernmental organization that is a Contracting Party to this Treaty, a national of one of the countries that is a member of that organization.

QUESTION

Consider the questions following articles 4, 5 and 6 of the Rome Convention, *supra*. What, if any, difference does the WPPT make to your answers?

3.1.3   Beijing Treaty

Article 3
Beneficiaries of Protection

(1) Contracting Parties shall accord the protection granted under this Treaty to performers who are nationals of other Contracting Parties.

(2) Performers who are not nationals of one of the Contracting Parties but who have their habitual residence in one of them shall, for the purposes of this Treaty, be assimilated to nationals of that Contracting Party.

QUESTIONS

What, if any, is the difference concerning the point of attachment retained by the Rome Convention and the WPPT for performers? What accounts for this development?

3.1.4   TRIPS Agreement

Article 1
Nature and Scope of Obligations

. . .

3. Members shall accord the treatment provided for in this Agreement to the nationals of other Members.[1] In respect of the relevant

intellectual property right, the nationals of other Members shall be understood as those natural or legal persons that would meet the criteria for eligibility for protection provided for in the Paris Convention (1967), the Berne Convention (1971), the Rome Convention and the Treaty on Intellectual Property in Respect of Integrated Circuits, were all Members of the WTO members of those conventions.[2] Any Member availing itself of the possibilities provided in paragraph 3 of Article 5 or paragraph 2 of Article 6 of the Rome Convention shall make a notification as foreseen in those provisions to the Council for Trade-Related Aspects of Intellectual Property Rights (the "Council for TRIPS").

Footnote 1 When "nationals" are referred to in this Agreement, they shall be deemed, in the case of a separate customs territory Member of the WTO, to mean persons, natural or legal, who are domiciled or who have a real and effective industrial or commercial establishment in that customs territory.

Footnote 2 In this Agreement, "Paris Convention" refers to the Paris Convention for the Protection of Industrial Property; "Paris Convention (1967)" refers to the Stockholm Act of this Convention of 14 July 1967. "Berne Convention" refers to the Berne Convention for the Protection of Literary and Artistic Works; "Berne Convention (1971)" refers to the Paris Act of this Convention of 24 July 1971. "Rome Convention" refers to the International Convention for the Protection of Performers, Producers of Phonograms and Broadcasting Organizations, adopted at Rome on 26 October 1961. "Treaty on Intellectual Property in Respect of Integrated Circuits" (IPIC Treaty) refers to the Treaty on Intellectual Property in Respect of Integrated Circuits, adopted at Washington on 26 May 1989. "WTO Agreement" refers to the Agreement Establishing the WTO.

WTO Arbitration in European Communities – Regime for the Importation, Sale and Distribution of Bananas, WT/DS27/ARB/ECU (26 November 2008)

[This arbitration decision was rendered in the context of WTO's dispute between Ecuador, Guatemala, Honduras, Mexico and the U.S. as complainants against the European Communities as respondent. European law being judged inconsistent with General Agreement on Tariffs and Trade of 1994, Ecuador requested authorization from the DSB (Dispute Settlement Body) to suspend the application of the European Communities of concessions or

other related obligations under the TRIPS Agreement, GATS and GATT*
pursuant to article 22.2 of the DSU (Dispute Settlement Understanding).
The European Communities therefore requested that the matter be referred
to arbitration pursuant to article 22.6 of the DSU. The following paragraphs
are excerpted from the arbitration decision.]

140. We first note that Article 1.3 of the TRIPS Agreement defines in general
the reach of the TRIPS Agreement: "Members shall accord the treatment
provided for in this Agreement to the *nationals* of other Members. In respect
of the *relevant intellectual property right*, the nationals of other Members shall
be understood as those *natural or legal persons* that would meet the criteria
for eligibility for protection provided for in the Paris Convention (1967),
the Berne Convention (1971), the Rome Convention and the Treaty on
Intellectual Property in Respect of Integrated Circuits, were all Members of
the WTO members of those conventions. . . ." [emphasis added, footnotes
omitted].

. . .

142. Article 1.3 of the TRIPS Agreement further specifies that the criteria
for determining which persons are entitled to the treatment provided for
under the TRIPS Agreement are those that meet the criteria for eligibility
for protection laid down in the main pre-existing intellectual property conventions, including the Paris Convention, the Berne Convention, the Rome
Convention, and the Treaty on Intellectual Property in Respect of Integrated
Circuits (IPIC Treaty) [footnote omitted].

. . .

144. In respect of the protection of performers, producers of phonograms
(sound recordings) and broadcasting organisations within the meaning of
Article 14 of the TRIPS Agreement, criteria for eligibility for protection of
persons are defined in the Rome Convention.

QUESTIONS

1. Is the nationality of the performer a relevant point of attachment under
   article 1(3) of the TRIPS Agreement? If not, what are the relevant points
   of attachment under the TRIPS for performers?

---

* Editors' note: The WTO Agreements cover goods, services and intellectual property by three different
agreements: the General Agreement on Tariffs and Trade (GATT) (for goods), the General Agreement on
Trade in Services (GATS) and the Trade-Related Aspects of Intellectual Property Rights (TRIPS).

2. Consider the questions following articles 4, 5 and 6 of the Rome Convention, supra. What, if any, difference does the TRIPS make to your answers.

Who is a "national"?

The following excerpt explains how to determine who is a "national" in order to ascertain if the point(s) of attachment for each international convention have been fulfilled. The excerpt shows that the question has to be resolved by the legislation of the state whose nationality is claimed. In the case that follows, the issue arose under the Paris Convention. The Paris Convention was drafted at the same time as the Berne Convention (1883) and applies to industrial property in the widest sense. The treaty's structure is generally identical to the Berne Convention's since it both applies the rule of national treatment and imposes some substantive minima.

WTO Panel in European Communities – Protection of Trademark and Geographical indications for agricultural products and foodstuffs, Panel Report, WT/DS174/R (15 March 2005)

VII.19   The issue for the Panel is how the less favourable treatment accorded under the Regulation with respect to the availability of protection affects the treatment accorded to the nationals of other Members and that accorded to the European Communities' own nationals for the purposes of Article 3.1 of the TRIPS Agreement. Article 1.3 defines "nationals of other Members" in order to determine the persons to whom Members shall accord treatment, which includes national treatment. It provides as follows:

> 3. Members shall accord the treatment provided for in this Agreement to the nationals of other Members. In respect of the relevant intellectual property right, the nationals of other Members shall be understood as those natural or legal persons that would meet the criteria for eligibility for protection provided for in the Paris Convention (1967), the Berne Convention (1971), the Rome Convention and the Treaty on Intellectual Property in Respect of Integrated Circuits, were all Members of the WTO members of those conventions (. . .) [footnote 1 omitted].

VII.20   In respect of the intellectual property rights relevant to this dispute, it is not disputed that the criteria for eligibility for protection that apply are those found in the Paris Convention (1967). Articles 2 and 3 of the Paris Convention (1967) provide how nationals and persons assimilated to nationals are to be treated. In the Panel's view, these are "criteria for eligibility for protection" for the purposes of the TRIPS Agreement.

VII.21   Articles 2 and 3 of the Paris Convention (1967) refer to "nationals" without defining that term. Article 3 of the Paris Convention (1967) provides for the assimilation of certain persons to nationals as follows:

> Nationals of countries outside the Union who are domiciled or who have real and effective industrial or commercial establishments in the territory of one of the countries of the Union shall be treated in the same manner as nationals of the countries of the Union.

VII.22   The rule in Article 3 of the Paris Convention (1967) only applies to nationals of countries outside the Paris Union. According to Article 1.3 of the TRIPS Agreement, these criteria shall be understood as if "all Members of the WTO" were members of that Convention. Therefore, for the purposes of the TRIPS Agreement, that rule of assimilation only applies to persons that are nationals of a country that is not a WTO Member. It does not apply to nationals of other WTO Members, such as the United States. Therefore, it does not mean that all persons who have a domicile or a real and effective industrial and commercial establishment in a WTO Member are necessarily nationals of that WTO Member for the purposes of the TRIPS Agreement.

VII.23   Otherwise, the Paris Convention (1967) contains no common rules on the meaning of "nationals". It can be noted that the original Paris Convention of 1883 appeared to use the term "subjects and citizens" and "nationals" interchangeably. The phrase "subjects and citizens" was replaced with "nationals" in Articles 2 and 3 in the Hague Act of 1925 without, apparently, changing the scope of the Convention.

VII.24   A leading commentator on the Paris Convention (1967) explains the practice under that Convention as follows:

> With respect to natural persons, nationality is a quality accorded or withdrawn by the legislation of the State whose nationality is claimed. Therefore, it is only the legislation of that State which can define the said nationality and which must be applied also in other countries where it is invoked.
> "With respect to legal persons, the question is more complicated because generally no 'nationality' as such is granted to legal persons by existing legislations. Where these legal persons are the State themselves, or State enterprises, or other bodies of public status, it would be logical to accord to them the nationality of their country. With regard to corporate bodies of private status, such as companies and associations, the authorities of

the countries where application of the Convention is sought will have to decide on the criterion of 'nationality' which they will employ. This 'nationality' can be made dependent upon the law according to which these legal persons have been constituted, or upon the law of their actual headquarters, or even on other criteria. Such law will also decide whether a legal person or entity really exists." [G.-H.-C. Bodenhausen, Guide to the Application of the Paris Convention for the Protection of Industrial property, BIRPI 1969, p. 27]

VII.25   This is consistent with the position under public international law. With respect to the meaning of "nationals of other Members" for the purposes of the TRIPS Agreement, WTO Members have, through Article 1.3 of the TRIPS Agreement, incorporated the meaning of "nationals" as it was understood in the Paris Convention (1967) and under public international law. With respect to natural persons, they refer first to the law of the Member of which nationality is claimed. 180 With respect to legal persons, each Member first applies its own criteria to determine nationality.

QUESTIONS

1. Arthur Author was born in the U.S. of Iraqi parents. He complains of an infringement of rights in his musical composition in Switzerland. Frieda Photographer was born in Switzerland of Iranian parents. She complains that the copyright in her photographs was infringed in the U.S. Under U.S. law, one is a citizen on the basis either of birth in the U.S. (*jus solis*) or of U.S. parentage (*jus sanguinis*). Swiss law recognizes only the *jus sanguinis*. Does the TRIPS require Switzerland to recognize Arthur's infringement claim? Does the TRIPS require the U.S. to recognize Frieda's?

2. Same as Questions 2 and 3 *supra*, pp. 168–69, but instead of Ethiopian creators, creators are from Cambodia.

3. An American producer, specialized in world music, signed a contract with an Ethiopian singer. The fixation of the performance of the songs was made in New York and the phonogram was first published in U.S. and in Canada. Meanwhile a German producer reproduced without authorization one of the Ethiopian's sound recordings in a compilation of the best world music. The American producer would like to sue in Germany. Which, if any, might be relevant points of attachment for neighboring rights treaties?

Table 3.1 Points of attachment for copyright and neighboring rights*

Berne Convention	WCT	Rome Convention	WPPT	Beijing Treaty	TRIPS
– authors who are **nationals** of a contracting state (Art. 3 (1)(a) Berne Convention)	– applying mutatis mutandis Art. 3, 4 Berne Convention (Art. 3 WCT)	– performance **taking place** in another contracting state (Art. 4 (a) Rome Convention)	– WPPT refers for performers to Art. 4 (a), (b), (c) Rome Convention (Art. 3 (1), (2) WPPT)	– performers who are **nationals** of another contracting party (Art. 3 (1) Beijing Treaty)	– natural or legal persons that meet the criteria for eligibility for protection of the Berne Convention or Rome Convention in respect of the relevant intellectual property right (Art. 1.3 TRIPS)
or		*or*	*or*	*or*	
– authors who have their **habitual residence** in a contracting state (Art. 3 (2) Berne Convention)		– performance incorporated in a phonogram which is protected under Art. 5 Rome Convention (Art. 4 (b) Rome Convention)	– WPPT refers for phonogram producers to Art. 5 (1), (2), (3) Rome Convention (Art. 3 (1), (2), (3) WPPT)	– performers who have their **habitual residence** in a contracting state (Art. 3 (2) Beijing Treaty)	
or		*or*			
– for works first or simultaneously **published** in at least one contracting state (Art. 3 (1)(b) Berne Convention)		– unfixed performance carried by a broadcast which is protected by Art. 6 Rome Convention (Art. 4 (c) Rome Convention)			
or					
– authors of cinematographic works, if the maker of which has his **headquarters or habitual residence**		– phonogram producers who are **nationals** of another contracting state (Art. 5 (1)(a) Rome Convention)			
		or			
		– first fixation of sound that was **made** in another contracting state (Art. 5 (1)(b) Rome Convention)*			
		or			

in a contracting state
(Art. 4 (a) Berne
Convention)

or

– authors of works of
architecture *erected* in
a contracting state
(Art. 4 (b) Berne
Convention)

or

– authors of artistic
works incorporated
in a building or other
structure *located* in
a contracting state
(Art. 4 (b) Berne
Convention)

– first or simultaneous
publication of a phonogram
in another contracting state
(Art. 5 (1)(c), (2) Rome
Convention)*

– *headquarters* of
broadcasting organization
is situated in another
contracting state (Art. 6 (1)(a)
Rome Convention)**

or

– *transmission* of broadcast
from a transmitter in another
contracting state (Art. 6 (1)(b)
Rome Convention)**

*contracting states can opt out
(Art. 5 (3) Rome Convention)
**contracting states can modify
the points of attachment (Art. 6
(2) Rome Convention)

* Many thanks to David Ruther, Columbia LLM 2014, for the preparation of this chart.

3.1.5   National implementation: U.S.

17 U.S.C. § 104. Subject matter of copyright: National origin

(a) Unpublished Works.—The works specified by sections 102 and 103, while unpublished, are subject to protection under this title without regard to the nationality or domicile of the author.

(b) Published Works.—The works specified by sections 102 and 103, when published, are subject to protection under this title if—

(1) on the date of first publication, one or more of the authors is a national or domiciliary of the United States, or is a national, domiciliary, or sovereign authority of a treaty party, or is a stateless person, wherever that person may be domiciled; or

(2) the work is first published in the United States or in a foreign nation that, on the date of first publication, is a treaty party; or

(3) the work is a sound recording that was first fixed in a treaty party; or

(4) the work is a pictorial, graphic, or sculptural work that is incorporated in a building or other structure, or an architectural work that is embodied in a building and the building or structure is located in the United States or a treaty party; or

(5) the work is first published by the United Nations or any of its specialized agencies, or by the Organization of American States; or

(6) the work comes within the scope of a Presidential proclamation. Whenever the President finds that a particular foreign nation extends, to works by authors who are nationals or domiciliaries of the United States or to works that are first published in the United States, copyright protection on substantially the same basis as that on which the foreign nation extends protection to works of its own nationals and domiciliaries and works first published in that nation, the President may by proclamation extend protection under this title to works of which one or more of the authors is, on the date of first publication, a national, domiciliary, or sovereign authority of that nation, or which was first published in that nation. The President may revise, suspend, or revoke any such proclamation or impose any conditions or limitations on protection under a proclamation.

For purposes of paragraph (2), a work that is published in the United States or a treaty party within 30 days after publication in a foreign nation that is not a treaty party shall be considered to be first published in the United States or such treaty party, as the case may be.

. . .

(d) Effect of Phonograms Treaties.—Notwithstanding the provisions of subsection (b), no works other than sound recordings shall be eligible for protection under this title solely by virtue of the adherence of the United States to the Geneva Phonograms Convention or the WIPO Performances and Phonograms Treaty.

Lafarge v. Lowrider Arte Magazine, 2012 U.S. Dist. LEXIS 120907 (C.D. Cal. August 24, 2012)

. . . The gravamen of Plaintiff Joaquin Lafarge's Complaint is that Defendant Source Interlink Magazines, LLC . . . infringed Plaintiff's copyrights by publishing photographs and images of Plaintiff's oil paintings in its August/ September 2010 issue of Lowrider Arte Magazine. . . .

b. Plaintiff alleges that the works in question were unpublished thereby rendering an allegation of first publication in the United States unnecessary.

Under the Copyright Act, unpublished works are subject to copyright protection "without regard to the nationality or domicile of the author." 17 U.S.C. § 102(a); see also 1–5 Nimmer on Copyright § 5.06 (explaining that if the work in question is unpublished, copyright protection is available to "any foreign author no less than to American nationals"). Published works, on the other hand, are subject to protection only if certain conditions are met. See 17 U.S.C. § 104(b). For example, Section 104(b)(2) explains that one way in which a published work is subject to protection is if "the work is first published in the United States or in a foreign nation that, on the date of first publication, is a treaty party." 17 U.S.C. § 104(b)(2).

"Publication" is defined under the Copyright Act as "the distribution of copies of a work to the public by sale or other transfer of ownership." 17 U.S.C. § 101. Although the statutory definition does not explicitly state that the distribution must be made under the authority of the copyright owner, "such authorization is undoubtedly implied." See 1–4 Nimmer on Copyright § 4.03[b] ("Congress could not have intended that the various legal consequences of publication under the current Act would be triggered by the unauthorized act of an infringer or other stranger to the copyright."); see also *Zito v. Steeplechase Films, Inc.,* 267 F. Supp. 2d 1022, 1026 (N.D. Cal. 2003).

Plaintiff sufficiently alleges that the works were unpublished prior to Defendant's magazine publication because Plaintiff alleges that the paintings-at-issue "had never been exposed to the public." Compl. at ¶10. Because Plaintiff pled that his works were unpublished, Plaintiff's works are subject to copyright protection without regard to his nationality or domicile.

Defendant argues that Section 104(b)(2) of the Copyright Act bars Plaintiff from suing for copyright infringement because Plaintiff has not alleged that the copyrightable works giving rise to the claim were first published in the United States. However, Section 104(b) is inapplicable because it applies only to published works. Thus, Defendant has failed to show that Plaintiff must plead publication to state a claim.

QUESTIONS

1. How do the U.S. points of attachment for protection differ from those of the Berne Convention or other copyright and neighboring rights treaties?
2. What is the point of section 104(d)?
3. In the absence of common membership in a multilateral treaty, under what circumstances will a foreign work be protected in the U.S.?

3.2   The general requirement of an international situation

We have seen that the international copyright and neighboring rights conventions will not apply unless the criteria for their attachment are met. But there is another condition as well: the controversy must present an element of internationality. The conventions do not govern disputes concerning local works or performances.

Although the requirement of internationality is shared by all copyright and neighboring rights conventions, modalities are nevertheless not the same. For neighboring rights conventions, the condition is satisfied as soon as one of the points of attachment retained is located in a different country than the country granting national treatment. For protected phonograms, the internationality may result either from the nationality of the producer, or from the first fixation or the first publication in another Contracting State than the one for which protection is sought (and therefore required to grant national treatment). For copyright and under the Berne Convention, the situation is different, the internationality of the situation may result only from a difference between the country for which protection is sought (granting national treatment) and the country of origin. The application of the Berne Convention is subordinated to the determination of the country of origin, which must be a country other than the state for which protection is sought.

This is clearly envisioned by article 5.1, specifying that national treatment and substantive minimum protections are granted in "countries other than the country of origin," point 3 of the same article reinforces this result by adding that "protection in the country of origin is governed by domestic law."

Berne Convention – Role and Definition of the Country of Origin

Berne Convention Article 5
Rights Guaranteed: 1. and 2. Outside the country of origin; 3. In the country of origin; 4. "Country of origin"

(1) Authors shall enjoy, in respect of works for which they are protected under this Convention, in countries of the Union other than the country of origin, the rights which their respective laws do now or may hereafter grant to their nationals, as well as the rights specially granted by this Convention.

. . .

(3) Protection in the country of origin is governed by domestic law. However, when the author is not national of the country of origin of the work for which he is protected under this Convention, he shall enjoy in that country the same rights as national authors.

(4) The country of origin shall be considered to be:

(a) in the case of works first published in a country of the Union, that country; in the case of works published simultaneously in several countries of the Union which grant different terms of protection, the country whose legislation grants the shortest term of protection;
(b) in the case of works published simultaneously in a country outside the Union and in a country of the Union, the latter country;
(c) in the case of unpublished works or of works first published in a country outside the Union, without simultaneous publication in a country of the Union, the country of the Union of which the author is a national, provided that:

(i) when these are cinematographic works the maker of which has his headquarters or his habitual residence in a country of the Union, the country of origin shall be that country, and
(ii) when these are works of architecture erected in a country of the Union or other artistic works incorporated in a building or other

structure located in a country of the Union, the country of origin shall be that country.

Berne Convention Article 3
Criteria of Eligibility for Protection

. . .

3. The expression "published works" means works published with the consent of their authors, whatever may be the means of manufacture of the copies, provided that the availability of such copies has been such as to satisfy the reasonable requirements of the public, having regard to the nature of the work. The performance of a dramatic, dramatico-musical, cinematographic or musical work, the public recitation of a literary work, the communication by wire or the broadcasting of literary or artistic works, the exhibition of a work of art and the construction of a work of architecture shall not constitute publication.

National situations submitted to domestic law

France's highest civil law court ruled clearly that the Berne Convention was not applicable to an alleged infringement of a French painting by a French auctioneer. The issue concerned the reproduction of paintings in reduced size in an auction catalog. In that particular case, the defendant tried to invoke the application of the Berne Convention's quotation exception (see *infra*, Part II, Chapter 5.5.1, pp. 437–38). The court rejected that invocation, as the situation could not be deemed an international one, thus excluding the application of the Berne Convention.

France, Cour de cassation, decision of February 10, 1992, n 95–19030

But whereas by virtue of article 5(3) of the Berne Convention . . . the protection of works in their country of origin is governed by national law, so that if there is no element of internationality whatsoever, the controversy would remain, in this instance, subject to French law. The court of appeals correctly applied that law, in deciding that the reproduction in full of a work, whatever its format, could not be deemed a "brief quotation" within the meaning of article L. 122–5.3.a of the Code of intellectual property [establishing an exception for "brief quotations"].

QUESTIONS

1. Reconsider the Questions in section 3.1.1, *supra* pp. 168–69, (point of attachment for application of the Berne Convention): on those facts, is the requirement of internationality satisfied?
2. Reconsider the first Question following Rome Conv. art. 6, in section 3.1.2, *supra* p. 172, (point of attachment for application of the Rome Convention): on those facts, is the requirement of internationality satisfied?
3. A famous French actor while in Marrakech is photographed by a French photographer. The picture was posted to a French website without the authorization of the photographer and reproduced as a thumbnail by the French website of a well-known search engine. The photographer would like to sue both the French website and the search engine. Does the Berne Convention apply? What is the work's country of origin? What if the French photographer resided in the U.S.? Or if the photographer had been an American living in Paris?
4. A Spanish photographer published her photographs in an Argentine newspaper. The photographs are subsequently copied and reprinted in Argentina without the photographer's authorization. Is the Spanish photographer entitled to national treatment in Argentina by virtue of the Berne Convention?
5. A French painter found a copy of one of his latest paintings (first displayed in France) in a German art newspaper published without the painter's authorization by a French company. Would the Berne Convention apply if the painter decided to litigate in Paris? (What is the painting's country of origin? What is the country for which protection is sought?)

Determination of the country of origin in the absence of any publication

QUESTIONS

1. The new Bollywood blockbuster of an Indian producer is available on a Canadian website (without authorization) prior to any authorized publication. The director is Canadian and the screenwriter is French; the music is composed by a German national. Does the Berne Convention apply to the infringement action brought in Canada by the film producer? (What is the film's country of origin?) Would it make a difference if the plaintiff were the director?
2. A folk group (a trio of Canadian, French and German composers all living in Paris) played the new songs of its forthcoming album in concert all over Europe; copies of the album have not yet been distributed for sale. Some unauthorized fixations of the concert were uploaded to a French website. The group would like to sue the French website in Paris. Does the Berne Convention apply? (What are the songs' country/ies of origin?)

Determination of the country of origin in the case of simultaneous publication

QUESTIONS

1. A famous French singer-songwriter distributed copies of his new album the first of January in France. He was invited mid-January to sing songs from his new album in a concert at Montreal, the concert being broadcast live by Radio Canada. Some unauthorized copies of the concert were sold in Canada at the end of January. The singer would like to sue the infringer in Canada, provided that the Berne Convention is applicable. The term of copyright in France is 70 years *post mortem auctoris* [pma]; in Canada it is 50 years *pma*. (What is the country of origin of the musical compositions?)

2. A novel written in English is published simultaneously in Canada, U.S., India and Seychelles where the author lives. In India, some unauthorized copies have been sold. The publisher would like to sue there provided that the Berne Convention is applicable. (What is the country of origin of the novel?)
   In U.S., the duration of protection is 70 years after the death of the author. In Canada, the duration of protection is 50 years after the death of the author. In India, the duration of protection is 60 years after the death of the author. In Seychelles, the duration is 25 years from the death of the author.

3. A novel written in French is published simultaneously in Canada, France, Côte d'Ivoire and Djibouti. The author is from the Côte d'Ivoire living in Djibouti. In France, some unauthorized copies have been sold. The publisher would like to sue there provided that the Berne Convention is applicable. (What is the country of origin of the novel?)
   In France, the duration of protection is 70 years after the death of the author. In Canada, the duration of protection is 50 years after the death of the author. In Côte d'Ivoire, the duration of protection is 99 years after the death of the author. In Djibouti, the duration is 25 years from the death of the author.

4. A novel written in English is simultaneously published in Canada and New Zealand; both have copyright terms of 50 years *pma*. What is the country of origin?

5. A photograph by a Swedish photographer is made available for downloading from a German website accessible to Internet users throughout the world. Assume the photograph has not previously been published. What is/are its country/ies of origin?

Determination of the country of origin when the work is made available on the Internet

Jane C. Ginsburg, *Berne Without Borders: Geographic Indiscretion and Digital Communications*, 2002 Intellectual Property Quarterly 111 (excerpts, footnotes omitted)

To understand what are the perverse effects [of simultaneous multinational publication], and how they may come about, it is necessary first to work one's way through the Berne concept of "publication." The member State in which first publication takes place is considered the "country of origin." Under art. 3.3's definition of "published works," a work will be considered "published" if copies are made available to the public in a manner that satisfies the public's reasonable requirements. If one interprets "copies" to include reproductions in RAM (a computer's temporary memory), then posting a work on a website makes "copies" available to anyone who accesses the website. If one rejects the RAM copying theory, one might contest the characterization of the posting as a "publication," on the ground that the website is simply making the material available as a public performance or display. These are not "publications" under the Berne Convention. Nonetheless, even if one interprets "copies" under art. 3.3 to mean more permanent embodiments, then any website that permits downloading (as opposed to streaming-only), would effect a publication because the downloading public can store the work to a more permanent format, such as hard disk or printout.

Let's now move to the second prong of the definition of publication: Internet disclosure makes copies available for downloading. Are these copies "made available to the public in a manner that satisfies its reasonable requirements"? The Internet culminates the passage from a model of communication of works to a public of passive recipients of a distribution or performance to a model where networks offer interactive consultation of works at the initiative of that very same public. Public access now can be immediate, individual and instantaneous. These copies are made available "on demand." Reversing the Rolling Stones' anthem, if you have a computer and Internet access, "you can[] always get what you want" (if it's made digitally available); this is probably at least as much as "what you need," for purposes of the Berne Convention. As a result, the posting of a work on a website can fulfill the reasonable requirements standard for publication, and thus effect publication in any country in which a sufficient portion of the public is computer-equipped. This, in turn, would mean that copies are simultaneously made available in every country of the world in which there is adequate Internet access at least for downloading. Currently, over [one hundred eighty-five] countries are Berne Union members. Many, if not all, will have sufficient computing resources to qualify as places of publication.

Now, if a work initially disclosed over the Internet is simultaneously "published" in up to [168] countries, does that mean that every one of those countries is the "country of origin"? The consequences of such a conclusion are bizarre indeed. Recall that the Berne Convention explicitly excuses Union members from according Berne-level protection to its members' domestic works of authorship. A Union member meets its Berne obligations if it accords protection consonant with Convention minima to foreign Berne-Union works. If, however, with simultaneous universal publication via the Internet, every work of authorship could be considered a domestic work in each country of the Berne Union, then, ironically, Berne Convention minimum standards of protection might never apply, because there will be no foreign works.

To avoid this preposterous result, one might apply article 5.4 of the Convention to conclude that, when there are multiple countries of first publication, the "country of origin" is the country whose term of protection is the shortest. . . . But if, in the case of multiple countries of first publication, the "country of origin" is the country whose term is the shortest, then all Internet-published works will be localized in the country with the shortest term. [Moreover, if multiple countries share the "shortest" Berne-compatible term, there still will be a plethora of countries to whose works the Berne Convention will not apply because the works, even if created by a foreign author and first disclosed on a foreign website, will still be deemed local works.]

These anomalies suggest that the notion of Internet "publication" should be limited to a single Berne Union country: but which one? One might designate as the country of first "publication" the country from which the author communicated the work to the server, but this characterization has some disadvantages. First, that country may have little relationship to the work, as the author may upload the work from a modem-equipped computer anywhere in the world (including from countries through which the author is merely traveling). Second, putting aside peer-to-peer file-sharing, the work is not yet available to the public until it arrives at its place of residence on the website that members of the public will access. This in turn suggests that the country of first publication is the one from which the work first becomes available to the public; that is, the country in which it is possible to localize the website through which members of the public (wherever located) access the work.

This choice, however, is not problem-free, either. Unlike countries of traditional, physical first publication, in which authors or publishers consciously organize the economic center of the exploitation of their work, the country in which the server that hosts the website is located may be completely indifferent, or even unknown, to the author. Moreover, the downloading web-user may not even be aware of the location of the website or its host server. Not only is the criterion of the physical location of the webserver irrelevant, but the location of the effective business establishment of the website operator may be insignificant to an author's selection of that site to disseminate the work. That is, if the conditions of publication are the same whatever the geographic location of the website operator's business establishment, then that country's relationship to the publication would seem purely fortuitous.

We have come a long way from the Berne drafters' preoccupation to enhance the likelihood that works of authorship would find some point of attachment to the Convention. At the time, multiple points of attachment helped ensure that a work would not be "stateless" in the Berne Union, but instead would find refuge on some Berne shore. Now we have the opposite problem: a plethora of contacts, but none of which may be particularly meaningful.

As the foregoing excerpt indicates, if "publication" is deemed to occur simultaneously in multiple countries, the consequence could be the designation of multiple countries of origin, as to which the Berne Convention, by virtue of arts. 5(1) and 5(3) does not apply. These countries, then, would be free to deny "local" works Berne-level substantive protections.

The problem has come to the fore in the U.S., whose courts have confronted this question through the interpretation of the provision of the U.S. copyright law that defines a "United States work" for purposes of determining whether the work must be registered with the Copyright Office before an infringement action may be brought. The Berne Convention prohibits imposition of this formality on foreign Berne Union works (see Part II, Chapter 5.1.1, pp. 261 et seq.): determination of the nationality of the work therefore was key to assessing whether pre-suit registration could be required.

17 U.S.C. § 101

For purposes of section 411, a work is a "United States work" only if—

(1) in the case of a published work, the work is first published—

(A) in the United States;
(B) simultaneously in the United States and another treaty party or parties, whose law grants a term of copyright protection that is the same as or longer than the term provided in the United States;
(C) simultaneously in the United States and a foreign nation that is not a treaty party; or
(D) in a foreign nation that is not a treaty party, and all of the authors of the work are nationals, domiciliaries, or habitual residents of, or in the case of an audiovisual work legal entities with headquarters in, the United States;

(2) in the case of an unpublished work, all the authors of the work are nationals, domiciliaries, or habitual residents of the United States, or, in the case of an unpublished audiovisual work, all the authors are legal entities with headquarters in the United States;
or
(3) in the case of a pictorial, graphic, or sculptural work incorporated in a building or structure, the building or structure is located in the United States.

QUESTIONS

1. What is a simultaneous publication? See 17 U.S.C. section 104(b):

    For purposes of paragraph (2), a work that is published in the United States or a treaty party within 30 days after publication in a foreign nation that is not a treaty party shall be considered to be first published in the United States or such treaty party, as the case may be.

2. Does the above text clarify the definition of "simultaneously"?
3. Is this definition consistent with Berne Convention articles 3(4) and 5(4)?

Moberg v. 33T LLC, 666 F. Supp. 2d 415 (D. Del. 2009)

Hillman, District Judge

This case concerns defendants' use of plaintiff's copyrighted photographs, and it raises issues of first impression with regard to foreign copyrighted works posted on the Internet . . . Defendants have moved to dismiss plaintiff's claims under the United States Copyright Act for lack of subject matter jurisdiction, . . . For the reasons expressed below, all of defendants' motions will be denied.

BACKGROUND

Plaintiff, Hakan Moberg, is a professional photographer living in Sweden. In 1993, he created a series of photographs of a woman, titled "Urban Gregorian I-IX." Plaintiff is the owner and exclusive copyright holder of these photographs. The photographs were first published in 2004 on a German website, blaugallery.com, which is an online art shop that offers copies of the works for sale as canvas prints stretched over a wooden framework. Each of the Urban Gregorian photographs attributed the works to plaintiff.

At some point prior to December 2007, five of plaintiff's photographs were posted on the websites dynamicfactory.us, flashtemplate.us and myflashxml.com. These websites sell website design templates, which customers purchase to avoid the costs associated with hiring a professional web developer to design their websites from the ground up. Once a customer purchases the template, the customer uploads its own graphics, pictures, and text. The websites dynamicfactory.us and myflashxml.com are registered to 33T LLC, a Delaware limited liability company, with a registered office in Delaware. . . .

From at least December 2007 through March 2008, these websites displayed the Urban Gregorian images. In March 2008, plaintiff's attorney contacted Cedric Leygues and 33T regarding their unauthorized use of plaintiff's photographs, and demanded that they cease their use. When plaintiff filed his complaint in September 2008, some of his images had been removed, but others still remained. Plaintiff claims that defendants have violated the United States Copyright Act, 17 U.S.C. § 501 et seq., . . .

Defendants have moved for the dismissal of these claims on several bases: (1) all defendants argue that this Court lacks subject matter jurisdiction to hear plaintiff's Copyright Act claims . . .

. . .

1. Whether this Court lacks subject matter jurisdiction to consider plaintiff's Copyright Act claims

In order for this Court to have subject matter jurisdiction over a plaintiff's Copyright Act claim for an alleged infringement of a "United States work," the work must be registered according to the provisions in the Copyright Act. 6 17 U.S.C. § 411(a) ("[N]o civil action for infringement of the copyright in any United States work shall be instituted until preregistration or registration of the copyright claim has been made in accordance with this title."). Defendants contend that plaintiff's Urban Gregorian photographs are "United States works," which plaintiff has failed to register. Because plaintiff's works are not registered, this Court lacks subject matter jurisdiction to hear plaintiff's Copyright Act claims against them.

What appears to be a simple premise actually joins an issue of first impression not addressed by any court. Defendants contend that plaintiff's photographs, which were created undisputably outside the United States, are United States works because when they were posted on a German website, they were "published" simultaneously in Germany and in the United States. . . . Defendants argue that it is "well settled that Internet publications are published everywhere simultaneously, regardless of the location of the server hosting the website." (Def. Br. at 7.) Therefore, because the posting of a photograph on a website simultaneously "publishes" the photograph "everywhere," including the United States, it is a "United States work," and as such, it must be registered prior to filing suit for infringement.

Plaintiff does not dispute that he has never registered his photographs in the United States. He contends, however, that defendants' premise is flawed because the posting of a photograph on a foreign country's website does not publish it simultaneously in the United States so as to transform the work into a "United States work." Because it is not a "United States work" as contemplated by our law, plaintiff argues that he is not required to follow the registration requirement of § 411(a) in order for this Court to have subject matter jurisdiction over his Copyright Act claims. The Court agrees with plaintiff, because, as explained below, the acceptance of defendants' position would overextend and pervert the United States copyright laws, and would be contrary to the Berne Convention.

As a primary matter, despite defendants' statement that it is "well settled" that "Internet publications are published everywhere simultaneously," the issue is far from settled. The two cases that defendants cite to support that proposition only make the observation that the Internet is located in no particular geographical location and it is available to anyone worldwide. (Def. Br. at 7, citing *Reno* v. *American Civil Liberties Union*, 521 U.S. 844, 849, 117 S. Ct. 2329, 138 L. Ed. 2d 874 (1997) (describing the Internet generally in the context of a challenge to the constitutionality of state statutes enacted to protect minors from "indecent" and "patently offensive" communications on the Internet) and *Nitke* v. *Gonzales*, 413 F. Supp. 2d 262, 264 (S.D.N.Y. 2005) (discussing the breadth of the Internet generally in the context of a constitutional challenge to the Communications Decency Act of 1996, which its obscenity provisions make it a crime to knowingly transmit obscenity by means of the Internet to a minor)). Indeed, defendants' citation to these cases, and not to any case that directly supports their proposition, evidences the lack of any court's consideration of the issue, let alone a consensus on it. Thus, in a case of first impression, this Court must consider the correlation between the posting of foreign copyrighted works on a foreign website and the copyright holder's ability to file suit for infringement in the United States pursuant to the United States Copyright Act.

Even though no court has addressed the issue, plaintiff has presented one legal scholar who has recognized the situation presented here. In his law journal article, *Toward a Functional Definition of Publication in Copyright Law*, 92 MINN. L. REV. 1724, 1749 (2008), Thomas Cotter considered, inter alia, the interrelation between the Copyright Act, the Berne Convention, and the Internet, and what constitutes "publication." First, Professor Cotter explains that "in 1988, the United States acceded to the 1971 Paris Act of the Berne Convention for the Protection of Literary and Artistic Works, an international copyright treaty that, among other things, reflects an unfavorable view of copyright formalities." Cotter, supra, at 1730–31. The effect of the United States' accession to the Convention "to exempt works the country of origin of which is not the United States from the registration requirement." Id. at 1743. Thus, at first blush, it appears that because plaintiff's photographs did not originate in the United States, they are not subject to the registration requirement, and such a formality is not a prerequisite to suit.

Professor Cotter explains, however, that the determination of the country of origin is not so simple, as that determination hinges on whether the work is "published," and, if so, where the work is published.

. . .

Thus, the determination of whether plaintiff's photographs are United States works depends on the resolution of two issues: (1) whether the posting of plaintiff's photographs on the Internet is considered "publishing," and, if so, (2) whether "publishing" on the Internet causes the photographs to be published only in the country where the Internet site is located, or in every country around the world simultaneously.

Under the United States Copyright Act, "publication" means "the distribution of copies or phonorecords of a work to the public by sale or other transfer of ownership, or by rental, lease, or lending. The offering to distribute copies or phonorecords to a group of persons for purposes of further distribution, public performance, or public display, constitutes publication. A public performance or display of a work does not of itself constitute publication. 17 U.S.C. § 101.

The Berne Convention provides, [omitted] Professor Cotter explains that the question of whether an Internet posting constitutes publication under U.S. law and the Berne Convention remains unresolved. Equating Internet postings with publication presents numerous issues, which are outlined by Professor Cotter. Id. at 1787–88 (summing up that "[o]n balance, despite some common-sense appeal to the notion that works transmitted over the Internet are necessarily published, and despite a plausible textual basis for reaching this result, it is hardly obvious that this result would be desirable"). The Court does not need to delve into yet another unsettled issue, however, because even assuming that the German website "published" plaintiff's photographs, the Court holds that as a matter of U.S. statutory law the photographs were not published simultaneously in the United States.

As mentioned above, defendants argue that because plaintiff's photographs were posted on a website, and because those photographs were visible instantaneously all over the world, they were published in not only Germany, but also the United States. This simultaneous publishing, defendants contend, subjected plaintiff to the formalities of the United States Copyright Act registration requirements, and those formalities must have been met prior to his ability to file suit against defendants for their infringement of his copyrighted works. As also mentioned above, however, this argument is untenable.

First, the proposition that publishing a work on a website automatically, instantaneously, and simultaneously causes that work to be published everywhere in the world, so that the copyright holder is subjected to the formalities of the copyright laws of every country which has such laws is contrary to the purpose of the Berne Convention. The overarching purpose of the Berne Convention is to provide protection to authors whose works will be published in many countries. Christopher Sprigman, *Reform(aliz) ing Copyright*, 57 STAN. L. REV. 485, 544 (2004). "Berne's proscription of mandatory formalities is a rational response to the difficulty of complying (and maintaining compliance) with differently administered formalities that may have been, absent the Convention, imposed in dozens of national systems, some with registries, some without, and none of which shares

information." Id. (explaining that "[e]vidence for this view can be found in the origins of the Berne Convention"). Thus, if the publishing of plaintiff's photographs on the German website simultaneously caused them to be published in the United States, and such publication transformed the work into a United States work, plaintiff would be subjected to the very formalities that the Berne Convention eschews. To hold otherwise would require an artist to survey all the copyright laws throughout the world, determine what requirements exist as preconditions to suits in those countries should one of its citizens infringe on the artist's rights, and comply with those formalities, all prior to posting any copyrighted image on the Internet. The Berne Convention was formed, in part, to prevent exactly this result.

Second, also based on the purpose of the Convention to constitute "a Union for the protection of the rights of authors in their literary and artistic works," Berne Convention art. 1, the transformation of plaintiff's photographs into United States works simply by posting them on the Internet would allow American citizens to infringe on foreign copyrighted works without fear of legal retribution, since the majority of foreign works are never registered in America. While not all Americans would exploit such an advantage, the misappropriation of intellectual property remains a significant problem and there is no principled reason why domestic users should be able to act with such impunity.

Third, the United States copyright laws, in accord with the Berne Convention, provide for protection of foreign works in the United States without requiring the artists to undertake any formalities in the United States. See 17 U.S.C. § 408(a) (2000) ('[R]egistration is not a condition of copyright protection.' [citations omitted] The adoption of defendants' point of view would be contrary to that law.

Here, plaintiff is a citizen of Sweden, who enlisted a German art gallery to sell his copyrighted photographs. That German art gallery advertised the sale of plaintiff's photographs on the Internet by posting an image of each of the photographs for sale. According to plaintiff's complaint, a United States company and two French citizens who purportedly operate U.S. websites digitally copied those images, and without authorization used those images on their websites. To require plaintiff to register his photographs in the United States prior to initiating suit against a United States company and the registrants of U.S.-based websites for their violation of United States law, which protects plaintiff's copyrights, would flout United States law and the international union the U.S. has joined voluntarily. Therefore, the Court finds that plaintiff's photographs are not "United States works," and, accordingly, his copyright infringement claims may stand without registration of the photographs.

Kernal Records OY v. Moseley, 694 F.3d 1294 (11th Cir. 2012)

Black, Circuit Judge

I. FACTS

In the summer of 2002, Glenn Rune Gallefoss created a Sound Interface Device (SID) file called Acidjazzed Evening [citations omitted]. Gallefoss based his musical work on a MOD file that had been previously created by Janne Suni. Suni's MOD file is playable on an Amiga computer or by using a newer computer running software that "emulates" the Amiga and its sounds. Gallefoss's SID file is playable on a Commodore 64 computer or with "emulator" software. The technical details of both the SID and MOD files are irrelevant to this opinion; all that is relevant is that during the summer of 2002, Suni's existing MOD file was modified by Gallefoss into a SID file called Acidjazzed Evening. On August 10, 2002, with Gallefoss's permission, Acidjazzed Evening appeared in the Australian disk magazine Vandalism News Issue #39. The parties disagree as to how this "disk magazine" was published. Kernel contends the disk magazine was published in August 2002 on a physical computer disk in Australia. Defendants contend the disk magazine was published in August 2002 "on the Internet." However published in August 2002, the parties agree that in December 2002, a Swedish website called High Voltage SID Collection uploaded Acidjazzed Evening to its own website, likely after obtaining a copy from Vandalism News Issue #39 (. . .)

II. PROCEDURAL HISTORY

Kernel filed this action in the United States District Court for the Southern District of Florida. Kernel's amended complaint alleged that defendants Timothy Z. Mosley, Mosley Music, LLC (Mosley Music), Universal Music Distribution Corp. (Universal), Nelly Furtado, UMG Recordings, Inc. (UMG), Interscope–Geffen–A&M (Interscope), EMI Music Publishing (EMI Publishing), EMI April Music, Inc. (EMI April), Virginia Beach Music (Virginia), WB Music Corp. (WB), and Warner Chappell Music, Inc. (Warner) (collectively, Defendants) infringed its copyright of Acidjazzed Evening. In the amended complaint, Kernel claimed Acidjazzed Evening was "first published outside the United States" and that "[c]opyright registration in the United States [was] not required as a prerequisite to bringing an infringement action as the sound recording and musical arrangement at issue is not a 'United States Work,' as defined in 17 U.S.C. § 101."

Defendants individually answered the complaint and pleaded affirmative defenses. Each defendant raised as an affirmative defense Kernel's failure to comply with the required statutory formalities prior to filing suit, including registration of the allegedly protected work with the Copyright Office.

On May 28, 2010, Mosley and Mosley Music (collectively Mosley) moved for summary judgment. Contemporaneously with the motion for summary judgment, Mosley filed a statement of material facts, which alleged the following was undisputed:

. . .

2. Gallefoss's work was first published on the Internet. "The first publication of Gallefoss's version of 'Acidjazzed Evening,' in any form, was in Australia as part of the disk magazine Vandalism News, issue 39, in August, 2002."

3. Gallefoss chose the Internet as the means to first publish his work (as is customary in the "demoscene" sub-culture of which he is a member).

4. The work at issue was not only "displayed" but was made available on more than one website for download, copying and for preparing derivative works by others.

In his motion, Mosley contended that Kernel lacked the statutorily required copyright registration for Acidjazzed Evening, and the copyright infringement action had to be dismissed. Mosley claimed it was undisputed that Acidjazzed Evening "was first published on the Internet" as part of the disk magazine Vandalism News Issue # 39. Mosley contended that by making Acidjazzed Evening available to download from an "Internet site," Gallefoss simultaneously published his work in every country in the world with Internet service. Mosley claimed such worldwide and simultaneous publication made Acidjazzed Evening a United States work subject to registration, and that Kernel's failure to register doomed its infringement claim (. . .)

IV. COPYRIGHT LAW

The Constitution authorizes federal regulation of copyright protection. U.S. Const. art. I, § 8, cl. 8. Congress overhauled federal copyright law by passing the Copyright Act of 1976, Pub.L. No. 94–553, 90 Stat. 2541 (codified at 17

U.S.C. § 101 et seq.). As part of that overhaul, Congress eliminated all statutory prerequisites to obtaining copyright protection. Instead, Congress provided "that a copyright exists the moment an original idea leaves the mind and finds expression in a tangible medium, be it words on a page, images on a screen, or paint on a canvas[ ]" [citations omitted].

A. Registration

Congress also created a new voluntary registration system. See 17 U.S.C. § 408(a) ("[R]egistration is not a condition of copyright protection."). Registration under the Copyright Act is relatively simple and inexpensive. A copyright owner who wishes to register must: (1) complete an application, id. § 409; (2) deposit with the Copyright Office a copy of the work to be copyrighted, id. § 408(b); and (3) pay a modest fee, id. § 708; 37 C.F.R. § 201.3(c) (listing fees ranging from $35 for a "basic claim" to $220 for a "claim in a vessel hull"). The Register of Copyrights examines the application and determines whether the deposited material is copyrightable, and if so, registers it. 17 U.S.C. § 410(a). Registration of a work may be obtained at any time during the subsistence of the work's copyright. Id. § 408(a).

"[R]egistration is not a condition of copyright protection," and is completely voluntary. Id. However, Congress created a substantial incentive for copyright owners to register United States works:

> [N]o civil action for infringement of the copyright in any United States work shall be instituted until preregistration or registration of the copyright claim has been made in accordance with this title. In any case, however, where the deposit, application, and fee required for registration have been delivered to the Copyright Office in proper form and registration has been refused, the applicant is entitled to institute a civil action for infringement if notice thereof, with a copy of the complaint, is served on the Register of Copyrights.

Id. § 411(a). Thus, although "registration is not a condition of copyright protection," see id. § 408(a), registration (or a refusal of registration) of a United States work "is a prerequisite for bringing an action for copyright infringements [citations omitted]. The plaintiff bears the burden of proving compliance with statutory formalities [citations omitted].

Courts have divided on whether the filing of an application for registration the Copyright Office is sufficient to comply with the statutory prerequisite, or whether a certificate of registration (or formal refusal) must be issued prior to suit. See Nimmer on Copyright § 7.16[B][3] (discussing "application" and "registration" approaches to registration timing problems). However, "[a]s an absolute limit, if the Copyright Office has failed to receive the necessary elements to issue a registration certificate [for a United States work] prior to the time that the court is called upon to issue final judgment, the action must be dismissed." Nimmer on Copyright § 7.16[B] [3][c]. "Given the lax standards involved . . . that requirement will never thwart a determined plaintiff." Id. Kernel, despite being a determined plaintiff, nevertheless failed to apply for registration prior to calling on the district court to issue final judgment. Thus, Kernel's infringement claim could survive only if Acidjazzed Evening is not a United States work, that is, if Acidjazzed Evening is a foreign work exempt from registration.

B. United States or Foreign Work

. . .

Although registration of "foreign works" (i.e., non-United States works) is not statutorily required, foreign works can also be registered. See Nimmer on Copyright § 7.16[C][1][a][iv]. Owners of foreign works may choose to apply for registration because Congress has granted substantial litigation benefits to owners of registered works. Id. A certificate of registration serves as prima facie evidence of copyright validity. 17 U.S.C. § 410(c). Further, only owners of registered works may collect statutory damages and attorney's fees. Id. §§ 412, 504, 505. Because the fee for a basic registration is only $35, see 37 C.F.R. § 201.3(c)(1), these benefits far outweigh the costs of registration.

Here, the parties agree that Acidjazzed Evening was published, but dispute whether Acidjazzed Evening is a United States work for which registration was required prior to suit. Thus, their dispute and our analysis focuses on subsection 1 of the definition of a "United States work." Subsection 1's definition hinges on the timing and locations of first publication. To determine where and when Acidjazzed Evening was first published, we must examine the law of publication.

C. Publication

"[P]ublication is a legal word of art, denoting a process much more esoteric than is suggested by the lay definition of the term." *Estate of Martin Luther King, Jr., Inc. v. CBS, Inc.,* 194 F.3d 1211, 1214 n. 3 (11th Cir.1999) (quotations omitted). The Copyright Act defines "publication" as:

the distribution of copies or phonorecords of a work to the public by sale or other transfer of ownership, or by rental, lease, or lending. The offering to distribute copies or phonorecords to a group of persons for purposes of further distribution, public performance, or public display, constitutes publication. A public performance or display of a work does not of itself constitute publication.

17 U.S.C. § 101. Publication also occurs "when an authorized offer is made to dispose of the work in any such manner[,] even if a sale or other such disposition does not in fact occur." *Brown* v. *Tabb*, 714 F.2d 1088, 1091 (11th Cir.1983) (quoting Nimmer on Copyright § 4.04). 9 Further, when copies are "given away" to the general public, a sufficient transfer of ownership has occurred. Id. Thus, proof of distribution or an offer of distribution is necessary to prove publication.

However, proof of distribution or an offer to distribute, alone, is insufficient to prove publication. Central to the determination of publication is the method, extent, and purpose of distribution. See *Estate of Martin Luther King, Jr., Inc.,* 194 F.3d at 1214–1216 (discussing general and limited publication); cf. 17 U.S.C. § 101 (defining publication as distribution to the public). Most publication disputes concern whether distribution of the subject work was sufficiently broad, or whether the purpose of the distribution included a transfer of the right of diffusion, reproduction, distribution, or sale [citations omitted].

D. Determining Whether First Publication Was Domestic or Foreign

Determining whether a work was first published domestically or abroad adds an additional level of complexity. Because the statutory definition of "United States work" contains strict temporal and geographic requirements (e.g., "first," "simultaneously," "in the United States," "foreign nation," and "treaty party"), see 17 U.S.C. § 101, a determination that a work was first published abroad requires both: (1) an examination of the method, extent, and purpose of the alleged distribution to determine whether that distribution was sufficient for publication, and (2) an examination of both the timing and geographic extent of the first publication to determine whether the work was published abroad.

For example, a free pamphlet distributed by mail to every household on the continent of North America would undoubtedly meet the statutory definition of "publication." See 17 U.S.C. § 101. However, to determine whether the very same pamphlet was first published abroad, the exact timing and geographic extent of the first publication must be known. Was the pamphlet first mailed to every household in Mexico, followed a week later by a separate mailing to the rest of the continent? If so, the pamphlet is a foreign work, first published abroad, and is not subject to the registration requirement. Or was the pamphlet first mailed to households in the United States and Mexico, followed a week later by a separate mailing to the rest of the continent? If so, the pamphlet was first published in the United States and a treaty party whose law grants a term of copyright protection longer than the United States, making the work a United States work that is subject to the registration requirement. See 17 U.S.C. §§ 101, 411(a). Without evidence of the exact timing and geographic extent of first publication, it would be impossible to determine whether the pamphlet met the statutory definition of a "United States work," or was instead a foreign work.

. . .

Thus, to proceed with a copyright infringement action, a plaintiff that claims his published work is exempt from the registration requirement must prove that the first publication occurred abroad. See 17 U.S.C. §§ 101, 411(a) [citations omitted.] This requires the plaintiff to first prove a publication: that the method, extent, and purpose of the distribution meets the Copyright Act's requirements for publication. Once the plaintiff has proven publication, he must then prove that the publication was, in fact, the first publication, and that the geographic extent of this first publication diverges from the statutory definition of a "United States work."

V. TECHNOLOGY REVIEW

. . .

To determine the countries to which these other online methods distribute material would require additional evidence, such as the country of residence of the users of a certain restricted website or peer-to-peer network, or the recipient of a certain e-mail. For example, if a restricted website has subscribers only in the United States, Germany, and Japan, placing a file on that website would not make the file simultaneously available to a worldwide audience. Similarly, if the software for a peer-to-peer network was downloaded only in Canada, Egypt, and the Netherlands, offering a file for download on the peer-to-peer network would not make the file simultaneously available to a worldwide audience. Finally, if the recipients of an e-mail are all located in Mexico, sending a file by e-mail attachment would not make the file simultaneously available to a worldwide audience. Each of these "online" distribution methods utilizes the Internet, but none of them can be presumed to result in simultaneous, worldwide distribution.

Throughout this case, the district court (as well as the parties) confounded "the Internet" and "online" with "World Wide Web" and "website." Because of the strict temporal and geographic requirements contained in the statutory definition of "United States work," conflating these terms had a profound impact on the district court's evidentiary analysis. By confounding "Internet" with "website," the district court erroneously assumed that all "Internet publication" must occur on the "World Wide Web" or a "website." The district court then erroneously assumed all "Internet publication" results in simultaneous, worldwide distribution. As outlined below, a proper separation of the terms yields a very different analysis.

VI. MOSLEY'S MOTION

Before the district court, Mosley claimed the evidence affirmatively established that Gallefoss, through Vandalism News, first offered Acidjazzed Evening to the public by "posting" it to an "Internet site" in August 2002. Mosley claimed that such a posting on the Internet amounted to a simultaneous, worldwide publication of Acidjazzed Evening, making Acidjazzed Evening a United States work, and requiring registration prior to suit. Drawing all justifiable inferences in favor of Kernel as the nonmoving party, we conclude that Mosley failed to meet his burden as the movant under Rule 56 to show that there was no genuine dispute as to whether Acidjazzed Evening is a United States work.

QUESTIONS

1. Which decision is most compatible with the Berne Convention? If one considers that making a work available from a website could be characterized as a "publication," does it mean that such a publication is always universal? How could one limit the publication to specific countries?
2. For purposes of determining a work's country of origin, should the domestic law definition of "publication" be read in light of the Berne Convention definition? What if domestic law defines "publication" more broadly?

Association Littéraire et Artistique Internationale (ALAI)

DETERMINATION OF COUNTRY OF ORIGIN WHEN A WORK IS FIRST PUBLICLY DISCLOSED OVER THE INTERNET

Report by the Country of Origin Study Group of the International Literary and Artistic Association (ALAI)

The problem

At the June 2011 ALAI Executive Committee meeting, the members designated the creation of a study group to examine the Berne Convention determination of the country of origin of a work first disclosed over the Internet. The study was prompted in part by the decision of a U.S. district court holding that the initial making a work available over a website for downloading by users located anywhere in the world, including the U.S., qualified the work as simultaneously "first published" in the US, and therefore subject to U.S. formalities [citations omitted]. Under Berne art. 5(3), protection in the country of origin is governed by local law, which under art. 5(1) need not, as to domestic authors, conform to Berne minima (such as the prohibition of formalities conditioning the exercise or existence of copyright). But if a work first disclosed over the Internet is considered "simultaneously first published" in every country where it may be downloaded, then the work could have over 160 countries of origin, and in effect might receive Berne minimum protections in none of them.

...

The Study Group determined that under the 1971 Paris Act articles 5(4) and 3(3), a work made available over the Internet for downloading is not "simultaneously published" all over the world because the copies referred to in art 3(3) are physical copies, not digital copies. We infer this from the words "manufacture of copies" or, in the authoritative French version, "fabrication d'exemplaires," and the term "availability of *such* copies" (emphasis supplied), which would seem to refer back to the material copies that are made available by the author or authorized intermediary distributor. Under a more permissive interpretation of article 3(3), the hallmark of publication would be the public availability of copies, regardless of how the copies are materialized. But the conclusion that the copies envisioned in article 3(3) are pre-existing physical copies also follows from the comparison of the first and second phrases of art 3(3): the exclusion from the definition of "published works" of literary or artistic works communicated by wire or broadcasting casts doubt on the characterization of works "made available" to the public over digital networks as "published." Moreover, in light of the purpose of the Berne Convention to promote the international protection of authors, it would be counterproductive (not to say perverse) to adopt a concept of "publication" that, by multiplying the work's countries of origin, would have the effect of disqualifying internet-disclosed works from the treaty's minimum standard of protection. The abandonment, during the 1996 Diplomatic Conference of the draft art. 3 of the WCT, which would have equated the making available of copies for public access with published works under Berne art. 3(3), presents a further impediment to extending the Berne text to encompass copies materialized only on receipt. Thus, works made available only on the Internet, even when globally accessible, are not "published" according to the definition in art. 3(3), because the required distribution of pre-existing physical copies to serve the needs of the general public has not taken place.

. . .

Given the absurdities that can arise from tying the country of origin to public disclosure in the digital environment, with the resulting multiplications of countries of origin, the Study Group concludes that the seemingly counter-intuitive result that a work disseminated only in dematerialized digital format is never "published" is the less problematic outcome. It is important in this respect to underscore that a work which, while technically "unpublished," has been publicly disclosed and made available to the public with its author's consent would, by virtue of its divulgation, be subject to the Union member copyright exceptions permitted under art. 10(1). In other words, "publication" (specifically in the context of first publication) is a term of art entailing particular consequences under the Berne Convention. In the sense of the Convention, the term should be employed with precision, and not conflated with the more colloquial meaning of "publicly disclosed."

QUESTION

If a work made available on the Internet is not characterized as published under the Berne Convention, how would one determine the country of origin when there is one author? When there is more than one author? See 17 USC section 104A(h)(8)(B)(ii) and C(ii), *infra* pp. 213–14.

3.3 Temporal scope: Effect of adherence to international convention

3.3.1 Article 18 Berne Convention*

Article 18
Works Existing on Convention's Entry Into Force:

1. Protectable where protection not yet expired in country of origin;
2. Non-protectable where protection already expired in country where it is claimed;
3. Application of these principles; 4. Special cases

(1) This Convention shall apply to all works which, at the moment of its coming into force, have not yet fallen into the public domain in the country of origin through the expiry of the term of protection.

(2) If, however, through the expiry of the term of protection which was previously granted, a work has fallen into the public domain of the country where protection is claimed, that work shall not be protected anew.

(3) The application of this principle shall be subject to any provisions contained in special conventions to that effect existing or to be concluded between countries of the Union. In the absence of such provisions, the respective countries shall determine, each in so far as it is concerned, the conditions of application of this principle.

(4) The preceding provisions shall also apply in the case of new accessions to the Union and to cases in which protection is extended by the application of Article 7 or by the abandonment of reservations.

QUESTIONS

1. What does "fallen into the public domain through the expiry of the term of protection" mean?
2. What does "the condition of application of that principle" mean?
3. To what extent might article 18 be applicable in France, which has been a member of the Berne Convention since 1887? For example, would

---

* See also WCT art 13: Contracting Parties shall apply the provisions of Article 18 of the Berne Convention to all protection provided for in this Treaty.

the work of Shostakovich (who died in 1975, when the Soviet Union had no international copyright relations with France) be protected in France after 1995 when the Russian Federation joined the Berne Convention?

WIPO Guide (2003) Article 18

"Retroactivity": a misnomer

BC-18.1. The effect of Article 18(1) and (2) of the Berne Convention is indicated quite frequently as "retroactive protection." This expression, however, is misleading. As discussed below, there is no retroactive protection required by these provisions, in the sense that certain acts, carried out before the entry into force of the Convention, which at that time, in the absence of protection, were allowed and free, would be considered infringements retroactively. The provisions of Article 18 only mean that the obligations under the Convention must be respected from the very moment of the entry into force of the Convention for a given country, including the obligation that all works must be protected (subject to the said provisions) for the term of protection which has not yet expired (it is only from that moment that, for the carrying out of acts covered by exclusive rights, authorization is needed, and that possible rights to remuneration apply).

BC-18.2. There is no retroactive obligation or liability involved in this, and, therefore, the application of Article 18(1) and (2) cannot raise any constitutional problem. Such problems may only emerge in respect of "acquired rights." Article 18(3) of the Convention, however – as discussed below – offers an appropriate solution to any such problem by allowing transitional provisions in order to respect the "acquired rights" of those who had relied on the legal situation before the entry into force of the Convention. These provisions and measures, however, may only serve the objectives indicated in the records of the various Diplomatic Conferences, as quoted below, and may not be applied beyond a reasonable time after the entry into the force of the Convention.

QUESTION

Why is it important for the WIPO Guide to avoid the use of the term "retroactivity"? What, if any is the difference between "application in time" and "retroactivity"? How would you characterize the restoration of protection for those who had relied on the legal situation before the entry into force of the Convention?

U.S. Implementation of Berne Convention Article 18

17 U.S.C. § 104A. Copyright in restored works

(a) Automatic Protection and Term.—

(1) Term.—
(A) Copyright subsists, in accordance with this section, in restored works, and vests automatically on the date of restoration.
(B) Any work in which copyright is restored under this section shall subsist for the remainder of the term of copyright that the work would have otherwise been granted in the United States if the work never entered the public domain in the United States.

(2) Exception.—Any work in which the copyright was ever owned or administered by the Alien Property Custodian and in which the restored copyright would be owned by a government or instrumentality thereof, is not a restored work.

(b) Ownership of Restored Copyright.—A restored work vests initially in the author or initial rightholder of the work as determined by the law of the source country of the work.

(c) Filing of Notice of Intent to Enforce Restored Copyright Against Reliance Parties.—On or after the date of restoration, any person who owns a copyright in a restored work or an exclusive right therein may file with the Copyright Office a notice of intent to enforce that person's copyright or exclusive right or may serve such a notice directly on a reliance party. Acceptance of a notice by the Copyright Office is effective as to any reliance parties but shall not create a presumption of the validity of any of the facts stated therein. Service on a reliance party is effective as to that reliance party and any other reliance parties with actual knowledge of such service and of the contents of that notice.

(d) Remedies for Infringement of Restored Copyrights.—

(1) Enforcement of copyright in restored works in the absence of a reliance party.—As against any party who is not a reliance party, the remedies provided in chapter 5 of this title shall be available on or after the date of restoration of a restored copyright with respect to an act of infringement of the restored copyright that is commenced on or after the date of restoration.

(2) Enforcement of copyright in restored works as against reliance parties.—As against a reliance party, except to the extent provided in paragraphs (3) and (4), the remedies provided in chapter 5 of this title shall be available, with respect to an act of infringement of a restored copyright, on or after the date of restoration of the restored copyright

if the requirements of either of the following subparagraphs are met:

(A)(i) The owner of the restored copyright (or such owner's agent) or the owner of an exclusive right therein (or such owner's agent) files with the Copyright Office, during the 24-month period beginning on the date of restoration, a notice of intent to enforce the restored copyright; and

(ii)(I) the act of infringement commenced after the end of the 12-month period beginning on the date of publication of the notice in the Federal Register;

(II) the act of infringement commenced before the end of the 12-month period described in subclause (I) and continued after the end of that 12-month period, in which case remedies shall be available only for infringement occurring after the end of that 12-month period; or

(III) copies or phonorecords of a work in which copyright has been restored under this section are made after publication of the notice of intent in the Federal Register.

(B)(i) The owner of the restored copyright (or such owner's agent) or the owner of an exclusive right therein (or such owner's agent) serves upon a reliance party a notice of intent to enforce a restored copyright; and

(ii)(I) the act of infringement commenced after the end of the 12-month period beginning on the date the notice of intent is received;

(II) the act of infringement commenced before the end of the 12-month period described in subclause (I) and continued after the end of that 12-month period, in which case remedies shall be available only for the infringement occurring after the end of that 12-month period; or

(III) copies or phonorecords of a work in which copyright has been restored under this section are made after receipt of the notice of intent.

In the event that notice is provided under both subparagraphs (A) and (B), the 12-month period referred to in such subparagraphs shall run from the earlier of publication or service of notice.

(3) Existing derivative works.—

(A) In the case of a derivative work that is based upon a restored work and is created—

(i) before the date of the enactment of the Uruguay Round Agreements Act, if the source country of the restored work is an eligible country on such date, or

(ii) before the date on which the source country of the restored work becomes an eligible country, if that country is not an eligible country on such date of enactment, a reliance party may continue to exploit that derivative work for the duration of the restored copyright if the reliance party pays to the owner of the restored copyright reasonable compensation for conduct which would be subject to a remedy for infringement but for the provisions of this paragraph.

(B) In the absence of an agreement between the parties, the amount of such compensation shall be determined by an action in United States district court, and shall reflect any harm to the actual or potential market for or value of the restored work from the reliance party's continued exploitation of the work, as well as compensation for the relative contributions of expression of the author of the restored work and the reliance party to the derivative work.

(4) Commencement of infringement for reliance parties.—For purposes of section 412, in the case of reliance parties, infringement shall be deemed to have commenced before registration when acts which would have constituted infringement had the restored work been subject to copyright were commenced before the date of restoration.

(e) Notices of Intent to Enforce a Restored Copyright.—

(1) Notice of Intent Filed With The Copyright Office. —

(A)(i) A notice of intent filed with the Copyright Office to enforce a restored copyright shall be signed by the owner of the restored copyright or the owner of an exclusive right therein, who files the notice under subsection (d)(2)(A)(i) (hereafter in this paragraph referred to as the "owner"), or by the owner's agent, shall identify the title of the restored work, and shall include an English translation of the title and any other alternative titles known to the owner by which the restored work may be identified, and an address and telephone number at which the owner may be contacted. If the notice is signed by an agent, the agency relationship must have been constituted in a writing signed by the owner before the filing of the notice. The Copyright Office may specifically require in regulations other information to be included in the notice, but failure to provide such other information shall not invalidate the notice or be a basis for refusal to list the restored work in the Federal Register.

(ii) If a work in which copyright is restored has no formal title, it shall be described in the notice of intent in detail sufficient to identify it.

(iii) Minor errors or omissions may be corrected by further notice at any time after the notice of intent is filed. Notices of corrections for such minor errors or omissions shall be accepted after the period established in subsection (d)(2)(A)(i). Notices shall be published in the Federal Register pursuant to subparagraph (B).

(B)(i) The Register of Copyrights shall publish in the Federal Register, commencing not later than 4 months after the date of restoration for a particular nation and every 4 months thereafter for a period of 2 years, lists identifying restored works and the ownership thereof if a notice of intent to enforce a restored copyright has been filed.

(ii) Not less than 1 list containing all notices of intent to enforce shall be maintained in the Public Information Office of the Copyright Office and shall be available for public inspection and copying during regular business hours pursuant to sections 705 and 708.

(C) The Register of Copyrights is authorized to fix reasonable fees based on the costs of receipt, processing, recording, and publication of notices of intent to enforce a restored copyright and corrections thereto.

(D)(i) Not later than 90 days before the date the Agreement on Trade-Related Aspects of Intellectual Property referred to in section 101(d)(15) of the Uruguay Round Agreements Act enters into force with respect to the United States, the Copyright Office shall issue and publish in the Federal Register regulations governing the filing under this subsection of notices of intent to enforce a restored copyright.

(ii) Such regulations shall permit owners of restored copyrights to file simultaneously for registration of the restored copyright.

(2) Notices of intent served on a reliance party.—

(A) Notices of intent to enforce a restored copyright may be served on a reliance party at any time after the date of restoration of the restored copyright.

(B) Notices of intent to enforce a restored copyright served on a reliance party shall be signed by the owner or the owner's agent, shall identify the restored work and the work in which the restored work is used, if any, in detail sufficient to identify them, and shall include an English translation of the title, any other alternative titles known to the owner by which the work may be identified, the use or uses to which the owner objects, and an address and telephone number at which the reliance party may contact the owner. If the notice is signed by an agent, the agency relationship must have been constituted in writing and signed by the owner before service of the notice.

. . .

(h) Definitions.—For purposes of this section and section 109(a):

(1) The term "date of adherence or proclamation" means the earlier of the date on which a foreign nation which, as of the date the WTO Agreement enters into force with respect to the United States, is not a nation adhering to the Berne Convention or a WTO member country, becomes—

(A) a nation adhering to the Berne Convention;

(B) a WTO member country;

(C) a nation adhering to the WIPO Copyright Treaty;

(D) a nation adhering to the WIPO Performances and Phonograms Treaty; or

(E) subject to a Presidential proclamation under subsection (g).

(2) The "date of restoration" of a restored copyright is—

(A) January 1, 1996, if the source country of the restored work is a nation adhering to the Berne Convention or a WTO member country on such date, or

(B) the date of adherence or proclamation, in the case of any other source country of the restored work.

(3) The term "eligible country" means a nation, other than the United States, that—

(A) becomes a WTO member country after the date of the enactment of the Uruguay Round Agreements Act [December 8, 1994];

(B) on such date of enactment is, or after such date of enactment becomes, a nation adhering to the Berne Convention;

(C) adheres to the WIPO Copyright Treaty;

(D) adheres to the WIPO Performances and Phonograms Treaty; or

(E) after such date of enactment becomes subject to a proclamation under subsection (g).

(4) The term "reliance party" means any person who—

(A) with respect to a particular work, engages in acts, before the source country of that work becomes an eligible country, which would have violated section 106 if the restored work had been subject to copyright protection, and who, after the source country becomes an eligible country, continues to engage in such acts;

(B) before the source country of a particular work becomes an eligible country, makes or acquires 1 or more copies or phonorecords of that work; or

(C) as the result of the sale or other disposition of a derivative work covered under subsection (d)(3), or significant assets of a person described in subparagraph (A) or (B), is a successor, assignee, or licensee of that person.

(5) The term "restored copyright" means copyright in a restored work under this section.

(6) The term "restored work" means an original work of authorship that—

(A) is protected under subsection (a);

(B) is not in the public domain in its source country through expiration of term of protection;

(C) is in the public domain in the United States due to—

(i) noncompliance with formalities imposed at any time by United States copyright law, including failure of renewal, lack of proper notice, or failure to comply with any manufacturing requirements;

(ii) lack of subject matter protection in the case of sound recordings fixed before February 15, 1972; or

(iii) lack of national eligibility;

(D) has at least one author or rightholder who was, at the time the work was created, a national or domiciliary of an eligible country, and if published, was first published in an eligible country and not published in the United States during the 30-day period following publication in such eligible country; and

(E) if the source country for the work is an eligible country solely by virtue of its adherence to the WIPO Performances and Phonograms Treaty, is a sound recording.[36]

(7) The term "rightholder" means the person—

(A) who, with respect to a sound recording, first fixes a sound recording with authorization, or

(B) who has acquired rights from the person described in subparagraph (A) by means of any conveyance or by operation of law.

(8) The "source country" of a restored work is—

(A) a nation other than the United States;

(B) in the case of an unpublished work—

(i) the eligible country in which the author or rightholder is a national or domiciliary, or, if a restored work has more than 1 author or rightholder, of which the majority of foreign authors or rightholders are nationals or domiciliaries; or

(ii) if the majority of authors or rightholders are not foreign, the nation other than the United States which has the most significant contacts with the work; and

(C) in the case of a published work—

(i) the eligible country in which the work is first published, or

(ii) if the restored work is published on the same day in 2 or more eligible countries, the eligible country which has the most significant contacts with the work.

17 U.S.C. § 109(a)

... Notwithstanding the preceding sentence, copies or phonorecords of works subject to restored copyright under section 104A that are manufactured before the date of restoration of copyright or, with respect to reliance parties, before publication or service of notice under section 104A(e), may be sold or otherwise disposed of without the authorization of the owner of the restored copyright for purposes of direct or indirect commercial advantage only during the 12-month period beginning on—
(1) the date of the publication in the Federal Register of the notice of intent filed with the Copyright Office under section 104A(d)(2)(A), or
(2) the date of the receipt of actual notice served under section 104A(d)(2)(B), whichever occurs first.

QUESTIONS

1. Work your way through the restoration provisions. For states that on the effective date of section 104A are Berne Union or WTO members, when is U.S. copyright restored? Who is the U.S. copyright owner? What must a restored copyright owner do in order to be vested with the U.S. copyright? In order to enforce the U.S. copyright?
2. Suppose a novel had been published in Italy in 1960; it was never registered in the U.S. Copyright Office. In 1989 a U.S. motion picture producer releases a film based on the novel. In 2013 a U.S. publisher distributes an unauthorized translation of the Italian novel. The Italian publisher would like to know what rights it has in the U.S. against either the U.S. film producer or publisher, and how it may enforce those rights.
3. Recall the difficulty of identifying the country of origin when an unpublished work's multiple authors are nationals of different Berne Union countries, or when there are multiple countries of simultaneous publication none of which has a shorter term. How does section 104A identify a single "source country?" Might section 104A's approach be useful in interpreting "country of origin" in Berne Convention article 5(4)?

Estate of Elkan v. Hasbro, Inc., 258 Fed. Appx. 125 (9ᵗʰ Cir. 2007) (unpublished)

O'Scannlain, Graber, and Callahan, Circuit Judges.

Plaintiff Estate of Gunter S. Elkan sued Defendants Hasbro, Inc., and its wholly owned subsidiary Milton Bradley Company for copyright infringement of Plaintiff's board game "Strategy," allegedly caused by Defendants' board game "Stratego." The district court granted Defendants' motion for summary judgment, ruling that Defendants lacked access to Plaintiff's work. Defendants moved for the award of attorney fees, which the district court denied. Plaintiff appeals the grant of summary judgment, and Defendants cross-appeal the denial of attorney fees.

. . .

1.   Under the Copyright Act, "[t]he legal . . . owner of an exclusive right under a copyright is entitled . . . to institute an action for any infringement of that particular right committed while he or she is the owner of it." 17 U.S.C. § 501(b). Plaintiff does not dispute that its United States copyright for Strategy expired in 1976, at which time Strategy passed into the public domain [citation omitted]. Plaintiff argues that its Canadian copyright for Strategy provides independent protection under the Copyright Act and restores the United States copyright under 17 U.S.C. § 104A. We disagree.

Although "[b]oth the Universal Copyright Convention . . . and the Berne Convention for the Protection of Literary and Artistic Works . . . mandate a policy of national treatment in which copyright holders are afforded the same protection in foreign nations that those nations provide their own authors," *Creative Tech., Ltd. v. Aztech Sys. PTE, Ltd.*, 61 F.3d 696, 700 (9th Cir. 1995), "[a]ny rights in a work eligible for protection under [the Copyright Act]. . . *shall not be expanded or reduced* by virtue of, or in reliance upon, the provisions of the Berne Convention, or the adherence of the United States thereto," 17 U.S.C. § 104(c) [emphasis added]. The rights to Strategy not only were eligible for protection under the Copyright Act, they were protected when Plaintiff obtained a United States copyright. Consequently, the Canadian copyright cannot expand the rights to Strategy here in the United States beyond those provided by the United States copyright, which Plaintiff admits expired but alleges has been restored.

In order for a foreign copyright to restore an expired United States copyright, a published work must have been published first in the foreign country and "not published in the United States *during the 30-day period following publication in such eligible country.*" Id. § 104A(h)(6)(D) [emphasis added]. The Canadian copyright and United States copyright each lists the initial publication date for Strategy in its respective country as May 25, 1948. Those publication dates preclude restoration of the United States copyright under § 104A(h)(6). Plaintiff does not have a valid, enforceable copyright under the Copyright Act.

. . .

QUESTIONS

1. Article 18.3 of the Berne Convention allows states to "determine the application" of the principle of restoration of copyright. May a member state decline altogether to restore copyright in a foreign Berne Union work? What transitional measures to accommodate those who previously and in good faith exploited the restored work are permissible?

2. Nora Novelist resides and published a work of fiction in a country which was not then a member of the Berne Convention. During that time, Trudy Translator published an unauthorized translation in a Berne member state. When Nora's state joins the Berne Convention, will Trudy's translation be ruled an infringement in Trudy's state?

3. A few years later, the publisher of Trudy's translation would like to publish the translation in electronic book (eBook) form. He considers that his reliance interest in the translation extends to an eBook version of the translation, meaning that he will have to pay to the copyright holder "reasonable compensation," but cannot be enjoined from disseminating the eBook version. Nora Novelist contends that the eBook is a new derivative work as to which the publisher is not a reliance party. What would be your position? See *Peter Mayer Pub'rs. Inc.* v. *Shilovskaya*, 11 F.Supp.3d 421 (SDNY 2014).

Hoepker v. Kruger, 200 F. Supp. 2d 340 (SDNY 2002)

Hellerstein, District Judge

...Plaintiff Thomas Hoepker is a well-known German photographer. In 1960, during the early days of his career, Hoepker created a photographic image of plaintiff Charlotte Dabney. The image, "Charlotte As Seen By Thomas," pictures Dabney from the waist up, holding a large magnifying glass over her right eye. Dabney's eye fills the lens of the magnifying glass, and the lens covers a large portion of Dabney's face. The image was published once in the German photography magazine *FOTO PRISMA* in 1960. Defendant Barbara Kruger also is a well-known artist, specializing in collage works combining photographs and text. In 1990, Kruger created an untitled work incorporating Hoepker's "Charlotte As Seen By Thomas." To create her work (the "Kruger Composite"), Kruger cropped and enlarged Hoepker's photographic image, transferred it to silkscreen and, in her characteristic style, superimposed three large red blocks containing words that can be read together as, "It's a small world but not if you have to clean it." In April of 1990, Kruger sold the Kruger Composite to defendant Museum of Contemporary Art L.A. ("MOCA"). MOCA thus acquired the right to display the Kruger Composite without violating Kruger's copyright by virtue of 17 U.S.C.

§ 109(c) and, by separate license, acquired a non-exclusive right to reproduce the work. From October 17, 1999 to February 13, 2000, MOCA displayed the Kruger Composite as one of sixty-four works of art in an exhibit dedicated to Kruger (the "Kruger Exhibit"). In conjunction with the exhibition, MOCA sold gift items in its museum shop featuring the Kruger Composite in the form of postcards, note cubes, magnets and t-shirts. MOCA also sold a book respecting Kruger's works and ideas entitled "Barbara Kruger" (the "Kruger Catalog") that was published jointly with defendant M.I.T. Press. The Kruger Catalog contains three depictions of the Kruger Composite among the hundreds of pictures in the 200–plus page book.

. . .

A. Status of Hoepker's [U.S.] Copyright

Hoepker, a German photographer, first published "Charlotte As Seen By Thomas" in Germany in 1960. Pursuant to the Uniform Copyright Convention (U.C.C.), to which both the United States and Germany are signatories,

> Published works of nationals of any Contracting State and works first published in that State shall enjoy in each other Contracting State the same protection as that other State accords to works of its nationals first published in its own territory.

U.C.C. Article II(1). Accordingly, . . . "Hoepker's work published in Germany was given 'in [the United States] the same protection as [the United States] accords to works of its nationals first published in its own territory.' U.C.C. Art. II(1). Thus, in 1960, when Hoepker gained a German copyright, he simultaneously gained a copyright in the United States." Under the terms of the U.C.C., Hoepker's copyright protection in the United States is governed by United States copyright laws. The laws in effect in 1960 afforded an initial copyright term of 28 years, subject to renewal at the end of the 28-year period for another 28 years. In Hoepker's case, his initial copyright term lasted from 1960 to 1988. Because Hoepker failed to renew protection as required by then-applicable United States law, his copyright terminated after this initial term. Thus, in 1988, "Charlotte As Seen by Thomas" fell into the public domain in the United States, and Kruger thereafter was free to incorporate the photographic image into her own work, as she did in 1990. In 1994, six years after Hoepker's United States copyright expired and four years after Kruger created the Kruger Composite, Congress amended the Copyright Act to restore copyright protection to works of foreign origin that had entered the public domain in the United States for failure to comply with certain formal requirements of United States copyright law. Section 104A of the Copyright Act, 17 U.S.C. § 104A, effectuates the restoration. Section 104(h)(6) defines a "restored work" as "an original work of authorship that . . . is not in the public domain in its source country . . . [but] is in the public domain in the United States." 17 U.S.C. § 104A(h)(6). "Charlotte As Seen By Thomas" qualifies as a restored work. When Hoepker's photographic image was first published in Germany in 1960, German law provided a copyright term of 25 years. The German law subsequently was revised to afford protection enduring for the life of the author plus seventy years. Since Hoepker's copyright is still extant in Germany, but had fallen into the public domain in the United States, his United States copyright was restored by virtue of Section 104A as of January 1, 1996. *See* 17 U.S.C. §§ 104A(a)(1)(A) & 104A(h)(2)(A) (Germany qualifies under this subsection). Hoepker's term of restored United States copyright endures through 2055, a period of 95 years as provided under the relevant statutes. *See* 17 U.S.C. §§ 104A(a)(1)(B) & 304.

B. Actions for Restored Copyrights

Recognizing that restoring copyright to works thought to be in the public domain could be problematic to those who had relied on the public domain status, Congress was careful to limit the restoration statute's potential for unanticipated infringement claims. First, the section provides a remedy only for infringing acts that occur after a copyright has been restored. *See* 17 U.S.C. § 104A(d)(1)–(2). More importantly, Section 104A provides safeguards to "reliance parties." . . . Infringement actions against reliance parties can be commenced (1) only after the restored copyright owner has provided notice of intent to enforce the restored copyright (either by filing a notice with the Copyright Office for publication in the Federal Register or by serving such a notice on the reliance party) and (2) only for those acts of infringement that either commence or continue 12 months or more after such notice is given. *See* 17 U.S.C. § 104A(d)(2)(A)–(B). Once notice is given and the grace period expires, Section 104A(d)(2) gives restored copyright holders full access to copyright remedies—except when the act of infringement is based on an "existing derivative work."[8] The only remedy for the "exploit[ation]" of

---

8 An "existing derivative work" is "a derivative work that is based upon a restored work and is created—(i) before the date of the enactment of the Uruguay Round Agreements Act [December 8, 1994], if the source country of the restored work is an eligible country on such date, or (ii) before the date on which the source country of the restored work becomes an eligible country, if that country is not an eligible country on such date of enactment." 17 U.S.C. § 104A(d)(3)(A).

an existing derivative work is the payment of "reasonable compensation for [the would-be infringing] conduct." 17 U.S.C. § 104A(d)(3). In other words, a person who created a new work of art by borrowing from a work then in the public domain but now protected by virtue of Section 104A restoration cannot be prohibited from exploiting that independent creation, but can be required to pay a licensing-type fee.[9]

C. Application

Hoepker has no cause of action for any infringement of "Charlotte, As Seen By Thomas" occurring between 1988 and 1994. At that time, his photographic image was in the public domain in the United States, and Section 104A restores copyright only for prospective acts of infringement. 17 U.S.C. § 104A(d)(1)–(2).

As for alleged acts of infringement occurring after the restoration of Hoepker's copyright, Kruger clearly is a reliance party. By creating the Kruger Composite in 1990, Kruger engaged in an act which would have violated Hoepker's copyright—specifically, his exclusive right to create derivative works—if Hoepker's photographic image had been subject to copyright protection at that time. According to the allegations of the complaint, she continued to engage in infringing acts post-restoration. Hence, she satisfies the requirements of a reliance party as set forth in 17 U.S.C. § 104(h)(4)(A). MOCA, too, is clearly a reliance party; having purchased the Kruger Composite, MOCA is, for some purposes, a successor to and, for other purposes, a licensee of Kruger. 17 U.S.C. § 104(h)(4)(B).

As reliance parties, Kruger and MOCA may engage in acts that infringe Hoepker's restored work until, and for 12 months after, Hoepker gives them formal notice, as required by subsections (d)(2)(A) and (d)(2)(B) and as specified in subsections (e)(1) and (e)(2). Hoepker never gave the requisite notice, neither filing a notice of intent with the Copyright Office nor serving such a notice on Kruger or MOCA. Therefore, at this time, Hoepker may not seek redress for any alleged acts of infringement by these parties.

---

9 Subsection (d)(3)(a) supposes that the existing derivative work owner and the restored copyright owner can agree on reasonable compensation. Where the parties are not able to arrive at a mutually acceptable agreement, either party, under subsection (d)(3)(b), may seek assistance from a district court to set an appropriate compensation fee.

QUESTIONS

1. Do you agree that, as the purchaser of the Kruger painting, and as Kruger's licensee, the museum is also a "reliance party"? When did the museum begin selling the various merchandizing properties "in the form of postcards, note cubes, magnets and t-shirts" based on the Kruger painting? Is an interpretation of section 104A that makes every reliance party's post-1994 licensee also a reliance party entitled to the derivative works exception consistent with Berne article 18?

2. In *Golan v. Holder*, 132 S. Ct. 873 (2012), *supra* page 133, the declaratory judgment plaintiff, who was the music director of the Denver Symphony, unsuccessfully challenged the restoration of U.S. copyrights in the works of Soviet composers, such as Prokofiev and Shostakovich, on the grounds that the removal of these works from the public domain violated the constitutional requirement that copyright endure for "limited times," and violated the musicians' freedom of expression. Before Russia (as successor to the USSR) joined the WTO and therefore became an "eligible country" for purposes of copyright restoration, the orchestra had performed and recorded the Soviet musical compositions without seeking authorization or paying the composers' estates. To what, if any, extent could the orchestra have relied on "reliance party" status to continue to perform and record those works, or to continue to disseminate prior recordings of those works?

3.3.2 Neighboring rights conventions

Rome Convention

> **Article 20**
> **Non–retroactivity**
>
> 1. This Convention shall not prejudice rights acquired in any Contracting State before the date of coming into force of this Convention for that State.
>
> 2. No Contracting State shall be bound to apply the provisions of this Convention to performances or broadcasts which took place, or to phonograms which were fixed, before the date of coming into force of this Convention for that State.

QUESTIONS

1. What are "rights acquired"?
2. Compare and explain the difference between article 20 of the Rome Convention and article 18 of the Berne Convention.
3. A French singer performed in Algeria in 2006. His performance was fixed without his authorization and beginning in April 2007 phonograms were sold only in Algeria. The French singer would like to sue the producer in Algeria. Does the Rome Convention apply?

TRIPS Agreement

Article 14
Protection of Performers, Producers of Phonograms (Sound Recordings) and Broadcasting Organizations

. . .

6. Any Member may, in relation to the rights conferred under paragraphs 1, 2 and 3, provide for conditions, limitations, exceptions and reservations to the extent permitted by the Rome Convention. However, the provisions of Article 18 of the Berne Convention (1971) shall also apply, mutatis mutandis, to the rights of performers and producers of phonograms in phonograms.

Article 70
Protection of Existing Subject Matter

. . .

2. Except as otherwise provided for in this Agreement, this Agreement gives rise to obligations in respect of all subject matter existing at the date of application of this Agreement for the Member in question, and which is protected in that Member on the said date, or which meets or comes subsequently to meet the criteria for protection under the terms of this Agreement. In respect of this paragraph and paragraphs 3 and 4, copyright obligations with respect to existing works shall be solely determined under Article 18 of the Berne Convention (1971), and obligations with respect to the rights of producers of phonograms and performers in existing phonograms shall be determined solely under Article 18 of the Berne Convention (1971) as made applicable under paragraph 6 of Article 14 of this Agreement.

QUESTIONS

1. Why does the TRIPS Agreement provide for the application in time to phonograms under the conditions provided for in article 18 of the Berne Convention?

2. A Canadian producer of phonograms specialized in Asian music discovered a lot of unauthorized copies of his phonograms while on holidays in the Laotian city of Luang Prabang in January 2013. Back in Montreal, he learned that Laos has recently adhered to the TRIPS Agreement. Does the adherence of Laos to TRIPS change the legal situation for the unauthorized reproduction in Laos?

3. In 1971, Japan began to protect the rights of performers and producers of sound recordings, but did not extend that protection to sound recordings fixed prior to 1971. Does Japan's subsequent adherence to the TRIPS Agreement require it to protect the pre-1971 sound recordings of WTO member state performers and producers?

Beijing Treaty

Article 19
Application in Time

(1) Contracting Parties shall accord the protection granted under this Treaty to fixed performances that exist at the moment of the entry into force of this Treaty and to all performances that occur after the entry into force of this Treaty for each Contracting Party.

(2) Notwithstanding the provisions of paragraph (1), a Contracting Party may declare in a notification deposited with the Director General of WIPO that it will not apply the provisions of Articles 7 to 11 of this Treaty, or any one or more of those, to fixed performances that existed at the moment of the entry into force of this Treaty for each Contracting Party. In respect of such Contracting Party, other Contracting Parties may limit the application of the said Articles to performances that occurred after the entry into force of this Treaty for that Contracting Party.

(3) The protection provided for in this Treaty shall be without prejudice to any acts committed, agreements concluded or rights acquired before the entry into force of this Treaty for each Contracting Party.

(4) Contracting Parties may in their legislation establish transitional provisions under which any person who, prior to the entry into force of this

Treaty, engaged in lawful acts with respect to a performance, may undertake with respect to the same performance acts within the scope of the rights provided for in Articles 5 and 7 to 11 after the entry into force of this Treaty for the respective Contracting Parties.

QUESTION

Compare article 19 of the Beijing Treaty with article 20 of the Rome Convention and article 18 of the Berne Convention. What accounts for the differences?

Part II

Application of international copyright and neighboring rights conventions

4

National treatment and most-favored-nation treatment

4.1 National treatment

Sam Ricketson and Jane C. Ginsburg, International Copyright and Neighbouring Rights: The Berne Convention and Beyond (Oxford 2006) (paras. 6.72–73, footnotes omitted)*

6.72 **A question of choice of laws:** There are three principal ways in which works from country A may be protected in country B pursuant to an international convention. . . . In essence, each embodies a fundamental choice in the area of private international law concerning the law to be applied in the protection of the works in question.

1.   Country B could apply the law of country A (the law of the country of origin of the work, or the *lex originis*, as this is often called in private international law). Under this approach the country of origin of the work might be defined by reference to the nationality of the author of the work, or, in the case of a published work, by reference to the place in which publication first took place. In the graphic words of Stewart, "[L]ike the person the work would then, so to speak, have a passport and take its nationality with it wherever it goes".** [A variant on this theme is reciprocity, in which works from Country A receive in Country B only as much protection as works from Country B would receive in Country A. This approach combines the laws of both countries, since Country B's law would apply only to the extent Country A's law is the same. If Country A's law offers greater protection, however, Country B's law still applies.]

---

* By permission of Oxford University Press.
** Editors' note: For an example, see the Montevideo Copyright Convention, 1889 on Literary and Artistic Property, art 2:
"Authors of a literary or artistic work and their successors shall enjoy in the Signatory States the rights granted to such authors by the laws of the State in which first publication or production of the work took place."

2.   Country B could treat the work in the same way as it treats the works of its own authors, that is, it could simply apply its national legislation to the foreign work (the law of the country where protection is claimed). This is often referred to as 'assimilation', or the application of the principle of national treatment. Strictly speaking, this approach is not concerned with the question of choice of laws, as it simply removes any differences between national and foreign authors, providing that both are to be treated in the same way under national law. . . .

3.   Country B could protect the foreign work in accordance with specific rules or standards contained in the international convention itself. In other words, the convention could embody a common code to be applied by each signatory state in the protection of works emanating from any of the other signatory states.

6.73   There are advantages and disadvantages in each approach. The first ensures that the work will receive the same treatment in each country which has signed the Convention. On the other hand, it can create considerable difficulties for the national courts of those countries as they have to apply laws which are foreign to them. For this reason, the second has clear practical advantages, as it means that national courts have only to apply their own laws. This, of course, means that works will receive differing treatment in each Convention country, and that in some cases works from country A will be more favourably treated in country B than are the works of country B in country A. Such imbalances can be corrected by requiring material reciprocity of protection, but this in turn involves the same difficulty as identified above in relation to the first approach, that is, the need to refer to the law of the country of origin of a work to ensure that there is equivalence of protection. By contrast, the third approach is simpler in that there is a common set of rules that is applied by each country which is party to the convention. However, it is unlikely that these rules will be all-embracing, and the filling of these gaps will therefore involve decisions as the law to be applied (perhaps either the *lex originis* or the law of the country where protection is claimed). All three approaches are to be found in the Berne Convention, although the first only applies in specific instances, such as duration of protection and the recognition of the *droit de suite*, and the treatment of works of applied art. Furthermore, while at the start of its life the principle of national treatment was the fundamental mainstay of the Convention, successive revisions of the Convention have now greatly augmented the substantive set of 'rights specially granted by the Convention,' making the conventional rules of far greater importance than at first.

4.1.1 Different treaties' different expressions of the principle of national treatment

Berne Convention

> **Article 5**
> **Rights Guaranteed**
>
> (1) Authors shall enjoy, in respect of works for which they are protected under this Convention, in countries of the Union other than the country of origin, the rights which their respective laws do now or may hereafter grant to their nationals, as well as the rights specially granted by this Convention.
>
> **Article 19**
> **Protection Greater than Resulting from Convention**
>
> The provisions of this Convention shall not preclude the making of a claim to the benefit of any greater protection which may be granted by legislation in a country of the Union.

Sam Ricketson and Jane C. Ginsburg, International Copyright and Neighbouring Rights: The Berne Convention and Beyond (Oxford 2006) (para. 6.95, footnotes omitted)*

6.95 There is clearly a need to define the field of application for the principle of national treatment, and this is best done by a consideration of the text of the Convention. This suggests the following conclusions. From the preamble and article 1, the object of the Convention is clearly indicated as being the protection of the "rights of authors in their literary and artistic works". This object, however, requires further clarification, as an examination of the substantive provisions of the Convention reveals that it is far from comprehensive in the protection which it accords. In essence, there are the following elements to this protection:

1. the identification of the persons who are eligible to claim this protection (namely, Union authors, and non-Union authors in particular circumstances);
2. the subject matter protected (namely, literary and artistic works);
3. the substantive rights protected;

---

* By permission of Oxford University Press.

4. the duration of this protection;
5. the exceptions to this protection;
6. the remedies afforded.

Each of these elements assists in defining and delimiting the field of application of the principle of national treatment, and has the effect of ensuring that it does not have an open-ended and indeterminate operation. Thus, an author claiming protection under the Convention should have the benefit of whatever are the provisions of national law concerning these matters, insofar as they go beyond what is required by a specific conventional rule. These matters can be briefly described as relating to the rights and subject-matter to be protected, the scope of this protection and its duration or termination. This is confirmed by article 19 which embodies the basic principle that the Convention only establishes the minimum of protection which is to be accorded to Union authors, and that the latter may claim whatever additional protection is provided to nationals. However, where a provision of national law lies entirely outside these matters, it cannot be the subject of any requirement to accord national treatment: there can be no automatic entitlement to the benefits of the law of the country where protection is claimed. For example, if a national law protects subject matter that is not a "work[] for which [authors] are protected under this Convention," i.e., subject matter that is not a "literary and artistic work," such as an author's commercial interest in controlling the marketing of her image, a foreign author would not, by virtue of the Berne Convention, be entitled to claim protection for her "publicity rights" in that jurisdiction. (This, of course, leaves open the question whether the author would enjoy that protection by virtue of that country's general private international law rules regarding the treatment of foreigners.)

QUESTIONS

May a Berne member state limit application of the rule of national treatment to matters covered by the Convention's substantive minima? For example, if recorded musical performances are not included within the subject matter of Berne Convention article 2 (see *infra*), may a Berne member state decline to protect sound recordings first published in another member state, or whose performers are nationals of another member state? Or, if the Berne Convention does not clearly or completely articulate a distribution right, may a Berne member state decline to grant distribution rights to works first published in another member state, or whose authors are nationals of another member state? How does article 19 affect the analysis?

Rome Convention

Article 2
Protection given by the Convention. Definition of National Treatment

1. For the purposes of this Convention, national treatment shall mean the treatment accorded by the domestic law of the Contracting State in which protection is claimed:

(a) to performers who are its nationals, as regards performances taking place, broadcast, or first fixed, on its territory;
(b) to producers of phonograms who are its nationals, as regards phonograms first fixed or first published on its territory;
(c) to broadcasting organisations which have their headquarters on its territory, as regards broadcasts transmitted from transmitters situated on its territory.

2. National treatment shall be subject to the protection specifically guaranteed, and the limitations specifically provided for, in this Convention.

Diplomatic Conference on the International Protection of Performers, Producers of Phonograms and Broadcasting Organizations (Rome, 10–26 October 1961), Report of Abraham L. Kaminstein, Rapporteur General (pp. 5–6)

In response to a proposal by Belgium and Switzerland, the Convention also contains a provision making national treatment subject to the protection specifically guaranteed by the Convention. This refers to the so-called minimum protection provided particularly in Articles 7, 10, 12 and 13, which the Contracting States undertake to grant – subject to permitted reservations and exceptions – even if they do not grant it to domestic performances, phonograms, or broadcasts. This idea is also expressed in paragraph 2 of Article 2, which also provides that national treatment shall be subject to the limitations specifically provided in the Convention. . .

In this connection, Czechoslovakia proposed that a State which granted rights other than the minima required by the Convention should not be bound to grant them to nationals of others States which did not grant such rights to nationals of the first States. This was not accepted by the Conference.

During the discussion several delegations expressed the view that Article 2, paragraph 2, was unnecessary as a matter of logic; they argued that the qualifications upon the principle of national treatment necessarily resulted from the various provisions of the Convention and needed no special mention. The majority believed, however, that a provision like paragraph 2 would facilitate the understanding of the Convention. They favoured a clear statement that what the Convention obligates the States to grant does not necessarily coincide exactly with national treatment, since Convention protection might, under the circumstances referred to above, be more or less than national treatment.

Guide to the Rome Convention and to the Phonograms Convention (1981 WIPO)

2.1   The protection given by the Convention consists mainly of national treatment. The General Report of the Rome Conference and the first paragraph of Article 2 have the aim of defining the national treatment as it applies to the three categories of beneficiaries . . . In short it is the treatment which a state accords to its national performers, phonograms and broadcasts. To demonstrate who are the beneficiaries of this treatment, the Convention, in Article 4, 5 and 6 sets out the respective point of attachment.

2.2   The treatment to be accorded is further defined in paragraph 2 of this Article which brings in the minimum protection specifically guaranteed by the Convention . . . Even if a Contracting State does not grant these minima to its own nationals, it must do so to nationals of other Contracting States

. . .

2.4   The formula in the Article has the advantage that it brings the level of treatment granted nationally at least as high as the conventional minima . . . since no country will wish to grant foreigners greater rights than its own national. But, the discussion in Rome made it clear that the protection which States are bound by the Convention to give may not always coincide exactly with national treatment since the former could be greater or less than the latter.

2.5   This provision, whereby foreigners are assimilated to nationals in all States party to the Convention is to be found in the multilateral copyright conventions, though in the Rome Convention its impact is less because the approach is different . . . the object of protection is not the thing, but specified beneficiaries. The copyright conventions on the other hand protect the work itself.

Guide to the Copyright and Related Rights Treaties Administered by WIPO (2003)

RC-2.3. There are certain views according to which the nature of the national treatment required under the Rome Convention would be different from that of the national treatment prescribed in the Berne Convention. The text of Article 2, together with the records of the Diplomatic Conference, however make it quite clear that, in all essential elements, the national treatment obligations are the same. Paragraph 1 of the Article defines national treatment as "the treatment accorded by the domestic law of the Contracting State in which protection is claimed: (a) to performers who are its nationals, as regards performances taking place, broadcast, or first fixed, on its territory; (b) to producers of phonograms who are its nationals, as regards phonograms first fixed or first published on its territory; (c) to broadcasting organisations which have their headquarters on its territory, as regards broadcasts transmitted from transmitters situated on its territory." In substance, this is the same kind of national treatment as the one prescribed in Article 5(1) of the Berne Convention for the countries of the Berne Union: "the rights which their respective laws do now or may hereafter grant to their nationals." The fact that Article 2 of the Rome Convention does not underline that the national treatment accorded by the Contracting States means both what they "do now or may hereinafter grant" to their nationals does not mean that not that treatment would be relevant which is granted at the time of the act in respect of which protection is claimed.

RC-2.4. The second structural element of the protection provided by the Rome Convention is also of the same nature as in the case of the Berne Convention. Paragraph 2 of Article 2 of the Rome Convention reads as follows: "National treatment shall be subject to the protection specifically guaranteed, and the limitations specifically provided for, in this Convention." "Protection specifically granted, and the limitations specifically provided for" means the minimum level of protection fixed by the Convention. National treatment is subject to this minimum level in the sense that, irrespective of what is granted to nationals, the protection granted to the beneficiaries of the Convention must not be lower than that. The "protection specifically granted" by the Convention must be granted in any case, and protection may only be restricted by any possible "limitations specifically provided for" in the Convention.

RC-2.5. The two elements contained in Article 2 of the Rome Convention: (i) "the treatment accorded [to nationals] by the domestic law of the Contracting State in which protection is claimed" (paragraph 1), and

(ii) "subject to the protection specifically guaranteed, and the limitations specifically provided for, in this Convention" (paragraph 2), have the same meaning and the same impact as the two elements in Article 5(1) of the Berne Convention: (i) "the rights which their respective laws do now or may hereafter grant to their nationals," and (ii) "as well as the rights specially granted by this Convention." The only difference is that the text of the Rome Convention more precisely expresses the same, for two reasons: first, obviously, from the viewpoint of the minimum obligation under either of the two conventions, not only the rights specifically granted should be taken into account but also the possibilities of limiting those rights permitted by the given convention; and, second, if a country grants at least those rights to its own nationals which correspond to the rights specifically granted by the given convention (that is, no less rights than what it must grant to foreigner under the convention; and undoubtedly this is the case in the overwhelming majority of countries), the second element "as well as the rights specifically granted by this Convention" is meaningless, since there are no "extra rights" beyond what is covered by national treatment. At the same time, in the Rome Convention, the second element of the provisions fixing the minimum level of protection to be granted is always meaningful, since it is always true that national treatment is subject to that level of protection.

RC-2.6. This interpretation of Article 2 of the Rome Convention is fully confirmed by the following statements expressing the understanding and agreement of the 1961 Rome Diplomatic Conference: "Simply stated, national treatment is the treatment that a State grants under its domestic law to domestic performances, phonograms, and broadcasts [. . .] In response to a proposal by Belgium [. . .] and Switzerland [. . .] the Convention also contains a provision making national treatment subject to the protection specifically guaranteed by the Convention. This refers to the so-called minimum protection provided particularly in Articles 7, 10, 12 and 13, which the Contracting States undertake to grant – subject to permitted reservations and exceptions – even if they do not grant it to domestic performances, phonograms, or broadcasts. This idea is expressed in paragraph 2 of Article 2, which also provides that national treatment shall be subject to the limitations specifically provided for in the Convention. For example, under Article 16 a Contracting State could deny or limit rights of secondary use with respect to phonograms (Article 12), regardless of whether its domestic law granted this protection [. . .] In this connection, Czechoslovakia proposed [. . .] that a State which granted rights other than the minima required by the Convention should not be bound to grant them to nationals of other States which did not grant such rights to nationals of the first State. This was not accepted by the Conference."

QUESTIONS

1. How does the rule of national treatment encompass the domestic protection of the contracting States? How does the scope of the rule of national treatment in the Berne Convention differ from the Rome Convention?

2. What is the value of the WIPO Guides as aides to treaty interpretation? (See *supra*, Part I, Chapter 2.1.5.) In the case of binding legal texts, the new law trumps the old one when their terms differ. Does the same apply to different versions of the *WIPO Guide*, so that the 2003 Guide displaces the 1981 *Guide*? If not, how would the conflict between different versions be resolved?

WPPT

Article 4
National Treatment

(1) Each Contracting Party shall accord to nationals of other Contracting Parties, as defined in Article 3(2), the treatment it accords to its own nationals with regard to the exclusive rights specifically granted in this Treaty, and to the right to equitable remuneration provided for in Article 15 of this Treaty.

(2) The obligation provided for in paragraph (1) does not apply to the extent that another Contracting Party makes use of the reservations permitted by Article 15(3) of this Treaty.

Guide to the Copyright and Related Rights Treaties Administered by WIPO (2003)

PPT-4.4. Treatment which only means the obligation to grant to the nationals of other Contracting Parties the rights specifically provided for in a treaty is not real national treatment; it is closer to the application of material reciprocity subject to certain minimum obligations under the treaty.

PPT-4.5. While Article 4 of the WPPT is in accordance with Article 3.1 of the TRIPS Agreement, it fundamentally differs from the provisions of Article 2 of the Rome Convention which, as discussed above in the comments to that Article – in spite of some views to the contrary [footnotes omitted] – provides for the same kind of real national treatment as the Berne Convention.

PPT-4.6. Article 4 permits Contracting Parties to deny national treatment, in respect of exclusive rights other than those "specifically granted in the Treaty," and rights to equitable remuneration other than the one provided for in Article 15 (also taking into account the exception in respect of the latter in paragraph (2) of that Article). "Specifically granted rights" are supposed to be granted by each Contracting State and, thus, the role of national treatment would only truly emerge when any further rights were granted in addition to the "specifically granted rights," but just in respect of such further rights, there is no obligation to grant national treatment. This replacement of national treatment with material reciprocity, however, is only allowed under the WPPT where one of the Contracting Parties is not party also to the Rome Convention. In a situation where both Contracting Parties are also party to the Rome Convention, the safeguard clause in Article 1(1) of the Treaty is applicable.

QUESTIONS

What is the difference between the rule of national treatment and material reciprocity? What do you think of the assertion in PPT 4.5?

Beijing Treaty

Article 4
National Treatment

(1) Each Contracting Party shall accord to nationals of other Contracting Parties the treatment it accords to its own nationals with regard to the exclusive rights specifically granted in this Treaty and the right to equitable remuneration provided for in Article 11 of this Treaty.

(2) A Contracting Party shall be entitled to limit the extent and term of the protection accorded to nationals of another Contracting Party under paragraph (1), with respect to the rights granted in Article 11(1) and 11(2) of this Treaty, to those rights that its own nationals enjoy in that other Contracting Party.

(3) The obligation provided for in paragraph (1) does not apply to a Contracting Party to the extent that another Contracting Party makes use of the reservations permitted by Article 11(3) of this Treaty, nor does it apply to a Contracting Party, to the extent that it has made such reservation.

QUESTION

How does the scope of the rule of national treatment in the Beijing Convention differ from the Rome Convention, WPPT and Berne Convention?

TRIPS Agreement

> **Article 3**
> **National Treatment**
>
> 1. Each Member shall accord to the nationals of other Members treatment no less favourable than that it accords to its own nationals with regard to the protection (3) of intellectual property, subject to the exceptions already provided in, respectively, the Paris Convention (1967), the Berne Convention (1971), the Rome Convention . . . . In respect of performers, producers of phonograms and broadcasting organizations, this obligation only applies in respect of the rights provided under this Agreement. . . .

QUESTION

How does the scope of the rule of national treatment in the TRIPS differ from the Berne Convention, the Rome Convention, WPPT and Beijing Convention?

4.1.2   Derogations from the rule of national treatment: exceptions in favor of the reciprocity rule

Berne Convention

> **Article 2**
> **Subject matter of protection**
>
> . . .
>
> (7) Subject to the provisions of Article 7(4) of this Convention, it shall be a matter for legislation in the countries of the Union to determine the extent of the application of their laws to works of applied art and industrial designs and models, as well as the conditions under which such works, designs and models shall be protected. Works [of applied art] protected in the country of origin solely as designs and models shall be entitled in another country of the Union only to such special protection as is granted in that country to designs and models; however, if no

such special protection is granted in that country, such works shall be protected as artistic works.

Article 7
Duration of protection

. . .

(8) In any case, the term shall be governed by the legislation of the country where protection is claimed; however, unless the legislation of that country otherwise provides, the term shall not exceed the term fixed in the country of origin of the work.

Article 14*ter*
Droit de suite

. . .

(2) The protection provided by the preceding paragraph may be claimed in a country of the Union only if legislation in the country to which the author belongs so permits, and to the extent permitted by the country where this protection is claimed.

QUESTIONS

1. What accounts for these exceptions to the rule of national treatment?
2. In Berne Convention articles 2(7) and 7(8), the rule of reciprocity is tempered in various ways. Under what circumstances will a work of applied art be protected as an artistic work (and therefore subject to the rule of national treatment)? Under what circumstances may a member State decline to apply the "rule of the shorter term"?
3. Compare the binding nature of the reciprocity rule under articles 2(7) and 7(8). To what extent does article 19 of the Berne Convention change the outcome?

Rome Convention

Article 12
Secondary Uses of Phonograms

If a phonogram published for commercial purposes, or a reproduction of such phonogram, is used directly for broadcasting or for any communication to the public, a single equitable remuneration shall be paid by the user to the performers, or to the producers of the phonograms, or to both. Domestic law may, in the absence of agreement between these parties, lay down the conditions as to the sharing of this remuneration.

Guide to the Copyright and Related Rights Treaties Administered by WIPO (2003)

RC-12.1. The report of the Diplomatic Conference states that the question of "what the Convention should provide in connection with the so-called secondary uses was doubtless the most difficult problem before the Conference." It also indicates that "secondary uses" was used as a generalized expression not found in the Convention to designate the use of phonograms in broadcasting and communication to the public. It should be stressed, however, that it no longer seems justified to qualify such uses as "secondary." With the advent of ever more numerous and ever-better quality broadcast programs which can now use perfect digital recordings, also in subscription systems in a near-on-demand manner, they have become basic, primary ways of exploiting phonograms and the performances embodied in them.

QUESTIONS

What does "secondary uses of phonograms" mean? Since the phrase appears only in the title of article 12, what weight should it receive?

Article 16
Reservations

1. Any State, upon becoming party to this Convention, shall be bound by all the obligations and shall enjoy all the benefits thereof. However, a State may at any time, in a notification deposited with the Secretary-General of the United Nations, declare that:
    (a) as regards Article 12:
        (i) it will not apply the provisions of that Article;
        (ii) it will not apply the provisions of that Article in respect of certain uses;
        (iii) as regards phonograms the producer of which is not a national of another Contracting State, it will not apply that Article;
        (iv) as regards phonograms the producer of which is a national of another Contracting State, it will limit the protection provided for by that Article to the extent to which, and to the term for which, the latter State grants protection to phonograms first fixed by a

national of the State making the declaration; however, the fact that the Contracting State of which the producer is a national does not grant the protection to the same beneficiary or beneficiaries as the State making the declaration shall not be considered as a difference in the extent of the protection;

(b) as regards Article 13, it will not apply item (d) of that Article; if a Contracting State makes such a declaration, the other Contracting States shall not be obliged to grant the right referred to in Article 13, item (d), to broadcasting organisations whose headquarters are in that State.

WIPO – Guide to the Rome Convention and to the Phonograms Convention (1981)

16–8 Finally, by the fourth option (a)(iv), a State which grants payment for secondary uses for phonograms the producers of which are nationals of another Contracting State, may limit protection to the extent to which the latter State protects nationals of the former. This is usually called material reciprocity. No contracting State must give more than it receives.

QUESTIONS

1. Suppose state A makes the declaration in (a)(iv), state B applies article 12 without reservation and state C rules article 12 out altogether. What would be the situation for a commercial phonogram made by national of state B and broadcast in state A? A commercial phonogram of state C broadcast in state A?
2. Work through article 16(1)(a)(iv), what does it mean in practice? How does it relate to article 12? How does it relate to the rule of national treatment?

The non-application of the rule of reciprocity in the E.U.

Article 18 TFEU (ex Article 12 TEC)

Within the scope of application of the Treaties, and without prejudice to any special provisions contained therein, any discrimination on grounds of nationality shall be prohibited.

The European Parliament and the Council, acting in accordance with the ordinary legislative procedure, may adopt rules designed to prohibit such discrimination.

a. Non-discrimination beyond the international obligations

C-92/92 and C-326/92 Joined Cases Phil Collins v. Imtrat Handelsgesellschaft mbH and Leif Emanuel Kraul v. EMI Electrola GmbH ECLI:EU:C:1993:847 [1993]

3. The questions which the Landgericht Muenchen I submitted in Case C-92/92 were raised in proceedings between Phil Collins, singer and composer of British nationality, and a phonogram distributer, Imtrat Handelsgesellschaft mbH ("Imtrat"), relating to the marketing, in Germany, of a compact disk containing the recording, made without the singer's consent, of a concert given in the United States.

4. According to Paragraphs 96(1) and 125(1) of the German Copyright Act of 9 September 1965 (Urheberrechtsgesetz, hereinafter "the UrhG") performing artists who have German nationality enjoy the protection granted by Paragraphs 73 to 84 of the UrhG in respect of all their performances. In particular, they may prohibit the distribution of those performances which are reproduced without their permission, irrespective of the place of performance. In contrast, the effect of the provisions of Paragraph 125(2) to (6) of the UrhG, relating to foreign performers, as interpreted by the Bundesgerichtshof and the Bundesverfassungsgericht (Federal Constitutional Court), is that those performers cannot avail themselves of the provisions of Paragraph 96(1), where the performance was given outside Germany.

5. Phil Collins applied to the Landgericht Muenchen I for an interim injunction prohibiting the marketing of the compact disk in question. The national court considered that the provisions of Paragraph 125 of the UrhG were applicable to the proceedings, to the exclusion, in particular, of the terms of the international Rome Convention of 26 October 1961 for the Protection of Performers, Producers of Phonograms and Broadcasting Organizations (Treaties Series, volume 496, No 7247), to which the United States, where the performance had taken place, had not acceded. It questioned, however, the conformity of those national provisions with the principle of non-discrimination laid down by the first paragraph of Article 7 of the Treaty.

. . .

7. In Case C-326/92 the questions were submitted by the Bundesgerichtshof in proceedings between EMI Electrola GmbH ("EMI Electrola") and Patricia Im- und Export Verwaltungsgesellschaft mbH ("Patricia") and its managing

director, Mr Kraul, relating to the marketing, in Germany, of phonograms containing recordings of shows given in Great Britain by Cliff Richard, a singer of British nationality, in 1958 and 1959.

8. EMI Electrola is the holder, in Germany, of exclusive rights to exploit the recordings of those shows. It maintains that Patricia infringed its exclusive rights by marketing phonograms reproducing those recordings without its consent.

9. The Bundesgerichtshof, before which the matter had come by way of an appeal on a point of law, considered that the proceedings fell within the provisions of Paragraph 125(2) to (6) of the UrhG, to the exclusion, in particular, of the terms of the Berne Convention for the Protection of Literary and Artistic Works of 9 September 1886, as last revised by the Paris Act of 24 July 1971 (WIPO, vol. 287), which concerns copyright in the strict sense, and not related performers' rights, and of the terms of the Rome Convention, which in its view could not be applied retroactively to performances given in 1958 and 1959.

. . .

Discrimination within the meaning of the first paragraph of Article 7 of the Treaty [now article 18 TFEU]

29. Imtrat and Patricia maintain that the differentiation which is made between German nationals and nationals of the other Member States in the cases referred to it by the national courts is objectively justified by the disparities which exist between national laws and by the fact that not all Member States have yet acceded to the Rome Convention. That differentiation is not, in those circumstances, contrary to the first paragraph of Article 7 of the Treaty [now article 18 TFEU].

30. It is undisputed that Article 7 [now article 18 TFEU] is not concerned with any disparities in treatment or the distortions which may result, for the persons and undertakings subject to the jurisdiction of the Community, from divergences existing between the laws of the various Member States, so long as those laws affect all persons subject to them, in accordance with objective criteria and without regard to their nationality.

31. Thus, contrary to what Imtrat and Patricia maintain, neither the disparities between the national laws relating to the protection of copyright and related rights nor the fact that not all Member States have yet acceded to the Rome Convention can justify a breach of the principle of non-discrimination

laid down by the first paragraph of Article 7 of the Treaty [now article 18 TFEU].

32.   In prohibiting "any discrimination on the grounds of nationality", Article 7 of the Treaty requires, on the contrary, that persons in a situation governed by Community law be placed on a completely equal footing with nationals of the Member State concerned [citations omitted]. In so far as that principle is applicable, it therefore precludes a Member State from making the grant of an exclusive right subject to the requirement that the person concerned be a national of that State.

33.   Accordingly, it should be stated in reply to the question put to the Court that the first paragraph of Article 7 of the Treaty [now article 18 TFEU] must be interpreted as precluding legislation of a Member State from denying, in certain circumstances, to authors and performers from other Member States, and those claiming under them, the right, accorded by that legislation the nationals of that State, to prohibit the marketing, in its national territory of a phonogram manufactured without their consent, where the performance was given outside its national territory.

The effects of the first paragraph of Article 7 of the Treaty [now article 18 TFEU]

34.   The Court has consistently held that the right to equal treatment laid down by the first paragraph of Article 7 of the Treaty [now article 18 TFEU], is conferred directly by Community law . . . . That right may, therefore, be relied upon before a national court as the basis for a request that it disapply the discriminatory provisions of a national law which denies to nationals of other Member States the protection which they accord to nationals of the State concerned.

35.   Accordingly, it should be stated in reply to the question put to the Court that the first paragraph of Article 7 of the Treaty [now article 18 TFEU] should be interpreted as meaning that the principle of non-discrimination which it lays down may be directly relied upon before a national court by an author or performer from another Member State, or by those claiming under them, in order to claim the benefit of protection reserved to national authors and performers.

QUESTIONS

1. Why do the international conventions not apply?
2. How do you understand the following expression (para. 32) "persons in a situation governed by Community law be placed on a completely equal

footing with nationals of the Member State concerned"? Is that coherent with paragraph 35 taking account of "author or performer from another Member State"?

3. What is the difference between the rule of national treatment and the non-discrimination rule?

b. Exclusion of international rules of reciprocity

i. Reciprocity as to duration: Berne Convention article 7(8)

C-360/00 Land Hessen v. Ricordi & Co. Bühnen-und Musikverlag GmbH ECLI:EU:C:2002:346 [2002]

2. The question of the interpretation of the first paragraph of Article 6 of the EC Treaty (now article 18 of the TFEU) was raised in proceedings between the Land Hessen and G. Ricordi & Co. Bühnen- und Musikverlag GmbH (hereinafter Ricordi), a firm publishing musical and dramatic works, concerning the right to have the opera La Bohème by the Italian composer Giacomo Puccini performed in the 1993/1994 and 1994/1995 seasons.

Legal background

National laws

3. At the material time, artistic and intellectual works were protected in Germany under the 1965 version of the Gezetz über Urheberrecht und verwandte Schutzrechte (Law on copyright and related rights, hereinafter the UrhG; Bundesgesetzblatt 1965 I, p. 1273). That legislation distinguished between the protection of the works of German nationals and that of the works of foreign authors.

4. Whilst the former enjoyed protection for all their works, whether published or not and regardless of where they were first published (Paragraph 120(1) of the UrhG), the latter were entitled to protection only for works published in Germany for the first time or within 30 days of their being first published (Paragraph 121(1) of the UrhG).

5. In other cases, foreign authors enjoyed the protection afforded to their rights by international treaties (Paragraph 121(4) of the UrhG).

6. The copyright protection granted by German legislation expires 70 years after the 1 January following the author's death (Paragraphs 64 and 69 of the UrhG).

7. Under Italian law, Article 25 of Law No 633 of 22 April 1941 on the protection of copyright and other rights relating to its exercise (GURI No 166 of 16 July 1941) and Article 1 of Legislative Decree No 440 of 20 July 1945 (GURI No 98 of 16 August 1945) provide that the term of copyright protection is 56 years from the time of the author's death.

International law

8. The principal international agreement governing copyright protection is the Berne Convention for the Protection of Literary and Artistic Works (Paris Act of 24 July 1971) which applies to the main proceedings in the version as amended on 28 September 1979 (the Berne Convention).

9. Under Article 7(1) of the Berne Convention, the term of protection granted thereby is to be the life of the author and 50 years after his death. Article 7(5) provides that the 50-year term is to be deemed to begin on 1 January of the year following the death. Under Article 7(6), the contracting parties may, however, grant a longer term of protection.

10. Article 7(8) of the Berne Convention institutes a scheme known as comparison of the terms of protection. Under that provision, the term of protection is, in any case, to be governed by the legislation of the country where protection is claimed. However, unless the legislation of that country otherwise provides, which German legislation has not, the term is not to exceed the term fixed in the country of origin of the work.

11. The limitations permitted under Article 7(8) of the Berne Convention were reproduced in Article 3(1) of the Agreement on trade-related aspects of intellectual property rights contained in Annex 1 C to the Agreement establishing the World Trade Organization approved on behalf of the European Community as regards matters within its competence by Council Decision 94/800/EC of 22 December 1994 (OJ 1994 L 336, p. 1). Article 9 of that agreement also provides that the signatory States are to comply with Articles 1 to 21 of the Berne Convention and the Appendix thereto.

. . .

13. Ricordi holds the rights of performance in the opera La Bohème by Puccini, who died on 29 November 1924 (see point 13 et seq. of the Opinion of the Advocate General). The Land Hessen operates the Staatstheater (State theatre) in Wiesbaden (Germany).

14.   During the 1993/1994 and 1994/1995 seasons, the Staatstheater in Wiesbaden staged a number of performances of that opera without Ricordi's consent.

15.   Ricordi argued before a Landgericht (Regional Court, Germany) that, in the light of the prohibition of discrimination on grounds of nationality in the EC Treaty, Puccini's works were necessarily protected in Germany until the expiry of the 70-year term prescribed by German law, that is, until 31 December 1994.

16.   The Land Hessen contended that the opera La Bohème was covered by the term of protection of 56 years prescribed by Italian law, so that the copyright in that work had expired on 31 December 1980.

17.   The Landgericht seised allowed Ricordi's application. The appeal brought by the Land Hessen was unsuccessful. The Land thus brought an appeal on points of law (Revision).

18.   In the order for reference, the Bundesgerichtshof points out that since, according to the findings made, the opera La Bohème was first published in Italy and not in Germany, it was, at the material time, protected in Germany solely to the extent provided by international treaties, pursuant to Paragraph 121(4) of the UrhG.

19.   Accordingly, in the light of Article 7(8) of the Berne Convention and the fact that German law does not contain any provision derogating from the principle according to which the term of protection must not exceed the term fixed in the country of origin of the work, the term of protection in Germany for the opera La Bohème was restricted by the term of protection prescribed by Italian law and thus expired in 1980.

20.   According to the Bundesgerichtshof, the outcome of the main proceedings depends on the applicability to the facts of the case of the prohibition of discrimination on grounds of nationality in the first paragraph of Article 6 of the EC Treaty.

. . .

27.   Lastly, it must be determined whether the difference of treatment at issue in the main proceedings, established by the UrhG between German and foreign authors, is contrary to Community law.

28.   The Land Hessen contends that this difference of treatment is due to the disparity between the laws of the Member States.

29.   It argues that comparison of the terms of protection, provided for in Article 7(8) of the Berne Convention, does not use nationality, but country of origin, as a criterion. The term of protection is fixed by each Member State, which remains free to extend the term of protection applicable under its legislation and thereby, by virtue of that provision, the term applicable in respect of its nationals living abroad. In those circumstances, the national legal situation constitutes a criterion of differentiation which is not arbitrary, but objective. The term of protection is only indirectly related to the nationality of the author.

30.   That interpretation cannot be accepted.

31.   Although it is undisputed that the first paragraph of Article 6 of the EC Treaty [now article 18 TFEU] is not concerned with any disparities in treatment or the distortions which may result, for the persons and undertakings subject to the jurisdiction of the Community, from divergences existing between the laws of the various Member States, so long as those laws affect all the persons subject to them, in accordance with objective criteria and without direct or indirect regard to nationality, it does prohibit any discrimination on grounds of nationality. Consequently, that provision requires each Member State to ensure that nationals of other Member States in a situation governed by Community law are placed on a completely equal footing with its own nationals (see, to that effect, *Phil Collins and Others*, cited above, paragraphs 30 and 32).

32.   Clearly, Paragraphs 120(1) and 121(1) of the UrhG discriminate directly on grounds of nationality.

33.   Moreover, since Article 7(8) of the Berne Convention permits the Federal Republic of Germany to extend to the rights of a foreign author the 70-year term of protection prescribed by German law, the mechanism of comparison of the terms of protection provided for in that provision cannot justify the difference of treatment as regards the term of protection, which is established by the abovementioned provisions of the UrhG, between the rights of a German author and those of an author who is a national of another Member State.

34.   In the light of the foregoing considerations, the answer to the question referred for a preliminary ruling must be that the prohibition of discrimination in the first paragraph of Article 6 of the EC Treaty [now article 18 TFEU] is also

applicable to the protection of copyright in cases where the author had died when the EEC Treaty entered into force in the Member State of which he was a national and it precludes the term of protection granted by the legislation of a Member State to the works of an author who is a national of another Member State being shorter than the term granted to the works of its own nationals.

QUESTIONS

The *La Bohème* case ruled that the German law distinguishing on the basis of nationality violates the non-discrimination principle. What about works first published in another E.U. country by a non-E.U. national? What about works first published outside the E.U. by an E.U. national? How does Berne Convention article 7(8) apply to those instances?

NOTE

In *The Royal Literary Fund* v. *Enokia SL, Audiencia Provicial de Madrid* sec. 28, Judgment 160/2013, the Madrid Court of Appeals ruled that the works of British author G. K. Chesterton, who died in 1936, were entitled to Spain's copyright term of 80 years *pma* for works under the 1879 Copyright Act, which was in effect when Chesterton died, and which the court held therefore applied to calculate the copyright term. The court referred to Berne Convention article 7(6): "The countries of the Union may grant a term of protection in excess of those provided by the preceding paragraphs," as well as to Berne Convention article 19. The court also held that the ECJ's *Phil Collins* and *Ricordi* decisions required Spain to extend its 80-year *pma* protection to works from other E.U. countries whose authors had died while the 80-year *pma* term was still in effect, even if their copyrights had expired in their countries of origin.

Directive 2006/116/EC of the European Parliament and of the Council of 12 December 2006 on the term of protection of copyright and certain related rights (codified version)

Article 3 – Duration of related rights*

1. The rights of performers shall expire 50 years after the date of the performance. However, if a fixation of the performance is lawfully published or lawfully communicated to the public within this period, the rights shall expire 50 years from the date of the first such publication or the first such communication to the public, whichever is the earlier.

---

* Editors' note: Directive 2011/77/EU added 20 years to the duration, see *infra* pp. 249–50.

Article 7 – Protection vis-à-vis third countries

1. Where the country of origin of a work, within the meaning of the Berne Convention, is a third country, and the author of the work is not a Community national, the term of protection granted by the Member States shall expire on the date of expiry of the protection granted in the country of origin of the work, but may not exceed the term laid down in Article 1.

2. The terms of protection laid down in Article 3* shall also apply in the case of rightholders who are not Community nationals, provided Member States grant them protection. However, without prejudice to the international obligations of the Member States, the term of protection granted by Member States shall expire no later than the date of expiry of the protection granted in the country of which the rightholder is a national and may not exceed the term laid down in Article 3.

3. Member States which, on 29 October 1993, in particular pursuant to their international obligations, granted a longer term of protection than that which would result from the provisions of paragraphs 1 and 2 may maintain this protection until the conclusion of international agreements on the term of protection of copyright or related rights.

QUESTIONS

1. How do you explain the difference between point 1 and point 2 of article 7 of the Directive?
2. Is article 7 of the Directive consistent with point 8 of article 7 of the Berne Convention? See *infra* page 294.

Directive 2011/77/EU of the European Parliament and of the Council of 27 September 2011 amending Directive 2006/116/EC on the term of protection of copyright and certain related rights

Article 1 – Amendments to Directive 2006/116/EC

Directive 2006/116/EC is hereby amended as follows:

. . .

    (2) Article 3 shall be amended as follows:
        (a) in paragraph 1, the second sentence shall be replaced by the following:

---

* Editors' note: Article 3 of the Directive is related to neighboring rights.

"However,

— if a fixation of the performance otherwise than in a phonogram is lawfully published or lawfully communicated to the public within this period, the rights shall expire 50 years from the date of the first such publication or the first such communication to the public, whichever is the earlier;

— if a fixation of the performance in a phonogram is lawfully published or lawfully communicated to the public within this period, the rights shall expire 70 years from the date of the first such publication or the first such communication to the public, whichever is the earlier.";

(b) in the second and third sentences of paragraph 2, the number "50" shall be replaced by "70". . . .

QUESTIONS

1. A Lebanese performer wishes to claim the benefits of the 2011 Directive. Assume that her performance has taken place and been fixed in Beirut. Under Lebanese law, the protection for related rights lasts for 50 years. Is the Lebanese performer protected in the E.U? What will be the duration of protection of her recorded performance under art. 7? What difference do the international treaties make?

2. Consider the same questions, but assume that the performer is a U.S. national and that the performance occurred in the U.S. under U.S. law, a sound recording fixed after February 15, 1972 is protected for 70 years from the death of the last surviving co-author, or, in the case of a work-made-for-hire, for 95 years from publication. (Sound recordings fixed before February 15, 1972 are protected by state law until no later than 15 February 2067.)

ii.   Reciprocity as to subject matter: Berne Convention article 2.7

C-28/04 Tod's SpA and Tod's France SARL v. Heyraud SA ECLI:EU:C:2005:418 [2005]

6.   It is apparent from the order for reference that Tod's is a company established under Italian law which claims to be the proprietor of artistic intellectual property rights in the shoes distributed under the Tod's and Hogan trade marks. Tod's France is the distributor of those shoes in France.

7.   Having learnt that Heyraud was offering for sale and selling under the Heyraud name designs of shoes which copied or at least imitated the prin-

cipal characteristics of the Tod's and Hogan designs, Tod's arranged for a bailiff's report to be drawn up on 8 February 2000. On 13 February 2002, the claimants in the main proceedings brought an action against Heyraud before the referring court. Technisynthèse, a subsidiary of the Eram group, entered the proceedings as a voluntary intervener in support of Heyraud.

8.   The subject-matter of the main proceedings consists, inter alia, of an action for infringement of registered designs of shoes bearing the Tod's and Hogan trade marks, against which Heyraud raises a plea of inadmissibility under Article 2(7) of the Berne Convention. Heyraud contends that, under that provision, Tod's is not entitled to claim copyright protection in France for designs that do not qualify for such protection in Italy.

9.   Tod's replies, inter alia, that application of the provision in question constitutes discrimination within the meaning of Article 12 EC [now article 18 TFEU].

10.   The referring court takes the view that the use of the phrase "shall be entitled . . . only" in the second sentence of Article 2(7) of the Berne Convention has the effect of depriving Union nationals who, in the country of origin of their work, enjoy only the protection granted in respect of designs and models, of the right to bring proceedings based on copyright in the countries of the Union which allow cumulation of protection.

11.   According to that court, while it appears that that provision makes no distinction based on the nationality of the proprietor of the copyright, it remains the case that its scope under Community law is debatable where the country of origin of the "published" work will most commonly be the country of which the author is a national or in which he has his habitual residence, and where the country of origin of an "unpublished" work will, under Article 5(4)(c) of that convention, be the country of which the author is a national.

. . .

18.   It should be recalled that copyright and related rights, which by reason in particular of their effects on intra-Community trade in goods and services fall within the scope of application of the EC Treaty, are necessarily subject to the general principle of non-discrimination laid down by the first paragraph of Article 12 EC [now article 18 TFEU] (Joined Cases C-92/92 and C-326/92 *Phil Collins and Others* [1993] ECR I-5145, paragraph 27, and Case C-360/00 *Ricordi* [2002] ECR I-5089, paragraph 24).

19. Moreover, as the Court has consistently held, the rules regarding equality of treatment between nationals and non-nationals prohibit not only overt discrimination by reason of nationality but also all covert forms of discrimination which, by the application of other distinguishing criteria, lead to the same result [citations omitted].

20. It is apparent from the order for reference that application, in the national law of a Member State, of Article 2(7) of the Berne Convention leads to a distinction based on the criterion of the country of origin of the work. In particular, the effect of such application is that no advantageous treatment, namely the enjoyment of twofold protection based, firstly, on the law relating to designs and, secondly, on the law of copyright, will be granted to the author of a work the country of origin of which is another Member State which affords that work only protection under the law relating to designs. By contrast, the abovementioned advantageous treatment is granted, in particular, to authors of a work the country of origin of which is the first Member State.

21. It is therefore necessary to examine whether, by adopting a distinguishing criterion based on the country of origin of the work, the application of rules such as those at issue in the main proceedings may constitute indirect discrimination by reason of nationality within the meaning of the case-law cited in paragraph 19 of the present judgment.

22. Heyraud and Technisynthèse, as well as the French Government, argue that that is not the case. The latter maintains, in particular, that, in view of the high mobility of designers and their successors in title in the field of the applied arts, the place of first publication of a design does not necessarily coincide with the nationality of its author and that, more often than not, the two do not coincide. It follows that the application of Article 2(7) of the Berne Convention does not substantially, or in the great majority of cases, operate to the detriment of nationals of other Member States and that that provision does not, therefore, give rise to indirect discrimination.

23. However, that argument cannot be accepted.

24. The existence of a link between the country of origin of a work within the meaning of the Berne Convention, on the one hand, and the nationality of the author of that work, on the other, cannot be denied.

25. In the case of unpublished works, that link is not in any doubt since it is expressly provided for in Article 5(4)(c) of the Berne Convention.

26. As regards published works, the country of origin is essentially, as Article 5(4)(a) of that convention indicates, the country where the work was first published. The author of a work first published in a Member State will, in the majority of cases, be a national of that State, whereas the author of a work published in another Member State will generally be a person who is not a national of the first Member State.

27. It follows that the application of rules such as those at issue in the main proceedings is liable to operate mainly to the detriment of nationals of other Member States and thus give rise to indirect discrimination on grounds of nationality [citations omitted].

28. However, that finding is not sufficient under the Court's case-law to justify the conclusion that the rules at issue are incompatible with Article 12 EC [now article 18 TFEU]. For that it would also be necessary for the application of those rules not to be justified by objective circumstances [citations omitted].

29. The French Government is of the opinion that Article 2(7) of the Berne Convention is in any event justified by a legitimate objective and that it is appropriate and necessary for the achievement of that objective.

30. It argues that the purpose of the Berne Convention is the protection of literary and artistic works and that Article 2(7) and Article 5(4) of that convention specify the conditions under which such works are to be protected by copyright on the basis of an objective criterion based on the law applicable to the classification of the work. In its view, where a design cannot aspire to classification as an artistic work in the country where it was first published, it is not entitled to such protection in the States party to the Berne Convention since it does not exist as an artistic work. Article 2(7) thus concerns not the detailed rules for the exercise of copyright, but the law applicable to the artistic classification of the work.

31. However, those considerations do not lead to the conclusion that there are objective circumstances capable of justifying the application of rules such as those at issue in the main proceedings.

32. As is apparent from Article 5(1) of the Berne Convention, the purpose of that convention is not to determine the applicable law on the protection of literary and artistic works, but to establish, as a general rule, a system of national treatment of the rights appertaining to such works.

33. Article 2(7) of that convention contains, for its part, as the Commission rightly observes, a rule of reciprocity under which a country of the Union

grants national treatment, that is to say, twofold protection, only if the country of origin of the work also does so.

34. It should be recalled that it is settled case-law that implementation of the obligations imposed on Member States by the Treaty or secondary legislation cannot be made subject to a condition of reciprocity [citations omitted].

35. Since no other objective circumstance capable of justifying rules such as those at issue in the main proceedings has been relied on, those rules must be considered to constitute indirect discrimination on grounds of nationality prohibited by Article 12 EC [now article 18 TFEU].

36. The answer to the question referred must therefore be that Article 12 EC [now article 18 TFEU], which lays down the general principle of non-discrimination on grounds of nationality, must be interpreted as meaning that the right of an author to claim in a Member State the copyright protection afforded by the law of that State may not be subject to a distinguishing criterion based on the country of origin of the work.

QUESTIONS

1. Does case C-28/04 comply with point 7 of article 2 of the Berne Convention? If not, does that mean that the E.U. does not comply with the Berne Convention?
2. How significant is the following assertion (para. 26): "The author of a work first published in a Member State will, in the majority of cases, be a national of that State, whereas the author of a work published in another Member State will generally be a person who is not a national of the first Member State"? Does it matter? Suppose Tod's shoes had first been published (sold) in the U.S.? Suppose Tod's employed shoe designers who were nationals of and resided in other Member States, or, indeed outside the E.U?
3. Architect and furniture designer Marcel Breuer was born in Hungary in 1902, worked in Germany during the 1920s, fled to London in 1933, and came to the U.S. in 1937. He died in New York City in 1981. His well-known furniture designs, featuring tubular and plywood elements, were created and first published in his various countries of then-residence. Suppose that aesthetic furniture design is protected as a "literary or artistic work" in Germany, but not in the U.K. or the U.S. Which of Breuer's furniture designs are protected under the Berne Convention? Which are protected under E.U. non-discrimination principles?

c. **The fate of article 14*ter* 2**

Directive 2001/84/EC of the European Parliament and of the Council of 27 September 2001 on the resale right for the benefit of the author of an original work of art

Recitals: Whereas

(6) The Berne Convention for the Protection of Literary and Artistic Works provides that the resale right is available only if legislation in the country to which the author belongs so permits. The right is therefore optional and subject to the rule of reciprocity. It follows from the case-law of the Court of Justice of the European Communities on the application of the principle of non-discrimination laid down in Article 12 of the Treaty [now article 18 TFEU], as shown in the judgment of 20 October 1993 in Joined Cases C-92/92 and C-326/92 *Phil Collins and Others*, that domestic provisions containing reciprocity clauses cannot be relied upon in order to deny nationals of other Member States rights conferred on national authors. The application of such clauses in the Community context runs counter to the principle of equal treatment resulting from the prohibition of any discrimination on grounds of nationality.

The Directive's substantive provisions include:

Article 7 – Third-country nationals entitled to receive royalties

1. Member States shall provide that authors who are nationals of third countries and, subject to Article 8(2), their successors in title shall enjoy the resale right in accordance with this Directive and the legislation of the Member State concerned only if legislation in the country of which the author or his/her successor in title is a national permits resale right protection in that country for authors from the Member States and their successors in title.

2. On the basis of information provided by the Member States, the Commission shall publish as soon as possible an indicative list of those third countries which fulfil the condition set out in paragraph 1. This list shall be kept up to date.

3. Any Member State may treat authors who are not nationals of a Member State but who have their habitual residence in that Member State in the same way as its own nationals for the purpose of resale right protection.

QUESTIONS

1. For which, if any, of the following is the artist entitled to resale royalties (assume the resale price exceeds the €3000 threshold established in article 3(2)):

   a. A work of art by a Colombian national sold in France.

   b. A work of art by a Colombian national habitually resident in France and sold in Germany.

   c. A work of art by a French national sold in the U.S?

4.2   Most-favored-nation treatment

WTO Principles of the trading system

http://www.wto.org/english/thewto_e/whatis_e/tif_e/fact2_e.htm

Under the WTO agreements, countries cannot normally discriminate between their trading partners. Grant someone a special favour (such as a lower customs duty rate for one of their products) and you have to do the same for all other WTO members.

This principle is known as most-favoured-nation (MFN) treatment. It is so important that it is the first article of the General Agreement on Tariffs and Trade (GATT), which governs trade in goods. MFN is also a priority in the General Agreement on Trade in Services (GATS) (Article 2) and the Agreement on Trade-Related Aspects of Intellectual Property Rights (TRIPS) (Article 4), although in each agreement the principle is handled slightly differently. Together, those three agreements cover all three main areas of trade handled by the WTO.

Editors' note. The TRIPS carves out certain exceptions to the MFN rule. Those exceptions are related to prior international treaties. Point b immunizes reciprocity rules encompassed by the Berne Convention from the MFN, which is coherent with the prior Berne integration into TRIPS by article 9. Point c subtracts the Rome Convention on neighboring rights from the scope of the MFN requirement. Finally, the last exception excludes prior international agreements from the MFN effect.

TRIPS Agreement Article 4
Most-Favoured-Nation Treatment

With regard to the protection of intellectual property, any advantage, favour, privilege or immunity granted by a Member to the nationals of any other country shall be accorded immediately and unconditionally to the nationals of all other Members. Exempted from this obligation are any advantage, favour, privilege or immunity accorded by a Member:

. . .

(b) granted in accordance with the provisions of the Berne Convention (1971) or the Rome Convention authorizing that the treatment accorded be a function not of national treatment but of the treatment accorded in another country;

(c) in respect of the rights of performers, producers of phonograms and broadcasting organizations not provided under this Agreement;

(d) deriving from international agreements related to the protection of intellectual property which entered into force prior to the entry into force of the WTO Agreement, provided that such agreements are notified to the Council for TRIPS and do not constitute an arbitrary or unjustifiable discrimination against nationals of other Members.

QUESTION

Article 4(c) of the TRIPS Agreement exempts from the MFN obligation rights of performers, producers of phonograms and broadcasting organizations for which the TRIPS does not already provide. Had the TRIPS not contained this limitation on the scope of the MFN rule, what would have been the consequences for the U.S. (recall that the U.S. is not a member of the Rome Convention); would the U.S. in effect have obtained Rome Convention rights via the "back door" of the MFN rule? Does TRIPS offer member states that have not adhered to the Berne Convention a "back-door" to that convention's protections?

Compare, Berne Convention Article 20

Special Agreements Among Countries of the Union

The Governments of the countries of the Union reserve the right to enter into special agreements among themselves, in so far as such agreements grant to authors more extensive rights than those granted by the Convention, or contain other provisions not contrary to this Convention. The provisions of existing agreements which satisfy these conditions shall remain applicable.

QUESTIONS

1. Under the MFN principle, any favor granted to one WTO member has to be given to all WTO members. Berne Convention, article 20, allows member states to make special agreements for the benefit only of the member states party to the agreement. What, if any, effect does the TRIPS MFN provision have on article 20 agreements? To what extent does Berne Convention article 20 apply, given the exceptions to the MFN principle? Recall, however, that TRIPs art 1(4) incorporates Berne Convention articles 1–21, and TRIPS art. 1(1) declares that the TRIPS is a special arrangement within the meaning of Article 20 of the Berne Convention . . ."

2. The rule of national treatment is generally understood as articulating a principle of non-discrimination against foreign authors relative to local authors. By contrast, the MFN principle prohibits discrimination amongst TRIPS member states; each advantage one TRIPS member state gives to another TRIPS member state must be offered to all other member states. Because of the rule of national treatment enshrined in the Berne Convention and integrated in the TRIPS, the MFN principle added no new obligations, because authors from all member states were already entitled to equal treatment with local authors. "For example, if the national law of a WTO Member vests in authors of musical work an exclusive distribution right that is not part of the TRIPS minimum, the Member in any case must extend this protection . . . to the 'nationals' of all other WTO Members on the mere basis of national treatment" (S. Von Lewinski, International Copyright Law and Policy, Oxford Press, 2008, 10.42). To what extent might the scope of the national treatment rule (full national treatment, or national treatment limited to conventional substantive minima) change your evaluation of the impact of the MFN principle? How might the MFN principle go further than a national treatment requirement limited to rights granted by the Convention? What if, pursuant to a bilateral agreement, a TRIPs member state applied a higher level of protection to foreign than to local authors (as we will see, Berne article 5.3 makes this result possible), and granted the authors of another TRIPS member protections in excess of those required by the Berne substantive minima, would the MFN principle require extending the benefits of that bilateral agreement to all TRIPS member states?

PROBLEMS

Vietnam is not a member of the WCT, Argentina is. Both are members of the WTO. To what extent could Vietnamese works of authorship benefit from the WCT in Argentina? On what grounds? Consider the same question but supposing that Argentine Law limits WCT's substantive minima to foreign works. To what extent could Vietnamese works of authorship benefit from the WCT's substantive minima in Argentina? If those minima do not apply to local authors would the rule of national treatment enshrined in the Berne Convention incorporated in the TRIPS Agreement entitle the Vietnamese author to the enhanced protection in Argentina? Would the TRIPS MFN rule require Argentina to extend that protection to Vietnamese works? Consider the same questions but with phonograms and the WPPT. To what extent could the WPPT's substantive minima, if applicable only to foreign works, benefit Vietnamese works of authorship? What is the outcome of applying article 4(c) of the TRIPS Agreement?

MFN and regional economic integration

While GATT and GATS contain specific exceptions in favor of regional economic integration,* point (d) of article 4 TRIPS allows exceptions for 'international agreements related to the protection of intellectual property which entered into force prior to the entry into force of the WTO Agreement, provided that such agreements are notified to the Council for TRIPS and do not constitute an arbitrary or unjustifiable discrimination against nationals of other Members'.

Treaties related to copyright and notified under this provision include: the Treaty Establishing the European Community, the Agreement Establishing the European Economic Area, the Cartagena Agreement, the Treaty of Asuncion and the Ouro Preto Protocol, European Convention on Transfrontier Television, European Agreement on the Protection of Television Broadcasts, Universal Copyright Convention and the North American Free Trade Agreement.

World Trade Organization IP/N/4/EEC/1 29 January 1996 (96–0351)

Council for Trade-Related Aspects

Rights NOTIFICATION UNDER ARTICLE 4(d) OF THE AGREEMENT European Communities and their Member States

The following communication, dated 19 December 1995, was received from the Head of the Permanent Delegation of the European Commission

---

* This exception in favor of regional economic integration allows discrimination for customs issues but not for IP issues.

and the Permanent Representative of Spain. Article 4, paragraph (d) of the Agreement on Trade-Related Aspects of Intellectual Property Rights provides the following: "With regard to the protection of intellectual property, any advantage, favour, privilege or immunity granted by a Member to the nationals of any other country shall be accorded immediately and unconditionally to the nationals of all other Members. Exempted from this obligation are any advantage, favour, privilege or immunity by a Member: [. . .] (d) deriving from international agreements related to the protection of intellectual property which entered into force prior to the entry into force of the WTO Agreement, provided that such agreements are notified to the Council for TRIPS and do not constitute an arbitrary or unjustifiable discrimination against nationals of other Members." We hereby notify on behalf of the European Community and its Member States to the Council for Trade-Related Aspects of Intellectual Property Rights, pursuant to Article 4, paragraph (d) of the Agreement on Trade-Related Aspects of Intellectual Property Rights, both the Treaty establishing the European Community and the Agreement establishing the European Economic Area. 1 Notification of these agreements covers not only those provisions directly contained therein, as interpreted by the relevant jurisprudence, but also existing or future acts adopted by the Community as such and/or by the Member States which conform with these agreements following the process of regional integration.

QUESTIONS

1. Why are E.U. copyright Directives promulgated and implemented after the WTO Agreement's entry into force not subject to the MFN rules?

2. The OHADA, French acronym for "Organisation pour l'Harmonisation en Afrique du Droit des Affaires", which translates into English as "Organisation for the Harmonization of Business Law in Africa", is a Regional Economic Organization linking 17 African States (Benin, Burkina Faso, Cameroon, Central African Republic, Chad, Comoro, Republic of the Congo, Côte d'Ivoire, Equatorial Guinea, Gabon, Guinea, Guinea-Bissau, Mali, Niger, Senegal, Togo, Democratic Republic of Congo). The harmonization is related to business under the supervision of a supranational court ensuring uniformity and consistent legal interpretations across the member countries. Suppose that the process of harmonization will encompass IP as a branch of business law. What would be the consequence as to the application of the MFN rule?

5

Substantive minima

We have seen that the two pillars of the Berne Convention are national treatment and substantive minima of protection. The previous chapter addressed the rule of national treatment; this chapter explores the substantive protection that Berne requires member states to extend to foreign authors. A cornerstone of Berne since the 1908 Berlin revision, and to a lesser extent since the 1886 original text, is the requirement that foreign authors' protection not be subject to any formality. Such prohibition of formalities was not achieved under the Rome Convention for neighboring rights. But later neighboring rights treaties, the Beijing Treaty and the TRIPS Agreement, now explicitly and implicitly prohibit formalities. We will first consider the development and application of that norm, and then will turn to the subject matter of protection, and to the exclusive rights member states must extend to foreign authors. Thereafter we will address the exceptions and limitations that member states may impose on exclusive rights, and finally, turn to the enforcement of rights.

5.1 Absence of formality

5.1.1 Copyright conventions

Berne Convention

> **Article 5**
>
> . . .
>
> (2) The enjoyment and the exercise of these rights [granted by member states to their nationals, or specially granted by the Berne Convention] shall not be subject to any formality; such enjoyment and such exercise shall be independent of the existence of protection in the country of origin of the work.

What is a "formality"?

Jane C. Ginsburg, "With untired spirits and formal constancy": Berne-Compatibility of Formal Declaratory Measures to Enhance Copyright Title-Searching, 28 Berkeley Tech. L.J. 1583 (2014) (excerpt; footnotes omitted)

History and interpretation of the Berne no-formalities rule

From the outset of the mid-19th century movement for international copyright, authors advocated the abolition or restriction of formalities. In the 19th century, to obtain protection at home and abroad, an author would have needed to comply with the formalities of each country in which he sought protection—assuming the country of which the author was not a national extended any protection at all to foreign claimants.

Proper compliance was cumbersome, costly, and often unsuccessful, hence authors' demand as early as the first international Congress aimed at securing authors' rights, held in Brussels in 1858, that authors be protected in all countries so long as they satisfied whatever formalities their home countries imposed. The 1886 and 1896 versions of the Berne Convention adopted this approach.

In practice, however, it turned out to be difficult to prove to foreign authorities that the author had complied with the country of origin's formalities. As a result, the 1908 Berlin revision prohibited the imposition of formalities on foreign authors altogether, although member states remained free to require that domestic authors affix notice, register claims, and/or deposit copies with local authorities. And, to ensure that an author's failure to carry out domestic formalities—with a consequent loss of protection in the country of origin—would not affect the availability of international protection, the Berlin revisers specified that "apart from the provisions of this Convention, the extent of protection, as well as the means of redress afforded to the author to protect his rights, shall be governed exclusively by the laws of the country where protection is claimed." The effect of this language was to confer copyright throughout the Berne Union, automatically and upon creation, on every Convention-covered work created by an author who was a national of a Berne Union member state, or first published within a member state. The no-formalities rule thus fundamentally undergirds the Berne Convention system of universal international authors' rights.

But what are "formalities" in the Berne sense? Article 5(2) declares that "the enjoyment and the exercise of these rights shall not be subject to any formality." Although earlier texts refer to "conditions and formalities," it has long been understood that the term "any formality" encompasses both "formal and material conditions" on the existence or enforcement of rights. "These rights" are "the rights which the[] respective laws [of the countries of the Union] do now or may hereafter grant to their nationals, as well as the rights specially granted by this Convention." Thus, a foreign author is entitled to national treatment in Berne member states (but without having to comply with any formalities the state may impose on its own authors), as well as to any additional Convention-guaranteed rights, even if these are not afforded to local authors.

The "enjoyment" of local or Berne minimum rights extends to "everything which must be complied with in order to ensure that the rights of the author with regard to his work may come into existence. These would include such requirements as registration, the deposit or filing of copies, the payment of fees, or the making of declarations." In addition to the initial attachment of protection (since 1908 automatic upon creation for authors from other Berne member states), the concept of "enjoyment" of copyright would include the persistence of protection for the minimum Berne term of copyright; obligations to register and renew copyrights thus would fall under the prohibition. The scope of rights (including any limitations or exceptions) also comes within the "enjoyment" of Berne and national rights. A member state may neither condition the initial attachment of copyright on compliance with formalities nor subsequently deny coverage of particular rights to authors who fail to meet declaratory obligations. Thus, for example, a member state may not make the adaptation right subject to registering the work or filing a notice of reservation of rights.

Berne precludes not only formalities that condition the existence of copyright, but also those that freight its "exercise." Without the second prohibition, an author might be *vested* with copyright, but unable to *enforce* her rights unless she complies with a variety of prerequisites to suit or to availability of remedies. Copyright-specific conditions on access to judicial process or to injunctive relief (including seizure and destruction of infringing articles) or to actual damages therefore contravene Berne norms. By contrast, general litigation obligations, such as payment of filing fees, or general procedural or evidentiary requirements, while they may affect the enforcement of a copyright claim, are not "formalities" in the Berne sense so long as they apply to all actions, whatever the subject matter.

WTO Panel, 26 January 2009 WT/DS 362/R – China – Measures Affecting the Protection and the Enforcement of Intellectual Property Rights, Report of the Panel

[This WTO Panel decision addressed the U.S. challenge to China's conditioning of copyright protection on censorship review of the content of works. The U.S. charged that the content review was a formality barred by Berne Convention article 5(2); China responded that it was a censorship measure permissible under Berne Convention article 17, which provides: "The provisions of this Convention cannot in any way affect the right of the Government of each country of the Union to permit, to control, or to prohibit, by legislation or regulation, the circulation, presentation, or exhibition of any work or production in regard to which the competent authority may find it necessary to exercise that right." As you read the decision, consider what is the difference between a formality conditioning the existence or enforcement of copyright, and a censorship measure prohibiting the circulation of works of authorship.]

(a)   Main arguments of the parties

7.145   The United States claims that China subjects the enjoyment and exercise of copyright to the formality of successful conclusion of content review, inconsistently with Article 5(2) of the Berne Convention (1971), as incorporated by Article 9.1 of the TRIPS Agreement. Works that have not successfully completed content review under the Regulation on the Administration of Films, the Regulation on the Management of Publications, the Regulation on the Management of Audiovisual Products or the Regulations on the Management of Electronic Publications may not legally be published or distributed within China. The United States submits that, consequently, works in this unauthorized status fall within the scope of Article 4(1) of the Copyright Law, and thus they are not protected by that Law. The United States submits that the Copyright Law's protection attaches only after such a work has been submitted for content review and, if it passes that review unchanged, an authorization to publish and distribute the work has issued. As a formal matter, therefore, copyright protection is dependent, in part, on the issuance of the authorization to publish and distribute resulting from successful conclusion of the content review process [citations omitted].

7.146   China responds that, under Article 2 of the Copyright Law and Article 6 of the Copyright Law Implementing Regulations, copyright protection vests upon creation of a work. While such works are pending review they enjoy the full panoply of copyright. In response to the Panel's questions, China asked the Panel to note that under the Chinese system of copyright, "copyright" and "copyright protection" are distinguishable. To the extent that Article 4(1) of the Copyright Law would come into play with respect to a work, it would operate not to remove copyright, but to deny the particularized rights of private copyright enforcement. Article 4(1) of the Copyright Law thus does not operate in any manner that would violate Article 5(2) of the Berne Convention (1971) as it is not a condition precedent to copyright formation, nor does it destroy the residual copyright granted under Article 2 of the Copyright Law

7.147   The United States responds that China's distinction between copyright and copyright enforcement lacks any legal effect under Article 5(2) of the Berne Convention (1971). Article 5(2) applies both to the enjoyment and "exercise" of rights so that a content review that affects the exercise of rights would still impose a "formality" within the meaning of that provision [citations omitted].

7.148   China further submits that the type of "formality" referred to in Article 5(2) of the Berne Convention (1971) is a condition precedent to the vesting of copyright. Given that Article 4(1) of the Copyright Law does not function as a condition precedent to copyright but rather as a condition subsequent, it is consistent with Article 5(2) of the Berne Convention (1971).

(b)   Main arguments of third parties

7.149   Australia considers that Article 5(2) of the Berne Convention (1971) prohibits the enjoyment and exercise of rights in a protected work being subject to any prior legal or administrative procedure, such as registration of the work or approval of its content [citations omitted].

7.150   Brazil does not consider that Article 5(2) of the Berne Convention (1971) requires that copyright arise "automatically" or "immediately" independently of what national legislation may dispose. The principle of automatic protection should be understood and limited to the fact that copyright protection is not conditional upon compliance with any formality, such as registration, deposit and the like [citations omitted].

7.151   Canada considers that the term "formality" extends to national laws that make copyright protection for foreign works contingent on compliance with administrative obligations. China seems to have laid down in its national laws the administrative obligation for exporters or importers to obtain approval to publish and distribute the work in China such that, if not fulfilled, it will lead to the loss of copyright or copyright-related protection.

7.152   The European Communities considers that if the enjoyment and exercise of copyright were contingent upon the dissemination approval by Chinese censorship authorities, this would be a "formality" inconsistent with Article 5(2) of the Berne Convention (1971). The European Communities does not comment upon the factual question of whether such a nexus exists under Chinese law but would be reticent to give specific instances of administrative enforcement too much weight in the assessment of an "as such" claim that appears to be based on the plain wording of the Chinese law [citations omitted].

(c)   Consideration by the Panel

7.153   The Panel notes that this claim concerns the denial of copyright protection under Article 4(1) of the Copyright Law. The Panel has already ruled on that issue in its consideration of the claim under Article 5(1) of the Berne Convention (1971), as incorporated by Article 9.1 of the TRIPS Agreement. Additional findings regarding this claim under Article 5(2) of the Berne Convention (1971), as incorporated by Article 9.1 of the TRIPS Agreement, would not contribute further to a positive solution to this dispute. Therefore, it is unnecessary for the Panel to rule on this claim.

QUESTIONS

1. In an earlier section of its decision, the Panel recognized the Chinese law's inconsistency with article 5.1 of the Berne Convention:

    7.118 ... the Panel recognizes that the potential denial of copyright protection, in the absence of a determination by the content review authorities, implies uncertainty with respect to works that do not satisfy the content criteria prior to a determination under Article 4(1) of the Copyright Law, with the consequent impact on enjoyment of rights described above. Therefore, the Panel reiterates for the record the firm position of China taken in these proceedings that: "Copyright vests at the time that a work is created, and is not contingent on publication. Unpublished works are protected, foreign works not yet released in the Chinese market are protected, and works never released in the Chinese market are protected" [footnote omitted]; and "Works that are unreviewed are decidedly not 'prohibited by law'" [footnote omitted].
    7.119 China has an international obligation to protect copyright in such

works in accordance with Article 5(1) of the Berne Convention (1971), as incorporated by Article 9.1 of the TRIPS Agreement.

Having ruled on the basis of article 5(1), the Panel considered it unnecessary to resolve the claim under article 5(2) of the Berne Convention. Do you think that the previous answer as to the Chinese law's consistency with article 5.1 (national treatment) of the Berne Convention (see Chapter 4) also applies with respect to article 5.2 (prohibition of formalities)?

2. Which arguments of the third-party states seem to you consistent with Berne Convention norms? And which seem inconsistent?

Combined application of articles 5.2 and 18 of the Berne Convention

France, Cour de cassation N° 07–21.115 07–21.553 [2009]*

[The French Cour de cassation, that nation's highest civil law court, has construed both articles 5(2) and 18 in a controversy concerning infringement in France of the classic American film "His Girl Friday" (with Rosalind Russell and Cary Grant). The plaintiffs, who were selling unauthorized DVDs and videocassettes of the film, sought a declaration that because the film had fallen into the public domain in the United States 28 years after its publication in 1939 due to non-renewal of registration of copyright, the U.S. film producer and its French licensee had no basis on which to object to plaintiffs' exploitation of the film in France. The copyright claimants rejoined that under article 18 of the Berne Convention, once the U.S. ratified that treaty, U.S. works that may previously have been in the public domain at home and accordingly in France, now would be protected anew in other Berne Union members, including France, even if the works remained in the public domain in the U.S. This seems a rather bold argument. After all, why should a foreign country extend coverage to a work that the country of origin will no longer protect?

[The answer turns on the text of article 18. Not every reason for the work being in the public domain in its country of origin permits another member state to withhold copyright protection. Another Berne member may decline to protect the new member's work only if its home copyright term has expired. If the work has fallen into the public domain for other reasons, particularly if the author failed to comply with formalities imposed by the country of origin, other Berne Union members may not deny protection. In the case of

---

* Translation: Jane C. Ginsburg

"His Girl Friday," the work fell out of copyright because of non-compliance with the renewal registration formality; thus, the French high court held that the condition for declining protection did not apply. According to the Cour de cassation]:

The Court of Appeals correctly held that the conditions for applying article 18.1 of the Berne Convention must be analyzed in light of article 5.2 of this same Convention, by virtue of which the enjoyment and exercise of copyright are not subject to any formality; the Court of Appeals correctly deduced that [the obligation of protection under] the Convention applied to works fallen into the public domain for any cause other than the expiration of the term of protection; thus the work "His Girl Friday" of Howard Hawks, which, registered in 1939, had not fallen into the public domain at the time of the entry into force of the Berne Convention in the USA, in 1989, "through the expiry of the term of protection," which, at the time, and setting aside any formalities, was 56 years. . . .

QUESTIONS

1. What is the relationship between article 18 and article 5(2)? If article 18 did not require restoration of copyright in foreign works in the public domain in their countries of origin because of non-compliance with formalities, would country of origin formalities then condition protection in other Union members? Does Berne generally require proof that the work seeking protection have satisfied country of origin formalities?
2. How, given that France and the U.S. are both members of the Berne Convention, could "His Girl Friday" be in the public domain in US, but not in France?

5.1.2 Neighboring rights conventions

Rome Convention

Article 11
Formalities for Phonograms
If, as a condition of protecting the rights of producers of phonograms, or of performers, or both, in relation to phonograms, a Contracting State, under its domestic law, requires compliance with formalities, these shall be considered as fulfilled if all the copies in commerce of the published phonogram or their containers bear a notice consisting of the symbol (P), accompanied by the year date of the first publication, placed in such a manner as to give reasonable notice of claim of protection; and if the

copies or their containers do not identify the producer or the licensee of the producer (by carrying his name, trade mark or other appropriate designation), the notice shall also include the name of the owner of the rights of the producer; and, furthermore, if the copies or their containers do not identify the principal performers, the notice shall also include the name of the person who, in the country in which the fixation was effected, owns the rights of such performers.

QUESTIONS

1. Could a member state of the Rome Convention impose formalities on foreign phonograms? In what way does the Rome Convention harmonize formalities?
2. Under article 3 of the Rome Convention, a "phonogram" means exclusively the aural fixation of the sounds of a performance or of other sounds; a "publication" means the offering of copies of a phonogram to the public in reasonable quantity. But the Convention does not define what is a "copy." As a result, the application of article 11 to the Internet becomes problematic. To what extent does article 11 apply to a phonogram made available on the Internet?

WPPT

Article 20
Formalities

The enjoyment and exercise of the rights provided for in this Treaty shall not be subject to any formality.

QUESTION

Belarus is member of the Rome Convention and the WPPT. One treaty allows member states to impose certain formalities, the other does not; how does Belarus comply with both?

Beijing Treaty

Article 17
Formalities

The enjoyment and exercise of the rights provided for in this Treaty shall not be subject to any formality.

QUESTION

The drafting of both the Beijing Convention and the WPPT moves away from the Rome Convention to align more closely with the Berne Convention. We have already encountered this shift with respect to transitional measures for newly adhering states. What inferences might you draw from this evolution?

TRIPS Agreement

Article 62

1. Members may require, as a condition of the acquisition or maintenance of the intellectual property rights provided for under Sections 2 through 6 of Part II [concerning trademarks, geographical indications, industrial designs, patents, and layouts of integrated circuits] [section 1 concerns copyright and neighboring rights], compliance with reasonable procedures and formalities. Such procedures and formalities shall be consistent with the provisions of this Agreement.

QUESTIONS

1. What bearing does this article have on copyright and neighboring rights?
2. Algeria and Morocco would like to impose formalities, such as notice and registration, on phonograms in the future. Would that comply with their international obligations?

5.2   Protectable subject matter

The Berne Convention defines protected works by explicitly introducing a list of protected works and implicitly imposing the specific conditions of originality and the idea-expression dichotomy. This Berne definition of protectable subject matter has been complemented by the TRIPS Agreement and the WCT, which specifically include computer programs and databases within copyrightable subject matter, and explicitly recognize the idea-expression dichotomy.

As to neighboring rights conventions, the treaties' approach shifts from the object of protection (the work) to the person protected (the performer, the producer, the broadcasting organization). But, at least with respect to the Rome Convention, a protected performance must pertain to a literary or artistic work.

5.2.1   In general

Berne Convention

> **Article 2**
> **Protected Works:**
>
> *1. "Literary and artistic works"; 2. Possible requirement of fixation;
> 3. Derivative works;
> 4. Official texts; 5. Collections; 6. Obligation to protect; beneficiaries
> of protection;
> 7. Works of applied art and industrial designs; 8. News*
>
> (1) The expression "literary and artistic works" shall include every
> production in the literary, scientific and artistic domain, whatever may
> be the mode or form of its expression, such as books, pamphlets and
> other writings; lectures, addresses, sermons and other works of the same
> nature; dramatic or dramatico-musical works; choreographic works and
> entertainments in dumb show; musical compositions with or without
> words; cinematographic works to which are assimilated works expressed
> by a process analogous to cinematography; works of drawing, painting,
> architecture, sculpture, engraving and lithography; photographic works
> to which are assimilated works expressed by a process analogous to pho-
> tography; works of applied art; illustrations, maps, plans, sketches and
> three-dimensional works relative to geography, topography, architecture
> or science.
>
> (2) It shall, however, be a matter for legislation in the countries of the
> Union to prescribe that works in general or any specified categories of
> works shall not be protected unless they have been fixed in some material
> form.
>
> (3) Translations, adaptations, arrangements of music and other altera-
> tions of a literary or artistic work shall be protected as original works
> without prejudice to the copyright in the original work.
>
> (4) It shall be a matter for legislation in the countries of the Union to
> determine the protection to be granted to official texts of a legislative,
> administrative and legal nature, and to official translations of such texts.
>
> (5) Collections of literary or artistic works such as encyclopaedias and
> anthologies which, by reason of the selection and arrangement of their

contents, constitute intellectual creations shall be protected as such, without prejudice to the copyright in each of the works forming part of such collections.

(6) The works mentioned in this Article shall enjoy protection in all countries of the Union. This protection shall operate for the benefit of the author and his successors in title.

(7) Subject to the provisions of Article 7(4) of this Convention, it shall be a matter for legislation in the countries of the Union to determine the extent of the application of their laws to works of applied art and industrial designs and models, as well as the conditions under which such works, designs and models shall be protected. Works protected in the country of origin solely as designs and models shall be entitled in another country of the Union only to such special protection as is granted in that country to designs and models; however, if no such special protection is granted in that country, such works shall be protected as artistic works.

(8) The protection of this Convention shall not apply to news of the day or to miscellaneous facts having the character of mere items of press information.

Article 2*bis*
Possible Limitation of Protection of Certain Works:

1. Certain speeches; 2. Certain uses of lectures and addresses; 3. Right to make collections of such works

(1) It shall be a matter for legislation in the countries of the Union to exclude, wholly or in part, from the protection provided by the preceding Article political speeches and speeches delivered in the course of legal proceedings.

(2) It shall also be a matter for legislation in the countries of the Union to determine the conditions under which lectures, addresses and other works of the same nature which are delivered in public may be reproduced by the press, broadcast, communicated to the public by wire and made the subject of public communication as envisaged in Article 11*bis*(1) of this Convention, when such use is justified by the informatory purpose.

(3) Nevertheless, the author shall enjoy the exclusive right of making a collection of his works mentioned in the preceding paragraphs.

QUESTIONS

1. Penelope Pyrotechnic produces fireworks displays. She is a national of a Berne Union country. Some of her displays employ classic elements in traditional displays, others combine traditional elements in new displays, and some of the displays are composed of newly designed bursts of light and color. Penelope first designs the displays on paper, then creates a computer program to command the firing of the various rockets at the appointed times.

   Outburst!, a rival fireworks producer in another Berne Union country, has emulated all of Penelope's displays. Does the Berne Convention require that her displays be protected?

2. In February 1996, the E.U. adopted a directive on the legal protection of databases. The directive created a new exclusive "sui generis" right for database producers, valid for 15 years, to protect their investment of time, money and effort, irrespective of whether the database is in itself innovative ("non-original" databases). The directive also harmonized copyright law applicable to the structure and arrangement of the contents of databases ("original" databases). In the absence of the directive, would the Berne Convention have obliged E.U. member states to protect original databases? Non-original databases?

   Article 11 of the directive determines its scope of application as to the sui generis right defined at article 7.

   > **Article 7 – Object of protection [of the sui generis right]**
   > 1. Member States shall provide for a right for the maker of a database which shows that there has been qualitatively and/or quantitatively a substantial investment in either the obtaining, verification or presentation of the contents to prevent extraction and/or re-utilization of the whole or of a substantial part, evaluated qualitatively and/or quantitatively, of the contents of that database.

   > **Article 11 – Beneficiaries of protection under the sui generis right**
   > 1. The right provided for in Article 7 shall apply to database whose makers or rightholders are nationals of a Member State [of the European Union] or who have their habitual residence in the territory of the Community.

   Does the identification of the beneficiaries of protection under the sui generis right comply with international obligations?

3. The Prime Minister of a Berne member delivers a speech; must other Berne members protect it? Years later, in retirement, the Prime

Minister assembles his speeches and publishes them: must Berne members protect the collection? Must they protect individual collected speeches?

4. On June 2006, the Dutch Supreme Court recognized that the scent of a perfume (Trésor, from Lancôme), if original, may qualify for protection under national copyright law. By contrast, the French highest civil jurisdiction refused in 2006 to protect the scent of a perfume by copyright, confirming the refusal in 2013 for the Perfume Trésor. As a result, are foreign perfumes entitled by virtue of the Berne Convention to local copyright protection in the Netherlands, but not in France?

TRIPS Agreement

Article 10
Computer Programs and Compilations of Data

1. Computer programs, whether in source or object code, shall be protected as literary works under the Berne Convention (1971).

2. Compilations of data or other material, whether in machine readable or other form, which by reason of the selection or arrangement of their contents constitute intellectual creations shall be protected as such. Such protection, which shall not extend to the data or material itself, shall be without prejudice to any copyright subsisting in the data or material itself.

WIPO Copyright Treaty

Article 4
Computer Programs

Computer programs are protected as literary works within the meaning of Article 2 of the Berne Convention. Such protection applies to computer programs, whatever may be the mode or form of their expression.

Agreed statement concerning Article 4: The scope of protection for computer programs under Article 4 of this Treaty, read with Article 2,* is consistent with Article 2 of the Berne Convention and on a par with the relevant provisions of the TRIPS Agreement.

---

* Editors' note: Article 2 of the WCT states: "Copyright protection extends to expressions and not to ideas, procedures, methods of operation or mathematical concepts as such." (see discussion *infra* pp. 284 et seq.).

Article 5
Compilations of Data (Databases)

Compilations of data or other material, in any form, which by reason of the selection or arrangement of their contents constitute intellectual creations, are protected as such. This protection does not extend to the data or the material itself and is without prejudice to any copyright subsisting in the data or material contained in the compilation.

> **Agreed statement concerning Article 5**: The scope of protection for compilations of data (databases) under Article 5 of this Treaty, read with Article 2, is consistent with Article 2 of the Berne Convention and on a par with the relevant provisions of the TRIPS Agreement.

QUESTIONS

1. What is the purpose of specifying in the WCT that computer programs "are protected as literary works within the meaning of article 2 of the Berne Convention" and in the TRIPS Agreement that they "shall be protected as literary works under the Berne Convention"? Does it imply that, absent these treaties' specifications, computer programs would not be covered by the Berne Convention? Does it on the contrary reinforce the prior coverage? See, *supra*, Part I, Chapter 2.1.3.
2. What inferences, relative to the Berne convention, might one draw with respect to the WCT and TRIPS inclusion of "compilations of data or other material"?

Rome Convention

Article 2
Protection given by the Convention

> . . .

> 1. For the purposes of this Convention, national treatment shall mean the treatment accorded by the domestic law of the Contracting State in which protection is claimed:

> (a) to performers who are its nationals, as regards performances taking place, broadcast, or first fixed, on its territory;
> (b) to producers of phonograms who are its nationals, as regards phonograms first fixed or first published on its territory;

(c) to broadcasting organisations which have their headquarters on its territory, as regards broadcasts transmitted from transmitters situated on its territory.

. . .

Article 3
Definitions: (a) Performers; (b) Phonogram; (c) Producers of Phonograms

For the purposes of this Convention:

(a) "performers" means actors, singers, musicians, dancers, and other persons who act, sing, deliver, declaim, play in, or otherwise perform literary or artistic works;
(b) "phonogram" means any exclusively aural fixation of sounds of a performance or of other sounds;
(c) "producer of phonograms" means the person who, or the legal entity which, first fixes the sounds of a performance or other sounds;
(f) "broadcasting" means the transmission by wireless means for public reception of sounds or of images and sounds;

. . .

Article 9
Variety and Circus Artists

Any Contracting State may, by its domestic laws and regulations, extend the protection provided for in this Convention to artists who do not perform literary or artistic works.

QUESTIONS

1. Rome Convention article 3 defines a phonogram as "any exclusively aural fixation of sounds of a performance." But what is a "fixation." Does it encompass works only in digital form?
2. What does the expression 'literary or artistic works' used in article 3(a) mean? What are the consequences for article 9?
3. To what extent might a figure skater or a runway model be characterized as a performer under article 3? If not, does article 9 allow contracting states to extend the protection? What guidance might one take from

the heading of article 9? See *supra*, Part I Chapter 2.1.5 (Supplementary means of interpretation).

4. Recall the materials on subsequent state practice, Part I, Chapter 2.1.3, concerning the clarification of subject matter for sound recordings. To what extent might the Rome Convention have an impact on the determination of what is a protected work under the Berne Convention?

PROBLEM

An African singer from the Ivory Coast is well known abroad, especially in Europe and North America. An American producer first fixes the sounds of the performance with the authorization of the singer in NYC. The performance is legally accessible from a German website and phonograms can be ordered from the website. Some illegal copies are distributed in the Côte d'Ivoire and in Germany. Does the Rome Convention apply if the producer sues in Germany? Does it apply in the Ivory Coast? Does it apply in the U.S.? How would the phonogram be protected in the latter country?

WPPT

Article 2
Definitions

For the purposes of this Treaty:

(a) "performers" are actors, singers, musicians, dancers, and other persons who act, sing, deliver, declaim, play in, interpret, or otherwise perform literary or artistic works or expressions of folklore;
(b) "phonogram" means the fixation of the sounds of a performance or of other sounds, or of a representation of sounds, other than in the form of a fixation incorporated in a cinematographic or other audiovisual work;

> **Agreed statement concerning Article 2(b):** It is understood that the definition of phonogram provided in Article 2(b) does not suggest that rights in the phonogram are in any way affected through their incorporation into a cinematographic or other audiovisual work.

(c) "fixation" means the embodiment of sounds, or of the representations thereof, from which they can be perceived, reproduced or communicated through a device;
(d) "producer of a phonogram" means the person, or the legal entity, who or which takes the initiative and has the responsibility for the first

fixation of the sounds of a performance or other sounds, or the representations of sounds. . . .

QUESTION

How does the WPPT enhance the scope of protection for performers and producers compared to the Rome Convention?

Beijing Treaty

Article 2
Definitions

For the purposes of this Treaty:
(a) "performers" are actors, singers, musicians, dancers, and other persons who act, sing, deliver, declaim, play in, interpret, or otherwise perform literary or artistic works or expressions of folklore;

> **Agreed statement concerning Article 2(a)**: It is understood that the definition of "performers" includes those who perform a literary or artistic work that is created or first fixed in the course of a performance.

(b) "audiovisual fixation" means the embodiment of moving images, whether or not accompanied by sounds or by the representations thereof, from which they can be perceived, reproduced or communicated through a device;

> **Agreed statement concerning Article 2(b)**: It is hereby confirmed that the definition of "audiovisual fixation" contained in Article 2(b) is without prejudice to Article 2(c) of the WPPT.

5.2.2   Originality

The Berne Convention does not explicitly announce a minimum threshold of creativity (compare E.U. Directives, discussed *infra*, pp. 280 et seq.), but article 2(3) refers to "original works." One may infer a standard of originality from article 2(5), which brings compilations of prior works within mandatory Berne subject matter so long as they "constitute intellectual creations" "by reason of the selection and arrangement of their contents." One may therefore infer that a work, to require protection in Berne member states, must not only come within the general ambit of article 2, but must also be an "intellectual creation." WCT article 5 and TRIPS Agreement article 10(2), both of which echo Berne article 2(5), reinforce this conclusion. In the E.U., the standard of creativity required for computer programs, databases, and photographs is that they constitute the author's "own intellectual creation." The ECJ has now generalized the "own intellectual creation" standard to works of authorship generally by interpreting the Berne Convention, as the following materials illustrate.

Berne Convention Article 2
Protected Works

(3) Translations, adaptations, arrangements of music and other alterations of a literary or artistic work shall be protected as original works without prejudice to the copyright in the original work.

. . .

(5) Collections of literary or artistic works such as encyclopaedias and anthologies which, by reason of the selection and arrangement of their contents, constitute intellectual creations shall be protected as such, without prejudice to the copyright in each of the works forming part of such collections.

. . .

(8) The protection of this Convention shall not apply to news of the day or to miscellaneous facts [*French version* "faits-divers"] having the character of mere items of press information.

QUESTIONS

To what extent could you infer from the above text an implicit definition of originality? What might be the relationship of the 'without prejudice' criterion of the condition of originality?

U.S. definition of originality

Feist v. Rural Telephone, 499 U.S. 340 (1991) [See *supra*, Part I, Chapter 2.5.1, pp. 154 et seq.]

QUESTION

To what extent is the U.S. definition of originality consistent with Berne Convention article 2.5?

E.U. definition of originality

Under E.U. law, a work is original if it is "the author's own intellectual creation." This standard, which echoes the Berne Convention, is enshrined in two E.U. Directives limited to specific subject matter, i.e., computer programs and databases. It also appears in the 1993 Term Directive (codified by Directive 2006/116) with respect to photographs. In the *Infopaq* case concerning the characterization of a data capture process, which consists of storing an extract of a protected work comprising 11 words, and posing the question whether those 11 words constituted a reproduction under the Information Society Directive 2001/29, the ECJ's broad definition of originality relied on and interpreted the Berne Convention.

Directive 2009/24/EC of the European Parliament and of the Council of 23 April 2009 on the legal protection of computer programs, codifying Directive 91/250 on the legal protection of computer programs

Article 1 – Object of protection

3. A computer program shall be protected if it is original in the sense that it is the author's own intellectual creation. No other criteria shall be applied to determine its eligibility for protection.

Directive 96/9/EC of the European Parliament and of the Council of 11 March 1996 on the legal protection of databases

Article 3 – Object of protection

1. In accordance with this Directive, databases which, by reason of the selection or arrangement of their contents, constitute the author's own intellectual creation shall be protected as such by copyright.

Directive 2006/116/EC of the European Parliament and of the Council of 12 December 2006 on the term of protection of copyright and certain related rights

Recital (16)

The protection of photographs in the Member States is the subject of varying regimes. A photographic work within the meaning of the Berne Convention is to be considered original if it is the author's own intellectual creation reflecting his personality, no other criteria such as merit or purpose being taken into account. The protection of other photographs should be left to national law

Article 6 – Protection of photographs

Photographs which are original in the sense that they are the author's own intellectual creation shall be protected in accordance with Article 1. No other criteria shall be applied to determine their eligibility for protection.

C-5/08 Infopaq International A/S v. Danske Dagblades Forening ECLI:EU:C:2009:465 [2009]

[The case concerned the question whether the reproduction of 11 words violates the exclusive right in article 2 Directive 2001/29 [Info Soc] to reproduce the work. InfoPaq monitors and analyses media articles, and supplies customers with summaries of word search queries. The summaries contain excerpts of media articles that match the search words. The excerpts contain the searched word and the preceding and succeeding five words.]

The first question

30   By its first question, the national court asks, essentially, whether the concept of "reproduction in part" within the meaning of Directive 2001/29 [Info Soc] is to be interpreted as meaning that it encompasses the storing and subsequent printing out on paper of a text extract consisting of 11 words.

31   It is clear that Directive 2001/29 [Info Soc] does not define the concept of either "reproduction" or "reproduction in part".

32   In those circumstances, those concepts must be defined having regard to the wording and context of Article 2 of Directive 2001/29 [Info Soc], where the reference to them is to be found and in the light of both the overall objectives of that directive and international law (see, to that effect, *SGAE*, paragraphs 34 and 35 and case-law cited).

33   Article 2(a) of Directive 2001/29 [Info Soc] provides that authors have the exclusive right to authorise or prohibit reproduction, in whole or in part, of their works. It follows that protection of the author's right to authorise or prohibit reproduction is intended to cover "work".

34   It is, moreover, apparent from the general scheme of the Berne Convention, in particular Article 2(5) and (8), that the protection of certain subject-matters as artistic or literary works presupposes that they are intellectual creations.

35   Similarly, under Articles 1(3) of Directive 91/250 [Computer Program], 3(1) of Directive 96/9 [Data Base] and 6 of Directive 2006/116 [Term of Protection], works such as computer programs, databases or photographs are protected by copyright only if they are original in the sense that they are their author's own intellectual creation.

. . .

44   As regards newspaper articles, their author's own intellectual creation [citations omitted] is evidenced clearly from the form, the manner in which the subject is presented and the linguistic expression. In the main proceedings, moreover, it is common ground that newspaper articles, as such, are literary works covered by Directive 2001/29 [Info Soc].

45   Regarding the elements of such works covered by the protection, it should be observed that they consist of words which, considered in isolation, are not as such an intellectual creation of the author who employs them. It is only through the choice, sequence and combination of those words that the author may express his creativity in an original manner and achieve a result which is an intellectual creation.

46   Words as such do not, therefore, constitute elements covered by the protection.

47   That being so, given the requirement of a broad interpretation of the scope of the protection conferred by Article 2 of Directive 2001/29 [Info Soc], the possibility may not be ruled out that certain isolated sentences, or even certain parts of sentences in the text in question, may be suitable for conveying to the reader the originality of a publication such as a newspaper article, by communicating to that reader an element which is, in itself, the expression of the intellectual creation of the author of that article. Such sentences or parts of sentences are, therefore, liable to come within the scope of the protection provided for in Article 2(a) of that directive.

48   In the light of those considerations, the reproduction of an extract of a protected work which, like those at issue in the main proceedings, comprises 11 consecutive words thereof, is such as to constitute reproduction

in part within the meaning of Article 2 of Directive 2001/29 [Info Soc], if that extract contains an element of the work which, as such, expresses the author's own intellectual creation; it is for the national court to make this determination.

49   It must be remembered also that the data capture process used by Infopaq allows for the reproduction of multiple extracts of protected works. That process reproduces an extract of 11 words each time a search word appears in the relevant work and, moreover, often operates using a number of search words because some clients ask Infopaq to draw up summaries based on a number of criteria.

50   In so doing, that process increases the likelihood that Infopaq will make reproductions in part within the meaning of Article 2(a) of Directive 2001/29 [Info Soc] because the cumulative effect of those extracts may lead to the reconstitution of lengthy fragments which are liable to reflect the originality of the work in question, with the result that they contain a number of elements which are such as to express the intellectual creation of the author of that work.

51   In the light of the foregoing, the answer to the first question is that an act occurring during a data capture process, which consists of storing an extract of a protected work comprising 11 words and printing out that extract, is such as to come within the concept of reproduction in part within the meaning of Article 2 of Directive 2001/29 [Info Soc], if the elements thus reproduced are the expression of the intellectual creation of their author; it is for the national court to make this determination.

QUESTIONS

1. If the *Infopaq* decision could be viewed as implicitly or explicitly construing the domestic definition of originality in the light of international copyright norms, *Infopaq* might contribute to a better understanding of the Berne Convention by exerting a reciprocal influence in the interpretation of article 2. Through what principle of treaty interpretation might that occur? See *supra*, Part I, Chapter 2.1.3 (subsequent practice).
2. The European Court of Justice (ECJ) interprets article 2(8) of the Berne Convention as a key element in favor of a pre-existing condition of originality under the Berne Convention. To what extent does the French formulation "*fait divers*" better support that understanding than does the English version's "*miscellaneous facts*"? See *supra*, Part I, Chapter 2.1.4 (prevailing language)
   In that light, which, if any, of the following acts does the Berne Convention exclude from the scope of copyright protection:

> a. A U.S. publisher reprints a story from Agence France Presse.
> b. A U.S. publisher reprints a story from Agence France Presse originally published last year.
> c. A U.S. blogger posts the headline of a story from Agence France Presse.

3. In 2013, the German Government published a new law which gives newspaper publishers the exclusive right to the commercial use of their publications on the Internet. This right will last until a year after the publication of the newspaper and will not cover single words or "very small text-snippets." The publishers lobbied for the law, pointing to the economic harm allegedly caused by certain search engines' practice of "news aggregation" (copying and collecting headlines and initial sentences of news stories carried on the newspapers' websites). To what extent might article 2(8) of the Berne Convention limit the scope or application of this new law?

5.2.3   Idea/expression dichotomy

The consecration of the dichotomy

The Berne Convention does not, unlike the later WIPO Copyright Treaty and the TRIPS Agreement, explicitly confine copyright protection to expressions. But such a limitation may well be implicit in article 2(1) of the Berne Convention, which requires member states to protect "every production in the literary, scientific and artistic domain, whatever may be the mode or form of its *expression*" (emphasis supplied). Similarly, where the WCT and the TRIPS distinguish facts from expression, and make clear that the protection of compilations "shall not extend to the data or material itself," the Berne Convention does not expressly preclude coverage of "data or material," but that result may be inferred both from the (implicit) requirement of originality, and from Berne Convention article 2(8), which excludes "news of the day" and "miscellaneous facts having the character of mere items of press information" from the scope of the Convention.

Berne Convention

See Article 2(1) and 2(8) of the Berne Convention, *supra*, pp. 271–72

QUESTION

To what extent is the idea/expression distinction independent from the originality condition?

TRIPS Agreement

> **Article 9**
> **Relation to the Berne Convention**
>
> . . .
>
> 2. Copyright protection shall extend to expressions and not to ideas, procedures, methods of operation or mathematical concepts as such.

WCT

> **Article 2**
> **Scope of Copyright Protection**
>
> Copyright protection extends to expressions and not to ideas, procedures, methods of operation or mathematical concepts as such.

QUESTIONS

1. Should the TRIPS Agreement and WCT's recognition of the idea and expression dichotomy be analyzed as a new rule or instead as the clarification of a preexisting implicit rule under the Berne Convention? Why does it matter?
2. What, if any, is the relationship between the idea/expression dichotomy and the recognition in the same text of copyright protection for computer programs?
3. Compare:

> **17 USC § 102**
>
> b) In no case does copyright protection for an original work of authorship extend to any idea, procedure, process, system, method of operation (. . .).

To what extent was TRIPS inspired by the U.S. Copyright law? Does it matter?

The application of the dichotomy

Computer programs

Directive 2009/24/EC of the European Parliament and of the Council of 23 April 2009 on the legal protection of computer programs (codifying Directive 91/250)

Recitals

(11) For the avoidance of doubt, it has to be made clear that only the expression of a computer program is protected and that ideas and principles which underlie any element of a program, including those which underlie its interfaces, are not protected by copyright under this Directive. In accordance with this principle of copyright, to the extent that logic, algorithms and programming languages comprise ideas and principles, those ideas and principles are not protected under this Directive. In accordance with the legislation and case-law of the Member States and the international copyright conventions, the expression of those ideas and principles is to be protected by copyright.

Article 1 – Object of protection

. . .

2. Protection in accordance with this Directive shall apply to the expression in any form of a computer program. Ideas and principles which underlie any element of a computer program, including those which underlie its interfaces, are not protected by copyright under this Directive.

C-406/10 SAS Institute Inc. v. World Programming Ltd ECLI:EU:C:2012:259 [2012]

[This case concerned the infringement of a computer program. The competitor studied how the program functioned and then wrote its own program to emulate that functionality. The issue was whether the copyright on the prior computer program was infringed by the second computer program. The analysis focused on the existence and scope of protection covering the functionality of the program.]

Questions 1 to 5

29 By these questions, the national court asks, in essence, whether Article 1(2) of Directive 91/250 [Equivalent to Directive 2009/24/EC of

the European Parliament and of the Council of 23 April 2009 on the legal protection of computer programs] must be interpreted as meaning that the functionality of a computer program and the programming language and the format of data files used in a computer program in order to exploit certain of its functions constitute a form of expression of that program and may, as such, be protected by copyright in computer programs for the purposes of that directive.

30   In accordance with Article 1(1) of Directive 91/250, computer programs are protected by copyright as literary works within the meaning of the Berne Convention.

31   Article 1(2) of Directive 91/250 extends that protection to the expression in any form of a computer program. That provision states, however, that the ideas and principles which underlie any element of a computer program, including those which underlie its interfaces, are not protected by copyright under that directive.

32   The 14th recital in the preamble to Directive 91/250* confirms, in this respect, that, in accordance with the principle that only the expression of a computer program is protected by copyright, to the extent that logic, algorithms and programming languages comprise ideas and principles, those ideas and principles are not protected under that directive. The 15th recital in the preamble to Directive 91/250 states that, in accordance with the legislation and jurisprudence of the Member States and the international copyright conventions, the expression of those ideas and principles is to be protected by copyright.

33   With respect to international law, both Article 2 of the WIPO Copyright Treaty and Article 9(2) of the TRIPS Agreement provide that copyright protection extends to expressions and not to ideas, procedures, methods of operation or mathematical concepts as such.

34   Article 10(1) of the TRIPS Agreement provides that computer programs, whether in source or object code, are to be protected as literary works under the Berne Convention.

. . .

---

* Editors' note: Recital 14 states: "Whereas, in accordance with this principle of copyright, to the extent that logic, algorithms and programming languages comprise ideas and principles, those ideas and principles are not protected under this Directive."

38   From this the Court [the Court of Justice] concluded that the source code and the object code of a computer program are forms of expression thereof which, consequently, are entitled to be protected by copyright as computer programs, by virtue of Article 1(2) of Directive 91/250. On the other hand, as regards the graphic user interface, the Court held that such an interface does not enable the reproduction of the computer program, but merely constitutes one element of that program by means of which users make use of the features of that program [citation omitted).

39   On the basis of those considerations, it must be stated that, with regard to the elements of a computer program which are the subject of Questions 1 to 5, neither the functionality of a computer program nor the programming language and the format of data files used in a computer program in order to exploit certain of its functions constitute a form of expression of that program for the purposes of Article 1(2) of Directive 91/250.

40   [Citations omitted], to accept that the functionality of a computer program can be protected by copyright would amount to making it possible to monopolise ideas, to the detriment of technological progress and industrial development.

41   Moreover, point 3.7 of the explanatory memorandum to the Proposal for Directive 91/250 [COM (88) 816] states that the main advantage of protecting computer programs by copyright is that such protection covers only the individual expression of the work and thus leaves other authors the desired latitude to create similar or even identical programs provided that they refrain from copying.

. . .

46   Consequently, the answer to Questions 1 to 5 is that Article 1(2) of Directive 91/250 must be interpreted as meaning that neither the functionality of a computer program nor the programming language and the format of data files used in a computer program in order to exploit certain of its functions constitute a form of expression of that program and, as such, are not protected by copyright in computer programs for the purposes of that directive.

QUESTIONS

1. How does the ECJ use international norms to draw the line between idea and expression? Is the court's approach useful beyond E.U. law? Does it create a reciprocal influence?
2. Article 9(2) of the TRIPS stems originally from a Japanese proposal as follows: "The copyright protection for computer programs works under the present Agreement shall not extend to any programming language, rule or algorithm used for making such works" (D. Gervais, THE TRIPS AGREEMENT, DRAFTING HISTORY AND ANALYSIS, (4th ed, n 2.140). The application of the European idea/expression dichotomy in the light of the TRIPS Agreement and the WCT leads to the exact same conclusion with respect to these works. Does the incorporation of the dichotomy into the text of the TRIPS and the WCT add anything more?

Conceptual art

France, Cour de cassation, N° 06–19021 [2008]*

[A conceptual artist stenciled the word "Paradise" over a crumbling door and doorframe, calling the result an artistic work titled "The Gates of Paradise." A photographer took and sold photographs of the doorway, showing the stenciled word.]

But whereas the decision below points out that the work at issue does not consist merely of a reproduction of the word "Paradise," but also of the affixation of this word in golden patinated letters in a particular graphic form, on an old and worn-out door, with a cross-shaped lock, embedded in a bare wall whose paint is peeling, that this combination entails aesthetic choices that convey the personality of the author; that from these observations and appreciations, which are the sovereign province of the lower court, it becomes apparent that through his conceptual approach, which consists of affixing one word in a particular place while turning it away from its normal meaning, the artist formally expressed himself in an original concrete realization, the court of appeals correctly concluded that the work benefitted from copyright protection.

---

* http://www.legifrance.com/affichJuriJudi.do?oldAction=rechJuriJudi&idTexte=JURITEXT00001977221 4&fastReqId=918821795&fastPos=1 [Translation: Jane C. Ginsburg].

QUESTION

Could France decline to extend its copyright coverage of (at least some) conceptual art to foreign works of authorship?

5.2.4 Optional limitations on protectable subject matter

Fixation

> **Berne Convention Article 2**
> **Protected Works**
>
> *. . . 2. Possible requirement of fixation*
>
> . . .
>
> (2) It shall, however, be a matter for legislation in the countries of the Union to prescribe that works in general or any specified categories of works shall not be protected unless they have been fixed in some material form.
>
> **17 U.S.C. sec. 102(a); 101**
>
> § 102. Subject matter of copyright: In general
>
> (a) Copyright protection subsists, in accordance with this title, in original works of authorship fixed in any tangible medium of expression, now known or later developed, from which they can be perceived, reproduced, or otherwise communicated, either directly or with the aid of a machine or device. . . .
>
> § 101. Definitions
>
> A work is "fixed" in a tangible medium of expression when its embodiment in a copy or phonorecord, by or under the authority of the author, is sufficiently permanent or stable to permit it to be perceived, reproduced, or otherwise communicated for a period of more than transitory duration. A work consisting of sounds, images, or both, that are being transmitted, is "fixed" for purposes of this title if a fixation of the work is being made simultaneously with its transmission.

France, Code of Intellectual Property

Article L112–1

The provisions of this Code shall protect the rights of authors in all works of the mind, whatever their kind, form of expression, merit or purpose.

Article L112–2

The following, in particular, shall be considered works of the mind within the meaning of this Code:

. . .

4° choreographic works, circus acts and feats and dumb-show works, the acting form of which is set down in writing or in other manner;

. . .

Editor's note: this French rule has been interpreted as referencing a rule of proof, rather than a substantive limitation on copyrightable subject matter.

UK Copyright, Patent and Designs Act 1988

1. Copyright and copyright works

(1) Copyright is a property right which subsists in accordance with this Part in the following descriptions of work—

(a) original literary, dramatic, musical or artistic works,

. . .

3. Literary, dramatic and musical works

. . .

(2) Copyright does not subsist in a literary, dramatic or musical work unless and until it is recorded, in writing or otherwise; and references in this Part to the time at which such a work is made are to the time at which it is so recorded.
(3) It is immaterial for the purposes of subsection (2) whether the work

is recorded by or with the permission of the author; and where it is not recorded by the author, nothing in that subsection affects the question whether copyright subsists in the record as distinct from the work recorded.

QUESTION

To what extent do the above national laws comply with the Berne Convention?

PROBLEM

An English dancer performs improvised break-dancing on the public square facing the Eiffel Tower in Paris, France. Without the dancer's authorization, an American photographer films the performance, and posts it to her website, which is hosted in the US. Under what copyright law may the dancer obtain redress against the photographer?

Official texts

Berne Convention Article 2
. . . 4. Official texts

It shall be a matter for legislation in the countries of the Union to determine the protection to be granted to official texts of a legislative, administrative and legal nature, and to official translations of such texts.

17 U.S.C. § 105. Subject matter of copyright: United States Government works

Copyright protection under this title is not available for any work of the United States Government, but the United States Government is not precluded from receiving and holding copyrights transferred to it by assignment, bequest, or otherwise.

17 U.S.C. § 101. Definitions

A "work of the United States Government" is a work prepared by an officer or employee of the United States Government as part of that person's official duties.

QUESTION

Can § 105 be "bilateralized" to bar U.S. copyright protection for works of foreign governments?

UK Copyright, Designs and Patents Act 1988

163. Crown copyright

(1) Where a work is made by Her Majesty or by an officer or servant of the Crown in the course of his duties—

(a) the work qualifies for copyright protection notwithstanding section 153(1) (ordinary requirement as to qualification for copyright protection), and
(b) Her Majesty is the first owner of any copyright in the work.

QUESTIONS

For which, if any, of the following acts does the Berne Convention require the copyright owner's authorization:

1. A U.S. publisher reprints the decisions of U.S. federal courts.
2. A U.S. publisher reprints the decisions of U.K. courts.
3. A U.K. publisher reprints the decisions of U.S. federal courts.

Applied art

[See *supra*, Part II, Chapter 4.1.2, pp. 237–38]

5.3 Duration

Duration delimits the term of protection. Highly disputed in domestic law, the term of protection differs among member states. For copyright and neighboring rights, the treaties adopt a reference point of 50 years. Nevertheless, the actual term of protection varies since the computation of 50 years starts from the death of the author for copyright and from the fixation of the performance for neighboring rights. The tendency in Europe and the U.S. is to offer a term of protection in excess of the ones set out in article 7 of the Berne Convention. Article 7(6) authorizes such augmentations of term. But because of article 7(8)'s reciprocity rule, this longer protection does not automatically benefit foreign works.

5.3.1 Copyright

Berne Convention

> **Article 7**
> **Term of Protection:**
>
> *1. Generally; 2. For cinematographic works; 3. For anonymous and pseudonymous works; 4. For photographic works and works of applied art; 5. Starting date of computation; 6. Longer terms; 7. Shorter terms; 8. Applicable law; "comparison" of terms*
>
> (1) The term of protection granted by this Convention shall be the life of the author and fifty years after his death.
>
> (2) However, in the case of cinematographic works, the countries of the Union may provide that the term of protection shall expire fifty years after the work has been made available to the public with the consent of the author, or, failing such an event within fifty years from the making of such a work, fifty years after the making.
>
> (3) In the case of anonymous or pseudonymous works, the term of protection granted by this Convention shall expire fifty years after the work has been lawfully made available to the public. However, when the pseudonym adopted by the author leaves no doubt as to his identity, the term of protection shall be that provided in paragraph (1). If the author of an anonymous or pseudonymous work discloses his identity during the above-mentioned period, the term of protection applicable shall be that provided in paragraph (1). The countries of the Union shall not be required to protect anonymous or pseudonymous works in respect of which it is reasonable to presume that their author has been dead for fifty years.
>
> (4) It shall be a matter for legislation in the countries of the Union to determine the term of protection of photographic works and that of works of applied art in so far as they are protected as artistic works; however, this term shall last at least until the end of a period of twenty-five years from the making of such a work.
>
> (5) The term of protection subsequent to the death of the author and the terms provided by paragraphs (2), (3) and (4) shall run from the date of death or of the event referred to in those paragraphs, but such terms shall

always be deemed to begin on the first of January of the year following the death or such event.

(6) The countries of the Union may grant a term of protection in excess of those provided by the preceding paragraphs.

. . .

(8) In any case, the term shall be governed by the legislation of the country where protection is claimed; however, unless the legislation of that country otherwise provides, the term shall not exceed the term fixed in the country of origin of the work.

Article 7*bis*
Term of Protection for Works of Joint Authorship

The provisions of the preceding Article shall also apply in the case of a work of joint authorship, provided that the terms measured from the death of the author shall be calculated from the death of the last surviving author.

QUESTIONS

1. What is a work of joint authorship? Does the Berne Convention define authorship, joint or otherwise?
2. Why, in the cases of photographic works, works of applied art, and cinematographic works, does the Berne Convention derogate from the otherwise applicable minimum duration?
3. The Berne Convention adopts two different computations of time. The general rule computes the time from the death of the author. Nevertheless, such a computation being impossible when the author is unknown, article 7(3) adopts for anonymous and pseudonymous works another computation, running from the lawful making available of the work. In U.S. copyright as seen below, such a computation is also adopted for works made for hire. The French law provisions on collective works provide the same result. To what extent do those countries comply with the Berne Convention? Consider the following two questions:
4. A creates a work made for hire which is published in 2000; suppose that A will die in 2050. To what extent does the rule laid down at article 7(8) derogate from the rule of national treatment? Does the article 7(8) rule apply in the E.U? Why not? (See *supra*, Part II, Chapter 4.1.2.)

5. Article 6 bis of the Berne Convention lays down the following rule: "(2) The rights granted to the author in accordance with the preceding paragraph shall, after his death, be maintained, at least until the expiry of the economic rights, and shall be exercisable by the persons or institutions authorized by the legislation of the country where protection is claimed". What, if any, is the relationship between article 7 and article 6 bis of the Berne Convention?

6. Applying Berne Convention article 7(8), determine the relevant duration in the cases below taking into account the following durations: France 70 *pma*, Canada 50 *pma* and India 60 *pma*.
   - a Canadian work of authorship for which protection is claimed in France.
   - a French work of authorship for which protection is claimed in Canada.
   - an Indian work of authorship for which protection is claimed in France.
   - a French work of authorship for which protection is claimed in India.

TRIPS Agreement

Article 12
Term of Protection

Whenever the term of protection of a work, other than a photographic work or a work of applied art, is calculated on a basis other than the life of a natural person, such term shall be no less than 50 years from the end of the calendar year of authorized publication, or, failing such authorized publication within 50 years from the making of the work, 50 years from the end of the calendar year of making.

QUESTIONS

1. Article 12 TRIPS Agreement deals with works whose author may be a juridical person. As seen previously, the Berne Convention does not encompass a specific computation rule of general application to those works (as opposed to cinematographic works). To what extent does article 12 TRIPS comply with article 20 Berne Convention?

2. Is publication under the TRIPS the equivalent of "making available" under the Berne Convention? What about works made available over the Internet?

WCT

Article 9
Duration of the Protection of Photographic Works

In respect of photographic works, the Contracting Parties shall not apply the provisions of Article 7(4) of the Berne Convention.

QUESTION

What is the consequence of WCT article 9? Could Brazil (Berne member) adopt a 25-year term of protection for foreign photographic works? What about Argentina (Berne and WCT member)?

U.S. Copyright Act

17 U.S.C. § 302. Duration of copyright: Works created on or after January 1, 1978

(a) In General. — Copyright in a work created on or after January 1, 1978, subsists from its creation and, except as provided by the following subsections, endures for a term consisting of the life of the author and 70 years after the author's death.

(b) Joint Works. — In the case of a joint work prepared by two or more authors who did not work for hire, the copyright endures for a term consisting of the life of the last surviving author and 70 years after such last surviving author's death.

(c) Anonymous Works, Pseudonymous Works, and Works Made for Hire. — In the case of an anonymous work, a pseudonymous work, or a work made for hire, the copyright endures for a term of 95 years from the year of its first publication, or a term of 120 years from the year of its creation, whichever expires first. If, before the end of such term, the identity of one or more of the authors of an anonymous or pseudonymous work is revealed in the records of a registration made for that work under subsections (a) or (d) of section 408, or in the records provided by this subsection, the copyright in the work endures for the term specified by subsection (a) or (b), based on the life of the author or authors whose identity has been revealed. Any person having an interest in the copyright in an anonymous or pseudonymous work may at any time record, in records to be maintained by the Copyright Office for that purpose, a statement identifying one or more authors of the work; the statement shall also identify the person filing it, the nature of that person's interest, the source of the information recorded, and the particular work affected, and shall comply in form and content with requirements that the Register of Copyrights shall prescribe by regulation.

. . .

QUESTION

The U.S. Copyright Act grants full national treatment to qualifying foreign works (see § 104, *supra*, Part II, Chapter 3.1.4). As a result, the U.S. copyright term will apply, even if it is longer than the copyright term in the country of origin. Does the U.S.' non application of the rule of the shorter term comply with the Berne Convention?

E.U. duration directives

Under domestic E.U. member states' laws, the term of protection granted was not initially unified, and therefore varied from 50 to 80 years *pma*. The initial Term Directive (Directive 93/98/EEC of 29 October 1993 harmonizing the term of protection of copyright and certain related rights) was adopted in 1993. At that time, the term unified was 70 years *post mortem* for copyright and 50 years for related rights. The term of protection is now 70 years for copyright and related rights. That Directive was codified in 2006 (Directive 2006/116/EC) and modified in 2011 (Directive 2011/77/EU of 27 September 2011 amending Directive 2006/116/EC on the term of protection of copyright and certain related rights).

Directive 2006/116/EC of the European Parliament and of the Council of 12 December 2006 on the term of protection of copyright and certain related rights (codified version)

Article 1 – Duration of authors' rights

1. The rights of an author of a literary or artistic work within the meaning of Article 2 of the Berne Convention shall run for the life of the author and for 70 years after his death, irrespective of the date when the work is lawfully made available to the public.

2. In the case of a work of joint authorship, the term referred to in paragraph 1 shall be calculated from the death of the last surviving author.

3. In the case of anonymous or pseudonymous works, the term of protection shall run for 70 years after the work is lawfully made available to the public. However, when the pseudonym adopted by the author leaves no doubt as to his identity, or if the author discloses his identity during the period referred to in the first sentence, the term of protection applicable shall be that laid down in paragraph 1.

4. Where a Member State provides for particular provisions on copyright in respect of collective works or for a legal person to be designated as the rightholder, the term of protection shall be calculated according to the provisions of paragraph 3, except if the natural persons who have created the work are identified as such in the versions of the work which are made available to the public. This paragraph is without prejudice to the rights of identified authors whose identifiable contributions are included in such works, to which contributions paragraph 1 or 2 shall apply.

5. Where a work is published in volumes, parts, instalments, issues or episodes and the term of protection runs from the time when the work was lawfully made available to the public, the term of protection shall run for each such item separately.

6. In the case of works for which the term of protection is not calculated from the death of the author or authors and which have not been lawfully made available to the public within 70 years from their creation, the protection shall terminate.

Article 2 – Cinematographic or audiovisual works

1. The principal director of a cinematographic or audiovisual work shall be considered as its author or one of its authors. Member States shall be free to designate other co-authors.

2. The term of protection of cinematographic or audiovisual works shall expire 70 years after the death of the last of the following persons to survive, whether or not these persons are designated as co-authors: the principal director, the author of the screenplay, the author of the dialogue and the composer of music specifically created for use in the cinematographic or audiovisual work.

Directive 2011/77/EU of 27 September 2011 amending Directive 2006/116/EC on the term of protection of copyright and certain related rights

Article 1 – Amendments to Directive 2006/116/EC

Directive 2006/116/EC is hereby amended as follows:

(1) The following paragraph shall be added to Article 1: "7. The term of protection of a musical composition with words shall expire 70 years after the death of the last of the following persons to survive, whether or not those persons are designated as co-authors: the author of the lyrics and the composer of the musical composition, provided that both contributions were specifically created for the respective musical composition with words."

QUESTIONS

1. To what extent can a musical composition with words or a cinematographic or audiovisual work be characterized as a joint work? Do the relevant E.U. provisions comply with the Berne Convention?
2. How do you explain the reference to the meaning of the Berne Convention at article 1 of the 2006 Directive?
3. In the U.S. and in Europe, the term of protection is 70 years *pma*, 20 years more than the minimum required under the Berne Convention. What implications does this difference have for the application of the Berne Convention?

5.3.2 Neighboring rights

Rome Convention

Article 14
Minimum Duration of Protection

The term of protection to be granted under this Convention shall last at least until the end of a period of twenty years computed from the end of the year in which:

(a) the fixation was made–for phonograms and for performances incorporated therein;
(b) the performance took place–for performances not incorporated in phonograms;
(c) the broadcast took place–for broadcasts.

WIPO Performances and Phonograms Treaty (WPPT)

Article 17
Term of Protection

(1) The term of protection to be granted to performers under this Treaty shall last, at least, until the end of a period of 50 years computed from the end of the year in which the performance was fixed in a phonogram.

(2) The term of protection to be granted to producers of phonograms under this Treaty shall last, at least, until the end of a period of 50 years computed from the end of the year in which the phonogram was published, or failing such publication within 50 years from fixation of the phonogram, 50 years from the end of the year in which the fixation was made.

Beijing Treaty

Article 14
Term of Protection

The term of protection to be granted to performers under this Treaty shall last, at least, until the end of a period of 50 years computed from the end of the year in which the performance was fixed.

TRIPS Agreement

Article 14
Protection of Performers, Producers of Phonograms (Sound Recordings) and Broadcasting Organizations

. . .

5. The term of the protection available under this Agreement to performers and producers of phonograms shall last at least until the end of a period of 50 years computed from the end of the calendar year in which the fixation was made or the performance took place. The term of protection granted pursuant to paragraph 3 shall last for at least 20 years from the end of the calendar year in which the broadcast took place.

QUESTION

How do you explain the differences between copyright and neighboring rights as to the computation of the term?

European implementation

Directive 2006/116/EC of the European Parliament and of the Council of 12 December 2006 on the term of protection of copyright and certain related rights (codified version)

Article 3 – Duration of related rights

1. The rights of performers shall expire 50 years after the date of the performance. However, if a fixation of the performance is lawfully published or lawfully communicated to the public within this period, the rights shall expire 50 years from the date of the first such publication or the first such communication to the public, whichever is the earlier.

Article 7 – Protection vis-à-vis third countries

1. Where the country of origin of a work, within the meaning of the Berne Convention, is a third country, and the author of the work is not a Community national, the term of protection granted by the Member States shall expire on the date of expiry of the protection granted in the country of origin of the work, but may not exceed the term laid down in Article 1.

2. The terms of protection laid down in Article 3 shall also apply in the case of rightholders who are not Community nationals, provided Member States grant them protection. However, without prejudice to the international obligations of the Member States, the term of protection granted by Member States shall expire no later than the date of expiry of the protection granted in the country of which the rightholder is a national and may not exceed the term laid down in Article 3.

3. Member States which, on 29 October 1993, in particular pursuant to their international obligations, granted a longer term of protection than that which would result from the provisions of paragraphs 1 and 2 may maintain this protection until the conclusion of international agreements on the term of protection of copyright or related rights.

Directive 2011/77/EU of the European Parliament and of the Council of 27 September 2011 amending Directive 2006/116/EC on the term of protection of copyright and certain related rights

Article 1 – Amendments to Directive 2006/116/EC

Directive 2006/116/EC is hereby amended as follows:

. . .

(2) Article 3 shall be amended as follows:

(a) in paragraph 1, the second sentence shall be replaced by the following:

'However,

- if a fixation of the performance otherwise than in a phonogram is lawfully published or lawfully communicated to the public within this period, the rights shall expire 50 years from the date of the first such publication or the first such communication to the public, whichever is the earlier,
- if a fixation of the performance in a phonogram is lawfully published or lawfully communicated to the public within this period, the rights shall expire 70 years from the date of the first such publication or the first such communication to the public, whichever is the earlier.';

(b) in the second and third sentences of paragraph 2, the number '50' shall be replaced by '70'. . . .

QUESTIONS

See *supra*, Chapter 4.1.2, p. 250.

5.4   Rights conferred

5.4.1   Moral rights

Moral rights have always been seen as a hallmark of the opposition between copyright protection and authors' right ("droit d'auteur") protection, accounting at least in part for the tardy adherence of the U.S. to the Berne Convention. The TRIPS Agreement's treatment of article 6*bis* of the Berne Convention illustrates how moral rights remain a vexing question in the process of harmonization of substantive copyright law. Similarly, no European harmonization of moral rights has yet taken place, whether by Directives or by case law.

Copyright treaties

Berne Convention

Article 6*bis*
Moral Rights

1. To claim authorship; to object to certain modifications and other derogatory actions;
2. After the author's death; 3. Means of redress

(1) Independently of the author's economic rights, and even after the transfer of the said rights, the author shall have the right to claim authorship of the work and to object to any distortion, mutilation or other modification of, or other derogatory action in relation to, the said work, which would be prejudicial to his honor or reputation.

(2) The rights granted to the author in accordance with the preceding paragraph shall, after his death, be maintained, at least until the expiry of the economic rights, and shall be exercisable by the persons or institutions authorized by the legislation of the country where protection is claimed. However, those countries whose legislation, at the moment of their ratification of or accession to this Act [1971], does not provide for the protection after the death of the author of all the rights set out in the preceding paragraph may provide that some of these rights may, after his death, cease to be maintained.

(3) The means of redress for safeguarding the rights granted by this Article shall be governed by the legislation of the country where protection is claimed.

QUESTIONS

1. Is the standard for determining violation of the author's rights under article 6*bis* subjective or objective? Why does it matter?
2. Does "any distortion, mutilation or other modification of, or other derogatory action in relation to, the said work . . ." include destruction of the original copy of a work?

3. May a Berne member state deny all *post-mortem* moral rights protection?
4. So long as a Berne member state achieves effective substantive protection of the attribution and integrity rights, do the legal labels under which the state accomplishes that goal matter? Then-Director-General of WIPO, Arpad Bogsch, endorsed this approach, claiming that the U.S. could ratify the Berne Convention in 1988 without amending its law to provide specific moral rights coverage. The U.S. took the position, and the Director-General agreed, that a "patchwork" of common law actions and other federal statutory claims together afforded the rough equivalent of formal moral rights provisions. Suppose, however, that subsequent caselaw developments eliminate some of the legal claims that formed the pieces of that "patchwork" (see *Dastar Corp. v. Twentieth Century Fox Film Corp.*, 539 U.S. 23 (2003) (no claim for non-attribution of intellectual origin of film under federal trademark act); if the non-copyright alternative coverage diminishes, is the U.S. still in compliance with its obligations under article 6*bis*?
5. Article 6*bis*(3) makes remedies for moral rights violations a matter for the legislation of the state where protection is sought. Is there any limit on how a Berne member state structures the remedies for a moral rights violation? For example, may a member state provide that, in the absence of specific moral rights legislation, all claims are to be brought under the national trademark law, or under general principles of tort law? Or may a member state restrict relief to an administrative determination by the national ministry of culture? For violations of the integrity right, may a member state, rather than awarding an injunction against the continued dissemination of the altered work, limit relief to requiring the defendant to providing the means to enable the public to compare the altered version with the original? Does it matter whether the restricted remedy results from judicial discretion or instead is imposed by legislation?

Note on the right of divulgation

One of the traditional components of moral rights protected in national laws is the right of disclosure (*'droit de divulgation'*).* There is no reference to this right in article 6*bis*, but it is possible to argue that other provisions of the Berne Convention bear on such a right. The argument derives by implication from the provisions dealing with exceptions to protection, notably articles 10 and 10*bis*. These provisions allow for certain instances of reproduction and

---

* The right of divulgation empowers the author to decide when and how to disclose the work of authorship. The author could also decide not to disclose it. Under French law, someone who finds the tatters of a painting destroyed by its author, could not sell those tatters, regardless of the physical property right he may have in the canvas. See Camoin (CA Paris, 6 mai 1931.DP 1931, 2, p. 88, note Nast.)

communication to the public of certain kinds of works, but in all cases, the work must have "already been lawfully made available to the public" (art. 10), or been "published" or "broadcast" (art. 10*bis*). Accordingly, a work not yet publicly disclosed by its author retains exclusive rights intact. It may not be too great a leap to infer further that the author's right to control the disclosure of his work to the world is one that the Berne Convention requires member states to protect, not only through national treatment in those member states which explicitly recognize a right of disclosure, but also as a matter of substantive minimum protection. In other words, member states lacking a separately articulated right of disclosure would be obliged to interpret their general provisions of copyright law to ensure foreign Berne authors' divulgation rights.

TRIPS Agreement

Article 9
Relation to the Berne Convention

(1) Members shall comply with articles 1 through 21 of the Berne Convention (1971) and the Appendix thereto. However, Members shall not have rights or obligations under this Agreement [i.e. Members shall have no recourse to WTO dispute settlement procedures] in respect of the rights conferred under Article 6*bis* of that Convention or of the rights derived therefrom.

Note

What does this text mean? On the one hand, members "shall comply" with article 6*bis*, but on the other hand, article 6*bis*, "or rights derived therefrom" cannot form the basis of a dispute resolution proceeding. TRIPS, in effect, ensures the unenforceability (at least in the WTO) of article 6*bis* attribution and integrity rights. But are all moral rights equally amputated? For example, the right of disclosure or divulgation is not comprehended within article 6*bis*; it finds a basis elsewhere in the Berne Convention. As discussed above, this right is arguably implicit in articles 10 and 10*bis*. As a result, it would appear that a TRIPS Agreement member state's failure to apply that right could give rise to a dispute settlement.

QUESTION

What accounts for the specific treatment of moral rights in the TRIPS Agreement?

DISCUSSION PROBLEM

Review the following draft statute and analyze the following problems:

State of Freedonia (English-speaking member of European Union, Berne Union and WTO):

Moral rights statute
WHEREAS the People of Freedonia, attentive to their international obligations, and solicitous of the rights of authors and of their public, desire to give full recognition to the moral rights of authors, while introducing flexibility sufficient to adapt them to society's current needs, especially in a digital age, do hereby enact the following amendment to the Freedonian Copyright Law:

Authors' Moral Rights Act
(1) For purposes of this Act, "author" means the human creator of a work of authorship. An employee who creates a work in furtherance of her employment is not an "author." A person who makes only minor contributions to a work principally created by another, or by others, is not an "author."

(2) Right of Attribution

  (a)   Authors are entitled to attribution of authorship of the works they create. The author's name must appear clearly and prominently in connection with all distributed copies of the work. Where the work is communicated by audio transmission, attribution shall be made to the extent reasonable under the circumstances.
  (b)   Authors may waive their rights to attribution. Waivers will be enforceable if they are in writing, signed by the author, and specify each use for which the attribution right is waived. Unspecified uses shall not be deemed waived.

(3) Right of Integrity

  (a)   Authors are entitled to object to the unjustified modification of their works. Unjustified modifications include alterations which are deleterious to the author's honour or reputation. Any translation of a work which has been authorized by the copyright owner, however, shall not be considered an "alteration" for purposes of this Act.

(b) Where the right has been infringed by the making available of copies or transmissions of the unjustifiably modified work, the author's remedies, in addition to those otherwise available for infringement of copyright, shall include an order to the defendant to do any or all of the following:

   (i) To incorporate a disclaimer indicating that the work has been altered without the author's consent;

   (ii) To make available an unaltered version of the work, for example by means of a hyperlink or other reference to a copy deposited by the author in the Freedonia National Archive.

(c) When the defendant's version exists only in digital form, the remedies set out in art. (3)(b)(i)(ii) shall constitute the author's exclusive relief.

QUESTIONS

Consider the following acts taken with respect to works of authorship. Do any of them violate the Freedonian Act? Insofar as any of the following acts are permissible under Freedonian law, are they nonetheless inconsistent with Berne Convention article 6bis?

1. The Freedonian Broadcasting Corporation, ever short of funds, seeks to maximize the airtime for advertisements. Its latest endeavors in this vein include, editing motion pictures to make them shorter as well as to allow for commercial breaks, and deleting the credit track at the end of the film. The Freedonian Broadcasting Corporate incorporates a disclaimer before the broadcasting of each truncated motion picture. When a copy has been deposited by the author in the Freedonia National Archive, the Freedonian Broadcasting Corporate creates a hyperlink to this copy.

2. Saygo, a videogame manufacturer, creates the bestselling game Sympleminded, known as Symp. Symp was developed for play on computers using the Windows or Mac operating systems. Johan Janssen, a Freedonian teenager, has developed a version for Linux. In this version, however, the play of the game is considerably faster than in the original versions.

3. During his lifetime, playwright Samuel Beckett consistently refused to permit the performance of Waiting for Godot by an all-female cast. The Freedonian players have produced an all female version at the National Theater. The program sold at the performances includes an article detailing the artistic and political reasons underlying the casting choice.

The article, written by a leading drama critic, contains an embarrassing number of typographical errors.

4. *The Uniform System of Citation*, the official rules of citation for Freedonian academic journals—known familiarly as the Blue Book after the color of its cover—sets out rules for authorship citations. In the cases of single authored works and of joint works created by two authors, the Blue Book instructs writers and editors to credit the full names of the author or authors, as they appear on the publications. Once a work has three or more authors, however, the Blue Book directs that only the first author's name shall appear, followed by 'et al'.

Neighboring rights treaties

WPPT

Article 5
Moral Rights of Performers

(1) Independently of a performer's economic rights, and even after the transfer of those rights, the performer shall, as regards his live aural performances or performances fixed in phonograms, have the right to claim to be identified as the performer of his performances, except where omission is dictated by the manner of the use of the performance, and to object to any distortion, mutilation or other modification of his performances that would be prejudicial to his reputation.

(2) The rights granted to a performer in accordance with paragraph (1) shall, after his death, be maintained, at least until the expiry of the economic rights, and shall be exercisable by the persons or institutions authorized by the legislation of the Contracting Party where protection is claimed. However, those Contracting Parties whose legislation, at the moment of their ratification of or accession to this Treaty, does not provide for protection after the death of the performer of all rights set out in the preceding paragraph may provide that some of these rights will, after his death, cease to be maintained.

(3) The means of redress for safeguarding the rights granted under this Article shall be governed by the legislation of the Contracting Party where protection is claimed.

Beijing Treaty

Article 5
Moral Rights

(1) Independently of a performer's economic rights, and even after the transfer of those rights, the performer shall, as regards his live performances or performances fixed in audiovisual fixations, have the right:

(i) to claim to be identified as the performer of his performances, except where omission is dictated by the manner of the use of the performance; and

(ii) to object to any distortion, mutilation or other modification of his performances that would be prejudicial to his reputation, taking due account of the nature of audiovisual fixations.

(2) The rights granted to a performer in accordance with paragraph (1) shall, after his death, be maintained, at least until the expiry of the economic rights, and shall be exercisable by the persons or institutions authorized by the legislation of the Contracting Party where protection is claimed. However, those Contracting Parties whose legislation, at the moment of their ratification of or accession to this Treaty, does not provide for protection after the death of the performer of all rights set out in the preceding paragraph may provide that some of these rights will, after his death, cease to be maintained.

(3) The means of redress for safeguarding the rights granted under this Article shall be governed by the legislation of the Contracting Party where protection is claimed.

Agreed statement concerning Article 5: For the purposes of this Treaty and without prejudice to any other treaty, it is understood that, considering the nature of audiovisual fixations and their production and distribution, modifications of a performance that are made in the normal course of exploitation of the performance, such as editing, compression, dubbing, or formatting, in existing or new media or formats, and that are made in the course of a use authorized by the performer, would not in themselves amount to modifications within the meaning of Article 5(1)(ii). Rights under Article 5(1)(ii) are concerned only with changes that are objectively prejudicial to the performer's reputation in a substantial way. It is also understood that the mere use of new or changed technology or media, as such, does not amount to modification within the meaning of Article 5(1)(ii).

QUESTIONS

1. Why do only performers benefit from moral rights?
2. Compare the WPPT and Beijing Treaty articles to Berne Convention article 6*bis*: how do they differ?

5.4.2   Economic rights

Copyright treaties

Reproduction right

Although the right to reproduce the work in copies has since the beginning of copyright (and even earlier, when sovereigns granted exclusive rights through printing privileges) been the primordial author's right, the Berne Convention did not expressly provide for the right of reproduction until the 1967 Stockholm and 1971 Paris Acts. But it was probably taken for granted that member states' domestic laws would generally provide for exclusive rights of reproduction, which Berne Union authors would have enjoyed by virtue of the rule of national treatment. Moreover, earlier versions of the Convention addressed the reproduction right indirectly, notably through provision of exceptions to it; were it not assumed that member states' laws covered the reproduction right, there would have been no call to permit or even require member states to allow for certain kinds of reproductions even without the authors' permission. Thus, article 7 of the original Berne Act created a mandatory exception for the lawful reproduction of articles from newspapers or periodicals in certain circumstances (this exception persists in art. 10(1) of the 1971 Paris Act). Older Berne texts evidence the background assumption of national reproduction rights in other ways as well: for example, article 12 of the 1886 Berne Act provided for the seizure of "pirated works" where these were imported into countries of the Union where the original work enjoyed protection (see art. 16 for the current version of this provision). In addition, as early as the 1908 Berlin revision, the Berne Convention explicitly covered reproduction of works in new media, such as mechanical reproductions of musical compositions (art. 13(1)) and reproductions of literary and artistic works by means of cinematography (art. 14(1)).

Berne Convention Article 9
Right of Reproduction

1. Generally; . . . ; 3. Sound and visual recordings

(1) Authors of literary and artistic works protected by this Convention shall have the exclusive right of authorizing the reproduction of these works, in any manner or form.

. . .

(3) Any sound or visual recording shall be considered as a reproduction for the purposes of this Convention.

WCT Agreed statement concerning Article 1(4):

The reproduction right, as set out in Article 9 of the Berne Convention, and the exceptions permitted thereunder, fully apply in the digital environment, in particular to the use of works in digital form. It is understood that the storage of a protected work in digital form in an electronic medium constitutes a reproduction within the meaning of Article 9 of the Berne Convention.

QUESTIONS

1. What does "any manner or form" in Berne Convention article 9(1) mean? Does it imply some level of permanence to the copy? Does the WCT agreed statement help resolve that question?
2. How closely must the alleged infringing reproduction hew to the original to be considered a "reproduction"?

Adaptation right

Berne Convention Article 12
Right of Adaptation, Arrangement and Other Alteration

Authors of literary or artistic works shall enjoy the exclusive right of authorizing adaptations, arrangements and other alterations of their works.

Berne Convention Article 8
Right of Translation

Authors of literary and artistic works protected by this Convention shall enjoy the exclusive right of making and of authorizing the translation of their works throughout the term of protection of their rights in the original works.

QUESTION

Compare these two articles with the treatment of translations and musical arrangements in the pre-Berne bilateral treaties and in the Austro-Sardinian treaty, articles 3 and 9. What inferences can you draw from the comparison?

Berne Convention Article 14
Cinematographic and Related Rights

(1) Authors of literary or artistic works shall have the exclusive right of authorizing:

(i) the cinematographic adaptation and reproduction of these works, and the distribution of the works thus adapted or reproduced;
(ii) the public performance and communication to the public by wire of the works thus adapted or reproduced.

(2) The adaptation into any other artistic form of a cinematographic production derived from literary or artistic works shall, without prejudice to the authorization of the author of the cinematographic production, remain subject to the authorization of the authors of the original works.

QUESTIONS

1. We have seen the operation of the "without prejudice" proviso in connection with the protectability of derivative works, see Berne Convention article 2(3). In effect, article 2(3) already implies the existence of an adaptation right: if translations, etc., were not subject to the authorization of the authors of the underlying work, there would be no need for the "without prejudice" proviso. How does the "without prejudice" proviso function in the context of article 14(2)?
2. What is the relationship between the adaption right and moral rights?

Public performance; communication to the public; making available rights

The Berne Convention and WIPO Copyright Treaty mandate protection for two kinds of public communications of works: performances *in public*, and "communication" of the work *to the public* by transmission. The first kind, covered in Berne Convention articles 11, 11*ter*, 14 and 14*bis*, concerns performances in places open to the public; the public is present at these performances and therefore apprehends them directly. The second kind, "communication to the public," provided for in the cited Berne Convention articles as well as in Berne Convention article 11*bis* and WCT art 8, reaches the members of the public through the intermediary of any manner of wired or wireless transmission.

The Berne Convention 1971 Paris Act covered public communications incompletely and imperfectly through a tangle of occasionally redundant or self-contradictory provisions on "public performance;" "communication to the public," "public communication," "broadcasting," and other forms of transmission. Worse, the scope of rights depended on the nature of the work, with musical and dramatic works receiving the broadest protection, and images the least; literary works, especially those adapted into cinematographic works, lying somewhere in between. The broadest right, with respect to subject matter, did not cover all kinds of transmissions; the broadest right, with respect to covered communications, did not extend to all types of works.

The 1996 WIPO Copyright Treaty rationalized and synthesized protection by establishing full coverage of the communication to the public right for all protected works of authorship. The WCT also introduced a new designation, the "right of making available to the public." This right corresponds to individualized communication of works over the Internet, whose users "access these works from a place and at a time individually chosen by them" (WCT art. 8). Significantly, the WCT resolved an important ambiguity regarding the scope of the Berne Convention right of communication to the public by wired or wireless transmissions. Under the Berne Convention, it was not clear whether the "public" to which the work is communicated must receive the work at the same time. While it is implicit in Berne's broadcasting and retransmissions rights that the members of the receiving public may be separated in *space*, the Berne Convention does not specify whether they may also be separated in *time*. Put another way, the question is: At whose impetus, the sender's or the recipient's, must the transmission occur?

Both articles 11 and 11*bis* address traditional "push" technologies: broadcast or wired transmissions from an originating (or retransmitting) entity to a passively receiving public. The transmitting entity selected the content and the timing of the communication; the public's choice was limited to selecting among pre-programmed communications, it did not extend to making up the programming to be received. While "broadcasting" may imply widely sending a communication simultaneously to many potential recipients, the more open-ended language in article 11*bis* covering "any other means of wireless diffusion of signs, sounds or images," as well as the broader concept of "communication to the public" in article 11, could indeed cover "pull technologies." Although those technologies may not have been contemplated in 1948, when the "any communication to the public right" was first introduced into article 11, and when the "any other means" language first appeared in article 11*bis*, nothing in the text of these articles prohibits their application to on-demand transmissions. On the other hand, given the historical context, it may be bold to assert that these articles *oblige* Member States to classify on-demand transmissions as communications to the public. Hence, the gap-filling role of WCT article 8.

i. Berne Convention

Article 11
Certain Rights in Dramatic and Musical Works

1. Right of public performance and of communication to the public of a performance; 2. In respect of translations

(1) Authors of dramatic, dramatico-musical and musical works shall enjoy the exclusive right of authorizing:

> (i) the public performance of their works, including such public performance by any means or process;
> (ii) any communication to the public of the performance of their works.

(2) Authors of dramatic or dramatico-musical works shall enjoy, during the full term of their rights in the original works, the same rights with respect to translations thereof.

Article 11*bis*
Broadcasting and Related Rights

1. Broadcasting and other wireless communications, public communi-
cation of broadcast by wire or rebroadcast, public communication of
broadcast by loudspeaker or analogous instruments;. . .

(1) Authors of literary and artistic works shall enjoy the exclusive right
of authorizing:

(i) the broadcasting of their works or the communication thereof to
the public by any other means of wireless diffusion of signs, sounds or
images;
(ii) any communication to the public by wire or by rebroadcasting of
the broadcast of the work, when this communication is made by an
organization other than the original one;
(iii) the public communication by loudspeaker or any other analogous
instrument transmitting, by signs, sounds or images, the broadcast of
the work.

. . .

Article 11*ter*
Certain Rights in Literary Works

1. Right of public recitation and of communication to the public of a
recitation; 2. In respect of translations

(1) Authors of literary works shall enjoy the exclusive right of
authorizing:

(i) the public recitation of their works, including such public recitation
by any means or process;
(ii) any communication to the public of the recitation of their
works.

(2) Authors of literary works shall enjoy, during the full term of their
rights in the original works, the same rights with respect to translations
thereof.

Article 14
Cinematographic and Related Rights

1. Cinematographic adaptation and reproduction; distribution; public performance and public communication by wire of works thus adapted or reproduced;...

(1) Authors of literary or artistic works shall have the exclusive right of authorizing:

(i) the cinematographic adaptation and reproduction of these works, and the distribution of the works thus adapted or reproduced;
(ii) the public performance and communication to the public by wire of the works thus adapted or reproduced.

...

Article 14*bis*
Special Provisions Concerning Cinematographic Works:

1. Assimilation to "original" works;...

(1) Without prejudice to the copyright in any work which may have been adapted or reproduced, a cinematographic work shall be protected as an original work. The owner of copyright in a cinematographic work shall enjoy the same rights as the author of an original work, including the rights referred to in the preceding Article.

...

ii. **WIPO Copyright Treaty**

Article 8
Right of Communication to the Public

Without prejudice to the provisions of Articles 11(1)(ii), 11*bis*(1)(i) and (ii), 11*ter*(1)(ii), 14(1)(ii) and 14*bis*(1) of the Berne Convention, authors of literary and artistic works shall enjoy the exclusive right of authorizing any communication to the public of their works, by wire or wireless means, including the making available to the public of their works in such a way that members of the public may access these works from a place and at a time individually chosen by them.

Agreed statements concerning Article 8: It is understood that the mere provision of physical facilities for enabling or making a communication does not in itself amount to communication within the meaning of this Treaty or the Berne Convention. . . .

QUESTIONS

1. For the "communication to the public" right to be triggered, must the person engaging in the communication in fact have transmitted the work to the public, or does an offer to transmit suffice to trigger the right? Is the "making available" right infringed by an offer to make works available, or must the work in fact have been communicated to a member of the public on demand? What difference does it make?

2. Jean Lafitte operates a website, music4free.com, that aggregates links to other websites from which users can download or stream unauthorized copies of recorded music. Some links are identified by the name of the music file; clicking on these links takes the user directly to another website and automatically downloads the named file from that website to the user's hard drive. Other links are identified by the names of the other websites; clicking on these sends the user to the website, from which she may elect to download or stream a variety of files. Does Jean's website violate any provisions of the Berne Convention? Of WCT article 8? (See the CJEU's decision in *Svensson*, infra this chapter.)

iii. National implementation of WCT article 8

WCT article 8 is expressed in technologically neutral terms; the technological means of "making available" were intended to be irrelevant. The records of the 1996 diplomatic conference indicate that member states may comply with the right either through local communication to the public rights, or, for those countries who have applied the distribution right to temporary digital copies, through the right to distribute copies, as the U.S. urged during the drafting period. (1996 Records at 675, paragraph 301.) In adopting what came to be known as the "umbrella solution,"* allowing member states to implement the making available right through any domestic law exclusive right, the drafters opted for an approach of juridical as well as technological neutrality. As you review the U.S. public performance right in this section and distribution right in the following section and the E.U. authorities in

---

* For extensive discussion of the "umbrella solution," by the coiner of the term, see; Mihaly Ficsor, The Law of Copyright and the Internet (Oxford 2002) at 204–9, 496–509.

both sections, consider whether their approaches fully implement their international obligations.

a. U.S. Copyright Law

§ 106. Exclusive rights in copyrighted works

Subject to sections 107 through 122, the owner of copyright under this title has the exclusive rights to do and to authorize any of the following:

. . .

(4) in the case of literary, musical, dramatic, and choreographic works, pantomimes, and motion pictures and other audiovisual works, to perform the copyrighted work publicly;

(5) in the case of literary, musical, dramatic, and choreographic works, pantomimes, and pictorial, graphic, or sculptural works, including the individual images of a motion picture or other audiovisual work, to display the copyrighted work publicly; and

(6) in the case of sound recordings, to perform the copyrighted work publicly by means of a digital audio transmission.

§ 101. Definitions

To "perform" a work means to recite, render, play, dance, or act it, either directly or by means of any device or process or, in the case of a motion picture or other audiovisual work, to show its images in any sequence or to make the sounds accompanying it audible.

To perform or display a work "publicly" means—

(1) to perform or display it at a place open to the public or at any place where a substantial number of persons outside of a normal circle of a family and its social acquaintances is gathered; or
(2) to transmit or otherwise communicate a performance or display of the work to a place specified by clause (1) or to the public, by means of any device or process, whether the members of the public capable of receiving the performance or display receive it in the same place or in separate places and at the same time or at different times.

To "transmit" a performance or display is to communicate it by any device or process whereby images or sounds are received beyond the place from which they are sent.

QUESTION

Is there a difference between "public performance" in U.S. law, and "communication to the public" within the meaning of the Berne Convention or WCT? Between "public performance" and "making available to the public"?

The meaning of "to perform"

U.S. v. American Society of Composers, Authors and Publishers (Applications of RealNetworks et al.), 627 F.3d 64 (2d Cir. 2010)

[This case involved a dispute between ASCAP, a collective that licenses public performance rights in musical works and Yahoo! and RealNetworks (the "Internet Companies") over the rate to be paid to license the right to perform music on Yahoo!'s and RealNetworks' online services. The parties disagreed, among other things, about whether song downloads from the Internet Companies' sites constituted performances for which an ASCAP license was needed.]

In answering the question of whether a download is a public performance, we turn to Section 101 of the Copyright Act, which states that "[t]o 'perform' a work means to recite, render, play, dance, or act it, either directly or by means of any device or process." A download plainly is neither a "dance" nor an "act." Thus, we must determine whether a download of a musical work falls within the meaning of the terms "recite," "render," or "play."

. . .

The ordinary sense of the words "recite," "render," and "play" refer to actions that can be perceived contemporaneously. To "recite" is "to repeat from memory or read aloud esp[ecially] before an audience," Webster's Third New International Dictionary 1895 (1981); to "render" is to "say over: recite, repeat," id. at 1922; and to "play" is to "perform on a musical instrument," "sound in performance," "reproduce sound of recorded material," or "act on a stage or in some other dramatic medium," id. at 1737. All three actions entail contemporaneous perceptibility.

. . . Music is neither recited, rendered, nor played when a recording (electronic or otherwise) is simply delivered to a potential listener.

The final clause of the § 101 definition of "to perform" further confirms our interpretation. It states that "[t]o 'perform' . . . a motion picture or other audiovisual work . . . [is] to show its images in any sequence or to make the sounds accompanying it audible." The fact that the statute defines performance in the audio-visual context as "show[ing]" the work or making it "audible" reinforces the conclusion that "to perform" a musical work entails contemporaneous perceptibility. ASCAP has provided no reason, and we can surmise none, why the statute would require a contemporaneously perceptible event in the context of an audio-visual work, but not in the context of a musical work.

The downloads at issue in this appeal are not musical performances that are contemporaneously perceived by the listener. They are simply transfers of electronic files containing digital copies from an on-line server to a local hard drive. The downloaded songs are not performed in any perceptible manner during the transfers; the user must take some further action to play the songs after they are downloaded. Because the electronic download itself involves no recitation, rendering, or playing of the musical work encoded in the digital transmission, we hold that such a download is not a performance of that work, as defined by § 101.

. . .

The Internet Companies' [streaming] transmissions, which all parties agree constitute public performances, illustrate why a download is not a public performance. A stream is an electronic transmission that renders the musical work audible as it is received by the client-computer's temporary memory. This transmission, like a television or radio broadcast, is a performance because there is a playing of the song that is perceived simultaneously with the transmission. [citation omitted] In contrast, downloads do not immediately produce sound; only after a file has been downloaded on a user's hard drive can he perceive a performance by playing the downloaded song. Unlike musical works played during radio broadcasts and stream transmissions, downloaded musical works are transmitted at one point in time and performed at another. Transmittal without a performance does not constitute a "public performance." . . .

Accordingly, we affirm the district court's grant of partial summary judgment on the basis that downloads do not constitute public performances of the downloaded musical works.

QUESTION

Does the court's interpretation of "to perform" place the U.S. in non-compliance with its obligations under the WCT? Does it matter?

American Broadcasting Cos., Inc. v. Aereo, Inc., 134 S. Ct. 2498, — U.S. — (2014)

[In 2012, a New York City company called Aereo began a service that allowed subscribers, for a monthly fee, to access live (or recorded) broadcast television via a Web browser from the subscriber's Internet-connected mobile device. The service worked by allowing a subscriber to connect to a very small antenna, located at Aereo's data center, that received broadcast television signals; no two subscribers were simultaneously connected to the same antenna. As a result, the same program could be received by multiple subscribers, but each transmission of the program was individualized, via the multiple personal antennae. Aereo claimed that it was not "performing" the television programming, but was merely providing equipment that enabled its subscribers to perform. A majority of the Supreme Court, 6–3, disagreed.]

▪ Justice Breyer delivered the opinion of the Court.

. . .

Does Aereo "perform"? See §106(4) ("[T]he owner of [a] copyright . . . has the exclusive righ[t] . . . to *perform* the copyrighted work publicly" (emphasis added)); §101 ("To *perform* . . . a work 'publicly' means [among other things] to transmit . . . a performance . . . of the work . . . to the public . . . " (emphasis added)). Phrased another way, does Aereo "transmit . . . a performance" when a subscriber watches a show using Aereo's system, or is it only the subscriber who transmits? In Aereo's view, it does not perform. It does no more than supply equipment that "emulate[s] the operation of a home antenna and [digital video recorder (DVR)]." Brief for Respondent 41. Like a home antenna and DVR, Aereo's equipment simply responds to its subscribers' directives. So it is only the subscribers who "perform" when they use Aereo's equipment to stream television programs to themselves.

Considered alone, the language of the Act does not clearly indicate when an entity "perform[s]" (or "transmit[s]") and when it merely supplies equipment that allows others to do so. But when read in light of its purpose, the Act is unmistakable: An entity that engages in activities like Aereo's performs.

[The court reviewed prior decisions in which it had held that cable television services were not "performing" the programming they retransmitted, and Congress' amendment of the Copyright Act in 1976 to clarify that the public performance right encompassed cable retransmissions.]

C.

This history makes clear that Aereo is not simply an equipment provider. Rather, Aereo, and not just its subscribers, "perform[s]" (or "transmit[s]"). Aereo's activities are substantially similar to those of the CATV companies that Congress amended the Act to reach. [citation omitted.] Aereo sells a service that allows subscribers to watch television programs, many of which are copyrighted, almost as they are being broadcast. In providing this service, Aereo uses its own equipment, housed in a centralized warehouse, outside of its users' homes. By means of its technology (antennas, transcoders, and servers), Aereo's system "receive[s] programs that have been released to the public and carr[ies] them by private channels to additional viewers." *Fortnightly*, 392 U. S., at 400. It "carr[ies] . . . whatever programs [it] receive[s]," and it offers "all the programming" of each over-the-air station it carries. *Id.*, at 392, 400.

Aereo's equipment may serve a "viewer function"; it may enhance the viewer's ability to receive a broadcaster's programs. It may even emulate equipment a viewer could use at home. But the same was true of the equipment that was before the Court, and ultimately before Congress, in *Fortnightly* and *Teleprompter.*

We recognize, and Aereo and the dissent emphasize, one particular difference between Aereo's system and the cable systems at issue in *Fortnightly* and *Teleprompter*. The systems in those cases transmitted constantly; they sent continuous programming to each subscriber's television set. In contrast, Aereo's system remains inert until a subscriber indicates that she wants to watch a program. Only at that moment, in automatic response to the subscriber's request, does Aereo's system activate an antenna and begin to transmit the requested program.

This is a critical difference, says the dissent. It means that Aereo's subscribers, not Aereo, "selec[t] the copyrighted content" that is "perform[ed]," (opinion of SCALIA, J.), and for that reason they, not Aereo, "transmit" the performance. Aereo is thus like "a copy shop that provides its patrons with a library card." A copy shop is not directly liable whenever a patron uses the shop's machines to "reproduce" copyrighted materials found in that library. . . . And by the same token, Aereo should not be directly liable whenever its patrons use its equipment to "transmit" copyrighted television programs to their screens.

In our view, however, the dissent's copy shop argument, in whatever form, makes too much out of too little. Given Aereo's overwhelming likeness to the cable companies targeted by the 1976 amendments, this sole technological difference between Aereo and traditional cable companies does not make a critical difference here. The subscribers of the *Fortnightly* and *Teleprompter* cable systems also selected what programs to display on their receiving sets. Indeed, as we explained in *Fortnightly*, such a subscriber "could choose any of the . . . programs he wished to view by simply turning the knob on his own television set." 392 U. S., at 392. The same is true of an Aereo subscriber. Of course, in *Fortnightly* the television signals, in a sense, lurked behind the screen, ready to emerge when the subscriber turned the knob. Here the signals pursue their ordinary course of travel through the universe until today's "turn of the knob"—a click on a website—activates machinery that intercepts and reroutes them to Aereo's subscribers over the Internet. But this difference means nothing to the subscriber. It means nothing to the broadcaster. We do not see how this single difference, invisible to subscriber and broadcaster alike, could transform a system that is for all practical purposes a traditional cable system into "a copy shop that provides its patrons with a library card."

In other cases involving different kinds of service or technology providers, a user's involvement in the operation of the provider's equipment and selection of the content transmitted may well bear on whether the provider performs within the meaning of the Act. But the many similarities between Aereo and cable companies, considered in light of Congress' basic purposes in amending the Copyright Act, convince us that this difference is not critical here. We conclude that Aereo is not just an equipment supplier and that Aereo "perform[s]."

. . .

▪ Justice Scalia, with whom Justice Thomas and Justice Alito join, dissenting.

. . .

The Networks claim that Aereo *directly* infringes their public-performance right. Accordingly, the Networks must prove that Aereo "perform[s]" copyrighted works, §106(4), when its subscribers log in, select a channel, and push the "watch" button. That process undoubtedly results in a performance;

the question is *who* does the performing. See *Cartoon Network LP, LLLP* v. *CSC Holdings, Inc.*, 536 F. 3d 121, 130 (CA2 2008). If Aereo's subscribers perform but Aereo does not, the claim necessarily fails.

The Networks' claim is governed by a simple but profoundly important rule: A defendant may be held directly liable only if it has engaged in volitional conduct that violates the Act [citation omitted]. This requirement is firmly grounded in the Act's text, which defines "perform" in active, affirmative terms: One "perform[s]" a copyrighted "audiovisual work," such as a movie or news broadcast, by "show[ing]" its images in any sequence" or "mak[ing] the sounds accompanying it audible." §101. And since the Act makes it unlawful to copy or perform copyrighted works, not to copy or perform in general, see §501(a), the volitional-act requirement demands conduct directed to the plaintiff 's copyrighted material [citation omitted]. Every Court of Appeals to have considered an automated-service provider's direct liability for copyright infringement has adopted that rule [citations omitted]. Although we have not opined on the issue, our cases are fully consistent with a volitional-conduct requirement. . . .

. . .

A comparison between copy shops and video-on-demand services illustrates the point. A copy shop rents out photocopiers on a per-use basis. One customer might copy his 10-year-old's drawings—a perfectly lawful thing to do—while another might duplicate a famous artist's copyrighted photographs—a use clearly prohibited by §106(1). Either way, *the customer* chooses the content and activates the copying function; the photocopier does nothing except in response to the customer's commands. Because the shop plays no role in selecting the content, it cannot be held directly liable when a customer makes an infringing copy [citation omitted].

Video-on-demand services, like photocopiers, respond automatically to user input, but they differ in one crucial respect: *They choose the content.* When a user signs in to Netflix, for example, "thousands of . . . movies [and] TV episodes" carefully curated by Netflix are "available to watch instantly" [citation omitted]. That selection and arrangement by the service provider constitutes a volitional act directed to specific copyrighted works and thus serves as a basis for direct liability.

The distinction between direct and secondary liability would collapse if there were not a clear rule for determining whether *the defendant* committed the infringing act [citation omitted]. The volitional-conduct requirement supplies that rule; its purpose is not to excuse defendants from account-ability, but to channel the claims against them into the correct analytical track [citation omitted]. Thus, in the example given above, the fact that the copy shop does not choose the content simply means that its culpability will be assessed using secondary-liability rules rather than direct-liability rules [citations omitted].

II. Application to Aereo

So which is Aereo: the copy shop or the video-on-demand service? In truth, it is neither. Rather, it is akin to a copy shop that provides its patrons with a library card. Aereo offers access to an automated system consisting of routers, servers, transcoders, and dime-sized antennae. Like a photocopier or VCR, that system lies dormant until a subscriber activates it. When a subscriber selects a program, Aereo's system picks up the relevant broadcast signal, translates its audio and video components into digital data, stores the data in a user-specific file, and transmits that file's contents to the subscriber via the Internet—at which point the subscriber's laptop, tablet, or other device displays the broadcast just as an ordinary television would. The result of that process fits the statutory definition of a performance to a tee: The sub-scriber's device "show[s]" the broadcast's "images" and "make[s] the sounds accompanying" the broadcast "audible." §101. The only question is whether those performances are the product of Aereo's volitional conduct.

They are not. Unlike video-on-demand services, Aereo does not provide a prearranged assortment of movies and television shows. Rather, it assigns each subscriber an antenna that—like a library card—can be used to obtain whatever broadcasts are freely available. Some of those broadcasts are copy-righted; others are in the public domain. The key point is that subscrib-ers call all the shots: Aereo's automated system does not relay any program, copyrighted or not, until a subscriber selects the program and tells Aereo to relay it. Aereo's operation of that system is a volitional act and a but-for cause of the resulting performances, but, as in the case of the copy shop, that degree of involvement is not enough for direct liability. . . .

QUESTION

What are the implications of the majority and dissenting views of "to perform" for U.S. consistency with the making available right? Is the dissent's "volition" approach incompatible with the making available right's basing of direct liability on the offering of access to copyrighted works?

What makes a performance "public"?

WNET v. Aereo, Inc., — U.S. —, 134 S. Ct. 2498 (2014)

▪ Justice Breyer delivered the opinion of the Court.

. . .

III

Next, we must consider whether Aereo performs petitioners' works "publicly," within the meaning of the Transmit Clause. Under the Clause, an entity performs a work publicly when it "transmit[s] . . . a performance . . . of the work . . . to the public." §101. Aereo denies that it satisfies this definition. It reasons as follows: First, the "performance" it "transmit[s]" is the performance created by its act of transmitting. And second, because each of these performances is capable of being received by one and only one subscriber, Aereo transmits privately, not publicly. Even assuming Aereo's first argument is correct, its second does not follow.

We begin with Aereo's first argument. What performance does Aereo transmit? Under the Act, "[t]o 'transmit' a performance . . . is to communicate it by any device or process whereby images or sounds are received beyond the place from which they are sent." *Ibid.* And "[t]o 'perform'" an audiovisual work means "to show its images in any sequence or to make the sounds accompanying it audible." *Ibid.*

Petitioners say Aereo transmits a *prior* performance of their works. Thus when Aereo retransmits a network's prior broadcast, the underlying broadcast (itself a performance) is the performance that Aereo transmits. Aereo, as discussed above, says the performance it transmits is the *new* performance created by its act of transmitting. That performance comes into existence when Aereo streams the sounds and images of a broadcast program to a subscriber's screen.

. . . As we have said, an Aereo subscriber receives broadcast television signals with an antenna dedicated to him alone. Aereo's system makes from those signals a personal copy of the selected program. It streams the content of the copy to the same subscriber and to no one else. One and only one subscriber has the ability to see and hear each Aereo transmission. The fact that each transmission is to only one subscriber, in Aereo's view, means that it does not transmit a performance "to the public."

In terms of the Act's purposes, these differences do not distinguish Aereo's system from cable systems, which do perform "publicly." Viewed in terms of Congress' regulatory objectives, why should any of these technological differences matter? They concern the behind-the-scenes way in which Aereo delivers television programming to its viewers' screens. They do not render Aereo's commercial objective any different from that of cable companies. Nor do they significantly alter the viewing experience of Aereo's subscribers. Why would a subscriber who wishes to watch a television show care much whether images and sounds are delivered to his screen via a large multisubscriber antenna or one small dedicated antenna, whether they arrive instantaneously or after a few seconds' delay, or whether they are transmitted directly or after a personal copy is made? And why, if Aereo is right, could not modern CATV systems simply continue the same commercial and consumer-oriented activities, free of copyright restrictions, provided they substitute such new technologies for old? Congress would as much have intended to protect a copyright holder from the unlicensed activities of Aereo as from those of cable companies.

The text of the Clause effectuates Congress' intent. Aereo's argument to the contrary relies on the premise that "to transmit . . . a performance" means to make a single transmission. But the Clause suggests that an entity may transmit a performance through multiple, discrete transmissions. That is because one can "transmit" or "communicate" something through a *set* of actions. Thus one can transmit a message to one's friends, irrespective of whether one sends separate identical e-mails to each friend or a single e-mail to all at once. So can an elected official communicate an idea, slogan, or speech to her constituents, regardless of whether she communicates that idea, slogan, or speech during individual phone calls to each constituent or in a public square.

. . . An entity may transmit a performance through one or several transmissions, where the performance is of the same work.

The Transmit Clause must permit this interpretation, for it provides that one may transmit a performance to the public "whether the members of the public capable of receiving the performance . . . receive it . . . at the same time or at different times." §101. Were the words "to transmit . . . a performance" limited to a single act of communication, members of the public could not receive the performance communicated "at different times." Therefore, in light of the purpose and text of the Clause, we conclude that when an entity communicates the same contemporaneously perceptible images and sounds to multiple people, it transmits a performance to them regardless of the number of discrete communications it makes.

We do not see how the fact that Aereo transmits via personal copies of programs could make a difference. The Act applies to transmissions "by means of any device or process." *Ibid.* And retransmitting a television program using user-specific copies is a "process" of transmitting a performance. A "cop[y]" of a work is simply a "material objec[t] . . . in which a work is fixed . . . and from which the work can be perceived, reproduced, or otherwise communicated." *Ibid.* So whether Aereo transmits from the same or separate copies, it performs the same work; it shows the same images and makes audible the same sounds. Therefore, when Aereo streams the same television program to multiple subscribers, it "transmit[s] . . . a performance" to all of them.

Moreover, the subscribers to whom Aereo transmits television programs constitute "the public." Aereo communicates the same contemporaneously perceptible images and sounds to a large number of people who are unrelated and unknown to each other. This matters because, although the Act does not define "the public," it specifies that an entity performs publicly when it performs at "any place where a substantial number of persons outside of a normal circle of a family and its social acquaintances is gathered." *Ibid.* The Act thereby suggests that "the public" consists of a large group of people outside of a family and friends.

Neither the record nor Aereo suggests that Aereo's subscribers receive performances in their capacities as owners or possessors of the underlying works. This is relevant because when an entity performs to a set of people, whether they constitute "the public" often depends upon their relationship to the underlying work. When, for example, a valet parking attendant returns cars to their drivers, we would not say that the parking service provides cars "to the public." We would say that it provides the cars to their owners. We would say that a car dealership, on the other hand, does provide cars to the public, for it sells cars to individuals who lack a pre-existing relationship to the cars. Similarly, an entity that transmits a performance to individuals in their capacities as owners or possessors does not perform to "the public," whereas an entity like Aereo that transmits to large numbers of paying subscribers who lack any prior relationship to the works does so perform.

Finally, we note that Aereo's subscribers may receive the same programs at different times and locations. This fact does not help Aereo, however, for the Transmit Clause expressly provides that an entity may perform publicly "whether the members of the public capable of receiving the performance . . . receive it in the same place or in separate places and at the same time or at different times." *Ibid.* In other words, "the public" need not be situated together, spatially or temporally. For these reasons, we conclude that Aereo transmits a performance of petitioners' copyrighted works to the public, within the meaning of the Transmit Clause.

IV

Aereo and many of its supporting *amici* argue that to apply the Transmit Clause to Aereo's conduct will impose copyright liability on other technologies, including new technologies, that Congress could not possibly have wanted to reach. We agree that Congress, while intending the Transmit Clause to apply broadly to cable companies and their equivalents, did not intend to discourage or to control the emergence or use of different kinds of technologies. But we do not believe that our limited holding today will have that effect.

For one thing, the history of cable broadcast transmissions that led to the enactment of the Transmit Clause informs our conclusion that Aereo "perform[s]," but it does not determine whether different kinds of providers in different contexts also "perform." For another, an entity only transmits a performance when it communicates contemporaneously perceptible images and sounds of a work. See Brief for Respondent 31 ("[I]f a distributor . . .sells [multiple copies of a digital video disc] by mail to consumers, . . . [its] distribution of the DVDs merely makes it possible for the recipients to perform the work themselves—it is not a 'device or process' by which the *distributor* publicly performs the work" (emphasis in original)).

Further, we have interpreted the term "the public" to apply to a group of individuals acting as ordinary members of the public who pay primarily to watch broadcast television programs, many of which are copyrighted. We have said that it does not extend to those who act as owners or possessors of the relevant product. And we have not considered whether the public performance right is infringed when the user of a service pays primarily for something other than the transmission of copyrighted works, such as the remote storage of content. See Brief for United States as *Amicus Curiae* 31 (distinguishing cloud based storage services because they "offer consumers more numerous and convenient means of playing back copies that the consumers have *already* lawfully acquired" (emphasis in original)). In addition, an entity does not transmit to the public if it does not transmit to a substantial number of people outside of a family and its social circle.

. . .

We cannot now answer more precisely how the Transmit Clause or other provisions of the Copyright Act will apply to technologies not before us. We agree with the Solicitor General that "[q]uestions involving cloud computing, [remote storage] DVRs, and other novel issues not before the Court, as to which 'Congress has not plainly marked [the] course,' should await a case in which they are squarely presented." Brief for United States as *Amicus Curiae* 34. . . . And we note that, to the extent commercial actors or other interested entities may be concerned with the relationship between the development and use of such technologies and the Copyright Act, they are of course free to seek action from Congress. . . .

QUESTIONS

1. Is the court's interpretation of "to perform publicly" consistent with the WCT making available right? Does the court require that the entity engaging in a public performance have in fact made a transmission, or does offering a transmission suffice?
2. Who is "the public" to which a public performance is transmitted? Do the international conventions provide any guidance?
3. What does the court mean by its distinction of "subscribers [who] receive performances in their capacities as owners or possessors of the underlying works."? Is this distinction relevant to the making available right?

b. E.U. Directives

Editors' note: Article 3 of the Info Soc Directive implements the right of making available by adopting verbatim the text of article 8 of the WCT. In interpreting article 3 of the Info Soc Directive, the Court takes into account the Berne Convention and the WCT. Moreover, as the following excerpts show, the Court in *SGAE* evokes a "new public"—a criterion drawn not from the text of a treaty but from a WIPO Guide. Subsequent ECJ caselaw has augmented the "new public" from a consideration to a condition, albeit with certain exceptions. In reviewing the caselaw, query whether a "new public" condition is consistent with the international norms that underpin the directive.

> **Directive 2001/29/EC of the European Parliament and of the Council of 22 May 2001 on the harmonisation of certain aspects of copyright and related rights in the information society**
>
> **Recitals**
> (23) This Directive should harmonise further the author's right of communication to the public. This right should be understood in a broad sense covering all communication to the public not present at the place

where the communication originates. This right should cover any such transmission or retransmission of a work to the public by wire or wireless means, including broadcasting. This right should not cover any other acts.

Article 3 – Right of communication to the public of works and right of making available to the public other subject-matter

1. Member States shall provide authors with the exclusive right to author-ise or prohibit any communication to the public of their works, by wire or wireless means, including the making available to the public of their works in such a way that members of the public may access them from a place and at a time individually chosen by them.

C-306/05 Sociedad General de Autores y Editores de España (SGAE) v. Rafael Hoteles SA ECLI:EU:C:2006:764 [2006]

32   By its first and third questions, which it is appropriate to examine together, the referring court asks, essentially, whether the distribution of a signal through television sets to customers in hotel rooms constitutes com-munication to the public within the meaning of Article 3(1) of Directive 2001/29 [Info Soc], and whether the installation of television sets in hotel rooms constitutes, in itself, an act of that nature.

33   In that respect, it should be noted that that Directive does not define "communication to the public".

. . .

37   The Court has held that, in the context of this concept, the term "public" refers to an indeterminate number of potential television viewers [citations omitted].

38   In a context such as that in the main proceedings, a general approach is required, making it necessary to take into account not only customers in hotel rooms, such customers alone being explicitly mentioned in the ques-tions referred for a preliminary ruling, but also customers who are present in any other area of the hotel and able to make use of a television set installed there. It is also necessary to take into account the fact that, usually, hotel cus-tomers quickly succeed each other. As a general rule, a fairly large number of persons are involved, so that they may be considered to be a public, having regard to the principal objective of Directive 2001/29 [Info Soc], as referred to in paragraph 36 of this judgment.

39   In view, moreover, of the cumulative effects of making the works available to such potential television viewers, the latter act could become very significant in such a context. It matters little, accordingly, that the only recipients are the occupants of rooms and that, taken separately, they are of limited economic interest for the hotel.

40   It should also be pointed out that a communication made in circumstances such as those in the main proceedings constitutes, according to Article 11bis(1)(ii) of the Berne Convention, a communication made by a broadcasting organisation other than the original one. Thus, such a transmission is made to a public different from the public at which the original act of communication of the work is directed, that is, to a new public.

41   As is explained in the Guide to the Berne Convention, an interpretative document drawn up by the WIPO which, without being legally binding, nevertheless assists in interpreting that Convention, when the author authorises the broadcast of his work, he considers only direct users, that is, the owners of reception equipment who, either personally or within their own private or family circles, receive the programme. According to the Guide, if reception is for a larger audience, possibly for profit, a new section of the receiving public hears or sees the work and the communication of the programme via a loudspeaker or analogous instrument no longer constitutes simple reception of the programme itself but is an independent act through which the broadcast work is communicated to a new public. As the Guide makes clear, such public reception falls within the scope of the author's exclusive authorisation right.

42   The clientele of a hotel forms such a new public. The transmission of the broadcast work to that clientele using television sets is not just a technical means to ensure or improve reception of the original broadcast in the catchment area. On the contrary, the hotel is the organisation which intervenes, in full knowledge of the consequences of its action, to give access to the protected work to its customers. In the absence of that intervention, its customers, although physically within that area, would not, in principle, be able to enjoy the broadcast work.

43   It follows from Article 3(1) of Directive 2001/29 [Info Soc] and Article 8 of the WIPO Copyright Treaty that for there to be communication to the public it is sufficient that the work is made available to the public in such a way that the persons forming that public may access it. Therefore, it is not decisive, contrary to the submissions of Rafael and Ireland, that customers who have not switched on the television have not actually had access to the works.

44   Moreover, it is apparent from the documents submitted to the Court that the action by the hotel by which it gives access to the broadcast work to its customers must be considered an additional service performed with the aim of obtaining some benefit. It cannot be seriously disputed that the provision of that service has an influence on the hotel's standing and, therefore, on the price of rooms. Therefore, even taking the view, as does the Commission of the European Communities, that the pursuit of profit is not a necessary condition for the existence of a communication to the public, it is in any event established that the communication is of a profit-making nature in circumstances such as those in the main proceedings.

45   With reference to the question whether the installation of television sets in hotel rooms constitutes, in itself, a communication to the public within the meaning of Article 3(1) of Directive 2001/29 [Info Soc], it should be pointed out that the 27th recital in the preamble to that directive states, in accordance with Article 8 of the WIPO Copyright Treaty, that "[t]he mere provision of physical facilities for enabling or making a communication does not in itself amount to communication within the meaning of [that] Directive."

46   While the mere provision of physical facilities, usually involving, besides the hotel, companies specialising in the sale or hire of television sets, does not constitute, as such, a communication within the meaning of Directive 2001/29 [Info Soc], the installation of such facilities may nevertheless make public access to broadcast works technically possible. Therefore, if, by means of television sets thus installed, the hotel distributes the signal to customers staying in its rooms, then communication to the public takes place, irrespective of the technique used to transmit the signal.

47   Consequently, the answer to the first and second questions is that, while the mere provision of physical facilities does not as such amount to a communication within the meaning of Directive 2001/29 [Info Soc], the distribution of a signal by means of television sets by a hotel to customers staying in its rooms, whatever technique is used to transmit the signal, constitutes communication to the public within the meaning of Article 3(1) of that directive.

QUESTIONS

1. How is the public that watches television programming from television sets in hotel guest rooms different from the public to which the broadcasters communicate the programming? Does the Berne Convention require that retransmissions of broadcast content be communicated to a new public?
2. What role did the WIPO Guide play in the court's decision?

C-403/08 and C-429/08 Joined Cases Football Association Premier League Ltd. and Others v. QC Leisure and Others and Karen Murphy v. Media Protection Services Ltd ECLI:EU:C:2011:631 and ECLI:EU:C:2011:43 [2010]

183 By its question, the referring court asks, in essence, whether "communication to the public" within the meaning of Article 3(1) of the Copyright Directive must be interpreted as covering transmission of the broadcast works, via a television screen and speakers, to the customers present in a public house.

. . .

200 In addition, in order for there to be communication to the public, the work broadcast must be transmitted to a "public not present at the place where the communication originates", within the meaning of recital 23 in the preamble to the Copyright Directive [Info Soc].

201 In this regard, it is apparent from Common Position No 48/2000* that this recital follows from the proposal of the European Parliament, which wished to specify, in the recital, that communication to the public within the meaning of that directive does not cover "direct representation or performance", a concept referring to that of "public performance" which appears in Article 11(1) of the Berne Convention and encompasses interpretation of the works before the public that is in direct physical contact with the actor or performer of those works (see the Guide to the Berne Convention, an interpretative document drawn up by WIPO which, without being binding, nevertheless assists in interpreting that convention, as the Court observed in *SGAE*, paragraph 41).

202 Thus, in order to exclude such direct public representation and performance from the scope of the concept of communication to the public in the context of the Copyright Directive [Info Soc], recital 23 in its preamble

---

* Editors' note:
Common Position (EC) No 48/2000 of 28 September 2000 adopted by the Council, acting in accordance with the procedure referred to in Article 251 of the Treaty establishing the European Community, with a view to adopting a Directive of the European Parliament and of the Council on the harmonisation of certain aspects of copyright and related rights in the information society
Recitals
(23) This Directive should harmonise further the author's right of communication to the public. This right should be understood in a broad sense covering all communication to the public not present at the place where the communication originates. This right should cover any such transmission or retransmission of a work to the public by wire or wireless means, including broadcasting. This right should not cover any other acts.
(24) The right to make available to the public subject-matter referred to in Article 3(2) should be understood as covering all acts of making available such subject-matter to members of the public not present at the place where the act of making available originates, and as not covering any other acts

explained that communication to the public covers all communication to the public not present at the place where the communication originates.

QUESTION

To what extent does the ECJ's decision enhance the understanding of article 11(1) of the Berne Convention?

C-607/11 ITV Broadcasting Ltd. and Others v. TVCatchup Ltd. ECLI:EU:C:2013:147 [2013]

[This case concerned an individualized retransmission technology very similar to the one at issue in the U.S. *Aereo* decision; the European court also found a violation of the right of communication to the public. While this European decision does not directly quote the international conventions, it flows from settled case law explicitly quoting those international conventions.]

19   By Question 1 and Question 2(a), the referring court asks, in essence, whether the concept of 'communication to the public', within the meaning of Article 3(1) of Directive 2001/29 [Info Soc], must be interpreted as meaning that it covers a retransmission of the works included in a terrestrial television broadcast:

- where the retransmission is made by an organisation other than the original broadcaster,
- by means of an internet stream made available to the subscribers of that other organisation who may receive the retransmission by logging on to its server,
- on the assumption that those subscribers are within the area of reception of the terrestrial television broadcast and may lawfully receive the broadcast on a television receiver.

20   First of all, it is to be noted that the principal objective of Directive 2001/29 [Info Soc] is to establish a high level of protection of authors, allowing them to obtain an appropriate reward for the use of their works, including on the occasion of communication to the public. It follows that 'communication to the public' must be interpreted broadly, as recital 23 in the preamble to the directive indeed expressly states [citations omitted].

21   In the first place, it is necessary to determine the meaning of the concept of 'communication' and reply to the question whether the activity at issue in the main proceedings comes within its scope.

22   In that connection, the Court notes that Directive 2001/29 [Info Soc] does not define the concept of "communication" exhaustively. Thus, the meaning and scope of that concept must be defined in the light of the context in which it occurs and also in the light of the objective referred to in paragraph 20 above.

23   It follows, in particular, from recital 23 in the preamble to Directive 2001/29 [Info Soc] that the author's right of communication to the public covers any transmission or retransmission of a work to the public not present at the place where the communication originates, by wire or wireless means, including broadcasting. In addition, it is apparent from Article 3(3) of that directive that authorising the inclusion of protected works in a communication to the public does not exhaust the right to authorise or prohibit other communications of those works to the public.

24   If follows that, by regulating the situations in which a given work is put to multiple use, the European Union legislature intended that each transmission or retransmission of a work which uses a specific technical means must, as a rule, be individually authorised by the author of the work in question.

25   Those findings are, moreover, supported by Articles 2 and 8 of Directive 93/83 [Satellite and Cable], which require fresh authorisation for a simultaneous, unaltered and unabridged retransmission by satellite or cable of an initial transmission of television or radio programmes containing protected works, even though those programmes may already be received in their catchment area by other technical means, such as by wireless means or terrestrial networks.

26   Given that the making of works available through the retransmission of a terrestrial television broadcast over the internet uses a specific technical means different from that of the original communication, that retransmission must be considered to be a 'communication' within the meaning of Article 3(1) of Directive 2001/29 [Info Soc]. Consequently, such a retransmission cannot be exempt from authorisation by the authors of the retransmitted works when these are communicated to the public.

27   That conclusion cannot be undermined by TVC's objection that the making of the works available over the Internet, as was done in the case in the main proceedings, is merely a technical means to ensure or improve reception of the terrestrial television broadcast in its catchment area.

28   Admittedly, it follows from the case-law of the Court that a mere technical means to ensure or improve reception of the original transmission in its

catchment area does not constitute a 'communication' within the meaning of Article 3(1) of Directive 2001/29 [citations omitted].

29   Thus, the intervention of such a technical means must be limited to maintaining or improving the quality of the reception of a pre-existing transmission and cannot be used for any other transmission.

30   In the present case, however, the intervention by TVC consists in a transmission of the protected works at issue which is different from that of the broadcasting organisation concerned. TVC's intervention is in no way intended to maintain or improve the quality of the transmission by that other broadcasting organisation. In those circumstances, that intervention cannot be considered to be a mere technical means within the meaning specified in paragraph 28 above.

31   In the second place, in order to be categorised as a 'communication to the public' within the meaning of Article 3(1) of Directive 2001/29 [Info Soc], the protected works must also in fact be communicated to a "public".

32   In that connection, it follows from the case-law of the Court that the term "public" in Article 3(1) of Directive 2001/29 [Info Soc] refers to an indeterminate number of potential recipients and implies, moreover, a fairly large number of persons (see, to that effect, *SGAE*, paragraphs 37 and 38 and the case law cited).

33   As regards that last criterion specifically, the cumulative effect of making the works available to potential recipients should be taken into account. In that connection, it is in particular relevant to ascertain the number of persons who have access to the same work at the same time and successively (*SGAE*, paragraph 39).

34   In that context, it is irrelevant whether the potential recipients access the communicated works through a one-to-one connection. That technique does not prevent a large number of persons having access to the same work at the same time.

35   In the present case, it should be noted that the retransmission of the works over the internet at issue in the main proceedings is aimed at all persons resident in the United Kingdom who have an Internet connection and who claim to hold a television licence in that State. Those people may access the protected works at the same time, in the context of the "live streaming" of television programmes on the Internet.

36   Thus, the retransmission in question is aimed at an indeterminate number of potential recipients and implies a large number of persons. Consequently, it must be held that, by the retransmission in question, the protected works are indeed communicated to a 'public' within the meaning of Article 3(1) of Directive 2001/29 [Info Soc].

37   However, TVC contends that the retransmission at issue in the main proceedings does not satisfy the requirement that there must be a new public, which is none the less necessary within the meaning of the judgments in SGAE (paragraph 40). . . . The recipients of the retransmission effected by TVC are, it submits, entitled to follow the televised broadcast, identical in content, using their own television sets.

38   In that connection, it should be noted that the situations examined in the cases which gave rise to the abovementioned judgments differ clearly from the situation at issue in the case in the main proceedings. In those cases, the Court examined situations in which an operator had made accessible, by its deliberate intervention, a broadcast containing protected works to a new public which was not considered by the authors concerned when they authorised the broadcast in question.

39   By contrast, the main proceedings in the present case concern the transmission of works included in a terrestrial broadcast and the making available of those works over the Internet. As is apparent from paragraphs 24 to 26 above, each of those two transmissions must be authorised individually and separately by the authors concerned given that each is made under specific technical conditions, using a different means of transmission for the protected works, and each is intended for a public. In those circumstances, it is no longer necessary to examine below the requirement that there must be a new public.

40   In the light of the foregoing, the answer to Question 1 and Question 2(a) is that the concept of "communication to the public", within the meaning of Article 3(1) of Directive 2001/29 [Info Soc], must be interpreted as meaning that it covers a retransmission of the works included in a terrestrial television broadcast

- where the retransmission is made by an organisation other than the original broadcaster,
- by means of an internet stream made available to the subscribers of that other organisation who may receive that retransmission by logging on to its server,

- even though those subscribers are within the area of reception of that terrestrial television broadcast and may lawfully receive the broadcast on a television receiver.

C-466/12 Nils Svensson and Others v. Retriever Sverige AB ECLI:EU:C:2014:76 [2014]

The dispute in the main proceedings and the questions referred for a preliminary ruling

8   The applicants in the main proceedings, all journalists, wrote press articles that were published in the Göteborgs-Posten newspaper and on the Göteborgs-Posten website. Retriever Sverige operates a website that provides its clients, according to their needs, with lists of clickable Internet links to articles published by other websites. It is common ground between the parties that those articles were freely accessible on the Göteborgs-Posten newspaper site. According to the applicants in the main proceedings, if a client clicks on one of those links, it is not apparent to him that he has been redirected to another site in order to access the work in which he is interested. By contrast, according to Retriever Sverige, it is clear to the client that, when he clicks on one of those links, he is redirected to another site.

9   The applicants in the main proceedings brought an action against Retriever Sverige before the Stockholms tingsrätt (Stockholm District Court) in order to obtain compensation on the ground that that company had made use, without their authorisation, of certain articles by them, by making them available to its clients.

. . .

13   In those circumstances, the Svea hovrätt decided to stay the proceedings and to refer the following questions to the Court of Justice for a preliminary ruling:

"(1) If anyone other than the holder of copyright in a certain work supplies a clickable link to the work on his website, does that constitute communication to the public within the meaning of Article 3(1) of Directive [2001/29]?

(2) Is the assessment under question 1 affected if the work to which the link refers is on a website on the Internet which can be accessed by anyone without restrictions or if access is restricted in some way?

(3) When making the assessment under question 1, should any distinction be drawn between a case where the work, after the user has clicked on the link, is shown on another website and one where the work, after the user has clicked on the link, is shown in such a way as to give the impression that it is appearing on the same website?

(4) Is it possible for a Member State to give wider protection to authors' exclusive right by enabling communication to the public to cover a greater range of acts than provided for in Article 3(1) of Directive 2001/29?"

The first three questions

14   By its first three questions, which it is appropriate to examine together, the referring court asks, in essence, whether Article 3(1) of Directive 2001/29 [Info Soc] must be interpreted as meaning that the provision, on a website, of clickable links to protected works available on another website constitutes an act of communication to the public as referred to in that provision, where, on that other site, the works concerned are freely accessible.

15   In this connection, it follows from Article 3(1) of Directive 2001/29 [Info Soc] that every act of communication of a work to the public has to be authorised by the copyright holder.

16   It is thus apparent from that provision that the concept of communication to the public includes two cumulative criteria, namely, an "act of communication" of a work and the communication of that work to a "public" (see, to that effect, Case C-607/11 *ITV Broadcasting and Others* [2013] ECR, paragraphs 21 and 31).

. . .

18   In the circumstances of this case, it must be observed that the provision, on a website, of clickable links to protected works published without any access restrictions on another site, affords users of the first site direct access to those works.

19   As is apparent from Article 3(1) of Directive 2001/29 [Info Soc], for there to be an "act of communication", it is sufficient, in particular, that a work is made available to a public in such a way that the persons forming that public may access it, irrespective of whether they avail themselves of that opportunity (see, by analogy, Case C-306/05 *SGAE* [2006] ECR I-11519, paragraph 43).

20   It follows that, in circumstances such as those in the case in the main proceedings, the provision of clickable links to protected works must be considered to be "making available" and, therefore, an "act of communication", within the meaning of that provision.

21   So far as concerns the second of the abovementioned criteria, that is, that the protected work must in fact be communicated to a "public", it follows from Article 3(1) of Directive 2001/29 [Info Soc] that, by the term "public", that provision refers to an indeterminate number of potential recipients and implies, moreover, a fairly large number of persons (SGAE, paragraphs 37 and 38, and ITV Broadcasting and Others, paragraph 32).

22   An act of communication such as that made by the manager of a website by means of clickable links is aimed at all potential users of the site managed by that person, that is to say, an indeterminate and fairly large number of recipients.

23   In those circumstances, it must be held that the manager is making a communication to a public.

24   None the less, according to settled case-law, in order to be covered by the concept of "communication to the public", within the meaning of Article 3(1) of Directive 2001/29 [Info Soc], a communication, such as that at issue in the main proceedings, concerning the same works as those covered by the initial communication and made, as in the case of the initial communication, on the Internet, and therefore by the same technical means, must also be directed at a new public, that is to say, at a public that was not taken into account by the copyright holders when they authorised the initial communication to the public (see, by analogy, SGAE, paragraphs 40 and 42; [citations omitted]).

25   In the circumstances of this case, it must be observed that making available the works concerned by means of a clickable link, such as that in the main proceedings, does not lead to the works in question being communicated to a new public.

26   The public targeted by the initial communication consisted of all potential visitors to the site concerned, since, given that access to the works on that site was not subject to any restrictive measures, all Internet users could therefore have free access to them.

27   In those circumstances, it must be held that, where all the users of another site to whom the works at issue have been communicated by means of a clickable link could access those works directly on the site on which they

were initially communicated, without the involvement of the manager of that other site, the users of the site managed by the latter must be deemed to be potential recipients of the initial communication and, therefore, as being part of the public taken into account by the copyright holders when they authorised the initial communication.

28   Therefore, since there is no new public, the authorisation of the copyright holders is not required for a communication to the public such as that in the main proceedings.

29   Such a finding cannot be called in question were the referring court to find, although this is not clear from the documents before the Court, that when Internet users click on the link at issue, the work appears in such a way as to give the impression that it is appearing on the site on which that link is found, whereas in fact that work comes from another site.

30   That additional circumstance in no way alters the conclusion that the provision on a site of a clickable link to a protected work published and freely accessible on another site has the effect of making that work available to users of the first site and that it therefore constitutes a communication to the public. However, since there is no new public, the authorisation of the copyright holders is in any event not required for such a communication to the public.

31   On the other hand, where a clickable link makes it possible for users of the site on which that link appears to circumvent restrictions put in place by the site on which the protected work appears in order to restrict public access to that work to the latter site's subscribers only, and the link accordingly constitutes an intervention without which those users would not be able to access the works transmitted, all those users must be deemed to be a new public, which was not taken into account by the copyright holders when they authorised the initial communication, and accordingly the holders' authorisation is required for such a communication to the public. This is the case, in particular, where the work is no longer available to the public on the site on which it was initially communicated or where it is henceforth available on that site only to a restricted public, while being accessible on another Internet site without the copyright holders' authorisation.

32   In those circumstances, the answer to the first three questions referred is that Article 3(1) of Directive 2001/29 [Info Soc] must be interpreted as meaning that the provision on a website of clickable links to works freely available on another website does not constitute an act of communication to the public, as referred to in that provision.

QUESTIONS

1. For the ECJ, there is an act of communication to the public either if there is a communication to "a new public" or if there is a use of "specific technical means different from that of the original communication" (*ITV Broadcasting Ltd.*, n 26). Do you find any basis in the international conventions for the condition of specific technical means? Concerning the condition of "a new public," the ECJ has presented this criterion in *SGAE* (n 40) as if it followed from article 11*bis*(1)(ii). Does the text of that article support this conclusion? Does deriving the "new public" criterion from the 1978 edition of the WIPO Guide to the Berne Convention lend support to that conclusion? What if that conclusion results from a misreading of the guide? To what extent do those misreadings result in interpretations inconsistent with the Berne Convention? To what extent are the interpretations inconsistent with the WCT? [See, *infra*, regarding the scope of the exhaustion doctrine]

2. If the "new public" prerequisite were inconsistent with the Berne Convention right of communication to the public, how might simple hyperlinks be justified within the Berne framework?

3. In *Svensson*, the Court considers that the condition of "a new public" is not fulfilled since the work is already freely accessible. The Court recognizes that the outcome would be different for a website offering only restricted access to the work. To what extent does this obligation to restrict access from the website on which the work was originally posted amount a formality prohibited by article 5(2) of the Berne Convention (see, *supra*, this Chapter, 5.1.1 (What is a "formality"?))?

4. Which, if any, of the following constitute "communication to the public" within the meaning of the Berne Convention and WIPO Copyright Treaty? The E.U. Info Soc Directive? "Making available to the public" within the meaning of the WIPO Treaties or the Info Soc Directive? Is there a difference? Does it matter?

   a. The installation by a condominium of TV sets in apartments connected to a central antenna.

   b. Communication of broadcast works, via television screen and speakers, to customers present in a building open to the public.

   c. The retransmission within the offices of private dental practices engaged in professional economic activity of free-to-air broadcasts of recorded songs.

   d. The performance of a magic show in a circus.

   e. Roger Jolly runs a website, Pirates-R-Us.com, from which he offers a variety of digital-format copyrighted works, including photographs, musical recordings, videogames, and text. Users accessing the site may listen to, view or download the desired files directly from the Pirates-R-Us.com site.

f. Secret-sharer.com distributes a software program, TotalShare, enabling end users to designate digital files of all kinds (text, image, sound, audiovisual) on their hard drives for other users of TotalShare to copy into their hard drives. Tracy Trader has accordingly designated files corresponding to the text and recorded reading of the 19th Harry Potter book, *Harry Potter and the Never-Ending Royalty Statement*, and a collection of great outtakes from all 74 Harry Potter films to date.

g. Sir Joseph Porter KCB, having acquired the various Harry Potter-related files from Tracy's hard drive, forwards them to a Facebook page accessible to his sisters and his cousins (whom he numbers by the dozens) and his aunts, as well as to all practitioners of Admiralty law, and the occasional Tar.

h. Oscar, an admiralty lawyer who is Sir Joseph's Facebook "friend," emails Lucinda the files he copied from Sir Joseph. Lucinda keeps her digital copies, but also sends the files on to Sybilla, who in turn sends them to Clancy, and so on.

i. A painting displayed in a museum in a place open to the public.

Distribution right—rights in physical (and digital?) copies

Copyright is generally considered an incorporeal right, regulating, inter alia, the creation of copies, but not the fate of the physical copies themselves. The latter belong to the realm of chattels, and generally come under the law pertaining to personal property. But there are significant points of intersection. First, the right to distribute the copies has historically accompanied the right to make copies. Hence, provisions going back to some early national copyright statutes entitling the right holder to "print, reprint, publish or vend" copies of the copyrighted work (U.S. Copyright Act of 1790, s 1). While Berne does not include a general right of distribution of hardcopies, the WCT does. Some national implementations of the distribution right, notably in the U.S., extend this right to digital copies.

Second, the burgeoning markets for rental of copies may deleteriously affect sales of copies; many member states accordingly provide for some control over rental as well as initial sale of copies; moreover, the WCT and the TRIPS explicitly cover some instances of rental, as does Directive 2006/115/EC on rental right and lending right (originally published as Directive 92/100/EEC) and § 109(b) of the current U.S. Copyright Act.

Third, some member states have enacted a more persistent form of control over the circulation of copies, by providing for a resale right (droit de suite) in manuscripts and original copies of artworks. Berne incorporates the droit de suite, but subjects it to a regime of reciprocity. Directive 2001/84/EC harmonizes the issue at a European level. Proposals for a U.S. droit de suite have been introduced in Congress and have been the subject of study and endorsement by the U.S. Copyright Office.

Fourth, unauthorized importation of copies furnishes another problem; while the Berne Convention does not mandate a general right to control the circulation of copies, it does require member states to provide for the seizure of copies traversing borders without the author's consent. The TRIPS set out elaborate provisions concerning infringing importations. Directive 2004/48/48 deals partially with this issue.

Finally, international texts address the exhaustion question. In both the U.S. and the E.U., the right to control the sale of copies generally is "exhausted" with the first sale: the distribution right does not extend to domestic resale markets. The question of the geographic scope of the exhaustion doctrine beyond domestic resale was highly disputed during the negotiations of the TRIPS and the WCT, with some countries favoring "international exhaustion" (once a lawfully made copy is sold anywhere in the world, it may be resold anywhere else in the world) and others preferring the more restrictive rule of "local exhaustion" (only copies made within the relevant national or regional territory may be freely resold there). International exhaustion effectively overrides the copyright owner's right to prohibit unauthorized importations of non-piratical copies; local exhaustion allows a member state or customs union (i.e., the E.U.) to keep out copies made abroad, while permitting the free recirculation within the territory of locally made copies. International exhaustion fosters the widest circulation of goods, while local exhaustion fragments the world into local markets, thus permitting copyright owners to price discriminate relative to the economic capacities of different national markets. Because the geographic scope of exhaustion was strongly contested, both the TRIPS and the WCT expressly decline to resolve the issue.

i.   Distribution in general

WCT Article 6
Right of Distribution

(1) Authors of literary and artistic works shall enjoy the exclusive right of authorizing the making available to the public of the original and copies of their works through sale or other transfer of ownership.

Agreed statements concerning Articles 6 and 7: As used in these Articles, the expressions "copies" and "original and copies," being subject to the right of distribution and the right of rental under the said Articles, refer exclusively to fixed copies that can be put into circulation as tangible objects.

QUESTIONS

1. Under the WCT, is the distribution right engaged if a work is offered for sale, but no one purchases it?
2. Under the WCT, what norms govern the sale of digital copies? Does it matter whether the digital object, e.g., a cinematographic work, is fixed in a tangible medium, such as a DVD, or is communicated by means of digital transmission to the buyer's hard drive or remote digital "storage locker"?
3. The agreed statement to WCT article 6 limits the distribution right to "tangible objects;" what about the communication of digital copies? See *supra*, communication to the public and making available rights.
4. The international norms cover the distribution of the original (initial fixation of the work) and of subsequent copies. In some author's right systems such as France, there is no autonomous distribution right, rather the right is considered an incident of the reproduction right. Does such a characterization comply with international obligations?

ii.   U.S. Copyright Act

§ 106. Exclusive rights in copyrighted works

Subject to sections 107 through 122, the owner of copyright under this title has the exclusive rights to do and to authorize any of the following

. . .

(3) to distribute copies or phonorecords of the copyrighted work to the public by sale or other transfer of ownership, or by rental, lease, or lending;. . . .

The "Umbrella Solution:" U.S. (non?) Implementation of the WCT making available right through the domestic law distribution right

The "umbrella solution" adopted at the 1996 Diplomatic Conference that yielded the WCT allows member states to implement the article 8 making available right through a variety of means, including, for example, an all-embracing "making available" right, or a combination of a public performance right covering streams and a digital distribution right covering downloads. Whatever the means chosen, however, the member state must ensure that its law covers the offering to the public of on-demand access to a work both as a stream and as a download.

U.S. compliance with its WCT obligations therefore turns on whether the U.S. Copyright Act, as interpreted by the courts, confers the exclusive right to offer on demand to the public a work for streaming and for downloading. The Supreme Court's *Aereo* decision (*supra*) alleviates some uncertainty regarding the U.S.' compliance with international norms with respect to coverage of on-demand streaming under the public performance right. With respect to the offer of downloads, the *Capitol Records v. Thomas* decision (*supra*, Part I, Chapter 2.3.1, pp. 125 et seq.), may render U.S. compliance even less certain.

At the time of ratification, however, U.S. authorities did not anticipate the difficulties that have subsequently ensued. As a study published by the U.S. Department of Commerce ("Green Paper") explains:

> When the United States implemented the WIPO Internet Treaties in the DMCA, it did not include an explicit "making available" right, as both Congress and the Administration concluded that the relevant acts were encompassed within the existing scope of exclusive rights. In addition to the existing reproduction and public performance rights, the distribution right, adopted in the 1976 Copyright Act, applied to digital transmissions as well as the distribution of physical copies. And the legislative history indicates that this right was intended to incorporate the prior law's "publication" right,[3] which included the mere offering of copies to the public.[4]

---

3 The right to "distribute" first emerged in the "Preliminary Draft for Revised U.S. Copyright Law" in late 1962, and was substituted for "publish" to avoid the confusion that had developed surrounding the term "publication" and courts' attempts to avoid the harsh effects of "publication" without proper notice (forfeiture of federal copyright protection). *See generally* Peter Menell, *In Search of Copyright's Lost Ark: Interpreting the Right to Distribute in the Internet Age*, 59 J. COPYRIGHT SOC'Y USA 1 (2011); Benjamin Kaplan, *Publication in Copyright Law: The Question of Phonograph Records*-103 U. PA. L. REV. 469, 488–9 (1955).

4 *See* Menell ibid. at 57; *see also* 2–8 NIMMER ON COPYRIGHT § 8.11[B][4][d]. At the time, the right to "publish" was understood to encompass the offering of copyright works to the public, and there was no requirement to prove actual distribution of copies. Ibid. *See* David O. Carson, *Making the "Making Available Right" Available: 22nd Annual Horace S Manges Lecture, February 3, 2009*, 33 COLUM. J.L. & ARTS 135, 160–61 (2010); RESTATEMENT (THIRD) OF THE FOREIGN RELATIONS LAW OF THE UNITED STATES § 114 (1986) ("Where fairly possible, a United States statute is to be construed so as not to conflict with international law or with an international agreement of the United States.").

Since that time, a number of U.S. courts have addressed the "making available" right, primarily in the context of individuals uploading a work to a shared folder on a computer connected to a peer-to-peer network. A number of courts have concluded that the distribution right incorporates the concept of "making available" reflected in the WIPO Treaties.[5] Some others have disagreed.[6] All of these cases, however, have focused solely on the scope of the distribution right and predate the recent academic scholarship described above, reviewing previously unanalyzed legislative history.[7]

U.S. Department of Commerce Internet Policy Task Force, Copyright Policy, Creativity, and Innovation in the Digital Economy (July 2013) ["Green Paper"] pp. 14–16 (footnotes partially omitted).

The Green Paper's hopeful coda ("All of these cases, however, have focused solely on the scope of the distribution right and predate the recent academic scholarship described above, reviewing previously unanalyzed legislative history") signals the problem: U.S. courts have inconsistently interpreted the scope of the distribution right. The Green Paper's hint to courts to heed academic commentators' exploration of legislative history reveals the U.S. Administration's fear that uncertain caselaw may be putting the U.S. out of step with international norms.

The U.S. encounters the danger of insufficient international compliance even though it has long been recognized in the U.S., as a matter of statute and caselaw, that the exclusive right to distribute the work in copies or phonorecords (17 U.S.C. s 106(3)) applies to digital as well as to material copies. *See, e.g.,* in addition to the sources cited in the "Green Paper," 17 U.S.C. § 115(a) ("digital phonorecord delivery"); § 115(c)(3)(A) ("compulsory licensee to *distribute* or authorize the distribution of a phonorecord of a non-dramatic musical work *by means of a digital transmission* which constitutes a digital phonorecord delivery" – emphasis supplied).

---

5 *A&M Records v. Napster, Inc.,* 239 F.3d 1004, 1014 (9th Cir. 2001) ("*Napster*"); *Universal City Studios Prods. LLLP v. Bigwood,* 441 F. Supp. 2d 185, 191 (D. Me. 2006); *Motown Records Co. . DiPietro,* No. 04-CV-2246, 2007 WL 576284 (E.D. Pa. Feb. 16, 2007); *UMG Recordings, Inc. v. Alburger,* Civil No. 07–3705, 2009 WL 3152153, at *3 (E.D. Pa. Sept. 29, 2009).

6 These cases have not, however, required direct evidence of the dissemination of copies, but have allowed proof based on circumstantial evidence or inference. *See Capitol Records, Inc. v. Thomas,* 579 F.Supp.2d 1210, 1225 (D. Minn. 2008); *London-Sire Records, Inc. v. Doe 1,*542 F.Supp.2d 153, 169 (D. Mass. 2008); *Atl. Recording Corp. v. Howell,* 554 F. Supp. 2d 976, 981–84 (D. Ariz. 2008).

7 Menell *supra* note 3; 2–8 NIMMER ON COPYRIGHT § 8.11[B][4][d].

But, as the "Green Paper" acknowledges, the authorities are inconsistent as to whether the distribution right extends both to offers as well as to actual deliveries of digital copies. For the moment, only federal district courts have ruled on the question, but their rulings have ranged from assimilating making available to "publication" (whose statutory definition encompasses offers to distribute) to requiring actual downloads. The latter group of decisions thus leaves a gap in U.S. coverage of the full range of the making available right.

QUESTIONS

Recall *Capitol Records* v. *Thomas*, 579 F.Supp.2d 1210 (D. Minn. 2008), *supra*, Part I, Chapter 2.3.1, pp. 125 et seq. In *Thomas*, the Court concluded that "the US compliance with the WIPO Treaties and the FTA's cannot override the clear congressional intent in § 106(3)." Assuming the *Thomas* court were correct that Congress unambiguously foreclosed interpreting § 106(3) to encompass offers to distribute and therefore that U.S. domestic law did not implement its obligations under the WIPO Treaties and Free Trade Agreements (as we have seen, those conclusions are in fact highly contested), what recourse might a foreign author denied protection in the U.S. against offers to distribute her works have? Is the WTO an available forum? As to Free Trade Agreements, if they include a Bilateral Investment Treaty, is the investment arbitration tribunal established by the BIT (see Chapter 1) an available forum? Christopher Wadlow describes investment arbitration tribunals as "wormhole between the public international law of states and the private law of persons" (*Intellectual Property as an 'Investment' in International Law*, in GLOBAL WRONGS AND PRIVATE LAW REMEDIES AND PROCEDURES (S. Banakas, ed., Wildy, Simmonds & Hills Publishing, 2011, p. 119). Under what circumstances might a non-U.S. private litigant sue the U.S. before an investment arbitration tribunal, and what remedies would be available?

iii.   E.U. directives

Directive 2009/24/EC of the European Parliament and of the Council of 23 April 2009 on the legal protection of computer programs

Article 4 – Restricted acts

1. Subject to the provisions of Articles 5 and 6, the exclusive rights of the rightholder within the meaning of Article 2 shall include the right to do or to authorise:

. . .

(c) any form of distribution to the public, including the rental, of the original computer program or of copies thereof.

Directive 96/9/EC of the European Parliament and of the Council of 11 March 1996 on the legal protection of databases

Article 5 – Restricted acts

In respect of the expression of the database which is protectable by copyright, the author of a database shall have the exclusive right to carry out or to authorize:

. . .

(c) any form of distribution to the public of the database or of copies thereof.

Directive 2001/29/EC of the European Parliament and of the Council of 22 May 2001 on the harmonisation of certain aspects of copyright and related rights in the information society

Article 4 – Distribution right

1. Member States shall provide for authors, in respect of the original of their works or of copies thereof, the exclusive right to authorise or prohibit any form of distribution to the public by sale or otherwise.

C-456/06 Peek & Cloppenburg KG v. Cassina SpA ECLI:EU:C:2008:232 [2008]

[The case concerned the displaying of counterfeit chairs at a rest area and in a display window of Peek & Cloppenburg, a leading department store. Cassina SpA, the authorized distributor of the well-known chairs designed by Charles-Édouard Jeanneret (Le Corbusier), sued Peek & Cloppenburg in Germany alleging infringement of the distribution right.]

14   Cassina manufactures chairs. Its collection includes furniture manufactured according to the designs of Charles-Édouard Jeanneret (Le Corbusier). That furniture includes armchairs and sofas in categories LC 2 and LC 3 and

the table system LC 10-P. Cassina has concluded a licensing agreement for the manufacture and sale of that furniture.

15 Peek & Cloppenburg operates menswear and womenswear shops throughout Germany. It has set up in one of its shops a rest area for customers, fitted out with armchairs and sofas from the LC 2 and LC 3 range and a low table from the LC 10-P table system. In a display window of its outlet, Peek & Cloppenburg placed an armchair from the LC 2 range for decorative purposes. Those items of furniture did not come from Cassina but were manufactured without Cassina's consent by an undertaking in Bologna (Italy). According to the referring court, such furniture was not protected at the time by copyright in the Member State in which it was manufactured.

16 As it considered that Peek & Cloppenburg had infringed its rights by so doing, Cassina brought an action against it before the Landgericht Frankfurt (Frankfurt Regional Court) (Germany) seeking an order that it must desist from that practice and provide Cassina with information, in particular as regards the distribution channels for those items of furniture. In addition, Cassina sought an order that Peek & Cloppenburg pay damages.

. . .

22 In those circumstances, the Bundesgerichtshof decided to stay the proceedings and to refer the following questions to the Court for a preliminary ruling:

"(1)(a) Can it be assumed that there is a distribution to the public otherwise than by sale, within the meaning of Article 4(1) of Directive 2001/29 [Info Soc] . . ., in the case where it is made possible for third parties to make use of items of copyright-protected works without the grant of user involving a transfer of de facto power to dispose of those items?

(b) Is there a distribution under Article 4(1) of [Directive 2001/29] also in the case in which items of copyright-protected works are shown publicly without the possibility of using those items being granted to third parties?

(2) If the answers are in the affirmative:

Can the protection accorded to the free movement of goods preclude, in the abovementioned cases, exercise of the distribution right if the items presented are not under copyright protection in the Member State in which they were manufactured and placed on the market?"

. . .

28   By Question 1(a) and (b), the referring court is essentially asking whether the concept of distribution to the public otherwise than through the sale of the original of a work or a copy thereof, for the purpose of Article 4(1) of Directive 2001/29 [Info Soc], must be interpreted as meaning that it includes, first, granting to the public the right to use reproductions of a work protected by copyright without that grant of use entailing a transfer of ownership and, secondly, exhibiting those reproductions to the public without actually granting a right to use them.

29   Neither Article 4(1) of Directive 2001/29 [Info Soc] nor any other provision of that directive gives a sufficient explanation of the concept of distribution to the public of a work protected by copyright. That concept is, on the other hand, defined more clearly by the CT [The World Intellectual Property Organisation (WIPO) Copyright Treaty (CT).] and the PPT [WIPO Performances and Phonograms Treaty (PPT)].

30   In this connection, it is settled case-law that Community legislation must, so far as possible, be interpreted in a manner that is consistent with international law, in particular where its provisions are intended specifically to give effect to an international agreement concluded by the Community [citations omitted].

31   It is common ground that, as recital 15* in the preamble to Directive 2001/29 [Info Soc] makes clear, that directive is intended to implement at Community level the Community's obligations under the CT and the PPT. In those circumstances, the concept of distribution in Article 4(1) of that directive must be interpreted, as far as is possible, in the light of the definitions given in those Treaties.

32   Article 6(1) of the CT defines the concept of the right of distribution enjoyed by the authors of literary and artistic works as the exclusive right of authorising the making available to the public of the original and copies of

---

* Editors' note: Recital 15 states:

The Diplomatic Conference held under the auspices of the World Intellectual Property Organization (WIPO) in December 1996 led to the adoption of two new Treaties, the "WIPO Copyright Treaty" and the "WIPO Performances and Phonograms Treaty", dealing respectively with the protection of authors and the protection of performers and phonogram producers. Those Treaties update the international protection for copyright and related rights significantly, not least with regard to the so-called "digital agenda", and improve the means to fight piracy worldwide. The Community and a majority of Member States have already signed the Treaties and the process of making arrangements for the ratification of the Treaties by the Community and the Member States is under way. This Directive also serves to implement a number of the new international obligations.

their works through sale or "other transfer of ownership". Moreover, Articles 8 and 12 of the PPT contain the same definitions of the right of distribution enjoyed by performers and producers of phonograms. Thus, the relevant international Treaties link the concept of distribution exclusively to that of transfer of ownership.

33   Since Article 4(1) of Directive 2001/29 [Info Soc] provides, in such a context, for "distribution by sale or otherwise", that concept should be interpreted in accordance with those Treaties as a form of distribution which entails a transfer of ownership.

. . .

36   It follows that the concept of distribution to the public, otherwise than through sale, of the original of a work or a copy thereof, for the purpose of Article 4(1) of Directive 2001/29 [Info Soc], covers acts which entail, and only acts which entail, a transfer of the ownership of that object. The information provided by the referring court shows that that clearly does not apply to the acts at issue in the main proceedings.

QUESTIONS

1. To what extent has the ECJ resorted to international norms in the process of interpreting the Directive?
2. How, if at all, does the interpretation enhance the process of harmonization internationally? See *supra* page 283, Question 1 following *Infopaq*. For the extension of the distribution right to digital copies see ECJ Case 128/11 *Usedsoft* [2012]; ECJ Case C–419/13 *Allposters* [2015], *infra*, pp. 395 et seq.

Rental

i.   International norms

TRIPS Agreement Article 11
Rental Rights

In respect of at least computer programs and cinematographic works, a Member shall provide authors and their successors in title the right to authorize or to prohibit the commercial rental to the public of originals or copies of their copyright works. A Member shall be excepted from this obligation in respect of cinematographic works unless such rental has led to widespread copying of such works which is materially impairing the exclusive right of reproduction conferred in that Member on authors and their successors in title. In respect of computer programs, this obligation does not apply to rentals where the program itself is not the essential object of the rental.

WCT Article 7
Right of Rental

(1) Authors of

(i) computer programs;
(ii) cinematographic works; and
(iii) works embodied in phonograms, as determined in the national law of Contracting Parties, shall enjoy the exclusive right of authorizing commercial rental to the public of the originals or copies of their works.

(2) Paragraph (1) shall not apply

(i) in the case of computer programs, where the program itself is not the essential object of the rental; and
(ii) in the case of cinematographic works, unless such commercial rental has led to widespread copying of such works materially impairing the exclusive right of reproduction.

(3) Notwithstanding the provisions of paragraph (1), a Contracting Party that, on April 15, 1994, had and continues to have in force a system of equitable remuneration of authors for the rental of copies of their works embodied in phonograms may maintain that system provided that the commercial rental of works embodied in phonograms is not giving rise to the material impairment of the exclusive right of reproduction of authors.

> **Agreed statements concerning Article 7**: It is understood that the obligation under Article 7(1) does not require a Contracting Party to provide an exclusive right of commercial rental to authors who, under that Contracting Party's law, are not granted rights in respect of phonograms. It is understood that this obligation is consistent with Article 14(4) of the TRIPS Agreement.

QUESTIONS

1. How would one prove the conditions prerequisite to attachment of an international obligation to extend rental rights to cinematographic works?
2. What does the agreed statement to WCT article 7 mean?

ii. U.S. Copyright Act

§ 109. Limitations on exclusive rights: Effect of transfer of particular copy or phonorecord

. . .

(b)(1)(A) Notwithstanding the provisions of subsection (a), unless authorized by the owners of copyright in the sound recording or the owner of copyright in a computer program (including any tape, disk, or other medium embodying such program), and in the case of a sound recording in the musical works embodied therein, neither the owner of a particular phonorecord nor any person in possession of a particular copy of a computer program (including any tape, disk, or other medium embodying such program), may, for the purposes of direct or indirect commercial advantage, dispose of, or authorize the disposal of, the possession of that phonorecord or computer program (including any tape, disk, or other medium embodying such program) by rental, lease, or lending, or by any other act or practice in the nature of rental, lease, or lending. Nothing in the preceding sentence shall apply to the rental, lease, or lending of a phonorecord for nonprofit purposes by a nonprofit library or nonprofit educational institution. The transfer of possession of a lawfully made copy of a computer program by a nonprofit educational institution to another nonprofit educational institution or to faculty, staff, and students does not constitute rental, lease, or lending for direct or indirect commercial purposes under this subsection.

(B) This subsection does not apply to—

(i) a computer program which is embodied in a machine or product and which cannot be copied during the ordinary operation or use of the machine or product; or
(ii) a computer program embodied in or used in conjunction with a limited purpose computer that is designed for playing video games and may be designed for other purposes.

. . .

Brilliance Audio, Inc. v. Haights Cross Communications, Inc., 474 F.3d 365 (6th Cir. 2007).

[Brilliance, which produces and sells audiobooks, sued Haights Cross for renting Brilliance's audiobooks without permission. The case was the first to consider whether section 109(b) bars rental, lease, and lending only of phonorecords that contain sound recordings of musical works or also applies to phonorecords, such as audiobooks, that contain sound recordings of other types of copyrighted works.]

We find that the language of § 109(b)(1)(A) is not unambiguous. One reading requires only the consent of the copyright owner in sound recordings containing musical works, as well as consent from the copyright owner in those musical works. The statute may also be read, however, to mandate obtaining permission from the copyright owners of all sound recordings and additionally to require the consent of the copyright owner in the work being recorded, if it is a musical work. Thus, the meaning of the statute cannot be determined merely by reference to the statutory text. To resolve the ambiguity, we must turn to the legislative history and policy rationales behind the § 109(b)(1)(A) exception.

The combination of the legislative history, the context in which the statute was passed, and the policy rationales behind both § 109 and copyright law in general provide strong evidence that Congress intended to exclude only sound recordings of musical works from the first sale doctrine.

[The court found that the legislative history indicated that Congress only sought to exempt from the first sale doctrine sound recordings of musical works. The court further found that the] statute at issue in this case . . . should be construed narrowly because it upsets the traditional bargain between the rights of copyright owners and the personal property rights of an individual who owns a particular copy. . . . The limited monopoly created by copyright law is needed to promote the creation of new works and ensure that the creator is properly compensated for this effort. Once a copyright holder has consented to distribution of a copy of that work, this monopoly is no longer needed because the owner has received the desired compensation for that copy. The first sale doctrine ensures that the copyright monopoly does not intrude on the personal property rights of the individual owner, given that the law generally disfavors restraints of trade and restraints on alienation. In passing the record rental exception, Congress made a specific policy choice that personal property rights in a certain type of work—sound recordings of musical works—should give way to ensure that copyright owners receive the protections envisioned by the Copyright Act as a whole.

By doing this, Congress effectively altered the traditional copyright bargain and extended the copyright monopoly for a limited set of works. In order to protect the bargain between copyright owners and personal property owners, we will not construe this exemption from the first sale doctrine any more broadly than explicitly mandated by Congress. The specific problem addressed by Congress in 1984—rampant piracy of popular musical recordings—does not apply to sound recordings of literary works. When evidence surfaced of a new class of works in need of § 109(b) protection—computer software—Congress amended the statute to explicitly exempt the works from the first sale doctrine. Absent such an express statement from Congress regarding audiobooks, there is no evidence that Congress intended to alter the copyright bargain, and we see no reason to extend § 109(b) beyond its original context.

. . . We hold that § 109(b)(1)(A) applies only to sound recordings of musical works and does not apply to sound recordings of literary works.

QUESTIONS

What is the scope of the rental right in the U.S.? To what works does it apply? In what kinds of works do international treaties oblige the U.S. to provide rental rights?

iii. E.U. Directives

Under European law, the rental right first appears in the Software Directive (the Directive 2009/24 being the codified version the 91/250 Directive). Then, the rental right was extended by a specific Directive to all works protected by copyright law. Directive 2006/115/EC of the European Parliament and of the Council of 12 December 2006 on rental right and lending right and on certain rights related to copyright in the field of intellectual property is the codified version of a previous directive (Directive 92/100/EEC of 19 November 1992 on rental right and lending right and on certain rights related to copyright in the field of intellectual property).

Directive 2009/24/EC of the European Parliament and of the Council of 23 April 2009 on the legal protection of computer programs

Article 4 – Restricted acts

1. Subject to the provisions of Articles 5 and 6, the exclusive rights of the rightholder within the meaning of Article 2 shall include the right to do or to authorise:

(c) any form of distribution to the public, including the rental, of the original computer program or of copies thereof.

Directive 2006/115/EC of the European Parliament and of the Council of 12 December 2006 on rental right and lending right and on certain rights related to copyright in the field of intellectual property

Article 1 – Object of harmonization

1. In accordance with the provisions of this Chapter, Member States shall provide, subject to Article 6, a right to authorise or prohibit the rental and lending of originals and copies of copyright works, and other subject matter as set out in Article 3(1).

C-200/96 Metronome Musik GmbH v. Music Point Hokamp GmbH ECLI:EU:C:1998:172 [1998]

[This case concerned the claim of a company whose business was the rental of compact discs. Its business was clearly affected by the German implementation of Directive 92/100/CE [Rental Right], since it could no longer rent out the compact discs it had lawfully purchased. The company challenged the compliance of the Directive with fundamental rights guaranteed by German Constitutional law and European law].

11 Metronome, the German, French, Italian and United Kingdom Governments, the Council and the Commission consider that the Directive [Rental Right] is valid. They maintain, essentially, that the exclusive rental right, which moreover is provided for in international conventions to which the Community and the Member States are parties, reflects objectives of general interest in the field of intellectual property and does not impair the substance of the right to pursue a trade or profession.

12   Hokamp contends, however, that the introduction of such a right by the Directive [Rental Right] must be regarded as void since it encroaches upon the fundamental rights of undertakings which operate rental businesses, including the right freely to pursue a trade or activity, and because it distorts competition in the Member States in which that activity was carried on independently of phonogram producers.

. . .

14   That principle is expressed in the settled case-law of the Court of Justice according to which, whilst Article 36 of the EC Treaty* allows derogations from the fundamental principle of the free movement of goods by reason of rights recognised by national legislation in relation to the protection of industrial and commercial property, such derogations are allowed only to the extent to which they are justified by the fact that they safeguard the rights which constitute the specific subject-matter of that property. However, the exclusive right guaranteed by the legislation of a Member State on industrial and commercial property is exhausted when a product has been lawfully distributed on the market in another Member State by the actual proprietor of the right or with his consent [citations omitted].

15   However, as the Court pointed out [citations omitted], literary and artistic works may be the subject of commercial exploitation by means other than the sale of the recordings made of them. That applies, for example, to the rental of video-cassettes, which reaches a different public from the market for their sale and constitutes an important potential source of revenue for makers of films.

16   In that connection, the Court observed that, by authorising the collection of royalties only on sales to private individuals and to persons hiring out video-cassettes, it is impossible to guarantee to makers of films a remuneration which reflects the number of occasions on which the video-cassettes are actually hired out and which secures for them a satisfactory share of the rental market. Laws which provide specific protection of the right to hire out video-cassettes are therefore clearly justified on grounds of the protection of industrial and commercial property pursuant to Article 36 of the Treaty [citations omitted].

---

* Editors' note: The question is now governed by article 36 of the TFEU stating that: "The provisions of Articles 34 and 35 shall not preclude prohibitions or restrictions on imports, exports or goods in transit justified on grounds of public morality, public policy or public security; the protection of health and life of humans, animals or plants; the protection of national treasures possessing artistic, historic or archaeological value; or the protection of industrial and commercial property. Such prohibitions or restrictions shall not, however, constitute a means of arbitrary discrimination or a disguised restriction on trade between Member States."

17   In the same judgment, the Court also rejected the argument that a maker of a film who has offered the video-cassette of that film for sale in a Member State whose legislation confers on him no exclusive right of hiring it out must accept the consequences of his choice and the exhaustion of his right to restrain the hiring-out of that video-cassette in any other Member State. Where national legislation confers on authors a specific right to hire out video-cassettes, that right would be rendered worthless if its owner were not in a position to authorise the operations for doing so (paragraphs 17 and 18).

19   Thus, the distinction drawn in the Directive between the effects of the specific rental and lending right, referred to in Article 1, and those of the distribution right, governed by Article 9 and defined as an exclusive right to make one of the objects in question available to the public, principally by way of sale, is justified. The former is not exhausted by the sale or any other act of distribution of the object, whereas the latter may be exhausted, but only and specifically upon the first sale in the Community by the rightholder or with his consent.

20   The introduction by the Community legislation of an exclusive rental right cannot therefore constitute any breach of the principle of exhaustion of the distribution right, the purpose and scope of which are different.

21   Furthermore, according to settled case-law, the freedom to pursue a trade or profession, and likewise the right to property, form part of the general principles of Community law. However, those principles are not absolute but must be viewed in relation to their social function. Consequently, the exercise of the right to property and the freedom to pursue a trade or profession may be restricted, provided that any restrictions in fact correspond to objectives of general interest pursued by the European Community and do not constitute in relation to the aim pursued a disproportionate and intolerable interference, impairing the very substance of the rights guaranteed [citations omitted].

. . .

25   Furthermore, as pointed out by most of those who have submitted observations, the obligation to establish, for the producers of phonograms and all other holders of rights in respect of phonograms, an exclusive right to authorise or prohibit the commercial rental of those products is in conformity with the combined provisions of Articles 11 and 14 of the Agreement on Trade-Related Aspects of Intellectual Property Rights (TRIPS), annexed to the agreement establishing the World Trade Organization, signed in

Marrakesh on 15 April 1994 and approved by Council Decision 94/800/EC of 22 December 1994 concerning the conclusion on behalf of the European Community, as regards matters within its competence, of the agreements reached in the Uruguay Round multilateral negotiations [citations omitted].

26   Thus, the general principle of freedom to pursue a trade or profession cannot be interpreted in isolation from the general principles relating to protection of intellectual property rights and international obligations entered into in that sphere by the Community and by the Member States. Since it does not appear that the objectives pursued could have been achieved by measures which preserved to a greater extent the entrepreneurial freedom of individuals or undertakings specialising in the commercial rental of phonograms, the consequences of introducing an exclusive rental right cannot be regarded as disproportionate and intolerable.

QUESTIONS

To what extent are the references to international norms useful? For the Court, the TRIPS Agreement imposes an obligation to establish an exclusive right to authorize or prohibit commercial rental. Does such an obligation solve the issue of temporal application raised by the defendant (recall that the defendant commenced its commercial CD rental business before the Directive was enacted)? (See *supra*, Part I, Chapter 3.3 (temporal scope).)

Droit de suite

i.   Berne Convention

Article 14*ter*
"Droit de suite" in Works of Art and Manuscripts
1. Right to an interest in resales; 2. Applicable law; 3. Procedure

(1) The author, or after his death the persons or institutions authorized by national legislation, shall, with respect to original works of art and original manuscripts of writers and composers, enjoy the inalienable right to an interest in any sale of the work subsequent to the first transfer by the author of the work.

(2) The protection provided by the preceding paragraph may be claimed in a country of the Union only if legislation in the country to which the author belongs so permits, and to the extent permitted by the country where this protection is claimed.

(3) The procedure for collection and the amounts shall be matters for determination by national legislation.

QUESTIONS

What does "original works of art" mean? Only works existing in a single copy? Limited editions? How limited? What does "the first transfer" mean? Why should the right to an interest in the resale be inalienable? Why is the right not subject to the rule of national treatment (see supra, Part II, Chapter 4.1.2)?

ii. U.S. Copyright Law

U.S. Copyright Office, Resale Royalties: An Updated Analysis (December 2013) (excerpts, footnotes omitted)

In general, visual artists do not share in the long-term financial success of their works. Instead, the financial gains from the resale of their works inure primarily to third parties such as auction houses, collectors, and art galleries. Moreover, the income typically available to other authors through reproduction and derivative uses of their works is more limited for artists. Although the Internet has provided artists with greater opportunities to exploit derivative images and/or sell mass-produced copies of their works, stakeholders agree that "for most visual artists . . . the amounts involved in reproduction or representation are generally insignificant." Indeed, it appears to be common ground that reproduction rights represent a "very minor aspect of [most artists'] careers" and that the first sale of a work is "the main or exclusive source of income for almost all American artists."

The Copyright Office agrees that these factors place many visual artists at a material disadvantage vis-à-vis other authors, and therefore the Office supports congressional consideration of a resale royalty right, or droit de suite, which would give artists a percentage of the amount paid for a work each time it is resold by another party. A large and growing number of countries around the world – more than seventy in total – now follow that approach. Other potential responses might include the facilitation of voluntary initiatives among stakeholders in the art market, amending the copyright law to give artists a continuing economic interest in their works through, for example, greater interests in public display or commercial rental rights, and increased federal grants for visual art programs.

That said, an "information problem" in the art market – something that many have acknowledged – does present certain challenges. Any assessment of the treatment of visual artists under U.S. law suffers from a lack of independently verifiable data about the operation of the art market and a resulting difficulty in determining whether a resale royalty in particular would truly operate to place artists on equal footing with other authors. At the same time, the Office recognizes that many of the arguments against the right are overblown. Moreover, according to the most recent studies, a number of the adverse consequences that this Office's previous report predicted might follow from implementation of the right have not materialized in countries that have adopted droit de suite since that time. Accordingly, the Office finds no clear impediment to implementation of a resale royalty right in the United States and supports the right as one alternative to address the disparity in treatment of artists under the copyright law.

A bill was proposed in Congress to institute an artist's resale royalty. Excerpts follow:

113th CONGRESS
2d Session

S. 2045

To amend title 17, United States Code, to secure the rights of visual artists to copyright, to provide for resale royalties, and for other purposes.

SECTION 1. SHORT TITLE.

This Act may be cited as the "American Royalties Too Act of 2014".

SEC. 2. DEFINITIONS.

Section 101 of title 17, United States Code, is amended—
 (1) by inserting after the definition of "architectural work" the following:
 "An 'auction' means a public sale at which a work of visual art is sold to the highest bidder and which is run by an entity that sold not less than $1,000,000 of works of visual art during the previous year.";

 (2) by inserting after the definition of "Pictorial, graphic, and sculptural works" the following:
 "For purposes of section 106(b), 'price' means the aggregate of all installments paid in cash or in-kind by or on behalf of a purchaser for a work of visual art as the result of the auction of that work.";

(3) by inserting after the definition of "registration" the following:
"For purposes of sections 106(b) and 701(b) (5), 'sale' means transfer of ownership or physical possession of a work of visual art as the result of the auction of that work."; and (4) in the definition of "work of visual art", by . . . inserting the following: "A 'work of visual art' is a painting, drawing, print, sculpture, or photograph, existing either in the original embodiment or in a limited edition of 200 copies or fewer that bear the signature or other identifying mark of the author and are consecutively numbered by the author, or, in the case of a sculpture, in multiple cast, carved, or fabricated sculptures of 200 or fewer that are consecutively numbered by the author and bear the signature or other identifying mark of the author.".

SEC. 3. EXCLUSIVE RIGHTS.

Section 106 of title 17, United States Code, is amended
. . .
(4) by adding at the end the following:

"(7) in the case of a work of visual art, to collect a royalty for the work if the work is sold by a person other than the author of the work for a price of not less than $5,000 as the result of an auction.
"(b) Collection of Royalty.—
"(1) In general.—The collection of a royalty under subsection (a) (7) shall be conducted in accordance with this subsection.
"(2) Calculation of royalty.—
"(A) In general.—The royalty shall be an amount equal to the lesser of—
"(i) 5 percent of the price paid for the work of visual art; or
"(ii) $35,000.

[the bill also requires annual cost-of-living increases of the $35,000 amount]

[the bill provides that the royalty is to be collected by the auction house and paid to a visual artists' collecting society, which is directed to make quarterly distributions. Failure to pay the royalty is an act of copyright infringement, subject to all remedies, including statutory damages]

(6) Eligibility to receive royalty payment.—The royalty shall be paid to—

"(A) any author of a work of visual art—
"(i) who is a citizen of or domiciled in the United States;

"(ii) who is a citizen of or domiciled in a country that provides resale royalty rights; or

"(iii) whose work of visual art is first created in the United States or in a country that provides resale royalty rights; or

"(B) the successor as copyright owner of an author described in subparagraph (A)."

QUESTIONS

1. Are the criteria for eligibility to receive royalty payments consistent with the U.S.' international obligations?
2. How does one ascertain where a work of visual art was "first created"?
3. What does subsection (6)(B) mean? Is that consistent with the Berne Convention?
4. The Copyright Office report proposed requiring copyright registration as a condition of receipt of artists' resale royalties. The bills establishing an artist's resale royalty did not include that condition. Would such a prerequisite have been consistent with the U.S' international obligations?

iii.   E.U. directive

Directive 2001/84/EC of the European Parliament and of the Council of 27 September 2001 on the resale right for the benefit of the author of an original work of art

See *supra*, Part II, Chapter 4.1.2, page 255, for the relevant text of the Directive.

Importation

i.   International norms

Berne Convention Article 16*
Infringing Copies

1. Seizure; 2. Seizure on importation; 3. Applicable law

(1) Infringing copies of a work shall be liable to seizure in any country of the Union where the work enjoys legal protection.

---

* Editors' note: See also article 13(3): "Recordings made in accordance with paragraphs (1) and (2) of this Article and imported without permission from the parties concerned into a country where they are treated as infringing recordings shall be liable to seizure."

(2) The provisions of the preceding paragraph shall also apply to reproductions coming from a country where the work is not protected, or has ceased to be protected.

(3) The seizure shall take place in accordance with the legislation of each country.

QUESTION

Copies of a work are made with authorization in country A, the country of origin. They are imported without authorization into country B. Both countries are Berne members. Does article 16 apply? Suppose only country B is a Berne member. Does article 16 apply?

TRIPS Agreement Article 46
Other Remedies

In order to create an effective deterrent to infringement, the judicial authorities shall have the authority to order that goods that they have found to be infringing be, without compensation of any sort, disposed of outside the channels of commerce in such a manner as to avoid any harm caused to the right holder, or, unless this would be contrary to existing constitutional requirements, destroyed. The judicial authorities shall also have the authority to order that materials and implements the predominant use of which has been in the creation of the infringing goods be, without compensation of any sort, disposed of outside the channels of commerce in such a manner as to minimize the risks of further infringements. In considering such requests, the need for proportionality between the seriousness of the infringement and the remedies ordered as well as the interests of third parties shall be taken into account. In regard to counterfeit trademark goods, the simple removal of the trademark unlawfully affixed shall not be sufficient, other than in exceptional cases, to permit release of the goods into the channels of commerce.

TRIPS Agreement Article 51
Suspension of Release by Customs Authorities

Members shall, in conformity with the provisions set out below, adopt procedures[13] to enable a right holder, who has valid grounds for suspecting that the importation of . . . pirated copyright goods[14] may take place, to lodge an application in writing with competent authorities, administrative or judicial, for the suspension by the customs authorities of the release into free circulation of such goods. Members may enable such an application to be made in respect of goods which involve other infringements of intellectual property rights, provided that the requirements of this Section are met. Members may also provide for corresponding procedures concerning the suspension by the customs authorities of the release of infringing goods destined for exportation from their territories.

Footnote 13 It is understood that there shall be no obligation to apply such procedures to imports of goods put on the market in another country by or with the consent of the right holder, or to goods in transit.

Footnote 14 For the purposes of this Agreement:

. . .

(b) "pirated copyright goods" shall mean any goods which are copies made without the consent of the right holder or person duly authorized by the right holder in the country of production and which are made directly or indirectly from an article where the making of that copy would have constituted an infringement of a copyright or a related right under the law of the country of importation.

TRIPS Agreement Article 59
Remedies

Without prejudice to other rights of action open to the right holder and subject to the right of the defendant to seek review by a judicial authority, competent authorities shall have the authority to order the destruction or disposal of infringing goods in accordance with the principles set out in Article 46. In regard to counterfeit trademark goods, the authorities shall not allow the re-exportation of the infringing goods in an unaltered state or subject them to a different customs procedure, other than in exceptional circumstances.

Article 69
International Cooperation

Members agree to cooperate with each other with a view to eliminating international trade in goods infringing intellectual property rights. For this purpose, they shall establish and notify contact points in their administrations and be ready to exchange information on trade in infringing goods. They shall, in particular, promote the exchange of information and cooperation between customs authorities with regard to trade in counterfeit trademark goods and pirated copyright goods.

QUESTIONS

1. What is the difference between an "infringing copy" under Berne article 16 and "pirated copyright goods" under TRIPS article 51, footnote 14(b)?
2. What are "goods in transit"? Does article 51 apply to "goods in transit"? To what extent may a TRIPS Member apply article 51 to "goods in transit"?

WTO Panel, 26 January 2009 WT/DS 362/R – China – Measures Affecting the Protection and the Enforcement of Intellectual Property Rights, Report of the Panel

[The following case concerned a complaint by the U.S. against China (for a summary description of this case see *supra*, Part I, Chapter 2.1.6.). One matter on which the U.S. requested consultation was the lack of authority under Chinese law to order the destruction or disposal of infringing goods required by article 59 of the TRIPS Agreement. For the U.S., China's Customs measures do not comply with article 59 of the TRIPS, mainly because the confiscated goods are not destroyed by the Customs authorities. As article 59 of the TRIPS Agreement on Border Measures integrates the requirement of article 46 specifying the remedies available, this case is also relevant to the materials on enforcement, *infra*, Chapter 5.6.]

Customs Measures

Description of the measures at issue

7.193 This Section of the Panel's findings concerns three of China's Customs measures. The Regulations on Customs Protection of Intellectual Property Rights ("Customs IPR Regulations") were enacted by the Standing Committee of the State Council in November 2003 and entered into force in March 2004. The Regulations were formulated in accordance with the Customs Law and provide a procedure for Customs to take protective measures against goods suspected of infringing trademark, copyright and related rights and patent rights upon importation or exportation. Article 27 provides for the confiscation of goods determined to have infringed an intellectual property right and, in the third paragraph, sets out different options for the disposal or destruction of such goods. The parties agreed to translate the relevant text as follows:

"Where the confiscated goods which infringe on intellectual property rights can be used for the social public welfare undertakings, Customs shall hand such goods over to relevant public welfare bodies for the use in social public welfare undertakings. Where the holder of the intellectual property rights intends to buy them, Customs can assign them to the holder of the intellectual property rights with compensation. Where the confiscated goods infringing on intellectual property rights cannot be used for social public welfare undertakings and the holder of the intellectual property rights has no intention to buy them, Customs can, after eradicating the infringing features, auction them off according to law. Where the infringing features are impossible to eradicate, Customs shall destroy the goods" [citations omitted].

7.240 . . . The terms of Article 59 do not indicate that the authority to order the specified types of remedies must be exclusive. This interpretation is confirmed by Article 46, which forms part of the context of Article 59, as Article 59 incorporates the principles of Article 46, and both Articles are phrased as obligations that authorities "shall have the authority" to order certain types of remedies. The first sentence of Article 46 provides, basically, that authorities shall have the authority to order that goods be disposed of outside the channels of commerce or destroyed. At the same time, the fourth sentence of Article 46 relates to release into the channels of commerce which does not correspond to either of the remedies required by the first sentence. This is an express recognition that the remedies set out in the first sentence of Article 46 are not exhaustive. The same position applies under Article 59.

. . .

7.246 The Panel observes that the reference to alternatives in Article 59 of the TRIPS Agreement implies a particular type of condition. Article 59 requires authority to order "destruction *or* disposal" (emphasis added). It is not disputed that where competent authorities have authority in any given situation within the scope of Article 59 to order either destruction or disposal (in accordance with applicable principles), this is sufficient to implement the obligation in the first sentence of Article 59. Therefore, a condition that precludes the authority to order one remedy (e.g. destruction) could be consistent with Article 59 as long as competent authorities still had the authority to order the other remedy (in this example, disposal).

. . .

7.249   The "authority" required by Article 59 concerns two types of remedies, namely "destruction or disposal". The meaning of "destruction" is not controversial. As for "disposal", the Panel notes that the English text of Article 59 does not qualify this word so that it could, in accordance with its ordinary meaning, refer both to disposal outside the channels of commerce as well as to release into the channels of commerce [citations omitted]. However, read in context, the word "disposal" could be a reference to an order that goods be "disposed of" outside the channels of commerce as set out in Article 46. This ambiguity is resolved by reference to the French and Spanish texts, which are equally authentic [citations omitted]. The French text of Article 59 refers to authority to order "la mise hors circuit" which is a reference to the authority to order that infringing goods be "écartées des circuits commerciaux" in Article 46. The Spanish text of Article 59 refers to authority to order "eliminación" which, read in its context as an alternative to "destrucción", is evidently a reference to the authority to order that infringing goods be "apartadas de los circuitos comerciales" in Article 46. Accordingly, the correct interpretation of the term "disposal" in the first sentence of Article 59 is disposal "outside the channels of commerce".

. . .

7.255   The first sentence of Article 59 provides that competent authorities shall have the authority to order the destruction or disposal of infringing goods "in accordance with the principles set out in Article 46". The phrase referencing the principles set out in Article 46 attaches to "the authority to order the destruction or disposal of infringing goods". This directs the treaty interpreter to those principles in Article 46 that attach to such authority.

7.256   The Panel makes the following observations. First, Article 59 refers to "authority". Second, Article 59 incorporates principles that attach to authority to order "destruction or disposal" (outside the channels of commerce for the reasons given at paragraph 7.249 above). Third, Article 59 relates to the authority to order destruction or disposal of "infringing goods" but not principles applicable to the disposition of materials and implements.

. . .

7.258   The first sentence of Article 46 refers to "authority" to order that "infringing goods" be "disposed of . . . or . . . destroyed". Therefore, it seems pertinent to Article 59.

7.259   The second sentence of Article 46 refers to disposal of materials and implements and is therefore inapposite. Indeed, materials and implements used to create infringing goods would not normally be suspended at the border with the infringing goods, unlike during enforcement actions within a Member's territory.

7.260   The third sentence of Article 46 refers to "such requests" although the previous sentences do not refer expressly to any requests. The content of the third sentence clearly relates to materials and implements as addressed in the second sentence but it could equally relate to infringing goods as addressed in the first sentence. The text is ambiguous on this point. This ambiguity can be resolved by reference to the records of the negotiation of the TRIPS Agreement [citations omitted].

7.261   The TRIPS Agreement was negotiated during the Uruguay Round in the Negotiating Group on Trade-Related Aspects of Intellectual Property Rights, including Trade in Counterfeit Goods (referred to below as the "TRIPS negotiating group"). The Chairman's draft text of the Agreement of 23 July 1990 included a draft article corresponding to what is Article 46 in the text as finally agreed [citations omitted]. In that draft article, the principle of proportionality and the interests of third parties were related to a request of the right holder under the previous sentence. That request could be for remedies with respect to infringing goods as well as materials and implements. In a later draft [citations omitted], the first sentence of the provision on remedies was divided into two separate sentences, one with respect to infringing goods and the other with respect to materials and implements. Both sentences included the phrase "upon request from the right holder". In the same draft, the phrase "[i]n considering such a request" was revised to read "[i]n considering such requests" (in the plural). This is the version of the third sentence that was retained in the so-called "Brussels Draft" [citations omitted] and the final text of Article 46 of the TRIPS Agreement.

7.262   Accordingly, the records of the negotiation of the TRIPS Agreement clarify that the terms of Article 46 in the third sentence refer inter alia to the consideration of requests for orders that infringing goods be disposed of outside the channels of commerce or destroyed. Therefore, the third sentence seems pertinent to Article 59 as well.

7.263   The fourth sentence refers to a category of infringing goods, i.e. counterfeit trademark goods. It does not refer expressly to authority to order destruction or disposal outside the channels of commerce. However, the context shows that the principle of proportionality in the previous sentence guides the competent authorities' choice between the remedies specified in the first sentence and any alternative remedies. Similarly, the fourth sentence of Article 46 sets out a consideration that the authorities must take into account when choosing between the required remedies, namely those specified in the first sentence, and release into the channels of commerce, if such an order is available. The fourth sentence attaches to the scope of authority to choose between destruction or disposal outside the channels of commerce and release into the channels of commerce, if that remedy is available. Therefore, the fourth sentence of Article 46 seems pertinent to Article 59.

7.264   Article 59 refers to the "principles" set out in Article 46. Therefore, it is necessary to determine what precisely that refers to in the first, third and fourth sentences of Article 46. The word "principles" can be defined as "a general law or rule adopted or professed as a guide to action." Each of these sentences of Article 46 contains language that is a guide to action by authorities and none dictate the precise terms of orders in specific cases.

7.265   The Panel does not consider that the choice of the word "principles" was intended to reflect a hierarchy of provisions within Article 46 that would include only the most general concepts and exclude the less general. There is a strong similarity in the language and purpose of the two provisions that both provide for authority to order destruction or disposal with respect to goods that have been found to infringe intellectual property rights at the conclusion of an enforcement procedure. However, there are also differences in the government agencies to which they relate ("competent authorities" to order remedies in border measures under Article 59 but "judicial authorities" under Article 46) and also in the scope of property to which the remedies apply ("infringing goods" under Article 59 and "infringing goods as well as materials and implements the predominant use of which has been in the creation of the infringing goods" under Article 46). These differences made it inappropriate simply to provide that the obligation in Article 59 applied "in accordance with Article 46" or otherwise incorporate the whole of Article 46. Instead, the cross-reference to "principles" avoided the duplication of a relatively large amount of text. Therefore, in the Panel's view, the reference to "principles" is a reference to language that is a guide to action by authorities with respect to orders for the destruction or disposal of infringing goods.

7.266   Accordingly, for the purposes of Article 59, the Panel considers that the first sentence of Article 46 sets out the following "principles":

(a)   authorities shall have the authority to order disposal or destruction in accordance with the first sentence "without compensation of any sort"; and

(b)   authorities shall have the authority to order disposal "outside the channels of commerce in such a manner as to avoid any harm caused to the right holder"; or

(c) authorities shall have the authority to order destruction "unless this would be contrary to existing constitutional requirements".

7.267   The third sentence sets out the following principle that applies inter alia to the authority to order disposal or destruction of infringing goods under the first sentence:

(d) in considering such requests "the need for proportionality between the seriousness of the infringement and the remedies ordered as well as the interests of third parties shall be taken into account".

7.268   The fourth sentence sets out the following principle that attaches to the authority to order destruction or disposal of infringing goods under the first sentence:

(e) in regard to counterfeit trademark goods, the simple removal of the trademark unlawfully affixed shall not be sufficient, other than in exceptional cases, to permit release of the goods into the channels of commerce.

7.269   The interpretation of all these principles is informed by the common objective set out at the beginning of Article 46, i.e. "to create an effective deterrent to infringement" which is, in itself, also a guide to action with respect to orders for the destruction or disposal of infringing goods and, hence, a principle set out in Article 46.

QUESTION

Identify the method(s) used by the Panel to interpret the TRIPS Agreement (Cf. Part I, Chapter 2): Are they all equivalent? To what extent does the selection of one method influence the outcome? Does the Vienna Convention create a hierarchy among these methods? Does the Panel explain how to select one method? Which interest does the interpretation favor? The infringer? The owner?

ii.   U.S. Copyright Act

§ 602. Infringing importation or exportation of copies or phonorecords

(a) Infringing Importation or Exportation.—

(1) Importation.—Importation into the United States, without the authority of the owner of copyright under this title, of copies or

phonorecords of a work that have been acquired outside the United States is an infringement of the exclusive right to distribute copies or phonorecords under section 106, actionable under section 501.

(2) Importation or exportation of infringing items.—Importation into the United States or exportation from the United States, without the authority of the owner of copyright under this title, of copies or phonorecords, the making of which either constituted an infringement of copyright, or which would have constituted an infringement of copyright if this title had been applicable, is an infringement of the exclusive right to distribute copies or phonorecords under section 106, actionable under sections 501 and 506.

(3) Exceptions.—This subsection does not apply to—

(A) importation or exportation of copies or phonorecords under the authority or for the use of the Government of the United States or of any State or political subdivision of a State, but not including copies or phonorecords for use in schools, or copies of any audiovisual work imported for purposes other than archival use;

(B) importation or exportation, for the private use of the importer or exporter and not for distribution, by any person with respect to no more than one copy or phonorecord of any one work at any one time, or by any person arriving from outside the United States or departing from the United States with respect to copies or phonorecords forming part of such person's personal baggage; or

(C) importation by or for an organization operated for scholarly, educational, or religious purposes and not for private gain, with respect to no more than one copy of an audiovisual work solely for its archival purposes, and no more than five copies or phonorecords of any other work for its library lending or archival purposes, unless the importation of such copies or phonorecords is part of an activity consisting of systematic reproduction or distribution, engaged in by such organization in violation of the provisions of section 108(g)(2).

(b) Import Prohibition.—In a case where the making of the copies or phonorecords would have constituted an infringement of copyright if this title had been applicable, their importation is prohibited. In a case where the copies or phonorecords were lawfully made, the United States Customs and Border Protection Service has no authority to prevent their importation. In either case, the Secretary of the Treasury is authorized to prescribe, by regulation, a procedure under which any person claiming an interest in the copyright in a particular work may, upon payment of a specified fee, be entitled to notification by the United States Customs and Border Protection Service of the importation of articles that appear to be copies or phonorecords of the work.

QUESTION

How does section 602 distinguish between copies made abroad without the copyright owner's authorization and those lawfully made abroad? Is the copyright owner's importation right limited to preventing the entry into the U.S. of the former kind of copies? Compare the text of section 602 with the U.S. Supreme Court's interpretation in *Kirtsaeng* v. *John Wiley & Sons, Inc.* 133 S Ct 1351 (2013), *infra*.

iii. E.U. Law

Border measures

As to European law, border measures issues have been harmonized by a specific regulation, Council Regulation (EC) No 1383/2003 of 22 July 2003 concerning customs actions against goods suspected of infringing certain intellectual property rights and the measures to be taken against goods found to have infringed such rights. This regulation was partially repealed by Regulation (EU) No 608/2013 concerning customs enforcement of intellectual property rights.

The ECJ had to interpret "counterfeit goods" and "pirated goods" in joined cases C-446/09 and C-495/09 concerning Regulation No 1383/2003. The definition retained by the Regulation being inspired by the TRIPS Agreement, the European interpretation may contribute to a better understanding of TRIPs article 51. The decision also offered an interesting application of TRIPS article 69. On this point, the new Regulation No 608/2013 does not change the solution.

C-446/09 and C-495/09 Joined Cases Koninklijke Philips Electronics NV v. Lucheng Meijing Industrial Co Ltd. and Others and Nokia Corporation v. Her Majesty's Commissioners of Revenue and Customs, ECLI:EU:C:2011:796 and ECLI:EU:C:2011:9 [2011]

[The case concerned the shipment of counterfeit goods via the E.U. Electric shavers from China resembling protected designs from Philips were discovered in Belgium. The destination of the shavers was unknown, and it could not be proven that they would be sold in countries of the

E.U. that protected Philips' designs. Also, mobile phones from Hong Kong, destined for Colombia, were detected in England. The mobile phones bore a sign identical to a community trade mark registered by Nokia.]

49   By their questions, which it is appropriate to consider together, the referring courts ask, in essence, whether goods coming from a non-member State which are imitations of goods protected in the European Union by a trade mark right or copies of goods protected in the European Union by copyright, a related right or a design can be classified as 'counterfeit goods' or 'pirated goods' within the meaning of Regulation No 1383/2003 and, before the entry into force of that regulation, within the meaning of Regulation No 3295/94 [of 22 December 1994 laying down measures to prohibit the release for free circulation, export, re-export or entry for a suspensive procedure of counterfeit and pirated goods] merely on the basis of the fact that they are brought into the customs territory of the European Union, without being released for free circulation there.

50   According to the definition of the terms 'counterfeit goods' and 'pirated goods' in Article 1(2) of Regulation No 3295/94 and Article 2(1) of Regulation No 1383/2003, they cover infringements of a trade mark, copyright, a related right or a design which applies pursuant to European Union legislation or pursuant to the domestic law of the Member State in which the application for action by the customs authorities is made. It follows that only infringements of intellectual property rights as conferred by European Union law and the national law of the Member States are covered.

51   In the main proceedings, it is not in dispute that the shavers detained in the port of Antwerp could, where appropriate, be classified as 'pirated goods' within the meaning of Regulation No 3295/94 if they were put on sale in Belgium or in another Member State where Philips holds a copyright and enjoys the design protection on which it relies, or that the mobile telephones inspected at London Heathrow Airport would infringe the Community trade mark relied on by Nokia and would therefore be 'counterfeit goods' within the meaning of Regulation No 1383/2003 if they were put on sale in the European Union. However, the parties to the main proceedings, the Member States which have submitted observations to the Court and the European Commission disagree on whether those goods can infringe those intellectual property rights by reason of the mere fact that they have been the subject, in the customs territory of the European Union, of a declaration seeking one of the suspensive procedures referred to in Article 84 of the

Customs Code,* namely, in Case C-446/09, customs warehousing and, in Case C-495/09, external transit.

. . .

56   Goods placed under a suspensive customs procedure cannot, merely by the fact of being so placed, infringe intellectual property rights applicable in the European Union [citations omitted].

57   On the other hand, those rights may be infringed where, during their placement under a suspensive procedure in the customs territory of the European Union, or even before their arrival in that territory, goods coming from non-member States are the subject of a commercial act directed at European Union consumers, such as a sale, offer for sale or advertising [citations omitted].

. . .

60   [A] customs authority which has established the presence in warehousing or in transit of goods which are an imitation or a copy of a product protected in the European Union by an intellectual property right can legitimately act when there are indications before it that one or more of the operators involved in the manufacture, consignment or distribution of the goods, while not having yet begun to direct the goods towards European Union consumers, are about to do so or are disguising their commercial intentions.

---

* Editors'Note: [Instrument] Article 84 states -
1. In Articles 85 to 90:
(a) where the term 'procedure' is used, it is understood as applying, in the case of non-Community goods, to the following arrangements:
— external transit;
— customs warehousing;
— inward processing in the form of a system of suspension;
— processing under customs control;
— temporary importation;
(b) where the term 'customs procedure with economic impact' is used, it is understood as applying to the following arrangements:
— customs warehousing;
— inward processing;
— processing under customs control;
— temporary importation;
— outward processing.
2. 'Import goods' means goods placed under a suspensive procedure and goods which, under the inward processing procedure in the form of the drawback system, have undergone the formalities for release for free circulation and the formalities provided for in Article 125.
3. 'Goods in the unaltered state' means import goods which, under the inward processing procedure or the procedures for processing under customs control, have undergone no form of processing.

61 [I]t is sufficient that there be material such as to give rise to suspicion. That material may include the fact that the destination of the goods is not declared whereas the suspensive procedure requested requires such a declaration, the lack of precise or reliable information as to the identity or address of the manufacturer or consignor of the goods, a lack of cooperation with the customs authorities or the discovery of documents or correspondence concerning the goods in question suggesting that there is liable to be a diversion of those goods to European Union consumers.

. . .

63 It should be borne in mind, in that regard, that imitations and copies coming from a non-member State and transported to another non-member State may comply with the intellectual property provisions in force in each of those States. In the light of the common commercial policy's main objective, set out in Article 131 EC and Article 206 TFEU* and consisting in the development of world trade through the progressive abolition of restrictions on trade between States, it is essential that those goods be able to pass in transit, via the European Union, from one non-member State to another without that operation being hindered, even by a temporary detention, by Member States' customs authorities. Precisely such hindrance would be created if Regulations No 3295/94 and No 1383/2003 were interpreted as permitting the detention of goods in transit without the slightest indication suggesting that they could be fraudulently diverted to European Union consumers.

. . .

65 Finally, with regard to goods in respect of which there is no indication as referred to in paragraph 61 of this judgment, but in respect

---

* Editors'Note:

Article 207 (ex Article 133 TEC) states -

1. The common commercial policy shall be based on uniform principles, particularly with regard to changes in tariff rates, the conclusion of tariff and trade agreements relating to trade in goods and services, and the commercial aspects of intellectual property, foreign direct investment, the achievement of uniformity in measures of liberalisation, export policy and measures to protect trade such as those to be taken in the event of dumping or subsidies. The common commercial policy shall be conducted in the context of the principles and objectives of the Union's external action.

2. The European Parliament and the Council, acting by means of regulations in accordance with the ordinary legislative procedure, shall adopt the measures defining the framework for implementing the common commercial policy.

3. Where agreements with one or more third countries or international organisations need to be negotiated and concluded, Article 218 shall apply, subject to the special provisions of this Article.

The Commission shall make recommendations to the Council, which shall authorise it to open the necessary negotiations. The Council and the Commission shall be responsible for ensuring that the agreements negotiated are compatible with internal Union policies and rules.

of which there are suspicions of infringement of an intellectual property right in the presumed non-member State of destination, it must be noted that the customs authorities of the Member States where those goods are in external transit are permitted to cooperate, pursuant to Article 69 of the TRIPS Agreement, with the customs authorities of that non-member State with a view to removing those goods from international trade where appropriate.

. . .

70　[T]he authority competent to take a substantive decision cannot classify as 'counterfeit goods' and 'pirated goods' or, more generally, 'goods infringing an intellectual property right' goods which a customs authority suspects of infringing an intellectual property right applicable in the European Union but in respect of which, after substantive examination, it is not proven that they are intended to be put on sale in the European Union.

71　With regard to the evidence which the authority competent to take a substantive decision must have in order to find that goods which are imitations or copies and have been brought into the customs territory of the European Union without being released for free circulation there are liable to infringe an intellectual property right applicable in the European Union, it must be stated that such evidence may include the existence of a sale of goods to a customer in the European Union, of an offer for sale or advertising addressed to consumers in the European Union, or of documents or corre-

---

The Commission shall conduct these negotiations in consultation with a special committee appointed by the Council to assist the Commission in this task and within the framework of such directives as the Council may issue to it. The Commission shall report regularly to the special committee and to the European Parliament on the progress of negotiations.

4. For the negotiation and conclusion of the agreements referred to in paragraph 3, the Council shall act by a qualified majority.

For the negotiation and conclusion of agreements in the fields of trade in services and the commercial aspects of intellectual property, as well as foreign direct investment, the Council shall act unanimously where such agreements include provisions for which unanimity is required for the adoption of internal rules.

The Council shall also act unanimously for the negotiation and conclusion of agreements:

(a) in the field of trade in cultural and audiovisual services, where these agreements risk prejudicing the Union's cultural and linguistic diversity;

(b) in the field of trade in social, education and health services, where these agreements risk seriously disturbing the national organisation of such services and prejudicing the responsibility of Member States to deliver them.

5. The negotiation and conclusion of international agreements in the field of transport shall be subject to Title VI of Part Three and to Article 218.

6. The exercise of the competences conferred by this Article in the field of the common commercial policy shall not affect the delimitation of competences between the Union and the Member States, and shall not lead to harmonisation of legislative or regulatory provisions of the Member States in so far as the Treaties exclude such harmonisation.

spondence concerning the goods in question showing that diversion of those goods to European Union consumers is envisaged.

. . .

78   Having regard to all the foregoing considerations, the answer to the questions referred is that Regulations No 3295/94 and No 1383/2003 must be interpreted as meaning that:

- goods coming from a non-member State which are imitations of goods protected in the European Union by a trade mark right or copies of goods protected in the European Union by copyright, a related right or a design cannot be classified as 'counterfeit goods' or 'pirated goods' within the meaning of those regulations merely on the basis of the fact that they are brought into the customs territory of the European Union under a suspensive procedure;
- those goods may, on the other hand, infringe the right in question and therefore be classified as 'counterfeit goods' or 'pirated goods' where it is proven that they are intended to be put on sale in the European Union, such proof being provided, inter alia, where it turns out that the goods have been sold to a customer in the European Union or offered for sale or advertised to consumers in the European Union, or where it is apparent from documents or correspondence concerning the goods that their diversion to European Union consumers is envisaged;
- in order that the authority competent to take a substantive decision may profitably examine whether such proof and the other elements constituting an infringement of the intellectual property right relied upon exist, the customs authority to which an application for action is made must, as soon as there are indications before it giving grounds for suspecting that such an infringement exists, suspend the release of or detain those goods; and
- those indications may include, inter alia, the fact that the destination of the goods is not declared whereas the suspensive procedure requested requires such a declaration, the lack of precise or reliable information as to the identity or address of the manufacturer or consignor of the goods, a lack of cooperation with the customs authorities or the discovery of documents or correspondence concerning the goods in question suggesting that there is liable to be a diversion of those goods to European Union consumers.

QUESTIONS

1. How does the ECJ draw the line between a good in transit and a counterfeit good? By drawing such a line, does the Court swing the balance in favor of free trade or in favor of intellectual property rights?

2. An Indian television producer has bought the catalog of an American producer of television series from the 1950s. Most of the series at that time were shot in black and white. The Indian producer decides to colorize them in order to sell copies in India. The copies travel from New York to Bombay with a stop in Paris CDG Airport. During that stop in Paris, the heirs of the director of one the colorized programs requests that French Customs authorities seize and destroy those copies on the ground that they infringe the director's moral rights. What should be the response of French Customs?

Exhaustion

i.   TRIPS Agreement

Article 6
Exhaustion

For the purposes of dispute settlement under this Agreement, subject to the provisions of Articles 3 [national treatment] and 4 [most favored nation] nothing in this Agreement shall be used to address the issue of the exhaustion of intellectual property rights.

QUESTIONS

1. What is the outcome of article 6? What are the differences between excluding the matter for the purpose of dispute settlement under this agreement and excluding the matter altogether from the agreement? What do the references to articles 3 and 4 mean?

2. According to paragraph 5(d) of the Doha Declaration on the TRIPS Agreement and Public Health: "(d) the effect of the provisions in the TRIPS Agreement that are relevant to the exhaustion of intellectual property rights is to leave each member free to establish its own regime for such exhaustion without challenge, subject to the MFN and the national treatment provisions of Article 3 and 4." Would you consider that the declaration illuminates article 6 of the TRIPS? What would be its binding nature? Could the declaration be characterized as a subsequent agreement [(see supra, Part I, Chapter 2.1.3)]?

ii. **WCT**

Article 6
Right of Distribution

. . .

(2) Nothing in this Treaty shall affect the freedom of Contracting Parties to determine the conditions, if any, under which the exhaustion of the right in paragraph (1) [Right of distribution] applies after the first sale or other transfer of ownership of the original or a copy of the work with the authorization of the author.

> **Agreed statements concerning Articles 6 and 7**: As used in these Articles, the expressions "copies" and "original and copies," being subject to the right of distribution and the right of rental under the said Articles, refer exclusively to fixed copies that can be put into circulation as tangible objects.

QUESTIONS

1. Compare the drafting of article 6 of the WCT and article 6 of the TRIPS: Which gives more freedom to contracting states as to exhaustion?
2. What does "nothing in the Treaty shall affect the freedom of Contracting Parties" mean? What articles in the Treaty could have "affect[ed] the freedom of Contracting Parties" with respect to exhaustion? (See *infra*, this Chapter 5.5.3 Generalization of the "three-step test" pp. 449 et seq.)
3. The text of article 6 leaves it to member states to determine the extent to which the copyright owner's rights in "the original or a copy" of a work may persist after its "first sale or other transfer of ownership." But the agreed statement limits the distribution right to physical copies. Does it follow that the exhaustion of the distribution right applies only to physical copies as well? In that event, does the WCT in fact "affect the freedom of Contracting Parties" by excluding digital copies from the scope of the exhaustion doctrine?

a. What is a sale or other transfer of ownership?

Article 6 of the WCT links exhaustion to the first sale or other transfer of ownership of the original or a copy of the work with the authorization of the author. Nevertheless, the text does not seem to define what a "sale or other transfer of ownership" means. Section 109(a) of the U.S. Copyright Act codifies the U.S. "first-sale doctrine," which entitles the "owner" of a copy to resell or "otherwise dispose of the possession" of her copy. Consider the difference between "owning" and "possessing" a copy. Only "owners" enjoy the rights set out in section 109(a). But what makes one an "owner"? Because a transfer of ownership is the predicate to the exhaustion of the author's distribution right, both U.S. and E.U. caselaw have debated the nature of a transaction that results in a transfer of ownership, and not merely of possession.

(1) US Copyright Act

§ 109. Limitations on exclusive rights: Effect of transfer of particular copy or phonorecord

(a) Notwithstanding the provisions of section 106(3), the owner of a particular copy or phonorecord lawfully made under this title, or any person authorized by such owner, is entitled, without the authority of the copyright owner, to sell or otherwise dispose of the possession of that copy or phonorecord. . . .

Vernor v. Autodesk, Inc. 621 F.3d 1102 (9th Cir. 2010)

Callahan, Circuit Judge:

Timothy Vernor purchased several used copies of Autodesk, Inc.'s AutoCAD Release 14 software ("Release 14") from one of Autodesk's direct customers, and he resold the Release 14 copies on eBay. Vernor brought this declaratory judgment action against Autodesk to establish that these resales did not infringe Autodesk's copyright. . . .

I.

A.   Autodesk's Release 14 software and licensing practices

The material facts are not in dispute. Autodesk makes computer-aided design software used by architects, engineers, and manufacturers. It has more than nine million customers. It first released its AutoCAD software in 1982. It holds registered copyrights in all versions of the software including the discontinued Release 14 version, which is at issue in this case. It provided Release 14 to customers on CD–ROMs.

Since at least 1986, Autodesk has offered AutoCAD to customers pursuant to an accompanying software license agreement ("SLA"), which customers must accept before installing the software. A customer who does not accept the SLA can return the software for a full refund. Autodesk offers SLAs with different terms for commercial, educational institution, and student users. The commercial license, which is the most expensive, imposes the fewest restrictions on users and allows them software upgrades at discounted prices.

The SLA for Release 14 first recites that Autodesk retains title to all copies. Second, it states that the customer has a nonexclusive and nontransferable license to use Release 14. Third, it imposes transfer restrictions, prohibiting customers from renting, leasing, or transferring the software without Autodesk's prior consent and from electronically or physically transferring the software out of the Western Hemisphere. Fourth, it imposes significant use restrictions:

> YOU MAY NOT: (1) modify, translate, reverse-engineer, decompile, or disassemble the Software . . . (3) remove any proprietary notices, labels, or marks from the Software or Documentation; (4) use . . . the Software outside of the Western Hemisphere; (5) utilize any computer software or hardware designed to defeat any hardware copy-protection device, should the software you have licensed be equipped with such protection; or (6) use the Software for commercial or other revenue-generating purposes if the Software has been licensed or labeled for educational use only.

Fifth, the SLA provides for license termination if the user copies the software without authorization or does not comply with the SLA's restrictions. Finally, the SLA provides that if the software is an upgrade of a previous version:

> [Y]ou must destroy the software previously licensed to you, including any copies resident on your hard disk drive . . . within sixty (60) days of the purchase of the license to use the upgrade or update. . . . Autodesk reserves the right to require you to show satisfactory proof that previous copies of the software have been destroyed.

Autodesk takes measures to enforce these license requirements. It assigns a serial number to each copy of AutoCAD and tracks registered licensees. It requires customers to input "activation codes" within one month after installation to continue using the software. The customer obtains the code by providing the product's serial number to Autodesk. Autodesk issues the activation code after confirming that the serial number is authentic, the copy is not registered to a different customer, and the product has not been upgraded. Once a customer has an activation code, he or she may use it to activate the software on additional computers without notifying Autodesk.

. . .

C.   Vernor's eBay business and sales of Release 14

Vernor has sold more than 10,000 items on eBay. In May 2005, he purchased an authentic used copy of Release 14 at a garage sale from an unspecified seller. He never agreed to the SLA's terms, opened a sealed software packet, or installed the Release 14 software. Though he was aware of the SLA's existence, he believed that he was not bound by its terms. He posted the software copy for sale on eBay. . . .

. . .

II.

In August 2007, Vernor brought a declaratory action against Autodesk to establish that his resales of used Release 14 software are protected by the first sale doctrine and do not infringe Autodesk's copyright. . . .

III.

. . .

This case requires us to decide whether Autodesk sold Release 14 copies to its customers or licensed the copies to its customers. If CTA [from whom Vernor purchased the copies] owned its copies of Release 14, then both its sales to Vernor and Vernor's subsequent sales were non-infringing under the first sale doctrine. However, if Autodesk only licensed CTA to use copies of Release 14, then CTA's and Vernor's sales of those copies are not protected by the first sale doctrine and would therefore infringe Autodesk's exclusive distribution right.

. . .

IV.

. . .

B.   Analysis

We hold today that a software user is a licensee rather than an owner of a copy where the copyright owner (1) specifies that the user is granted a license; (2) significantly restricts the user's ability to transfer the software; and (3) imposes notable use restrictions. Applying our holding to Autodesk's SLA, we conclude that CTA was a licensee rather than an owner of copies of Release 14 and thus was not entitled to invoke the first sale doctrine or the essential step defense.

Autodesk retained title to the software and imposed significant transfer restrictions: it stated that the license is nontransferable, the software could not be transferred or leased without Autodesk's written consent, and the software could not be transferred outside the Western Hemisphere. The SLA also imposed use restrictions against the use of the software outside the Western Hemisphere and against modifying, translating, or reverse-engineering the software, removing any proprietary marks from the software or documentation, or defeating any copy protection device. Furthermore, the SLA provided for termination of the license upon the licensee's unauthorized copying or failure to comply with other license restrictions. Thus, because Autodesk reserved title to Release 14 copies and imposed significant transfer and use restrictions, we conclude that its customers are licensees of their copies of Release 14 rather than owners.

CTA was a licensee rather than an "owner of a particular copy" of Release 14, and it was not entitled to resell its Release 14 copies to Vernor under the first sale doctrine. Therefore, Vernor did not receive title to the copies from CTA and accordingly could not pass ownership on to others. Both CTA's and Vernor's sales infringed Autodesk's exclusive right to distribute copies of its work. . . .

UMG Recordings, Inc. v. Augusto, 628 F.3d 1175 (9th Cir. 2011)

Canby, Circuit Judge:

UMG Recordings appeals the district court's grant of summary judgment in favor of defendant Troy Augusto on UMG's claim of copyright infringement in violation of § 501 of the Copyright Act, which entitles copyright owners to institute an action for infringement of the exclusive right to distribute copies of the copyrighted work. The copies in issue comprise eight specially-produced compact discs, each embodying a copyrighted sound recording. UMG, the copyright owner, used the discs solely for marketing purposes, sending them unsolicited to individuals such as music critics and radio disc jockeys. Although Augusto was not one of those individuals, he managed to obtain the discs from various sources. He later sold them at auction, an act which UMG contends infringed its exclusive right to distribute the discs.

Augusto asserts that UMG's initial distribution of the discs effected a transfer of ownership of the discs to the recipients, rendering the discs subject to the "first sale" doctrine, which permits one who has acquired ownership of a copy to dispose of that copy without the permission of the copyright owner. UMG argues that the statements on the discs and the circumstances of their distribution granted only a license to each recipient, not a transfer of ownership (or "sale") of the copy. Absent a sale, UMG remained the owner of the discs and, accordingly, the defense of the first sale doctrine would be out of Augusto's reach. We conclude that the mailing indeed did effect a sale of the discs to the recipients for purposes of the first sale doctrine, and we affirm the order of the district court.

BACKGROUND

. . .

The material facts of the case are undisputed. UMG is among the world's largest music companies. One of its core businesses is the creation, manufacture, and sale of recorded music, or phonorecords, the copyrights of which are owned by UMG. These phonorecords generally take the form of compact discs ("CDs").

Like many music companies, UMG ships specially-produced promotional CDs to a large group of individuals ("recipients"), such as music critics and radio programmers, that it has selected. There is no prior agreement or request by the recipients to receive the CDs. UMG does not seek or receive payment for the CDs, the content and design of which often differs from that of their commercial counterparts. UMG ships the promotional CDs by means of the United States Postal Service and United Parcel Service. Relatively few of the recipients refuse delivery of the CDs or return them to UMG, and UMG destroys those that are returned.

Most of the promotional CDs in issue in this case bore a statement (the "promotional statement") similar to the following:

> This CD is the property of the record company and is licensed to the intended recipient for personal use only. Acceptance of this CD shall constitute an agreement to comply with the terms of the license. Resale or transfer of possession is not allowed and may be punishable under federal and state laws.

Some of the CDs bore a more succinct statement, such as "Promotional Use Only—Not for Sale."

Augusto was not among the select group of individuals slated to receive the promotional CDs. He nevertheless managed to acquire numerous such CDs, many of which he sold through online auctions at eBay.com. Augusto regularly advertised the CDs as "rare . . . industry editions" and referred to them as "Promo CDs."

After several unsuccessful attempts at halting the auctions through eBay's dispute resolution program, UMG filed a complaint against Augusto in the United States District Court for the Central District of California, alleging that Augusto had infringed UMG's copyrights in eight promotional CDs for which it retained the "exclusive right to distribute." The district court granted summary judgment in favor of Augusto, and UMG appealed.

. . .

DISCUSSION

. . .

The Distribution of the Promotional CDs Effected a Sale

. . . Notwithstanding its distinctive name, the [first sale] doctrine applies not only when a copy is first sold, but when a copy is given away or title is otherwise transferred without the accouterments of a sale. "[O]nce the copyright owner places a copyrighted item in the stream of commerce . . ., he has exhausted his exclusive statutory right to control its distribution." *Quality King*, 523 U.S. at 152. . . .

. . . [A] copyright owner who transfers title in a particular copy to a purchaser or donee cannot prevent resale of that particular copy. We have recognized, however, that not every transfer of possession of a copy transfers title. Particularly with regard to computer software, we have recognized that copyright owners may create licensing arrangements so that users acquire only a license to use the particular copy of software and do not acquire title that permits further transfer or sale of that copy without the permission of the copyright owner. Our most recent example of that rule is *Vernor v. Autodesk, Inc.*, 621 F.3d 1102 (9th Cir. 2010). . . . All of these [software] cases dealt with the question whether arrangements with consumers amounted to sales of copies, or succeeded in awarding only licenses. They recognized that the mere labeling of an arrangement as a license rather than a sale, although it was a factor to be considered, was not by itself dispositive of the issue. See, e.g., *Vernor*, 621 F.3d at 1109).

The same question is presented here. Did UMG succeed in creating a license in recipients of its promotional CDs, or did it convey title despite the restrictive labeling on the CDs? We conclude that, under all the circumstances of the CDs' distribution, the recipients were entitled to use or dispose of them in any manner they saw fit, and UMG did not enter a license agreement for the CDs with the recipients. Accordingly, UMG transferred title to the particular copies of its promotional CDs and cannot maintain an infringement action against Augusto for his subsequent sale of those copies.

Our conclusion that the recipients acquired ownership of the CDs is based largely on the nature of UMG's distribution. First, the promotional CDs are dispatched to the recipients without any prior arrangement as to those particular copies. The CDs are not numbered, and no attempt is made to keep track of where particular copies are or what use is made of them. As explained in greater detail below, although UMG places written restrictions in the labels of the CDs, it has not established that the restrictions on the CDs create a license agreement.

. . .

There are additional reasons for concluding that UMG's distribution of the CDs did not involve a consensual licensing operation. Some of the statements on the CDs and UMG's purported method of securing agreement to licenses militate against a conclusion that any licenses were created. The sparest promotional statement, "Promotional Use Only—Not for Sale," does not even purport to create a license. But even the more detailed statement is flawed in the manner in which it purports to secure agreement from the recipient. The more detailed statement provides:

> This CD is the property of the record company and is licensed to the intended recipient for personal use only. Acceptance of this CD shall constitute an agreement to comply with the terms of the license. Resale or transfer of possession is not allowed and may be punishable under federal and state laws.

It is one thing to say, as the statement does, that "acceptance" of the CD constitutes an agreement to a license and its restrictions, but it is quite another to maintain that "acceptance" may be assumed when the recipient makes no response at all. This record reflects no responses. Even when the evidence is viewed in the light most favorable to UMG, it does not show that any recipients agreed to enter into a license agreement with UMG when they received the CDs.

Because the record here is devoid of any indication that the recipients agreed to a license, there is no evidence to support a conclusion that licenses were established under the terms of the promotional statement. Accordingly, we conclude that UMG's transfer of possession to the recipients, without meaningful control or even knowledge of the status of the CDs after shipment, accomplished a transfer of title.

. . .

Because we conclude that UMG's method of distribution transferred the ownership of the copies to the recipients, we have no need to parse the remaining provisions in UMG's purported licensing statement; UMG dispatched the CDs in a manner that permitted their receipt and retention by the recipients without the recipients accepting the terms of the promotional statements. UMG's transfer of unlimited possession in the circumstances present here effected a gift or sale within the meaning of the first sale doctrine, as the district court held. . . .

QUESTIONS

How do you ascertain whether a particular copy has been "sold" or "licensed"? How, if at all, do the 9th Circuit's two decisions relate to the contours of the exhaustion doctrine evoked in TRIPS article 6 and WCT article 6?

(2) E.U. Law

Note on exhaustion of rights in the E.U.

In Europe, the doctrine of exhaustion of rights was originally created by the confrontation between IP and the European principle of free circulation of goods.* The way for the ECJ reconciled these principles by limiting IP rights by the rule of exhaustion of the distribution right. As a result, once the

---

* See the following article of the TFEU:Article 28
1. The Union shall comprise a customs union which shall cover all trade in goods and which shall involve the prohibition between Member States of customs duties on imports and exports and of all charges having equivalent effect, and the adoption of a common customs tariff in their relations with third countries.
2. The provisions of Article 30 and of Chapter 3 of this Title shall apply to products originating in Member States and to products coming from third countries which are in free circulation in Member States.
Article 34
Quantitative restrictions on imports and all measures having equivalent effect shall be prohibited between Member States.
Article 35
Quantitative restrictions on exports, and all measures having equivalent effect, shall be prohibited between Member States.

distribution of the copy has been authorized in one European country, that copy may be imported into any other E.U. country. The exhaustion principle being related to the creation of a European single market, its scope is limited to countries that are members of the E.U; the distribution right continues fully to apply with respect to copies imported from outside the E.U. The exhaustion doctrine has been integrated in European Directives, and especially in Directive 2001/29/EC on the harmonisation of certain aspects of copyright and related rights in the information society.

Directive 2009/24/EC of the European Parliament and of the Council of 23 April 2009 on the legal protection of computer programs

Article 4 – Restricted acts

2. The first sale in the Community of a copy of a program by the rightholder or with his consent shall exhaust the distribution right within the Community of that copy, with the exception of the right to control further rental of the program or a copy thereof.

Directive 96/9/EC of the European Parliament and of the Council of 11 March 1996 on the legal protection of databases

Article 5 – Restricted acts

(c) . . . The first sale in the Community of a copy of the database by the rightholder or with his consent shall exhaust the right to control resale of that copy within the Community; . . .

Directive 2001/29/EC of the European Parliament and of the Council of 22 May 2001 on the harmonisation of certain aspects of copyright and related rights in the information society

Recitals

(28) Copyright protection under this Directive includes the exclusive right to control distribution of the work incorporated in a tangible article.

Article 36
The provisions of Articles 34 and 35 shall not preclude prohibitions or restrictions on imports, exports or goods in transit justified on grounds of public morality, public policy or public security; the protection of health and life of humans, animals or plants; the protection of national treasures possessing artistic, historic or archaeological value; or the protection of industrial and commercial property. Such prohibitions or restrictions shall not, however, constitute a means of arbitrary discrimination or a disguised restriction on trade between Member States.

The first sale in the Community of the original of a work or copies thereof by the rightholder or with his consent exhausts the right to control resale of that object in the Community. This right should not be exhausted in respect of the original or of copies thereof sold by the rightholder or with his consent outside the Community. Rental and lending rights for authors have been established in Directive 92/100/EEC. The distribution right provided for in this Directive is without prejudice to the provisions relating to the rental and lending rights contained in Chapter I of that Directive.

(29) The question of exhaustion does not arise in the case of services and on-line services in particular. This also applies with regard to a material copy of a work or other subject-matter made by a user of such a service with the consent of the rightholder. Therefore, the same applies to rental and lending of the original and copies of works or other subject-matter which are services by nature. Unlike CD-ROM or CD-I, where the intellectual property is incorporated in a material medium, namely an item of goods, every on-line service is in fact an act which should be subject to authorisation where the copyright or related right so provides.

Article 4 – Distribution right

2. The distribution right shall not be exhausted within the Community in respect of the original or copies of the work, except where the first sale or other transfer of ownership in the Community of that object is made by the rightholder or with his consent.

QUESTION

Under E.U. directives, what is the predicate of the exhaustion? A sale or any transfer of the right of ownership? What, if any, are the consequences as to compliance with international norms?

b. What is a "copy" subject to the first sale doctrine?

(1) U.S. Copyright Act

Capitol Records v. ReDigi 934 F. Supp. 2d 640 (SDNY 2013)

[Capitol Records charged ReDigi with infringement of the reproduction and distribution rights. ReDigi contended that its system offered the digital equivalent of the used record market, and accordingly should benefit from the first sale doctrine. The district court disagreed and granted summary judgment for Capitol Records. It held that ReDigi reproduced the files on its servers and distributed copies to its customers. The court found no statutory basis for a digital first sale doctrine; rather the text of the statute clearly precluded the doctrine's application to dematerialized copies. The court declined ReDigi's invitation to craft such an exception:]

[T]he first sale doctrine does not protect ReDigi's distribution of Capitol's copyrighted works. This is because, as an unlawful reproduction, a digital music file sold on ReDigi is not "lawfully made under this title." 17 U.S.C. § 109(a). Moreover, the statute protects only distribution by "the owner of a particular copy or phonorecord . . . of that copy or phonorecord." Here, a ReDigi user owns the phonorecord that was created when she purchased and downloaded a song from iTunes to her hard disk. But to sell that song on ReDigi, she must produce a new phonorecord on the ReDigi server. Because it is therefore impossible for the user to sell her "particular" phonorecord on ReDigi, the first sale statute cannot provide a defense. Put another way, the first sale defense is limited to material items, like records, that the copyright owner put into the stream of commerce. Here, ReDigi is not distributing such material items; rather, it is distributing reproductions of the copyrighted code embedded in new material objects, namely, the ReDigi server in Arizona and its users' hard drives. The first sale defense does not cover this any more than it covered the sale of cassette recordings of vinyl records in a bygone era.

. . . ReDigi effectively requests that the Court amend the statute to achieve ReDigi's broader policy goals—goals that happen to advance ReDigi's economic interests. However, ReDigi's argument fails for two reasons. First, while technological change may have rendered Section 109(a) unsatisfactory to many contemporary observers and consumers, it has not rendered it ambiguous. The statute plainly applies to the lawful owner's "particular" phonorecord, a phonorecord that by definition cannot be uploaded and sold on ReDigi's website. Second, amendment of the Copyright Act in line with ReDigi's proposal is a legislative prerogative that courts are unauthorized and ill suited to attempt.

Nor are the policy arguments as straightforward or uncontested as ReDigi suggests. Indeed, when confronting this precise subject in its report on the Digital Millenium Copyright Act, 17 U.S.C. § 512, the United States Copyright Office . . . rejected extension of the first sale doctrine to the distribution of digital works, noting that the justifications for the first sale doctrine in the physical world could not be imported into the digital domain. . . . Thus, while ReDigi mounts attractive policy arguments, they are not as one-sided as it contends.

Finally, ReDigi feebly argues that the Court's reading of Section 109(a) would in effect exclude digital works from the meaning of the statute. That is not the case. Section 109(a) still protects a lawful owner's sale of her "particular" phonorecord, be it a computer hard disk, iPod, or other memory device onto which the file was originally downloaded. While this limitation clearly presents obstacles to resale that are different from, and perhaps even more onerous than, those involved in the resale of CDs and cassettes, the limitation is hardly absurd—the first sale doctrine was enacted in a world where the ease and speed of data transfer could not have been imagined. There are many reasons, some discussed herein, for why such physical limitations may be desirable. It is left to Congress, and not this Court, to deem them outmoded.

Accordingly, the Court concludes that the first sale defense does not permit sales of digital music files on ReDigi's website.

QUESTION

Is the *ReDigi* court's interpretation of section 109(a) consistent with WCT article 6? Consider the agreed statement and the inferences to draw from it.

(2) E.U. Law

C-128/11 UsedSoft GmbH v. Oracle International Corp. ECLI:EU:C:2012:407 [2012]

[This case concerned the extent of the distribution right under the computer program Directive, and its corollary, the exhaustion of the right to distribute digital copies. In order to apply the exhaustion doctrine, the court also had to determine what constitutes a "sale."]

21   Oracle distributes the software at issue in the main proceedings, namely databank software, in 85% of cases by downloading from the internet. The customer downloads a copy of the software directly to his computer from Oracle's website. The software is what is known as 'client-server-software'. The user right for such a program, which is granted by a licence agreement, includes the right to store a copy of the program permanently on a server and to allow a certain number of users to access it by downloading it to the main memory of their work-station computers. On the basis of a maintenance agreement, updated versions of the software ('updates') and programs for correcting faults ('patches') can be downloaded from Oracle's website.

. . .

24   UsedSoft markets used software licences, including user licences for the Oracle computer programs at issue in the main proceedings. For that purpose UsedSoft acquires from customers of Oracle such user licences, or parts of them, where the original licences relate to a greater number of users than required by the first acquirer.

25   In October 2005 UsedSoft promoted an 'Oracle Special Offer' in which it offered for sale 'already used' licences for the Oracle programs at issue in the main proceedings. In doing so it pointed out that the licences were all 'current' in the sense that the maintenance agreement concluded between the original licence holder and Oracle was still in force, and that the lawfulness of the original sale was confirmed by a notarial certificate.

26   Customers of UsedSoft who are not yet in possession of the Oracle software in question download a copy of the program directly from Oracle's website, after acquiring such a used licence. Customers who already have that software and then purchase further licences for additional users are induced by UsedSoft to copy the program to the work stations of those users.

. . .

35   By its second question, which should be addressed first, the referring court [the German Federal Court of Justice] essentially seeks to know whether and under what conditions the downloading from the internet of a copy of a computer program, authorised by the copyright holder, can give rise to exhaustion of the right of distribution of that copy in the European Union within the meaning of Article 4(2) of Directive 2009/24 [Computer Program].

36   It should be recalled that under Article 4(2) of Directive 2009/24 [Computer Program] the first sale in the European Union of a copy of a computer program by the rightholder or with his consent exhausts the distribution right within the European Union of that copy.

37   According to the order for reference, the copyright holder itself, in this case Oracle, makes available to its customers in the European Union who wish to use its computer program a copy of that program which can be downloaded from its website.

38   To determine whether, in a situation such as that at issue in the main proceedings, the copyright holder's distribution right is exhausted, it must

be ascertained, first, whether the contractual relationship between the right-holder and its customer, within which the downloading of a copy of the program in question has taken place, may be regarded as a 'first sale . . . of a copy of a program' within the meaning of Article 4(2) of Directive 2009/24 [Computer Program].

. . . .

42   According to a commonly accepted definition, a 'sale' is an agreement by which a person, in return for payment, transfers to another person his rights of ownership in an item of tangible or intangible property belonging to him. It follows that the commercial transaction giving rise, in accordance with Article 4(2) of Directive 2009/24 [Computer Program], to exhaustion of the right of distribution of a copy of a computer program must involve a transfer of the right of ownership in that copy.

. . .

44   It must be observed that the downloading of a copy of a computer program and the conclusion of a user licence agreement for that copy form an indivisible whole. Downloading a copy of a computer program is point-less if the copy cannot be used by its possessor. Those two operations must therefore be examined as a whole for the purposes of their legal classification [citations omitted].

45   As regards the question whether, in a situation such as that at issue in the main proceedings, the commercial transactions concerned involve a transfer of the right of ownership of the copy of the computer program, it must be stated that, according to the order for reference, a customer of Oracle who downloads the copy of the program and concludes with that company a user licence agreement relating to that copy receives, in return for payment of a fee, a right to use that copy for an unlimited period. The making available by Oracle of a copy of its computer program and the con-clusion of a user licence agreement for that copy are thus intended to make the copy usable by the customer, permanently, in return for payment of a fee designed to enable the copyright holder to obtain a remuneration cor-responding to the economic value of the copy of the work of which it is the proprietor.

46   In those circumstances, the operations mentioned in paragraph 44 above, examined as a whole, involve the transfer of the right of ownership of the copy of the computer program in question.

. . .

48 Consequently, in a situation such as that at issue in the main proceedings, the transfer by the copyright holder to a customer of a copy of a computer program, accompanied by the conclusion between the same parties of a user licence agreement, constitutes a 'first sale . . . of a copy of a program' within the meaning of Article 4(2) of Directive 2009/24 [Computer Program].

. . .

52 Moreover, as stated in paragraph 46 above, in a situation such as that at issue in the main proceedings, the copyright holder transfers the right of ownership of the copy of the computer program to his customer. [citations omitted], it follows from Article 6(1) of the Copyright Treaty [WCT], in the light of which Articles 3 and 4 of Directive 2001/29 [Info Soc] must, so far as possible, be interpreted (see, to that effect, Case C-456/06 *Peek & Cloppenburg* [2008] ECR I-2731, paragraph 30), that the existence of a transfer of ownership changes an 'act of communication to the public' provided for in Article 3 of that directive into an act of distribution referred to in Article 4 of the directive which, if the conditions in Article 4(2) of the directive are satisfied, can, like a 'first sale . . . of a copy of a program' referred to in Article 4(2) of Directive 2009/24 [Computer Program], give rise to exhaustion of the distribution right.

53 [I]t must also be examined whether, as argued by Oracle, the governments which have submitted observations to the Court, and the Commission, the exhaustion of the distribution right referred to in Article 4(2) of Directive 2009/24 [Computer Program] relates only to tangible property and not to intangible copies of computer programs downloaded from the internet. They refer in this respect to the wording of Article 4(2) of Directive 2009/24 [Computer Program], recitals 28 and 29 in the preamble to Directive 2001/29 [Info Soc], Article 4 of Directive 2001/29 [Info Soc] read in conjunction with Article 8 of the Copyright Treaty [WCT], and the agreed statement concerning Articles 6 and 7 of the Copyright Treaty [WCT], whose transposition is one of the aims of Directive 2001/29 [Info Soc].

54 Furthermore, according to the Commission, recital 29 in the preamble to Directive 2001/29 [Info Soc] confirms that '[t]he question of exhaustion does not arise in the case of services and on-line services in particular'.

55   On this point, it must be stated, first, that it does not appear from Article 4(2) of Directive 2009/24 [Computer Program] that the exhaustion of the right of distribution of copies of computer programs mentioned in that provision is limited to copies of programmes on a material medium such as a CD-ROM or DVD. On the contrary, that provision, by referring without further specification to the 'sale . . . of a copy of a program', makes no distinction according to the tangible or intangible form of the copy in question.

56   Next, it must be recalled that Directive 2009/24 [Computer Program], which concerns specifically the legal protection of computer programs, constitutes a lex specialis in relation to Directive 2001/29 [Info Soc].

57   Article 1(2) of Directive 2009/24 [Computer Program] states that '[p]rotection in accordance with this Directive shall apply to the expression in any form of a computer program'. Recital 7 in the preamble to that directive specifies that the 'computer programs' it aims to protect 'include programs in any form, including those which are incorporated into hardware'.

58   Those provisions thus make abundantly clear the intention of the European Union legislature to assimilate, for the purposes of the protection laid down by Directive 2009/24 [Computer Program], tangible and intangible copies of computer programs.

59   In those circumstances, it must be considered that the exhaustion of the distribution right under Article 4(2) of Directive 2009/24 [Computer Program] concerns both tangible and intangible copies of a computer program, and hence also copies of programs which, on the occasion of their first sale, have been downloaded from the internet onto the first acquirer's computer.

60   It is true that the concepts used in Directives 2001/29 [Info Soc] and 2009/24 [Computer Program] must in principle have the same meaning [citations omitted], indicated that, for the works covered by that directive, the exhaustion of the distribution right concerned only tangible objects, that would not be capable of affecting the interpretation of Article 4(2) of Directive 2009/24 [Computer Program], having regard to the different intention expressed by the European Union legislature in the specific context of that directive.

61   It should be added that, from an economic point of view, the sale of a computer program on CD-ROM or DVD and the sale of a program by downloading from the internet are similar. The on-line transmission method is the functional equivalent of the supply of a material medium. . . .

. . .

70   An original acquirer who resells a tangible or intangible copy of a computer program for which the copyright holder's right of distribution is exhausted in accordance with Article 4(2) of Directive 2009/24 [Computer Program] must, in order to avoid infringing the exclusive right of reproduction of a computer program which belongs to its author, laid down in Article 4(1)(a) of Directive 2009/24 [Computer Program], make his own copy unusable at the time of its resale. In a situation such as that mentioned in the preceding paragraph, the customer of the copyright holder will continue to use the copy of the program installed on his server and will not thus make it unusable. . . .

ECJ: C–419/13 Art & Allposters International BV v. Stichting Pictoright ECLI:EU:C:2015:27 [2015]

[Plaintiff Pictoright is a Netherlands copyright collecting society mandated to exploit and enforce copyright in visual works on behalf of the rightholders. Defendant Allposters, markets posters and other reproductions depicting the works of famous painters, which are covered by the copyright exploited by Pictoright. Among other products, Allposters sells canvasses bearing images transferred from paper posters. In order to produce an image on canvas, a synthetic coating (laminate) is first applied to a paper poster depicting the chosen work. Next, the image on the poster is transferred from the paper to a canvas by means of a chemical process. Finally, that canvas is stretched over a wooden frame. The image of the work disappears from the paper backing during the process. Pictoright alleged that Allposters' 'canvas transfers' infringed its right to distribute copies of the work; Allposters replied that copyright in the images was exhausted with the sale of the paper posters, and that the canvass transfers did not create any additional copies of the images.]

. . .

29   With regard to the conditions of application of the exhaustion rule, it follows from Article 4(2) of Directive 2001/29 [Info Soc] that the distribution right is not exhausted in respect of the original or copies of a work, except where the first sale or other transfer of ownership in the European Union of that object is made by the rightholder or with his consent.

32   In the case in the main proceedings, it is undisputed that posters reproducing works of famous painters, which are covered by the copyright the holders of which are represented by Pictoright, have been placed on the

market in the EEA [European Economic Area] with the consent of those rightholders.

33   However, the parties in the main proceedings are in disagreement, first, as to whether exhaustion of the distribution right covers the tangible object into which a work or its copy is incorporated or the author's own intellectual creation and, secondly, as to whether the alteration of the medium, as undertaken by Allposters, has an impact on exhaustion of the exclusive distribution right.

34   With regard, first, to the purpose of the distribution right, Article 4(2) of Directive 2001/29 [Info Soc] refers to the first sale or other transfer of ownership of 'that object'.

. . .

37   . . . the E.U. legislature, by using the terms 'tangible article' and 'that object', wished to give authors control over the initial marketing in the European Union of each tangible object incorporating their intellectual creation.

38   That finding, as the European Commission correctly states, is supported by international law, and in particular by the WIPO Copyright Treaty, in the light of which Directive 2001/29 [Info Soc] must be interpreted as far as possible [citations omitted].

39   Article 6(1) of that Treaty provides that authors of literary and artistic works are to enjoy the exclusive right of authorising the making available to the public of the original and copies of their works through sale or other transfer of ownership. In that regard, the significance of the term 'copy' was explained by the Contracting Parties by an agreed statement concerning Articles 6 and 7 of the Treaty adopted by the Diplomatic Conference of 20 December 1996, at which the Treaty itself was also adopted. According to that statement, 'the expressions "copies" and "original and copies" being subject to the right of distribution and the right of rental under the said Articles, refer exclusively to fixed copies that can be put into circulation as tangible objects'.

40   Accordingly, it should be found that exhaustion of the distribution right applies to the tangible object into which a protected work or its copy is incorporated if it has been placed onto the market with the copyright holder's consent.

41   In the second place, it must be assessed whether the fact that the object, which was marketed with the copyright holder's consent, has undergone subsequent alterations to its physical medium has an impact on exhaustion of the distribution right within the meaning of Article 4(2) of Directive 2001/29 [Info Soc].

. . .

44   Allposters . . . maintains that the transfer onto canvas cannot be categorised as reproduction on the ground that there is no multiplication of copies of the protected work since the image is transferred and no longer appears on the poster. It explains that the ink which reproduces the work is not altered and that the work itself is not affected in any way.

45   That argument cannot be accepted. The fact that the ink is saved during the transfer cannot affect the finding that the image's medium has been altered. What is important is whether the altered object itself, taken as a whole, is, physically, the object that was placed onto the market with the consent of the rightholder. That does not appear to be the case in the dispute in the main proceedings.

46   Consequently, the consent of the copyright holder does not cover the distribution of an object incorporating his work if that object has been altered after its initial marketing in such a way that it constitutes a new reproduction of that work. . . .

QUESTIONS

1. Based on these decisions, to what extent does the E.U. exhaustion doctrine apply to non tangible copies?
2. What role do international norms play in each of these decisions? Are the decisions consistent with international norms?

c. What is the territorial scope of exhaustion?

(1) International exhaustion under U.S. Law

Kirtsaeng v. John Wiley & Sons, Inc. 133 S Ct 1351 (2013)

▪ Justice Breyer delivered the opinion of the Court.

Section 106 of the Copyright Act grants "the owner of copyright under this title" certain "exclusive rights," including the right "to distribute copies . . . of

the copyrighted work to the public by sale or other transfer of ownership."
17 U.S.C. § 106(3). These rights are qualified, however, by the application
of various limitations set forth in the next several sections of the Act, §§ 107
through 122. . . .

Section 109(a) sets forth the "first sale" doctrine as follows:

> "Notwithstanding the provisions of section 106(3), the owner of a par-
> ticular copy or phonorecord *lawfully made under this title* . . . is entitled,
> without the authority of the copyright owner, to sell or otherwise dispose
> of the possession of that copy or phonorecord." (Emphasis added.)

Thus, even though § 106(3) forbids distribution of a copy of, say, the copyrighted novel *Herzog* without the copyright owner's permission, § 109(a)
adds that, once a copy of *Herzog* has been lawfully sold (or its ownership otherwise lawfully transferred), the buyer of *that copy* and subsequent owners
are free to dispose of it as they wish. In copyright jargon, the "first sale" has
"exhausted" the copyright owner's § 106(3) exclusive distribution right.

What, however, if the copy of *Herzog* was printed abroad and then initially
sold with the copyright owner's permission? Does the "first sale" doctrine
still apply? Is the buyer, like the buyer of a domestically manufactured copy,
free to bring the copy into the United States and dispose of it as he or she
wishes?

To put the matter technically, an "importation" provision, § 602(a)(1), says
that

> "[i]mportation into the United States, without the authority of the
> owner of copyright under this title, of copies . . . of a work that have been
> acquired outside the United States is an infringement of the exclusive
> right to distribute copies . . . *under section 106* . . . ." 17 U.S.C. § 602(a)(1)
> (emphasis added).

Thus § 602(a)(1) makes clear that importing a copy without permission
violates the owner's exclusive distribution right. But in doing so, § 602(a)(1)
refers explicitly to the *§ 106(3)* exclusive distribution right. As we have just
said, § 106 is by its terms "[s]ubject to" the various doctrines and principles
contained in §§ 107 through 122, including § 109(a)'s "first sale" limitation.
Do those same modifications apply—in particular, does the "first sale" modification apply—when considering whether § 602(a)(1) prohibits importing
a copy?

In *Quality King Distribs. v. L'anza Research Int'l*, 523 U.S. 135, 145 (1998), we held that § 602(a)(1)'s reference to § 106(3)'s exclusive distribution right incorporates the later subsections' limitations, including, in particular, the "first sale" doctrine of § 109. Thus, it might seem that, § 602(a)(1) notwithstanding, one who buys a copy abroad can freely import that copy into the United States and dispose of it, just as he could had he bought the copy in the United States.

But *Quality King* considered an instance in which the copy, though purchased abroad, was initially manufactured in the United States (and then sent abroad and sold). This case is like *Quality King* but for one important fact. The copies at issue here were manufactured abroad. That fact is important because § 109(a) says that the "first sale" doctrine applies to "a particular copy or phonorecord *lawfully made under this title*." And we must decide here whether the five words, "lawfully made under this title," make a critical legal difference.

Putting section numbers to the side, we ask whether the "first sale" doctrine applies to protect a buyer or other lawful owner of a copy (of a copyrighted work) lawfully manufactured abroad. Can that buyer bring that copy into the United States (and sell it or give it away) without obtaining permission to do so from the copyright owner? Can, for example, someone who purchases, say at a used bookstore, a book printed abroad subsequently resell it without the copyright owner's permission?

In our view, the answers to these questions are, yes. We hold that the "first sale" doctrine applies to copies of a copyrighted work lawfully made abroad.

I.

[John Wiley publishes textbooks in a variety of countries. In some countries the books are printed on lower-quality paper and are stamped with a notice that they are not to be resold. Kirtsaeng nonetheless purchased substantial quantities of Wiley text books in Thailand and imported them to the U.S., where he sold them for prices considerably lower than the U.S. publisher's price. The lower courts held that the first sale doctrine did not apply to copies made outside of the U.S. and therefore found Kirtsaeng liable for infringement of Wiley's distribution right. Kirtsaeng sought certiorari, arguing that copies lawfully made anywhere in the world could be resold in the U.S. without the U.S. copyright owner's authorization.]

II.

We must decide whether the words "lawfully made under this title" restrict the scope of § 109(a)'s "first sale" doctrine geographically [to copies made in the United States]. . . .

In our view, § 109(a)'s language, its context, and the common-law history of the "first sale" doctrine, taken together, favor a *non*-geographical interpretation. We also doubt that Congress would have intended to create the practical copyright-related harms with which a geographical interpretation would threaten ordinary scholarly, artistic, commercial, and consumer activities. We consequently conclude that Kirtsaeng's nongeographical reading is the better reading of the Act.

A.

The language of § 109(a) read literally favors Kirtsaeng's nongeographical interpretation, namely, that "lawfully made under this title" means made "in accordance with" or "in compliance with" the Copyright Act. The language of § 109(a) says nothing about geography. The word "under" can mean "[i]n accordance with." 18 Oxford English Dictionary 950 (2d ed. 1989). See also Black's Law Dictionary 1525 (6th ed. 1990) ("according to"). And a nongeographical interpretation provides each word of the five-word phrase with a distinct purpose. The first two words of the phrase, "lawfully made," suggest an effort to distinguish those copies that were made lawfully from those that were not, and the last three words, "under this title," set forth the standard of "lawful[ness]." Thus, the nongeographical reading is simple, it promotes a traditional copyright objective (combatting piracy), and it makes word-by-word linguistic sense.

The geographical interpretation, however, bristles with linguistic difficulties. It gives the word "lawfully" little, if any, linguistic work to do. (How could a book be *un*lawfully "made under this title"?) It imports geography into a statutory provision that says nothing explicitly about it. And it is far more complex than may at first appear.

To read the clause geographically, Wiley, like the Second Circuit and the Solicitor General, must first emphasize the word "under." Indeed, Wiley reads "under this title" to mean "in conformance with the Copyright Act *where the Copyright Act is applicable*." Wiley must then take a second step, arguing that the Act "is applicable" only in the United States. . . .

One difficulty is that neither "under" nor any other word in the phrase means "where." See, *e.g.*, 18 Oxford English Dictionary, *supra*, at 947–952 (definition of "under"). It might mean "subject to," but as this Court has repeatedly acknowledged, the word evades a uniform, consistent meaning.

A far more serious difficulty arises out of the uncertainty and complexity surrounding the second step's effort to read the necessary geographical limitation into the word "applicable" (or the equivalent). Where, precisely, is the Copyright Act "applicable"? The Act does not instantly *protect* an American copyright holder from unauthorized piracy taking place abroad. But that fact does not mean the Act is *inapplicable* to copies made abroad. As a matter of ordinary English, one can say that a statute imposing, say, a tariff upon "any rhododendron grown in Nepal" applies to *all* Nepalese rhododendrons. And, similarly, one can say that the American Copyright Act is *applicable* to *all* pirated copies, including those printed overseas. Indeed, the Act itself makes clear that (in the Solicitor General's language) foreign-printed pirated copies are "subject to" the Act. § 602(a)(2) (referring to importation of copies "the making of which either constituted an infringement of copyright, or which would have constituted an infringement of copyright if this title had been applicable"); Brief for United States.

The appropriateness of this linguistic usage is underscored by the fact that § 104 of the Act itself says that works *"subject to protection under this title"* include unpublished works "without regard to the nationality or domicile of the author," and works "first published" in any one of the nearly 180 nations that have signed a copyright treaty with the United States. §§ 104(a), (b) (emphasis added); § 101 (defining "treaty party"); U.S. Copyright Office, Circular No. 38A, International Copyright Relations of the United States (2010). Thus, ordinary English permits us to say that the Act "applies" to an Irish manuscript lying in its author's Dublin desk drawer as well as to an original recording of a ballet performance first made in Japan and now on display in a Kyoto art gallery. . . .

The Ninth Circuit's geographical interpretation produces still greater linguistic difficulty. As we said, that Circuit interprets the "first sale" doctrine to cover both (1) copies manufactured in the United States and (2) copies manufactured abroad but first sold in the United States with the American copyright owner's permission. . . .

We can understand why the Ninth Circuit may have thought it necessary to add the second part of its definition. As we shall later describe, without some such qualification a copyright holder could prevent a buyer from domestically reselling or even giving away copies of a video game made in Japan, a film made in Germany, or a dress (with a design copyright [sic]) made in China, *even* if the copyright holder has granted permission for the foreign manufacture, importation, and an initial domestic sale of the copy. A publisher such as Wiley would be free to print its books abroad, allow their importation and sale within the United States, but prohibit students from later selling their used texts at a campus bookstore. We see no way, however, to reconcile this half-geographical/half-nongeographical interpretation with the language of the phrase, "lawfully made under this title." As a matter of English, it would seem that those five words either do cover copies lawfully made abroad or they do not.

In sum, we believe that geographical interpretations create more linguistic problems than they resolve. And considerations of simplicity and coherence tip the purely linguistic balance in Kirtsaeng's, nongeographical, favor.

. . .

D.

. . .

[R]eliance upon the "first sale" doctrine is deeply embedded in the practices of those, such as booksellers, libraries, museums, and retailers, who have long relied upon its protection. Museums, for example, are not in the habit of asking their foreign counterparts to check with the heirs of copyright owners before sending, *e.g.*, a Picasso on tour. That inertia means a dramatic change is likely necessary before these institutions, instructed by their counsel, would begin to engage in the complex permission-verifying process that a geographical interpretation would demand. And this Court's adoption of the geographical interpretation could provide that dramatic change. These intolerable consequences (along with the absurd result that the copyright owner can exercise downstream control even when it authorized the import or first sale) have understandably led the Ninth Circuit, the Solicitor General as *amicus*, and the dissent to adopt textual readings of the statute that attempt to mitigate these harms. But those readings are not defensible, for they require too many unprecedented jumps over linguistic and other hurdles that in our view are insurmountable. . . .

Finally, the fact that harm has proved limited so far may simply reflect the reluctance of copyright holders so far to assert geographically based resale rights. They may decide differently if the law is clarified in their favor.

Regardless, a copyright law that can work in practice only if unenforced is not a sound copyright law. It is a law that would create uncertainty, would bring about selective enforcement, and, if widely unenforced, would breed disrespect for copyright law itself.

Thus, we believe that the practical problems that petitioner and his *amici* have described are too serious, too extensive, and too likely to come about for us to dismiss them as insignificant—particularly in light of the ever-growing importance of foreign trade to America. The upshot is that copyright-related consequences along with language, context, and interpretive canons argue strongly against a geographical interpretation of § 109(a).

. . .

. . . Wiley and the dissent claim that a nongeographical interpretation will make it difficult, perhaps impossible, for publishers (and other copyright holders) to divide foreign and domestic markets. We concede that is so. A publisher may find it more difficult to charge different prices for the same book in different geographic markets. But we do not see how these facts help Wiley, for we can find no basic principle of copyright law that suggests that publishers are especially entitled to such rights.

. . .

To the contrary, Congress enacted a copyright law that (through the "first sale" doctrine) limits copyright holders' ability to divide domestic markets. And that limitation is consistent with antitrust laws that ordinarily forbid market divisions. Whether copyright owners should, or should not, have more than ordinary commercial power to divide international markets is a matter for Congress to decide. We do no more here than try to determine what decision Congress has taken.

Fourth, the dissent and Wiley contend that our decision launches United States copyright law into an unprecedented regime of "international exhaustion." But they point to nothing indicative of congressional intent in 1976. The dissent also claims that it is clear that the United States now opposes adopting such a regime, but the Solicitor General as *amicus* has taken no such position in this case. In fact, when pressed at oral argument, the Solicitor General stated that the consequences of Wiley's reading of the statute (perpetual downstream control) were "worse" than those of Kirtsaeng's reading (restriction of market segmentation). And the dissent's reliance on the Solicitor General's position in *Quality King* is undermined by his agreement in that case with our reading of § 109(a). Brief for United States as *Amicus Curiae* in *Quality King*, O. T. 1996, No. 1470, p. 30 ("When ... Congress wishes to make the location of manufacture relevant to Copyright Act protection, it does so expressly"); *ibid.* (calling it "distinctly unlikely" that Congress would have provided an incentive for overseas manufacturing).

Moreover, the exhaustion regime the dissent apparently favors would provide that "the sale in one country of a good" does not "exhaus[t] the intellectual-property owner's right to control the distribution of that good elsewhere." But our holding in *Quality King* that § 109(a) is a defense in U.S. courts even when "the first sale occurred abroad," 523 U.S., at 145, n. 14, has already significantly eroded such a principle.

. . .

▪ Justice Kagan, with whom Justice Alito joins, concurring. [omitted]

▪ Justice Ginsburg, with whom Justice Kennedy joins, and with whom Justice Scalia joins except as to Parts III and V-B-1, dissenting.

"In the interpretation of statutes, the function of the courts is easily stated. It is to construe the language so as to give effect to the intent of Congress." *United States v. American Trucking Assns., Inc.*, 310 U.S. 534, 542 (1940). Instead of adhering to the Legislature's design, the Court today adopts an interpretation of the Copyright Act at odds with Congress' aim to protect copyright owners against the unauthorized importation of low-priced, foreign-made copies of their copyrighted works. The Court's bold departure from Congress' design is all the more stunning, for it places the United States at the vanguard of the movement for "international exhaustion" of copyrights—a movement the United States has steadfastly resisted on the world stage.

. . .

I.

Because economic conditions and demand for particular goods vary across the globe, copyright owners have a financial incentive to charge different prices for copies of their works in different geographic regions. Their ability to engage in such price discrimination, however, is undermined if arbitrageurs are permitted to import copies from low-price regions and sell them in high-price regions. The question in this case is whether the unauthorized importation of foreign-made copies constitutes copyright infringement under U.S. law.

To answer this question, one must examine three provisions of Title 17 of the U.S. Code: § § 106(3), 109(a), and 602(a)(1). Section 106 sets forth the "exclusive rights" of a copyright owner, including the right "to distribute copies or phonorecords of the copyrighted work to the public by sale or other transfer of ownership, or by rental, lease, or lending." § 106(3). This distribution right is limited by § 109(a), which . . . codifies the "first sale doctrine," a doctrine articulated in *Bobbs–Merrill Co. v. Straus*, 210 U.S. 339, 349–351 (1908), which held that a copyright owner could not control the price at which retailers sold lawfully purchased copies of its work. . . .

Section 602(a)(1)—last, but most critical, of the three copyright provisions bearing on this case—is an importation ban. . . .

In *Quality King Distribs. v. L'anza Research Int'l*, 523 U.S. 135, 143–154 (1998), the Court held that a copyright owner's right to control importation under § 602(a)(1) is a component of the distribution right set forth in § 106(3) and is therefore subject to § 109(a)'s codification of the first sale doctrine. *Quality King* thus held that the importation of copies *made in the United States* but sold abroad did not rank as copyright infringement under § 602(a)(1). Important to the Court's holding, the copies at issue in *Quality King* had been "'lawfully made under [Title 17]'"—a prerequisite for application of § 109(a). Section 602(a)(1), the Court noted, would apply to "copies that were 'lawfully made' not under the United States Copyright Act, but instead, under the law of some other country." *Id.*, at 147. Drawing on an example discussed during a 1964 public meeting on proposed revisions to the U.S. copyright laws, the Court stated:

> "If the author of [a] work gave the exclusive United States distribution rights—enforceable under the Act—to the publisher of the United States edition and the exclusive British distribution rights to the publisher of the British edition, . . . presumably only those [copies] made by the publisher of the United States edition would be 'lawfully made under this title' within the meaning of § 109(a). The first sale doctrine would not provide the publisher of the British edition who decided to sell in the American market with a defense to an action under § 602(a) (or, for that matter, to an action under § 106(3), if there was a distribution of the copies)." *Id.*, at 148.

As the District Court and the Court of Appeals concluded, application of the *Quality King* analysis to the facts of this case would preclude any invocation of

§ 109(a). Petitioner Supap Kirtsaeng imported and then sold at a profit over 600 copies of copyrighted textbooks printed outside the United States by the Asian subsidiary of respondent John Wiley & Sons, Inc. (Wiley). In the words the Court used in *Quality King*, these copies "were 'lawfully made' not under the United States Copyright Act, but instead, under the law of some other country." Section 109(a) therefore does not apply, and Kirtsaeng's unauthorized importation constitutes copyright infringement under § 602(a)(1).

. . .

II.

The text of the Copyright Act demonstrates that Congress intended to provide copyright owners with a potent remedy against the importation of foreign-made copies of their copyrighted works. As the Court recognizes, this case turns on the meaning of the phrase "lawfully made under this title" in § 109(a). In my view, that phrase is most sensibly read as referring to instances in which a copy's creation is governed by, and conducted in compliance with, Title 17 of the U.S. Code. This reading is consistent with the Court's interpretation of similar language in other statutes.

Section 109(a), properly read, affords Kirtsaeng no defense against Wiley's claim of copyright infringement. The Copyright Act, it has been observed time and again, does not apply extraterritorially. The printing of Wiley's foreign-manufactured textbooks therefore was not governed by Title 17. The textbooks thus were not "lawfully made under [Title 17]," the crucial precondition for application of § 109(a). And if § 109(a) does not apply, there is no dispute that Kirtsaeng's conduct constituted copyright infringement under § 602(a)(1).

The Court's point of departure is similar to mine. According to the Court, the phrase "'lawfully made under this title' means made 'in accordance with' or 'in compliance with' the Copyright Act." But the Court overlooks that, according to the very dictionaries it cites, the word "under" commonly signals a relationship of subjection, where one thing is governed or regulated by another. See Black's Law Dictionary 1525 (6th ed. 1990) ("under" "frequently" means "inferior" or "subordinate" (internal quotation marks omitted)); 18 Oxford English Dictionary 950 (2d ed. 1989) ("under" means, among other things, "[i]n accordance with (*some regulative power or principle*)" (emphasis added)). Only by disregarding this established meaning of "under" can the Court arrive at the conclusion that Wiley's foreign-manufactured textbooks were "lawfully made under" U.S. copyright law, even though that law did not govern their creation. It is anomalous, however, to speak of particular conduct as "lawful" under an inapplicable law. For example, one might say that driving on the right side of the road in England is "lawful" under U.S. law, but that would be so only because U.S. law has nothing to say about the subject. The governing law is English law, and English law demands that driving be done on the left side of the road.

The logical implication of the Court's definition of the word "under" is that *any* copy manufactured abroad—even a piratical one made without the copyright owner's authorization and in violation of the law of the country where it was created—would fall within the scope of § 109(a). Any such copy would have been made "in accordance with" or "in compliance with" the U.S. Copyright Act, in the sense that manufacturing the copy did not violate the Act (because the Act does not apply extraterritorially).

The Court rightly refuses to accept such an absurd conclusion. Instead, it interprets § 109(a) as applying only to copies whose making actually complied with Title 17, or would have complied with Title 17 had Title 17 been applicable (*i.e.*, had the copies been made in the United States). ("§ 109(a)'s 'first sale' doctrine would apply to copyrighted works as long as their manufacture met the requirements of American copyright law."). Congress, however, used express language when it called for such a counterfactual inquiry in 17 U.S.C. §§ 602(a)(2) and (b). See § 602(a)(2) ("Importation into the United States or exportation from the United States, without the authority of the owner of copyright under this title, of copies or phonorecords, the making of which either constituted an infringement of copyright, or *which would have constituted an infringement of copyright if this title had been applicable*, is an infringement of the exclusive right to distribute copies or phonorecords under section 106." (emphasis added)); § 602(b) ("In a case where the making of the copies or phonorecords *would have constituted an infringement of copyright if this title had been applicable*, their importation is prohibited." (emphasis added)). Had Congress intended courts to engage in a similarly hypothetical inquiry under § 109(a), Congress would presumably have included similar language in that section.

Not only does the Court adopt an unnatural construction of the § 109(a) phrase "lawfully made under this title." Concomitantly, the Court reduces § 602(a)(1) to insignificance. . . .

The far more plausible reading of §§ 109(a) and 602(a), then, is that Congress intended § 109(a) to apply to copies made in the United States, not to copies manufactured and sold abroad. That reading of the first sale and importation provisions leaves § 602(a)(3)'s exceptions with real, meaningful work to do. . . . In the range of circumstances covered by the exceptions, § 602(a)(3) frees individuals and entities who purchase foreign-made copies abroad from the requirement they would otherwise face under § 602(a)(1) of obtaining the copyright owner's permission to import the copies into the United States.

. . .

IV.

Unlike the Court's holding, my position is consistent with the stance the United States has taken in international-trade negotiations. This case bears on the highly contentious trade issue of interterritorial exhaustion. The issue arises because intellectual property law is territorial in nature, which means that creators of intellectual property "may hold a set of parallel" intellectual property rights under the laws of different nations. Chiappetta, The Desirability of Agreeing to Disagree: The WTO, TRIPS, International IPR Exhaustion and a Few Other Things, 21 Mich. J. Int'l L. 333, 340–341 (2000) There is no international consensus on whether the sale in one country of a good incorporating protected intellectual property exhausts the intellectual property owner's right to control the distribution of that good elsewhere. Indeed, the members of the World Trade Organization, "agreeing to disagree," provided in Article 6 of the Agreement on Trade-Related Aspects of Intellectual Property Rights (TRIPS), Apr. 15, 1994, 33 I.L.M. 1197, 1200, that "nothing in this Agreement shall be used to address the issue of . . . exhaustion."

In the absence of agreement at the international level, each country has been left to choose for itself the exhaustion framework it will follow. One option is a national-exhaustion regime, under which a copyright owner's right to control distribution of a particular copy is exhausted only within the country in which the copy is sold. Another option is a rule of international exhaustion, under which the authorized distribution of a particular copy anywhere in the world exhausts the copyright owner's distribution right everywhere with respect to that copy. The European Union has adopted the intermediate approach of regional exhaustion, under which the sale of a copy anywhere within the European Economic Area exhausts the copyright owner's distribution right throughout that region. Section 602(a)(1), in my view, ties the United States to a national-exhaustion framework. The Court's decision, in contrast, places the United States solidly in the international-exhaustion camp.

Strong arguments have been made both in favor of, and in opposition to, international exhaustion. International exhaustion subjects copyright-protected goods to competition from lower priced imports and, to that extent, benefits consumers. Correspondingly, copyright owners profit from a national-exhaustion regime, which also enlarges the monetary incentive to create new copyrightable works.

Weighing the competing policy concerns, our Government reached the conclusion that widespread adoption of the international-exhaustion framework would be inconsistent with the long-term economic interests of the United States. See Brief for United States as *Amicus Curiae* in *Quality King*, O. T. 1997, No. 96–1470, pp. 22–26 (hereinafter *Quality King* Brief). Accordingly, the United States has steadfastly "taken the position in international trade negotiations that domestic copyright owners should . . . have the right to prevent the unauthorized importation of copies of their work sold abroad." *Id.* at 22. The United States has "advanced this position in multilateral trade negotiations," including the negotiations on the TRIPS Agreement. *Id.* at 24. It has also taken a dim view of our trading partners' adoption of legislation incorporating elements of international exhaustion.

Even if the text and history of the Copyright Act were ambiguous on the answer to the question this case presents—which they are not—I would resist a holding out of accord with the firm position the United States has taken on exhaustion in international negotiations. *Quality King*, I acknowledge, discounted the Government's concerns about potential inconsistency with United States obligations under certain bilateral trade agreements. That decision, however, dealt only with copyright-protected products made in the United States. *Quality King* left open the question whether owners of U.S. copyrights could retain control over the importation of copies manufactured and sold abroad—a point the Court obscures (arguing that *Quality King* "significantly eroded" the national-exhaustion principle that, in my view, § 602(a)(1) embraces). The Court today answers that question with a resounding "no," and in doing so, it risks undermining the United States' credibility on the world stage. While the Government has urged our trading partners to refrain from adopting international-exhaustion regimes that could benefit consumers within their borders but would impact adversely on intellectual-property producers in the United States, the Court embraces an international-exhaustion rule that could benefit U.S. consumers but would likely disadvantage foreign holders of U.S. copyrights. This dissonance scarcely enhances the United States' "role as a trusted partner in multilateral endeavors." *Vimar Seguros y Reaseguros, S. A. v. M/V Sky Reefer*, 515 U. S. 528, 539 (1995).

. . .

VI.

To recapitulate, the objective of statutory interpretation is "to give effect to the intent of Congress." Here, two congressional aims are evident. First, in enacting § 602(a)(1), Congress intended to grant copyright owners permission to segment international markets by barring the importation of foreign-made copies into the United States. Second, as codification of the first sale doctrine underscores, Congress did not want the exclusive distribution right conferred in § 106(3) to be boundless. Instead of harmonizing these objectives, the Court subordinates the first entirely to the second. It is unsurprising that none of the three major treatises on U.S. copyright law embrace the Court's construction of § 109(a). See 2 Nimmer § 8.12[B][6][c], at 8–184.34 to 8–184.35; 2 Goldstein § 7.6.1.2(a), at 7:141; 4 Patry §§ 13:22, 13:44, 13:44.10.

Rather than adopting the very international-exhaustion rule the United States has consistently resisted in international-trade negotiations, I would adhere to the national-exhaustion framework set by the Copyright Act's text and history. Under that regime, codified in § 602(a)(1), Kirtsaeng's unauthorized importation of the foreign-made textbooks involved in this case infringed Wiley's copyrights. I would therefore affirm the Second Circuit's judgment.

QUESTIONS

1. Compare the majority's and dissent's understandings of the territorial application of the U.S. copyright law. What does "under this title [the U.S. Copyright Act]" mean? Are both understandings consistent with the TRIPS agreement? Are they consistent with the Berne Convention?
2. What are the consequences of the *Kirtsaeng* case as to the importation right? In the U.S.? In Europe? For example, suppose a U.K. publisher engaged in price discrimination, segmenting the English-language market, and selling the same books for a higher price in the North American market relative to the European or Asian or Australian-New Zealand markets: how does *Kirtsaeng* affect the U.K. publisher's business model? Does *Kirtsaeng's* rule of international exhaustion apply only to works first published abroad by U.S. enterprises? Does TRIPS require the U.S. to exclude the international exhaustion of copies of works lacking any point of attachment with the U.S. (other than their prospective importation into the U.S.)? Would TRIPS *permit* such a national limitation?
3. In *Quality King Distribs. v. L'anza* Research Int'l, 523 U.S. 135, 143–154 (1998), the Supreme Court wrote that the Free Trade Agreement "sheds no light on the proper interpretation of a statute that was enacted in

1976." Subsequently, in *Kirtsaeng*, the Court interpreted the copyright act in favor of international exhaustion.

In the interim between *L'Anza* and *Kirtsaeng*, Article 4(11) of the AGREEMENT BETWEEN THE UNITED STATES OF AMERICA AND THE HASHEMITE KINGDOM OF JORDAN ON THE ESTABLISHMENT OF A FREE TRADE AREA [2000] lays down the following rule:

11. Each Party shall provide to authors and their successors in interest, to performers and to producers of phonograms the exclusive right to authorize or prohibit the importation into each Party's territory of copies of works and phonograms, even where such copies were made with the authorization of the author, performer or producer of the phonogram or a successor in interest.

Should the Court have taken this FTA into account?

(2) Regional exhaustion under E.U. Law

C-479/04 Laserdisken ApS v. Kulturministeriet ECLI:EU:C:2006:549 [2006]

11   Laserdisken is a commercial company which sells inter alia copies of cinematographic works to individual purchasers through its sales outlets in Denmark.

12   Until the end of 2002, those copies were mostly imported by the company from other Member States of the European Union but also from non-member countries. The products included special editions, such as original American editions, or editions filmed using special techniques. Another major part of the product range consisted of cinematographic works which were not or would not be available in Europe.

13   Having registered a significant drop in its operations following the abovementioned legislative amendment, on 19 February 2003 Laserdisken brought legal proceedings against the Kulturministeriet before the Østre Landsret (Eastern Regional Court), claiming that section 19 of the Law on copyright, as amended in the context of the transposition of Article 4(2) of Directive 2001/29, [InfoSoc] did not apply. According to Laserdisken, the new provisions of section 19 have a significant effect on its imports and sales of DVDs lawfully marketed outside the EEA [European Economic Area].

. . .

16   Since the abovementioned pleas in law were contested in their entirety by the Kulturministeriet, the Østre Landsret decided to stay the proceedings and to refer the following two questions to the Court for a preliminary ruling:

1.   Is Article 4(2) of Directive [2001/29] invalid?
2.   Does Article 4(2) of Directive [2001/29] preclude a Member State from retaining international exhaustion in its legislation?

17   By its second question, which it is appropriate to consider first, the national court asks whether Article 4(2) of Directive 2001/29 [Info Soc] precludes national rules which provide that the distribution right in respect of the original or copies of a work is exhausted where the first sale or other transfer of ownership is made by the holder of that right or with his consent outside the Community.

18   Laserdisken and the Polish Government claim that Article 4(2) of Directive 2001/29 [Info Soc] does not preclude a Member State from retaining such a rule of exhaustion in its legislation. The Commission of the European Communities maintains the opposite view.

19   Article 4(1) of Directive 2001/29 [Info Soc] enshrines the exclusive right for authors, in respect of the original of their works or of copies thereof, to authorise or prohibit any form of distribution to the public by sale or otherwise.

20   Article 4(2) contains the rule pertaining to exhaustion of that right. According to that provision, the distribution right is not to be exhausted in respect of the original or copies of the work, except where the first sale or other transfer of ownership in the Community of that object is made by the rightholder or with his consent.

21   It follows that for the right in question to be exhausted, two conditions must be fulfilled: first, the original of a work or copies thereof must have been placed on the market by the rightholder or with his consent and, second, they must have been placed on the market in the Community.

22   Laserdisken and the Polish Government argue, essentially, that Article 4(2) of the Directive leaves it open to the Member States to introduce or maintain in their respective national laws a rule of exhaustion in respect of works placed on the market not only in the Community but also in non-member countries.

23   Such an interpretation cannot be accepted. According to the twenty-eighth recital in the preamble to Directive 2001/29 [Info Soc], copyright protection under that directive includes the exclusive right to control distribution of the work incorporated in a tangible article. The first sale in the Community of the original of a work or copies thereof by the rightholder or with his consent exhausts the right to control resale of that object in the Community. According to the same recital, that right should not be exhausted in respect of the original of the work or of copies thereof sold by the rightholder or with his consent outside the Community.

24   It follows from the clear wording of Article 4(2) of Directive 2001/29 [Info Soc], in conjunction with the twenty-eighth recital in the preamble to that directive, that that provision does not leave it open to the Member States to provide for a rule of exhaustion other than the Community-wide exhaustion rule.

25   That finding is supported by Article 5 of Directive 2001/29 [Info Soc], which allows Member States to provide for exceptions or limitations to the reproduction right, the right of communication to the public of works, the right of making available to the public other subject-matter and the distribution right. Nothing in that article indicates that the exceptions or limitations authorised might relate to the rule of exhaustion laid down in Article 4(2) of Directive 2001/29 [Info Soc] and, therefore, allow Member States to derogate from that rule.

26   This, moreover, is the only interpretation which is fully consistent with the purpose of Directive 2001/29 [Info Soc] which, according to the first recital in the preamble thereto, is to ensure the functioning of the internal market. A situation in which some Member States will be able to provide for international exhaustion of distribution rights whilst others will provide only for Community-wide exhaustion of those rights will inevitably give rise to barriers to the free movement of goods and the freedom to provide services.

27   In the light of the foregoing, the answer to the second question must be that Article 4(2) of Directive 2001/29 [Info Soc] is to be interpreted as precluding national rules providing for exhaustion of the distribution right in respect of the original or copies of a work placed on the market outside the Community by the rightholder or with his consent.

. . .

– Infringement of international agreements concluded by the Community on copyright and related rights

36 The national court does not state which agreements binding the Community might be infringed by the rule of Community-wide exhaustion of distribution rights laid down in Article 4(2) of Directive 2001/29 [Info Soc].

37 In its observations, Laserdisken states, although without providing further explanations, that the distribution right and the exhaustion rule laid down in Article 4(2) of Directive 2001/29 [Info Soc] are contrary to Articles 1(c) and 2(a) of the Convention on the Organisation for Economic Co-operation and Development (OECD), signed in Paris on 14 December 1960. Those provisions state respectively that '[t]he aims of the [OECD] shall be to promote policies designed . . . to contribute to the expansion of world trade on a multilateral, non-discriminatory basis' and that, in pursuit of those aims inter alia, 'the [Member States] agree that they will . . . promote the efficient use of their economic resources'.

38 The Court finds that not only is that argument vague, but also that the provisions referred to by Laserdisken, even if they do bind the Community, are not intended to regulate the issue of exhaustion of distribution rights.

39 Moreover, the fifteenth recital in the preamble to Directive 2001/29 [Info Soc] states that the Directive implements the international obligations resulting from the adoption, in Geneva on 20 December 1996, under the auspices of the World Intellectual Property Organisation ('WIPO'), of the WIPO Copyright Treaty and the WIPO Performances and Phonograms Treaty, which treaties were approved on behalf of the Community by Council Decision 2000/278/EC of 16 March 2000 (OJ 2000 L 89, p. 6).

40 Regarding the right of distribution, neither Article 6(2) of the WIPO Copyright Treaty nor Articles 8(2) and 12(2) of the WIPO Performances and Phonograms Treaty impose an obligation on the Community, as a contracting party, to provide for a specific rule concerning the exhaustion of that right.

41 It follows from the purpose of those treaties, as formulated inter alia in the first recitals in the preambles thereto, that they tend towards a harmonisation of the rules pertaining to copyright and related rights.

42 More specifically, regarding the right of distribution, the WIPO Copyright Treaty fulfils its harmonisation objective in providing for the exclusive right of authors to authorise the making available to the public of

the originals of their works and copies thereof through sale or other transfer of ownership. The Treaty does not, however, affect the contracting parties' power to determine the conditions governing how exhaustion of that exclusive right may apply after the first sale. It thus allows the Community to pursue further harmonisation of national laws also in relation to the rule of exhaustion. The abovementioned provisions of the WIPO Copyright Treaty and those of Directive 2001/29 [Info Soc] are therefore complementary, in the light of the harmonisation objective pursued.

43   It follows from all the above considerations that the submission that Article 4(2) of Directive 2001/29 [Info Soc] infringes the international agreements concluded by the Community in the field of copyright and related rights cannot be upheld.

QUESTIONS

1. In the *Laserdisken* decision, to what extent does the Court apply international norms? To interpret the European norm in the light of those international norms? To verify the compliance of the European norm with those international norms?
2. As we have seen, the ECJ and the U.S. Supreme Court reached opposite results pertaining to the geographic scope of the exhaustion doctrine. Nevertheless, each approach may comply with international norms. How do you explain this apparent paradox?

iii.   **Marrakesh Treaty to Facilitate Access to Published Works for Persons Who are Blind, Visually Impaired, or Otherwise Print Disabled, Marrakesh, June 17 to 28, 2013**

Article 5
Cross-Border Exchange of Accessible Format Copies

1. Contracting Parties shall provide that if an accessible format copy is made under a limitation or exception or pursuant to operation of law, that accessible format copy may be distributed or made available by an authorized entity to a beneficiary person or an authorized entity in another Contracting Party.

. . .

5. Nothing in this Treaty shall be used to address the issue of exhaustion of rights.

Article 6
Importation of Accessible Format Copies

To the extent that the national law of a Contracting Party would permit a beneficiary person, someone acting on his or her behalf, or an authorized entity, to make an accessible format copy of a work, the national law of that Contracting Party shall also permit them to import an accessible format copy for the benefit of beneficiary persons, without the authorization of the rightholder.

> **Agreed statement concerning Article 5(1):** It is further understood that nothing in this Treaty reduces or extends the scope of exclusive rights under any other treaty.
> **Agreed statement concerning Article 6:** It is understood that the Contracting Parties have the same flexibilities set out in Article 4 when implementing their obligations under Article 6.

QUESTIONS

1. To what extent does the Marrakesh Treaty create a specific and regional exhaustion exception? Is that consistent with TRIPS article 51? Consistent with the Marrakesh Treaty's article 5(5)?
2. Whose law determines if the accessible format copy referred to in article 5(1) was lawfully made? That of the country of where the copy was made, or of the country receiving the copy?
3. What is the relationship between articles 5(1) and 6? May a contracting party import an accessible format copy even if it was not lawfully made in the country from which the copy was sent?

Neighboring rights treaties

General presentation

See Table 5.1, on following pages.

Table 5.1 Comparison of Treaty Provisions*

	Rome Convention	TRIPS	WPPT	Beijing Treaty
Protected Persons or Entities and Subject Matter	**Performing Artists:** • performances of literary or artistic works (see Art. 2 (1)(a), Art. 3 (a))	**Performing Artists:** • performances (Art. 14 (1))	**Performing Artists:** performances of literary or artistic works or expressions of folklore (see Art. 2 (a), Art. 3 (1))	**Performing Artists:** • audiovisual fixation of performances of literary or artistic works or expressions of folklore
	Producers of Phonograms: • first, and exclusively aural, fixation of sounds of a performance or of other sounds (see Art. 2 (1)(b), Art. 3 (b), (c))	**Producers of Phonograms:** • phonograms (Art. 14(2))	**Producers of Phonograms:** • first fixation of sounds of a performance or of other sounds, or a representation of sounds (see Art. 2 (b), (d), Art. 3 (1))	
	broadcasting organizations: • transmissions by wireless means for public reception of sounds or of images and sounds (see Art. 2 (1)(c), Art. 3 (f))	**broadcasting organizations:** • broadcasts (Art. 14 (3) TRIPS)		

* Many thanks to David Rüther, Columbia LLM 2014, for the preparation of the chart.

Economic Rights				
Right of fixation of unfixed performances	performers in their performances (Art. 7 (1)(b)) phonogram producers [N/A] broadcasting organizations in their broadcasts (Art. 13 (a))	performers in their performances (limited to sounds) (Art. 14 (1)) phonogram producers [N/A] broadcasting organizations in their broadcasts (Art. 14(3))	⊕ performers in their performances (Art. 6 (ii)) phonogram producers [N/A] Broadcasting orgs N/A	⊕ performers in their performances (Art. 6 (ii)) phonogram producers N/A Broadcasting orgs N/A
Right of broadcasting and communication to the public for unfixed works	N/A	N/A	performers, except where performance is already a broadcast performance (Art. 6 (i))	performers, except where performance is already a broadcast performance (Art. 6 (i))
Reproduction Right	performers in their performances (Art. 7 (1)(c) (i)-(iii)) [performer waives right once he has consented to the incorporation of his performance in a visual or audiovisual fixation, Art. 19] phonogram producers in their phonograms (Art. 10) broadcasting organizations regarding broadcasts (Art. 13 (c) Rome Convention)	performers in their fixed performances (Art. 14 (1)) phonogram producers in their phonograms (Art. 14 (2)) broadcasting organizations regarding fixed broadcasts (Art. 14 (3) TRIPS)	performers in their performances fixed in phonograms (Art. 7) phonogram producers in their phonograms (Art. 11) Broadcasting orgs N/A	performers in their performances fixed in audiovisual fixations (Art. 7) phonogram producers N/A Broadcasting orgs N/A

Table 5.1 (continued)

	Rome Convention	TRIPS	WPPT	Beijing Treaty
Distribution Right	N/A	N/A	performers in original and copies of performances fixed in phonograms (Art. 8 (1))	performers in original and copies of performances fixed in audiovisual fixations (Art. 8 (1))
			phonogram producers regarding original and copies of phonograms (Art. 12 (1))	phonogram producers N/A
			Broadcasting orgs N/A	Broadcasting orgs N/A
Rental Right	N/A	Performers [N/A]	performers regarding commercial rental to the public of original and copies of performances fixed in phonograms (Art. 9 (1); Art. 9 (2) equitable remuneration)	performers regarding commercial rental to the public of original and copies of performances fixed in audiovisual fixations (Art. 9 (1); but see exception in Art. 9 (2))
		phonogram producers regarding commercial rental to the public of originals or copies of phonograms (Art. 14 (4); Art. 14 (4) second sentence: equitable remuneration)	phonogram producers regarding commercial rental to the public of original and copies of phonograms (Art. 13 (1); Art. 13 (2) equitable remuneration)	phonogram producers N/A
		Broadcasting orgs [N/A]	Broadcasting orgs N/A	Broadcasting orgs N/A

Broadcasting Right	performers in their performances (Art. 7 (1) (a)); but see exception in Art. 7 (1)(a)) [and performer waives right once he has consented to the incorporation of his performance in a visual or audiovisual fixation, Art. 19]	performers in their live performance (Art. 14 (1))	performers regarding performances fixed in audiovisual fixations (Art. 11 (1)) [State may notify Director General of WIPO that it will not abide, Art. 11 (2), (3)]
	phonogram producers or performers regarding phonogram have only the right to a single equitable remuneration (Art. 12) [State may notify Secretary General of UN that it will not abide, Art. 16 (1)(a)]	phonogram producers [N/A]	phonogram producers or performers regarding phonograms have only the right to a single equitable remuneration (Art. 15 (1)) [State may notify Director General of WIPO that it will not abide, Art. 15 (3)]
	broadcasting organizations regarding rebroadcasts (Art. 13 (a))	broadcasting organizations regarding rebroadcasts by wireless means (Art. 14 (3))	phonogram producers N/A
		Broadcasting orgs N/A	Broadcasting orgs N/A

Table 5.1 (continued)

	Rome Convention	TRIPS	WPPT	Beijing Treaty
Communication to the Public Right	performers in their performances (Art. 7 (1)(a); but see exception in Art. 7 (1)(a))	performers in their live performances (Art. 14 (1))	phonogram producers or performers regarding phonogram have only the right to a single equitable remuneration (Art. 15 (1)) [State may notify Director General of WIPO that it will not abide, Art. 15 (3)]	performers regarding performances fixed in audiovisual fixations (Art. 11 (1)) [State may notify Director General of WIPO that it will not abide, Art. 11 (2), (3)]
	phonogram producers or performers regarding phonogram have right only to a single equitable remuneration (Art. 12) [State may notify Secretary General of UN that it will not abide, Art. 16 (1)(a)]	phonogram producers [N/A]	phonogram producers [N/A]	phonogram producers N/A

	broadcasting organizations regarding television broadcasts if such communication is made in places accessible to the public against payment of an entrance fee (Art. 13 (d); matter of domestic law to determine conditions of exercise (Art. 13 (d)) [State may notify Secretary General of UN that it will not abide, Art. 16 (1)(a)]	broadcasting organizations regarding television broadcasts (Art. 14 (3))	Broadcasting orgs N/A	Broadcasting orgs N/A
			performers regarding performances fixed in phonograms (Art. 10)	performers regarding performances fixed in audiovisual fixations (Art. 10)
			phonogram producers regarding phonograms (Art. 14)	phonogram producers N/A
Making Available Right	N/A	N/A	Broadcasting orgs N/A	Broadcasting orgs N/A

QUESTIONS

Note: To respond to the following questions, it will be necessary to consult the text of the various conventions, set out in the appendix to this casebook.

1. What role does the Rome Convention give to domestic law?
2. Compare the drafting of article 7 of the Rome Convention "shall include the possibility" and that of article 10 "shall enjoy;" what is the difference, and what accounts for it?
3. To what extent is the right of fixation under the TRIPS Agreement equivalent to the right of fixation under the WPPT or the Beijing Treaty?
4. What, if any, are the differences between the rental right under the WPPT and the Beijing Treaty and the rental right under the WCT?
5. How does the right of communication to the public under the WPPT compare with that under the WCT?

PROBLEMS

1. A performance by an American singer is fixed on a phonogram by an American producer. A French producer includes one of those recorded performances in a multi-artist compilation phonogram distributed in French supermarkets. Which neighboring rights text is or are applicable to determine France's national treatment obligation? Does it matter whether the plaintiff is the producer or the singer?
2. Consider the same question, but now the performer and producer are Brazilian.
3. A French phonogram producer has noticed that some copies of its latest phonograms (the public fixation of the concert of a French rock star in Paris) have been distributed without its authorization in Iceland. He would like to know whether distribution rights are protected there and if yes under which convention?
4. Consider the same facts but against an Icelandic Company offering commercial rental of those phonograms in Iceland. The producer would like to know whether rental rights are protected there and if so, under which convention? What about the performers?

European interpretations

C-245/00 Stichting ter Exploitatie van Naburige Rechten (SENA) v. Nederlandse Omroep Stichting (NOS) ECLI:EU:C:2003:68 [2003]

[This case concerned a proceeding between the Stichting ter Exploitatie van Naburige Rechten (Association for the Exploitation of Related Rights, hereinafter SENA) and the Nederlandse Omroep Stichting (Netherlands Broadcasting Association, hereinafter NOS) relating to the determination of the equitable remuneration to be paid to performing artists and phonogram producers for the broadcasting of phonograms by radio and television. The question raised concerned the existence of an autonomous concept of "equitable remuneration."]

The first question

21   By its first question the national court is asking, essentially, whether the concept of equitable remuneration within the meaning of Article 8(2) of Directive 92/100* [Rental Right] must, firstly, be interpreted in the same way in all Member States, and secondly, be applied using the same criteria in all Member States.

. . .

33   It must be recalled that the directive requires the Member States to lay down rules ensuring that users pay an equitable remuneration when a phonogram is broadcast. It also states that the manner in which that remuneration is shared between performing artists and producers of phonograms is normally to be determined by agreement between them. It is only if their negotiations do not produce agreement as to how to distribute the remuneration that the Member State must intervene to lay down the conditions.

34   In the absence of any Community definition of equitable remuneration, there is no objective reason to justify the laying down by the Community judicature of specific methods for determining what constitutes uniform equitable remuneration, which would necessarily entail its acting in the place of the Member States, which are not bound by any particular criteria under Directive 92/100 [Rental Right] [citations omitted]. It is therefore for the Member States alone to determine, in their own territory, what are the most relevant criteria for ensuring, within the limits imposed by Community law, and particularly Directive 92/100 [Rental Right], adherence to that Community concept.

---

* Editors' Note: Council Directive 92/100/EEC of 19 November 1992 on rental right and lending right and on certain rights related to copyright in the field of intellectual property. This Directive has been codified the Directive 2006/115/EC.

35   In that connection, it is apparent that the source of inspiration for Article 8(2)* of Directive 92/100 is Article 12** of the International Convention for the Protection of Performers, Producers of Phonograms and Broadcasting Organisations signed in Rome on 26 October 1961. That convention provides that the payment of equitable remuneration, and the conditions for sharing that remuneration are, in the absence of agreement between the various parties concerned, to be established by domestic law and simply lists a number of factors, which it states to be non-exhaustive, non-binding and potentially relevant, for the purposes of deciding what is equitable in each case.

36   In those circumstances, the Court's role, in the context of a dispute brought before it, can only be to call upon the Member States to ensure the greatest possible adherence throughout the territory of the Community to the concept of equitable remuneration, a concept which must, in the light of the objectives of Directive 92/100 [Rental Directive], as specified in particular in the preamble thereto, be viewed as enabling a proper balance to be achieved between the interests of performing artists and producers in obtaining remuneration for the broadcast of a particular phonogram, and the interests of third parties in being able to broadcast the phonogram on terms that are reasonable.

37   As the Commission points out, whether the remuneration, which represents the consideration for the use of a commercial phonogram, in particular for broadcasting purposes, is equitable is to be assessed, in particular, in the light of the value of that use in trade.

38   The reply to the first question must therefore be that the concept of equitable remuneration in Article 8(2) of Directive 92/100 [Rental Directive] must be interpreted uniformly in all the Member States and applied by each Member State; it is for each Member State to determine, in its own territory, the most appropriate criteria for assuring, within the limits imposed by Community law and Directive 92/100 [Rental Directive] in particular, adherence to that Community concept.

---

* Editors' Note: "Member States shall provide a right in order to ensure that a single equitable remuneration is paid by the user, if a phonogram published for commercial purposes, or a reproduction of such phonogram, is used for broadcasting by wireless means or for any communication to the public, and to ensure that this remuneration is shared between the relevant performers and phonogram producers. Member States may, in the absence of agreement between the performers and phonogram producers, lay down the conditions as to the sharing of this remuneration between them."

** Editors' Note: "If a phonogram published for commercial purposes, or a reproduction of such phonogram, is used directly for broadcasting or for any communication to the public, a single equitable remuneration shall be paid by the user to the performers, or to the producers of the phonograms, or to both. Domestic law may, in the absence of agreement between these parties, lay down the conditions as to the sharing of this remuneration."

The second and third questions

39   By its second and third questions, the national court is asking, essentially, what criteria are to be used for determining the amount of the equitable remuneration, and what limits are imposed on the Member States in laying down those criteria.

. . .

46   ... [T]he reply to the second and third questions must be that Article 8(2) of Directive 92/100 does not preclude a model for calculating what constitutes equitable remuneration for performing artists and phonogram producers that operates by reference to variable and fixed factors, such as the number of hours of phonograms broadcast, the viewing and listening densities achieved by the radio and television broadcasters represented by the broadcast organisation, the tariffs fixed by agreement in the field of performance rights and broadcast rights in respect of musical works protected by copyright, the tariffs set by the public broadcast organisations in the Member States bordering on the Member State concerned, and the amounts paid by commercial stations, provided that that model is such as to enable a proper balance to be achieved between the interests of performing artists and producers in obtaining remuneration for the broadcast of a particular phonogram, and the interests of third parties in being able to broadcast the phonogram on terms that are reasonable, and that it does not contravene any principle of Community law.

QUESTIONS

1. For the ECJ, the source of inspiration for article 8(2) of Directive 92/100 was article 12 of the International Convention for the Protection of Performers, Producers of Phonograms and Broadcasting Organizations signed in Rome on 26 October 1961. How on-point is article 12 of the Rome Convention? What, if any, are the differences between the two texts?
2. For the ECJ, article 12 of the Rome Convention "lists a number of factors, which it states to be non-exhaustive, non-binding and potentially relevant, for the purposes of deciding what is equitable in each case." Do you agree?
3. To what extent is the European interpretation of article 8(2) of Directive 92/100 consistent with article 12 of the Rome Convention?

C-135/10 Società Consortile Fonografici (SCF) v. Marco Del Corso ECLI:EU:C:2012:140 [2012]

57   The referring court asks whether the broadcasting, free of charge, of phonograms within private dental practices engaged in professional

economic activity, for the benefit of patients of those practices and enjoyed by them without any active choice on their part, constitutes 'communication to the public' or 'making available to the public' for the purposes of the application of Article 3(2)(b)* of Directive 2001/29 [Info Soc] and whether such an act of transmission entitles the phonogram producers to the payment of remuneration?

. . .

70   As regards the concept of 'communication to the public', it must be observed at the outset that it appears not only in Article 8(2) of Directive 92/100 [Rental Right Directive], a provision which is relevant to the main proceedings, but also in Article 3(1)** of Directive 2001/29 [Info Soc Directive] and, inter alia, in Article 12 of the Rome Convention, Article 15 of the WPPT and Article 14(1) of the TRIPS agreement.

71   . . .[T]he concept of 'communication to the public' must be interpreted in the light of the equivalent concepts contained in the Rome Convention, the TRIPS agreement and the WPPT and in such a way that it is compatible with those agreements, taking account of the context in which those concepts are found and the purpose of the provisions of those agreements.

72   It must be recalled that, under Article 3(1) of Directive 2001/29 [Info Soc], Member States are to provide authors with the exclusive right to authorise or prohibit any communication to the public of their works, by wire or wireless means, including the making available to the public of their works in such a way that members of the public may access them from a place and at a time individually chosen by them. That provision is inspired by Article 8 of the WCT, the wording of which it reproduces almost verbatim.

73   Article 8(2) of Directive 92/100 [Rental Right] requires Member States to provide a right in order to ensure that a single equitable remuneration is paid by the user if a phonogram published for commercial purposes, or a reproduction of such phonogram, is used for broadcasting by wireless means or for any communication to the public and to ensure that this remuneration

---

* Editors' Note: "Member States shall provide for the exclusive right to authorise or prohibit the making available to the public, by wire or wireless means, in such a way that members of the public may access them from a place and at a time individually chosen by them: (b) for phonogram producers, of their phonograms."
** Editors' Note: "Member States shall provide authors with the exclusive right to authorise or prohibit any communication to the public of their works, by wire or wireless means, including the making available to the public of their works in such a way that members of the public may access them from a place and at a time individually chosen by them."

is shared between the relevant performers and phonogram producers. That provision is inspired by Article 12 of the Rome Convention the wording of which it likewise reproduces almost verbatim [citations omitted].

74   It is clear from a comparison of Article 3(1) of Directive 2001/29 [Info Soc] and Article 8(2) of Directive 92/100 [Rental Right] that the concept of communication to the public appearing in those provisions is used in contexts which are not the same and pursue objectives which, while similar, are none the less different to some extent.

. . .

83   Second, the Court has already identified certain aspects of the concept of public.

84   In that regard, the Court has held that the term 'public' within the meaning of Article 3(1) of Directive 2001/29 [Info Soc] refers to an indeterminate number of potential listeners, and, in addition, implies a fairly large number of persons [citations omitted].

85   As regards, to begin with, the 'indeterminate' nature of the public, the Court has observed that, according to the definition of the concept of 'communication to the public' given by the WIPO glossary, which, while not legally binding, none the less sheds light on the interpretation of the concept of public, it means 'making a work . . . perceptible in any appropriate manner to persons in general, that is, not restricted to specific individuals belonging to a private group'.

86   Next, as regards, the criterion of 'a fairly large number of people', this is intended to indicate that the concept of public encompasses a certain de minimis threshold, which excludes from the concept groups of persons which are too small, or insignificant.

87   In order to determine that number, the Court took account of the cumulative effects of making works available to potential audiences (*SGAE*, paragraph 39). In that connection, not only is it relevant to know how many persons have access to the same work at the same time but it is also necessary to know how many of them have access to it in succession.

88   Third, in paragraph 204 of the judgment in *Football Association Premier League and Others*, the Court held that it is not irrelevant that a 'communication' within the meaning of Article 3(1) of Directive 2001/29 [Info Soc] is of a profit-making nature.

89   It follows that this must be all the more true in the case of the right to equitable remuneration provided for in Article 8(2) of Directive 92/100 [Rental Right] given its essentially financial nature.

90   More specifically, the Court has held that the action by a hotel operator by which it gives access to a broadcast work to its customers must be considered an additional service performed with the aim of obtaining some benefit, since the provision of that service has an influence on the hotel's standing and, therefore, on the price of rooms. Similarly, the Court has held that the transmission of broadcast works by the operator of a public house is made with the intention that it should, and is likely to, have an effect upon the number of people going to that establishment and, ultimately, on its financial results (see, to that effect, *SGAE*, paragraph 44, and *Football Association Premier League and Othe s*, paragraph 205).

91   It is thus understood that the public which is the subject of the communication is both targeted by the user and receptive, in one way or another, to that communication, and not merely 'caught' by chance.

92   It is in the light of those criteria in particular that it must be determined whether, in a case such as that at issue in the main proceedings, a dentist who broadcasts phonograms to his patients, by way of background music, is making a communication to the public within the meaning of Article 8(2) of Directive 92/100 [Rental Right].

. . .

96   As regards, further, having regard to paragraph 84 of the present judgment, the number of persons to whom the same broadcast phonogram is made audible by the dentist, it must be held that, in the case of the patients of a dentist, the number of persons is not large, indeed it is insignificant, given that the number of persons present in his practice at the same time is, in general, very limited. Moreover, although there are a number of patients in succession, the fact remains that, as those patients attend one at a time, they do not generally hear the same phonograms, or the broadcast phonograms, in particular.

97   Finally, it cannot be disputed that, in a situation such as that in the main proceedings, a dentist who broadcasts phonograms, by way of background music, in the presence of his patients cannot reasonably either expect a rise in the number of patients because of that broadcast alone or increase the price of the treatment he provides. Therefore, such a broadcast is not liable, in itself, to have an impact on the income of that dentist.

98   The patients of a dentist visit a dental practice with the sole objective of receiving treatment, as the broadcasting of phonograms is in no way a part of dental treatment. They have access to certain phonograms by chance and without any active choice on their part, according to the time of their arrival at the practice and the length of time they wait and the nature of the treatment they undergo. Accordingly, it cannot be presumed that the usual customers of a dentist are receptive as regards the broadcast in question.

99   Consequently such a broadcast is not of a profit-making nature, and thus does not fulfil the criterion set out in paragraph 90 of the present judgment.

100   It follows from all the foregoing considerations that a dentist such as the one in question in the case in the main proceedings who broadcasts phonograms free of charge in his dental practice, for the benefit of his clients and enjoyed by them without any active choice on their part, is not making a 'communication to the public' for the purposes of the application of Article 8(2) of Directive 92/100 [Rental Right].

101   It follows that the requirement set out in Article 8(2) of Directive 92/100 [Rental Right] for the payment of equitable remuneration by the user, namely that the user makes a 'communication to the public' within the meaning of that provision, is not met in a situation such as that in the main proceedings.

102   Accordingly, the answer to the fourth and fifth questions is that the concept of 'communication to the public' for the purposes of Article 8(2) of Directive 92/100 [Rental Right] must be interpreted as meaning that it does not cover the broadcasting, free of charge, of phonograms within private dental practices engaged in professional economic activity, such as the one at issue in the main proceedings, for the benefit of patients of those practices and enjoyed by them without any active choice on their part. Therefore such an act of transmission does not entitle the phonogram producers to the payment of remuneration.

QUESTIONS

1. Compare the uniform concept of "communication to the public" with the uniform concept of "equitable remuneration" seen previously in *Sena* [cross-reference]. Although both concepts are defined in the WIPO glossary, the ECJ quoted the WIPO glossary only in *Del Corso* decision. Why? What difference does it make?
2. In *Del Corso*, the ECJ was asked to interpret article 3(2) of Directive 2001/29 concerning neighboring rights. The Court mentions that the

notion of communication to the public also appears in article 8(2) of Directive 92/100, as well as in article 3(1) of Directive 2001/29. For the Court, "the concept of 'communication to the public' must be interpreted in the light of the equivalent concepts contained in the Rome Convention, the TRIPS agreement and the WPPT and in such a way that it is compatible with those agreements, taking account of the context in which those concepts are found and the purpose of the provisions of those agreements" (n 70). Finally, the Court applied to this case the concept of "public" based on previous cases concerning copyright law. Despite noting that in light of the previous criteria a dentist who broadcasts phonograms to his patients is making the recorded performances available to the public (n 92), the Court, taking into account other criteria, concluded that *Del Corso* was not engaged in a communication to the public under Directive 92/100. In a subsequent decision concerning a spa establishment's placement of radio and television receivers in guest rooms (C-351/12 [2014], paragraph 35), the Court limited its prior conclusion to neighboring rights. The Court distinguished *Del Corso*, stating:

> In that respect, it suffices to note that the principles developed in SCF are not relevant in the present case, since SCF does not concern the copyright referred to in Article 3(1) of Directive 2001/29, but rather the right to remuneration of performers and producers of phonograms provided for in Article 8(2) of Council Directive 92/100/EEC of 19 November 1992 on rental right and lending right and on certain rights related to copyright in the field of intellectual property (OJ 1992 L 346, p. 61).

As a result, for the Court there are at least two different concepts of communication to the public in European law. Because these concepts are interpreted in light of international norms, does it mean that for the ECJ the concept of communication to the public enshrined in article 8 of the WCT is different from the one enshrined in article 12 of the Rome Convention? Or of article 15 of the WPPT? Is such an interpretation consistent with the evolution of neighboring rights treaties since the Rome Convention?

5.5 Exceptions and limitations

International agreements set a framework for the interaction of exclusive rights on the one hand and limitations and exceptions on the other. The conventional substantive minima therefore also comprehend exceptions, in order to allow member states to fix a fair balance between the respective interests of authors and users.

While earlier texts of the Berne Convention included some specific exceptions and limitations on the reproduction and communication to the public rights, the broadest statement of a framework for national laws' derogations from the scope of copyright appears in the most recent revision (Paris 1971), in relation to the right of reproduction. This mechanism, known as the "three-step test" was subsequently included and generalized in the TRIPS Agreement and the WIPO Treaties.

This section of the Casebook will first explore the Berne Convention exceptions and limitations, and then will turn to their influence on subsequent agreements. The presentation will focus on the three-step test as a constraint on member states' diminution of the scope of economic rights. Finally, this section will consider the extent to which U.S. law and E.U. law implement exceptions consistently with international norms.

5.5.1 Copyright conventions

Berne Convention

> **Article 9**
> **Right of Reproduction**
>
> *. . . 2. Possible exceptions*
>
> . . .
>
> (2) It shall be a matter for legislation in the countries of the Union to permit the reproduction of such works in certain special cases, provided that such reproduction does not conflict with a normal exploitation of the work and does not unreasonably prejudice the legitimate interests of the author.
>
> **Article 10**
> **Certain Free Uses of Works**
>
> *1. Quotations; 2. Illustrations for teaching; 3. Indication of source and author*
>
> (1) It shall be permissible to make quotations from a work which has already been lawfully made available to the public, provided that their making is compatible with fair practice, and their extent does not exceed

that justified by the purpose, including quotations from newspaper articles and periodicals in the form of press summaries.

(2) It shall be a matter for legislation in the countries of the Union, and for special agreements existing or to be concluded between them, to permit the utilization, to the extent justified by the purpose, of literary or artistic works by way of illustration in publications, broadcasts or sound or visual recordings for teaching, provided such utilization is compatible with fair practice.

(3) Where use is made of works in accordance with the preceding paragraphs of this Article, mention shall be made of the source, and of the name of the author if it appears thereon.

Article 10*bis*
Further Possible Free Uses of Works

1. Of certain articles and broadcast works; 2. Of works seen or heard in connection with current events

(1) It shall be a matter for legislation in the countries of the Union to permit the reproduction by the press, the broadcasting or the communication to the public by wire of articles published in newspapers or periodicals on current economic, political or religious topics, and of broadcast works of the same character, in cases in which the reproduction, broadcasting or such communication thereof is not expressly reserved. Nevertheless, the source must always be clearly indicated; the legal consequences of a breach of this obligation shall be determined by the legislation of the country where protection is claimed.

(2) It shall also be a matter for legislation in the countries of the Union to determine the conditions under which, for the purpose of reporting current events by means of photography, cinematography, broadcasting or communication to the public by wire, literary or artistic works seen or heard in the course of the event may, to the extent justified by the informatory purpose, be reproduced and made available to the public.

QUESTIONS

1. Recall the exclusions from the scope of copyright subject matter in article 2 of the Berne Convention, as well as the general statement of the idea/expression dichotomy in WCT article 2 and TRIPS article 9(2). How do these interact with exceptions from the scope of rights?

2. What is the scope of the article 9(2) exception? What is its relationship to the exceptions in articles 10 and 10*bis*?
3. The third step of the "three-step test" set out in article 9(2) permits member states, in appropriate circumstances (as to what those may be, see, *infra*, discussion following WTO Panel Decision), to impose compulsory licenses so that authors may be remunerated for the uses that the member states remove from their control. The Berne Convention also specifically authorizes compulsory licenses in article 11*bis*(2) and 13(1), below. In light of these specific provisions, how general is the authorization afforded by article 9(2)?

Article 11*bis*
Broadcasting and Related Rights

. . . 2. Compulsory licenses; 3. Recording; ephemeral recordings

. . .

(2) It shall be a matter for legislation in the countries of the Union to determine the conditions under which the rights mentioned in the preceding paragraph [broadcasting and other wireless communications, public communication of broadcast by wire or rebroadcast, public communication of broadcast by loudspeaker or analogous instruments] may be exercised, but these conditions shall apply only in the countries where they have been prescribed. They shall not in any circumstances be prejudicial to the moral rights of the author, nor to his right to obtain equitable remuneration which, in the absence of agreement, shall be fixed by competent authority.

(3) In the absence of any contrary stipulation, permission granted in accordance with paragraph (1) of this Article shall not imply permission to record, by means of instruments recording sounds or images, the work broadcast. It shall, however, be a matter for legislation in the countries of the Union to determine the regulations for ephemeral recordings made by a broadcasting organization by means of its own facilities and used for its own broadcasts. The preservation of these recordings in official archives may, on the ground of their exceptional documentary character, be authorized by such legislation.

QUESTIONS

How do you understand the following expression "it shall be a matter for the legislation" or "it shall be permissible"? To what extent do the articles employing those phrases impose rather than merely permit exceptions? See

Question 1 under ECJ *TV2 Danmark* A/S C-510/10 [2012], *supra*, Part I, Chapter 2.4.2, page 145.

Article 13
Possible Limitation of the Right of Recording of Musical Works and Any Words Pertaining Thereto

1. Compulsory licenses; . . .

(1) Each country of the Union may impose for itself reservations and conditions on the exclusive right granted to the author of a musical work and to the author of any words, the recording of which together with the musical work has already been authorized by the latter, to authorize the sound recording of that musical work, together with such words, if any; but all such reservations and conditions shall apply only in the countries which have imposed them and shall not, in any circumstances, be prejudicial to the rights of these authors to obtain equitable remuneration which, in the absence of agreement, shall be fixed by competent authority.

. . .

QUESTIONS

1. What is the justification for this permissible limitation on the right of making sound recordings?
2. Under article 13, reservations and conditions may be imposed only if the first recording has been authorized. Who should give the authorization for the initial recording of the musical work together with any words?
3. In addition to the requirement of an initial authorized recording, if a member state avails itself of the possibility accorded by article 13, how will it comply with the other conventional restrictions on the "reservations and conditions" that member states may impose?

Marrakesh Treaty

[For the TRIPs Agreement and the WCT see below Section 5.5.3: Generalization of the Three-Step-Test pp. 449 et seq.]

Article 4
National Law Limitations and Exceptions Regarding Accessible Format Copies

1. (a) Contracting Parties shall provide in their national copyright laws for a limitation or exception to the right of reproduction, the right of distribution, and the right of making available to the public as provided by the WIPO Copyright Treaty (WCT), to facilitate the availability of works in accessible format copies for beneficiary persons. The limitation or exception provided in national law should permit changes needed to make the work accessible in the alternative format.

(b) Contracting Parties may also provide a limitation or exception to the right of public performance to facilitate access to works for beneficiary persons.

2. A Contracting Party may fulfill Article 4(1) for all rights identified therein by providing a limitation or exception in its national copyright law such that:

(a) Authorized entities shall be permitted, without the authorization of the copyright rightholder, to make an accessible format copy of a work, obtain from another authorized entity an accessible format copy, and supply those copies to beneficiary persons by any means, including by non-commercial lending or by electronic communication by wire or wireless means, and undertake any intermediate steps to achieve those objectives, when all of the following conditions are met:
   (i) the authorized entity wishing to undertake said activity has lawful access to that work or a copy of that work;
   (ii) the work is converted to an accessible format copy, which may include any means needed to navigate information in the accessible format, but does not introduce changes other than those needed to make the work accessible to the beneficiary person;
   (iii) such accessible format copies are supplied exclusively to be used by beneficiary persons; and
   (iv) the activity is undertaken on a non-profit basis; and
(b) A beneficiary person, or someone acting on his or her behalf including a primary caretaker or caregiver, may make an accessible format copy of a work for the personal use of the beneficiary person or otherwise may assist the beneficiary person to make and use accessible format copies where the beneficiary person has lawful access to that work or a copy of that work.

3. A Contracting Party may fulfill Article 4(1) by providing other limitations or exceptions in its national copyright law pursuant to Articles 10 and 11.

4. A Contracting Party may confine limitations or exceptions under this Article to works which, in the particular accessible format, cannot be obtained commercially under reasonable terms for beneficiary persons in that market. Any Contracting Party availing itself of this possibility shall so declare in a notification deposited with the Director General of WIPO at the time of ratification of, acceptance of or accession to this Treaty or at any time thereafter.

5. It shall be a matter for national law to determine whether limitations or exceptions under this Article are subject to remuneration.

Agreed statement concerning Article 4(3): It is understood that this paragraph neither reduces nor extends the scope of applicability of limitations and exceptions permitted under the Berne Convention, as regards the right of translation, with respect to persons with visual impairments or with other print disabilities.

Agreed statement concerning Article 4(4): It is understood that a commercial availability requirement does not prejudge whether or not a limitation or exception under this Article is consistent with the three-step test.

Article 10
General Principles on Implementation

1. Contracting Parties undertake to adopt the measures necessary to ensure the application of this Treaty.

2. Nothing shall prevent Contracting Parties from determining the appropriate method of implementing the provisions of this Treaty within their own legal system and practice.

3. Contracting Parties may fulfill their rights and obligations under this Treaty through limitations or exceptions specifically for the benefit of beneficiary persons, other limitations or exceptions, or a combination thereof, within their national legal system and practice. These may include judicial, administrative or regulatory determinations for the

benefit of beneficiary persons as to fair practices, dealings or uses to meet their needs consistent with the Contracting Parties' rights and obligations under the Berne Convention, other international treaties, and Article 11.

> **Agreed statement concerning Article 10(2)**: It is understood that when a work qualifies as a work under Article 2(a), including such works in audio form, the limitations and exceptions provided for by this Treaty apply mutatis mutandis to related rights as necessary to make the accessible format copy, to distribute it and to make it available to beneficiary persons.

Article 11
General Obligations on Limitations and Exceptions

In adopting measures necessary to ensure the application of this Treaty, a Contracting Party may exercise the rights and shall comply with the obligations that that Contracting Party has under the Berne Convention, the Agreement on Trade-Related Aspects of Intellectual Property Rights and the WIPO Copyright Treaty, including their interpretative agreements so that:

(a) in accordance with Article 9(2) of the Berne Convention, a Contracting Party may permit the reproduction of works in certain special cases provided that such reproduction does not conflict with a normal exploitation of the work and does not unreasonably prejudice the legitimate interests of the author;

(b) in accordance with Article 13 of the Agreement on Trade-Related Aspects of Intellectual Property Rights, a Contracting Party shall confine limitations or exceptions to exclusive rights to certain special cases which do not conflict with a normal exploitation of the work and do not unreasonably prejudice the legitimate interests of the rightholder;

(c) in accordance with Article 10(1) of the WIPO Copyright Treaty, a Contracting Party may provide for limitations of or exceptions to the rights granted to authors under the WCT in certain special cases, that do not conflict with a normal exploitation of the work and do not unreasonably prejudice the legitimate interests of the author;

(d) in accordance with Article 10(2) of the WIPO Copyright Treaty, a Contracting Party shall confine, when applying the Berne Convention, any limitations of or exceptions to rights to certain special cases that do not conflict with a normal exploitation of the work and do not unreasonably prejudice the legitimate interests of the author.

Article 12
Other Limitations and Exceptions

1. Contracting Parties recognize that a Contracting Party may implement in its national law other copyright limitations and exceptions for the benefit of beneficiary persons than are provided by this Treaty having regard to that Contracting Party's economic situation, and its social and cultural needs, in conformity with that Contracting Party's international rights and obligations, and in the case of a least-developed country taking into account its special needs and its particular international rights and obligations and flexibilities thereof.

2. This Treaty is without prejudice to other limitations and exceptions for persons with disabilities provided by national law.

QUESTIONS

1. The Marrakesh Treaty limits the rights of authors. How does the Treaty try to prevent economic abuse of the exceptions to the authors' rights by third parties? What about the moral rights of authors, does the Marrakesh Treaty mention them? May moral rights be limited by this treaty? Consider article 2(b):

> "accessible format copy" means a copy of a work in an alternative manner or form which gives a beneficiary person access to the work, including to permit the person to have access as feasibly and comfortably as a person without visual impairment or other print disability. The accessible format copy is used exclusively by beneficiary persons and it must respect the integrity of the original work, taking due consideration of the changes needed to make the work accessible in the alternative format and of the accessibility needs of the beneficiary persons;. . .

2. Article 4(1)(b) grants contracting parties the right to "provide a limitation or exception to the right of public performance" for beneficiary persons. How does this relate to the limited definition of works in article 2(a)?

Article 2

For the purposes of this Treaty:

(a) "works" means literary and artistic works within the meaning of Article 2(1) of the Berne Convention for the Protection of Literary and Artistic Works, in the form of text, notation and/or related illustrations, whether published or otherwise made publicly available in any media

. . .

Agreed statement concerning Article 2(a): For the purposes of this Treaty, it is understood that this definition includes such works in audio form, such as audiobooks.

Why is the definition of "works" extended to audiobooks by an agreed statement when the Marrakesh Treaty should benefit the blind, visually impaired, *or otherwise print disabled*?

3. Country C has a relatively high population of visually impaired persons. Therefore the government has ratified the Marrakesh Treaty (assume the Marrakesh Treaty is in force). After the ratification and the implementation into national law, closely following the suggestions in the Marrakesh Treaty, the government authorizes an entity to produce accessible format copies (AFC). Shortly after, the first AFCs of copyrighted books are distributed. Two copyright owners whose books are made available as AFCs intervene. The first copyright owner alleges that AFCs of his book are not allowed because a commercially available, unabridged audiobook of his work exists in country C. This audiobook suffices for the visually impaired, according to the copyright owner. The second copyright owner objects to the third-party production of AFCs of his copyrighted book, on the ground that he already has entered the market for the visually impaired and made commercially available a version similar to the AFCs made by the authorized entity. However, the authorized entity asserts that those AFCs are too expensive. The authorized entity can produce AFCs of the book for one-fifth of the price. Are the objections of the copyright owners valid, if country C's national law has implemented verbatim the Marrakesh Treaty's suggestions?
4. Marrakesh Treaty article 4 obliges member states to enact appropriate exceptions into their domestic law. Articles 11 and 12 outline the contours of permissible exceptions. What is WIPO's authority to intervene

in national copyright law, as opposed to administering treaties that impose certain norms respecting the treatment of foreign authors? What is WIPO's authority to promulgate a treaty concerning exceptions to copyright, as opposed to the protection of authors? Consider the following provisions of the Convention Establishing the World Intellectual Property Organization (Signed at Stockholm on July 14, 1967 and as amended on September 28, 1979):

Article 3 – Objectives of the Organization

The objectives of the Organization are:

(i) to promote the protection of intellectual property throughout the world through cooperation among States and, where appropriate, in collaboration with any other international organization,
(ii) to ensure administrative cooperation among the Unions.

Article 4 – Functions

In order to attain the objectives described in Article 3, the Organization, through its appropriate organs, and subject to the competence of each of the Unions:

(i) shall promote the development of measures designed to facilitate the efficient protection of intellectual property throughout the world and to harmonize national legislation in this field;
(ii) shall perform the administrative tasks of the Paris Union, the Special Unions established in relation with that Union, and the Berne Union;
(iii) may agree to assume, or participate in, the administration of any other international agreement designed to promote the protection of intellectual property;
(iv) shall encourage the conclusion of international agreements designed to promote the protection of intellectual property;
(v) shall offer its cooperation to States requesting legal–technical assistance in the field of intellectual property;
(vi) shall assemble and disseminate information concerning the protection of intellectual property, carry out and promote studies in this field, and publish the results of such studies;
(vii) shall maintain services facilitating the international protec-

tion of intellectual property and, where appropriate, provide for registration in this field and the publication of the data concerning the registrations;

(viii) shall take all other appropriate action.

See also, Berne Convention Article 20:

> **Berne Convention Article 20**
> **Special Agreements among countries of the Union**
>
> The Governments of the countries of the Union reserve the right to enter into special agreements among themselves, in so far as such agreements grant to authors more extensive rights than those granted by the Convention, or contain other provisions not contrary to this Convention. The provisions of existing agreements which satisfy these conditions shall remain applicable.

Is the Marrakesh Treaty a Berne article 20 "special agreement"?

5. How do you explain article 11 of the Marrakesh Treaty? In domestic law, a new law may change or abrogate a prior law. May a new international copyright convention modify or abrogate a prior convention? If not, does that mean that international obligations pertaining to copyright law may never be changed, at least if the change entails a reduction in the prior conventional level of protection?

5.5.2 Neighboring rights

Rome Convention

> **Article 15**
> **Permitted Exceptions**
>
> *1. Specific Limitations; 2. Equivalents with copyright*
>
> 1. Any Contracting State may, in its domestic laws and regulations, provide for exceptions to the protection guaranteed by this Convention as regards:
>
> (a) private use;
> (b) use of short excerpts in connection with the reporting of current events;

(c) ephemeral fixation by a broadcasting organisation by means of its own facilities and for its own broadcasts;

(d) use solely for the purposes of teaching or scientific research.

2. Irrespective of paragraph 1 of this Article, any Contracting State may, in its domestic laws and regulations, provide for the same kinds of limitations with regard to the protection of performers, producers of phonograms and broadcasting organisations, as it provides for, in its domestic laws and regulations, in connection with the protection of copyright in literary and artistic works. However, compulsory licences may be provided for only to the extent to which they are compatible with this Convention.

QUESTION

How do the exceptions authorized by Rome Convention article 15(1) compare with the exceptions authorized by international copyright conventions?

TRIPS

Article 14
Protection of Performers, Producers of Phonograms (Sound Recordings) and Broadcasting Organizations

. . .

6. Any Member may, in relation to the rights conferred under paragraphs 1, 2 and 3, provide for conditions, limitations, exceptions and reservations to the extent permitted by the Rome Convention. However, the provisions of Article 18 of the Berne Convention (1971) shall also apply, mutatis mutandis, to the rights of performers and producers of phonograms in phonograms.

QUESTION

TRIPS Agreement authorizes Members to apply the exceptions and limitations to the extent permitted by the Rome Convention. The first paragraphs of article 14 are covered but not the fourth (concerning Rental Right). Do you see any reason to exclude the rental right from the scope of article 14(6)?

WPPT

> **Article 16**
> **Limitations and Exceptions**
>
> (1) Contracting Parties may, in their national legislation, provide for the same kinds of limitations or exceptions with regard to the protection of performers and producers of phonograms as they provide for, in their national legislation, in connection with the protection of copyright in literary and artistic works.

Beijing Treaty

> **Article 13**
> **Limitations and Exceptions**
>
> (1) Contracting Parties may, in their national legislation, provide for the same kinds of limitations or exceptions with regard to the protection of performers as they provide for, in their national legislation, in connection with the protection of copyright in literary and artistic works.

QUESTIONS

How do you explain the relationship between the Rome Convention, the WPPT and the Beijing Treaty? Why is an identity of exceptions between neighboring rights and copyright required? Could it be related to the clause that safeguards copyright proper (see article 1 of the Rome Convention, article 1 of the WPPT and article 1 of the Beijing Treaty)?

5.5.3 Generalization of the "three-step test"

International conventions

TRIPS

> **Article 13**
> **Limitations and Exceptions**
>
> Members shall confine limitations or exceptions to exclusive rights to certain special cases which do not conflict with a normal exploitation of the work and do not unreasonably prejudice the legitimate interests of the right holder.

WCT

Article 10
Limitations and Exceptions

(1) Contracting Parties may, in their national legislation, provide for limitations of or exceptions to the rights granted to authors of literary and artistic works under this Treaty in certain special cases that do not conflict with a normal exploitation of the work and do not unreasonably prejudice the legitimate interests of the author.

(2) Contracting Parties shall, when applying the Berne Convention, confine any limitations of or exceptions to rights provided for therein to certain special cases that do not conflict with a normal exploitation of the work and do not unreasonably prejudice the legitimate interests of the author.

Agreed statement concerning Article 10: It is understood that the provisions of Article 10 permit Contracting Parties to carry forward and appropriately extend into the digital environment limitations and exceptions in their national laws which have been considered acceptable under the Berne Convention. Similarly, these provisions should be understood to permit Contracting Parties to devise new exceptions and limitations that are appropriate in the digital network environment.
It is also understood that Article 10(2) neither reduces nor extends the scope of applicability of the limitations and exceptions permitted by the Berne Convention.

QUESTIONS

1. What is the difference in the application of the three-step test to works covered by the Berne Convention, and works newly covered by the WCT? Is it clear that the works covered by the WCT were not already embraced within Berne?
2. What is the difference in the application of the three-step test to rights previously established in the Berne Convention, and rights newly-articulated in the WCT? Is it clear that the WCT establishes rights not already embraced within Berne?
3. Under the Agreed Statement concerning article 10, member states may "appropriately extend" exceptions admitted for the analog environment to the digital environment. Do all analog environment exceptions "appropriately extend" to the digital environment? For example, what about private copying?

WPPT

Article 16
Limitations and Exceptions

. . .

(2) Contracting Parties shall confine any limitations of or exceptions to rights provided for in this Treaty to certain special cases which do not conflict with a normal exploitation of the performance or phonogram and do not unreasonably prejudice the legitimate interests of the performer or of the producer of the phonogram.

> **Agreed statement concerning Articles 7, 11 and 16**: The reproduction right, as set out in Articles 7 and 11, and the exceptions permitted thereunder through Article 16, fully apply in the digital environment, in particular to the use of performances and phonograms in digital form. It is understood that the storage of a protected performance or phonogram in digital form in an electronic medium constitutes a reproduction within the meaning of these Articles.
>
> **Agreed statement concerning Article 16**: The agreed statement concerning Article 10 (on Limitations and Exceptions) of the WIPO Copyright Treaty is applicable mutatis mutandis also to Article 16 (on Limitations and Exceptions) of the WIPO Performances and Phonograms Treaty. [The text of the agreed statement concerning Article 10 of the WCT reads as follows: "It is understood that the provisions of Article 10 permit Contracting Parties to carry forward and appropriately extend into the digital environment limitations and exceptions in their national laws which have been considered acceptable under the Berne Convention. Similarly, these provisions should be understood to permit Contracting Parties to devise new exceptions and limitations that are appropriate in the digital network environment."]

QUESTIONS

1. To what extent does article 16(2) of the WPPT innovate compared to the TRIPS Agreement?
2. Article 16(1) permits member states to "provide for the same kinds of limitations or exceptions with regard to the protection of performers and producers of phonograms as they provide for, in their national legislation, in connection with the protection of copyright in literary and artistic works." The three-step test being already encompassed in WCT or the TRIPS Agreement, was it necessary to add it in the WPPT?

Beijing Treaty

Article 13
Limitations and Exceptions

. . .

(2) Contracting Parties shall confine any limitations of or exceptions to rights provided for in this Treaty to certain special cases which do not conflict with a normal exploitation of the performance and do not unreasonably prejudice the legitimate interests of the performer.

> **Agreed statement concerning Article 13**: The Agreed statement concerning Article 10 (on Limitations and Exceptions) of the WIPO Copyright Treaty (WCT) is applicable mutatis mutandis also to Article 13 (on Limitations and Exceptions) of the Treaty.

QUESTIONS

Article 11(1) of the Beijing Treaty grants performers "the exclusive right of authorizing the broadcasting and communication to the public of their performances fixed in audiovisual fixations." Under article 11(2), however, member states may nonetheless enter a reservation and instead "establish a right to equitable remuneration for the direct or indirect use of performances fixed in audiovisual fixations for broadcasting or for communication to the public." Article 11(3) also allows member states to declare that they will not apply either the exclusive right or the remuneration right "at all." To what extent do paragraphs 2 and 3 color the analysis of the three-step test? Do they imply that audiovisual performers have a "legitimate interest" in remuneration that a broad, uncompensated, fair use right would "unreasonably prejudice"? Or does a member state's freedom to deny any rights mean that it may implement a remuneration right, but still provide for unremunerated exceptions?

Interpretation

WTO Panel, WT/DS160/R – 15 June 2000 United States – Section 110(5) of the U.S. Copyright Act Report of the Panel

[The U.S. exemption under scrutiny and condemned by the Panel (17 U.S.C. s 110(5)(B)) applied to the public performance of radio or television transmissions of nondramatic musical works by:

- any business establishment with less than 2000 gross square feet of space, and
- any food service or drinking establishment that has less than 3750 gross square feet of space,
- If the establishment is 2000 gross square feet or more, or if the food service or drinking establishment is 3750 gross square feet or more, the establishment will nonetheless be exempt, if:
  - the performance of the radio transmission incorporating nondramatic musical compositions is "communicated by means of a total of not more than six loudspeakers, of which not more than four loudspeakers are located in any one room or adjoining outdoor space," or
  - the performance of a television transmission incorporating nondramatic musical compositions is "communicated by means of a total of not more than four audiovisual devices, of which not more than one audiovisual device is located in any one room, and no such audiovisual device has a diagonal screen size greater than 55 inches, and any audio portion of the performance or display is communicated by means of a total of not more than six loudspeakers, of which not more than four loudspeakers are located in any one room or adjoining outdoor space."

[The 1998 exception significantly enlarged a preexisting "homestyle" exemption, for the "communication of a transmission embodying a performance or display of a work by the public reception of the transmission on a single receiving apparatus of a kind commonly used in private homes . . ." The E.U. also, but unsuccessfully, challenged this exception.

[The E.U. contended that the U.S. section 110(5) exemptions violated U.S. TRIPS obligations because they conflicted with articles 11 (1)(ii) and 11*bis*(1)(iii) of the Berne Convention (incorporated through article 9.1 of TRIPS). Article 11 (1)(ii) of the Berne Convention grants to authors of dramatic and musical works the exclusive right to authorize "any communication to the public of the performance of their works". Article 11*bis*(1) (iii) grants to authors of artistic works (which includes nondramatic and other musical works) the exclusive right of authorizing "the public communication by loudspeaker or any other analogous instrument transmitting, by signs, sounds or images, the broadcast of the work". Article 11*bis* (2) permits member countries to determine how the transmission right shall be exercised, but, in preserving the author's "right to obtain equitable remuneration," appears to preclude outright exemptions.

[The U.S. responded that the apparent inconsistency of section 110(5) with Berne Convention articles 11 (1)(ii) and 11*bis* (1)(iii) did not constitute a violation of TRIPS because the exceptions came within the scope of TRIPS article 13. As a threshold matter, this defense required the Panel to address the relationship between exceptions set forth in the Berne Convention, as incorporated in TRIPS, and the general TRIPS article 13 exception. The E.U. had asserted that article 13 should apply only to the rights newly introduced into TRIPS; it should not provide an additional or broader defense to a violation of a preexisting Berne Convention right. To expand the exceptions previously set out or implied into the Berne Convention would violate that Treaty's article 20, which permits Union member countries to enter into agreements granting more extensive rights, but which, by implication, prohibits agreements reducing Berne Convention rights, argued the E.U.

[The E.U. further claimed that, under the Berne Convention, the disputed exception could not exceed the scope of the "minor exceptions" implied into the public performance right. The Panel determined that TRIPS article 9.1 incorporated not only the Berne Convention text, but also its *acquis*, that is, the context of each provision's enactment, and their prevailing interpretations. Thus, the "minor exceptions" doctrine should be deemed incorporated as well. On the question whether the scope of TRIPS article 13 exceeds the scope of "minor exceptions," the Panel agreed with the U.S. position that article 13 "clarifies and articulates the standards applicable to minor exceptions under the Berne Convention" but does not enlarge it. (Panel decision ¶ 6.82)

[Having equated performance rights "minor exceptions" with exceptions permitted under the three-step test, the Panel went on to assess the merits of § 110(5) in light of that test. The panel determined that § 110(5)(B) failed to meet any of the test's criteria. (See *supra*, Part I, Chapter 2.1.3, subsequent agreements and practices.)]

. . .

2. The three criteria test under Article 13 of the TRIPS Agreement

(a) General introduction

6.97   Article 13 of the TRIPS Agreement requires that limitations and exceptions to exclusive rights (1) be confined to certain special cases, (2) do not conflict with a normal exploitation of the work, and (3) do not unreasonably prejudice the legitimate interests of the right holder. The principle of effective treaty interpretation requires us to give a distinct meaning to each of the three conditions and to avoid a reading that could

reduce any of the conditions to "redundancy or inutility". The three conditions apply on a cumulative basis, each being a separate and independent
requirement that must be satisfied. Failure to comply with any one of the
three conditions results in the Article 13 exception being disallowed. Both
parties agree on the cumulative nature of the three conditions. The Panel
shares their view. It may be noted at the outset that Article 13 cannot have
more than a narrow or limited operation. Its tenor, consistent as it is with
the provisions of Article 9(2) of the Berne Convention (1971), discloses
that it was not intended to provide for exceptions or limitations except for
those of a limited nature. The narrow sphere of its operation will emerge
from our discussion and application of its provisions in the paragraphs
which follow.

. . .

6.99   The parties have largely relied on similar factual information in sub-
stantiating their legal arguments under each of the three conditions of Article
13. We are called upon to evaluate this information from different angles
under the three conditions, which call for different requirements for justifying exceptions or limitations. We will look at the defined and limited scope
of the exemptions at issue under the first condition, and focus on the degree
of conflict with normal exploitation of works under the second condition. In
relation to the third condition, we will examine the extent of prejudice caused
to the legitimate interests of the right holder in the light of the information
submitted by the parties.

6.100   In providing such factual information, the United States has focused
on describing the immediate and direct impact on copyright holders caused
by the introduction of the exemptions into its law; this can be characterized
as the *actual* effects of the exemptions. The United States argues that while
both actual losses and potential losses may be relevant to the analysis, the key
is a realistic appraisal of the conditions that prevail in the market; the only
way to avoid the danger of arbitrariness is to base the analysis on realistic
market conditions.

6.101   The European Communities emphasizes the importance of taking
into account the way that the exemptions affect the right holders' opportunities to exercise their exclusive rights as well as the indirect impact of the
exemptions; this can be characterized as the *potential* effects of the exemptions. We will address below the question to what extent we should focus on
the actual impact on the right holder and to what extent we should also take
into account the potential impact.

(b) "Certain special cases"

(i) General interpretative analysis

. . .

6.103   The United States submits that the fact that the TRIPS Agreement does not elaborate on the criteria for a case to be considered "special" provides Members flexibility to determine for themselves whether a particular case represents an appropriate basis for an exception. But it acknowledges that the essence of the first condition is that the exceptions be well-defined and of limited application.

. . .

6.107   We start our analysis of the first condition of Article 13 by referring to the ordinary meaning of the terms in their context and in the light of its object and purpose. It appears that the notions of "exceptions" and "limitations" in the introductory words of Article 13 overlap in part in the sense that an "exception" refers to a derogation from an exclusive right provided under national legislation in some respect, while a "limitation" refers to a reduction of such right to a certain extent.

6.108   The ordinary meaning of "certain" is "known and particularised, but not explicitly identified", "determined, fixed, not variable; definitive, precise, exact". In other words, this term means that, under the first condition, an exception or limitation in national legislation must be clearly defined. However, there is no need to identify explicitly each and every possible situation to which the exception could apply, provided that the scope of the exception is known and particularised. This guarantees a sufficient degree of legal certainty.

6.109   We also have to give full effect to the ordinary meaning of the second word of the first condition. The term "special" connotes "having an individual or limited application or purpose", "containing details; precise, specific", "exceptional in quality or degree; unusual; out of the ordinary" or "distinctive in some way". This term means that more is needed than a clear definition in order to meet the standard of the first condition. In addition, an exception or limitation must be limited in its field of application or exceptional in its scope. In other words, an exception or limitation should be narrow in quantitative as well as a qualitative sense. This suggests a narrow scope as well as an exceptional or distinctive objective. To put this aspect of the first condition into the context of the second condition ("no conflict with a normal exploitation"), an exception or limitation should be the opposite of a non-special, i.e., a normal case.

6.110   The ordinary meaning of the term "case" refers to an "occurrence", "circumstance" or "event" or "fact". For example, in the context of the dispute at hand, the "case" could be described in terms of beneficiaries of the exceptions, equipment used, types of works or by other factors.

6.111   As regards the parties' arguments on whether the public policy purpose of an exception is relevant, we believe that the term "certain special cases" should not lightly be equated with "special purpose". It is difficult to reconcile the wording of Article 13 with the proposition that an exception or limitation must be justified in terms of a legitimate public policy purpose in order to fulfill the first condition of the Article. We also recall in this respect that in interpreting other WTO rules, such as the national treatment clauses of the GATT and the GATS, the Appellate Body has rejected interpretative tests which were based on the subjective aim or objective pursued by national legislation.

6.112   In our view, the first condition of Article 13 requires that a limitation or exception in national legislation should be clearly defined and should be narrow in its scope and reach. On the other hand, a limitation or exception may be compatible with the first condition even if it pursues a special purpose whose underlying legitimacy in a normative sense cannot be discerned. The wording of Article 13's first condition does not imply passing a judgment on the legitimacy of the exceptions in dispute. However, public policy purposes stated by law-makers when enacting a limitation or exception may be useful from a factual perspective for making inferences about the scope of a limitation or exception or the clarity of its definition.

6.113   In the case at hand, in order to determine whether subparagraphs (B) . . . of Section 110(5) are confined to "certain special cases", we first examine whether the exceptions have been clearly defined. Second, we ascertain whether the exemptions are narrow in scope, *inter alia*, with respect to their reach. In that respect, we take into account what percentage of eating and drinking establishments and retail establishments may benefit from the business exemption under subparagraph (B), . . .

(ii) The business exemption of subparagraph (B)

. . .

6.117   It appears that the European Communities does not dispute the fact that subparagraph (B) is clearly defined in respect of the size limits of establishments and the type of equipment that may be used by establishments above the applicable limits. The primary bone of contention between the parties is whether the business exemption, given its scope and reach, can be considered as a "special" case within the meaning of the first condition of Article 13.

6.118   The Congressional Research Service ("CRS") estimated in 1995 the percentage of the US eating and drinking establishments and retail establishments that would have fallen at that time below the size limits of 3,500 square feet and 1,500 square feet respectively. Its study found that:

65.2 per cent of all eating establishments;

71.8 per cent of all drinking establishments; and

27 per cent of all retail establishments would have fallen below these size limits.

6.119   The United States confirms these figures as far as eating and drinking establishments are concerned.

6.120   We note that this study was made in 1995 using the size limit of 3,500 square feet for eating and drinking establishments, and the size limit of 1,500 square feet for retail establishments, while the size limits under subparagraph (B) now are 3,750 square feet for eating and drinking establishments and 2,000 square feet for retail establishments. Therefore, in our view, it is safe to assume that the actual percentage of establishments which may fall within the finally enacted business exemption in the Fairness in Music Licensing Act of 1998 is higher than the above percentages.

. . .

6.127   We agree with the European Communities that it is the scope in respect of potential users that is relevant for determining whether the coverage of the exemption is sufficiently limited to qualify as a "certain *special* case". While it is true, as the United States argues, that some establishments might turn off the radio or television if they had to pay fees, other establishments which have not previously played music might do the opposite, because under the business exemption the use of music is free. Some establishments that have used recorded music may decide to switch to broadcast music in order to avoid paying licensing fees. It is clear that, in examining the exemption, we have to also consider its impact on the use of other substitutable sources of music. . . .

. . .

6.131   We note that, according to its preparatory works, Article 11*bis*(iii) of the Berne Convention (1971) was intended to provide right holders with a right to authorize the use of their works in the types of establishments covered by the exemption contained in Section 110(5)(B). Specifically, the preparatory works for the 1948 Brussels Conference indicate that the establishments that were intended to be covered were places "above all, where people meet: in the cinema, in restaurants, in tea rooms, railway carriages . . .". The preparatory works also refer to places such as factories, shops and offices. We fail to see how a law that exempts a major part of the users that were specifically intended to be covered by the provisions of Article 11*bis*(1) (iii) could be considered as a *special* case in the sense of the first condition of Article 13 of the TRIPS Agreement.

6.132   We are aware that eating, drinking and retail establishments are not the only potential users of music covered by the exclusive rights conferred under Articles 11*bis*(1)(iii) and 11(1)(ii) of the Berne Convention (1971). The United States has mentioned, *inter alia*, conventions, fairs and sporting events as other potential users of performances of works in the meaning of the above Articles. However, we believe that these examples of other potential users do not detract from the fact that eating, drinking and retail establishments are among the major groups of potential users of the works in the ways that are covered by the above-mentioned Articles.

6.133   The factual information presented to us indicates that a substantial majority of eating and drinking establishments and close to half of retail establishments are covered by the exemption contained in subparagraph (B) of Section 110(5) of the US Copyright Act. Therefore, we conclude that the exemption does not qualify as a "certain special case" in the meaning of the first condition of Article 13.

. . .

(c) "Not conflict with a normal exploitation of the work"

(i) General interpretative analysis

. . .

6.164   In interpreting the second condition of Article 13, we first need to define what "exploitation" of a "work" means. More importantly, we have to determine what constitutes a "normal" exploitation, with which a derogation is not supposed to "conflict".

6.165   The ordinary meaning of the term "exploit" connotes "making use of" or "utilising for one's own ends". We believe that "exploitation" of musical works thus refers to the activity by which copyright owners employ the exclusive rights conferred on them to extract economic value from their rights to those works.

6.166   We note that the ordinary meaning of the term "normal" can be defined as "constituting or conforming to a type or standard; regular, usual, typical, ordinary, conventional . . .". In our opinion, these definitions appear to reflect two connotations: the first one appears to be of an empirical nature, i.e., what is regular, usual, typical or ordinary. The other one reflects a somewhat more normative, if not dynamic, approach, i.e., conforming to a type or standard. We do not feel compelled to pass a judgment on which one of these connotations could be more relevant. Based on Article 31 of the Vienna Convention, we will attempt to develop a harmonious interpretation which gives meaning and effect to both connotations of "normal".

6.167   If "normal" exploitation were equated with full use of all exclusive rights conferred by copyrights, the exception clause of Article 13 would be left devoid of meaning. Therefore, "normal" exploitation clearly means something less than full use of an exclusive right.

6.168   In the US view, it is necessary to look to the ways in which an author might reasonably be expected to exploit his work in the normal course of events, when one determines what constitutes a normal exploitation. In this respect, it is relevant that Article 13 does not refer to particular specific rights but to "the work" as a whole. This implies that, in examining an exception under the second condition, consideration should be given to the scope of the exception *vis-à-vis* the panoply of all the rights holders' exclusive rights, as well as *vis-à-vis* the exclusive right to which it applies. In its view, the most important forms of exploitation of musical works, namely, "primary" performance and broadcasting, are not affected by either subparagraph of Section 110(5). The business and homestyle exemptions only affect what the United States considers "secondary" uses of broadcasts, and that too, subject to size and equipment limitations. In the US view, right holders normally obtain the main part of their remuneration from "primary" uses and only a minor part from "secondary" uses.

6.169   The European Communities rejects the idea that there could be a hierarchical order between "important" and "unimportant" rights under the TRIPS Agreement. For the European Communities, there are no "secondary" rights and the exclusive rights provided for in Articles 11*bis*(1)(iii) and 11(1)(ii) of the Berne Convention (1971) are all equally important separate rights.

6.170   The United States itself clarifies that it does not imply that a legal hierarchy exists between different exclusive rights conferred under Articles 11, 11*bis* or any other provision of the Berne Convention (1971) and that a country cannot completely eliminate an exclusive right even if that right be economically unimportant. But it takes the view that when a possible conflict with a normal exploitation of the work is analysed, it is relevant whether the exception applies to one or several exclusive rights. Similarly, the degree to which the exception affects a particular exclusive right is also relevant for the analysis of the second condition of Article 13.

6.171   It is true, as the United States points out, that Article 13 refers to a normal exploitation of "the work." However, the TRIPS Agreement and the Berne Convention provide exclusive rights in relation to the work. These exclusive rights are the legal means by which exploitation of the work, i.e., the commercial activity for extracting economic value from the rights to the work, can be carried out. The parties do not in principle question that the term "works" should be understood as referring to the "exclusive rights" in those works. In our view, Article 13's second condition does not explicitly refer *pars pro toto* to exclusive rights concerning a "work" given that the TRIPS Agreement (or the Berne Convention (1971) as incorporated into it) confers a considerable number of exclusive rights to all of which the exception clause of Article 13 may apply. Therefore, we believe that the "work" in Article 13's second condition means all the exclusive rights relating to it.

6.172   While we agree with the United States that the degree to which an exception affects a particular right is relevant for our analysis under the second condition, we emphasize that a possible conflict with a normal exploitation of a particular exclusive right cannot be counter-balanced or justified by the mere fact of the absence of a conflict with a normal exploitation of another exclusive right (or the absence of any exception altogether with respect to that right), even if the exploitation of the latter right would generate more income.

6.173   We agree with the European Communities that whether a limitation or an exception conflicts with a normal exploitation of a work should be judged for each exclusive right individually. We recall that this dispute primarily concerns the exclusive right under Article 11*bis*(1)(iii) of the Berne Convention

(1971) as incorporated into the TRIPS Agreement, but also the exclusive right under Article 11(1)(ii). In our view, normal exploitation would presuppose the possibility for right holders to exercise separately all three exclusive rights guaranteed under the three subparagraphs of Article 11*bis*(1), as well as the rights conferred by other provisions, such as Article 11, of the Berne Convention (1971). If it were permissible to limit by a statutory exemption the exploitation of the right conferred by the third subparagraph of Article 11*bis*(1) simply because, in practice, the exploitation of the rights conferred by the first and second subparagraphs of Article 11*bis*(1) would generate the lion's share of royalty revenue, the "normal exploitation" of each of the three rights conferred separately under Article 11*bis*(1) would be undermined.

. . .

6.175   We also note that the amplification of broadcast music will occur in establishments such as bars, restaurants and retail stores for the commercial benefit of the owner of the establishment. Both parties agree on the commercial nature of playing music even when customers are not directly charged for it. It may be that the amount yielded from any royalty payable as a consequence of this exploitation of the work will not be very great if one looks at the matter in the context of single establishments. But it is the accumulation of establishments which counts. It must be remembered that a copyright owner is entitled to exploit each of the rights for which a treaty, and the national legislation implementing that treaty, provides. If a copyright owner is entitled to a royalty for music broadcast over the radio, why should the copyright owner be deprived of remuneration which would otherwise be earned, when a significant number of radio broadcasts are amplified to customers of a variety of commercial establishments no doubt for the benefit of the businesses being conducted in those establishments. We also note that although, in a sense, the amplification which is involved is additional to and separate from the broadcast of a work, it is tied to the broadcast. The amplification cannot occur unless there is a broadcast. If an operator of an establishment plays recorded music, there is no legislative exception to the copyright owners' rights in that regard. But the amplification of a broadcast adds to the broadcast itself because it ensures that a wider audience will hear it. Clearly Article 11*bis*(iii) contemplates the use which is in question here by conferring rights on copyright owners in respect of the amplification of broadcasts.

6.176   That leaves us with the question of how to determine whether a particular use constitutes a normal exploitation of the exclusive rights provided under Articles 11*bis*(1)(iii) and 11(1)(ii) of the Berne Convention (1971). In academic literature, one approach that has been suggested would be to rely on "the ways in which an author might reasonably be expected to exploit his work in the normal course of events".

6.177   The main thrust of the US argumentation is that, for judging "normal exploitation", Article 13's second condition implies an economic analysis of the degree of "market displacement" in terms of foregone collection of remuneration by right owners caused by the free use of works due to the exemption at issue. In the US view, the essential question to ask is whether there are areas of the market in which the copyright owner would ordinarily expect to exploit the work, but which are not available for exploitation because of this exemption. Under this test, uses from which an owner would not ordinarily expect to receive compensation are not part of the normal exploitation.

6.178   In our view, this test seems to reflect the empirical or quantitative aspect of the connotation of "normal", the meaning of "regular, usual, typical or ordinary". We can, therefore, accept this US approach, but only for the empirical or quantitative side of the connotation. We have to give meaning and effect also to the second aspect of the connotation, the meaning of "conforming to a type or standard". We described this aspect of normalcy as reflecting a more normative approach to defining normal exploitation, that includes, *inter alia*, a dynamic element capable of taking into account technological and market developments. The question then arises how this normative aspect of "normal" exploitation could be given meaning in relation to the exploitation of musical works.

6.179   In this respect, we find persuasive guidance in the suggestion by a study group, composed of representatives of the Swedish Government and the United International Bureaux for the Protection of Intellectual Property ("BIRPI"), which was set up to prepare for the Revision Conference at Stockholm in 1967 ("Swedish/BIRPI Study Group"). In relation to the reproduction right, this Group suggested to allow countries:

> "[to] limit the recognition and the exercising of that right, for specified purposes and *on the condition that these purposes should not enter into economic competition with these works*" in the sense that "*all forms of exploiting a work, which have, or are likely to acquire, considerable economic or practical importance, must be reserved to the authors*" (emphasis added).

6.180   Thus it appears that one way of measuring the normative connotation of normal exploitation is to consider, in addition to those forms of exploitation that currently generate significant or tangible revenue, those forms of exploitation which, with a certain degree of likelihood and plausibility, could acquire considerable economic or practical importance.

6.181   In contrast, exceptions or limitations would be presumed not to conflict with a normal exploitation of works if they are confined to a scope or degree that does not enter into economic competition with non-exempted uses. In this respect, the suggestions of the Swedish/BIRPI Study Group are useful:

> "In this connection, the Study Group observed that, on the one hand, it was obvious that *all forms of exploiting a work which had, or were likely to acquire, considerable economic or practical importance must in principle be reserved to the authors*; exceptions that might restrict the possibilities open to the authors in these respects were unacceptable. On the other hand, it should not be forgotten that *domestic laws already contained a series of exceptions in favour of various public and cultural interests* and that it would be vain to suppose that countries would be ready at this stage to abolish these exceptions to any appreciable extent" (emphasis added).

6.182   We recall that the European Communities proposes to measure the impact of exceptions by using a benchmark according to which, at least, all those forms of use of works that create an economic benefit for the user should be considered as normal exploitation of works. We can accept that the assessment of normal exploitation of works, from an empirical or quantitative perspective, requires an economic analysis of the commercial use of the exclusive rights conferred by the copyrights in those works. However, in our view, not every use of a work, which in principle is covered by the scope of exclusive rights and involves commercial gain, necessarily conflicts with a normal exploitation of that work. If this were the case, hardly any exception or limitation could pass the test of the second condition and Article 13 might be left devoid of meaning, because normal exploitation would be equated with full use of exclusive rights.

6.183   We believe that an exception or limitation to an exclusive right in domestic legislation rises to the level of a conflict with a normal exploitation of the work (i.e., the copyright or rather the whole bundle of exclusive rights conferred by the ownership of the copyright), if uses, that in principle are covered by that right but exempted under the exception or limitation, enter into economic competition with the ways that right holders normally extract economic value from that right to the work (i.e., the copyright) and thereby deprive them of significant or tangible commercial gains.

6.184   In developing a benchmark for defining the normative connotation of normal exploitation, we recall the European Communities' emphasis on the potential impact of an exception rather than on its actual effect on the market at a given point in time, given that, in its view, it is the potential effect that determines the market conditions.

. . .

6.186   Therefore, in respect of the exclusive rights related to musical works, we consider that normal exploitation of such works is not only affected by those who actually use them without an authorization by the right holders due to an exception or limitation, but also by those who may be induced by it to do so at any time without having to obtain a licence from the right holders or the CMOs representing them. Thus we need to take into account those whose use of musical works is free as a result of the exemptions, and also those who may choose to start using broadcast music once its use becomes free of charge.

6.187   We base our appraisal of the actual and potential effects on the commercial and technological conditions that prevail in the market currently or in the near future. What is a normal exploitation in the market-place may evolve as a result of technological developments or changing consumer preferences. Thus, while we do not wish to speculate on future developments, we need to consider the actual and potential effects of the exemptions in question in the current market and technological environment.

6.188   We do acknowledge that the extent of exercise or non-exercise of exclusive rights by right holders at a given point in time is of great relevance for assessing what is the normal exploitation with respect to a particular exclusive right in a particular market. However, in certain circumstances, current licensing practices may not provide a sufficient guideline for assessing the potential impact of an exception or limitation on normal exploitation. For example, where a particular use of works is not covered by the exclusive rights conferred in the law of a jurisdiction, the fact that the right holders do not license such use in that jurisdiction cannot be considered indicative of what constitutes normal exploitation. The same would be true in a situation where, due to lack of effective or affordable means of enforcement, right holders may not find it worthwhile or practical to exercise their rights.

6.189   Both parties are of the view that the "normalcy" of a form of exploitation should be analysed primarily by reference to the market of the WTO Member whose measure is in dispute, i.e., the US market in this dispute. The European Communities is also of the view that comparative references to other countries with a similar level of socio-economic development could be relevant to corroborate or contradict data from the country primarily concerned. We note that while the WTO Members are free to choose the method of implementation, the minimum standards of protection are the same for all of them. In the present case it is enough for our purposes to take account of the specific conditions applying in the US market in assessing whether the measure in question conflicts with a normal exploitation in that market, or whether the measure meets the other conditions of Article 13.

(ii) The business exemption of subparagraph (B)

. . .

6.206   We recall that a substantial majority of eating and drinking establishments and close to half of retail establishments are eligible to benefit from the business exemption. This constitutes a major potential source of royalties for the exercise of the exclusive rights contained in Articles 11(1)*bis*(iii) and 11(1)(ii) of the Berne Convention (1971), as demonstrated by the figures of the D&B studies referred to under our analysis of the first condition of Article 13.

6.207   We recall that subparagraph (B) of Section 110(5) exempts communication to the public of radio and television broadcasts, while the playing of musical works from CDs and tapes (or live music) is not covered by it. Given that we have not been provided with reasons other than historical ones for this distinction, we see no logical reason to differentiate between broadcast and recorded music when assessing what is a normal use of musical works.

. . .

6.210   Right holders of musical works would expect to be in a position to authorize the use of broadcasts of radio and television music by many of the establishments covered by the exemption and, as appropriate, receive compensation for the use of their works. Consequently, we cannot but conclude that an exemption of such scope as subparagraph (B) conflicts with the "normal exploitation" of the work in relation to the exclusive rights conferred by Articles 11*bis*(1)(iii) and 11(1)(ii) of the Berne Convention (1971).

6.211   In the light of these considerations, we conclude that the business exemption embodied in subparagraph (B) conflicts with a normal exploitation of the work within the meaning of the second condition of Article 13.

. . .

(d) "Not unreasonably prejudice the legitimate interests of the right holder"

(i) General interpretative analysis

6.220   The United States defines "prejudice [to] the legitimate interests of the right holder" in terms of the economic impact caused by subparagraphs (A) and (B) of Section 110(5). In the US view, while the second condition of Article 13 of the TRIPS Agreement looks to the degree of market displacement caused by a limitation or exception, the "unreasonable prejudice" standard measures how much the right holder is harmed by the effects of the exception. Given that any exception to exclusive rights may technically result in some degree of prejudice to the right holder, the key question is whether that prejudice is unreasonable.

6.221   The European Communities submits that the legitimate interests of a right holder consist in being able to prevent all instances of a certain use of his or her work protected by a specific exclusive right undertaken by a third party without his or her consent. The legitimate interests include, at a minimum, all commercial uses by a third party of the right holder's exclusive rights. For the European Communities, both empirical and normative elements are relevant for the examination of the third condition of Article 13. In practice, economic prejudice to right holders should be assessed primarily on the basis of the economic effects in the country applying the exception. In the EC's view, it is sufficient to demonstrate the potentiality to prejudice; it is not necessary to quantify the actual financial losses suffered by the right holders concerned.

6.222   We note that the analysis of the third condition of Article 13 of the TRIPS Agreement implies several steps. First, one has to define what are the "interests" of right holders at stake and which attributes make them "legitimate". Then, it is necessary to develop an interpretation of the term "prejudice" and what amount of it reaches a level that should be considered "unreasonable".

6.223   The ordinary meaning of the term "interests" may encompass a legal right or title to a property or to use or benefit of a property (including intellectual property). It may also refer to a concern about a potential detriment or advantage, and more generally to something that is of some importance to a natural or legal person. Accordingly, the notion of "interests" is not necessarily limited to actual or potential economic advantage or detriment.

6.224   The term "legitimate" has the meanings of

(a)   "conformable to, sanctioned or authorized by, law or principle; lawful; justifiable; proper;
(b)   normal, regular, conformable to a recognized standard type."

Thus, the term relates to lawfulness from a legal positivist perspective, but it has also the connotation of legitimacy from a more normative perspective, in the context of calling for the protection of interests that are justifiable in the light of the objectives that underlie the protection of exclusive rights.

6.225   We note that the ordinary meaning of "prejudice" connotes damage, harm or injury. "Not unreasonable" connotes a slightly stricter threshold than "reasonable". The latter term means "proportionate", "within the limits of reason, not greatly less or more than might be thought likely or appropriate", or "of a fair, average or considerable amount or size".

6.226   Given that the parties do not question the "legitimacy" of the interest of right holders to exercise their rights for economic gain, the crucial question becomes which degree or level of "prejudice" may be considered as "unreasonable". Before dealing with the question of what amount or which kind of prejudice reaches a level beyond reasonable, we need to find a way to measure or quantify legitimate interests.

6.227   In our view, one – albeit incomplete and thus conservative – way of looking at legitimate interests is the economic value of the exclusive rights conferred by copyright on their holders. It is possible to estimate in economic terms the value of exercising, e.g., by licensing, such rights. That is not to say that legitimate interests are necessarily limited to this economic value.

6.228   In examining the second condition of Article 13, we have addressed the US argument that the prejudice to right holders caused by the exemptions at hand are minimal because they already receive royalties from broadcasting stations. We concluded that each exclusive right conferred by copyright, *inter alia*, under each subparagraph of Articles 11*bis* and 11 of the Berne Convention (1971), has to be considered separately for the purpose of examining whether a possible conflict with a "normal exploitation" exists.

6.229   The crucial question is which degree or level of "prejudice" may be considered as "unreasonable",[204] given that, under the third condition, a certain amount of "prejudice" has to be presumed justified as "not unreasonable".[205] In our view, prejudice to the legitimate interests of right holders reaches an unreasonable level if an exception or limitation causes or has the potential to cause an unreasonable loss of income to the copyright owner.

Legitimate interests of right holders of EC, US and third-country origin

. . .

[After assessing the information on market conditions provided by the parties, and taking into account the actual as well as the potential prejudice caused by the exemptions, the Panel determined that the prejudice caused by the business exemption of subparagraph (B) to the legitimate interests of the right holder was unreasonable. By contrast, the Panel accepted the homestyle exception because it exempted only a relatively small number of establishments, and the evidence showed that secondary transmissions of dramatic works were not a significant source of income for right holders.]

---

204 The term used in the French version of the Berne Convention is *"injustifié"*. According to article 37(1 (c) of the Berne Convention, both the English and the French text of the Convention are equally authentic, but "in case of differences of opinion on the interpretation of the various texts, the French text shall prevail."

However, article 37 of the Berne Convention has not been incorporated into the TRIPS Agreement. To the extent that articles 1–21 of the Berne Convention have been incorporated into the TRIPS Agreement by virtue of its article 9.1, the general rule of article XVI of the Agreement Establishing the WTO applies, i.e., that the English, French and Spanish versions of the covered agreements are equally authentic.

Article 33 of the Vienna Convention on the Law of Treaties stipulates that treaties which are authentic in several languages should be interpreted harmoniously, i.e., presuming that expressions in the treaty have the same meaning in all authentic languages.

205 In respect of what could be the dividing line between "unreasonable" and "not unreasonable" prejudice, we consider the explanation of the Guide to the Berne Convention to be of persuasive value. It states in the context of the third condition of article 9(2) of the Berne Convention, which is worded almost identically to article 13 of the TRIPS Agreement but refers to exceptions to the reproduction right:

"Note that it is not a question of prejudice or no: all copying is damaging to some degree . . .". The paragraph goes on to discuss whether photocopying "prejudices the circulation of the review", whether it "might seriously cut in on its sales " and says that "[i]n cases where there would be serious loss of profit for the copyright owner, the law should provide him with some compensation (a system of compulsory licensing with equitable remuneration)." *See* the Guide to the Berne Convention, paragraph 9.8., pp. 55–56. We do not believe that in this respect the benchmark has to be substantially different for reproduction rights, performance rights or broadcasting rights in the meanings of Articles 9, 11 or 11*bis* of the Berne Convention (1971).

NOTES AND QUESTIONS

1. Under the Panel's decision, to survive scrutiny under TRIPS article 13, the member state defending the challenged exemption or limitation bears the burden of showing each of the following:

    (1) That the exemption is limited to a narrow and specifically defined class of uses ["certain special cases"], but the member state need not demonstrate or justify the local policy that underlies the exception;

    (2) That the exempted use does not compete with an actual or potential source of economic gain from the ways rightholders normally exercise rights under copyright ["conflict with a normal exploitation of the work"]; and

    (3) That the exempted use does not unreasonably harm rightholder interests that are justifiable in light of general copyright objectives ["not unreasonably prejudice the legitimate interests of the rightholder"]; the unreasonableness of the harm may be allayed if the member state imposes a compensation-ensuring compulsory license in lieu of an outright exemption.

Significantly, "The three conditions apply on a cumulative basis, each being a separate and independent requirement that must be satisfied. Failure to comply with any one of the three conditions results in the Article 13 exception being disallowed." (Panel decision ¶ 6.97) Thus, for example, if the exploitation at issue is "normal," then subjecting it to a compulsory license would not be permissible. As a result, if educational uses constitute the principal market for a book (such as a collection of grammar exercises), then a member state would violate article 13 if it imposed a compulsory license to permit the book's reproduction. By the same token, a member state would not comply with article 13 if its exception or limitation were not confined to "certain special cases," even if the impact of the exception or limitation did not "conflict with a normal exploitation" nor "unreasonably prejudice the legitimate interests of the rightholder."

Some commentators have disputed the WTO Panel's requirement that each step be satisfied. For example the Wittem Project "European Copyright Code" http://www.copyrightcode.eu/, article 5.5, essentially foregoes the first step:

> Any other use that is comparable to the uses enumerated in article 5.1 to 5.4(1) [Uses with minimal economic significance; Uses for the purpose of freedom of expression and information; Uses Permitted to Promote Social, Political and Cultural Objectives; Uses for the purpose

of enhancing competition (advertising and reverse engineering)] is permitted provided that the corresponding requirements of the relevant limitation are met and the use does not conflict with the normal exploitation of the work and does not unreasonably prejudice the legitimate interests of the author or rightholder, taking account of the legitimate interests of third parties.

Is the Panel correct that the proponent of the exception or limitation must prove its compliance with each step? Is the U.S. fair use exception (17 U.S.C. s 107) consistent with the Panel's interpretation of article 13?

2. What in the Panel's view is a "normal exploitation"? The Panel focused initially on what it called the "empirical" aspect of the term "normal exploitation." The issue seems to be whether today the right owner is, or tomorrow will be, in fact exploiting a particular market. But the Panel also perceived a "normative" dimension in the second step. That said, having announced the existence of a normative dimension, the Panel did not clearly articulate its content. In fact, the Panel's suggestion that one might discern the normative connotations of the second step by considering "those forms of exploitation which, with a certain degree of likelihood and plausibility, could acquire considerable economic or practical importance," (Panel decision ¶ 6.180.) seems more like a direction to anticipate what the empirical situation will be, than an explanation of what the rightholder's markets *should* cover. Admittedly, the case before the WTO Panel did not present significant normative difficulties, since the pork barrel exception at issue (favoring the business interests of restaurants and retail establishments) did not further speech, scholarship, or other creative activities often fostered by copyright exceptions.

The absence of a genuine normative problem in the dispute before the Panel could lead one to oversimplify the synthesis of the Panel decision. Arguably, any economically significant exploitation that the right holder realistically can, or will be able to, individually license comes within the scope of a "normal exploitation." So stated, however, there is a risk that even traditionally privileged uses, such as scholarship or parody, could be deemed "normal exploitations," assuming copyright owners could develop a low transactions cost method of charging for them. Is it sufficient to reply that the desirability of charging for these uses may be addressed as part of the step three inquiry into the "legitimate" interests of the author? Not if one does not get to step three because the exception conflicts with a "normal exploitation." As a result, it is all the more important to bear in mind the factual context of the Panel decision. Should a controversy requiring examination of a speech- or scholarship-motivated exception under the three-step test come before a WTO Panel, or, for that matter, a member state court, that institution should consider whether, as a normative matter, there is a "market" for criticism and similar kinds of uses that the copyright owner should control.

3. In ¶ 6.80 (not included in the above excerpt of the WTO Panel decision), the Panel stated: "In our view, neither the express wording nor the context of Article 13 or any other provision of the TRIPS Agreement supports the interpretation that the scope of application of Article 13 is limited to the exclusive rights newly introduced under the TRIPS Agreement." How does this statement compare with the agreed statements to WCT article 10? Is there a difference, and does it matter?

4. Compare the French and English versions of the third step: "ni ne cause un préjudice injustifié" with "not unreasonably prejudice": the French "not cause an unjustified prejudice" may be more restrictive since it implies that the proponent of the exception must justify any harm it causes. As a matter of interpretation of the Berne Convention, article 37 provides that the French text prevails. The WTO Panel, however, in n 204, observing that the TRIPS does not incorporate article 37, held the English text equally authentic. Does it follow that a national exception or limitation may pass muster under the TRIPS, but not under Berne? Does it matter?

5. In March 2012, the French Intellectual Property Code was amended in order to authorize the exploitation of twentieth-century "Unavailable books." An unavailable book is "a book published in France before January 1, 2001, which is commercially unavailable and is not currently published in paper or digital format." The definition appears designed to limit the universe of affected works to works of French origin (as to which the Berne prohibition of formalities does not apply). But the definition is not confined to books first published in France, nor does it exclude French translations of foreign works. As a result, the law may still affect works to which Berne minima apply. The books deemed unavailable following the deadline for opposition are registered in a public database. Both the author and the publisher may oppose the registration of the book in the database. Absent opposition, a collective management society approved by the Ministry of Culture is authorized to grant the original publisher an exclusive license, or if the original publisher declines, to grant another publisher a non-exclusive license for digital exploitation of the book for a period of five years, which will be renewable. Once the license is granted, both the author and the original publisher may still notify that they want to exploit the book. However, their decision will not void the licenses already granted.

To what extent, does the French law comply with the three-step test? If not, does the ability to opt out of the digitization scheme change the analysis? Would the opt-out be deemed a formality prohibited under article 5(1) of the Berne Convention? (See, *supra*, this Chapter, 5.1.1 (What is a "formality"?))

5.5.4   U.S. approach

In addition to a variety of compulsory licenses (e.g., cable and satellite retransmissions, 17 USC §§ 111, 119; reproduction and distribution of sound recordings of musical compositions, § 115; non interactive transmissions of sound recordings, § 114) and specific exceptions to the public performance right set out in section 110, the U.S. Copyright Act includes an unremunerated exception of overarching general application: fair use. Section 107 provides:

> **§ 107. Limitations on exclusive rights: Fair use**
>
> Notwithstanding the provisions of sections 106 and 106A, the fair use of a copyrighted work, including such use by reproduction in copies or phonorecords or by any other means specified by that section, for purposes such as criticism, comment, news reporting, teaching (including multiple copies for classroom use), scholarship, or research, is not an infringement of copyright. In determining whether the use made of a work in any particular case is a fair use the factors to be considered shall include—
>
> (1) the purpose and character of the use, including whether such use is of a commercial nature or is for nonprofit educational purposes;
> (2) the nature of the copyrighted work;
> (3) the amount and substantiality of the portion used in relation to the copyrighted work as a whole; and
> (4) the effect of the use upon the potential market for or value of the copyrighted work.
>
> The fact that a work is unpublished shall not itself bar a finding of fair use if such finding is made upon consideration of all the above factors.

U.S. copyright law has long recognized fair use as an exception favoring new creativity. Justice Story's 1841 decision in *Folsom* v. *Marsh*, 9 F. Cas. 342 (C.C.D. Mass. 1841), to which many assign the doctrine's ancestor attribution, refined the British rule of "fair abridgement" to emphasize the authorship contributions of the alleged infringer, as well as their impact on the market for the copied work. Justice Story distinguished between "real, substantial condensation of the materials, and intellectual labor and judgment bestowed thereon" and "merely the facile use of the scissors; or extracts of the essential parts, constituting the chief value of the original work." The ensuing century and a half of fair use cases almost exclusively debated the nature of the second author's additions or alterations, pitted against the first author or copyright owner's prospects for exploiting the work. In controversies involving scholarship, criticism and commentary (including parody), the caselaw thus calibrated the basic moving parts of the traditional fair use doctrine: authorship, public benefit, economic impact. The progress of learning advances when the law allows follow-on authors to bestow their intellectual labor and judgment in reworking selections from a prior work, without prejudicing the profits or prospects of that work.

Over the last 20 years, U.S. fair use cases involving follow-on authorship have largely turned on the "transformative" character of the contribution, as well as on economic impact, though U.S. courts sometimes conflate the two factors, equating "transformative" works or purposes with those that do not substitute for the copyright owner's normal markets for the work. Indeed, the Second Circuit has developed the concept of a transformative market, for exploitations that fall outside the copyright owner's zone of exclusivity: "transformative uses do[] not count because such uses, by definition, do not serve as substitutes for the original work."* The counterpoint to a transformative market (favoring fair use) is a traditional license market, that is, a "traditional, reasonable, or likely to be developed market"** (disfavoring fair use). Courts inquire into whether the plaintiff is currently exploiting the market, or whether the market is one that similarly situated copyright owners would normally exploit. Thus, the traditional fair use inquiry balances the new expressive use (promoting the second-comer's authorship) against the first author's returns for her intellectual labors.

More recently, however, U.S. courts have extended the fair use exception to exempt enterprises or uses that make the work more widely available. These redistribution "fair uses" are different from traditional fair uses. They do not directly produce new works. What motivations therefore underlie non authorship-based exceptions? The caselaw and legislative history of the 1976 Copyright Act indicate two broad impetuses. First, a category one might call "subsidy," in which redistributive copying for non-commercial purposes (generally by educational institutions or libraries) receives a free

---

* Authors Guild v. HathiTrust, 755 F.3d 87, 99 (2d Cir. 2014).
** American Geophysical Union v. Texaco Inc., 60 F. 3d 913, 930 (2d Cir. 1994); *see also HathiTrust* at 96.

pass (subject to a variety of limitations). Second, and primarily in the case of redistributive uses developed by new (generally commercial and technological) market entrants, "market failure" may justify uses that are as a practical matter insusceptible to licensing, notably because of their volume. The following decision exemplifies the application of the fair use exception to a redistributive use.

Authors Guild, Inc. v. HathiTrust, 755 F.3d 87 (2d Cir. 2014)

Barrington D. Parker, Circuit Judge:

Beginning in 2004, several research universities including the University of Michigan, the University of California at Berkeley, Cornell University, and the University of Indiana agreed to allow Google to electronically scan the books in their collections. In October 2008, thirteen universities announced plans to create a repository for the digital copies and founded an organization called HathiTrust to set up and operate the HathiTrust Digital Library (or "HDL"). Colleges, universities, and other nonprofit institutions became members of HathiTrust and made the books in their collections available for inclusion in the HDL. HathiTrust currently has 80 member institutions and the HDL contains digital copies of more than ten million works, published over many centuries, written in a multitude of languages, covering almost every subject imaginable. This appeal requires us to decide whether the HDL's use of copyrighted material is protected against a claim of copyright infringement under the doctrine of fair use.

BACKGROUND

A.   The HathiTrust Digital Library

. . . HathiTrust allows the general public to search for particular terms across all digital copies in the repository. Unless the copyright holder authorizes broader use, the search results show only the page numbers on which the search term is found within the work and the number of times the term appears on each page. The HDL does not display to the user any text from the underlying copyrighted work (either in "snippet" form or otherwise). Consequently, the user is not able to view either the page on which the term appears or any other portion of the book. . . .

The HDL stores digital copies of the works in four different locations. One copy is stored on its primary server in Michigan, one on its secondary server in Indiana, and two on separate backup tapes at the University of Michigan.[3] Each copy contains the full text of the work, in a machine readable format, as well as the *images* of each page in the work as they appear in the print version.

. . .

C. Proceedings in the District Court

This case began when twenty authors and authors' associations (collectively, the "Authors") sued HathiTrust, one of its member universities, and the presidents of four other member universities (collectively, the "Libraries") for copyright infringement seeking declaratory and injunctive relief. . . .

. . .

The district court granted the Libraries' . . . motions for summary judgment on the infringement claims on the basis that the three uses permitted by the HDL were fair uses. In this assessment, the district court gave considerable weight to what it found to be the "transformative" nature of the three uses and to what it described as the HDL's "invaluable" contribution to the advancement of knowledge, *Authors Guild, Inc. v. HathiTrust*, 902 F.Supp.2d 445, 460–64 (S.D.N.Y.2012). The district court explained:

Although I recognize that the facts here may on some levels be without precedent, I am convinced that they fall safely within the protection of fair use such that there is no genuine issue of material fact. I cannot imagine a definition of fair use that would not encompass the transformative uses made by [the HDL] and would require that I terminate this invaluable contribution to the progress of science and cultivation of the arts that at the same time effectuates the ideals espoused by the [Americans With Disabilities Act of 1990 (codified as amended at 42 U.S.C. §§ 12101, et seq.)].

Id. at 464.

. . . [T]his appeal followed.

---

3 Separate from the HDL, one copy is also kept by Google. Google's use of its copy is the subject of a separate lawsuit currently pending in this Court. *See Authors Guild, Inc. v. Google, Inc.*, 721 F.3d 132 (2d Cir.2013), *on remand*, 954 F.Supp.2d 282 (S.D.N.Y.2013), *appeal docketed*, No. 13–4829 (2d Cir. Dec. 23, 2013).

DISCUSSION

. . .

I.   Fair Use

. . .

B.

. . .

1. Full–Text Search

It is not disputed that, in order to perform a full-text search of books, the Libraries must first create digital copies of the entire books. Importantly, as we have seen, the HDL does not allow users to view any portion of the books they are searching. Consequently, in providing this service, the HDL does not add into circulation any new, human-readable copies of any books. Instead, the HDL simply permits users to "word search"—that is, to locate where specific words or phrases appear in the digitized books. Applying the relevant factors, we conclude that this use is a fair use.

i.

Turning to the first factor, we conclude that the creation of a full-text searchable database is a quintessentially transformative use. As the example, *supra*, demonstrates, the result of a word search is different in purpose, character, expression, meaning, and message from the page (and the book) from which it is drawn. Indeed, we can discern little or no resemblance between the original text and the results of the HDL full-text search.

There is no evidence that the Authors write with the purpose of enabling text searches of their books. Consequently, the full-text search function does not "supersede[ ] the objects [or purposes] of the original creation," *Campbell,* 510 U.S. at 579 [internal quotation marks omitted]. The HDL does not "merely repackage[ ] or republish[ ] the original[s]," Leval, 103 HARV. L.REV.. at 1111, or merely recast "an original work into a new mode of presentation," *Castle Rock Entm't, Inc. v. Carol Publ'g Grp., Inc.,* 150 F.3d 132, 143 (2d Cir.1998). Instead, by enabling full-text search, the HDL adds to the original something new with a different purpose and a different character.

Full-text search adds a great deal more to the copyrighted works at issue than did the transformative uses we approved in several other cases. For example, in *Cariou v. Prince*, we found that certain photograph collages were transformative, even though the collages were cast in the same medium as the copyrighted photographs. 714 F.3d at 706. Similarly, in *Bill Graham Archives v. Dorling Kindersley Ltd.*, we held that it was a transformative use to include in a biography copyrighted concert photos, even though the photos were unaltered (except for being reduced in size). 448 F.3d 605, 609–11 (2d Cir.2006); *see also Blanch v. Koons*, 467 F.3d 244, 252–53 (2d Cir.2006) (transformative use of copyrighted photographs in collage painting); *Leibovitz v. Paramount Pictures Corp.*, 137 F.3d 109, 114 (2d Cir.1998) (transformative use of copyrighted photograph in advertisement).

Cases from other Circuits reinforce this conclusion. In *Perfect 10, Inc.*, the Ninth Circuit held that the use of copyrighted thumbnail images in internet search results was transformative because the thumbnail copies served a different function from the original copyrighted images. 508 F.3d at 1165. And in *A.V. ex rel. Vanderhye v. iParadigms, LLC*, a company created electronic copies of unaltered student papers for use in connection with a computer program that detects plagiarism. Even though the electronic copies made no "substantive alteration to" the copyrighted student essays, the Fourth Circuit held that plagiarism detection constituted a transformative use of the copyrighted works. 562 F.3d 630, 639–40.

ii.

The second fair-use factor—the nature of the copyrighted work—is not dispositive. The HDL permits the full-text search of every type of work imaginable. Consequently, there is no dispute that the works at issue are of the type that the copyright laws value and seek to protect. However, "this factor 'may be of limited usefulness where,' as here, 'the creative work . . . is being used for a transformative purpose.'" *Cariou*, 714 F.3d at 710 (quoting *Bill Graham Archives*, 448 F.3d at 612). Accordingly, our fair-use analysis hinges on the other three factors.

iii.

The third factor asks whether the copying used more of the copyrighted work than necessary and whether the copying was excessive. As we have noted, "[t]here are no absolute rules as to how much of a copyrighted work may be copied and still be considered a fair use." *Maxtone–Graham v. Burtchaell*, 803 F.2d 1253, 1263 (2d Cir.1986). "[T]he extent of permissible copying varies with the purpose and character of the use." *Campbell*, 510 U.S. at 586–87. The crux of the inquiry is whether "no more was taken than necessary." For some purposes, it may be necessary to copy the entire copyrighted work, in which case Factor Three does not weigh against a finding of fair use.

In order to enable the full-text search function, the Libraries, as we have seen, created digital copies of all the books in their collections. Because it was reasonably necessary for the HDL to make use of the entirety of the works in order to enable the full-text search function, we do not believe the copying was excessive.

. . .

iv.

The fourth factor requires us to consider "the effect of the use upon the potential market for or value of the copyrighted work," 17 U.S.C. § 107(4), and, in particular, whether the secondary use "usurps the market of the original work," *NXIVM Corp.*, 364 F.3d at 482.

The Libraries contend that the full-text-search use poses no harm to any existing or potential traditional market and point to the fact that, in discovery, the Authors admitted that they were unable to identify "any specific, quantifiable past harm, or any documents relating to any such past harm," resulting from any of the Libraries' uses of their works (including full-text search). The district court agreed with this contention, as do we.

At the outset, it is important to recall that the Factor Four analysis is concerned with only one type of economic injury to a copyright holder: the harm that results because the secondary use serves as a substitute for the original work. *See Campbell*, 510 U.S. at 591 ("cognizable market harm" is limited to "market substitution"). In other words, under Factor Four, any economic "harm" caused by transformative uses does not count because such uses, by definition, do not serve as substitutes for the original work.

To illustrate why this is so, consider how copyright law treats book reviews. Book reviews often contain quotations of copyrighted material to illustrate the reviewer's points and substantiate his criticisms; this is a paradigmatic fair use. And a negative book review can cause a degree of economic injury to the author by dissuading readers from purchasing copies of her book, even when the review does not serve as a substitute for the original. But, obviously, in that case, the author has no cause for complaint under Factor Four:

The only market harms that count are the ones that are caused because the secondary use serves as a substitute for the original, not when the secondary use is transformative (as in quotations in a book review). *See Campbell,* 510 U.S. at 591–92 ("[W]hen a lethal parody, like a scathing theater review, kills demand for the original, it does not produce a harm cognizable under the Copyright Act.").

The Authors assert two reasons why the full-text-search function harms their traditional markets. The first is a "lost sale" theory which posits that a market for licensing books for digital search could possibly develop in the future, and the HDL impairs the emergence of such a market because it allows patrons to search books without any need for a license. Thus, according to the Authors, every copy employed by the HDL in generating full-text searches represents a lost opportunity to license the book for search.

This theory of market harm does not work under Factor Four, because the full-text search function does not serve as a substitute for the books that are being searched. Thus, it is irrelevant that the Libraries might be willing to purchase licenses in order to engage in this transformative use (if the use were deemed unfair). Lost licensing revenue counts under Factor Four only when the use serves as a substitute for the original and the full-text-search use does not.

. . .

Without foreclosing a future claim based on circumstances not now predictable, and based on a different record, we hold that the balance of relevant factors in this case favors the Libraries. In sum, we conclude that the doctrine of fair use allows the Libraries to digitize copyrighted works for the purpose of permitting full-text searches.

. . .

QUESTION

Among the millions of in-copyright books scanned from the University of Michigan library, some substantial number would have been works whose country of origin was not the U.S. Is the fair use exception, as applied in this case, consistent with the three-step test, as applied by the WTO Panel?

5.5.5 E.U. approach

European harmonization of exceptions

Exceptions and limitations were first harmonized in specific directives related to specific objects, such as computer program, or specific rights, such as the rental right. The Info Soc Directive adopted a general approach to limitations and exceptions, creating one compulsory exception, some optional exceptions and subordinating all domestic exceptions to the three-step test.

Directive 2009/24/EC of the European Parliament and of the Council of 23 April 2009 on the legal protection of computer programs

Article 5 – Exceptions to the restricted acts

1. In the absence of specific contractual provisions, the acts referred to in points (a) and (b) of Article 4(1) shall not require authorisation by the rightholder where they are necessary for the use of the computer program by the lawful acquirer in accordance with its intended purpose, including for error correction.

2. The making of a back-up copy by a person having a right to use the computer program may not be prevented by contract in so far as it is necessary for that use.

3. The person having a right to use a copy of a computer program shall be entitled, without the authorisation of the rightholder, to observe, study or test the functioning of the program in order to determine the ideas and principles which underlie any element of the program if he does so while performing any of the acts of loading, displaying, running, transmitting or storing the program which he is entitled to do.

Directive 2006/115/EC of the European Parliament and of the Council of 12 December 2006 on rental right and lending right and on certain rights related to copyright in the field of intellectual property

Article 10 – Limitations to rights

1. Member States may provide for limitations to the rights referred to in this Chapter in respect of:

    (a) private use;
    (b) use of short excerpts in connection with the reporting of current events;

(c) ephemeral fixation by a broadcasting organisation by means of its own facilities and for its own broadcasts;

(d) use solely for the purposes of teaching or scientific research.

2. Irrespective of paragraph 1, any Member State may provide for the same kinds of limitations with regard to the protection of performers, producers of phonograms, broadcasting organisations and of producers of the first fixations of films, as it provides for in connection with the protection of copyright in literary and artistic works.

However, compulsory licences may be provided for only to the extent to which they are compatible with the Rome Convention.

3. The limitations referred to in paragraphs 1 and 2 shall be applied only in certain special cases which do not conflict with a normal exploitation of the subject matter and do not unreasonably prejudice the legitimate interests of the rightholder.

Directive 2001/29/EC of the European Parliament and of the Council of 22 May 2001 on the harmonisation of certain aspects of copyright and related rights in the information society

Article 5 – Exceptions and limitations

1. Temporary acts of reproduction referred to in Article 2, which are transient or incidental [and] an integral and essential part of a technological process and whose sole purpose is to enable:

(a) a transmission in a network between third parties by an intermediary, or

(b) a lawful use of a work or other subject-matter to be made, and which have no independent economic significance, shall be exempted from the reproduction right provided for in Article 2.

2. Member States may provide for exceptions or limitations to the reproduction right provided for in Article 2 in the following cases:

(a) in respect of reproductions on paper or any similar medium, effected by the use of any kind of photographic technique or by some other process having similar effects, with the exception of sheet music, provided that the rightholders receive fair compensation;

(b) in respect of reproductions on any medium made by a natural person for private use and for ends that are neither directly nor indirectly commercial, on condition that the rightholders receive fair compensation which takes account of the application or non-application of technological measures referred to in Article 6 to the work or subject-matter concerned;

(c) in respect of specific acts of reproduction made by publicly accessible libraries, educational establishments or museums, or by archives, which are not for direct or indirect economic or commercial advantage;

(d) in respect of ephemeral recordings of works made by broadcasting organisations by means of their own facilities and for their own broadcasts; the preservation of these recordings in official archives may, on the grounds of their exceptional documentary character, be permitted;

(e) in respect of reproductions of broadcasts made by social institutions pursuing non-commercial purposes, such as hospitals or prisons, on condition that the rightholders receive fair compensation.

3. Member States may provide for exceptions or limitations to the rights provided for in Articles 2 and 3 in the following cases:

(a) use for the sole purpose of illustration for teaching or scientific research, as long as the source, including the author's name, is indicated, unless this turns out to be impossible and to the extent justified by the non-commercial purpose to be achieved;

(b) uses, for the benefit of people with a disability, which are directly related to the disability and of a non-commercial nature, to the extent required by the specific disability;

(c) reproduction by the press, communication to the public or making available of published articles on current economic, political or religious topics or of broadcast works or other subject-matter of the same character, in cases where such use is not expressly reserved, and as long as the source, including the author's name, is indicated, or use of works or other subject-matter in connection with the reporting of current events, to the extent justified by the informatory purpose and as long as the source, including the author's name, is indicated, unless this turns out to be impossible;

(d) quotations for purposes such as criticism or review, provided that they relate to a work or other subject-matter which has already been lawfully made available to the public, that, unless this turns out to be impossible, the source, including the author's name, is indicated, and that their use is in accordance with fair practice, and to the extent required by the specific purpose;

(e) use for the purposes of public security or to ensure the proper performance or reporting of administrative, parliamentary or judicial proceedings;

(f) use of political speeches as well as extracts of public lectures or similar works or subject-matter to the extent justified by the informatory purpose and provided that the source, including the author's name, is indicated, except where this turns out to be impossible;

(g) use during religious celebrations or official celebrations organised by a public authority;

(h) use of works, such as works of architecture or sculpture, made to be located permanently in public places;

(i) incidental inclusion of a work or other subject-matter in other material;

(j) use for the purpose of advertising the public exhibition or sale of artistic works, to the extent necessary to promote the event, excluding any other commercial use;

(k) use for the purpose of caricature, parody or pastiche;

(l) use in connection with the demonstration or repair of equipment;

(m) use of an artistic work in the form of a building or a drawing or plan of a building for the purposes of reconstructing the building;

(n) use by communication or making available, for the purpose of research or private study, to individual members of the public by dedicated terminals on the premises of establishments referred to in paragraph 2(c) of works and other subject-matter not subject to purchase or licensing terms which are contained in their collections;

(o) use in certain other cases of minor importance where exceptions or limitations already exist under national law, provided that they only concern analogue uses and do not affect the free circulation of goods and services within the Community, without prejudice to the other exceptions and limitations contained in this Article.

4. Where the Member States may provide for an exception or limitation to the right of reproduction pursuant to paragraphs 2 and 3, they may provide similarly for an exception or limitation to the right of distribution as referred to in Article 4 to the extent justified by the purpose of the authorised act of reproduction.

5. The exceptions and limitations provided for in paragraphs 1, 2, 3 and 4 shall only be applied in certain special cases which do not conflict with a normal exploitation of the work or other subject-matter and do not unreasonably prejudice the legitimate interests of the rightholder.

C-145/10 Eva-Maria Painer v. Standard VerlagsGmbH and Others ECLI:EU:C:2013:138 [2011]

[This case has already been presented, see *supra*, Part I, Chapter 2.1.4 (prevailing language), pp. 110–11]

The second question

Preliminary observations

[Paras. 118–127, see *supra*, Part I, Chapter 2.1.4 (prevailing language), pp. 111–12]

128   In those circumstances, the French expression 'mis[e] à la disposition du public [d'une oeuvre]' (making a work available to the public), in the sense of Article 5(3)(d) of Directive 2001/29, must be understood as meaning the act of making that work available to the public. That interpretation is also confirmed not only by the expression 'made available to the public' but also by the expression 'der Öffentlichkeit zugänglich gemacht' used unvaryingly in the English and German versions of both Article 5(3)(d) of Directive 2001/29 and Article 10(1) of the Berne Convention.

QUESTION

Does the European Directive 2001/29 require that the work quoted has to be already lawfully made available to the public? Why does the ECJ add this requirement? On that basis, should other requirements be added?

Three-step test and the European Court of Justice

C-435/12 ACI Adam BV and Others v. Stichting de Thuiskopie and Others ECLI:EU:C:2014:254 [2014]

[This case concerned the scope of the exception for copying for private use under European law and more specifically whether the exception for copying for private use can be applied only to reproductions that are made from legitimate sources. Many E.U. countries provide for a levy imposed on manufacturers and importers of media designed for the reproduction of literary, scientific or artistic works; the surcharge, paid by the consumer, is designed to compensate rightholders and creators for the consumer's use of the media to make private copies. Private copying levies pose a variety of problems, particularly in the digital environment, because the relationship of the levy to the making of private copies may fail to correspond to consumers' actual use, in effect overcharging those consumers who engage in little private copying, and undercharging those who make many private copies. The underlying issue in the ACI Adam case, however, was whether the amount of the levy could lawfully take into account copies made through unauthorized downloading.]

1   This request for a preliminary ruling concerns the interpretation of Article 5(2)(b) and (5) of Directive 2001/29/EC of the European Parliament and of the Council of 22 May 2001 on the harmonisation of certain aspects of copyright and related rights in the information society (OJ 2001 L 167, p. 10), and of Directive 2004/48/EC of the European Parliament and of the Council of 29 April 2004 on the enforcement of intellectual property rights (OJ 2004 L 157, p. 45 and corrigenda in OJ 2004 L 195, p. 16 and OJ 2007 L 204, p. 27).

2   The request has been made in proceedings between, on the one hand, ACI Adam BV and a certain number of other undertakings ('ACI Adam and Others') and, on the other, Stichting de Thuiskopie ('Thuiskopie') and Stichting Onderhandelingen Thuiskopie vergoeding ('SONT') — two foundations responsible for, first, collecting and distributing the levy imposed on manufacturers and importers of media designed for the reproduction of literary, scientific or artistic works with a view to private use ('the private copying levy'), and, secondly, determining the amount of that levy — regarding the fact that SONT, in determining the amount of that levy, takes into account the harm resulting from copies made from an unlawful source.

. . .

19. . . . the Hoge Raad der Nederlanden (Supreme Court of the Netherlands) . . . refer[red] the following questions to the Court of Justice for a preliminary ruling:

'(1) Should Article 5(2)(b) — whether or not in conjunction with Article 5(5) — of Directive [2001/29] be interpreted as meaning that the limitation on copyright referred to therein applies to reproductions which satisfy the requirements set out in that provision, regardless of whether the copies of the works from which the reproductions were taken became available to the natural person concerned lawfully — that is to say: without infringing the copyright of the rightholders — or does that limitation apply only to reproductions taken from works which have become available to the person concerned without infringement of copyright?'

(2) a. If the answer to question 1 is that expressed at the end of the question, can the application of the "three-stage test" referred to in Article 5(5) of Directive [2001/29] form the basis for the expansion of the scope of the exception of Article 5(2), or can its application only lead to the reduction of the scope of the limitation?

b. If the answer to question 1 is that expressed at the end of the question, is a rule of national law which provides that in the case of reproductions made by a natural person for private use and without any direct or indirect commercial objective, fair compensation is payable, regardless of whether the making of those reproductions is authorised under Article 5(2) of Directive [2001/29] — and without there being any infringement by that rule of the prohibition right of the rightholder and his entitlement to damages — contrary to Article 5 of [that] Directive, or to any other rule of E.U. law?

. . .

22   As regards the scope of those exceptions and limitations, it must be pointed out that, according to the settled case-law of the Court, the provisions of a directive which derogate from a general principle established by that directive must be interpreted strictly (Case C 5/08 *Infopaq International* EU:C:2009:465, paragraph 56 and the case-law cited).

23   It follows that the different exceptions and limitations provided for in Article 5(2) of Directive 2001/29 [Info Soc] must be interpreted strictly.

24   Furthermore, it must be pointed out that Article 5(5) of Directive 2001/29 [Info Soc] requires that the exceptions and limitations to the reproduction right are to be applied only in certain special cases which do not conflict with a normal exploitation of the work or other subject-matter and do not unreasonably prejudice the legitimate interests of the rightholder.

25   As is apparent from its wording, that provision of Directive 2001/29 [Info Soc] simply specifies the conditions for the application of the exceptions and limitations to the reproduction right which are authorised by Article 5(2) of that directive, namely that those exceptions and limitations are to be applied only in certain special cases, which do not conflict with a normal exploitation of the work or other subject-matter and do not unreasonably prejudice the legitimate interests of the rightholder. Article 5(5) of that directive does not therefore define the substantive content of the different exceptions and limitations set out in Article 5(2) of that directive, but takes effect only at the time when they are applied by the Member States.

26   Consequently, Article 5(5) of Directive 2001/29 [Info Soc] is not intended either to affect the substantive content of provisions falling within the scope of Article 5(2) of that directive or, inter alia, to extend the scope of the different exceptions and limitations provided for therein.

27   Furthermore, it is apparent from recital 44 in the preamble to Directive 2001/29 [Info Soc] that the E.U. legislature meant to envisage, when Member States provide for the exceptions or limitations referred to by that directive, that the scope of those exceptions or limitations could be limited even more when it comes to certain new uses of copyright works and other subject-matter. By contrast, neither that recital nor any other provision of that directive envisages the possibility of the scope of such exceptions or limitations being extended by the Member States.

28   In particular, under Article 5(2)(b) of Directive 2001/29 [Info Soc], Member States may provide for an exception to the author's exclusive reproduction right in his work in respect of reproductions on any medium made by a natural person for private use and for ends that are neither directly nor indirectly commercial ('the private copying exception').

29   That provision does not address expressly the lawful or unlawful nature of the source from which a reproduction of the work may be made.

30   The wording of that provision must therefore be interpreted by applying the principle of strict interpretation, as referred to in paragraph 23 of the present judgment.

31   Such an interpretation requires Article 5(2)(b) of Directive 2001/29 [Info Soc] to be understood as meaning that the private copying exception admittedly prohibits copyright holders from relying on their exclusive right to authorise or prohibit reproductions with regard to persons who make private copies of their works; however, it precludes that provision from being understood as requiring, beyond that limitation which is provided for expressly, copyright holders to tolerate infringements of their rights which may accompany the making of private copies.

. . .

35   If the Member States had the option of adopting legislation which also allowed reproductions for private use to be made from an unlawful source, the result of that would clearly be detrimental to the proper functioning of the internal market.

36   Secondly, it is apparent from recital 22 in the preamble to Directive 2001/29 [Info Soc], that the objective of proper support for the dissemination of culture must not be achieved by sacrificing strict protection of rights or by tolerating illegal forms of distribution of counterfeited or pirated works.

37   Consequently, national legislation which makes no distinction between private copies made from lawful sources and those made from counterfeited or pirated sources cannot be tolerated.

38   Furthermore, when it is applied, national legislation, such as that at issue in the main proceedings, which does not draw a distinction according to whether the source from which a reproduction for private use is made is lawful or unlawful, may infringe certain conditions laid down by Article 5(5) of Directive 2001/29 [Info Soc].

39   First, to accept that such reproductions may be made from an unlawful source would encourage the circulation of counterfeited or pirated works, thus inevitably reducing the volume of sales or of other lawful transactions relating to the protected works, with the result that a normal exploitation of those works would be adversely affected.

40   Secondly, the application of such national legislation may, having regard to the finding made in paragraph 31 of the present judgment, unreasonably prejudice copyright holders.

41   It is apparent from the foregoing considerations that Article 5(2)(b) of Directive 2001/29 [Info Soc] must be interpreted as not covering the case of private copies made from an unlawful source.

QUESTIONS

1. In recommending that private copying exceptions be limited to legal source copies, Advocate General Pedro Cruz Villalón's opinion in the *ACI Adam* case referred at several points to international constraints on the scope of exceptions:

   > 55   In contrast to this, it must be observed that Directive 2001/29 contains no explicit reference to the second condition laid down in Article 5(5) of Directive 2001/29, according to which the exception or restriction of the exclusive reproduction rights may not conflict with the *normal exploitation* of protected work or material. This case therefore affords the Court the opportunity to express its views on this

point, and to allow itself to be inspired by international practice, to the extent that this is possible.[38]

. . .

59 Furthermore, the actions of Union law must be interpreted as far as possible in the light of international law, in particular where it is intended to implement an international legal agreement entered into by the Community.

60 In that regard, Point 15 of the preamble of Directive 2001/29 makes precise that this Directive implements the international obligations arising from the Union's adoption of the WIPO treaty, in particular with regard to the means of controlling piracy in the digital environment worldwide. Furthermore, the Court has found that within the scope of Directive 2001/29, the Union has replaced the Member States for the implementation of the provisions of the Berne Convention.

. . .

72 In any event, the interpretation defended by the Dutch government conflicts with the provisions of Article 5(5) of Directive 2001/29, as interpreted in the light of the Berne Convention, the WCT and the TRIPS and in particular, against the background of the condition concerning the need not to prejudice the normal exploitation of the protected work or material.

In basing its reasoning on the text of the Directive and on the effect of the Dutch exception on the internal market, has the ECJ divorced its interpretation of the Directive from international norms? Do the Berne Convention, the WCT and/or the TRIPS limit the application of a private copying exception to legal source copies?

2. To what extent does authorizing downloads as private copies (whatever the legality of the source) conflict with the three-step test? If private copying is incompatible, is that because it is inconsistent with the condition of normal exploitation or with the absence of unreasonable prejudice to the legitimate interests of the author? Does it matter which step is at issue? With respect to the legality of the source, does it matter that the Dutch

---

38 I refer in particular to the report of the Special Group of the WTO of 15 June 2000, United States – Section 110(5) of the US Copyright Act, WT/DS160/R. This report states (§ 6.181) that 'exceptions or limitations would be presumed not to conflict with a normal exploitation of works if they are confined to a scope or degree that does not enter into economic competition with non-exempted uses'. The report refers to the suggestions of a Study Group formed for the preparation of the Conference for the revision of the Berne Convention held in Stockholm in 1967. These suggestions state precisely that 'it is obvious that all forms of exploiting a work which had, or were likely to acquire, considerable economic or practical importance must in principle be reserved to the authors; exceptions that might restrict the possibilities open to the authors in these respects are unacceptable.

law's inclusion of illegal source copies would at least produce compensation to the right holders, while their exclusion from the private copying exception will deprive authors of private copying royalties, with little current prospect of effective enforcement against illegal downloading?

C-117/13 Technische Universitat Darmstadt v. Eugen Ulmer KG ECLI:EU:C:2014:2196 [2014]

[The case, considered a "test case" by Advocate General Jaaskinen, concerned the scope of the exception for digitization of hardcopy books owned by an academic library for the purpose of making those works available to users, by means of dedicated terminals within those establishments. The library also allowed users to download the digital file on a personal USB stick or to print the work out on paper. The court was asked to determine whether the Directive's exceptions permitted the library to engage in these acts.]

1   This request for a preliminary ruling concerns the interpretation of Article 5(3)(n) of Directive 2001/29/EC of the European Parliament and of the Council of 22 May 2001 on the harmonisation of certain aspects of copyright and related rights in the information society [citation omitted].

2   The request was made in proceedings between the Technical University of Darmstadt (Technische Universität Darmstadt, 'TU Darmstadt') and Eugen Ulmer KG ('Ulmer'), concerning TU Darmstadt's making available to the public, by terminals installed within a library, of a book contained in its collection, the user rights to which are held by Ulmer.

Legal context

European Union law

3   Recitals 31, 34, 36, 40, 44, 45 and 51 in the preamble to Directive 2001/29 [Info Soc] are worded as follows:

'(31) A fair balance of rights and interests between the different categories of rightholders, as well as between the different categories of rightholders and users of protected subject-matter must be safeguarded. . . .

. . .

(34) Member States should be given the option of providing for certain exceptions or limitations for cases such as educational and scientific purposes, for

the benefit of public institutions such as libraries and archives, for purposes of news reporting, for quotations, for use by people with disabilities, for public security uses and for uses in administrative and judicial proceedings.

. . .

(36) The Member States may provide for fair compensation for rightholders also when applying the optional provisions on exceptions or limitations which do not require such compensation.

. . .

(40) Member States may provide for an exception or limitation for the benefit of certain non-profit making establishments, such as publicly accessible libraries and equivalent institutions, as well as archives. However, this should be limited to certain special cases covered by the reproduction right. . . . Therefore, specific contracts or licences should be promoted which, without creating imbalances, favour such establishments and the disseminative purposes they serve.

. . .

(44) When applying the exceptions and limitations provided for in this Directive, they should be exercised in accordance with international obligations. Such exceptions and limitations may not be applied in a way which prejudices the legitimate interests of the rightholder or which conflicts with the normal exploitation of his work or other subject-matter. . . .

(45) The exceptions and limitations referred to in Article 5(2), (3) and (4) should not, however, prevent the definition of contractual relations designed to ensure fair compensation for the rightholders insofar as permitted by national law.

. . .

(51) . . . Member States should promote voluntary measures taken by rightholders, including the conclusion and implementation of agreements between rightholders and other parties concerned, to accommodate achieving the objectives of certain exceptions or limitations provided for in national law in accordance with this Directive. . . .'

4   Article 2 of that directive, entitled 'Reproduction right', provides:

'Member States shall provide for the exclusive right to authorise or prohibit direct or indirect, temporary or permanent reproduction by any means and in any form, in whole or in part:

(a) for authors, of their works;

. . .'

5   Article 3 of the same directive, entitled 'Right of communication to the public of works and right of making available to the public other subject-matter', provides in paragraph 1:

'Member States shall provide authors with the exclusive right to authorise or prohibit any communication to the public of their works, by wire or wireless means, including the making available to the public of their works in such a way that members of the public may access them from a place and at a time individually chosen by them.'

6   Article 5 of the same directive, entitled 'Exceptions and limitations', provides in paragraph 2:

'Member States may provide for exceptions or limitations to the reproduction right provided for in Article 2 in the following cases:

(a) in respect of reproductions on paper or any similar medium, effected by the use of any kind of photographic technique or by some other process having similar effects, with the exception of sheet music, provided that the rightholders receive fair compensation;

(b) in respect of reproductions on any medium made by a natural person for private use and for ends that are neither directly nor indirectly commercial, on condition that the rightholders receive fair compensation which takes account of the application or non-application of technological measures referred to in Article 6 to the work or subject-matter concerned;

(c) in respect of specific acts of reproduction made by publicly accessible libraries, educational establishments or museums, or by archives, which are not for direct or indirect economic or commercial advantage;

. . .'

7   Article 5(3) of that directive provides:

'Member States may provide for exceptions or limitations to the rights provided for in Articles 2 and 3 in the following cases:

. . .

(n) use by communication or making available, for the purpose of research or private study, to individual members of the public by dedicated terminals on the premises of establishments referred to in paragraph 2(c) of works and other subject-matter not subject to purchase or licensing terms which are contained in their collections;

. . .'

8   According to Article 5(5) of the same directive:

'The exceptions and limitations provided for in paragraphs 1, 2, 3 and 4 shall only be applied in certain special cases which do not conflict with a normal exploitation of the work or other subject-matter and do not unreasonably prejudice the legitimate interests of the rightholder.'

German law

9   Paragraph 52b of the German Law on copyright (Urheberrechtsgesetz, 'UrhG') of 9 September 1965 (BGBl. I, p. 1273), in the version applicable at the date of the facts in the main proceedings, is worded as follows:

'Reproduction of works at electronic reading points in public libraries, museums and archives

So far as there are no contractual provisions to the contrary, it shall be permissible to make published works available from the holdings of publicly accessible libraries, museums or archives, which neither directly nor indirectly serve economic or commercial purposes, exclusively on the premises of the relevant establishment at electronic reading points dedicated to the purpose of research and for private study. The number of copies of a work made available at electronic reading points shall not, in principle, be higher than the number held by the establishment. Equitable remuneration shall be paid in consideration of their being made available. The claim may be asserted only by a collecting society.'

  The dispute in the main proceedings and the questions referred for a preliminary ruling

10 TU Darmstadt operates a regional and academic library in which it installed electronic reading points that allow the public to consult works contained in the collection of that library.

11 Since January or February 2009, those works have included the textbook of Schulze W., Einführung in die neuere Geschichte ('the textbook at issue'), published by Ulmer, a scientific publishing house established in Stuttgart (Germany).

12 TU Darmstadt did not take up Ulmer's offer of 29 January 2009 of an opportunity to purchase and use the textbooks it publishes as electronic books ('e-books'), including the textbook at issue.

13 TU Darmstadt digitised that textbook so as to make it available to users on electronic reading points installed in its library. Those points did not allow for a greater number of copies of that work to be consulted at any one time than the number owned by the library. Users of the reading points could print out the work on paper or store it on a USB stick, in part or in full, and take it out of the library in that form.

. . .

22 In those circumstances, the Bundesgerichtshof decided to stay the proceedings and refer the following questions to the Court for a preliminary ruling:

'(1) Is a work subject to purchase or licensing terms, within the meaning of Article 5(3)(n) of Directive 2001/29 [Info Soc], where the rightholder offers to conclude with the establishments referred to therein licensing agreements for the use of that work on appropriate terms?

(2) Does Article 5(3)(n) of Directive 2001/29 [Info Soc] entitle the Member States to confer on those establishments the right to digitise the works contained in their collections, if that is necessary in order to make those works available on terminals?

(3) May the rights which the Member States lay down pursuant to Article 5(3)(n) of Directive 2001/29 [Info Soc] go so far as to enable users of the terminals to print out on paper or store on a USB stick the works made available there?'

Consideration of the questions referred for a preliminary ruling

The first question

23   By its first question, the referring court is essentially asking whether a work is subject to 'purchase or licensing terms', within the meaning of Article 5(3)(n) of Directive 2001/29 [Info Soc], where the rightholder has offered to conclude with an establishment referred to in that provision, such as a publicly accessible library, on appropriately worded terms a licensing agreement in respect of that work.

24   All of the interested parties that have presented written observations, with the exception of Ulmer, propose that the first question be answered in the negative and essentially support an interpretation to the effect that the concept of 'purchase or licensing terms', mentioned in Article 5(3)(n) of Directive 2001/29 [Info Soc], must be understood to mean that the right-holder and establishment concerned must have concluded a licensing agreement in respect of the work in question that sets out the conditions in which that establishment may use the work.

25   Ulmer argues that the mere fact that the rightholder offers to conclude a licensing agreement with a publicly accessible library is sufficient for ruling out the application of Article 5(3)(n) of Directive 2001/29 [Info Soc], provided always that such offer is 'appropriate'.

26   In that regard, first of all, a comparison of the language versions of Article 5(3)(n) of Directive 2001/29 [Info Soc], particularly the English, French, German and Spanish versions — which use the words 'terms', 'conditions', 'Regelung' and 'condiciones', respectively — shows that, in that provision, the E.U. legislature used the concepts 'terms' or 'provisions', which refer to contractual terms actually agreed as opposed to mere contractual offers.

27   Next, it should be recalled that the limitation under Article 5(3)(n) of Directive 2001/29 [Info Soc] aims to promote the public interest in promoting research and private study, through the dissemination of knowledge, which constitutes, moreover, the core mission of publicly accessible libraries.

28   The interpretation favoured by Ulmer implies that the rightholder could, by means of a unilateral and essentially discretionary action, deny the establishment concerned the right to benefit from that limitation and thereby prevent it from realising its core mission and promoting the public interest.

29   Moreover, recital 40 in the preamble to Directive 2001/29 [Info Soc] states that specific contracts or licences should be promoted which, without

creating imbalances, favour such establishments and the disseminative purposes they serve.

30   As noted by the Advocate General in points 21 and 22 of his Opinion, recitals 45 and 51 in the preamble to Directive 2001/29 [Info Soc] confirm (including in their German version)* that, in the context, inter alia, of the exceptions and limitations listed in Article 5(3) of Directive 2001/29, it is *existing* contractual relations and the conclusion and implementation of *existing* contractual agreements that are at issue, and not mere prospects of contracts or licences.

31   Furthermore, the interpretation proposed by Ulmer is difficult to reconcile with the aim pursued by Article 5(3)(n) of Directive 2001/29 [Info Soc], which is to maintain a fair balance between the rights and interests of rightholders, on the one hand, and, on the other hand, users of protected works who wish to communicate them to the public for the purpose of research or private study undertaken by individual members of the public.

32   In addition, if the mere act of offering to conclude a licensing agreement were sufficient to rule out the application of Article 5(3)(n) of Directive 2001/29 [Info Soc], such an interpretation would be liable to negate much of the substance of the limitation provided for in that provision, or indeed its effectiveness, since, were it to be accepted, the limitation would apply, as Ulmer has maintained, only to those increasingly rare works of which an electronic version, primarily in the form of an e-book, is not yet offered on the market.

33   Lastly, the interpretation to the effect that there must be contractual terms actually agreed also cannot be ruled out — contrary to what is maintained by Ulmer — by reason of the fact that it would conflict with the three-fold condition provided for in Article 5(5) of Directive 2001/29 [Info Soc].

---

* Editors' Note: The referenced paragraphs of the Advocate General's Opinion state:

21. As TU Darmstadt rightly points out, some light is shed on the relationship between exploitation rights, on the one hand, and limitation rules, on the other, by a reading of recitals 45 and 51 in the preamble to Directive 2001/29. Those recitals state, inter alia, that '[t]he exceptions and limitations . . . should not, however, prevent the definition of *contractual relations* designed to ensure fair compensation for the rightholders insofar as permitted by national law' and that 'Member States should promote voluntary measures taken by rightholders, *including the conclusion and implementation of agreements between rightholders and other parties concerned*, to accommodate achieving the objectives of certain exceptions or limitations provided for in national law in accordance with this Directive' [Footnote omitted].

22. These two recitals plainly refer, in their German version, to *existing* contractual relations and the conclusion and implementation of *existing* contractual agreements, and not mere prospects of licences. The different language versions of those recitals also corroborate this view [Footnote omitted].

34   In that regard, it is sufficient to state that the limitation provided for in Article 5(3)(n) of Directive 2001/29 [Info Soc] is accompanied by a number of restrictions that guarantee — even though the application of that provision is ruled out only in the event that contractual terms have actually been concluded — the continuing applicability of such a limitation in special cases which do not conflict with a normal exploitation of the works and do not unreasonably prejudice the legitimate interests of the rightholder.

35   In the light of the foregoing considerations, the answer to the first question is that the concept of 'purchase or licensing terms' provided for in Article 5(3)(n) of Directive 2001/29 [Info Soc] must be understood as requiring that the rightholder and an establishment, such as a publicly accessible library, referred to in that provision must have concluded a licensing agreement in respect of the work in question that sets out the conditions in which that establishment may use that work.

The second question

36   By its second question, the referring court is essentially asking whether Article 5(3)(n) of Directive 2001/29 [Info Soc] must be interpreted to mean that it precludes Member States from granting to publicly accessible libraries covered by that provision the right to digitise the works contained in their collections, if such act of reproduction is necessary for the purpose of making those works available to users, by means of dedicated terminals, within those establishments.

37   The first point to be noted is that the digitisation of a work, which essentially involves the conversion of the work from an analogue format into a digital one, constitutes an act of reproduction of the work.

38   The question therefore arises whether Article 5(3)(n) of Directive 2001/29 permits Member States to grant that reproduction right to publicly accessible libraries, since, under Article 2 of that directive, it is the authors that have the exclusive right to authorise or prohibit the reproduction of their works.

39   In that regard, it should first be stated that, according to the first sentence of Article 5(3) of Directive 2001/29 [Info Soc], the exceptions and limitations set out in that paragraph relate to the rights provided for in Articles 2 and 3 of that directive and thus both the exclusive reproduction right enjoyed by the rightholder and the right of communication to the public of works.

40　However, Article 5(3)(n) of the directive limits the use of works, within the meaning of that provision, to the 'communication or making available' of those works and thus to acts which fall under the sole exclusive right of communication to the public of works referred to in Article 3 of that directive.

41　Next, it should be recalled that for there to be an 'act of communication' for the purposes of Article 3(1) of Directive 2001/29 [Info Soc], it is sufficient, in particular, that those works are made available to a public in such a way that the persons forming that public may access them, irrespective of whether they avail themselves of that opportunity (judgment in *Svensson and Others*, C-466/12, EU:C:2014:76, paragraph 19).

42　It follows that, in circumstances such as those of the case in the main proceedings, where an establishment, such as a publicly accessible library, which falls within Article 5(3)(n) of Directive 2001/29 [Info Soc], gives access to a work contained in its collection to a 'public', namely all of the individual members of the public using the dedicated terminals installed on its premises for the purpose of research or private study, that must be considered to be 'making [that work] available' and, therefore, an 'act of communication' for the purposes of Article 3(1) of that directive (see, to that effect, judgment in *Svensson and Others*, EU:C:2014:76, paragraph 20).

43　Such a right of communication of works enjoyed by establishments such as publicly accessible libraries covered by Article 5(3)(n) of Directive 2001/29 [Info Soc], within the limits of the conditions provided for by that provision, would risk being rendered largely meaningless, or indeed ineffective, if those establishments did not have an ancillary right to digitise the works in question.

44　Those establishments are recognised as having such a right pursuant to Article 5(2)(c) of Directive 2001/29 [Info Soc], provided that 'specific acts of reproduction' are involved.

45　That condition of specificity must be understood as meaning that, as a general rule, the establishments in question may not digitise their entire collections.

46　However, that condition is, in principle, observed where the digitisation of some of the works of a collection is necessary for the purpose of the 'use by communication or making available, for the purpose of research or private study, to individual members of the public by dedicated terminals', as provided in Article 5(3)(n) of Directive 2001/29.

47   Furthermore, the scope of that ancillary right of digitisation must be determined by interpreting Article 5(2)(c) of Directive 2001/29 [Info Soc] in the light of Article 5(5) of that directive, under which that limitation is applicable only in certain special cases which do not prejudice the normal exploitation of the work or other protected object or cause unjustified harm to the legitimate interests of the rightholder, the latter provision, however, not being intended to extend the scope of the exceptions and limitations provided for in Article 5(2) of the directive [citation omitted] and *ACI Adam and Others*, C-435/12, EU:C:2014:254, paragraph 26).

48   In the present case, it must be stated that the applicable national legislation takes due account of the conditions provided for in Article 5(5) of the directive, since it follows, first, from Article 52b of the UrhG, that the digitisation of works by publicly accessible libraries cannot have the result of the number of copies of each work made available to users by dedicated terminals being greater than that which those libraries have acquired in analogue format. Secondly, although, by virtue of that provision of national law, the digitisation of the work is not, as such, coupled with an obligation to provide compensation, the subsequent making available of that work in digital format, on dedicated terminals, gives rise to a duty to make payment of adequate remuneration.

49   Having regard to the foregoing considerations, the answer to the second question is that Article 5(3)(n) of Directive 2001/29 [Info Soc], read in conjunction with Article 5(2)(c) of that directive, must be interpreted to mean that it does not preclude Member States from granting to publicly accessible libraries covered by those provisions the right to digitise the works contained in their collections, if such act of reproduction is necessary for the purpose of making those works available to users, by means of dedicated terminals, within those establishments.

The third question

50   By its third question, the referring court is essentially asking whether Article 5(3)(n) of Directive 2001/29 [Info Soc] must be interpreted to mean that it precludes Member States from granting to publicly accessible libraries covered by that provision the right to make works available to users by dedicated terminals which permit the printing out of those works on paper or their storage on a USB stick.

51   As is clear from paragraphs 40 and 42 of the present judgment, the limitation laid down in Article 5(3)(n) of Directive 2001/29 [Info Soc] covers, in principle, only certain acts of communication normally falling under the

exclusive right of the author provided for in Article 3 of that directive, namely those by which the establishments in question make a work available to individual members of the public, for the purpose of research or private study, by dedicated terminals installed on their premises.

52   It is undisputed that acts such as the printing out of a work on paper or its storage on a USB stick, even if made possible by the specific features of the dedicated terminals on which that work can be consulted, are not acts of 'communication', within the meaning of Article 3 of Directive 2001/29 [Info Soc], but rather of 'reproduction', within the meaning of Article 2 of that directive.

53   What is involved is the creation of a new analogue or digital copy of the work that an establishment makes available to users by means of dedicated terminals.

54   Such acts of reproduction, unlike some operations involving the digitisation of a work, also cannot be permitted under an ancillary right stemming from the combined provisions of Articles 5(2)(c) and 5(3)(n) of Directive 2001/29 [Info Soc], since they are not necessary for the purpose of making the work available to the users of that work, by dedicated terminals, in accordance with the conditions laid down by those provisions. Moreover, since those acts are carried out not by the establishments referred to in Article 5(3)(n) of Directive 2001/29 [Info Soc], but rather by the users of the dedicated terminals installed within those establishments, they cannot be authorised under that provision.

55   By contrast, such acts of reproduction on analogue or digital media may, if appropriate, be authorised under the national legislation transposing the exceptions or limitations provided for in Article 5(2)(a) or (b) of Directive 2001/29 [Info Soc] since, in each individual case, the conditions laid down by those provisions, in particular as regards the fair compensation which the rightholder must receive, are met.

56   Furthermore, such acts of reproduction must observe the conditions set out in Article 5(5) of Directive 2001/29 [Info Soc]. Consequently, the extent of the texts reproduced may not, in particular, unreasonably prejudice the legitimate interests of the rightholder.

57   Having regard to the foregoing considerations, the answer to the third question is that Article 5(3)(n) of Directive 2001/29 [Info Soc] must be interpreted to mean that it does not extend to acts such as the printing out

of works on paper or their storage on a USB stick, carried out by users from dedicated terminals installed in publicly accessible libraries covered by that provision. However, such acts may, if appropriate, be authorised under national legislation transposing the exceptions or limitations provided for in Article 5(2)(a) or (b) of that directive provided that, in each individual case, the conditions laid down by those provisions are met.

QUESTIONS

With the above decision, the ECJ goes further than the US court in *Authors Guild v. HathiTrust*, 755 F.3d 87 (2d Cir.2014) (see above). An academic library owning a tangible book for which an e-book is commercialized by the publisher is authorized to digitize the book for the purpose of making those works available to users by means of dedicated terminals, users being permitted at the end to print or to store part of the book on a USB stick. For the ECJ, these acts comply with various exceptions and satisfy the European three-step test integrated in article 5(5). Whereas the ECJ does not directly quote the relevant international norms in its reasoning, it quotes as part of the legal context Recital (44) stating that: "When applying the exceptions and limitations provided for in this Directive, they should be exercised in accordance with international obligations. Such exceptions and limitations may not be applied in a way which prejudices the legitimate interests of the rightholder or which conflicts with the normal exploitation of his work or other subject-matter. . . ."

1. Whereas the ECJ applies literally the same rule as the one enshrined in the international norms (InfoSoc Directive article 5(5) incorporating the three-step test in article 13 of the TRIPS), is the court's ruling consistent with any step of that test, as construed by the WTO Panel? For example, the Court disregarded the availability of the library-digitized book as an e-book from the publisher. And it did not address the impact on the market for e-books were library patrons to make their own digital copies from digitized versions made available on dedicated library terminals.

2. The practical consequence of the decision is to allow an academic library that owns a tangible copy of a book to create by digitization its own e-book for the purpose of making those works available to users on dedicated terminals. While the Court in paragraph 45 stated that the "condition of specificity [in art. 5(2)(c)] must be understood as meaning that, as a general rule, the establishments in question may not digitise their entire collections" do you see a limiting principle in the court's opinion? Does the condition of "dedicated terminals" in any way constrain the operation of the exception? How do these considerations affect the inquiry whether the court has limited the application of article 5(3)(n) to "certain special cases"?

3. The ECJ noted that "although, by virtue of that provision of national law, the digitisation of the work is not, as such, coupled with an obligation to provide compensation, the subsequent making available of that work in digital format, on dedicated terminals, gives rise to a duty to make payment of adequate remuneration" (point 48). Because the library's digitization is a necessary predicate to the making available on dedicated terminals, a single compensation suffices. Should the amount of the compensation take into account the making of the copy (in lieu of purchasing the e-book version), or merely the communication of the copy on a dedicated terminal? What difference does it make, and what impact might the difference have on the analysis of the three-step test?

4. Suppose the publisher's version of the e-book included a technological protection measure limiting the number of copies that can be made from the source copy. The version of the e-book that the library will have made by digitizing its own copy, however, may not include the technological measure, and therefore may permit an unlimited number of further copies to be made. Would the library have thus circumvented a technological protection measure? Would its technological protection-free source copy of the e-book unreasonably prejudice the legitimate interest of the rightholder?

5.6   Enforcement

5.6.1   Copyright

The Berne Convention bears most clearly on protected subject matter and rights, largely neglecting their enforcement. This issue is indirectly treated in articles 5, 15 and 16. We have seen, or we will see, those articles with respect to other issues such as the distribution right (*supra*, Part II, Chapter 5.4.2), copyright ownership (*infra*, Part II, Chapter 6.2, 6.3), or private international law (*infra*, Part III). Enforcement issues appear only as an accessory to those questions. With the WCT or the WPPT and the TRIPS Agreement, however, the focus of attention has shifted. In those texts, enforcement appears as a major issue directly treated.

Berne Convention

> **Article 5**
> **Rights Guaranteed**
>
> (2) . . . the means of redress afforded to the author to protect his rights, shall be governed exclusively by the laws of the country where protection is claimed.

QUESTIONS

1. Apart from article 16 (presented with the study of the importation right), does the Berne Convention specify any "means of redress"? Is a member state free, for example, systematically to deny injunctive relief, thus making damages the sole remedy for infringement?
2. May the laws of the country where protection is claimed condition the "means of redress" on compliance with formalities?
3. Consider the relationship between article 5(2) and articles 41 et seq. of the TRIPS Agreement, *infra*, mandating certain remedies.

WCT: New obligations

Article 11
Obligations concerning Technological Measures

Contracting Parties shall provide adequate legal protection and effective legal remedies against the circumvention of effective technological measures that are used by authors in connection with the exercise of their rights under this Treaty or the Berne Convention and that restrict acts, in respect of their works, which are not authorized by the authors concerned or permitted by law.

QUESTIONS

1. What is an "effective technological measure"?
2. What does "used by authors" mean?
3. What does "in connection with the exercise of their rights under this Treaty or the Berne Convention" mean? Does it apply to technological measures controlling access to works of authorship?
4. How does WCT article 11 reconcile protection of technological controls with exceptions and limitations to copyright?
5. Ursula User purchases a DVD containing a copyrighted videogame. To play the game, she needs to load the game into her computer or videogame player; a technological measure included on the DVD does not permit her to play her copy of the game unless, she enters a password, and plays the game only on certain designated computers. What kind of technological measure is involved; do any of the texts require its protection against circumvention?
6. Michael Merchant advertises and distributes the Copy Champion, promoted as a device designed to allow consumers to make back-up copies of DVDs and other copy-protected works by bypassing copy

controls embedded in the DVDs. Is Michael in violation of any of the texts?

7. Raver Automobiles has entered into an exclusive agreement with Robot Radio Corp. to install Robot digital radios in all cars that Raver manufactures. Computer programs included in the radio and the car communicate with one another to link the radio to the car's control system. To prevent substitutions, Raver has included an access protocol programmed to "recognize" only computer programs contained in Robot radios. Next Wave Radios offers a cheaper car radio, but its radio will not work in a Raver car unless Next Wave devises a means to "fool" the Raver access protocol into thinking it is communicating with a Robot Radio. Next Wave reverse engineers the Robot software in order to discover the corresponding protocol. Is Next Wave in violation of the obligations member states incur under WCT article 11?

Article 12
Obligations concerning Rights Management Information

(1) Contracting Parties shall provide adequate and effective legal remedies against any person knowingly performing any of the following acts knowing, or with respect to civil remedies having reasonable grounds to know, that it will induce, enable, facilitate or conceal an infringement of any right covered by this Treaty or the Berne Convention:

> (i) to remove or alter any electronic rights management information without authority;
> (ii) to distribute, import for distribution, broadcast or communicate to the public, without authority, works or copies of works knowing that electronic rights management information has been removed or altered without authority.

(2) As used in this Article, "rights management information" means information which identifies the work, the author of the work, the owner of any right in the work, or information about the terms and conditions of use of the work, and any numbers or codes that represent such information, when any of these items of information is attached to a copy of a work or appears in connection with the communication of a work to the public.

> **Agreed statements concerning Article 12:** It is understood that the reference to "infringement of any right covered by this Treaty or

the Berne Convention" includes both exclusive rights and rights of remuneration.

It is further understood that Contracting Parties will not rely on this Article to devise or implement rights management systems that would have the effect of imposing formalities which are not permitted under the Berne Convention or this Treaty, prohibiting the free movement of goods or impeding the enjoyment of rights under this Treaty.

QUESTIONS

1. What policies underlie WCT article 12?
2. What kind of information must member states protect under article 12? Are member states obliged to require the affixation of copyright management information?
3. What does "attached to a copy of a work or appears in connection with the communication of a work to the public" mean? Are copyright notices on print copies included? Is information in a government or collecting society's registry included?
4. Article 12 requires proof of two levels of knowledge on the part of the alleged infringer. How would one establish these?
5. How would copyright management information "prohibit[] the free movement of goods or imped[e] the enjoyment of rights under [the WCT]"? Would it have any such effects on the enjoyment of rights under the Berne Convention?

Article 14
Provisions on Enforcement of Rights

(1) Contracting Parties undertake to adopt, in accordance with their legal systems, the measures necessary to ensure the application of this Treaty.

(2) Contracting Parties shall ensure that enforcement procedures are available under their law so as to permit effective action against any act of infringement of rights covered by this Treaty, including expeditious remedies to prevent infringements and remedies which constitute a deterrent to further infringements.

QUESTIONS

1. Does WCT article 14 require enforcement of Berne Convention rights?
2. How does WCT article 14(2) compare with Part III of the TRIPS Agreement, *infra*?

5.6.2 Neighboring rights

WPPT

Article 18
Obligations concerning Technological Measures

Contracting Parties shall provide adequate legal protection and effective legal remedies against the circumvention of effective technological measures that are used by performers or producers of phonograms in connection with the exercise of their rights under this Treaty and that restrict acts, in respect of their performances or phonograms, which are not authorized by the performers or the producers of phonograms concerned or permitted by law.

Article 19
Obligations concerning Rights Management Information

(1) Contracting Parties shall provide adequate and effective legal remedies against any person knowingly performing any of the following acts knowing, or with respect to civil remedies having reasonable grounds to know, that it will induce, enable, facilitate or conceal an infringement of any right covered by this Treaty:

(i) to remove or alter any electronic rights management information without authority;
(ii) to distribute, import for distribution, broadcast, communicate or make available to the public, without authority, performances, copies of fixed performances or phonograms knowing that electronic rights management information has been removed or altered without authority.

(2) As used in this Article, "rights management information" means information which identifies the performer, the performance of the performer, the producer of the phonogram, the phonogram, the owner of any right in the performance or phonogram, or information about the terms and conditions of use of the performance or phonogram, and any numbers or codes that represent such information, when any of these items of information is attached to a copy of a fixed performance or a phonogram or appears in connection with the communication or making available of a fixed performance or a phonogram to the public.

Agreed statement concerning Article 19: The agreed statement concerning Article 12 (on Obligations concerning Rights Management Information) of the WIPO Copyright Treaty is applicable mutatis mutandis also to Article 19 (on Obligations concerning Rights Management Information) of the WIPO Performances and Phonograms Treaty.

Editors' note: The text of the Agreed statement concerning article 12 of the WCT reads as follows:

"It is understood that the reference to 'infringement of any right covered by this Treaty or the Berne Convention' includes both exclusive rights and rights of remuneration. It is further understood that Contracting Parties will not rely on this Article to devise or implement rights management systems that would have the effect of imposing formalities which are not permitted under the Berne Convention or this Treaty, prohibiting the free movement of goods or impeding the enjoyment of rights under this Treaty."

Article 23
Provisions on Enforcement of Rights

(1) Contracting Parties undertake to adopt, in accordance with their legal systems, the measures necessary to ensure the application of this Treaty.

(2) Contracting Parties shall ensure that enforcement procedures are available under their law so as to permit effective action against any act of infringement of rights covered by this Treaty, including expeditious remedies to prevent infringements and remedies which constitute a deterrent to further infringements.

Beijing Treaty

Article 15
Obligations concerning Technological Measures
Contracting Parties shall provide adequate legal protection and effective legal remedies against the circumvention of effective technological measures that are used by performers in connection with the exercise of their rights under this Treaty and that restrict acts, in respect of their performances, which are not authorized by the performers concerned or permitted by law.

Agreed statement concerning Article 15 as it relates to Article 13:*
It is understood that nothing in this Article prevents a Contracting Party from adopting effective and necessary measures to ensure that a beneficiary may enjoy limitations and exceptions provided in that Contracting Party's national law, in accordance with Article 13, where technological measures have been applied to an audiovisual perform-ance and the beneficiary has legal access to that performance, in cir-cumstances such as where appropriate and effective measures have not been taken by rights holders in relation to that performance to enable the beneficiary to enjoy the limitations and exceptions under that Contracting Party's national law. Without prejudice to the legal protection of an audiovisual work in which a performance is fixed, it is further understood that the obligations under Article 15 are not appli-cable to performances unprotected or no longer protected under the national law giving effect to this Treaty.
Agreed statement concerning Article 15: The expression "techno-logical measures used by performers" should, as this is the case regard-ing the WPPT, be construed broadly, referring also to those acting on behalf of performers, including their representatives, licensees or assignees, including producers, service providers, and persons engaged in communication or broadcasting using performances on the basis of due authorization.

Article 16
Obligations concerning Rights Management Information

(1) Contracting Parties shall provide adequate and effective legal rem-edies against any person knowingly performing any of the following acts knowing, or with respect to civil remedies having reasonable grounds to know, that it will induce, enable, facilitate, or conceal an infringement of any right covered by this Treaty:

(i) to remove or alter any electronic rights management information without authority;
(ii) to distribute, import for distribution, broadcast, communicate or make available to the public, without authority, performances or copies of performances fixed in audiovisual fixations knowing that electronic rights management information has been removed or altered without authority.

---

* Editors' note: article 13 of the Beijing Treaty addresses limitations and exceptions.

(2) As used in this Article, "rights management information" means information which identifies the performer, the performance of the performer, or the owner of any right in the performance, or information about the terms and conditions of use of the performance, and any numbers or codes that represent such information, when any of these items of information is attached to a performance fixed in an audiovisual fixation.

> **Agreed statement concerning Article 16:** The Agreed statement concerning Article 12 (on Obligations concerning Rights Management Information) of the WCT is applicable mutatis mutandis also to Article 16 (on Obligations concerning Rights Management Information) of the Treaty.

Article 20
Provisions on Enforcement of Rights

(1) Contracting Parties undertake to adopt, in accordance with their legal systems, the measures necessary to ensure the application of this Treaty.

(2) Contracting Parties shall ensure that enforcement procedures are available under their law so as to permit effective action against any act of infringement of rights covered by this Treaty, including expeditious remedies to prevent infringements and remedies which constitute a deterrent to further infringements.

QUESTIONS

While the drafting of the WCT, the WPPT and the Beijing Treaty are the same, the Agreed statements are not always the same. The same Agreed statement is applicable as to the text of the article pertaining to obligations concerning rights management information. Nevertheless, the Beijing Treaty added new Agreed statements to the obligation concerning Technological Measures. What explains those differences? Are those new Agreed statements limited to the Beijing Treaty? Is it appropriate to draw negative inferences from the comparison of the Beijing Treaty's Agreed statement on technological protection measures with the Agreed statements in the WCT and WPPT?

5.6.3   TRIPS Part III

Section 1: General obligations

Article 41

1. Members shall ensure that enforcement procedures as specified in this Part are available under their law so as to permit effective action against any act of infringement of intellectual property rights covered by this Agreement, including expeditious remedies to prevent infringements and remedies which constitute a deterrent to further infringements. These procedures shall be applied in such a manner as to avoid the creation of barriers to legitimate trade and to provide for safeguards against their abuse.

2. Procedures concerning the enforcement of intellectual property rights shall be fair and equitable. They shall not be unnecessarily complicated or costly, or entail unreasonable time-limits or unwarranted delays.

3. Decisions on the merits of a case shall preferably be in writing and reasoned. They shall be made available at least to the parties to the proceeding without undue delay. Decisions on the merits of a case shall be based only on evidence in respect of which parties were offered the opportunity to be heard.

4. Parties to a proceeding shall have an opportunity for review by a judicial authority of final administrative decisions and, subject to jurisdictional provisions in a Member's law concerning the importance of a case, of at least the legal aspects of initial judicial decisions on the merits of a case. However, there shall be no obligation to provide an opportunity for review of acquittals in criminal cases.

5. It is understood that this Part does not create any obligation to put in place a judicial system for the enforcement of intellectual property rights distinct from that for the enforcement of law in general, nor does it affect the capacity of Members to enforce their law in general. Nothing in this Part creates any obligation with respect to the distribution of resources as between enforcement of intellectual property rights and the enforcement of law in general.

The scope of application of article 41

The following case concerned a complaint by the U.S. against China. One matter on which the U.S. requested consultation was the denial of enforcement with respect to works locally denied copyright protection (because of censorship). The issue turned on the scope of article 41 and whether it applies to all works of art covered by the Berne Convention or only to those protected on a domestic basis.

WTO Panel, 26 January 2009 WT/DS 362/R – China – Measures Affecting the Protection and the Enforcement of Intellectual Property Rights, Report of the Panel

6.   Claim under Article 41.1 of the TRIPS Agreement

(a) Main arguments of the parties

7.161   The United States claims that the enforcement provisions of Chapter V of China's Copyright Law are unavailable with respect to works denied copyright protection under Article 4 of that Law. Therefore, China fails to ensure that enforcement procedures as specified in Part III of the TRIPS Agreement are available under its law, as required by Article 41.1 of the TRIPS Agreement.

7.162   China responds that this claim fails in light of the fact that copyright is not in fact denied under the Copyright Law as alleged by the United States, for the reasons set out above in relation to Article 5(1) of the Berne Convention (1971) [citations omitted].

7.163   The United States notes China's defence – that Article 4(1) of the Copyright Law only denies "copyright protection" not "copyright" – and argues that, therefore, authors of the works for which copyright protection is denied do not benefit from the enforcement remedies specified in Chapter V of the Copyright Law.

7.164   China submits that Article 41.1 of the TRIPS Agreement only requires enforcement procedures to be provided for rights covered by the TRIPS Agreement. If a right is not covered by the Agreement, then there is no obligation to enforce it. China also submits that the standard for enforcement procedures is that they permit "effective action". Given that China prohibits publication of the content at issue entirely, and rigorously enforces that prohibition, it has provided a procedure for "effective action" against any attempt to publish that content. Lastly, China submits that its copyright enforcement procedures are "available", in the sense in which that term was interpreted in US – Section 211 Appropriations Act, because the author of any work may go to court and seek remedies, regardless of what judgment a court eventually reaches [citations omitted].

(b) Main arguments of third parties

7.165   Canada submits that as a result of Article 4 of the Copyright Law, that Law does not apply to works that have been banned from publication or distribution in China and that, as a result, none of the required enforcement procedures is applicable. Therefore, Article 4 of the Copyright Law is also inconsistent with Article 41.1 of the TRIPS Agreement [citations omitted].

(c) Consideration by the Panel

7.166   The Panel observes that Chapter V of the Copyright Law, titled "Legal Liabilities and Enforcement Measures", includes Articles 46 and 47. Article 46 provides for civil liability for 11 types of acts of infringement, many of which correspond to the rights set out in Article 10. Article 47 provides for civil and administrative liability and investigation of criminal liability for eight specific types of action, many of which correspond to rights set out in Article 10.

7.167   It is undisputed that Chapter V of the Copyright Law provides for enforcement procedures against acts of infringement of copyright, including orders to cease infringement, to pay compensation for damages and to confiscate the products of infringement, and provisional measures to order discontinuation of the infringement and to preserve property.

7.168   The Panel recalls its conclusion [citations omitted] above that the Copyright Law, specifically the first sentence of Article 4, is inconsistent with China's obligations (with respect to the rights specially granted by the Berne Convention) under Article 5(1) of that Convention, as incorporated by Article 9.1 of the TRIPS Agreement. In the absence of protection of the rights specially granted by the Berne Convention, there can be no enforcement procedures against any act of infringement of such rights with respect to the relevant works.

7.169   The Panel recalls that, in reaching that conclusion, it dismissed China's argument that Article 4(1) of the Copyright Law does not remove copyright but only "the particularized rights of private copyright enforcement" [citations omitted]. However, the Panel will accept that argument arguendo for the purposes of the claim under Article 41.1 of the TRIPS Agreement.

7.170   Article 41.1 of the TRIPS Agreement provides as follows:

"1. Members shall ensure that enforcement procedures as specified in this Part are available under their law so as to permit effective action against any act of infringement of intellectual property rights covered by this Agreement, including expeditious remedies to prevent infringements and remedies which constitute a deterrent to further infringements. These procedures shall be applied in such a manner as to avoid the creation of barriers to legitimate trade and to provide for safeguards against their abuse."

7.171   This claim is made under the first sentence of Article 41.1. This raises certain interpretative issues. The first concerns the scope of application of this sentence, as expressed by the phrase "any act of infringement of intellectual property rights covered by this Agreement".

7.172   The term "intellectual property" is defined in Article 1.2 of the TRIPS Agreement as follows: "For the purposes of this Agreement, the term 'intellectual property' refers to all categories of intellectual property that are the subject of Sections 1 through 7 of Part II."

7.173   The subject of Section 1 of Part II is "Copyright and Related Rights". Within Section 1, Article 9.1 incorporates Articles 1 through 21 of the Berne Convention (1971) and the Appendix thereto, with the exception of rights conferred under, or derived from, Article 6bis. Those provisions provide for the grant of various rights to authors in respect of their literary and artistic works. Any act falling within the scope of those rights carried out with respect to protected works without the authorization of the right holder or outside the scope of an applicable exception is a priori an act of infringement. Accordingly, an act of infringement of copyright in a literary or artistic work, as provided for in those provisions of the Berne Convention (1971) that are incorporated by Article 9.1 of the TRIPS Agreement, is an "act of infringement of intellectual property rights covered by this Agreement" within the meaning of the first sentence of Article 41.1 of the TRIPS Agreement [citations omitted].

7.174   China acknowledges that a right holder of a work denied copyright protection under Article 4(1) of the Copyright Law is denied "the particularized rights of private copyright enforcement" [citations omitted]. China has explained Article 4(1) in the following terms: "Its core principle is that the Copyright Law shall not enforce the protections of the copyright law for works the contents of which are illegal."

7.175   In the Panel's view, this is an acknowledgement that, despite the alleged existence of "copyright" under Article 2 of the Copyright Law, there are no enforcement procedures against any act of infringement of copyright in the relevant works, as required by Article 41.1 of the TRIPS Agreement.

7.176   China contested that the rights denied by Article 4(1) of the Copyright Law were "covered by [the TRIPS] Agreement". This defence stems from China's view that it is entitled, under Article 17 of the Berne Convention (1971),* to deny the rights provided for in Article 5(1) of that Convention. The Panel recalls its findings at paragraphs 7.122 to 7.139 above in which it rejected that view. Accordingly, that view provides no defence to the claim that the rights denied by Article 4(1) of the Copyright Law include protection against "act[s] of infringement of intellectual property rights covered by [the TRIPS] Agreement", within the meaning of the first sentence of Article 41.1 of the TRIPS Agreement either.

7.177   The second issue concerns the nature of the obligation to ensure that "enforcement procedures as specified in this Part are available under their law so as to permit effective action". Article 41 is found in Part III of the TRIPS Agreement. Therefore, the reference to the enforcement procedures as specified in "this Part" is a reference to the enforcement procedures as specified in Part III of the TRIPS Agreement.

7.178   China asserts that the enforcement procedures in Chapter V of the Copyright Law are "available" in the sense that the authors of all works have "access" to enforcement process irrespective of whether they have adequate evidence or a valid right to enforce. The Panel observes that this argument, in effect, asserts that a Member may make available the enforcement procedures as specified in Part III of the TRIPS Agreement simply by not preventing right holders from filing and pursuing claims in vain.

7.179   The Panel notes that, whilst right holders whose works are denied protection under Article 4(1) of the Copyright Law may or may not have access to process, the enforcement procedures "as specified in [Part III]"

---

*   Editors' note: Berne Convention article 17 provides:
The provisions of this Convention cannot in any way affect the right of the Government of each country of the Union to permit, to control, or to prohibit, by legislation or regulation, the circulation, presentation, or exhibition of any work or production in regard to which the competent authority may find it necessary to exercise that right.

of the TRIPS Agreement are far more extensive. This is clear, among other things, from the text of Article 41.1 of the TRIPS Agreement which specifies that these procedures include "remedies". For example, Articles 44, 45, 46 and 50 of the TRIPS Agreement specify that the judicial authorities shall have the authority to make certain orders, such as injunctions, orders to pay damages, orders for the disposal or destruction of infringing goods, and provisional measures. Where copyright protection is denied to a work under Article 4(1) of the Copyright Law, the judicial authorities have no such authority under Chapter V of the Copyright Law. It is not asserted that they are available in China under any other law. Citations omitted Therefore, this set of enforcement procedures, including remedies, is not available to the right holders as required by Article 41.1 of the TRIPS Agreement.

7.180   China asserts that an entire ban on publication of a work is a form of "effective action" and that "it is in a sense an alternative form of enforcement against infringement". The Panel notes that the range of exclusive rights recognized under the Berne Convention (1971) that may be infringed is broader than simply a right to authorize publication. In any event, the effectiveness of a government ban on publication is beside the point. Part III of the TRIPS Agreement includes a multilaterally agreed minimum set of enforcement procedures that Members must make available to right holders against any infringement of intellectual property rights covered by the TRIPS Agreement. Where a Member chooses to make available other procedures – for enforcement of intellectual property rights or for enforcement of other policies with respect to certain subject matter – that policy choice does not diminish the Member's obligation under Article 41.1 of the TRIPS Agreement to ensure that enforcement procedures as specified in Part III are available [citations omitted].

7.181   For the above reasons, the Panel concludes that the Copyright Law, specifically the first sentence of Article 4, is inconsistent with China's obligations under Article 41.1 of the TRIPS Agreement.

QUESTIONS

What subject matter does TRIPS article 41 require member states to protect? Which rights? What is the relevance of the Berne Convention?

Section 2: Civil and administrative procedures and remedies

Article 42
Fair and Equitable Procedures

Members shall make available to right holders[11] civil judicial procedures concerning the enforcement of any intellectual property right covered by this Agreement. Defendants shall have the right to written notice which is timely and contains sufficient detail, including the basis of the claims. Parties shall be allowed to be represented by independent legal counsel, and procedures shall not impose overly burdensome requirements concerning mandatory personal appearances. All parties to such procedures shall be duly entitled to substantiate their claims and to present all relevant evidence. The procedure shall provide a means to identify and protect confidential information, unless this would be contrary to existing constitutional requirements.

Footnote 11 For the purpose of this Part, the term "right holder" includes federations and associations having legal standing to assert such rights.

. . .

Article 44
Injunctions

1. The judicial authorities shall have the authority to order a party to desist from an infringement, inter alia to prevent the entry into the channels of commerce in their jurisdiction of imported goods that involve the infringement of an intellectual property right, immediately after customs clearance of such goods. Members are not obliged to accord such authority in respect of protected subject matter acquired or ordered by a person prior to knowing or having reasonable grounds to know that dealing in such subject matter would entail the infringement of an intellectual property right.

2. Notwithstanding the other provisions of this Part and provided that the provisions of Part II specifically addressing use by governments, or by third parties authorized by a government, without the authorization of the right holder are complied with, Members may limit the remedies available against such use to payment of remuneration in accordance with subparagraph (h) of Article 31. In other cases, the remedies under this Part shall apply or, where these remedies are inconsistent with a Member's law, declaratory judgments and adequate compensation shall be available.

Article 45
Damages

1. The judicial authorities shall have the authority to order the infringer to pay the right holder damages adequate to compensate for the injury the right holder has suffered because of an infringement of that person's intellectual property right by an infringer who knowingly, or with reasonable grounds to know, engaged in infringing activity.

2. The judicial authorities shall also have the authority to order the infringer to pay the right holder expenses, which may include appropriate attorney's fees. In appropriate cases, Members may authorize the judicial authorities to order recovery of profits and/or payment of pre-established damages even where the infringer did not knowingly, or with reasonable grounds to know, engage in infringing activity.

Article 46
Other Remedies

In order to create an effective deterrent to infringement, the judicial authorities shall have the authority to order that goods that they have found to be infringing be, without compensation of any sort, disposed of outside the channels of commerce in such a manner as to avoid any harm caused to the right holder, or, unless this would be contrary to existing constitutional requirements, destroyed. The judicial authorities shall also have the authority to order that materials and implements the predominant use of which has been in the creation of the infringing goods be, without compensation of any sort, disposed of outside the channels of commerce in such a manner as to minimize the risks of further infringements. In considering such requests, the need for proportionality between the seriousness of the infringement and the remedies ordered as well as the interests of third parties shall be taken into account. In regard to counterfeit trademark goods, the simple removal of the trademark unlawfully affixed shall not be sufficient, other than in exceptional cases, to permit release of the goods into the channels of commerce.

QUESTIONS

Which, if any, of the following incentives to compliance with non-mandatory formalities are compatible with the TRIPS Agreement (see, *supra*, this Chapter, 5.1.1 (What is a "formality"?) pp. 262 et seq.):

1. Conferring evidentiary advantages on a certificate of copyright registration, for example, a legal presumption that the statements in the certificate are true and that the copyright is valid.
2. Conditioning statutory damages and attorneys fees on registration prior to the alleged infringement.
3. Denying injunctive relief unless the work was registered prior to the alleged infringement.

Article 47
Right of Information

Members may provide that the judicial authorities shall have the authority, unless this would be out of proportion to the seriousness of the infringement, to order the infringer to inform the right holder of the identity of third persons involved in the production and distribution of the infringing goods or services and of their channels of distribution.

C-275/06 Productores de Música de España (Promusicae) v. Telefónica de España SAU ECLI:EU:C:2008:54 [2008]

[This case concerned the disclosure of the identities and physical addresses of users of P2P software. Promusicae (a not for profit organization of producers and publishers of musical and audiovisual recordings) asked that Telefonica (whose activities include the provision of Internet access service) to be ordered to disclose those identities. The requested disclosure put in issue the balance of IP protection with other fundamental rights such as protection of personal data.]

Legal context

International law

3   Part III of the Agreement on Trade-Related Aspects of Intellectual Property Rights ('the TRIPS Agreement'), which constitutes Annex 1C to the Agreement establishing the World Trade Organization ('the WTO'), signed at Marrakesh on 15 April 1994 and approved by Council Decision 94/800/EC of 22 December 1994 concerning the conclusion on behalf of the European Community, as regards matters within its competence, of the agreements reached in the Uruguay Round multilateral negotiations (1986–1994) (OJ 1994 L 336, p. 1), is headed 'Enforcement of intellectual property rights'. [The Court cited TRIPS articles 41 and 47]

. . .

The three directives mentioned by the national court

57   It should first be noted that . . . the purpose of the directives mentioned by the national court is that the Member States should ensure, especially in the information society, effective protection of industrial property, in particular copyright. However, it follows from Article 1(5)(b) of Directive 2000/31 [Directive on electronic commerce*], Article 9 of Directive 2001/29 [Information Society Directive] and Article 8(3)(e) of Directive 2004/48 [Directive on the enforcement of intellectual property] that such protection cannot affect the requirements of the protection of personal data.

58   Article 8(1) of Directive 2004/48 admittedly requires Member States to ensure that, in the context of proceedings concerning an infringement of an intellectual property right and in response to a justified and proportionate request of the claimant, the competent judicial authorities may order that information on the origin and distribution networks of the goods or services which infringe an intellectual property right be provided. However, it does not follow from those provisions, which must be read in conjunction with those of paragraph 3(e) of that article, that they require the Member States to lay down, in order to ensure effective protection of copyright, an obligation to communicate personal data in the context of civil proceedings.

59   Nor does the wording of Articles 15(2) and 18 of Directive 2000/31 [E–Commerce] or that of Article 8(1) and (2) of Directive 2001/29 [Info Soc] require the Member States to lay down such an obligation.

60   As to Articles 41, 42 and 47 of the TRIPS Agreement, relied on by Promusicae, in the light of which Community law must as far as possible be interpreted where – as in the case of the provisions relied on in the context of the present reference for a preliminary ruling – it regulates a field to which that agreement applies [Citations omitted], while they require the effective protection of intellectual property rights and the institution of judicial remedies for their enforcement, they do not contain provisions which require those directives to be interpreted as compelling the Member States to lay down an obligation to communicate personal data in the context of civil proceedings.

* Editors' note: The Electronic Commerce Directive, adopted in 2000, sets up an Internal Market framework for electronic commerce, which provides legal certainty for business and consumers alike. It establishes harmonized rules on issues such as the transparency and information requirements for online service providers, commercial communications, electronic contracts and limitations of liability of intermediary service providers. (http://ec.europa.eu/internal_market/e-commerce/directive/index_en.htm).

QUESTIONS

1. For the ECJ, nothing in the TRIPS Agreement obliges the member states to lay down an obligation to communicate personal data. Do you agree? How do you interpret article 47 of the TRIPS Agreement?

2. After the *Promusicae* case, the ECJ streamlined its position pertaining to injunctions ordered against service providers in the following cases (C-70/10 *Scarlett* and C-360/10 *Netlog*). The Court had to draw a balance between the protection of IP and other fundamental rights. In those cases, the Court no longer referred to the TRIPS Agreement, although it did quote Directive 2004/48 [Enforcement] implementing the TRIPS Agreement. What accounts for the reference to the TRIPS in *Promusicae* but not in *Scarlett* or *Netlog*? Would it be more difficult to draw the balance between IP and other fundamental rights by quoting the TRIPS? Why? Do you think that European fundamental rights could be interpreted as "existing constitutional requirements" that article 42 does not purport to override?

Section 3: Provisional measures

Article 50

1. The judicial authorities shall have the authority to order prompt and effective provisional measures:

(a) to prevent an infringement of any intellectual property right from occurring, and in particular to prevent the entry into the channels of commerce in their jurisdiction of goods, including imported goods immediately after customs clearance;

(b) to preserve relevant evidence in regard to the alleged infringement.

2. The judicial authorities shall have the authority to adopt provisional measures *inaudita altera parte* where appropriate, in particular where any delay is likely to cause irreparable harm to the right holder, or where there is a demonstrable risk of evidence being destroyed.

3. The judicial authorities shall have the authority to require the applicant to provide any reasonably available evidence in order to satisfy themselves with a sufficient degree of certainty that the applicant is the right holder and that the applicant's right is being infringed or that such infringement is imminent, and to order the applicant to provide a security or equivalent assurance sufficient to protect the defendant and to prevent abuse.

4. Where provisional measures have been adopted *inaudita altera parte*, the parties affected shall be given notice, without delay after the execution of the measures at the latest. A review, including a right to be heard, shall take place upon request of the defendant with a view to deciding, within a reasonable period after the notification of the measures, whether these measures shall be modified, revoked or confirmed.

5. The applicant may be required to supply other information necessary for the identification of the goods concerned by the authority that will execute the provisional measures.

6. Without prejudice to paragraph 4, provisional measures taken on the basis of paragraphs 1 and 2 shall, upon request by the defendant, be revoked or otherwise cease to have effect, if proceedings leading to a decision on the merits of the case are not initiated within a reasonable period, to be determined by the judicial authority ordering the measures where a Member's law so permits or, in the absence of such a determination, not to exceed 20 working days or 31 calendar days, whichever is the longer.

7. Where the provisional measures are revoked or where they lapse due to any act or omission by the applicant, or where it is subsequently found that there has been no infringement or threat of infringement of an intellectual property right, the judicial authorities shall have the authority to order the applicant, upon request of the defendant, to provide the defendant appropriate compensation for any injury caused by these measures.

8. To the extent that any provisional measure can be ordered as a result of administrative procedures, such procedures shall conform to principles equivalent in substance to those set forth in this Section.

C-53/96 Hermès International v. FHT Marketing Choice BV ECLI:EU:C:1998:292 [1998]

[This case concerned unauthorized distribution of copies bearing infringing trademarks. The owner of the trademark asked for an interim order to cease infringement and the adoption of all measures necessary to bring the infringement definitively to an end. A dispute arose as to the time-limit of provisional measures. The solution turned on the interpretation of article 50 of the TRIPS Agreement.]

34   The national court asks whether a measure whose purpose is to put an end to alleged infringements of a trade-mark right and which is adopted in the course of a procedure distinguished by the following features:

- the measure is characterised under national law as an 'immediate provisional measure' and its adoption must be made 'on grounds of urgency',
- the opposing party is summoned and is heard if he appears before the court,
- the decision adopting the measure is reasoned and given in writing following an assessment of the substance of the case by the judge hearing the interim application,
- an appeal may be lodged against the decision, and
- although the parties remain free to initiate proceedings on the merits of the case, the decision is usually accepted by the parties as a 'final' resolution of their dispute,

is to be regarded as a 'provisional measure' within the meaning of Article 50 of the TRIPS Agreement.

35   It should be stressed at the outset that, although the issue of the direct effect of Article 50 of the TRIPS Agreement has been argued, the Court is not required to give a ruling on that question, but only to answer the question of interpretation submitted to it by the national court so as to enable that court to interpret Netherlands procedural rules in the light of that article.

36   According to Article 50(1) of the TRIPS Agreement, that article applies to 'prompt and effective' measures, whose purpose is to 'prevent an infringement of any intellectual property right from occurring'.

37   A measure such as the order made by the national court in the main proceedings meets that definition. Its purpose is to put an end to an infringement of trade-mark rights; it is expressly characterised in national law as an 'immediate provisional measure'; and it is adopted 'on grounds of urgency'.

38   Furthermore, it is common ground that the parties have the right, whether or not they make use of it, to initiate, following the adoption of the measure in question, proceedings on the merits of the case. Thus, in law, the measure is not regarded as definitive.

39   The conclusion that a measure such as the order made by the national court is a 'provisional measure' within the meaning of Article

50 of the TRIPS Agreement is not affected by the other characteristics of that order.

40   First, as to the fact that the other party is summoned and is entitled to be heard, it should be observed that Article 50(2) of the Agreement provides that 'where appropriate' provisional measures may be ordered '*inaudita altera parte*' and that Article 50(4) lays down specific procedures in that regard. Although those provisions allow for the adoption, where appropriate, of provisional measures *inaudita altera parte* that cannot mean that only measures adopted in that way are to be characterised as provisional for the purposes of Article 50 of the TRIPs Agreement. It is, on the contrary, clear from those provisions that in all other cases provisional measures are to be adopted in accordance with the principle *audi alteram partem*.

41   Second, the fact that the judge hearing the application for interim measures gives a reasoned decision in writing does not preclude that decision being characterised as a 'provisional measure' within the meaning of Article 50 of the TRIPS Agreement, since that provision lays down no rule as to the form of the decision ordering such a measure.

42   Third, there is nothing in the wording of Article 50 of the TRIPS Agreement to indicate that the measures to which that article refers must be adopted without an assessment by the judge of the substantive aspects of the case. On the contrary, Article 50(3), in terms of which the judicial authorities are to have authority to require the applicant to provide any reasonably available evidence in order to satisfy themselves with a sufficient degree of certainty that his right is being infringed or that such infringement is imminent, implies that the 'provisional measures' are based, at least to a certain extent, upon such an assessment.

43   Fourth, as regards the fact that an appeal may be brought against a measure such as that in question in the main proceedings in this case, it should be observed that, although Article 50(4) of the TRIPS Agreement expressly provides for the possibility of requesting a 'review' where the provisional measure has been adopted *inaudita altera parte*, no provision of that article precludes that 'provisional measures' should in general be open to appeal.

44   Lastly, any possible willingness of the parties to accept the interim judgment as a 'final' resolution of their dispute cannot alter the legal nature of a measure characterised as 'provisional' for the purposes of Article 50 of the TRIPS Agreement.

45   The answer to the question submitted must therefore be that a measure whose purpose is to put an end to alleged infringements of a trade-mark right and which is adopted in the course of a procedure distinguished by the following features:

- the measure is characterised under national law as an 'immediate provisional measure' and its adoption must be required 'on grounds of urgency',
- the opposing party is summoned and is heard if he appears before the court,
- the decision adopting the measure is reasoned and given in writing following an assessment of the substance of the case by the judge hearing the interim application,
- an appeal may be lodged against the decision, and
- although the parties remain free to initiate proceedings on the merits of the case, the decision is usually accepted by the parties as a 'final' resolution of their dispute,

is to be regarded as a 'provisional measure' within the meaning of Article 50 of the TRIPS Agreement.

QUESTIONS

What, according to the ECJ, is the role of the domestic law as to the characterization of a provisional measure under the TRIPS Agreement? What is the relationship of provisional measures to the proceedings on the merits?

Section 5: Criminal procedures

Article 61

Members shall provide for criminal procedures and penalties to be applied at least in cases of wilful trademark counterfeiting or copyright piracy on a commercial scale. Remedies available shall include imprisonment and/or monetary fines sufficient to provide a deterrent, consistently with the level of penalties applied for crimes of a corresponding gravity. In appropriate cases, remedies available shall also include the seizure, forfeiture and destruction of the infringing goods and of any materials and implements the predominant use of which has been in the commission of the offence. Members may provide for criminal procedures and penalties to be applied in other cases of infringement of intellectual property rights, in particular where they are committed wilfully and on a commercial scale.

WTO Panel, 26 January 2009 WT/DS 362/R – China – Measures Affecting the Protection and the Enforcement of Intellectual Property Rights, Report of the Panel

[The following case concerned a complaint by the U.S. against China. One matter on which the U.S. requested consultation was the threshold established by the reference to "commercial scale."]

(v) "on a commercial scale"

7.532   The parties adopt different approaches to the task of interpreting the phrase "on a commercial scale". The Panel will examine each of these approaches in turn, beginning with that of the complainant.

7.533   The ordinary meaning of the word "scale" is uncontroversial. It may be defined as "relative magnitude or extent; degree, proportion. Freq. in on a grand, lavish, small, etc. scale" [citations omitted]. The ordinary meaning of the word includes both the concept of quantity, in terms of magnitude or extent, as well as the concept of relativity. Both concepts are combined in the notions of degree and proportion. Therefore, a particular "scale" compares certain things or actions in terms of their size. Some things or actions will be of the relevant size and others will not.

7.534   The relevant size is indicated by the word "commercial". The ordinary meaning of "commercial" may be defined in various ways. The following two definitions have been raised in the course of these proceedings:

"1. Engaged in commerce; of, pertaining to, or bearing on commerce.

2. (. . .)

3. Interested in financial return rather than artistry; likely to make a profit; regarded as a mere matter of business."

7.535   The Panel considers the first definition to be apposite. It includes the term "commerce" which may, in turn, be defined as "buying and selling; the exchange of merchandise or services, esp. on a large scale" [citations omitted]. Reading this definition into the definition of "commercial" indicates that "commercial" means, basically, engaged in buying and selling, or pertaining to, or bearing on, buying and selling [citations omitted]. A combination of that expanded definition of "commercial" and the definition of "scale" would render a meaning in terms of a relative magnitude or extent (of those) engaged in buying and selling, or a relative magnitude or extent pertaining to, or bearing on, buying and selling. This draws a link to the commercial marketplace.

7.536   The United States also submits that the word "commercial" scale draws a link to the commercial marketplace. However, it refers to elements of the first and third meanings in definition 3, but dismisses the relevance of the second meaning, "likely to make a profit", because it is different from the other two [citations omitted].

7.537   The Panel notes that the third definition, which includes the qualifiers "rather than artistry" and "mere", refers to usages such as a "commercial artist", "commercial film" or "commercial writing" in the sense of those who are more interested in financial return than the artistic merit of a work, works that are of such a nature that they are likely to make a profit and works that are regarded as a mere matter of business rather than as expressions of other values. This definition is not apposite in the first sentence of Article 61.

7.538   Therefore, the Panel considers that the first definition set out at paragraph 7.534 above is appropriate. However, the combination of that definition of "commercial" with the definition of "scale" presents a problem in that scale is a quantitative concept whilst commercial is qualitative, in the sense that it refers to the nature of certain acts. Some acts are in fact commercial, whilst others are not. Any act of selling can be described as commercial in this primary sense, irrespective of its size or value. If "commercial" is simply read as a qualitative term, referring to all acts pertaining to, or bearing on commerce, this would read the word "scale" out of the text. Acts on a commercial scale would simply be commercial acts. The phrase "on a commercial scale" would simply mean "commercial". Such an interpretation fails to give meaning to all the terms used in the treaty and is inconsistent with the rule of effective treaty interpretation [citations omitted].

7.539   There are no other uses of the word "scale" in the TRIPS Agreement, besides the first and fourth sentences of Article 61. However, the wider context shows that the TRIPS Agreement frequently uses the word "commercial" with many other nouns, although nowhere else with "scale". The other uses of the word "commercial" include "commercial rental", "commercial purposes" [citations omitted] "commercial exploitation" [citations omitted], "commercial terms" [citations omitted], "public non-commercial use" [citations omitted], "first commercial exploitation" [citations omitted], "honest commercial practices" [citations omitted], "commercial value" [citations omitted], "unfair commercial use" [citations omitted], "non-commercial nature" [citations omitted] and "legitimate commercial interests" [citations omitted].

7.540   The provisions of the Paris Convention (1967) incorporated by Article 2.1 of the TRIPS Agreement include uses of the word "commercial" in the phrase "industrial or commercial establishment" (in the singular or plural) [citations omitted] and in the phrases "industrial or commercial matters" and "industrial or commercial activities" [citations omitted]. The provisions of the Berne Convention (1971) incorporated by Article 9.1 of the TRIPS Agreement include the phrase "any commercial purpose" [citations omitted]. The provisions of the IPIC Treaty incorporated by Article 35 of the TRIPS Agreement include the phrase "commercially exploited" and "exploits ordinarily commercially" [citations omitted].

7.541   The context shows that the negotiators chose to qualify certain activities, such as rental, exploitation and use, as "commercial". They also chose to qualify various nouns, such as "terms", "value", "nature" and "interests", as "commercial" or "non-commercial". In a similar way, they could have agreed that the obligation in the first sentence of Article 61 would apply to cases of wilful and "commercial" trademark counterfeiting or copyright piracy. This would have included all commercial activity. Indeed, the records of the negotiation of the TRIPS Agreement show that this formulation was in fact suggested (by the United States) at an early stage [citations omitted].

7.542   The context shows that the negotiators used the term "commercial purposes" in two provisions on the scope of protection of certain categories of intellectual property rights, and that the Appendix to the Berne Convention (1971) already did use that term in the singular in provisions on possible limitations to particular rights. However, the negotiators did not agree that the obligation in the first sentence of Article 61 would apply to cases of wilful trademark counterfeiting or copyright piracy "for commercial purposes". This would have included all activity for financial gain or profit.

7.543   Instead, the negotiators agreed in Article 61 to use the distinct phrase "on a commercial scale". This indicates that the word "scale" was a deliberate choice and must be given due interpretative weight. "Scale" denotes a relative size, and reflects the intention of the negotiators that the limitation on the obligation in the first sentence of the Article depended on the size of acts of counterfeiting and piracy. Therefore, whilst "commercial" is a qualitative term, it would be an error to read it solely in those terms. In context it must indicate a quantity [citations omitted].

7.544   A review of the uses of the word "commercial" throughout the TRIPS Agreement indicates that it links various activities, not simply selling, to the marketplace. It also shows that "commercial" activities cannot be presumed to be on a larger scale than others, such as "public non-commercial" activities, even though they would generally be larger than, say, "personal" or "domestic" use. The distinguishing characteristic of a commercial activity is that it is carried out for profit [citations omitted]. The review of the uses of the word "commercial" also shows that, unlike all the others, Article 61 uses the word "commercial" to qualify a notion of size.

7.545   In the Panel's view, the combination of the primary definition of "commercial" and the definition of "scale" can be reconciled with the context of Article 61 if it is assessed not solely according to the nature of an activity but also in terms of relative size, as a market benchmark. As there is no other qualifier besides "commercial", that benchmark must be whatever "commercial" typically or usually connotes. In quantitative terms, the benchmark would be the magnitude or extent at which engagement in commerce, or activities pertaining to or bearing on commerce, are typically or usually carried on, in other words, the magnitude or extent of typical or usual commercial activity. Given that the phrase uses the indefinite article "a", it refers to more than one magnitude or extent of typical or usual commercial activity. The magnitude or extent will vary in the different "cases" of counterfeiting and piracy to which the obligation applies. In the Panel's view, this reflects the fact that what is typical or usual varies according to the type of commerce concerned.

. . .

7.558   The Panel observes that the general rule of treaty interpretation in Article 31 of the Vienna Convention refers in paragraph 1 to the ordinary meaning of the terms of the treaty, read in context. Where the terms are a single term, or ordinarily used together, then the treaty interpreter should refer to the ordinary meaning of that single term, or of each term in the particular context of each other. This is a distinct exercise from that in paragraph 4 of Article 31 of the Vienna Convention which requires a "special meaning" to be given to a term if it is established that the parties so intended. No party to this dispute considers that a "special meaning" should be given to the phrase "on a commercial scale", and nor does the Panel.

. . .

7.562   The term "on a commercial scale" was also used in the specific context of trademark counterfeiting and copyright piracy in the WIPO Committee of Experts on Measures Against Counterfeiting and Piracy in 1988 contemporaneously with the earlier part of the negotiations of the TRIPS Agreement. Draft Model Provisions for National Laws set out in a Memorandum by the International Bureau of WIPO for that Committee included, in Article A(1), (2) and (3), three draft Model Provisions on manufacturing as an act of counterfeiting, manufacturing as an act of piracy and additional acts of counterfeiting and piracy, respectively. Each of those draft Model Provisions contained a proviso that such goods were manufactured, or the act was committed, "on a commercial scale". An explanatory observation accompanied the term "commercial scale" as a phrase [citations omitted].

7.563   The evidence on the record includes many other uses of the words "commercial scale" and "on a commercial scale" in a variety of contexts. Accordingly, the Panel considers that the words "commercial" and "scale" provide important context for the ordinary meaning of each other when used together in the phrase "on a commercial scale" as in the first sentence of Article 61 of the TRIPS Agreement.

. . .

7.567   The Panel notes that the explanatory observation did not purport to be a definition but was prepared by the International Bureau of WIPO for the specific purpose of accompanying a provision on manufacturing in the draft Model Provisions. The Report of the WIPO Committee of Experts on Measures against Counterfeiting and Piracy of April 1988 shows that the concept of "commercial scale" proved controversial [citations omitted]. Accordingly, it is not an example of ordinary usage. In any event, the draft Model Provisions of the Committee of Experts themselves were never agreed [citations omitted]. Therefore, it would not be appropriate to select an explanatory observation that accompanied them and elevate it to the status of the proper interpretation of a treaty text that was negotiated in another forum and that was finally agreed.

. . .

7.577   The Panel recalls its view at paragraph 7.545 above and, in light of the evidence considered above, finds that a "commercial scale" is the magnitude or extent of typical or usual commercial activity. Therefore, counterfeiting or piracy "on a commercial scale" refers to counterfeiting or piracy carried on at the magnitude or extent of typical or usual commercial activity with respect to a given product in a given market. The magnitude or extent of typical or usual commercial activity with respect to a given product in a given market forms a benchmark by which to assess the obligation in the first sentence of Article 61. It follows that what constitutes a commercial scale for counterfeiting or piracy of a particular product in a particular market will depend on the magnitude or extent that is typical or usual with respect to such a product in such a market, which may be small or large. The magnitude or extent of typical or usual commercial activity relates, in the longer term, to profitability.

QUESTIONS

1. To what extent does the use of the ordinary meaning of the words seem suitable to interpret notions encompassed in the TRIPS Agreement? Is the use of the ordinary meaning still relevant when the same notion is encompassed in domestic laws? How does the Panel take into account the explanatory observation from the International Bureau of WIPO?

2. Under European law, Directive 2004/48 [Enforcement Directive] deals with enforcement for all IP issues including copyright issues. It is the first transversal IP directive, clearly inspired by the TRIPS Agreement. What do you understand by the following recital from the Enforcement Directive:

   > "(7) It emerges from the consultations held by the Commission on this question that, in the Member States, and despite the TRIPS Agreement, there are still major disparities as regards the means of enforcing intellectual property rights"?

   If some Member States had not at the time of the Enforcement Directive (2004) conformed their domestic laws to the TRIPS' requirements, is the Directive now in effect constraining them to implement TRIPS norms through E.U-wide equivalent standards? Does international norm-making provide a means to modify domestic norms in ways that the domestic legislator, left to its own devices, might not or would not? Is this desirable?

6

Lacunae – authorship and ownership

Who is the "author" of a work covered by the international treaties? Who is a "rightholder" either from the outset or by transfer? These questions are essential to the international protection of works of authorship, but the Berne Convention and other multilateral accords barely confront them. Article 1 of the Berne Convention declares that its "protection shall operate for the benefit of the author and his successors in title," but the Convention neither designates who is an "author," nor establishes general rules concerning the transfer of title. As a result, it generally leaves the determination of authorship, ownership, and transfer of rights to national law. Because these often diverge, however, the absence of supranational norms of authorship and ownership means that claimants may encounter varying outcomes depending on which domestic rule a court finds competent to resolve a conflict of authorship or ownership. We will consider the choice of law issues in Part III of this casebook. This chapter will first expose the lacunae in the Conventional treatment of individual authors and joint works, then will take up the special treatment the Convention reserves for the "makers" of cinematographic works, before turning to questions of ownership and transfer of copyright, with particular attention to the elaborate rules set out for cinematographic works. In addition, we will address the extent to which U.S. law and European Directives resolve questions of authorship and ownership at the national and regional level. This examination will also serve as a prelude to the private international law analysis in Part III of this casebook.

6.1 Authorship

6.1.1 Berne Convention

While Berne provides no general definition of authorship, its provisions permit the inference of at least certain characteristics of authorship. These derive in part from the concept of originality (see *supra* Part II, Chapter 5.2.2), and in part from other indices, such as the protection of the "honor or reputation" of the author both during his lifetime and *post-mortem* (art 6*bis*), and the calculation of the term of copyright based on the life of the author (art 7(1)). With respect to authorship, key questions are whether the Berne Convention assumes that the "author" will be a human being, rather than a juridical entity, and if so, whether that assumption may be rebutted in the case of national laws that make explicit provision for non-human "authorship." As we will see, both the U.S., and to a more limited extent, the E.U. extend the "author" title to juridical entities in certain cases.

Article 2
Protected Works

. . .; 5. Collections; . . .

. . .

(5) Collections of literary or artistic works such as encyclopaedias and anthologies which, by reason of the selection and arrangement of their contents, constitute intellectual creations shall be protected as such, without prejudice to the copyright in each of the works forming part of such collections.

Article 2*bis*
Possible Limitation of Protection of Certain Works

1. Certain speeches; 2. Certain uses of lectures and addresses; 3. Right to make collections of such works

(1) It shall be a matter for legislation in the countries of the Union to exclude, wholly or in part, from the protection provided by the preceding Article political speeches and speeches delivered in the course of legal proceedings.

(2) It shall also be a matter for legislation in the countries of the Union to determine the conditions under which lectures, addresses and other works of the same nature which are delivered in public may be reproduced by the press, broadcast, communicated to the public by wire and made the subject of public communication as envisaged in Article 11*bis* (1) of this Convention, when such use is justified by the informatory purpose.

(3) Nevertheless, the author shall enjoy the exclusive right of making a collection of his works mentioned in the preceding paragraphs.

Article 4
Criteria of Eligibility for Protection of Cinematographic Works, . . .

. . .

(a) authors of cinematographic works the maker of which has his headquarters or habitual residence in one of the countries of the Union . . .

Article 6*bis*
Moral Rights

(1) Independently of the author's economic rights, and even after the transfer of the said rights, the author shall have the right to claim authorship of the work and to object to any distortion, mutilation or other modification of, or other derogatory action in relation to, the said work, which would be prejudicial to his honor or reputation.

(2) The rights granted to the author in accordance with the preceding paragraph shall, after his death, be maintained, at least until the expiry of the economic rights . . .

Article 7
Term of Protection

(1) The term of protection granted by this Convention shall be the life of the author and fifty years after his death.

. . .

(3) In the case of anonymous or pseudonymous works, the term of protection granted by this Convention shall expire fifty years after the work has been lawfully made available to the public. However, when the pseudonym adopted by the author leaves no doubt as to his identity, the term of protection shall be that provided in paragraph (1). If the author of an anonymous or pseudonymous work discloses his identity during the above-mentioned period, the term of protection applicable shall be that provided in paragraph (1). The countries of the Union shall not be required to protect anonymous or pseudonymous works in respect of which it is reasonable to presume that their author has been dead for fifty years.

Article 7*bis*
Term of Protection for Works of Joint Authorship

The provisions of the preceding Article shall also apply in the case of a work of joint authorship, provided that the terms measured from the death of the author shall be calculated from the death of the last surviving author.

Article 14t*er*
Droit de suite in Works of Art and Manuscripts

(1) The author, or after his death the persons or institutions authorized by national legislation, shall, with respect to original works of art and original manuscripts of writers and composers, enjoy the inalienable right to an interest in any sale of the work subsequent to the first transfer by the author of the work.

Article 15
Right to Enforce Protected Rights

1. Where author's name is indicated or where pseudonym leaves no doubt as to author's identity; 2. In the case of cinematographic works; 3. In the case of anonymous and pseudonymous works; 4. In the case of certain unpublished works of unknown authorship

(1) In order that the author of a literary or artistic work protected by this Convention shall, in the absence of proof to the contrary, be regarded as such, and consequently be entitled to institute infringement proceedings in the countries of the Union, it shall be sufficient for his name to appear on the work in the usual manner. This paragraph shall be applicable even if this name is a pseudonym, where the pseudonym adopted by the author leaves no doubt as to his identity.

(2) The person or body corporate whose name appears on a cinematographic work in the usual manner shall, in the absence of proof to the contrary, be presumed to be the maker of the said work.

(3) In the case of anonymous and pseudonymous works, other than those referred to in paragraph (1) above, the publisher whose name appears on the work shall, in the absence of proof to the contrary, be deemed to represent the author, and in this capacity he shall be entitled to protect and enforce the author's rights. The provisions of this paragraph shall cease

to apply when the author reveals his identity and establishes his claim to authorship of the work.

(4)

(a) In the case of unpublished works where the identity of the author is unknown, but where there is every ground to presume that he is a national of a country of the Union, it shall be a matter for legislation in that country to designate the competent authority which shall represent the author and shall be entitled to protect and enforce his rights in the countries of the Union.

(b) Countries of the Union which make such designation under the terms of this provision shall notify the Director General by means of a written declaration giving full information concerning the authority thus designated. The Director General shall at once communicate this declaration to all other countries of the Union.

QUESTIONS

1. What is "the usual manner" for the author's name to appear on the work?
2. Article 15(1) and (3) establish presumptions. Who bears the burden of proving what?
3. Why, do you suppose, does the Berne Convention not specify who is an "author"?
4. Consider the following definitions of "author" proposed in connection with a WIPO Draft Model Law: what benefits do you see? What problems? Why, do you suppose that WIPO in fact never promulgated either?

   "Author" is the physical person who has created the work. Reference to "author" also means the successors in title of the author as well as the original owner of rights other than the author, where applicable.*
   "Author" is the physical person who has created the work. Reference to "author" includes, in addition to the author, where applicable, also the successors in title of the author and where the original owner of the rights in the work is a person other than the author, such a person.**

5. A video game is published on the Internet. The producer is American, the director is Canadian, the graphic designers are French and the software

---

* See Committee of Experts on Model Provisions in the Field of Copyright, Third Session, Geneva July 2–13, 1990, preparatory document and summary of meeting, [1990] *Copyright* 241, 251, para. 74.
** Ibid. at 253, para. 89.

programmers are German. On the Internet, the name of the director appears in connection with the video game as the author. Recall the question of the determination of the country of origin when a work by multiple authors of multiple nationalities or residences is first disclosed over the Internet (see *supra*, Part I, Chapter 3.1.1): do you think that article 15 might help resolve that determination?

Deemed authorship

Some Berne member states provide for the vesting of authorship status in persons or entities who are not the actual human creator of the work. This attribution of authorship applies particularly to works created on commission or pursuant to an employment relationship, as well as to computer programs and databases—works that the WCT and the TRIPS have now explicitly included within the subject matter of copyright.

17 USC § 101

A "work made for hire" is—

(1) a work prepared by an employee within the scope of his or her employment; or

(2) a work specially ordered or commissioned for use as a contribution to a collective work, as a part of a motion picture or other audiovisual work, as a translation, as a supplementary work, as a compilation, as an instructional text, as a test, as answer material for a test, or as an atlas, if the parties expressly agree in a written instrument signed by them that the work shall be considered a work made for hire. For the purpose of the foregoing sentence, a "supplementary work" is a work prepared for publication as a secondary adjunct to a work by another author for the purpose of introducing, concluding, illustrating, explaining, revising, commenting upon, or assisting in the use of the other work, such as forewords, afterwords, pictorial illustrations, maps, charts, tables, editorial notes, musical arrangements, answer material for tests, bibliographies, appendixes, and indexes, and an "instructional text" is a literary, pictorial, or graphic work prepared for publication and with the purpose of use in systematic instructional activities.

. . .

Directive No. 2009/24/EC of the European Parliament and of the Council of 23 April 2009 on the legal protection of computer programs

Article 2 – Authorship of computer programs

(1) The author of a computer program shall be the natural person or group of natural persons who has created the program or, where the legislation of the Member State permits, the legal person designated as the rightholder by that legislation. Where collective works are recognized by the legislation of a Member State, the person considered by the legislation of the Member State to have created the work shall be deemed to be its author.

Directive 96/9/EC of the European Parliament and of the Council of 11 March 1996 on the legal protection of databases

Article 4 – Database authorship

(1) The author of a database shall be the natural person or group of natural persons who created the base or, where the legislation of the Member States so permits, the legal person designated as the rightholder by that legislation.

QUESTIONS

1. Are these provisions consistent with the Berne Convention?
2. Does it matter, in that respect, that computer programs and databases may not, prior to the WCT and the TRIPS, have come within the ambit of Berne minimum subject matter? What, if any, difference does their inclusion in the WCT and the TRIPS make?

Works with multiple authors

Just as the Berne Convention does not explicitly identify indicia of authorship, so it does not, as a general matter, determine whether those who collaborate on a work's creation should each be deemed an author of the resulting work. Thus, the Berne Convention neither illuminates what kind of contribution makes one a co-author, nor does it determine whether a work is properly classified as a joint work, or as two separate, albeit interdependent works. A notable example of the latter problem is a musical composition with accompanying words: is it one work with two authors (assuming a single composer and a single lyricist), or two works each with one author? The characterization matters not least because Berne article 7*bis* provides that duration of copyright in a joint work runs from the death of the last surviving co-author. Thus, Berne attaches consequences to the characterization of a work, yet declines to instruct member states how to determine whether a work is a joint work. (Cf. Directive 2011/77/EU of 27 September 2011 amending Directive 2006/116/EC on the term of protection of copyright and certain related rights, art 1(1), *supra*, Part II, Chapter 5.3.1) Further consequences of characterization concern control and compensation. If a work which combines the creative efforts of several contributors is a joint work of co-authorship, then its authors jointly control the work's exploitation and share in its profits. If the work instead is deemed a composite work consisting of separately exploitable components, then no creative contributor will control the whole, nor will she be compensated for the exploitation of her co-creator's contributions (absent contractual agreement).

6.2   Initial ownership

Authorship should be distinguished from first ownership, as to which the Berne Convention establishes elaborate presumptions in the unique context of cinematographic works (art 14*bis*).

In this area, the Berne Convention does set out—very complicated—rules for allocation of ownership in multiply-authored works: cinematographic works. Article 14*bis* (immediately below) sidesteps the attribution of "authorship" status to any of the creative participants in a cinematographic work, but it does endeavor to allocate one of the principal consequences of authorship status: ownership of rights in the work as a whole, as well as of its component parts.

> **Article 14*bis***
> **Special Provisions Concerning Cinematographic Works:**
>
> *1. Assimilation to "original" works; 2. Ownership; limitation of certain rights of certain contributors; 3. Certain other contributors*
>
> (1) Without prejudice to the copyright in any work which may have been adapted or reproduced, a cinematographic work shall be protected as an original work. The owner of copyright in a cinematographic work shall enjoy the same rights as the author of an original work, including the rights referred to in the preceding Article.

(2)

(a) Ownership of copyright in a cinematographic work shall be a matter for legislation in the country where protection is claimed.

(b) However, in the countries of the Union which, by legislation, include among the owners of copyright in a cinematographic work authors who have brought contributions to the making of the work, such authors, if they have undertaken to bring such contributions, may not, in the absence of any contrary or special stipulation, object to the reproduction, distribution, public performance, communication to the public by wire, broadcasting or any other communication to the public, or to the subtitling or dubbing of texts, of the work.

(c) The question whether or not the form of the undertaking referred to above should, for the application of the preceding sub-paragraph (b), be in a written agreement or a written act of the same effect shall be a matter for the legislation of the country where the maker of the cinematographic work has his headquarters or habitual residence. However, it shall be a matter for the legislation of the country of the Union where protection is claimed to provide that the said undertaking shall be in a written agreement or a written act of the same effect. The countries whose legislation so provides shall notify the Director General by means of a written declaration, which will be immediately communicated by him to all the other countries of the Union.

(d) By "contrary or special stipulation" is meant any restrictive condition which is relevant to the aforesaid undertaking.

(3) Unless the national legislation provides to the contrary, the provisions of paragraph (2)(b) above shall not be applicable to authors of scenarios, dialogues and musical works created for the making of the cinematographic work, or to the principal director thereof. However, those countries of the Union whose legislation does not contain rules providing for the application of the said paragraph (2)(b) to such director shall notify the Director General by means of a written declaration, which will be immediately communicated by him to all the other countries of the Union.

QUESTIONS

1. Work through the various provisions:
   a. How does article 14*bis* identify who is the owner of copyright in a cinematographic work?

    b. Which contributors to the creation of a cinematographic work are covered by article 14*bis*? Do the same rules apply to all?

    c. How, if at all, does article 14*bis* address the ownership of the separate contributions in the event of their exploitation in works other than cinematographic works, for example, the creation and sale of phonograms reproducing the soundtrack (or portions of it), or the recording by other artists of songs first performed on the soundtrack?

2. An author who resides in Country A writes the screenplay for a cinematographic work produced by a resident of Country B. The cinematographic work is exploited in Country C, as well as in A and B. Countries A and C vest initial ownership of copyright in the contributions to a cinematographic work in the creators of those contributions. Country B vests initial copyright ownership in the film producer. Suppose the author contends that the cinematographic work deleteriously alters the screenplay in a manner injurious to his reputation? Or that the author claims that the film is being exploited in media not covered by his contract with the producer? What rights does article 14*bis* afford the author? Where?

3. Does article 14*bis* apply to audiovisual works generally?

4. What, if any, negative inferences may one draw from article 14*bis* with respect to the attribution of initial ownership to works other than cinematographic works?

5. Consider the following critique of article 14*bis*(2) and (3): do you agree?

> These provisions have been aptly described as 'devoid of practically any real substance', and this must surely be correct: a vast amount of time was spent [in the Revision Conference that produced this text] to secure a very meagre advance. The stated purpose of the exercise was the production of a uniform international code to regulate the exploitation of cinematographic works so as to promote the free circulation of films. This objective was hardly achieved, and the provisions adopted are the most obscure and least useful in the whole Convention. (Sam Ricketson and Jane C. Ginsburg, *International Copyright and Neighbouring Rights: The Berne Convention and Beyond*, para 7.31 (2006)).

C-277/10 Martin Luksan v. Petrus Van der Let ECLI:EU:C:2012:65 [2012]

[This case concerned a dispute between the principal director of a documentary and his producer. The dispute arose because the producer made the movie available on the Internet without the authorization of the director. The producer considered that, as producer and under Austrian law applicable to the contract, all exclusive exploitation rights in the film vest in him. The director rejoined that Austrian law did not comply with European law, under which he claimed the right should vest in him.]

Question 1

37   By its first question, the national court asks, in essence, whether Articles 1 and 2 of Directive 93/83 [Satellite and Cable Directive], and Articles 2 and 3 of Directive 2001/29 [Info Soc Directive] in conjunction with Articles 2 and 3 of Directive 2006/115 [Rental and lending rights Directive] and with Article 2 of Directive 2006/116 [Copyright term Directive], must be interpreted as meaning that rights to exploit a cinematographic work such as those at issue in the main proceedings (satellite broadcasting right, reproduction right and any other right of communication to the public through the making available to the public) vest by operation of law, directly and originally, in the principal director, in his capacity as author of that work. It asks whether, consequently, the abovementioned provisions preclude national legislation which allocates the rights in question by operation of law exclusively to the producer of the work.

. . .

53   Thus, the provisions referred to in the previous three paragraphs allot, by way of original grant, to the principal director in his capacity as author the rights to exploit a cinematographic work that are at issue in the main proceedings.

54   However, notwithstanding these provisions of secondary legislation, the Austrian Government relies in its observations submitted to the Court upon paragraph 2(b), in conjunction with paragraph 3, of Article 14*bis* of the Berne Convention, an article which relates to cinematographic works and which, in its submission, authorises it to grant those rights to the producer of the work alone.

55   It is apparent from those provisions of the Berne Convention, read together, that, by way of derogation, it is permitted for national legislation to deny the principal director certain rights to exploit a cinematographic work, such as, in particular, the reproduction right and the right of communication to the public.

56   In this connection, it should be noted first of all that all the Member States of the European Union have acceded to the Berne Convention, some

before 1 January 1958 and others before the date of their accession to the European Union.

57 As regards, more specifically, Article 14*bis* of the Berne Convention, relating to cinematographic works, it is to be observed that this article was inserted following the revisions to the convention adopted in Brussels in 1948, then in Stockholm in 1967.

58 Thus, the Berne Convention displays the characteristics of an international agreement for the purposes of Article 351 TFEU, which provides inter alia that the rights and obligations arising from agreements concluded before 1 January 1958, or, for acceding States, before the date of their accession, between one or more Member States, on the one hand, and one or more third countries, on the other, are not to be affected by the provisions of the Treaties.

59 It should also be observed that the European Union, which is not a party to the Berne Convention, is nevertheless obliged, under Article 1(4) of the WIPO Copyright Treaty, to which it is a party, which forms part of its legal order and which Directive 2001/29 [Info Soc] is intended to implement, to comply with Articles 1 to 21 of the Berne Convention (see, to this effect, Football Association Premier League and Others, paragraph 189 and the case-law cited). Consequently, the European Union is required to comply inter alia with Article 14bis of the Berne Convention.

60 Accordingly, the question arises whether the provisions of Directives 93/83 [Satellite and Cable] and 2001/29 [Info Soc] referred to in paragraphs 50 to 52 of the present judgment must be interpreted, in the light of Article 1(4) of the WIPO Copyright Treaty, as meaning that a Member State may in its national legislation, on the basis of Article 14*bis* of the Berne Convention and in reliance upon the power which that convention article is said to accord to it, deny the principal director the rights to exploit a cinematographic work that are at issue in the main proceedings.

61 In this regard, it should be recalled first of all that the purpose of the first paragraph of Article 351 TFEU is to make clear, in accordance with the principles of international law, that application of the Treaty does not affect the commitment of the Member State concerned to respect the rights of third countries under an agreement preceding its accession and to comply with its corresponding obligations [citations omitted].

62 However, when such an agreement allows, but does not require, a Member State to adopt a measure which appears to be contrary to European

Union law, the Member State must refrain from adopting such a measure [citations omitted].

63   That case-law must also be applicable mutatis mutandis when, because of a development in European Union law, a legislative measure adopted by a Member State in accordance with the power offered by an earlier international agreement appears contrary to European Union law. In such a situation, the Member State concerned cannot rely on that agreement in order to exempt itself from the obligations that have arisen subsequently from European Union law.

64   In providing that the principal director of a cinematographic work is to be considered its author or one of its authors, the European Union legislature exercised the competence of the European Union in the field of intellectual property. In those circumstances, the Member States are no longer competent to adopt provisions compromising that European Union legislation. Accordingly, they can no longer rely on the power granted by Article 14*bis* of the Berne Convention.

65   Next, a legislative measure as described in paragraph 60 of the present judgment does not prove compatible with the aim pursued by Directive 2001/29 [Info Soc].

. . .

71   It follows from the foregoing that the provisions of Directives 93/83 [Satellite and Cable] and 2001/29 [Info Soc] referred to in paragraphs 50 to 52 of the present judgment cannot be interpreted, in the light of Article 1(4) of the WIPO Copyright Treaty, as meaning that a Member State might in its national legislation, on the basis of Article 14*bis* of the Berne Convention and in reliance upon the power which that convention article is said to accord to it, deny the principal director the rights to exploit a cinematographic work that are at issue in the main proceedings, because such an interpretation, first, would not respect the competence of the European Union in the matter, second, would not be compatible with the aim pursued by Directive 2001/29 and, finally, would not be consistent with the requirements flowing from Article 17(2) of the Charter of Fundamental Rights guaranteeing the protection of intellectual property.

QUESTIONS

1. Do you agree with the Austrian Government's interpretation of Berne Convention as authorizing member states to grant rights in cinematographic works to the producer? How does the Court solve the apparent conflict with three different kinds of norms, i.e., national, European, international? What is the Court's interpretation, at point 55, of the Berne Convention? Is that the same as the Austrian Government's?
2. Would a provision of national law vesting copyright in the principal director but then presumptively transferring all rights of cinematographic exploitation to the producer be consistent with the Berne Convention? With European norms?

6.3   Transfers of ownership

6.3.1   Berne Convention

> **Article 2**
> **Protected Works**
>
> . . .; *6. Obligation to protect; beneficiaries of protection; . . .*
>
> . . .
>
> (6) The works mentioned in this Article shall enjoy protection in all countries of the Union. This protection shall operate for the benefit of the author and his successors in title.

As the foregoing text indicates, the Berne Convention anticipates that persons other than the author may come to own rights initially vested in authors. This outcome is ineluctable in the case of rights owned after the author's death, since the minimum Conventional term is 50 years *pma*. But "successors in title" may also include the author's transferees. Apart from the rather opaque provisions of article 14*bis*, however, the Berne Convention addresses transfers of rights, obliquely, only in article 6*bis* (1):

> Independently of the author's economic rights, and even after the transfer of the said rights, the author shall have the right to claim authorship of the work and to object to any distortion, mutilation or other modification of, or other derogatory action in relation to, the said work, which would be prejudicial to his honor or reputation.

QUESTIONS

1. Are moral rights transferrable? Waivable? At all? Only under certain conditions? What are they?
2. What, if anything, does the Berne Convention provide with respect to the transfer of economic rights? Does the Convention limit the scope of the grant with respect to its duration? The rights covered? Does the Convention require that any transfer be in writing?
3. To the extent that the Convention does not answer the above questions, one must look to national law. But what national law applies? To which questions? For further exploration of these issues, see Part III: Private International Law, *infra*.

6.3.2 Mandatory remuneration of authors and performers

As we have seen, the Berne Convention says very little about transfers of authors' rights, and nothing about how (or if) authors are to be remunerated for those transfers. By contrast, neighboring rights conventions do contain provisions regarding transferability of and remuneration of performers' rights. In addition, E.U. Directives bring some authors' rights within the regimes the conventions design for performers' rights.

Rome Convention

Article 7
Minimum Protection for Performers:

. . .;2. Relations between Performers and Broadcasting Organizations

. . .

2.

(1) If broadcasting was consented to by the performers, it shall be a matter for the domestic law of the Contracting State where protection is claimed to regulate the protection against rebroadcasting, fixation for broadcasting purposes and the reproduction of such fixation for broadcasting purposes.
(2) The terms and conditions governing the use by broadcasting organisations of fixations made for broadcasting purposes shall be determined in accordance with the domestic law of the Contracting State where protection is claimed.

(3) However, the domestic law referred to in sub–paragraphs (1) and (2) of this paragraph shall not operate to deprive performers of the ability to control, by contract, their relations with broadcasting organisations.

Article 12
Secondary Uses of Phonograms

If a phonogram published for commercial purposes, or a reproduction of such phonogram, is used directly for broadcasting or for any communication to the public, a single equitable remuneration shall be paid by the user to the performers, or to the producers of the phonograms, or to both. Domestic law may, in the absence of agreement between these parties, lay down the conditions as to the sharing of this remuneration.

WPPT

Article 15
Right to Remuneration for Broadcasting and Communication to the Public

(1) Performers and producers of phonograms shall enjoy the right to a single equitable remuneration for the direct or indirect use of phonograms published for commercial purposes for broadcasting or for any communication to the public

(2) Contracting Parties may establish in their national legislation that the single equitable remuneration shall be claimed from the user by the performer or by the producer of a phonogram or by both. Contracting Parties may enact national legislation that, in the absence of an agreement between the performer and the producer of a phonogram, sets the terms according to which performers and producers of phonograms shall share the single equitable remuneration.

(3) Any Contracting Party may, in a notification deposited with the Director General of WIPO, declare that it will apply the provisions of paragraph (1) only in respect of certain uses, or that it will limit their application in some other way, or that it will not apply these provisions at all.

. . .

Beijing Treaty

Article 11
Right of Broadcasting and Communication to the Public

(1) Performers shall enjoy the exclusive right of authorizing the broadcasting and communication to the public of their performances fixed in audiovisual fixations.

(2) Contracting Parties may in a notification deposited with the Director General of WIPO declare that, instead of the right of authorization provided for in paragraph (1), they will establish a right to equitable remuneration for the direct or indirect use of performances fixed in audiovisual fixations for broadcasting or for communication to the public. Contracting Parties may also declare that they will set conditions in their legislation for the exercise of the right to equitable remuneration.

(3) Any Contracting Party may declare that it will apply the provisions of paragraphs (1) or (2) only in respect of certain uses, or that it will limit their application in some other way, or that it will not apply the provisions of paragraphs (1) and (2) at all.

Article 12
Transfer of Rights

(1) A Contracting Party may provide in its national law that once a performer has consented to fixation of his or her performance in an audiovisual fixation, the exclusive rights of authorization provided for in Articles 7 to 11 of this Treaty shall be owned or exercised by or transferred to the producer of such audiovisual fixation subject to any contract to the contrary between the performer and the producer of the audiovisual fixation as determined by the national law.

(2) A Contracting Party may require with respect to audiovisual fixations produced under its national law that such consent or contract be in writing and signed by both parties to the contract or by their duly authorized representatives.

(3) Independent of the transfer of exclusive rights described above, national laws or individual, collective or other agreements may provide the performer with the right to receive royalties or equitable

remuneration for any use of the performance, as provided for under this Treaty including as regards Articles 10 and 11.

QUESTIONS

1. A U.S. musician's performance is fixed in France and broadcast there and in the U.K.; do the neighboring rights conventions entitle her to equitable remuneration?
2. A French musician's performance is fixed in the U.S. and broadcast there and in Canada and in Costa Rica; do the neighboring rights conventions entitle him to equitable remuneration?
3. A U.S. musician's performance is fixed in France and distributed in phonograms there and in the UK; do the neighboring rights conventions entitle her to equitable remuneration?
4. A French musician's performance is fixed in the U.S. and distributed in phonograms there and in Canada and in Costa Rica; do the neighboring rights conventions entitle him to equitable remuneration?

Part III

Application of national norms: Private international law

Introduction to international private law and its application to copyright and neighboring rights

Edouard Treppoz, International Intellectual Property Litigation and Private International Law (excerpts;* footnotes omitted) in J. de Werra, Ed., LA RÉSOLUTION DES LITIGES DE PROPRIÉTÉ INTELLECTUELLE (Schulthess, 2010)

Internationality is at the heart of intellectual property because of the intangible nature of its object. While tangible goods can be physically apprehended and therefore fixed in a particular place, (even if capable of subsequent displacement), intangible goods can be everywhere at once. As others have observed, intangible goods are ubiquitous. This ubiquitous nature is its force, but also a weakness to the extent that it underscores the limits of a purely national protection of this kind of property. The response to the problem was to establish international treaties.

With the internet, the possibilities of international litigation are multiplied. Structurally, the causes of the internationalization of litigation are three-fold. The international character may derive from the creation, from the infringer, or from the infringement. The first example concerns the infringement in country A of a creation foreign to that country. The second example is based on the foreign nationality of the infringer. Finally, the infringement may, in its geographic extent, cover many locations. Copies may be made in country A, and subsequently distributed in country B. The internet does not change the causes of internationality. But it has transformed these examples from exceptional instances to almost commonplace ones. This reversal of the principle/exception dialectic is particularly evident with respect to the third cause of internationality. An infringement committed over the internet is in its essence international, the *Cristal* case perfectly illustrates this inversion of perspective. The case concerned the potential infringement of the trademark CRISTAL owned by a French producer of Champagne in France by a Spanish company owning the same trademark for its Cava in Spain and using the trademark on its website. Before the internet, each designation, the Spanish one for Cava, and the French one for Champagne peacefully coexisted on each side of the border. With the internet, coexistence becomes more fraught, as each designation is accessible in both countries. This internationalization of litigation is attested to in caselaw and in commentary by the increased attention

---

* Original title: *Les litiges internationaux de propriété intellectuelle et le droit international privé* (translation, Jane C. Ginsburg). Reprinted with permission.

intellectual property scholars are paying to the perspective of international law scholars.

Nonetheless, recourse to private international law method to resolve this international dimension of intellectual property litigation is controversial for two reasons. The first bears on the substantive harmonization effected by the major international conventions, today incorporated in the TRIPS Accord. This harmonization excludes any divergence and as a result excludes any role for the determination of applicable law. Conflict of laws is evolving into false conflicts because of the substantial equivalence of the laws at issue. This description is of course exaggerated and attributes far too much significance to these treaties. One might immediately observe that these treaties impose only minimum standards of protection. As a result, despite the existence of Berne art. 6bis on moral rights, the choice between the application of French law and U.S. law remains a true conflict. In addition, these treaties do not harmonize the totality of copyright or intellectual property issues. Thus, to remain in the copyright context, nothing is said regarding the determination of the original owner of the rights. One must therefore recognize the persistence of true conflicts of law in copyright notwithstanding the efforts at harmonization.

The second reason undermining recourse to private international law is more profound and is grounded in the dogma, in this field, of the principle of territoriality. The apparent internationality of these lawsuits is disputed by some secondary authorities who perceive in them only purely domestic situations requiring no recourse to private international law. According to these scholars, an infringement in one country involves only a property right in that country, and not any property rights in any foreign country. The reason for this would derive from the principle of territoriality which geographically limits the application of domestic intellectual property laws. According to this theory, as well, infringement would be limited to the borders of one country, and cannot extend to multiple other countries. The supposed international infringement resulting from the production in country A of an infringing work, and the work's dissemination in country B, gives rise to two distinct domestic infringements, as demonstrated by the existence of a distinct violation of the distribution right. Albeit provocative, this thesis should nonetheless not diminish the significance of private international law. First, the principle of territoriality that underlies this inward-looking analysis of the cases is itself a response supplied by private international law. Second, and most importantly, the principle of territoriality is not the only response private international law affords in these cases. On the contrary, we believe that this principle of territoriality today can no longer answer all the issues raised by the internet. We will see that a judge, other than the judge of the country where the intellectual property right is registered, can be competent to rule on an infringement occurring outside the territory of the forum. We will also see that a law other than the law governing the infringement can apply, thus conferring on that law an extraterritoriality. There remains, as [the German scholar] Zwiegert observed, "between conflict of laws and territoriality the same relationship as between fire and water: either the water of territoriality extinguishes the fire, or the fire of conflict of laws makes the water of territoriality evaporate." It is far from certain that territoriality has extinguished the flames of conflict of laws.

As a result, if recourse to private international law method is necessary, each country will be called upon to resolve these international disputes. Thus, if the French judge is competent, French private international law will apply, which is distinct from the Swiss private international law which would apply were a Swiss judge to be deciding the case. There again, one must inquire whether there is a possible harmonization, no longer of domestic substantive rules, but of private international law rules. This harmonization would derive from the major international conventions, especially the Berne Convention and its article 5. We will see that the interpretation of these articles is controversial. If harmonization exists, it is today limited to the European Union. One should recall that within that region, the determination of judicial competence depends on criteria that are harmonized by the Brussels I Regulation, while applicable law turns on the Rome I and II Regulations. Even so, this harmonization remains limited to the domain of these regulations' application. As a result, the crucial question of ownership of rights is not governed by European private international law; this leaves room for the private international law rules of the member states. Beyond these three normative levels (national, regional and international), harmonization might come from learned codifications (soft law rules). While the influence of the latter is real, it is nonetheless insufficient, leaving persistent divergences within the rules of private international law.

This absence of uniformity at the level of rules of private international law underscores the importance of the determination of the forum. It is, in fact, in ascertaining the forum that the parties will know what private international law system will apply to their essentially international dispute. It is indeed well known today that the determination of the forum does not entail the application of the forum's substantive rules. As section 103 of the American Law Institute PRINCIPLES GOVERNING JURISDICTION, CHOICE OF LAW AND JUDGMENTS IN TRANSNATIONAL DISPUTES correctly notes, "competence to adjudicate does not imply application of the forum State's substantive law." The questions are distinct and call for distinct methods. While one, the determination of the forum, is necessarily unilateral, the other, the determination of applicable law, is, in principle, bilateral. These distinct questions are nonetheless subject to the same issues, which are the role of territoriality and the analysis of "complex wrongful acts". Even so, while the issues are common, the responses will diverge depending on whether the question in the end concerns judicial or legislative competence.

7

Jurisdiction to adjudicate (judicial competence)

As employed in this casebook, the term "jurisdiction" refers to a national court's competence to hear a claim of copyright infringement arising out of an international situation. Judicial competence is distinct from legislative competence, which concerns applicable law. The first question in a transnational litigation is "what court decides?" and only subsequently, "whose law applies?" Moreover, as we have seen, the choice of forum will affect the choice of law. For now, we focus on the power of a national court to hear the case in the first place. This power is determined locally. The method is unilateral. French law determines if French courts have jurisdiction, while U.S. law determines if U.S. courts have jurisdiction. Nevertheless, as applied in national law, the method might vary as we will see. That power to adjudicate could be justified over the subject matter of the claim or/and over the person of the defendant. A court generally has jurisdiction to hear claims concerning copyright infringements that occur within the forum, but does it also have authority to hear infringement claims arising out of acts occurring abroad? A court generally has jurisdiction over its own citizens or residents, but under what circumstances may a court compel a foreign defendant to appear before the court (or enter a default judgment should she not appear)? Are the criteria cumulative or alternative? Does a court have authority to hear local infringements that occurred between a foreign plaintiff and a foreign defendant?

We will first consider whether the international treaties have anything to say about judicial competence, and then will turn to U.S. caselaw, and regional norms, the E.U.'s Brussels I Regulation. Finally we will address two international "soft law" instruments that propose rules of judicial competence, the American Law Institute's *Intellectual Property: Principles Governing Jurisdiction, Choice of Law, and Judgments in Transnational Disputes* (2008), and the Max Planck Institut's CLIP project, *Principles on Conflict of Laws in Intellectual Property* (2011).

7.1 International conventions

7.1.1 IP conventions

Berne Convention

Does the Berne Convention in any way address judicial competence? Article 5(2) refers to "the country where protection is claimed" as the country whose laws "exclusively" govern "the extent of protection, as well as the means of redress afforded to the author to protect his rights." The phrase "where protection is claimed" may imply that the forum will be one in which an alleged infringement has occurred or impacted. If that country's laws are to govern the claim, it would follow that they have some relationship to the claim, for example, because the harmful act occurred or caused harm in that territory. The occurrence or impact of a wrongful act in the territory, moreover, is a well-recognized basis for judicial competence.

But reading Berne article 5(2) as a forum-designator is ultimately unconvincing, for several reasons. First, it makes jurisdiction, normally the predicate question, turn on determination of the applicable law, and therefore analytically puts the cart before the horse. Second, the country "where" protection is claimed is not necessarily the country where the infringement occurred. A copyright owner may choose to pursue a defendant in her country of residence, even though the infringing acts may have occurred elsewhere, because only in the country of the defendant's residence may she have sufficient assets to satisfy a judgment. If the country of her residence is otherwise unrelated to the claim, the application of its substantive law seems questionable. Third, suppose the infringement is multi-territorial, with infringing acts committed or impacting in many states. To read Berne article 5(2) as designating the judicial competence of the country "where protection is claimed" based on an equivalence between the application of the law of the place of the infringement and the competence of its courts would mean that multi-territorial infringement claims would have to be litigated separately in as many national fora as there are infringing acts or impacts. This costly and inefficient result clashes with the overall objective of the Berne Convention, to "constitute a Union for the protection of the rights of authors in their literary and artistic works" (art 1); since the text of article 5(2) hardly commands such a result, it would be best to avoid an interpretation that would yield such a counter-productive outcome.

The likely conclusion, then, is that the Berne Convention does not supply a rule designating a forum for copyright actions. The question thus will be left to member state law. Where Berne member states are also party to a multilateral instrument on jurisdiction, such as the E.U. Brussels I Regulation, its general rules (or specific rules, if any) will determine the competent forum or fora. Otherwise, the domestic law of member states will determine both whether the court had power over the person of the defendant, and authority to hear a copyright claim (particularly copyright claims arising under foreign laws).

7.1.2 Private international law conventions

Hague Convention on Choice of Court Agreements (2005)
(this Convention is not yet in force)

CHAPTER I – SCOPE AND DEFINITIONS

Article 1 – Scope

(1) This Convention shall apply in international cases to exclusive choice of court agreements concluded in civil or commercial matters.

(2) For the purposes of Chapter II, a case is international unless the parties are resident in the same Contracting State and the relationship of the parties and all other elements relevant to the dispute, regardless of the location of the chosen court, are connected only with that State.

(3) For the purposes of Chapter III, a case is international where recognition or enforcement of a foreign judgment is sought.

Article 2 – Exclusions from scope

. . .

(2) This Convention shall not apply to the following matters –

. . .

    n) the validity of intellectual property rights other than copyright and related rights;
    o) infringement of intellectual property rights other than copyright and related rights, except where infringement proceedings are brought for breach of a contract between the parties relating to such rights, or could have been brought for breach of that contract;

. . .

CHAPTER II – JURISDICTION

Article 5 – Jurisdiction of the chosen court

(1) The court or courts of a Contracting State designated in an exclusive choice of court agreement shall have jurisdiction to decide a dispute to which the agreement applies, unless the agreement is null and void under the law of that State.

(2) A court that has jurisdiction under paragraph 1 shall not decline to exercise jurisdiction on the ground that the dispute should be decided in a court of another State.

(3) The preceding paragraphs shall not affect rules –

a) on jurisdiction related to subject matter or to the value of the claim;
b) on the internal allocation of jurisdiction among the courts of a Contracting State. However, where the chosen court has discretion as to whether to transfer a case, due consideration should be given to the choice of the parties.

Article 6 – Obligations of a court not chosen

A court of a Contracting State other than that of the chosen court shall suspend or dismiss proceedings to which an exclusive choice of court agreement applies unless –

a) the agreement is null and void under the law of the State of the chosen court;
b) a party lacked the capacity to conclude the agreement under the law of the State of the court seised;
c) giving effect to the agreement would lead to a manifest injustice or would be manifestly contrary to the public policy of the State of the court seised;
d) for exceptional reasons beyond the control of the parties, the agreement cannot reasonably be performed; or
e) the chosen court has decided not to hear the case.

QUESTION

Compare the Hague Convention with *London Film Production, Ltd v. International Communications, Inc,* 580 F. Supp 47 (S.D.N.Y 1984) *and*

LucasFilm Ltd & Ors v. *Ainsworth & Anor* [2011] UKSC 39, below. To what extent does the convention adopt the same approach?

7.2   The U.S. approach

Under the U.S. approach, the power to adjudicate the case must be two-fold. The court must have jurisdiction over the subject matter of the claim and have jurisdiction over the person of the defendant. Those criteria are cumulative. While the parties cannot confer subject-matter jurisdiction by agreement, a forum-selection clause in the parties' contract can provide *in personam* jurisdiction. Even if the court has subject-matter jurisdiction over the claim and personal jurisdiction over the parties, the court may, in appropriate circumstances, decline to exercise its power to hear the case, and to desist in favor of a forum that may be better situated to try the facts and provide a remedy. In those instances, the judge will be exercising her discretion under the *forum non conveniens* doctrine.

7.2.1   Subject-matter jurisdiction

28 U.S.C. § 1338

(a) The district courts shall have original jurisdiction of any civil action arising under any Act of Congress relating to patents, plant variety protection, copyrights and trademarks. No State court shall have jurisdiction over any claim for relief arising under any Act of Congress relating to patents, plant variety protection, or copyrights. For purposes of this subsection, the term "State" includes any State of the United States, the District of Columbia, the Commonwealth of Puerto Rico, the United States Virgin Islands, American Samoa, Guam, and the Northern Mariana Islands.
(b) The district courts shall have original jurisdiction of any civil action asserting a claim of unfair competition when joined with a substantial and related claim under the copyright, patent, plant variety protection or trademark laws.

28 U.S.C. § 1332 – Diversity of citizenship; amount in controversy; costs

(a) The district courts shall have original jurisdiction of all civil actions where the matter in controversy exceeds the sum or value of $75,000, exclusive of interest and costs, and is between—
    (1) citizens of different States;

(2) citizens of a State and citizens or subjects of a foreign state, . . .;

(3) citizens of different States and in which citizens or subjects of a foreign state are additional parties; . . .

. . .

(c) For the purposes of this section . . .—

(1) a corporation shall be deemed to be a citizen of every State and foreign state by which it has been incorporated and of the State or foreign state where it has its principal place of business, except that in any direct action against the insurer of a policy or contract of liability insurance, whether incorporated or unincorporated, to which action the insured is not joined as a party-defendant, such insurer shall be deemed a citizen of—

(A) every State and foreign state of which the insured is a citizen;

(B) every State and foreign state by which the insurer has been incorporated; and

(C) the State or foreign state where the insurer has its principal place of business; . . .

QUESTIONS

1. Suppose that two companies incorporated in Delaware but headquartered in California have a dispute over an alleged infringement of a foreign copyright outside the U.S. Do either article 28 USC § 1338 or § 1332 apply?

2. If the claim alleges infringement of a foreign copyright owner's rights outside the U.S., how is the amount in controversy requirement satisfied? What if the foreign copyright owner seeks only injunctive relief against the U.S. defendant? What if the foreign copyright owner alleges infringement of its work in the U.S., does the amount in controversy requirement still apply?

NOTE

As these Questions indicate, the U.S. federal courts will have subject-matter jurisdiction over claims alleging infringement of copyright occurring in the U.S., because those claims "arise under" the U.S. copyright act. We will discuss later the territorial scope of the U.S. Copyright Act. At this point, it is important to note that federal jurisdiction over the subject matter requires allegations either of infringing acts occurring in the U.S., or of acts outside the U.S. infringing a foreign copyright interest, but in that case, jurisdiction will be based on diversity of citizenship; in other words, in that case, jurisdiction will lie only if the parties are citizens of different U.S. states or one is a citizen of a U.S, state and the other is a citizen or subject of a foreign state.

London Film Productions, Ltd. v. Intercontinental Communications, Inc., 580 F.Supp. 47 (S.D.N.Y. 1984)

▪ Robert L. Carter, District Judge.

This case presents a novel question of law. Plaintiff, London Film Productions, Ltd. ("London"), a British corporation, has sued Intercontinental Communications, Inc. ("ICI"), a New York corporation based in New York City, for infringements of plaintiff's British copyright. The alleged infringements occurred in Chile and other South American countries. In bringing the case before this Court, plaintiff has invoked the Court's diversity jurisdiction. 28 U.S.C. § 1332(a)(2). Defendant has moved to dismiss plaintiff's complaint, arguing that the Court should abstain from exercising jurisdiction over this action.

Background

London produces feature motion pictures in Great Britain, which it then distributes throughout the world. ICI specializes in the licensing of motion pictures, produced by others, that it believes are in the public domain. London's copyright infringement claim is based mainly on license agreements between ICI and Dilatsa S.A., a buying agent for Chilean television stations. The agreements apparently granted the latter the right to distribute and exhibit certain of plaintiff's motion pictures on television in Chile. London also alleges that ICI has marketed several of its motion pictures in Venezuela, Peru, Equador, Costa Rica and Panama, as well as in Chile.

Plaintiff alleges that the films that are the subjects of the arrangements between Dilatsa S.A. and defendant are protected by copyright in Great Britain as well as in Chile and most other countries (but not in the United States) by virtue of the terms and provisions of the Berne Convention.* The license agreements, it maintains, have unjustly enriched defendants and deprived plaintiff of the opportunity to market its motion pictures for television use.

Defendant questions this Court's jurisdiction because plaintiff has not alleged any acts of wrongdoing on defendant's part that constitute violations of United States law,[3] and, therefore, defendant claims that this Court lacks a vital interest in the suit. In addition, assuming jurisdiction, defendant argues that because the Court would have to construe "alien treaty rights," with

---

* Editors' note: At the time of this decision the U.S. was not party to the Berne Convention.
3 The films named, although formerly subject to United States copyrights, are no longer so subject.

which it has no familiarity, the suit would violate, in principle, the doctrine of *forum non conveniens.* In further support of this contention, defendant maintains that the law would not only be foreign, but complex, since plaintiff's claims would have to be determined with reference to each of the South American states in which the alleged copyright infringements occurred.

Determination

There seems to be no dispute that plaintiff has stated a valid cause of action under the copyright laws of a foreign country. Also clear is the fact that this Court has personal jurisdiction over defendant; in fact, there is no showing that defendant may be subject to personal jurisdiction in another forum. Under these circumstances, one authority on copyright law has presented an argument pursuant to which this Court has jurisdiction to hear the matter before it. M. Nimmer, 3 Nimmer on Copyright (1982). It is based on the theory that copyright infringement constitutes a transitory cause of action,[4] and hence may be adjudicated in the courts of a sovereign other than the one in which the cause of action arose. *Id.* at § 1703. That theory appears sound in the absence of convincing objections by defendant to the contrary.

Although plaintiff has not alleged the violation of any laws of this country by defendant, this Court is not bereft of interest in this case. The Court has an obvious interest in securing compliance with this nation's laws by citizens of foreign nations who have dealings within this jurisdiction. A concern with the conduct of American citizens in foreign countries is merely the reciprocal of that interest. An unwillingness by this Court to hear a complaint against its own citizens with regard to a violation of foreign law will engender, it would seem, a similar unwillingness on the part of a foreign jurisdiction when the question arises concerning a violation of our laws by one of its citizens who has since left our jurisdiction. This Court's interest in adjudicating the controversy in this case may be indirect, but its importance is not thereby diminished.

Of course, not every violation of foreign law by a citizen of this country must be afforded a local tribunal, and defendants cite several cases in which, basically under general principles of comity, it would be inappropriate for this Court to exercise its jurisdiction. *Cf. Kalmich v. Bruno,* 404 F.Supp. 57, 61 (N.D.Ill. 1975), *rev'd on other grounds,* 553 F.2d 549 (7th Cir. 1977), *cert. denied,* 434 U.S. 940 (1977). This is not one of those. The line of cases on

---

4 *See* 3 Nimmer, *supra* at § 12.01[C] (copyright is intangible incorporeal right; it has no situs apart from domicile of proprietor).

which defendants rely can be distinguished on significant points. The Court in *Vanity Fair Mills, Inc. v. T. Eaton, Ltd.*, 234 F.2d 633 (2d Cir.), *cert. denied*, 352 U.S. 871 (1956), the principal case of those cited, found that the district court had not abused its discretion in declining to assume jurisdiction over a claim for acts of alleged trademark infringement and unfair competition arising in Canada under Canadian law. As defendant here has acknowledged, the complaint raised a "crucial issue" as to the validity of Canadian trademark law. This factor weighed heavily in the Court's decision.

> We do not think it the province of United States district courts to determine the validity of trademarks which officials of foreign countries have seen fit to grant. To do so would be to welcome conflicts with the administrative and judicial officers of the Dominion of Canada.

Id. at 647. But as Nimmer has noted, "[i]n adjudicating an infringement action under a foreign copyright law there is . . . no need to pass upon the validity of acts of foreign government officials," 3 Nimmer, *supra*, at § 1703, since foreign copyright laws, by and large, do not incorporate administrative formalities which must be satisfied to create or perfect a copyright. *Id.*

The facts in this case confirm the logic of Nimmer's observation. The British films at issue here received copyright protection in Great Britain simply by virtue of publication there. Copinger, Law of Copyright (9th ed. 1958), 21 et seq. Chile's adherence to the Berne Convention in 1970 automatically conferred copyright protection on these films in Chile. Therefore, no "act of state" is called into question here. Moreover, there is no danger that foreign courts will be forced to accept the inexpert determination of this Court, nor that this Court will create "an unseemly conflict with the judgment of another country." *See Packard Instrument Co. v. Beckman Instruments, Inc.*, 346 F.Supp. 408, 410 (N.D.Ill. 1972). The litigation will determine only whether an American corporation has acted in violation of a foreign copyright, not whether such copyright exists, nor whether such copyright is valid.

With respect to defendant's *forum non conveniens* arguments, it is true that this case will likely involve the construction of at least one, if not several foreign laws.[6] However, the need to apply foreign law is not in itself reason to dismiss or transfer the case. *Manu Int'l S.A. v. Avon Products, Inc.*, 641 F.2d 62,

---

6 Plaintiff has alleged infringements in Chile, Venezuela, Peru, Ecuador, Costa Rica and Panama. Since, under the Berne Convention, the applicable law is the copyright law of the state in which the infringement occurred, [sic] defendant seems correct in its assumption that the laws of several countries will be involved in the case. 3 Nimmer, *supra* at § 17.05.

67–68 (2d Cir. 1981). Moreover, there is no foreign forum in which defendant is the subject of personal jurisdiction, and an available forum is necessary to validate dismissal of an action on the ground of *forum non conveniens*, for if there is no alternative forum "the plaintiff might find himself with a valid claim but nowhere to assert it." *Farmanfarmaian v. Gulf Oil Corp.*, 437 F.Supp. 910, 915 (S.D.N.Y. 1977) (Carter, J.), *aff'd*, 588 F.2d 880 (2d Cir. 1978).

While this Court might dismiss this action subject to conditions that would assure the plaintiff of a fair hearing, *Mizokami Bros. of Ariz. v. Mobay Chemical Corp.*, 660 F.2d 712, 719 (8th Cir. 1981), neither plaintiff nor defendant has demonstrated the relative advantage in convenience that another forum, compared to this one, would provide. *Overseas Programming Companies v. Cinematographische Commerz–Anstalt*, 684 F.2d 232, 235 (2d Cir. 1982). The selection of a South American country as an alternative forum, although it would afford greater expertise in applying relevant legal principles, would seem to involve considerable hardship and inconvenience for both parties. A British forum might similarly provide some advantages in the construction of relevant law, however, it would impose additional hardships upon defendant, and would raise questions, as would the South American forum, regarding enforceability of a resulting judgment. *See American Rice, Inc. v. Arkansas Rice Growers Co-op. Ass'n*, 701 F.2d 408, 417 (5th Cir. 1983). Where the balance does not tip strongly in favor of an alternative forum it is well-established that the plaintiff's choice of forum should not be disturbed.

For all of the above reasons, the Court finds it has jurisdiction over the instant case and defendant's motion to dismiss is denied, as is its motion to have the Court abstain from exercising its jurisdiction here. . . .

Armstrong v. Virgin Records, 91 F.Supp.2d 628 (S.D.N.Y. 2000).

[The plaintiff, a U.S. resident performing artist, brought a copyright infringement action against British performers and record producers, alleging that defendants' work unlawfully "sampled" his recorded performances. Defendants' recordings had been distributed in the U.K. and the U.S., but were made in the U.K. The defendants moved to dismiss for lack of subject-matter jurisdiction, on the ground that U.S. copyright law did not apply to the making of the recordings in the U.K, and that the U.S. court lacked jurisdiction to apply English copyright law to the acts committed in the U.K. The court agreed that, absent a "predicate act" in the U.S. (see infra [cross-reference]), U.S. copyright law did not reach U.K. acts. Nonetheless, the court ruled that it was competent to hear plaintiff's claim regarding alleged copyright infringements in England:]

The question presented is whether, if any of the defendants committed acts of infringement abroad actionable under the laws of foreign nations, this Court may exercise subject matter jurisdiction over such claims—not whether it is advisable, convenient, or wise to hear such claims. . . .

While certain courts have, at times, demonstrated their reluctance to "enter the bramble bush of ascertaining and applying foreign law without an urgent reason to do so," [citation omitted] there is no principled reason to bar, in absolute fashion, copyright claims brought under foreign law for lack of subject matter jurisdiction. Not only is this Court called upon to enter bramble bushes, briar patches, and other thorny legal thickets on a routine basis, but a number of persuasive authorities and commentators have also indicated that the exercise of subject matter jurisdiction is appropriate in cases of transnational copyright infringement [citations omitted]. As Professor Nimmer has explained:

> Even if the United State Copyright Act is clearly inoperative with respect to acts occurring outside of its jurisdiction, it does not necessarily follow that American courts are without [subject matter] jurisdiction in such a case. If the plaintiff has a valid cause of action under the copyright laws of a foreign country, and if personal jurisdiction of the defendant can be obtained in an American court, it is arguable that an action may be brought in such court for infringement of a foreign copyright law. This would be on a theory that copyright infringement constitutes a transitory cause of action, and hence, may be adjudicated in the courts of a sovereign other than the one in which the cause of action arose.

3 Nimmer § 17.03; see 3 Goldstein § 16.2 ("Causes of action for copyright infringement are transitory and may be brought in any court that has jurisdiction over the defendant. Subject to jurisdictional requirements, a copyright owner may sue an infringer in United States courts even though the only alleged infringement occurred in another country. Under the territoriality principle, the copyright law of the other country, and not United States copyright law, will govern the action in the United States.").

. . .

In the present case, this Court would unquestionably have subject matter jurisdiction over any claims properly arising under United States copyright law, potentially allowing the Court to exercise pendent jurisdiction over claims arising under foreign law. Moreover, there would appear to be complete diversity as among the parties to this action.

For other examples of adjudication of multiple territory copyright claims, see *Monroig* v. *RMM Records & Video Corp.*, 196 F.R.D. 214, 220 (D.P.R. 2000), in which plaintiff's song was modified and reproduced without authorization in phonorecords and on the sound track of a film distributed in Puerto Rico, Venezuela, Chile, Panama, Nicaragua, Costa Rica, Guatemala, Ecuador, Peru, Mexico, Spain, Portugal, Japan, Uruguay and Colombia. Plaintiff did not receive authorship credit as the composer. The court found violations not only of the songwriter's reproduction rights under the U.S. Copyright Act, but also of his moral rights in each of the countries of distribution. The court awarded $5,000,000 for the combined foreign moral rights violations. *See also*, *Carell* v. *Shubert Org.*, 104 F.Supp.2d 236 (S.D.N.Y. 2000) (makeup designer for musical *Cats* alleged infringement of her designs by producers of the musical in U.S., Australia, Canada, Japan and U.K.; court sustains its subject-matter jurisdiction over foreign claims); *Well–Made Toy Mfg. Corp.* v. *Lotus Onda Indus. Co.*, 2003 WL 42001 (S.D.N.Y. 2003) (fabric design allegedly infringed in Hong Kong).

QUESTIONS

1. Why would the foreign copyright owners in *London Film*; *Armstrong*; and the cases cited in the last paragraph of *Armstrong, supra,* want to sue in the U.S.?
2. Why would a U.S. court decline to adjudicate a claim involving infringement of a foreign trademark outside the U.S.? Why are claims alleging infringement of foreign copyrights outside the U.S. different?

7.2.2   Personal jurisdiction

While U.S. federal courts have exclusive subject-matter jurisdiction over claims alleging violations of U.S. copyright law, Federal Rule of Civil Procedure 4 directs the federal court to apply the personal jurisdiction rules of the state in which the federal district court is situated. A court always has personal jurisdiction over a defendant resident in the forum. By contrast, in a case involving a foreign alleged infringer, the federal court would apply the forum state's "long-arm statute" setting out the bases for asserting jurisdiction over out-of-state defendants. The following decision applies the New York long-arm statute in a case involving alleged copyright infringement over the Internet. The out-of-state defendants resided and operated their websites from other states within the U.S., but the analysis would likely be the same had the defendants been operating from outside the U.S.

Contacts with the forum

Penguin Group (USA) Inc. v. American Buddha, 16 N.Y.3d 295 (N.Y. 2011)

[The New York Court of Appeals, on a question certified from the Second Circuit, considered whether, in a New York publisher's copyright infringement action, a court situated in New York could assert personal jurisdiction under the New York "long-arm" statute over the operator of an "online library" whose business or servers were located in Arizona or Colorado. While the case concerned a defendant from another U.S. state, the court's analysis would appear to apply equally to a defendant from a foreign state. The New York statute, N.Y. C.P.L.R. § 302(a)(3)(ii), authorizes personal jurisdiction over an out-of-state defendant with no other contacts with New York, who, "commits a tortious act outside of the state that causes an injury to a person or property within the state, provided that the party ... expects or reasonably should expect the act to have consequences in the state and derives substantial revenue from interstate or international commerce." Jurisdiction turned on whether the defendant's copyright-infringing activities in Arizona or Colorado "caused the requisite injury in New York." The complaint apparently specifically alleged neither that the defendant distributed works in New York by making them available for downloading by New York residents, nor that New York residents had engaged in infringing downloads caused by defendant's website offer. As a result, no act of infringement occurred in New York, though a New York resident allegedly sustained the impact of the out-of-state act.]

▪ Graffeo, J.

In copyright infringement cases involving the uploading of a copyrighted printed literary work onto the Internet, is the situs of injury for purposes of determining long-arm jurisdiction under N.Y. C.P.L.R. § 302 (a) (3) (ii) the location of the infringing action or the residence or location of the principal place of business of the copyright holder? In answer to this ... question and under the circumstances of this case, we conclude it is the location of the copyright holder.

. . .

The injury in the case before us is ... difficult to identify and quantify because the alleged infringement involves the Internet, which by its nature is intangible and ubiquitous. But the convergence of two factors persuades us that a New York copyright owner alleging infringement sustains an in-state injury pursuant to CPLR 302(a)(3)(ii) when its printed literary work is uploaded without permission onto the Internet for public access. First, it is clear that the Internet itself plays an important role in the jurisdictional analysis in the specific context of this case. It is widely recognized that "the digital environment poses a unique threat to the rights of copyright owners" and that "digital technology enables pirates to reproduce and distribute perfect copies of works—at virtually no cost at all to the pirate" [citations omitted].

The crux of Penguin's copyright infringement claim is not merely the unlawful electronic copying or uploading of the four copyrighted books. Rather, it is the intended consequence of those activities—the instantaneous availability of those copyrighted works on American Buddha's Web sites for anyone, in New York or elsewhere, with an Internet connection to read and download the books free of charge. . . . [T]he alleged injury in this case involves online infringement that is dispersed throughout the country and perhaps the world. In cases of this nature, identifying the situs of injury is not as simple as turning to "the place where plaintiff lost business" because there is no singular location that fits that description.

As a result, although it may make sense in traditional commercial tort cases to equate a plaintiff's injury with the place where its business is lost or threatened, it is illogical to extend that concept to online copyright infringement cases where the place of uploading is inconsequential and it is difficult, if not impossible, to correlate lost sales to a particular geographic area. In short, the out-of-state location of the infringing conduct carries less weight in the jurisdictional inquiry in circumstances alleging digital piracy and is therefore not dispositive.

The second critical factor that tips the balance in favor of identifying New York as the situs of injury derives from the unique bundle of rights granted to copyright owners. The Copyright Act gives owners of copyrighted literary works five "exclusive rights," which include the right of reproduction; the right to prepare derivative works; the right to distribute copies by sale, rental, lease or lending; the right to perform the work publicly; and the right to display the work publicly (see 17 U.S.C. § 106). Hence, a copyright holder possesses an overarching "right to exclude others from using his property" (*eBay Inc. v. MercExchange, L.L.C.,* 547 U.S. 388, 392 [2006] [internal quotation marks and citation omitted]).

Based on the multifaceted nature of these rights, a New York copyright holder whose copyright is infringed suffers something more than . . . indirect financial loss . . . . For instance, one of the harms arising from copyright infringement is the loss or diminishment of the incentive to publish or write (*see Twentieth Century Music Corp. v. Aiken,* 422 U.S. 151, 156 [1975]; *see also*

Princeton Univ. Press v. Michigan Document Servs., Inc., 99 F.3d 1381, 1391 [6th Cir. 1996], cert denied 520 U.S. 1156 [1997] ["[P]ublishers obviously need economic incentives to publish scholarly works . . . If publishers cannot look forward to receiving permission fees, why should they continue publishing marginally profitable books at all? And how will artistic creativity be stimulated if the diminution of economic incentives for publishers to publish academic works means that fewer academic works will be published?"]). And, the harm to a plaintiff's property interest in copyright infringement cases "has often been characterized as irreparable in light of possible market confusion" (*Salinger v. Colting*, 607 F.3d 68, 81 [2d Cir. 2010]).

Moreover, the absence of any evidence of the actual downloading of Penguin's four works by users in New York is not fatal to a finding that the alleged injury occurred in New York. In [the past], we made clear that a tort committed outside the state that was likely to cause harm through the loss of business inside the state was sufficient to establish personal jurisdiction regardless of whether damages were likely recoverable or even ascertainable. Courts often issue injunctive relief in copyright infringement cases to halt impermissible uses because "to prove the loss of sales due to infringement is . . . notoriously difficult" (*Salinger*, 607 F.3d at 81 [internal quotation marks and citation omitted]). In any event, it is undisputed that American Buddha's Web sites are accessible by any New Yorker with an Internet connection and, as discussed, an injury allegedly inflicted by digital piracy is felt throughout the United States, which necessarily includes New York.

In sum, the role of the Internet in cases alleging the uploading of copyrighted books distinguishes them from traditional commercial tort cases where courts have generally linked the injury to the place where sales or customers are lost. The location of the infringement in on-line cases is of little import inasmuch as the primary aim of the infringer is to make the works available to anyone with access to an Internet connection, including computer users in New York. In addition, the injury to a New York copyright holder, while difficult to quantify, is not as remote as a purely indirect financial loss due to the broad spectrum of rights accorded by copyright law. The concurrence of these two elements—the function and nature of the Internet and the diverse ownership rights enjoyed by copyright holders situated in New York—leads us to . . . conclude that the alleged injury in this case occurred in New York for purposes of CPLR 302(a)(3)(ii).[5]

---

5 We do not find it necessary to address whether a New York copyright holder sustains an in-state injury pursuant to CPLR 302(a)(3)(ii) in a copyright infringement case that does not allege digital piracy and, therefore, express no opinion on that question.

Finally, contrary to American Buddha's assertion, our decision today does not open a Pandora's box allowing any nondomiciliary accused of digital copyright infringement to be haled into a New York court when the plaintiff is a New York copyright owner of a printed literary work. Rather, CPLR 302(a) (3)(ii) incorporates built-in safeguards against such exposure by requiring a plaintiff to show that the nondomiciliary both "expects or should reasonably expect the act to have consequences in the state" and, importantly, "derives substantial revenue from interstate or international commerce." There must also be proof that the out-of-state defendant has the requisite "minimum contacts" with the forum state and that the prospect of defending a suit here comports with "traditional notions of fair play and substantial justice," as required by the Federal Due Process Clause. These issues are beyond the scope of this certified question and their resolution awaits further briefing before the federal courts.

NOTE

On remand, however, the Southern District of New York held that defendant did not derive substantial revenue from interstate commerce "because it 'operates on a strictly eleemosynary model' and has no revenue whatsoever." *Penguin Group (USA) Inc. v. American Buddha*, 106 U.S.P.Q.2D (BNA) 1306 (SDNY 2013). The court acknowledged that:

> It is true that Internet companies can operate without any costs or even revenue. It is also true that an online library such as American Buddha's is indeed far from an industry with a "local character;" and that its reach, like that of other Internet sites, is inherently global in nature. Nonetheless, the statutory language remains the same, requiring proof of "substantial" revenue to apply New York's long-arm statute.

Thus, while the New York Court of Appeals interpreted the statutory criterion of "injury within the state" flexibly in light of the characteristics of the Internet, the Southern District of New York did not find the New York long-arm statute permitted a lower threshold of revenue substantiality, even though the Internet enables a non-profit (or unprofitable) defendant to wreak substantial injury on New York businesses. Unless the SDNY's reading of the long-arm statute is reversed, the Court of Appeals' expansive interpretation will apply only to commercial actors on the Internet, and perhaps only to commercial actors whose for-profit endeavors prove successful.

Doe v. Geller, 533 F.Supp.2d 996 (N.D.Cal. 2008).

[The court held it lacked personal jurisdiction over a U.K. resident who, plaintiff alleged, had, in violation of 17 US.C. § 512(f), knowingly misrepresented that material posted to You Tube infringed the defendant's copyrights. Although the take-down notice was sent to California resident You Tube, the court ruled that the location of the host did not determine whether the defendant had "purposefully directed" its allegedly tortuous activity to California. Rather, because the person who posted the allegedly infringing material resided in Pennsylvania, the court considered that the defendant's communication was best characterized as targeting Pennsylvania. (In fact, the defendant had already initiated an infringement action against the plaintiff in Pennsylvania.) The court held that asserting personal jurisdiction over the U.K. defendant in California would be unreasonable. Weighing several factors going to reasonableness, the court observed:]

The fourth factor—the forum state's interest in adjudicating the dispute—weighs against personal jurisdiction. [Plaintiff] Sapient resides in Pennsylvania, not California. "Because the plaintiff is not a California resident, California's legitimate interests in the dispute have considerably diminished" [citation omitted]. Sapient alleges no violations of California law. YouTube is a California company but is not a party to this litigation. California has little interest in the outcome of this case.

Sapient's only argument to the contrary is that "California has an abiding interest in protecting YouTube videos from improper takedown notices," citing the free speech clause in the California constitution and a California statute banning the use of lawsuits to chill free speech. See Cal Const art I, § 2(a); Cal Code Civ Proc § 425.16(a). Those provisions apply to California residents, not Pennsylvania internet users, inanimate computer files or lawsuits filed by British residents against a Pennsylvania resident in Pennsylvania federal court asserting claims under British law. California is not the world-wide regulator of free speech in the digital age.

QUESTIONS

1. Has the NY Court of Appeals held that a federal court in New York State may exercise jurisdiction over out-of-state (including off-shore) alleged "pirates" so long as the alleged infringement occurs over the Internet and the plaintiff copyright holder is a New York domiciliary? Does the court define "piracy"? How is "piracy" different from other kinds of infringement online?

2. The plaintiffs are the composers of the successful Broadway musical "Grease." They allege that the defendant cruise ship operators have been performing numbers from the show on shipboard during voyages. Do the court's personal and subject-matter jurisdiction turn on where the ships were located when the performances took place? On the nationality of the registration of the ship? On the residence of the operator? *See Jacobs* v. *Carnival Corp.*, 2009 WL 856637 (S.D.N.Y. 2009).

Nationwide contacts

The New York Court of Appeals' assessment of the nexus between the New York forum and an infringement originating over the Internet gives special emphasis to the plaintiff's forum residence. A more conventional analysis of whether the foreign defendant has "purposefully directed" its activities toward the forum might find insufficient contacts with the forum. An insignificant number of infringements in any given state could nonetheless, when viewed nationwide, cumulatively establish the requisite nexus with the U.S. as a whole. Where the defendant's communications to any one state may be too insubstantial to meet constitutional "minimum contacts" standards for personal jurisdiction, but the claim requires application of federal law, F.R.Civ.P. 4(k)(2) permits a federal court to assert personal jurisdiction over a foreign national actor on the basis of adequate nationwide contacts.*

Graduate Mgt. Admission Council v. Raju, 241 F.Supp.2d 589 (E.D.Va. 2003)

[The defendant—the operator of a website in India—carried on its website the text of questions from GMAT examinations, whose copyright was owned by the Virginia plaintiff. The federal court, although holding that jurisdiction could not properly be asserted under the Virginia state long-arm statute because of lack of sufficient business activities within that state, found that there was an independent source of federal in personam jurisdiction under Federal Rule of Civil Procedure 4(k)(2). The court also held that the proper substantive law governing the claim was U.S. copyright law.]

Honorable T. S. Ellis, III, United States District Judge.

MEMORANDUM OPINION

---

* Editors' note: F.R.Civ.P. 4(k)(2) states:
Federal Claim Outside State-Court Jurisdiction. For a claim that arises under federal law, serving a summons or filing a waiver of service establishes personal jurisdiction over a defendant if:
(A) the defendant is not subject to jurisdiction in any state's courts of general jurisdiction; and
(B) exercising jurisdiction is consistent with the United States Constitution and laws.

This copyright and trademark action against a citizen of India grows out of defendant's use of a foreign Internet website with an infringing domain name to sell plaintiff's copyrighted materials throughout the world including the United States. Defendant has defaulted and plaintiff has demonstrated a right to copyright and trademark relief provided there is personal jurisdiction over defendant. Thus, explored and resolved here is the question whether there is personal jurisdiction over a citizen of India who registers and operates a foreign website selling plaintiff's test preparation materials in apparent violation of United States copyright and trade-mark laws, where (i) the copyright and trademark holder is located in Virginia, (ii) the website contains a purported testimonial from a Virginia citizen, (iii) infringing materials were sold and delivered to two individuals in Virginia, and (iv) the website contains ordering information for United States citizens.

. . .

The determination of *in personam* jurisdiction involves a two-step inquiry [citations omitted]. A court must first determine whether the facts of the case fall within the reach of Virginia's long-arm statute [citation omitted]. Second, a court must determine "whether the long-arm statute's reach in the case exceeds its constitutional grasp," by considering whether the exercise of personal jurisdiction is consistent with "traditional notions of fair play and substantial justice" under the Due Process clause [citations omitted].

1. Virginia long-arm statute

The conduct alleged by GMAC clearly places Raju within the reach of the Virginia long-arm statute. The Virginia long-arm statute provides for personal jurisdiction over a person "causing tortious injury in this Commonwealth by an act or omission outside this Commonwealth if he regularly does or solicits business, or engages in any other persistent course of conduct, or derives substantial revenue from goods used or consumed or services rendered, in this Commonwealth." Va. Code § 8.01-328.1(A)(4). Raju's actions in operating his website and selling the GMATplus materials caused tortious injury to GMAC in Virginia through his alleged actions in violation of federal trademark and copyright law [citation omitted]. Moreover, it is well established that soliciting business through a website accessible by Virginians satisfies the remaining requirement of the long-arm statute, namely that the person "does or solicits business, or engages in any other persistent course of conduct" in Virginia [citations omitted].

Thus, the magistrate judge properly concluded that the requirements of the Virginia long-arm statute were met.

2. Due Process analysis

The second prong of the personal jurisdictional inquiry requires a consideration of the constitutionality of personal jurisdiction under the Due Process clause. Under the well-established *International Shoe* formulation, the exercise of personal jurisdiction over a defendant requires that the defendant "have certain minimum contacts with [the forum] such that the maintenance of a suit does not offend 'traditional notions of fair play and substantial justice.'" "See *Int'l Shoe Co. v. Washington*, 326 U.S. 310, 316, 90 L. Ed. 95, 66 S. Ct. 154 (1945); see also *ALS Scan*, 293 F.3d at 710–12 (discussing the modern development of personal jurisdiction doctrine). Personal jurisdiction can be established under either general or specific jurisdiction [citations omitted]. Where, as here, the defendant's contacts with the forum are also the basis for the suit, specific jurisdiction is appropriate [citation omitted]. In determining whether specific jurisdiction exists, courts must consider "(1) the extent to which the defendant 'purposefully availed' itself of the privilege of conducting activities in the State; (2) whether the plaintiff's claims arise out of those activities directed at the State; and (3) whether the exercise of personal jurisdiction would be constitutionally 'reasonable'"[9] [citations omitted].

As the Fourth Circuit noted in *ALS*, this due process analysis must take account of the modern reality of widespread Internet electronic communications [citation omitted]. Accordingly, the Fourth Circuit recently adopted the Zippo "slid-ing-scale" approach for determining whether Internet activity can serve as a basis for personal jurisdiction. See *ALS*, 293 F.3d at 713-14 (discussing *Zippo Manufacturing Co. v. Zippo Dot Com, Inc.*, 952 F. Supp. 1119 (W.D. Pa. 1997)).

Under the now-familiar *Zippo* test, the likelihood that personal jurisdiction can be constitutionally exercised is determined by focusing on "the nature and the quality of commercial activity that an entity conducts over the Internet." Passive websites, that do "little more" than make information available to users in other jurisdictions, cannot support personal jurisdiction everywhere that information is accessed. At the other end of the spectrum are situations where a defendant "clearly does business over the Internet," for

---

9 General jurisdiction, which is necessary when the contacts with the forum are not the basis for the suit, is analyzed under the more demanding "continuous and systematic" standard.

example through the "knowing and repeated transmission of files over the Internet," which clearly do support personal jurisdiction. In between is the "middle ground" of "interactive Web sites" which are not passive, because they allow a user to exchange information with the host computer, but also do not constitute "clearly doing business over the Internet." To determine whether an "interactive" website is grounds for personal jurisdiction, a court must consider the "level of interactivity and the commercial nature of the exchange of information that occurs on the Web site."

In this regard, the Fourth Circuit "adopted and adapted the *Zippo* model" as follows:

[A] State may, consistent with due process, exercise judicial power over a person outside of the State when that person: (1) directs electronic activity into the State, (2) with the manifested intent of engaging in business or other interactions within the State, and (3) that activity creates, in a person within the State, a potential cause of action cognizable in the State's courts.

ALS, 293 F.3d at 714. A comparison of this formulation to the original *Zippo* test indicates that the *ALS* test emphasizes that requirement of purposeful targeting of a particular forum, not just the level of interactivity. Under the *ALS* test, the defendant must direct activity into the forum state, with the intent to engage in business within the state. As the *ALS* panel makes clear, personal jurisdiction requires "purposeful availment," that is "purposeful conduct directed at the State."

. . .

In this case, GMAC asserts that the following contacts support a finding of personal jurisdiction based on Raju's contacts with Virginia: First, Raju's site is not merely passive; through it, he solicited orders of his infringing materials from Virginia residents. Second, Raju specifically targeted Virginia residents, by listing a testimonial from a Virginia customer and by selling and shipping materials to at least two Virginia residents. Third, Raju's activities were targeted at and infringed the rights of GMAC, a Virginia corporation. Fourth, colleges and universities in Virginia rely on the GMAT. . . .

These contacts, evaluated in light of the three-part *ALS* test, point ultimately to the absence of personal jurisdiction. Although some parts of the test are met, it is doubtful whether Raju can be said to have "directed electronic activity into the state" with the "intent of engaging in business . . . within the State," as required by the first and second elements of the *ALS* test. . . . [T]he potential indirect injury suffered by the colleges and universities which rely on GMAT scores in their admissions process is too indirect and too diffuse to support a finding that the defendant specifically targeted Virginia. Significantly, over 1700 programs worldwide use the GMAT to evaluate candidates, thus there is no basis to conclude that Raju was knowingly targeting Virginia institutions. . . . [B]ased on the circumstances of this case, the shipment of materials to two Virginia customers is not a sufficient basis for personal jurisdiction, although the question is close. . . . [T]he interaction in this case with Virginia residents was minimal; Raju simply shipped the materials to the two customers at the addresses they provided. Two shipments and one purported customer testimonial are not a sufficient basis on which to conclude that Raju was intentionally directing his website at a Virginia audience. . . .

Finally, GMAC also relies on the fact that the tortious conduct was targeted at GMAC, which is located in Virginia. In some circumstances, the location of the plaintiff, as the "focal point . . . of the harm suffered" can form the basis for personal jurisdiction. . . . In this regard, "although the place that the plaintiff feels the alleged injury is plainly relevant to the [jurisdictional] inquiry, it must ultimately be accompanied by the defendant's own [sufficient minimum] contacts with the state if jurisdiction . . . is to be upheld" [citation omitted]. Here, there is no indication that Raju purposefully directed his tortious activity at Virginia. Indeed, Raju's GMAT plus site consistently refers to "ETS" as the entity that administers the GMAT and publishes test questions. Thus, there is no indication that Raju should "reasonably anticipate being hauled into court" in Virginia based on GMAC's location there, when there is no showing that he was even aware of GMAC, let alone GMAC's location in Virginia.

In sum, the magistrate judge correctly concluded that there is no basis for personal jurisdiction in Virginia under Rule 4(k)(1)(A) based on the contacts with Virginia asserted by GMAC.

B.

. . . [T]here is an alternate basis for personal jurisdiction in this case under Rule 4(k)(2), Fed. R. Civ. P. This Rule provides for personal jurisdiction through nationwide service of process over any defendant provided (i) exercise of jurisdiction is consistent with the Constitution and the laws of the United States, (ii) the claim arises under federal law, and (iii) the defendant is not subject to the jurisdiction of the courts of general jurisdiction of any state [citations omitted]. Rule 4(k)(2) was added in 1993 to deal with a gap in federal personal jurisdiction law in situations where a defendant does not reside in the United States, and lacks contacts with a single state sufficient to justify personal jurisdiction, but has enough contacts with the United States as a whole to satisfy the due process requirements [citations omitted]. Precisely this situation is presented here.

1. Due Process analysis

The first element of the Rule 4(k)(2) analysis requires the same minimum contacts due process analysis as is conducted under Rule 4(k)(1)(A), with the significant difference that the relevant forum is the United States as a whole, not an individual State. . . .

In considering Raju's contacts with the United States in this case, the *ALS* test for determining personal jurisdiction based on electronic activities, must be adapted for the purpose of national contacts analysis. Substituting the United States as the relevant forum, the test requires a showing in this case (i) that Raju directed his electronic activity into the United States, (ii) that he did so with the manifest intent of engaging in business or other interactions within the United States, and (iii) that his activity creates a potential cause of action in a person within the United States that is cognizable in the United States' courts.

Raju's alleged activity plainly creates a potential cause of action in a person within the United States which is cognizable in federal courts, satisfying the third element of the *ALS* test. GMAC is a Virginia non-profit corporation and thus a "person" within the United States. GMAC's causes of action are based on federal law, and thus are clearly cognizable in federal courts. It is also clear that Raju's intent is to "engage in business," namely the business of selling his GMAT test preparation materials to buyers for a substantial fee. Thus, the second element of the *ALS* test is fulfilled in part. All that remains is a showing that Raju "directed his electronic activity" into the United States, with the intent of engaging in business "within the United States," as required by the first and second elements of the *ALS* test.

The record clearly indicates that Raju directed his activity at the United States market and specifically targeted United States customers. The intended market for business conducted through a website can be determined by considering the apparent focus of the website as a whole. . . . The relevant question is whether the website is "designed to attract or serve a [United States] audience."

In sum, it is quite clear upon review of the GMAT-plus website and the record as a whole that while Raju may have aimed his website at the entire, worldwide market of GMAT test takers, he specifically directed his electronic activity at the United States market and did in fact ship materials in the United States. Thus, GMAT has shown under the *ALS* test that Raju "directed his electronic activity into [the United States] with the manifested intent of engaging in business . . . within [the United States]," satisfying the remaining elements of the ALS test. It follows that the exercise of personal jurisdiction based on nationwide contacts under [Rule] 4(k)(2) comports with constitutional due process requirements in this case.

2. Remaining issues under Rule 4(k)(2)

The second element of Rule 4(k)(2)—that the claim arise under federal law—is readily shown. See Rule 4(k)(2), Fed R. Civ. P. GMAC's five claims, for copyright infringement, trademark infringement, dilution, cyberpiracy, and unfair competition, all arise under and are expressly predicated on federal statutes.

The final element of Rule 4(k)(2) requires a showing that the defendant is not subject to the jurisdiction of the courts of general jurisdiction of any state. See Rule 4(k)(2), Fed R. Civ. P. Federal courts have struggled in determining how fairly to assign the burden of making this showing, since it apparently places a burden on plaintiffs, who bear the burden of establishing personal jurisdiction, to "prove a negative," namely that the defendant is not subject to personal jurisdiction, in all fifty states [citations omitted]. Yet, on this record, it is readily apparent that personal jurisdiction is unavailable in any state. There are no specific contacts with any state other than Virginia, and the Virginia contacts are not sufficient to support jurisdiction in Virginia. Moreover, plaintiffs have no access to evidence that might provide more detail on Raju's possible contacts with other states; the defendant is in default and has neither appeared nor been subject to discovery. Accordingly, the proper conclusion on this record is that there is no personal jurisdiction over Raju in any district.

QUESTIONS

1. Compare the *American Buddha* court's assessment of the relevance of the plaintiff's forum residence to the *Raju* court's evaluation. Which do you find more persuasive? Why?
2. In *American Buddha*, the court localizes the injury in the New York State in order to assert jurisdiction over the person of the defendant. In *Raju*,

the court aggregated contacts throughout the U.S. in order to meet the criteria of F.R.Civ.P. 4(k)(2). When the claim arises under federal copyright law (a law of uniform national application, and of exclusive federal jurisdiction), why should federal courts have first to ascertain if minimum contacts exist in the forum state, rather than looking solely to nationwide contacts?

3. To what extent might the determination of jurisdiction over the claim affect the analysis of applicable law? (See *infra*, Part III, Chapter 8)

4. In *Metro–Goldwyn–Mayer Studios v. Grokster, Ltd.*, 243 F.Supp.2d 1073 (C.D.Cal. 2003), the district court upheld the assertion of jurisdiction in a contributory infringement claim against KaZaA, an Australian–Vanuatan entrepreneur of peer-to-peer file-sharing software that facilitated the copying of music and motion picture files by U.S. end-users. The court held that the extensive downloading engaged in by California residents using the KaZaA software met minimum contacts and fairness standards. The court also upheld California's jurisdiction on the theory that KaZaA had "targeted" California movie studios for economic harm. Finally, the court offered Fed. R. Civ. Pro. 4(k)(2) as an alternative basis for jurisdiction. What difference does it make whether personal jurisdiction is founded on state or federal grounds?

7.2.3   Forum non conveniens

The *London Films* court referred to the doctrine of *forum non conveniens*, to which a court may resort in order to decline to exercise its subject-matter jurisdiction over an action. Courts applying the doctrine inquire whether there is a more convenient foreign court in which the action might be tried. Considerations courts take into account include the applicable law (or laws), the location of the events at issue, the location and convenience of the parties and the witnesses, and the availability of another forum in which the claim maybe tried. As the *London Films* court emphasized, the need to apply a foreign law in an action over which the court has jurisdiction generally does not suffice to justify a court's abstention.

Boosey & Hawkes Music Publrs., Ltd. v. Walt Disney Co., 145 F.3d 481 (2d Cir. 1998)

[In this case, the Second Circuit forcefully reiterated the lesson of London Films. The Second Circuit reversed the district court's dismissal of a claim which would have required the court to apply 18 foreign countries' copyright laws to a copyright and contract dispute over the coverage of videocassettes by Igor Stravinsky's 1939 contract granting motion picture synchronization rights in the Rite of Spring to Disney for the soundtrack of the motion picture Fantasia.]

Foreign Copyright Claims. Invoking the doctrine of forum non conveniens, the district court dismissed Boosey's [Stravinsky's publisher's] second cause of action, which sought damages for copyright infringement deriving from Disney's sales of videocassettes of Fantasia in at least eighteen foreign countries. *Boosey & Hawkes,* 934 F. Supp. at 125. The court below concluded that these claims should be tried "in each of the nations whose copyright laws are invoked." Id. at 124. Boosey appeals, seeking remand to the district court for trial.

District courts enjoy broad discretion to decide whether to dismiss an action under the doctrine of forum non conveniens [citation omitted]. Nevertheless, this discretion is subject to "meaningful appellate review." *R. Maganlal & Co. v. M.G. Chem. Co., Inc.,* 942 F.2d 164, 167 (2d Cir. 1991). A dismissal for forum non conveniens will be upset on appeal where a defendant has failed to demonstrate that "an adequate alternative forum exists" and that "the balance of convenience tilts strongly in favor of trial in the foreign forum." Id.; see also *Manu Int'l S.A. v. Avon Products Inc.,* 641 F.2d 62, 65 (2d Cir. 1981) (emphasizing appellate obligation to enforce principle that "unless the balance is strongly in favor of the defendant, the plaintiff's choice of forum should rarely be disturbed") (quoting *Gulf Oil Corp. v. Gilbert,* 330 U.S. 501, 508, 67 S. Ct. 839, 843, 91 L. Ed. 1055 (1947)).

We recently explained that a motion to dismiss under forum non conveniens is decided in two steps [citation omitted]. The district court first must determine whether there exists an alternative forum with jurisdiction to hear the case. If so, the court then weighs the factors set out in *Gilbert,* 330 U.S. at 508-09, 67 S. Ct. at 843 ("the *Gilbert* factors"), to decide which "forum . . . will be most convenient and will best serve the ends of justice" [citation omitted].

The district court failed to consider whether there were alternative fora capable of adjudicating Boosey's copyright claims. It made no determination whether Disney was subject to jurisdiction in the various countries where the court anticipated that trial would occur and did not condition dismissal on Disney's consent to jurisdiction in those nations.

Furthermore, consideration of the *Gilbert* factors makes plain that forum non conveniens is inappropriate here. The district court must carefully weigh the private and public interests set forth in *Gilbert* and may grant the forum non conveniens motion only if these considerations strongly support dismissal [citations omitted]. Relevant private interests of the litigants include access to proof, availability of witnesses and "all other practical problems that make trial of a case easy, expeditious and inexpensive." *Gilbert*, 330 U.S. at 508, 67 S. Ct. at 843.

The private interests of the litigants favor conducting the litigation in New York where the plaintiff brought suit. Disney does not allege that a New York forum is inconvenient. The necessary evidence and witnesses are available and ready for presentation. A trial here promises to begin and end sooner than elsewhere, and would allow the parties to sort out their rights and obligations in a single proceeding. This is not a circumstance where the plaintiff's choice of forum is motivated by harassment. *Gilbert*, 330 U.S. 507, 67 S. Ct. at 842. Indeed, it seems rather more likely that Disney's motion seeks to split the suit into 18 parts in 18 nations, complicate the suit, delay it, and render it more expensive.

In dismissing the cases, the court relied on the "public interests" identified in *Gilbert*. It reasoned that the trial would require extensive application of foreign copyright and antitrust jurisprudence, bodies of law involving strong national interests best litigated "in their respective countries." The court concluded as well that these necessary inquiries into foreign law would place an undue burden on our judicial system."

While reluctance to apply foreign law is a valid factor favoring dismissal under *Gilbert*, standing alone it does not justify dismissal. See *Piper Aircraft Co. v. Reyno*, 454 U.S. 235, 260 n.29, 102 S. Ct. 252, 268 n.29, 70 L. Ed. 2d 419 (1968) ("The need to apply foreign law . . . . alone is not sufficient to warrant dismissal."). District courts must weigh this factor along with the other relevant considerations. See id.; see also *Manu Int'l*, 641 F.2d at 68 ("Proof of foreign law . . . is not alone enough to push the balance of convenience strongly in favor of the defendant. The other forum non conveniens factors must do that."). Numerous countervailing considerations suggest that New York venue is proper: defendant is a U.S. corporation, the 1939 agreement was substantially negotiated and signed in New York, and the agreement is governed by New York law. The plaintiff has chosen New York and the trial is ready to proceed here. Everything before us suggests that trial would be more "easy, expeditious and inexpensive" in the district court than dispersed to 18 foreign nations [citations omitted]. We therefore vacate the dismissal of the foreign copyright claims and remand for trial.

QUESTIONS

1. Why does Boosey favor the New York venue? Why does Disney contest this venue on the ground of the *forum non conveniens*?
2. What are the arguments of the court in support of its refusal to dismiss? Would the solution be different if Disney had been able to prove that another forum had jurisdiction over the entirety of the claim?
3. A New York publisher discovers that a French website is offering free downloads of its latest published book. Would a U.S. federal court have personal jurisdiction over the French website operator? Could the French defendant contest the U.S. venue on the ground of *forum non conveniens*, pleading that the French courts are more appropriate for pursuit of the action? Does it make a difference if the website proposes to deliver tangible copies, and the New York publisher orders one copy for delivery to its office in NY?

7.3 The E.U. approach (a study of the Brussels I Regulation Recast)

7.3.1 General rules

The Brussels Regulation Recast is applicable in all E.U. member states (with the exception of Denmark), provided that the defendant has its domicile in a E.U. member state. Thus, for litigation between a U.S. plaintiff and a French defendant before an E.U. member state's courts, judicial competence in all E.U. members would depend on the European Regulation. On the contrary, if the U.S. party is the defendant, and if the French party wants to sue in an E.U. country, the Regulation does not apply. The determination of the court's competence to hear the case would then depend on each national court's domestic private international law.

The Brussels Regulation retains the general jurisdiction of the courts of the country of the domicile of the defendant. The Regulation also designates some optional bases of jurisdiction; the most disputed being jurisdiction over tort claims. For those claims, the plaintiff has an option between alternative bases of jurisdiction; the availability of alternative bases of jurisdiction allows the plaintiff to choose the basis most suitable for his case. But the Regulation eliminates alternative bases in two instances: article 24 provides for exclusive jurisdiction over claims concerning registered rights (patents and trademarks) and when the parties have signed a choice of court agreement. If the court does have jurisdiction, any discretion to desist from exercising jurisdiction on the ground of the *forum non conveniens* doctrine is prohibited under the Brussels Regulation.

Regulation (EU) No 1215/2012 of the European Parliament and of the Council of 12 December 2012 on jurisdiction and the recognition and enforcement of judgments in civil and commercial matters (recast)

SECTION 1 – General provisions

Article 4

1. Subject to this Regulation, persons domiciled in a Member State shall, whatever their nationality, be sued in the courts of that Member State.

2. Persons who are not nationals of the Member State in which they are domiciled shall be governed by the rules of jurisdiction applicable to nationals of that Member State.

SECTION 6 – Exclusive jurisdiction

Article 24

The following courts of a Member State shall have exclusive jurisdiction, regardless of the domicile of the parties:

. . .

(4) in proceedings concerned with the registration or validity of patents, trade marks, designs, or other similar rights required to be deposited or registered, irrespective of whether the issue is raised by way of an action or as a defence, the courts of the Member State in which the deposit or registration has been applied for, has taken place or is under the terms of an instrument of the Union or an international convention deemed to have taken place.

Without prejudice to the jurisdiction of the European Patent Office under the Convention on the Grant of European Patents, signed at Munich on 5 October 1973, the courts of each Member State shall have exclusive jurisdiction in proceedings concerned with the registration or validity of any European patent granted for that Member State;

General Provisions
Article 62

1. In order to determine whether a party is domiciled in the Member State whose courts are seised of a matter, the court shall apply its internal law.

2. If a party is not domiciled in the Member State whose courts are seised of the matter, then, in order to determine whether the party is domiciled in another Member State, the court shall apply the law of that Member State.

Article 63

1. For the purposes of this Regulation, a company or other legal person or association of natural or legal persons is domiciled at the place where it has its:

(a) statutory seat, or
(b) central administration, or
(c) principal place of business.

2. For the purposes of the United Kingdom and Ireland "statutory seat" means the registered office or, where there is no such office anywhere, the place of incorporation or, where there is no such place anywhere, the place under the law of which the formation took place.

3. In order to determine whether a trust is domiciled in the Member State whose courts are seised of the matter, the court shall apply its rules of private international law.

QUESTION

Article 62(1) directs the E.U. member state forum to "apply its internal law" in order to ascertain whether a party is domiciled in the forum. Article 63 (3) directs the forum to "apply its rules of private international law" to ascertain whether a trust is domiciled in the forum. What is the difference?

LucasFilm Ltd & Ors v. Ainsworth & Anor, [2011] UKSC 39

[This case concerned the alleged infringement of the design of the Helmet of the Imperial Stormtroopers in the movie Star Wars Episode IV – A new hope. The plaintiff is Lucasfilm (regrouping three companies related to Lucas, two being from U.S. and one from U.K.). The defendant is a U.K. domiciliary who distributed copies of the helmet in the U.K. and the U.S.. One of the issues was whether a U.K. court has jurisdiction over claims alleging infringements committed in the U.S. The Brussels Regulation was applicable because of the U.K. domicile of the defendant.]

Lord Walker and Lord Collins (with whom Lord Phillips and Lady Hale agree)

Part II: Whether a claim against a defendant domiciled in England for infringement of a foreign copyright is justiciable

The decision of the Court of Appeal and the issue on the appeal

51.   The issue on this aspect of the appeal is a narrow one, whether the English court may exercise jurisdiction in a claim against persons domiciled in England for infringement of copyright committed outside the European Union in breach of the copyright law of that country. That issue has raised two questions. The first question is whether a claim for infringement of a foreign copyright is non-justiciable. The second question only arises if the answer to the first question is in the affirmative: the question would then arise whether the English court is in any event required to accept jurisdiction by virtue of Council Regulation (EC) No 44/2001 on jurisdiction and the enforcement of judgments in civil and commercial matters (the Brussels I Regulation), article 2 [recast 4], which provides that, subject to the terms of the Regulation, persons domiciled in a Member State shall be sued in the courts of that Member State.

. . .

The act of state doctrine

82.   In the United States the act of state doctrine has been used as a basis for non-justiciability of foreign trademark and patent rights. The Court of Appeals for the Second Circuit held in *Vanity Fair Mills Inc v. T Eaton Co Ltd*, 234 F 2d 633, 646 (2d Cir 1956), cert den, 352 US 871 (1956) that a United States federal court should not rule on the validity of a Canadian trade mark because (among other reasons) the act of state doctrine precluded determination of the acts of a foreign sovereign done within its own territory, and to rule on validity would create conflicts with Canadian administrative and judicial officers.

83.   The act of state doctrine was also invoked more recently in the United States as a ground for refusing to allow the addition of claims for infringement of parallel foreign patents to claims for infringement of United States patents, in litigation in which validity was in issue: *Voda v. Cordis Corp*, 476 F 3d 887 (Fed Cir 2007). The majority of the court (Gajarsa CJ, Prost CJ concurring) said (at p 904):

> "the act of state doctrine may make the exercise of supplemental jurisdiction over foreign patent infringement claims fundamentally unfair. As "a 'principle of decision binding on federal and state courts alike,' " the act of state doctrine "requires that, in the process of deciding, the acts of foreign sovereigns taken within their own jurisdictions shall be deemed valid." *W S Kirkpatrick & Co, Inc v. Envtl Tectonics Corp, Int'l*, 493 U.S. 400, 406, 409 . . . (1990) . . . In this case, none of the parties or amicus curiae have persuaded us that the grant of a patent by a sovereign is not an act of state. . . . Therefore, assuming arguendo that the act of state doctrine applies, the doctrine would prevent our courts from inquiring into the validity of a foreign patent grant and require our courts to adjudicate patent claims regardless of validity or enforceability."

84.   The act of state doctrine was held not to apply where, in a dispute arising out of a patent licence, the issue was one of interpretation of the patent, and not of validity: *Fairchild Semiconductor Corpn v. Third Dimension (3D) Semiconductor Inc*, 589 F Supp 2d 84, 98 (D Me 2008).

85.   So also, in the case of copyright infringement, it has been held that the act of state doctrine has no application because there is no need to pass on the validity of acts of foreign government officials. In *London Film Productions, Ltd v. Intercontinental Communications, Inc*, 580 F Supp 47, 49 (SDNY 1984) the District Court held that the plaintiff could sue for infringement of its foreign copyright in films. The court accepted Professor Nimmer's view that the act of state doctrine was not engaged: in adjudicating an infringement action under a foreign copyright law there was no need to pass upon the validity of acts of foreign governmental officials, since foreign copyright laws did not generally incorporate administrative formalities which had to be satisfied to create or perfect a copyright. In *Frink America, Inc v. Champion Road Machinery Ltd*, 961 F Supp 398 (NDNY 1997) it was held that dismissal of a claim for infringement of Canadian copyright was not warranted because US and Canada were signatories to the Berne Convention, which bars administrative formalities, and therefore there was no question of passing on acts of foreign government. Contrast *ITSI TV Productions, Inc v California Authority of Racing Fairs, Inc*, 785 F Supp 854, 866 (ED Cal 1992).

. . .

87.   It has been said that the grant of a national patent is "an exercise of national sovereignty" (Jenard Report on the Brussels Convention (OJ 1979 C59 pp 1, 36), and the European Court has emphasised that the issue of patents necessitates the involvement of the national administrative authorities (Case C-4/03 *Gesellschaft für Antriebstechnik mbH & Co KG (GAT) v Lamellen und Kupplungsbau Beteiligungs KG (LuK)* [2006] ECR I-6509, para [23]). But in England the foreign act of state doctrine has not been applied to any acts other than foreign legislation or governmental acts of officials such as requisition, and it should not today be regarded as an impediment to an action for infringement of foreign intellectual property rights, even if validity of a grant is in issue, simply because the action calls into question the decision of a foreign official.

European law and intellectual property rights

88.   Two important developments in European law have undermined any argument that there is a substantial policy reason for the view that actions for infringement of intellectual property rights cannot be brought outside the State in which they are granted or subsist.

89.   First, article 22(4) [24(4) Recast] of the Brussels I Regulation (formerly article 16(4) of the Brussels Convention) provides that, in proceedings concerned with the registration or validity of patents, trade marks, designs, or other similar rights required to be deposited or registered, the courts of the Member State in which the deposit or registration has been applied for, has taken place or is deemed to have taken place, have exclusive jurisdiction irrespective of the domicile of the defendant. This is an exception to the general domicile rule of jurisdiction, and has to be construed strictly. It applies only to intellectual property rights which are required to be deposited or registered, and does not apply to infringement actions in which there is no issue as to validity.

90.   The European Court has emphasised that article 22(4) [24(4) Recast] is only concerned with cases in which a question of validity arises. It has made the following points: the basis for article 22(4) [24(4) Recast] is that the courts of the Contracting State in which the deposit or registration has been applied for or made are best placed to adjudicate upon cases in which the dispute itself concerns the validity of the patent or the existence of the deposit or registration; but it does not apply in proceedings which do not concern the validity of the intellectual property right or the existence of the

deposit or registration and these matters are not disputed by the parties, for example, a patent infringement action, in which the question of the validity of the patent allegedly infringed is not called into question; it would apply if the question of validity were raised by way of defence in infringement proceedings; the concern for the sound administration of justice is all the more important in the field of patents since, given the specialised nature of this area, a number of Contracting States have set up a system of specific judicial protection, to ensure that these types of cases are dealt with by specialised courts; the exclusive jurisdiction is also justified by the fact that the issue of patents necessitates the involvement of the national administrative authorities: Case C-4/03 *Gesellschaft für Antriebstechnik mbH & Co KG (GAT) v Lamellen und Kupplungsbau Beteiligungs KG (LuK)* [2006] ECR I-6509, para [16] et seq.

91. Article 22(4) [24(4) Recast] does not in terms apply to intellectual property rights outside the Member States. It is not necessary for present purposes to delve into the question whether it may be applied by analogy (or "reflexively") to non-Member States. What it shows is that there is a fundamental distinction between intellectual property claims which involve the registration or validity of intellectual property rights which are required to be deposited or registered, and those which are not.

92. The second relevant piece of European legislation does not apply to the present proceedings because it came into force only on 11 January 2009, but it also shows clearly that there is no European public policy against the litigation of foreign intellectual property rights. Regulation (EC) No 864/2007 of the European Parliament and of the Council on the law applicable to non-contractual obligations (Rome II) applies wherever in the world a tort was committed. It plainly envisages that actions may be brought in Member States for infringement of foreign intellectual property rights, including copyright. Recital (26) states:

> "Regarding infringements of intellectual property rights, the universally acknowledged principle of the lex loci protectionis should be preserved. For the purposes of this Regulation, the term 'intellectual property rights' should be interpreted as meaning, for instance, copyright, related rights, the sui generis right for the protection of databases and industrial property rights."

93. As regards choice of law, article 8 provides:

> "Infringement of intellectual property rights

1. The law applicable to a non-contractual obligation arising from an infringement of an intellectual property right shall be the law of the country for which protection is claimed.
2. In the case of a non-contractual obligation arising from an infringement of a unitary Community intellectual property right, the law applicable shall, for any question that is not governed by the relevant Community instrument, be the law of the country in which the act of infringement was committed.

. . ."

Other proposals

94.   These developments in European law are mirrored in proposals within the American Law Institute, which favour adjudication of foreign intellectual property rights, at least where issues of validity are not in issue. The American Law Institute's Intellectual Property: Principles Governing Jurisdiction, Choice of Law, and Judgments in Transnational Disputes (2008) apply to transnational civil disputes which involve (inter alia) copyrights, patents, trademarks, and other intellectual property rights (section 102) and note the controversy over the question of the justiciability of intellectual property rights (Reporters' Notes 4 and 5). Section 211 provides that the court must have subject-matter and personal jurisdiction. Comment b states:

> "There is substantial sentiment that issues regarding the validity of a registered right, particularly a patent right, should be adjudicated in the courts of the State in which the right is registered. Only this State is competent to cancel the registration. . . . Nonetheless, the Principles do not include a blanket prohibition on the adjudication of matters involving a foreign State's registered rights, because separating adjudication of validity from infringement can have substantive ramifications. Separate resolutions can prevent a court from hearing all of the evidence relevant to the action and from using its understanding of how a technology is utilized to inform its decision on the scope of the right. Bifurcating validity and infringement can also increase the parties' costs."

95.   The draft Principles for Conflict of Laws in Intellectual Property, 2011, prepared by the European Union Max Planck Group on Conflict of Laws in Intellectual Property contain no specific provision for actions for infringement of foreign rights abroad, but it is implicit in the Principles that they envisage such actions: (a) the primary rule of jurisdiction in the Principles is habitual residence (Part 2, section 1), and (b) the primary law applicable

to infringement is the law of the State for which protection is sought (Part 3, section 6).

. . .

99.   In *Pearce v Ove Arup Partnership Ltd* [2000] Ch 403 Mr Pearce claimed that the defendants had infringed his English and Dutch copyrights in his drawings and plans for a town hall by copying them in designing the Kunsthal in Rotterdam. There was no issue about existence or validity of the copyrights. The sole factual question was whether his drawings and plans had been copied. On the question of the justiciability of the claim for infringement of the Dutch copyright, the court had personal jurisdiction over the defendants by virtue of their domicile in England (because they were additional parties for the purposes of what is now article 6(1) [Article 8(1)] of the Brussels I Regulation). It was not suggested that what is now article 22(4) [24(4) Recast] applied, since the proceedings were for infringement of copyright and no question of deposit or registration arose. The effect of what is now article 22(1)) [24(1) Recast] was that the Moçambique rule no longer applied within the Member States, and that where proceedings in relation to intellectual property fell outside what is now article 22(1) [24(1) Recast], the general rules of jurisdiction applied, and there was no room for an objection of non-justiciability. The common law rule of choice of law applied because the relevant events occurred before section 11 of the Private International law (Miscellaneous Provisions) Act 1995 came into force in 1996, but (as mentioned above) the court disapplied the first limb of the rule in *Phillips v. Eyre* in favour of the law of the country which with respect to that issue had the most significant relationship with the occurrence and with the parties, which was Dutch law.

Foreign authorities

100.   In the United States the local action [under which foreign property right claims, including IP, are not justiciable] rule has been used as a ground for refusal to add claims for infringement of foreign patents to a United States patent infringement action: *Voda v Cordis Corp*, 476 F 3d 887 (Fed Cir 2007), discussed above in connection with the act of state doctrine. The majority said (at pp. 901–902):

> "the local action doctrine informs us that exercising supplemental jurisdiction in this case appears to violate our own norms of what sovereigns ordinarily expect. Courts derived the local action doctrine from the distinction between local and transitory actions beginning with *Livingston v. Jefferson*, written by Justice John Marshall riding Circuit.

15 F. Cas. 660 (C.C.D.Va. 1811). . . . [T]he local action doctrine served to prevent courts from adjudicating claims for trespass or title to real property.
The territorial limits of the rights granted by patents are similar to those conferred by land grants. A patent right is limited by the metes and bounds of the jurisdictional territory that granted the right to exclude. . . .
Therefore, a patent right to exclude only arises from the legal right granted and recognized by the sovereign within whose territory the right is located. It would be incongruent to allow the sovereign power of one to be infringed or limited by another sovereign's extension of its jurisdiction. . . ."

101.   Claims for infringement of foreign copyright have been held in New Zealand and South Africa to be non-justiciable. In *Atkinson Footwear Ltd v Hodgskin International Services Ltd*, (1994) 31 IPR 186 (High Court of New Zealand) Tipping J followed the *Tyburn Productions Ltd* decision and in *Gallo Africa Ltd v Sting Music (Pty) Ltd* [2010] ZASCA 96, 2010 (6) SA 329 the Supreme Court of Appeal of South Africa applied the decision of the Court of Appeal in the present case. But in *KK Sony Computer Entertainment v Van Veen* (2006) 71 IPR 179 MacKenzie J in the High Court of New Zealand declined to follow *Atkinson Footwear* and held that a claim for infringement of foreign intellectual property rights (in that case breach of United Kingdom and Hong Kong copyright in PlayStation 2) was justiciable if no question of the existence or validity of those rights was in issue.

Conclusions on the justiciability question

. . .

103.   As recorded by Mann J, the trial judge ([2008] EWHC 1878 (Ch), [2009] FSR 103, at [272]), the dispute relating to the United States copyright was as follows. The subsistence of copyright and ownership of all drawings was accepted by Mr Ainsworth, although the existence of some drawings was disputed. Infringement was denied so far as some drawings are concerned, on the footing that they were not copied, or not copied closely enough. Because three-dimensional items were produced, it was argued that under United States law there was no infringement because copyright in the drawings would not be infringed by the production of a utilitarian or functional device. Lucasfilm claimed copyright in physical helmets and armour, which was disputed by Mr Ainsworth because they were said to be functional or utilitarian. According to the judge, at one stage it had also been suggested that if there was copyright it was vested in Mr Ainsworth and not in Lucasfilm, but this point was not ultimately persisted in.

104.   Although at trial the infringement arguments sometimes merged into a subsistence argument, the substantial dispute has always been about the ownership of the relevant copyrights and their infringement rather than about their subsistence.

105.   Were these claims justiciable? Mr Ainsworth argued that the principle behind the [local action rule] still subsists and applies to claims for infringement of all foreign intellectual property rights, including copyright, because such claims are essentially "local" and must be brought in the place where the rights have been created, irrespective as to whether there is any claim to title. But to describe the claims as "local" is simply to beg the question whether as a matter of law they must be brought in the place where the rights originate and are effective.

106.   We have come to the firm conclusion that, in the case of a claim for infringement of copyright of the present kind, the claim is one over which the English court has jurisdiction, provided that there is a basis for in personam jurisdiction over the defendant, or, to put it differently, the claim is justiciable. . . .

108.   [. . .] There is no room for the application of the act of state doctrine in relation to copyright in this case, even if actions of officials involved with registration and grant of intellectual property rights were acts of state. The requirement to apply for copyright registration in the United States is limited to the "copyright in any United States work" which in practice means that published works first published outside the United States are exempted from compliance with US registration provisions. In the present case the copyrights were treated as United States works and were registered. Registration is a pre-requisite to proceedings in the United States: United States Copyright Act, section 411. But the unchallenged evidence before the judge in this case was that registration was not a prerequisite to subsistence but only to suit, and it was possible to register at the time of suit. Consequently the provision is purely procedural. That has been confirmed recently by the United States Supreme Court, which has held that federal courts have subject matter jurisdiction to approve a class action settlement where some of the authors are not registered, because section 411 is not a jurisdictional rule: *Reed Elsevier Inc v. Muchnick*, 130 S Ct 1237 (2010).

109.   There is no doubt that the modern trend is in favour of the enforcement of foreign intellectual property rights. First, article 22(4) of the Brussels I Regulation only assigns exclusive jurisdiction to the country where the right originates in cases which are concerned with registration or validity of rights

which are "required to be deposited or registered" and does not apply to infringement actions in which there is no issue as to validity. This can rarely, if ever, apply to copyright. Second, the Rome II Regulation also plainly envisages the litigation of foreign intellectual property rights and, third, the professional and academic bodies which have considered the issue, the American Law Institute and the Max Planck Institute, clearly favour them, at any rate where issues of validity are not engaged.

110.   There are no issues of policy which militate against the enforcement of foreign copyright. States have an interest in the international recognition and enforcement of their copyrights, as the Berne Convention on the International Union for the Protection of Literary and Artistic Works shows. . . . It was also said by the Court of Appeal that enforcement of foreign intellectual property law might involve a clash of policies such that a defendant may be restrained by injunction from doing acts in this country which are lawful in this country. But such an injunction will be granted only if the acts are anticipated to achieve fruition in another country, and there is no objection in principle to such an injunction. Nor is there any objection in principle, as the Court of Appeal thought, to a restraint on acts in another country. Extra-territorial injunctions are commonly granted here against defendants subject to the in personam jurisdiction. The Court of Appeal also thought that it was relevant that there was no international regime for the mutual recognition of copyright jurisdiction and of copyright judgments, but this is no reason for the English court refusing to take jurisdiction over an English defendant in a claim for breach of foreign copyright.

. . .

QUESTIONS

1. Why does the court quote U.S. case law? What about the ALI Principles? Why would the solution have been different had it been based on trademark law?
2. Imagine that the defendant had distributed copies of the helmet only in the U.S., would the claim have been justiciable in the U.K. courts? Imagine the opposite situation: the plaintiff is from U.K., the defendant from U.S. and the copies are distributed in the U.K., would the claim have been justiciable in the U.S.?

7.3.2   Multiple defendants

Regulation (EU) No 1215/2012 of the European Parliament and of the Council of 12 December 2012 on jurisdiction and the

recognition and enforcement of judgments in civil and commercial matters (recast) (Brussels Regulation Recast)

Article 8

A person domiciled in a Member State may also be sued:

(1) where he is one of a number of defendants, in the courts for the place where any one of them is domiciled, provided the claims are so closely connected that it is expedient to hear and determine them together to avoid the risk of irreconcilable judgments resulting from separate proceedings;

. . .

QUESTION

Does article 8 apply to a co-defendant whose domicile is in a non-EU Country?

C-539/03 Roche Nederland BV and Others v. Frederick Primus and Others ECLI:EU:C:2006:458 [2006]

[This case concerned the application of article 8 in order to consolidate a patent infringement action against multiple defendants at the place of the domicile of one of the defendants. The infringed patent was a European patent granted by the Convention on the Grant of European Patent (Munich Convention). The aim of the Munich Convention, not limited to E.U. members, is to harmonize the criteria for granting a patent. Once granted, the European Patent devolves into national titles. As such, the protection given is still a national one. In this decision, the court expressed a restricted interpretation of the notion of irreconcilable judgments, excluding the application of article 8.]

13   Drs Primus and Goldenberg, who are domiciled in the United States of America, are the proprietors of European patent No 131 627.

14   On 24 March 1997, they brought an action before the Rechtbank te s'-Gravenhage against Roche Nederland BV, a company established in the Netherlands, and eight other companies in the Roche group established in the United States of America, Belgium, Germany, France, the United Kingdom, Switzerland, Austria and Sweden ('Roche and Others'). The

applicants claimed that those companies had all infringed the rights conferred on them by the patent of which they are the proprietors. That alleged infringement consisted in the placing on the market of immuno-assay kits in countries where the defendants are established.

. . .

18   By those questions, which it is appropriate to consider together, the national court asks essentially whether Article 6(1) [8.1 recast] of the Brussels Convention must be interpreted as meaning that it is to apply to European patent infringement proceedings involving a number of companies established in various Contracting States in respect of acts committed in one or more of those States and, in particular, where those companies, which belong to the same group, have acted in an identical or similar manner in accordance with a common policy elaborated by one of them.

26   . . . in order that decisions may be regarded as contradictory it is not sufficient that there be a divergence in the outcome of the dispute, but that divergence must also arise in the context of the same situation of law and fact.

27   However, in the situation referred to by the national court in its first question referred for a preliminary ruling, that is in the case of European patent infringement proceedings involving a number of companies established in various Contracting States in respect of acts committed in one or more of those States, the existence of the same situation of fact cannot be inferred, since the defendants are different and the infringements they are accused of, committed in different Contracting States, are not the same.

28   Possible divergences between decisions given by the courts concerned would not arise in the context of the same factual situation.

29   Furthermore, although the Munich Convention lays down common rules on the grant of European patents, it is clear from Articles 2(2) and 64(1) of that convention that such a patent continues to be governed by the national law of each of the Contracting States for which it has been granted.

30   In particular, it is apparent from Article 64(3) of the Munich Convention that any action for infringement of a European patent must be examined in the light of the relevant national law in force in each of the States for which it has been granted.

31 It follows that, where infringement proceedings are brought before a number of courts in different Contracting States in respect of a European patent granted in each of those States, against defendants domiciled in those States in respect of acts allegedly committed in their territory, any divergences between the decisions given by the courts concerned would not arise in the context of the same legal situation.

32 Any diverging decisions could not, therefore, be treated as contradictory.

QUESTIONS

To what extent is the ruling of the *Roche* decision applicable to the following case:
A company in Luxembourg reproduces and distributes copies of Indian movies, without authorization from the Indian producer. These copies are distributed locally in other E.U. countries by local entities, subsidiaries of the Luxembourg company. To what extent will article 8 allow an Indian copyright owner to adjudicate in one country claims for all distributions made by local entities? What may be the consequence of the *Roche* ruling?

C-145/10 Eva-Maria Painer v. Standard VerlagsGmbH and Others ECLI:EU:C:2013:138 [2011]

[We have already encountered the *Painer* case (see *supra*, Part I, Chapter 2.1.4, pp. 110–12; Part II, Chapter 5.5.5, p. 485). The case concerned the unauthorized reproduction of a photograph by an Austrian newspaper and by a German newspaper. The issue at stake was whether the courts of the domicile of one defendant were also competent to decide on the infringement claim made against the other defendant.]

43 . . . the Handelsgericht Wien decided to stay the proceedings and to refer the following questions to the Court of Justice for a preliminary ruling:

'(1) Is Article 6(1) [8(1) Recast] of Regulation No 44/2001] to be interpreted as meaning that its application and therefore joint legal proceedings are not precluded where actions brought against several defendants for copyright infringements identical in substance are based on differing national legal grounds the essential elements of which are nevertheless identical in substance – such as applies to all European States in proceedings for a prohibitory injunction, not based on fault, in claims for reasonable remuneration for copyright infringements and in claims in damages for unlawful exploitation?'

. . .

72   By its first question, the referring court asks, in essence, whether Article 6(1) [8(1) Recast] of Regulation No 44/2001 must be interpreted as precluding its application if actions against several defendants for substantially identical copyright infringements are brought on national legal grounds which vary according to the Member States concerned.

73   The rule of jurisdiction laid down in Article 6(1) [8(1) Recast] of Regulation No 44/2001 provides that a person may, where he is one of a number of defendants, be sued in the courts for the place where any one of them is domiciled, provided the claims are so closely connected that it is expedient to hear and determine them together to avoid the risk of irreconcilable judgments resulting from separate proceedings.

. . .

76   It is not apparent from the wording of Article 6(1) [8(1) Recast] of Regulation No 44/2001 that the conditions laid down for application of that provision include a requirement that the actions brought against different defendants should have identical legal bases [citations omitted].

. . .

79   In that regard, the Court has stated that, in order for judgments to be regarded as irreconcilable within the meaning of Article 6(1) [8(1) Recast] of Regulation No 44/2001, it is not sufficient that there be a divergence in the outcome of the dispute, but that divergence must also arise in the same situation of fact and law [citations omitted].

80   However, in assessing whether there is a connection between different claims, that is to say a risk of irreconcilable judgments if those claims were determined separately, the identical legal bases of the actions brought is only one relevant factor among others. It is not an indispensable requirement for the application of Article 6(1) [8(1) Recast] of Regulation No 44/2001 [citations omitted].

81   Thus, a difference in legal basis between the actions brought against the various defendants, does not, in itself, preclude the application of Article 6(1) [8(1) Recast] of Regulation No 44/2001, provided however that it was foreseeable by the defendants that they might be sued in the Member State where at least one of them is domiciled [citations omitted].

82   That reasoning is stronger if, as in the main proceedings, the national laws on which the actions against the various defendants are based are, in the referring court's view, substantially identical.

83   It is, in addition, for the referring court to assess, in the light of all the elements of the case, whether there is a connection between the different claims brought before it, that is to say a risk of irreconcilable judgments if those claims were determined separately. For that purpose, the fact that defendants against whom a copyright holder alleges substantially identical infringements of his copyright did or did not act independently may be relevant.

84   In the light of the foregoing considerations, the answer to the first question is that Article 6(1) of Regulation No 44/2001 [8.1 Recast] must be interpreted as not precluding its application solely because actions against several defendants for substantially identical copyright infringements are brought on national legal grounds which vary according to the Member States concerned. It is for the referring court to assess, in the light of all the elements of the case, whether there is a risk of irreconcilable judgments if those actions were determined separately.

QUESTIONS

Would you say that *Painer* overruled *Roche*? What does the expression "substantially identical" mean? Would you say that in the previous hypothetical following *Roche*, concerning the Indian films, the national laws are substantially identical? If yes, may the defendant choose the domicile of any defendant in order to decide the entire case?

C-616/10 Solvay SA v. Honeywell Fluorine Products EuropeBV and Others ECLI:EU:C:2012:445 [2012]

12   On 6 March 2009, Solvay, the proprietor of European patent EP 0 858 440, brought an action in the Rechtbank 's-Gravenhage for infringement of the national parts of that patent, as in force in Denmark, Ireland, Greece, Luxembourg, Austria, Portugal, Finland, Sweden, Liechtenstein and Switzerland, against the Honeywell companies for marketing a product HFC-245 fa, manufactured by Honeywell International Inc. and identical to the product covered by that patent.

13   Specifically, Solvay accuses Honeywell Flourine Products Europe BV and Honeywell Europe NV of performing the reserved actions in the whole

of Europe and Honeywell Belgium NV of performing the reserved actions in Northern and Central Europe.

14   In the course of its action for infringement, on 9 December 2009 Solvay also lodged an interim claim against the Honeywell companies, seeking provisional relief in the form of a cross-border prohibition against infringement until a decision had been made in the main proceedings.

15   In the interim proceedings, the Honeywell companies raised the defence of invalidity of the national parts of the patent concerned without, however, having brought or even declared their intention of bringing proceedings for the annulment of the national parts of that patent, and without contesting the competence of the Dutch court to hear both the main proceedings and the interim proceedings.

. . .

The first question

17   By its first question, the referring court asks, in essence, whether Article 6(1) [8(1) Recast] of Regulation No 44/2001 must be interpreted as meaning that a situation where two or more companies established in different Member States, in proceedings pending before a court of one of those Member States, are each separately accused of committing an infringement of the same national part of a European patent which is in force in yet another Member State by virtue of their performance of reserved actions with regard to the same product, is capable of leading to 'irreconcilable judgments' resulting from separate proceedings as referred to in that provision.

18   First of all, it must be observed that Article 6(1) [8(1) Recast] of Regulation No 44/2001 provides, in order to avoid irreconcilable judgments resulting from separate proceedings, that a defendant may be sued, where he is one of a number of defendants, in the courts for the place where any one of them is domiciled, provided the claims are so closely connected that it is expedient to hear and determine them together.

. . .

24   The Court has however stated in this connection that, in order for judgments to be regarded as at risk of being irreconcilable within the meaning of Article 6(1) [8(1) Recast] of Regulation No 44/2001, it is not sufficient that there be a divergence in the outcome of the dispute, but that divergence must

also arise in the same situation of fact and law (see Case C-539/03 *Roche Nederland and Others* [2006] ECR I-6535, paragraph 26; [citations omitted] and *Painer*, paragraph 79).

. . .

27   It follows from the specific features of a case such as that in the main proceedings that potential divergences in the outcome of the proceedings are likely to arise in the same situation of fact and law, so that it is possible that they will culminate in irreconcilable judgments resulting from separate proceedings.

28   As the Advocate General observed in point 25 of his Opinion, were Article 6(1) [8(1) Recast] of Regulation No 44/2001 not applicable, two courts would each have to examine the alleged infringements in the light of the different national legislation governing the various national parts of the European patent alleged to have been infringed. They would, for instance, be called upon to assess according to the same Finnish law the infringement of the Finnish part of the European patent by the Honeywell companies as a result of the marketing of an identical infringing product in Finland.

29   In order to assess, in a situation such as that at issue in the main proceedings, whether there is a connection between the different claims brought before it and thus whether there is a risk of irreconcilable judgments if those claims were determined separately, it is for the national court to take into account, inter alia, the dual fact that, first, the defendants in the main proceeding are each separately accused of committing the same infringements with respect to the same products and, secondly, such infringments were committed in the same Member States, so that they adversely affect the same national parts of the European patent at issue.

30   In the light of the foregoing, the answer to the first question is that Article 6(1) [8(1) Recast] of Regulation No 44/2001 must be interpreted as meaning that a situation where two or more companies from different Member States, in proceedings pending before a court of one of those Member States, are each separately accused of committing an infringement of the same national part of a European patent which is in force in yet another Member State by virtue of their performance of reserved actions with regard to the same product, is capable of leading to 'irreconcilable judgments' resulting from separate proceedings as referred to in that provision. It is for the referring court to assess whether such a risk exists, taking into account all the relevant information in the file.

QUESTIONS

1. To what extent, if any, are the facts different here than in *Painer* or *Roche*? Does *Solvay* follow the path drawn by *Painer*?
2. Suppose that following *Roche*, the copies made by the Luxembourg company are no longer distributed locally but in all E.U. member States by three subsidiaries of the Luxembourg company, one being in France, the other in Germany and the last one in the U.K. Does article 8 apply?

7.3.3 Jurisdiction over tort claims

Regulation (EU) No 1215/2012 of the European Parliament and of the Council of 12 December 2012 on jurisdiction and the recognition and enforcement of judgments in civil and commercial matters (recast) (Brussels Regulation Recast)

SECTION 2 – Special jurisdiction

Article 7

A person domiciled in a Member State may be sued in another Member State: ... (2) in matters relating to tort, delict or quasi-delict, in the courts for the place where the harmful event occurred or may occur;. . .

This rule has given rise to questions concerning its application to intellectual property and more specifically to copyright. The more difficult issue concerned the application of the connecting factor for ubiquitous infringement. If the infringement spans multiple countries, in which countri(es) may it be said that the harmful event occurred? This issue, which already arose in the context of older technologies implicating cross-border communications, such as radio, television, and satellite transmissions, has become particularly vexing with the advent of the Internet. Another difficult issue concerned the scope of this alternate ground of jurisdiction and whether a declaratory judgment could be characterized as raising 'matters relating to the tort'.

Infringement actions

While the European Court of Justice (ECJ) had confronted the problem of determining the connecting factor in cases involving transnational torts, notably in the case of a defamation claim arising out of an internationally distributed newspaper (see immediately below), it seems that the arrival of the

Internet has blurred the line the court initially drew, leading the court in later cases to distinguish between the media used and the right infringed.

Pre-Internet cases

The main case decided by the ECJ concerned a defamation action brought by a U.K. national against a French newspaper. The court addressed the determination of the place of the harmful event when the tort is committed by a newspaper distributed in more than one country.

C-68/93 Fiona Shevill and Others v. Presse Alliance SA ECLI:EU:C:1995:61 [1995]

[The case concerned the interpretation of "place where the harmful event occurred" in article 5 (3) Brussels I [7(2) Recast]. Ms Shevill, an English national and domiciliary, worked in a currency exchange office in France at the time the police searched the premises. Press Alliance SA, a press company registered in France, published an article about the police operation naming Ms Shevill and her employer Chequepoint. "Miss Shevill [and] Chequepoint [. . .] considered that the [. . .] article was defamatory in that it suggested that they were part of a drug-trafficking network for which they had laundered money. On 17 October 1989 they issued a writ in the High Court of England and Wales claiming damages for libel from Presse Alliance SA".]

19   It is settled case-law [citations omitted] that that rule of special jurisdiction, the choice of which is a matter for the plaintiff, is based on the existence of a particularly close connecting factor between the dispute and courts other than those of the State of the defendant' s domicile which justifies the attribution of jurisdiction to those courts for reasons relating to the sound administration of justice and the efficacious conduct of proceedings.

20   It must also be emphasized that in *Mines de Potasse d'Alsace* the Court held (at paragraphs 24 and 25) that, where the place of the happening of the event which may give rise to liability in tort, delict or quasi-delict and the place where that event results in damage are not identical, the expression "place where the harmful event occurred" in Article 5(3) of the Convention [7(2) Recast] must be understood as being intended to cover both the place where the damage occurred and the place of the event giving rise to it, so that the defendant may be sued, at the option of the plaintiff, either in the courts for the place where the damage occurred or in the courts for the place of the event which gives rise to and is at the origin of that damage.

21   In that judgment, the Court stated (at paragraphs 15 and 17) that the place of the event giving rise to the damage no less than the place where the damage occurred could constitute a significant connecting factor from the point of view of jurisdiction, since each of them could, depending on the circumstances, be particularly helpful in relation to the evidence and the conduct of the proceedings.

22   The Court added (at paragraph 20) that to decide in favour only of the place of the event giving rise to the damage would, in an appreciable number of cases, cause confusion between the heads of jurisdiction laid down by Articles 2 and 5(3) of the Convention [4 and 7(2) Recast], so that the latter provision would, to that extent, lose its effectiveness.

23   Those observations, made in relation to physical or pecuniary loss or damage, must equally apply, for the same reasons, in the case of loss or damage other than physical or pecuniary, in particular injury to the reputation and good name of a natural or legal person due to a defamatory publication.

24   In the case of a libel by a newspaper article distributed in several Contracting States, the place of the event giving rise to the damage, within the meaning of those judgments, can only be the place where the publisher of the newspaper in question is established, since that is the place where the harmful event originated and from which the libel was issued and put into circulation.

25   The court of the place where the publisher of the defamatory publication is established must therefore have jurisdiction to hear the action for damages for all the harm caused by the unlawful act.

26   However, that forum will generally coincide with the head of jurisdiction set out in the first paragraph of Article 2 of the Convention [4 Recast].

27   As the Court held in *Mines de Potasse d'Alsace*, the plaintiff must consequently have the option to bring proceedings also in the place where the damage occurred, since otherwise Article 5(3) [7(2) Recast] of the Convention would be rendered meaningless.

28   The place where the damage occurred is the place where the event giving rise to the damage, entailing tortious, delictual or quasi-delictual liability, produced its harmful effects upon the victim.

29   In the case of an international libel through the press, the injury caused by a defamatory publication to the honour, reputation and good name

of a natural or legal person occurs in the places where the publication is distributed, when the victim is known in those places.

30   It follows that the courts of each Contracting State in which the defamatory publication was distributed and in which the victim claims to have suffered injury to his reputation have jurisdiction to rule on the injury caused in that State to the victim's reputation.

31   In accordance with the requirement of the sound administration of justice, the basis of the rule of special jurisdiction in Article 5(3) [7(2) Recast], the courts of each Contracting State in which the defamatory publication was distributed and in which the victim claims to have suffered injury to his reputation are territorially the best placed to assess the libel committed in that State and to determine the extent of the corresponding damage.

32   Although there are admittedly disadvantages to having different courts ruling on various aspects of the same dispute, the plaintiff always has the option of bringing his entire claim before the courts either of the defendant's domicile or of the place where the publisher of the defamatory publication is established.

33   In light of the foregoing, the answer to the first, second, third and sixth questions referred by the House of Lords must be that, on a proper construction of the expression "place where the harmful event occurred" in Article 5(3) of the Convention [7(2) Recast], the victim of a libel by a newspaper article distributed in several Contracting States may bring an action for damages against the publisher either before the courts of the Contracting State of the place where the publisher of the defamatory publication is established, which have jurisdiction to award damages for all the harm caused by the defamation, or before the courts of each Contracting State in which the publication was distributed and where the victim claims to have suffered injury to his reputation, which have jurisdiction to rule solely in respect of the harm caused in the State of the court seised.

QUESTIONS

1. What might be the difference between the place of publication and the place where the publisher is established?
2. Why may the forum of the place of distribution of the newspaper have a limited jurisdiction compared to the forum of the publisher's establishment?
3. To what extent could this ruling apply to an infringement of copyright over the Internet?

Cases arising since the advent of the Internet

Shevill was used by national courts as a general framework for analysis of claims of copyright infringement over the Internet. Accordingly, the plaintiff may have a choice of fora on the ground of article 5.3 [7.2 Recast] between the country where the owner of the website is established and the countries where the infringing content was received. While the courts of the country of establishment of the website may have general jurisdiction, allowing the judge to decide on the entire geographic scope of the case (taking account of all territories of impact of the harm), the judge in the country where the infringing content is received may have a limited jurisdiction encompassing only the harm caused in that specific state. From a practical point of the view, the place of the event giving rise to the damage was the same as the place of the domicile of the defendant. In fact, the option offered by article 5.3 [7.2 Recast] was thus limited to countries where damages occurred. But that place is not so easily identified. Scholars and courts strongly dispute the localization of the place where damages occurred. Some of them adopted a technical approach, retaining the criterion of forum accessibility of the infringing content. Following this tendency, mere technical accessibility sufficed to locate the damage, without proving actual receipt of the infringing content. The contrary view held that more than mere accessibility was required. At the least, the website should have targeted the audience of a country, i.e., forum-state users, in order to identify that state as the place of the harm. Different criteria might be used to establish such a targeting.

Under the accessibility approach, the damage is spread over, at least, all the European countries, thus allowing the defendant to initiate an action in any of those countries. Nevertheless, the court's authority to adjudicate is limited to the damage suffered in the forum. Under the targeting criterion, the damage could be limited to one country, if the website has targeted only this country. The French highest civil court was originally in favor of the accessibility criterion, moving finally in favor of the targeting one. Nevertheless, the ECJ decided not to use *Shevill* as a framework for jurisdiction over claims alleging torts committed over the Internet, preferring an approach that distinguishes between the media used and the right infringed.

The first case decided by the ECJ concerning a cyber-tort was the *e-date* and *Martinez* joined Cases. *e-Date* concerned an action by two German residents against an Austrian Internet portal that refused to desist from reporting about a crime committed more than ten years ago by the two German residents, or to give an undertaking that it would refrain from future publication. The German residents brought their action in Germany, whose international jurisdiction was contested by the defendant. The second case concerned the action of a French actor against a U.K. publisher for the publication of an article infringing his personality rights. The French actor brought his action before the French courts, whose jurisdiction the defendant challenged.

C-509/09 and C-161/10 Joined Cases eDate Advertising GmbH v. X and Olivier Martinez and Others v. MGN Ltd, ECLI:EU:C:2011:685 and ECLI:EU:C:2010:656 [2011]

Interpretation of Article 5(3) of the Regulation [7(2) Recast]

37   By the first two questions in Case C-509/09 and the single question in Case C-161/10, which it is appropriate to examine together, the national courts ask the Court, in essence, how the expression 'the place where the harmful event occurred or may occur', used in Article 5(3) of the Regulation [7(2) Recast], is to be interpreted in the case of an alleged infringement of personality rights by means of content placed online on an internet website.

. . . .

41   It must also be borne in mind that the expression 'place where the harmful event occurred' is intended to cover both the place where the damage occurred and the place of the event giving rise to it. Those two places could constitute a significant connecting factor from the point of view of jurisdiction, since each of them could, depending on the circumstances, be particularly helpful in relation to the evidence and the conduct of the proceedings (see Case C-68/93 *Shevill and Others* [1995] ECR I-415, paragraphs 20 and 21).

42   In relation to the application of those two connecting criteria to actions seeking reparation for non-material damage allegedly caused by a defamatory publication, the Court has held that, in the case of defamation by means of a newspaper article distributed in several Contracting States, the victim may bring an action for damages against the publisher either before the courts of the Contracting State of the place where the publisher of the defamatory publication is established, which have jurisdiction to award damages for all of the harm caused by the defamation, or before the courts of each Contracting State in which the publication was distributed and where the victim claims to have suffered injury to his reputation, which have jurisdiction to rule solely in

respect of the harm caused in the State of the court seised (*Shevill and Others*, paragraph 33).

43   In that regard, the Court has also stated that, while it is true that the limitation of the jurisdiction of the courts in the State of distribution solely to damage caused in that State presents disadvantages, the plaintiff always has the option of bringing his entire claim before the courts either of the defendant's domicile or of the place where the publisher of the defamatory publication is established (*Shevill and Others*, paragraph 32).

44   Those considerations may, as was noted by the Advocate General at point 39 of his Opinion, also be applied to other media and means of communication and may cover a wide range of infringements of personality rights recognised in various legal systems, such as those alleged by the applicants in the main proceedings.

45   However, as has been submitted both by the referring courts and by the majority of the parties and interested parties which have submitted observations to the Court, the placing online of content on a website is to be distinguished from the regional distribution of media such as printed matter in that it is intended, in principle, to ensure the ubiquity of that content. That content may be consulted instantly by an unlimited number of internet users throughout the world, irrespective of any intention on the part of the person who placed it in regard to its consultation beyond that person's Member State of establishment and outside of that person's control.

46   It thus appears that the internet reduces the usefulness of the criterion relating to distribution, in so far as the scope of the distribution of content placed online is in principle universal. Moreover, it is not always possible, on a technical level, to quantify that distribution with certainty and accuracy in relation to a particular Member State or, therefore, to assess the damage caused exclusively within that Member State.

47   The difficulties in giving effect, within the context of the internet, to the criterion relating to the occurrence of damage which is derived from *Shevill and Others* contrasts, as the Advocate General noted at point 56 of his Opinion, with the serious nature of the harm which may be suffered by the holder of a personality right who establishes that information injurious to that right is available on a world-wide basis.

48   The connecting criteria referred to in paragraph 42 of the present judgment must therefore be adapted in such a way that a person who has

suffered an infringement of a personality right by means of the internet may bring an action in one forum in respect of all of the damage caused, depending on the place in which the damage caused in the European Union by that infringement occurred. Given that the impact which material placed online is liable to have on an individual's personality rights might best be assessed by the court of the place where the alleged victim has his centre of interests, the attribution of jurisdiction to that court corresponds to the objective of the sound administration of justice, referred to in paragraph 40 above.

49   The place where a person has the centre of his interests corresponds in general to his habitual residence. However, a person may also have the centre of his interests in a Member State in which he does not habitually reside, in so far as other factors, such as the pursuit of a professional activity, may establish the existence of a particularly close link with that State.

. . .

51   Moreover, instead of an action for liability in respect of all of the damage, the criterion of the place where the damage occurred, derived from *Shevill and Others*, confers jurisdiction on courts in each Member State in the territory of which content placed online is or has been accessible. Those courts have jurisdiction only in respect of the damage caused in the territory of the Member State of the court seised.

52   Consequently, the answer to the first two questions in Case C-509/09 and the single question in Case C-161/10 is that Article 5(3) of the Regulation [7(2) Recast] must be interpreted as meaning that, in the event of an alleged infringement of personality rights by means of content placed online on an internet website, the person who considers that his rights have been infringed has the option of bringing an action for liability, in respect of all the damage caused, either before the courts of the Member State in which the publisher of that content is established or before the courts of the Member State in which the centre of his interests is based. That person may also, instead of an action for liability in respect of all the damage caused, bring his action before the courts of each Member State in the territory of which content placed online is or has been accessible. Those courts have jurisdiction only in respect of the damage caused in the territory of the Member State of the court seised.

QUESTIONS

1. Why does the ECJ refuse to extend *Shevill* to cyber-torts? Do you find that distinction relevant?
2. Before which courts(s) could a French novelist assert a cyber-infringement of his personality right by a Belgian website? Imagine that the French novelist lives eight months per year in Dublin where he is completely unknown?
3. To what extent might this ruling be applicable to copyright infringement over the Internet?

C-523/10 Wintersteiger AG v. Products 4U Sondermaschinenbau GmbH ECLI:EU:C:2012:220 [2012]

10   Wintersteiger is an undertaking established in Austria which manufactures and sells worldwide ski and snowboard servicing tools, together with replacement parts and accessories. Since 1993 it is the proprietor of the Austrian trade mark Wintersteiger.

11   Products 4U, which is established in Germany, also develops and sells ski and snowboard servicing tools. In addition, it sells accessories for tools made by other manufacturers, in particular Wintersteiger. Those accessories, which Products 4U describes as 'Wintersteiger-Zubehör' ('Wintersteiger accessories') are neither produced by, nor are they authorised by, Wintersteiger. Like the applicant, Products 4U operates on a worldwide basis and also sells its goods in Austria.

12   Since 1 December 2008, Products 4U has reserved the keyword ('AdWord') 'Wintersteiger' in the advertising system developed by the referencing service provider on Google Internet. Following that reservation, which was limited to Google's German top-level domain, namely the website 'google.de', an internet user who enters the keyword 'Wintersteiger' into the search engine of that referencing service receives a link to Wintersteiger's website as the first search result. However, doing a search of that same term also leads to an advertisement for Products 4U appearing on the right-hand side of the screen with the heading 'Anzeige' ('advertisement'). The text of the advertisement bears the heading 'Skiwerkstattzubehör' ('Ski workshop accessories'), underlined and in blue font. It also contains the words 'Ski und Snowboardmaschinen' ('ski and snowboard tools') and 'Wartung und Reparatur' ('maintenance and repair') in two lines. Products 4U's website address is given in green lettering in the last line. Clicking on the heading 'Skiwerkstattzubehör' ('Ski workshop accessories') brings up the

'Wintersteiger-Zubehör' ('Wintersteiger accessories') on offer on Products 4U's website. The advertisement on 'google.de' does not give any indication that there are no economic links between Wintersteiger and Products 4U. On the other hand, Products 4U has not entered any advertisement linked to the search term 'Wintersteiger' in Google's Austrian top-level domain, namely the website 'google.at'.

13   Wintersteiger brought an action for injunction in the Austrian courts claiming that, by placing the advertisement on 'google.de', Products 4U infringed its Austrian trade mark. In respect of the jurisdiction of those courts to hear its application, Wintersteiger relied on Article 5(3) of Regulation No 44/2001 [7(2) Recast]. It argued that 'google.de' can also be accessed in Austria and that the referencing service is configured in German.

. . . .

17   By its questions, which it is appropriate to examine together, the national court is asking, in essence, what criteria are to be used to determine jurisdiction under Article 5(3) of Regulation No 44/2001 [7(2) Recast] to hear an action relating to an alleged infringement of a trade mark registered in a Member State through the use, by an advertiser, of a keyword identical to that trade mark on the website of an internet search engine operating under a top-level domain different from that of the Member State where the trade mark is registered.

. . . .

19   It should also be noted that the expression 'place where the harmful event occurred or may occur' in Article 5(3) of Regulation No 44/2001 [7(2) Recast] is intended to cover both the place where the damage occurred and the place of the event giving rise to it, so that the defendant may be sued, at the option of the applicant, in the courts for either of those places (*eDate Advertising and Others*, paragraph 41 and the case-law cited).

. . .

The place where the damage occurred

. . .

22   In the context of the internet, the Court has . . . held that, in the event of an alleged infringement of personality rights, the person who considers that his rights have been infringed by means of content placed online on a website

has the option of bringing an action for liability, in respect of all the damage caused, before the courts of the Member State in which the centre of his interests is based (see *eDate Advertising and Others*, paragraph 52).

23 As the Court noted on that occasion, the criterion of centre of interests of the person whose rights have been infringed is in accordance with the objective of foreseeability of jurisdiction in so far as it enables the applicant to identify easily the court in which he may sue and the defendant reasonably to foresee before which court he may be sued (*eDate Advertising and Others*, paragraph 50).

24 However, as the Advocate General pointed out at paragraph 20 of his Opinion, that assessment, made in the particular context of infringements of personality rights, does not apply also to the determination of jurisdiction in respect of infringements of intellectual property rights, such as those alleged in the main proceedings.

25 Contrary to the situation of a person who considers that there has been an infringement of his personality rights, which are protected in all Member States, the protection afforded by the registration of a national mark is, in principle, limited to the territory of the Member State in which it is registered, so that, in general, its proprietor cannot rely on that protection outside the territory.

27 With regard to jurisdiction to hear a claim of infringement of a national mark in a situation such as that in the main proceedings, it must be considered that both the objective of foreseeability and that of sound administration of justice militate in favour of conferring jurisdiction, in respect of the damage occurred, on the courts of the Member State in which the right at issue is protected.

28 It is the courts of the Member State in which the trade mark at issue is registered which are best able to assess, taking account of the interpretation of Directive 2008/95 [Trademark Directive] in, inter alia [citations omitted], whether a situation such as that in the main proceedings actually infringes the protected national mark. Those courts have the power to determine all the damage allegedly caused to the proprietor of the protected right because of an infringement of it and to hear an application seeking cessation of all infringements of that right.

29 Therefore it must be held that an action relating to infringement of a trade mark registered in a Member State through the use, by an advertiser, of

a keyword identical to that trade mark on a search engine website operating under a country-specific top-level domain of another Member State may be brought before the courts of the Member State in which the trade mark is registered.

The place where the event giving rise to the damage occurred

30   As regards, second, the place where the event occurred which gives rise to an alleged infringement of a national mark through the use of a keyword identical to that trade mark on a search engine operating under a country-specific top-level domain of another Member State, it should be noted that the territorial limitation of the protection of a national mark is not such as to exclude the international jurisdiction of courts other than the courts of the Member State in which that trade mark is registered.

. . .

34   In the case of an alleged infringement of a national trade mark registered in a Member State because of the display, on the search engine website, of an advertisement using a keyword identical to that trade mark, it is the activation by the advertiser of the technical process displaying, according to pre-defined parameters, the advertisement which it created for its own commercial communications which should be considered to be the event giving rise to an alleged infringement, and not the display of the advertisement itself.

. . .

36   It is true that the technical display process by the advertiser is activated, ultimately, on a server belonging to the operator of the search engine used by the advertiser. However, in view of the objective of foreseeability, which the rules on jurisdiction must pursue, the place of establishment of that server cannot, by reason of its uncertain location, be considered to be the place where the event giving rise to the damage occurred for the purpose of the application of Article 5(3) of Regulation No 44/2001 [7(2) Recast].

37   By contrast, since it is a definite and identifiable place, both for the applicant and for the defendant, and is therefore likely to facilitate the taking of evidence and the conduct of the proceedings, it must be held that the place of establishment of the advertiser is the place where the activation of the display process is decided.

. . .

39   In view of all the foregoing considerations, Article 5(3) of Regulation No 44/2001[7(2) Recast] must be interpreted as meaning that an action relating to infringement of a trade mark registered in a Member State because of the use, by an advertiser, of a keyword identical to that trade mark on a search engine website operating under a country-specific top-level domain of another Member State may be brought before either the courts of the Member State in which the trade mark is registered or the courts of the Member State of the place of establishment of the advertiser.

QUESTIONS

1. Why does the Court refuse to apply the ruling of *eDate* to trademark infringement claims? What are the consequences?
2. A French producer of Champagne has registered in all E.U. countries PURE as a trademark, with one notable exception, Spain, where a local producer of Cava has already registered PURE as a trademark for his Cava. The Spanish producer exploits a website solely written in Spanish in order to promote its Cava in Spain. Consumers may order his Cava provided that the address of distribution is in Spain. The French producer considers that the Spanish website infringes his French trademark and brings an action before the French court. Does *Wintersteiger* authorize the French court to hear the case?

C-173/11 Football Dataco Ltd. And Others v. Sportradar GmbH and Others ECLI:EU:C:2012:642 [2012]

[This case concerns the infringement of the sui generis right in databases. Football Dataco, a U.K. company, alleged that Sportradar, a German company which provides results and other statistics relating to the English League football matches via the Internet, infringed its sui generis right. Football Dataco brought the action before the U.K. courts. The dispute concerned the localization of the act of transmission: whether it must be regarded as taking place not, or not only, in the member state from which the data has been sent by Sportradar, but also in the member state in which the persons receiving those transmissions are located, i.e., in the U.K.]

26   To that end, the directive requires all the Member States to make provision in their national law for the protection of databases by a sui generis right.

27   In that context, the protection by the sui generis right provided for in the legislation of a Member State is limited in principle to the territory of

that Member State, so that the person enjoying that protection can rely on it only against unauthorised acts of re-utilisation which take place in that territory (see, by analogy, Case C-523/10 *Wintersteiger* [2012] ECR I -0000, paragraph 25).

28   According to the order for reference, the referring court, in the main proceedings, has to assess the validity of the claims of Football Dataco and Others alleging infringement of the sui generis right they claim to hold, under United Kingdom law, in the Football Live database. For that assessment, it is thus necessary to know whether the acts of sending data at issue in the main proceedings fall, as acts taking place within the United Kingdom, within the territorial scope of the protection by the sui generis right afforded by the law of that Member State.

29   Secondly, Article 5(3) of Regulation No 44/2001 [7(2) Recast] establishes, in cases which, like that at issue in the main proceedings, concern tortious liability, special jurisdiction on the part of 'the courts for the place where the harmful event occurred or may occur'.

30   It follows that the question of the localisation of the acts of sending at issue in the main proceedings, which Football Dataco and Others claim have caused damage to the substantial investment involved in creating the Football Live database, is liable to have an influence on the question of the jurisdiction of the referring court, with respect in particular to the action seeking to establish the principal liability of Sportradar in the dispute before that court.

31   Thirdly, in accordance with Article 8 of Regulation No 864/2007 [Rome II Regulation], in the case of an infringement of an intellectual property right which, like the sui generis right established by Directive 96/9, is not a 'unitary Community' right within the meaning of Article 8(2) of that regulation (see paragraphs 24 to 26 above), the law applicable to a non-contractual obligation arising from such an infringement is, under Article 8(1), 'the law of the country for which protection is claimed'.

32   That conflict-of-laws rule confirms that it is relevant to know whether, regardless of the possible localisation of the acts of sending at issue in the main proceedings in the Member State in which the web server of the person doing those acts is situated, the acts took place in the United Kingdom, the Member State in which Football Dataco and Others claim protection of the Football Live database by the sui generis right.

33   In this respect, the localisation of an act of 're-utilisation' within the meaning of Article 7 of Directive 96/9 [Database Directive] must, like the definition of that concept, correspond to independent criteria of European Union law [citation omitted].

34   In the case of re-utilisation carried out, as in the main proceedings, by means of a web server, it must be observed, as the Advocate General does in points 58 and 59 of his Opinion, that this is characterised by a series of successive operations, ranging at least from the placing online of the data concerned on that website for it to be consulted by the public to the transmission of that data to the interested members of the public, which may take place in the territory of different Member States [citations omitted].

36   . . . the mere fact that the website containing the data in question is accessible in a particular national territory is not a sufficient basis for concluding that the operator of the website is performing an act of re-utilisation caught by the national law applicable in that territory concerning protection by the sui generis right [citations omitted].

37   If the mere fact of being accessible were sufficient for it to be concluded that there was an act of re-utilisation, websites and data which, although obviously targeted at persons outside the territory of the Member State concerned, were nevertheless technically accessible in that State would wrongly be subject to the application of the relevant law of that State [citations omitted].

. . .

39   The localisation of an act of re-utilisation in the territory of the Member State to which the data in question is sent depends on there being evidence from which it may be concluded that the act discloses an intention on the part of its performer to target persons in that territory [citations omitted].

40   In the dispute in the main proceedings, the circumstance that the data on Sportradar's server includes data relating to English football league matches, which is such as to show that the acts of sending at issue in the main proceedings proceed from an intention on the part of Sportradar to attract the interest of the public in the United Kingdom, may constitute such evidence.

41   The fact that Sportradar granted, by contract, the right of access to its server to companies offering betting services to that public may also be evidence of its intention to target them, if – which will be for the referring court to ascertain – Sportradar was aware, or must have been aware, of that specific

destination [citations omitted]. It could be relevant in this respect if it were the case that the remuneration fixed by Sportradar as consideration for the grant of that right of access took account of the extent of the activities of those companies in the United Kingdom market and the prospects of its website betradar.com subsequently being consulted by internet users in the United Kingdom.

42   Finally, the circumstance that the data placed online by Sportradar is accessible to the United Kingdom internet users who are customers of those companies in their own language, which is not the same as those commonly used in the Member States from which Sportradar pursues its activities, might, if that were the case, be supporting evidence for the existence of an approach targeting in particular the public in the United Kingdom [citations omitted].

43   Where such evidence is present, the referring court will be entitled to consider that an act of re-utilisation such as those at issue in the main proceedings is located in the territory of the Member State of location of the user to whose computer the data in question is transmitted, at his request, for purposes of storage and display on screen (Member State B).

44   The argument put forward by Sportradar that an act of re-utilisation within the meaning of Article 7 of Directive 96/9 [Database Directive] must in all circumstances be regarded as located exclusively in the territory of the Member State in which the web server from which the data in question is sent is situated cannot be accepted.

45   Besides the fact that, as Football Dataco and Others observe, it is sometimes difficult to localise such a server with certainty (see *Wintersteiger*, paragraph 36), such an interpretation would mean that an operator who, without the consent of the maker of the database protected by the sui generis right under the law of a particular Member State, proceeds to re-utilise online the content of that database, targeting the public in that Member State, would escape the application of that national law solely because his server is located outside the territory of that State. That would have an impact on the effectiveness of the protection under the national law concerned conferred on the database by that law [citations omitted].

46   Moreover, as Football Dataco and Others submit, the objective of protection of databases by the sui generis right pursued by Directive 96/9 [Database Directive] would, in general, be compromised if acts of re-utilisation aimed at the public in all or part of the territory of the European

Union were outside the scope of that directive and the national legislation transposing it, merely because the server of the website used by the person doing that act was located in a non-member country [citations omitted].

47 In the light of the above considerations, the answer to the question is that Article 7 of Directive 96/9 [Database Directive] must be interpreted as meaning that the sending by one person, by means of a web server located in Member State A, of data previously uploaded by that person from a database protected by the sui generis right under that directive to the computer of another person located in Member State B, at that person's request, for the purpose of storage in that computer's memory and display on its screen, constitutes an act of 're-utilisation' of the data by the person sending it. That act takes place, at least, in Member State B, where there is evidence from which it may be concluded that the act discloses an intention on the part of the person performing the act to target members of the public in Member State B, which is for the national court to assess.

QUESTIONS

1. Why does the ECJ refuse to locate the jurisdiction-triggering act at the place of the server?
2. Why does the Court refuse to use the criterion of accessibility? Can you reconcile the approach in *Football Dataco* with the Court's emphasis on accessibility in *eDate*? Consider this question again after you read *Pez Hejduk*, immediately following.
3. How could a court determine whether a website is targeting particular countries? To what extent does the analysis concern judicial competence? Legislative competence (applicable law)?

C-441/13 Pez Hejduk v. EnergieAgentur.NRW GmbH
ECLI:EU:C:2015:28 [2015]

10 According to the order for reference, Ms Hejduk is a professional photographer of architecture and is the creator of photographic works depicting the buildings of the Austrian architect, Georg W. Reinberg. As part of a conference organised on 16 September 2004 by EnergieAgentur, Mr Reinberg used Ms Hejduk's photographs in order to illustrate his buildings, which he was authorised to do by Ms Hejduk.

11 Subsequently, EnergieAgentur, without Ms Hejduk's consent and without providing a statement of authorship, made those photographs available on its website for viewing and downloading.

12   Taking the view that her copyright had been infringed by EnergieAgentur, Ms Hejduk brought an action before the Handelsgericht Wien for damages in the sum of EUR 4 050 . . .

13   . . . EnergieAgentur raised an objection that the Handelsgericht Wien lacked international and local jurisdiction, claiming that its website is not directed at Austria and that the mere fact that a website may be accessed from Austria is insufficient to confer jurisdiction on that court.

14   Accordingly, the Handelsgericht Wien decided to stay the proceedings and to refer the following question to the Court for a preliminary ruling:

'Is Article 5(3) of Regulation No 44/2001 [article 7(2) Recast] to be interpreted as meaning that, in a dispute concerning an infringement of rights related to copyright which is alleged to have been committed by keeping a photograph accessible on a website, the website being operated under the top-level domain of a Member State other than that in which the proprietor of the right is domiciled, there is jurisdiction only

–   in the Member State in which the alleged perpetrator of the infringement is established; and

–   in the Member State(s) to which the website, according to its content, is directed?'

. . .

18   It is clear from the Court's case-law that the expression 'place where the harmful event occurred or may occur' in Article 5(3) of Regulation No 44/2001 [7(2) Recast] is intended to cover both the place where the damage occurred and the place of the event giving rise to it, so that the defendant may be sued, at the option of the applicant, in the courts for either of those places [citation omitted].

19   In that connection, according to settled case-law, the rule of special jurisdiction laid down in Article 5(3) of that regulation is based on the existence of a particularly close linking factor between the dispute and the courts of the place where the harmful event occurred or may occur, which justifies the attribution of jurisdiction to those courts for reasons relating to the sound administration of justice and the efficacious conduct of proceedings [citation omitted].

20   Since identification of one of the linking factors recognised by the case-law referred to in paragraph 18 above thus establishes the jurisdiction of the court objectively best placed to determine whether the elements establishing the liability of the person sued are present, it follows that only the court in whose jurisdiction the relevant linking factor is situated may validly be seised [citation omitted]

. . .

22   . . . it must be observed that, although copyright rights must be automatically protected, in particular in accordance with Directive 2001/29 [Info Soc], in all Member States, they are subject to the principle of territoriality. Those rights are thus capable of being infringed in each Member State in accordance with the applicable substantive law [citation omitted].

. . .

24   In a situation such as that at issue in the main proceedings, in which the alleged tort consists in the infringement of copyright or rights related to copyright by the placing of certain photographs online on a website without the photographer's consent, the activation of the process for the technical display of the photographs on that website must be regarded as the causal event. The event giving rise to a possible infringement of copyright therefore lies in the actions of the owner of that site (see, by analogy, judgment in *Wintersteiger*, C-523/10, EU:C:2012:220, paragraphs 34 and 35).

25   In a case such as that in the main proceedings, the acts or omissions liable to constitute such an infringement may be localised only at the place where EnergieAgentur has its seat, since that is where the company took and carried out the decision to place photographs online on a particular website. It is undisputed that that seat is not in the Member State from which the present reference is made.

26   It follows that in circumstances such as those at issue in the main proceedings, the causal event took place at the seat of that company and therefore does not attribute jurisdiction to the court seised.

27   It is therefore necessary to examine, secondly, whether that court may have jurisdiction on the basis of the place where the alleged damage occurred.

28   Thus, the Court must determine the conditions in which, for the purposes of Article 5(3) of Regulation No 44/2001 [7(2) Recast], the damage

arising out of an alleged infringement of copyright occurs or is likely to occur in a Member State other than the one in which the defendant took and carried out the decision to place photographs online on a particular website.

29 In that regard, the Court has stated not only that the place where the alleged damage occurred within the meaning of that provision may vary according to the nature of the right allegedly infringed, but also that the likelihood of damage occurring in a particular Member State is subject to the condition that the right whose infringement is alleged is protected in that Member State [citation omitted].

30 . . . It is not disputed, as is clear in particular from paragraph 22 above, that the rights on which [Ms. Hejduk] relies are protected in Austria.

31 With regard to the likelihood of the damage occurring in a Member State other than the one where EnergieAgentur has its seat, that company states that its website, on which the photographs at issue were published, operating under a country-specific German top-level domain, that is to say 'de', is not directed at Austria and that consequently the damage did not occur in that Member State.

32 It is clear from the Court's case-law that . . . Article 5(3) [7(2) Recast] does not require, in particular, that the activity concerned be 'directed to' the Member State in which the court seised is situated [citation omitted].

33 Therefore, . . . it is irrelevant that the website at issue in the main proceedings is not directed at the Member State in which the court seised is situated.

34 In circumstances such as those at issue in the main proceedings, it must thus be held that the occurrence of damage and/or the likelihood of its occurrence arise from the accessibility in the Member State of the referring court, via the website of EnergieAgentur, of the photographs to which the rights relied on by Ms Hejduk pertain.

35 The issue of the extent of the damage alleged by Ms Hejduk is part of the examination of the substance of the claim and is not relevant to the stage in which jurisdiction is verified.

36 However, given that the protection of copyright and rights related to copyright granted by the Member State of the court seised is limited to the territory of that Member State, a court seised on the basis of the place where

the alleged damage occurred has jurisdiction only to rule on the damage caused within that Member State [citation omitted].

37   The courts of other Member States in principle retain jurisdiction, in the light of Article 5(3) of Regulation No 44/2001 and the principle of territoriality, to rule on the damage to copyright or rights related to copyright caused in their respective Member States, given that they are best placed, first, to ascertain whether those rights guaranteed by the Member State concerned have in fact been infringed and, secondly, to determine the nature of the damage caused [citation omitted].

38   Having regard to all the foregoing considerations, the answer to the question referred is that Article 5(3) of Regulation No 44/2001 [7(2) Recast] must be interpreted as meaning that, in the event of an allegation of infringement of copyright and rights related to copyright guaranteed by the Member State of the court seised, that court has jurisdiction, on the basis of the place where the damage occurred, to hear an action for damages in respect of an infringement of those rights resulting from the placing of protected photographs online on a website accessible in its territorial jurisdiction. That court has jurisdiction only to rule on the damage caused in the Member State within which the court is situated.

QUESTIONS

1. Does the Court follow the ruling in *Football Dataco*? If not, why not?
2. Why does the Court apply the *Wintersteiger* ruling to copyright infringement by means of the Internet? How does this decision compare with the NY Court of Appeals' decision in *Penguin Group (USA) Inc. v. American Buddha*? Why does the Court not follow the ruling in *eDate* ?
3. Would the *Pez Hejduk* court's approach apply to moral rights? In an earlier decision endorsing the accessibility criterion in assessing judicial competence in copyright infringement cases, C-170/12 *Peter Pinckney v. KDG Mediatech AG* ECLI:EU:C:2013:635 [2013], the English version of the ECJ's judgment in *Pinckney* mentioned 'the alleged infringement of a copyright' (para 43); the original French version, however, specified 'la violation alléguée d'un droit patrimonial d'auteur' ['the alleged violation of an economic right under copyright']. In *Pinckney*, French was the language of proceedings, French being also the internal working language at the Court. If the French version prevails, what does that imply for claims asserting violations of moral rights?
4. *Pez Hejduk* stated: 'The issue of the extent of the damage alleged by Ms Hejduk is part of the examination of the substance of the claim and is

not relevant to the stage in which jurisdiction is verified (para. 35)'. In other words, the court's competence derives from the accessibility in the forum of the infringing copies or communications, not from the proof that infringements occurred there. Nevertheless, in the following paragraph, the ECJ ruled that 'a court seised on the basis of the place where the alleged damage occurred has jurisdiction only to rule on the damage caused within that Member State.' Thus, the forum may not take into account infringements culminating in other Member States. Suppose the infringing communication is accessible in the forum, but no one has accessed it. For example, suppose the forum is the author's residence, and defendant's website is accessible in the forum, but, by its language, currency, and advertising, the website is "targeting" a Member State other than the forum. In the absence of actual access to the website, would the forum no longer be competent to hear the case? But if the plaintiff must prove actual access, does that mean (para. 35 notwithstanding) that the court must determine the merits of the infringement claim in order to ascertain if it has jurisdiction to hear the claim?

5. What is the difference between basing jurisdiction on "targeting" and basing it on accessibility? On actual access?

6. Given the ECJ's focus on 'a particularly close linking factor between the dispute and the courts of the place where the harmful event occurred or may occur, which justifies the attribution of jurisdiction to those courts for reasons relating to the sound administration of justice and the efficacious conduct of proceedings' (para. 19), and on the courts 'best placed ... to ascertain whether [the] rights guaranteed by the Member State concerned have in fact been infringed' (para. 37) should it not follow that courts in the state of the event giving rise to the damage are not competent to determine whether an infringement has occurred in the state or states where the damage occurred? What about the courts of the state of the defendant's residence (which often may be the state of the event giving rise to the damage)?

7. The ECJ twice evokes the "principle of territoriality" (paras. 22 and 37). What is the legal basis for this principle? (See *infra*, Chapter 8.) While, as we shall see, courts generally adhere to the principle of territoriality when they apply the law of the place of the harm to determine whether a wrongful act occurred in that place, legislative competence (applicable law) need not command judicial competence (jurisdiction). For example, under the Brussels I Regulation [Recast], art. 2, the courts of defendant's residence have jurisdiction over all claims against the defendant, wherever the acts were committed or caused harm. As we will see, it is expected that defendant's forum will apply the laws of the countries where the wrongful act occurred, even if the forum state is not one of those countries. Why,

then, should another forum, such as one of the countries where the harm was incurred, not be competent to adjudicate infringements transpiring in other countries, so long as it applies the law of those countries?

8. Suppose that in *Football Dataco*, the English sports fans targeted by the online service included not only English persons who received the communications at home in England, but also English persons wherever located. That group includes transient English persons, but also those with second homes in various E.U. member or foreign states, as well as those domiciled abroad. After *Pez Hejduk*, which court(s) are competent to hear claims against the online service? For which damage does the court have jurisdiction?

PROBLEM

A UK newspaper's website offers free downloads of its content to members of the public who subscribe to the newspaper's print version. Everyone else may access up to ten articles per month for free, but thereafter must pay per article, or purchase an online subscription. A Swedish website written in Swedish aggregates every article on the UK newspaper's website that mentions a Swede. The aggregator's site is accessible all over the world in a version that offers only the titles and the sentences that include the names of Swedish persons. Full access requires a subscription in Swedish Krona. After *Pez Hejduk* does the UK court have jurisdiction to hear a claim by the UK newspaper against the Swedish site? For which damages? For what scope of injunctive relief? Do the Swedish courts have jurisdiction? For which damages? For what scope of injunctive relief?

How would you analyze this problem under *Football Dataco*? Which approach seems to you the most effective to resolve a multi-territorial dispute? Why?

Declaratory judgment

The following case concerned the scope of article 7.2 and whether this article encompasses an action for a declaratory judgment of non-infringement. The case concerned patent law and competition law and addressed whether the refusal to grant a patent license might be contrary to competition law. The owner of the patent brought a declaratory judgment action in Germany. Because Germany was not the place of defendant's residence, the sole basis for jurisdiction was article 7.2.

C-133/11 Folien Fischer AG and Others v. Ritrama SpA ECLI:EU:C:2012:664 [2012]

[Folien Fischer and Fofitec are partner companies established in Switzerland who distribute their products among other countries also in Germany. Folien Fischer and Fofitec brought an action for a negative declaration against Ritrama, a company established in Italy. With the action for a negative declaration in front of a German court, Folien Fischer and Fofitec sought the declaration that their distribution policy and refusal in granting patent licenses to third parties did not violate competition law.]

The scope of point (3) of Article 5 [7(2) recast] of Regulation No 44/2001

36   It should be noted that, according to the wording of point (3) of Article 5 [7(2) Recast] of Regulation No 44/2001, the rule establishing special jurisdiction which is laid down in that provision is envisaged, in general terms, for 'matters relating to tort, delict or quasi-delict'. Given that formulation, therefore, the possibility that an action for a negative declaration might fall within the scope of that provision cannot automatically be excluded.

. . .

41   It is therefore a question of deciding whether, notwithstanding the special nature of an action for a negative declaration, jurisdiction to hear such an application can be attributed on the basis of the criteria laid down out in point (3) of Article 5 Regulation No 44/2001[7(2) Recast].

42   In that regard, it should be noted that the special nature of an action for a negative declaration arises from the fact that the claimant is seeking to establish that the pre-conditions for liability, as a result of which the defendant would have a right of redress, are not satisfied.

43   In that context, . . . an action for a negative declaration entails a reversal of the normal roles in matters relating to tort or delict, since, in such an action, the claimant is the party against whom a claim based on a tort or delict might be made, while the defendant is the party whom that tort or delict may have adversely affected.

44   However, that reversal of roles is not such as to exclude an action for a negative declaration from the scope of point (3) of Article 5 Regulation No 44/2001 [7(2) Recast].

45   The objectives, pursued by that provision and repeatedly stressed in case-law [citations omitted], of ensuring that the court with jurisdiction is foreseeable and of preserving legal certainty are not connected either to the allocation of the respective roles of claimant and defendant or to the protection of either.

46   Specifically, point (3) of Article 5 of Regulation No 44/2001 [7(2) Recast] does not pursue the same objective as the rules on jurisdiction laid down in Sections 3 to 5 of Chapter II of that regulation, which are designed to offer the weaker party stronger protection [citations omitted].

47   In consequence, as has been correctly pointed out by Folien Fischer, Fofitec, the German, French, Dutch and Portuguese Governments, and by the European Commission, the application of point (3) of Article 5 is not contingent upon the potential victim initiating proceedings.

48   Admittedly, there is a difference between, on the one hand, the interests of the applicant in an action for a negative declaration and, on the other, the interests of the applicant in proceedings seeking to have the defendant held liable for causing loss and ordered to pay damages. In both cases, however, the examination undertaken by the court seised essentially relates to the same matters of law and fact.

49   Furthermore, . . . an action seeking to have the defendant held liable for causing loss and ordered to pay damages has the same cause of action as an action brought by that defendant seeking a declaration that he is not liable for that loss.

50   It should further be stated that, during the stage at which jurisdiction is verified, the court seised does not examine either the admissibility or the substance of the application for a negative declaration in the light of national law, but identifies only the points of connection with the State in which that court is sitting, which support its claim to jurisdiction under point (3) of Article 5 of Regulation No 44/2001 [7(2) Recast].

51   In those circumstances, the special nature of the action for a negative declaration, referred to in paragraph 42 above, has no bearing on the examination that the national court must carry out in order to determine whether it has jurisdiction in matters relating to tort, delict or quasi-delict, since the only matter to be established is whether there is a point of connection with the Member State in which the court seised is sitting.

52   If, therefore, the relevant elements in the action for a negative declaration can either show a connection with the State in which the damage
occurred or may occur or show a connection with the State in which the
causal event giving rise to that damage took place, in accordance with the
case-law set out in paragraph 39 above, then the court in one of those two
places, as the case may be, can claim jurisdiction to hear such an action,
pursuant to point (3) of Article 5 of Regulation No 44/2001 [7(2) Recast],
irrespective of whether the action in question has been brought by a party
whom a tort or delict may have adversely affected or by a party against whom
a claim based on that tort or delict might be made.

53   Where, on the other hand, the court cannot identify, in the State in
which that court is sitting, one of the two points of connection referred to
in paragraph 39 above, it cannot claim jurisdiction without failing to have
regard for the objectives of point (3) of Article 5 of Regulation No 44/2001
[7(2) Recast].

54   It follows from the foregoing that, for the purposes of determining the
jurisdiction of national courts, an action for a negative declaration cannot be
excluded from the scope of point (3) of Article 5 of Regulation No 44/2001
[7(2) Recast].

55   Consequently, the answer to the question referred is that point (3) of
Article 5 of Regulation No 44/2001 [7(2) Recast] must be interpreted as
meaning that an action for a negative declaration seeking to establish the
absence of liability in tort, delict, or quasi-delict falls within the scope of that
provision.

**Regulation (EU) No 1215/2012 of the European Parliament and of
the Council of 12 December 2012 on jurisdiction and the recognition and enforcement of judgments in civil and commercial matters
(recast) (Brussels Regulation Recast)**

SECTION 9 – Lis pendens — related actions

Article 29

1. . . . where proceedings involving the same cause of action and between
the same parties are brought in the courts of different Member States,
any court other than the court first seised shall of its own motion stay its
proceedings until such time as the jurisdiction of the court first seised is
established.

QUESTION

Taking into account article 29 of the Recast Regulation, what are the consequences of the ruling in *Folien Fischer* for potential defendants in copyright infringement actions? For the copyright owner?

PROBLEM

An Italian journalist has published an article concerning French political personalities and their behavior in Italy. The article was published only in an Italian newspaper. A French journalist copied from this article in order to write his own article, published both in a French newspaper and on its website. The newspaper is distributed in hard copy all over Europe and its website is accessible throughout Europe as well.

The French newspaper received a letter from the Italian journalist threatening to sue if the newspaper did not compensate him for the infringement of his article. Advised by its lawyer, the French newspaper decided to bring an action in Italy seeking a declaratory judgment of non-infringement. Could the French newspaper have brought the claim in other fora? With the same consequences? What about a claim brought in the U.K.?

7.3.4 Contract

Article 7(1) offers an optional forum to the plaintiff, who may choose between the defendant's domicile under article 2 and the contractual forum under article 7(1). Article 7(1) applies if the claim between the plaintiff and the defendant relates to contractual issues; it therefore is necessary to distinguish between tort claims under article 7(2) and contract actions under article 7(1). Once the claim is characterized as one in contract, another characterization is required in order to determine if point (b) or point (a) applies. Point (b) applies for contracts for sales of goods or for the provision of services. In that case, the competent court is determined by the place of delivery of the goods or of the service; these are considered as being the characteristic performance of the contract. If the contract is neither a contract for sales of goods nor for the provision of services, point (a) applies, determining the court by the place of performance of the obligation in question regardless of the characteristic performance. The place of performance is determined pursuant to the substantive law applicable to the claim in question. Concerning IP contracts, the ECJ refused to characterize a license as contract for the provision of services, meaning that point (a) applies. As a result, the determination of the forum requires first to determine which obligation is litigated, and once the claim is characterized, to apply the substantive law applicable to determine the place of performance of the specific obligation. Thus, the same contract can be the object of litigation in different fora, depending on the obligation at issue.

> **Regulation (EU) No 1215/2012 of the European Parliament and of the Council of 12 December 2012 on jurisdiction and the recognition and enforcement of judgments in civil and commercial matters (recast) (Brussels Regulation Recast)**
>
> **Article 7**
>
> (1) (a) in matters relating to a contract, in the courts for the place of performance of the obligation in question;
> (b) for the purpose of this provision and unless otherwise agreed, the place of performance of the obligation in question shall be:
>   - in the case of the sale of goods, the place in a Member State where, under the contract, the goods were delivered or should have been delivered,
>   - in the case of the provision of services, the place in a Member State where, under the contract, the services were provided or should have been provided;
> (c) if point (b) does not apply then point (a) applies;. . .

Applicability of article 7(1) Brussels I Regulation Recast

The ECJ has construed the Regulation's boundary between contract and tort. It has held that the concept of "matters relating to tort, delict or quasi-delict" within the meaning of article 5(3) [article 7(2)] of Regulation No 44/2001 covers all actions which seek to establish the liability of a defendant and which do not concern "matters relating to a contract" within the meaning of article 5(1)(a) [article 7(1)(a)] of the Regulation. But what are "matters related to a contract"? Are they any claims that arise between contractual parties? Recently, in (C-548/12 *Brogsitter* ECLI:EU:C:2014:148 [2014]) the ECJ recognized that:

> 23 . . . the mere fact that one contracting party brings a civil liability claim against the other is not sufficient to consider that the claim concerns 'matters relating to a contract' within the meaning of Article 5(1)(a) [Article 7(1)(a)] of Regulation No 44/2001.

24   That is the case only where the conduct complained of may be considered a breach of contract, which may be established by taking into account the purpose of the contract.

25   That will a priori be the case where the interpretation of the contract which links the defendant to the applicant is indispensable to establish the lawful or, on the contrary, unlawful nature of the conduct complained of against the former by the latter.

QUESTION

A motion picture producer licenses a toy manufacturer to make and distribute 10 000 copies of a toy based on a character in the movie producer's latest animated cartoon. The licensee instead manufactures 20 000 copies. Is the manufacturer's conduct a breach of the terms of the license agreement? Does article 7(1) apply? Why might the motion picture producer prefer the jurisdictional bases of article 7(1) to those of article 7(2)?

Application of article 7(1) Brussels I Regulation Recast

C-533/07 Falco Privatstiftung and Others v. Gisela Weller-Lindhorst ECLI:EU:C:2009:257 [2009]

12   It is apparent from the order for reference that the applicants in the main proceedings request payment of royalties, calculated by reference to the, partially known, amount of sales of video recordings of a concert. They also request that the defendant in the main proceeding be ordered to provide an account of all sales of video and audio recordings and to pay the resulting supplementary royalties. In support of their claims, the applicants in the main proceedings rely on, with regard to the video recordings, the provisions of the contract between them and their contractual partner and, with regard to the sales of audio recordings, a copyright infringement, there being no contractual basis in that regard.

. . .

The first question

18   By its first question, the national court asks, essentially, whether a contract under which the owner of an intellectual property right grants its contractual partner the right to use the right in return for remuneration, is

a contract for the provision of services within the meaning of the second indent of Article 5(1)(b) of Regulation No 44/2001 [Recast 7(1)(b)].

. . .

29 . . . the concept of service implies, at the least, that the party who provides the service carries out a particular activity in return for remuneration.

30 It cannot be inferred from a contract under which the owner of an intellectual property right grants its contractual partner the right to use that right in return for remuneration that such an activity is involved.

31 By such a contract, the only obligation which the owner of the right granted undertakes with regard to its contractual partner is not to challenge the use of that right by the latter. As pointed out by the Advocate General in point 58 of her Opinion, the owner of an intellectual property right does not perform any service in granting a right to use that property and undertakes merely to permit the licensee to exploit that right freely.

QUESTION

If a copyright license is not a contract for the provision of services, how is the place of performance determined? Is there one or various places of performance for a European license, for a worldwide license? What about an assignment of all rights?

C-128/11 UsedSoft GmbH v. Oracle International Corp. ECLI:EU:C:2012:407 [2012]

See *supra*, Part II, Chapter 5.4.2, pp. 396–98, from point 35 to 48.

QUESTIONS

1. To what extent might this characterization of sale under article 4(2) of Directive 2009/24 [Software Directive] be relevant to the Brussels Regulation Recast?
2. How would you ascertain the place of delivery for digital copies?

7.3.5 Forum selection clauses

Regulation (EU) No 1215/2012 of the European Parliament and of the Council of 12 December 2012 on jurisdiction and the recognition and enforcement of judgments in civil and commercial matters (recast) (Brussels Regulation Recast)

Article 25

1. If the parties, regardless of their domicile, have agreed that a court or the courts of a Member State are to have jurisdiction to settle any disputes which have arisen or which may arise in connection with a particular legal relationship, that court or those courts shall have jurisdiction, unless the agreement is null and void as to its substantive validity under the law of that Member State. Such jurisdiction shall be exclusive unless the parties have agreed otherwise. The agreement conferring jurisdiction shall be either:

(a) in writing or evidenced in writing;
(b) in a form which accords with practices which the parties have established between themselves; or
(c) in international trade or commerce, in a form which accords with a usage of which the parties are or ought to have been aware and which in such trade or commerce is widely known to, and regularly observed by, parties to contracts of the type involved in the particular trade or commerce concerned.

2. Any communication by electronic means which provides a durable record of the agreement shall be equivalent to 'writing'.

3. The court or courts of a Member State on which a trust instrument has conferred jurisdiction shall have exclusive jurisdiction in any proceedings brought against a settlor, trustee or beneficiary, if relations between those persons or their rights or obligations under the trust are involved.

4. Agreements or provisions of a trust instrument conferring jurisdiction shall have no legal force if they are contrary to Articles 15, 19 or 23, or if the courts whose jurisdiction they purport to exclude have exclusive jurisdiction by virtue of Article 24.

5. An agreement conferring jurisdiction which forms part of a contract shall be treated as an agreement independent of the other terms of the contract.

The validity of the agreement conferring jurisdiction cannot be contested solely on the ground that the contract is not valid.

The Recast's innovations here are not only formal. The text of article 25 Recast is much more developed than the prior version's article 23.

The Regulation is applicable as soon as a member state is designated by the selection clause regardless of the parties' domicile. As to substance, article 25 determines the law applicable to the validity of the clause and the independence of the clause from the contract. The following case was decided under prior article 23, but the solution would be unchanged under new article 25.

Skype Technologies SA v. Joltid LTD, [2009] EWHC 2783 (Ch)

Mr Justice Lewison:

1. The Skype Group offers software which can be downloaded from the internet for free and allows users to communicate through free voice and video calls, by sending instant messages, SMS (text messages) or files, and by making or receiving low-cost calls to and from landline and mobile numbers. Skype has proved very successful: as at 31 December 2008, Skype had 405.3 million registered users throughout the world. The Claimant, Skype Technologies SA, is a member of the Skype Group. It is domiciled in Luxembourg.

2. The Defendant, Joltid Ltd, is a company incorporated in the British Virgin Islands. It is the owner of the copyright in certain software called the Global Index software. This software is fundamental to Skype's business. On 20 November 2003 Skype Technologies and Joltid entered into a written licence agreement. The License Agreement recorded the terms upon which Joltid would grant to Skype Technologies a world-wide licence to use a compiled object code form (in essence, a form of software which is machine-readable rather than human-readable) of the Global Index software. It is referred to in the License Agreement as the "Joltid Software". The object code is to be distinguished from the source code which is a human-readable form of the software. Under the License Agreement Joltid retained sole control over the source code.

3. Clause 19.1 of the License Agreement contained a jurisdiction clause which stated:

Governing Law and Jurisdiction. Any claim arising under or relating to this Agreement shall be governed by the internal substantive laws of England and Wales and the parties submit to the exclusive jurisdiction of the English courts.

. . .

11.   Skype Technologies claims that in so far as the US proceedings make claims against it, the claim is a breach of clause 19.1 of the License Agreement, and seek an anti-suit injunction to restrain any further steps being taken against it in the USA.

12.   Article 23 [25 Recast] of Council Regulation (EC) No 44/2001 ("the Judgments Regulation") provides:

"1. If the parties, one or more of who is domiciled in a Member State, have agreed that a court or the courts of a member State are to have jurisdiction to settle any disputes which have arisen or which may arise in connection with a particular legal relationship, that court or those courts shall have jurisdiction. Such jurisdiction shall be exclusive unless the parties have agreed otherwise."

13.   Since Skype Technologies is domiciled in Luxembourg, there is no doubt that this article applies. Since clause 19.1 of the License Agreement confers exclusive jurisdiction on the courts of this country, there is equally no doubt that this court has jurisdiction to determine all claims between Skype Technologies and Joltid arising under or relating to the License Agreement. That gives rise to two questions:

    i)   In so far as the US proceedings concern Skype Technologies, do they fall within the scope of the exclusive jurisdiction agreement;

    ii) If they do, how does that affect the court's willingness to grant an anti-suit injunction?

14.   Whether a claim falls within an agreed jurisdiction clause is a question of interpretation of the clause in question. That question is to be decided according to national law, even in the context of the Judgments Regulation (see *Benincasa v. Dentalkit Srl* [1997] E.T.M.R. 447; *Knorr-Bremse Systems for Commercial Vehicles Ltd v Haldex Brake Products GmbH* [2008] FSR 30). In my judgment there is no distinction to be drawn between the approach to the interpretation of a clause in an agreement which confers jurisdiction on the courts of a particular territory and a clause in an agreement which confers jurisdiction on a particular tribunal, such as an arbitrator. Both types of clause represent the parties' agreement about how disputes are to be resolved. Both should be interpreted in accordance with the same principles. The correct approach to the interpretation of arbitration agreements has been considered recently by both the Court of Appeal and the House of Lords. In *Fiona Trust & Holdings Corporation v Privalov* [2007] 2 Lloyd's Rep 267 a charterparty contained a clause which referred "any dispute arising under this charter" to arbitration. Longmore LJ said (§ 17):

Ordinary businessmen would be surprised at the nice distinctions drawn in the cases and the time taken up by argument in debating whether a particular case falls within one set of words or another very similar set of words. If businessmen go to the trouble of agreeing that their disputes be heard in the courts of a particular country or by a tribunal of their choice they do not expect (at any rate when they are making the contract in the first place) that time and expense will be taken in lengthy argument about the nature of particular causes of action and whether any particular cause of action comes within the meaning of the particular phrase they have chosen in their arbitration clause.

15. He added (§ 18):

As it seems to us any jurisdiction or arbitration clause in an international commercial contract should be liberally construed. The words "arising out of" should cover "every dispute except a dispute as to whether there was ever a contract at all". . .

. . .

17. . . . Mr Calver QC, appearing with Mr Brandreth for Joltid, lays stress on that part of clause 19.1 which speaks of any "claim" rather than any "dispute". He says that Joltid's *claim* in the US proceedings does not arise out of the License Agreement. On the contrary it is predicated on the assumption that the License Agreement has been terminated. Mr Calver says that his proposition can be tested in the following way:

[Had] the UK litigation been concluded in Joltid's favour before the commencement of the US proceedings, could [Skype Technologies] claim that Joltid's US copyright infringement claims relating to acts done after the termination of the Agreement arose under or were related to the Agreement? The answer must be: plainly not.

18. If the question is put in that way, then Mr Calver may be right, although Mr Hollander QC, appearing with Mr Singla for Skype Technologies, would dispute that. But the heart of the current dispute between the parties is whether the License Agreement has or has not been validly terminated. That issue has not been determined, and it is the issue which this court will decide. The fact is that if Skype Technologies is right in saying that the License Agreement remains in force and that it has the effect that it says it has, then Joltid's claims against Skype Technologies in the US proceedings will fail. It is only if Joltid succeeds in this court that the claims made in the US pro-

ceedings get off the ground against Skype Technologies. Mr Calver relied on part of the speech of Lord Scott of Foscote in *Donohue v Armco Inc* [2002] 1 Lloyd's Rep 425 § 60 in which his Lordship appeared to distinguish between a clause which covered "any dispute" between the parties and one which covered "any claim against" one of the parties. But this was both hypothetical and *obiter*, and none of the other Law Lords associated themselves with it. More to the point, Lord Scott's observations were made five years before the House of Lords in *Fiona Trust* drew a line under the authorities and made a fresh start (per Lord Hoffmann § 12). In *Fiona Trust* Lord Scott himself said that he was in complete agreement both with Lord Hoffmann's conclusion and his reasoning (§ 36).

19. Mr Calver's argument is, in my judgment, based on an unduly narrow reading of the clause. It is exactly the kind of fine distinction that both Longmore LJ and Lord Hoffmann deplored in *Fiona Trust*. Whether the contention that the License Agreement is still in force is pleaded by way of Complaint or by way of defence is, in my judgment, irrelevant. Rational businessmen would not envisage that their choice of jurisdiction would depend on who issued proceedings first, or whether an ingenious pleader could frame a cause of action without actually mentioning the License Agreement.

20. Accordingly, in my judgment the claims against Skype Technologies made in the US proceedings fall within the scope of clause 19.1 of the License Agreement.

QUESTIONS

1. How would jurisdiction over this litigation have been determined in the absence of a forum selection clause? Which court(s) may have jurisdiction to decide the case?
2. Assume that the same forum selection clause is incorporated in worldwide license between an Indian company and an American company. What would have been the solution of an English judge based on the article 25 Recast?

7.3.6 The prohibition of the *forum non conveniens* doctrine under the Brussels I Regulation Recast

As we have seen above, the *forum non conveniens* doctrine is a well-established principle in common law. But when it comes to the civil law system, the *forum non conveniens* doctrine does not exist. The denial of *forum non conveniens* in civil law systems is supposedly justified by due process concerns, foreseeability and the right to a court hearing which includes the hearing at a predetermined venue. The harmonization of the law of judicial competence in the E.U. confronted the different perspectives on *forum non conveniens* between the U.K. as a common law country and continental Europe with its civil law system. The 1968 Brussels Convention on Jurisdiction and the Enforcement of Judgments in Civil and Commercial Matters, the Brussels I Regulation from 2001, and the most recent Brussels I Recast did not explicitly prohibit the use of *forum non conveniens*, even though such a mechanism seems not very coherent with the system established in those instruments. In 2005 the ECJ rendered a judgment in the *Owusu* case setting the fate of the *forum non conveniens*.

C-281/02 Andrew Owusu v. N.B. Jackson, trading as 'Villa Holidays Bal-Inn Villas' and Others ECLI:EU:C:2005:120 [2005]

[Mr Owusu, an English national, vacationed in Jamaica where he was severely injured in a swimming accident. Back home in England Mr Owusu sued the British lessor of the Jamaican vacation home, a Jamaican company, which was responsible for the safety of the beach where the accident occurred, and the Jamaican beach resorts which were licensed to use the beach. The Court of Appeal for England and Wales forwarded to the ECJ the question on the applicability of *forum non conveniens*:]

35   It follows from the foregoing that Article 2 of the Brussels Convention [4 Recast] applies to circumstances such as those in the main proceedings, involving relationships between the courts of a single Contracting State and those of a non-Contracting State rather than relationships between the courts of a number of Contracting States.

36   It must therefore be considered whether, in such circumstances, the Brussels Convention precludes a court of a Contracting State from applying the forum non conveniens doctrine and declining to exercise the jurisdiction conferred on it by Article 2 of that Convention [4 Recast].

The compatibility of the forum non conveniens doctrine with the Brussels Convention

37   It must be observed, first, that Article 2 of the Brussels Convention [4 Recast] is mandatory in nature and that, according to its terms, there can be no derogation from the principle it lays down except in the cases expressly provided for by the Convention [citations omitted]. It is common ground

that no exception on the basis of the forum non conveniens doctrine was provided for by the authors of the Convention, . . .

38 Respect for the principle of legal certainty, which is one of the objectives of the Brussels Convention [citations omitted], would not be fully guaranteed if the court having jurisdiction under the Convention had to be allowed to apply the forum non conveniens doctrine.

39 According to its preamble, the Brussels Convention is intended to strengthen in the Community the legal protection of persons established therein, by laying down common rules on jurisdiction to guarantee certainty as to the allocation of jurisdiction among the various national courts before which proceedings in a particular case may be brought [citations omitted].

40 The Court has thus held that the principle of legal certainty requires, in particular, that the jurisdictional rules which derogate from the general rule laid down in Article 2 of the Brussels Convention [4 Recast] should be interpreted in such a way as to enable a normally well-informed defendant reasonably to foresee before which courts, other than those of the State in which he is domiciled, he may be sued [citations omitted].

41 Application of the forum non conveniens doctrine, which allows the court seised a wide discretion as regards the question whether a foreign court would be a more appropriate forum for the trial of an action, is liable to undermine the predictability of the rules of jurisdiction laid down by the Brussels Convention, in particular that of Article 2 [4 Recast], and consequently to undermine the principle of legal certainty, which is the basis of the Convention.

42 The legal protection of persons established in the Community would also be undermined. First, a defendant, who is generally better placed to conduct his defence before the courts of his domicile, would not be able, in circumstances such as those of the main proceedings, reasonably to foresee before which other court he may be sued. Second, where a plea is raised on the basis that a foreign court is a more appropriate forum to try the action, it is for the claimant to establish that he will not be able to obtain justice before that foreign court or, if the court seised decides to allow the plea, that the foreign court has in fact no jurisdiction to try the action or that the claimant does not, in practice, have access to effective justice before that court, irrespective of the cost entailed by the bringing of a fresh action before a court of another State and the prolongation of the procedural time-limits.

43   Moreover, allowing forum non conveniens in the context of the Brussels Convention would be likely to affect the uniform application of the rules of jurisdiction contained therein in so far as that doctrine is recognised only in a limited number of Contracting States, whereas the objective of the Brussels Convention is precisely to lay down common rules to the exclusion of derogating national rules.

44   The defendants in the main proceedings emphasise the negative consequences which would result in practice from the obligation the English courts would then be under to try this case, inter alia as regards the expense of the proceedings, the possibility of recovering their costs in England if the claimant's action is dismissed, the logistical difficulties resulting from the geographical distance, the need to assess the merits of the case according to Jamaican standards, the enforceability in Jamaica of a default judgment and the impossibility of enforcing cross-claims against the other defendants.

45   In that regard, genuine as those difficulties may be, suffice it to observe that such considerations, which are precisely those which may be taken into account when forum non conveniens is considered, are not such as to call into question the mandatory nature of the fundamental rule of jurisdiction contained in Article 2 of the Brussels Convention [4 Recast], for the reasons set out above.

46   In the light of all the foregoing considerations, the answer to the first question must be that the Brussels Convention precludes a court of a Contracting State from declining the jurisdiction conferred on it by Article 2 of that convention [4 Recast] on the ground that a court of a non-Contracting State would be a more appropriate forum for the trial of the action even if the jurisdiction of no other Contracting State is in issue or the proceedings have no connecting factors to any other Contracting State.

QUESTION

Why does the Brussels Recast Regulation prohibit a U.K. judge from exercising her discretion? In what situations does the judge still have discretion?

7.4   Soft law

Edouard Treppoz, A Comparative Study of the Principles of the American Law Institute and the Max Planck Institute on Private International and Intellectual Property (excerpts; footnotes omitted), C. Nourissat & E. Treppoz eds., ***Droit international privé et propriété***

intellectuelle – un nouveau cadre pour des nouvelles strategies, (**Lamy Kluwer, 2009**).

To offer another perspective of private international law and intellectual property law issues presupposes stepping back for a moment from the European Community [European Union] context. The objective of this excursion outside of the Community [Union] is not just to seek the relaxing exoticism of faraway places. It targets a more in-depth, more precise and thus more convincing analysis of Community [EU] law, ending with a review of the Brussels I Regulation. As we know, one of the difficulties facing the E.U. lawmaker indeed relates to intellectual property. That said, focusing on the private international law of intellectual property undeniably requires us to look more closely at the remarkable work conducted by the American Law Institute under the aegis of Professors Dessemontet, Dreyfuss and Ginsburg.

A brief review of the origins of this work is crucial. One remembers, at the end of 1999, the ambitious draft Convention on the jurisdiction of foreign courts for civil and criminal matters conducted under the aegis of The Hague Conference and perceived for a long time as a worldwide extension of the Brussels and Lugano Conventions. This project, perhaps because it was so ambitious, failed. And one of the reasons for this failure related directly to intellectual property, whose supposed specificities, for some, were not taken sufficiently into consideration. Professors Ginsburg and Dreyfuss, under the auspices of WIPO, then proposed to adapt this work to the specificities of intellectual property. Rather than accept the "one size fits all" version offered by the Hague Conference, WIPO's "made-to-measure" version certainly seemed more attractive. So the jurisdictional conflict aspect remained to be completed by a conflict-of-laws aspect in order to offer a full text on issues that were particularly lacking and delicate, those of intellectual property and private international law, at a time when the Internet was starting to emerge. That said, while the Community [EU] origin of conflicts of jurisdictions can be argued, that of the conflicts of laws could, with some benevolence, be attributed to Lyon. We in fact learned that the joint proposal of a hierarchical appurtenance structure published by Professors Dessemontet and Ginsburg in 1996 took shape after a conference in Lyon, which joint proposal came to play an important role in the first draft of the ALI Principles. The interest of the American Law Institute was rapidly drawn to the projects of Professors Ginsburg and Dreyfuss, while Professor Dessemontet was appointed the third reporter. Finally, these "principles governing jurisdiction, choice of law and judgments in transnational disputes" on intellectual property were adopted by the American Law Institute on 14 May 2007 at its Annual Meeting in San Francisco.

The objective of these ALI Principles was threefold: to provide a text for international bodies seeking to regulate this matter, such as the WIPO and WTO, as well as regional and national bodies called upon to regulate this issue and, finally, to allow for a discussion and renewed debate amongst the highest academic milieus on these questions. In brief, this was a "soft law", non-binding text, with its persuasive effect resulting exclusively from its quality. An analogy could then be made with the famous UNIDROIT Principles of International Commercial Contracts, the significant difference being that the will of the parties in this case had no power to impose the application of the ALI Principles. The persuasive impact of the quality must be acknowledged, however, as only the first of its objectives has not been achieved to date! And American courts no longer hesitate to draw on these principles to strengthen their position. In particular, the doctrine has adopted these principles, also to compare them to national and regional solutions. The success was so resounding that these principles are subject to competition. . . . Since April 2009, in fact, one must now take into consideration the Principles proposed by the European Group at the Max Planck Institute on the conflict of laws in intellectual property matters, the version of 6 June 2009 being the last version reviewed for this publication. The objective is the same: to be a model for the "interpreter", and for the legislator. Japanese principles on this very question will soon be added. So it seems difficult to walk away from these new proposals, and a new vision, or multiple visions, seems more appropriate to us, especially in the current context of the Community's [EU's] revision of the text.

Therefore, this study moves from the ALI Principles towards a comparative study of these principles with the Principles established under the aegis of the Max Planck Institute. The objective consists in seeking convergences among these texts on doctrine, which provide as many areas for reflection by Community lawmakers in their revision of the Brussels I Regulation. Yet, these converging solutions, although numerous, cannot overshadow the differences in the approaches of these two principles, which highlight the very relativity of the starting point. This comparative study of the ALI Principles and the CLIP Principles will therefore start by reviewing the divergent approaches and then the converging solutions.

During the last century, the international intellectual property scheme was the subject of a well-known debate between proponents of a restrictive territorialism and proponents of a broad universalism, a controversy that only ended with the "weariness of the fighters". A century later, the debate is not over, and the place of the territoriality principle is still under discussion, as illustrated by a comparison between the Max Planck Principles and the ALI Principles. While the former still focus on a territorialist and dogmatic approach, the latter are more pragmatic and internationalist.

7.4.1 ALI Principles

Part II – JURISDICTION
Chapter One: Personal Jurisdiction over the Defendant

§ 201. Defendant's Residence

(1) A person may be sued in the courts in any State where that person is resident.

(2) For the purposes of these Principles:

(a) a natural person is resident where he or she is habitually found and maintains durable professional and personal connections;
(b) a juridical person is resident in any State or States in which it:
(i) has a statutory seat;
(ii) is incorporated or formed;
(iii) has its central administration or chief executive office; or
(iv) has its principal place of business.

QUESTION

A software company that devises and distributes office management applications has its principal place of business in Switzerland and is incorporated in the Bahamas. It also has sales representatives resident in the U.K and the U.S. A competitor would like to sue the software company for infringement. Where could it sue the software company under § 201 ALI Principles?

§ 204. Infringement Activity by a Defendant Not Resident in the Forum

(1) A person may be sued in any State in which that person has substantially acted, or taken substantial preparatory acts, to initiate or to further an alleged infringement. The court's jurisdiction extends to claims respecting all injuries arising out of the conduct within the State that initiates or furthers the alleged infringement, wherever the injuries occur.

(2) A person may be sued in any State in which its activities give rise to an infringement claim, if it reasonably can be seen as having directed those activities to that State. The court's jurisdiction extends to claims respecting injuries occurring in that State.

(3) A person who cannot be sued in a WTO-member State through the application of §§ 201–202 or 204(1) may be sued in any State in which its activities give rise to an infringement claim if:

(a) it reasonably can be seen as having directed those activities to that State, and

(b) it solicits or maintains contacts, business, or an audience in that State on a regular basis, whether or not those contacts initiate or further the infringing activity or activities.

The court's jurisdiction extends to claims respecting injuries arising out of conduct outside the State that relates to the alleged infringement in the State, wherever the injuries occur.

QUESTIONS

1. A, a resident of Portugal, runs a Portuguese-language website offering Portuguese-language popular music. Prices are in U.S. dollars and the site hosts advertisements for local businesses in Newark, N.J., which has a sizeable Portuguese and Brazilian population. B, a resident of New York, is the composer of some of the music offered on A's website. B sues A for copyright infringement in New York. Under the ALI Principles, is A amenable to suit in the U.S.?

2. Reconsider the following case under the ALI Principles: a French producer of Champagne has registered in all E.U. countries PURE as a trademark, with one notable exception, Spain where a local producer of Cava has already registered the PURE as a trademark for his Cava. The Spanish producer exploits a website solely written in Spanish in order to promote its Cava in Spain. Consumers could order some Sava provided that the address of distribution is in Spain. The French producer considers that the Spanish website infringes his French trademark and brings an action before the French Court. Do the ALI Principles authorize the French court to hear the case?

3.

(a) A U.S. website seeks to avoid being subject to personal jurisdiction in Italy. Its website eschews the Italian language, currency, and content. Nonetheless, it still carries content that is likely to attract Italian users. To avoid amenability to suit, the U.S. website installs a filter that blocks access from Italian Internet-connection services. It also requires its subscribers to provide credit card and residence information. Italian residents are automatically excluded.

(b) A U.S. website seeks to avoid being subject to the jurisdiction of courts outside the U.S. Its website is accessible throughout the world, but the website's home page states that access will be granted only to those users who can show that they have a U.S. postal code. The home page asks users to type in their U.S. postal code. The home page also lists the address, with postal code, of the U.S. website's headquarters.

In which case could the U.S. website be haled into court in Italy? Under the ALI Principles?

§ 206. Personal Jurisdiction over Multiple Defendants

(1) A plaintiff bringing an action against a person in a State in which that person is resident may also proceed in that State against one or more other defendants not resident in that State if the claims against the person resident in that State and such other defendants are so closely connected that they should be adjudicated together to avoid a risk of inconsistent judgments, and

> (a) there is a substantial, direct, and foreseeable connection between the forum's intellectual property rights at issue and each nonresident defendant; or
> (b) as between the forum and the States in which the added defendants are resident, there is no forum that is more closely related to the entire dispute.

(2) There is a risk of inconsistent judgments if it appears that:

> (a) the judgments would impose redundant liability;
> (b) the judgment in one case would undermine the judgment in another case; or
> (c) a party cannot conform its behavior to both judgments.

(3) Subsection (1) does not apply to a codefendant invoking an exclusive choice-of-court clause agreed with the plaintiff and conforming with § 202.

(4) If an action is brought in a State on the basis of this section, then that court has jurisdiction with respect to injuries, wherever occurring,

that arise out of the activities that allegedly create the risk of inconsistent judgments.

QUESTIONS

1. A, a Canadian resident, streams television signals from Canada over the Internet without authorization. A chooses the materials to be streamed and has subcontracted maintenance of its Canadian servers to an outside technician, F, a Canadian. A U.S. television station sues A in the U.S. for copyright infringement and seeks to join F. Would the ALI Principles authorize such consolidation?

2. Balthazar Inc., an e-book publisher and resident of the U.S., travels to England, where it enters into an agreement with an author whose works were previously published in print format by Ariane, Inc., which is located in India. The agreement obligates Balthazar to disseminate the works in the new format. Ariane is neither a party to the contract nor aware of it. Ariane sues Balthazar in the U.S. for injunctive relief, claiming that the transfer of copyright ownership Ariane received from the English author covered publication in all media for all countries. Ariane seeks to join the author to the action. Would the ALI Principles authorize the joinder?

7.4.2 CLIP Principles

PART 2: JURISDICTION
Section 1: General jurisdiction

Article 2:101: General jurisdiction

Subject to these Principles, a person may be sued in the courts of any State in which the person is habitually resident (Article 2:601).

Article 2:202: Infringement

In disputes concerned with infringement of an intellectual property right, a person may be sued in the courts of the State where the alleged infringement occurs or may occur, unless the alleged infringer has not acted in that State to initiate or further the infringement and her/his activity cannot reasonably be seen as having been directed to that State.

Article 2:203: Extent of jurisdiction over infringement claims

(1) Subject to paragraph 2, a court whose jurisdiction is based on Article 2:202 shall have jurisdiction in respect of infringements that

occur or may occur within the territory of the State in which that court is situated.

(2) In disputes concerned with infringement carried out through ubiquitous media such as the Internet, the court whose jurisdiction is based on Article 2:202 shall also have jurisdiction in respect of infringements that occur or may occur within the territory of any other State, provided that the activities giving rise to the infringement have no substantial effect in the State, or any of the States, where the infringer is habitually resident and

(a) substantial activities in furtherance of the infringement in its entirety have been carried out within the territory of the State in which the court is situated, or

(b) the harm caused by the infringement in the State where the court is situated is substantial in relation to the infringement in its entirety.

QUESTION

Consider the questions that followed section 204 of the ALI Principles, above; what would be the responses under article 2:203 of the CLIP Principles?

Article 2:206: Multiple defendants

(1) A person who is one of a number of defendants may also be sued in the courts of the State where any of the defendants is habitually resident, provided the claims are so closely connected that it is appropriate to hear and determine them together to avoid the risk of incompatible judgments resulting from separate proceedings.

(2) For the purposes of paragraph 1, a risk of incompatible judgments requires a risk of divergence in the outcome of the actions against the different defendants which arises in the context of essentially the same situation of law and fact. In particular in infringement disputes and subject to the individual circumstances of the case,

(a) disputes involve essentially the same factual situation if the defendants have, even if in different States, acted in an identical or similar manner in accordance with a common policy;

(b) disputes may involve essentially the same legal situation even if different national laws are applicable to the claims against the different defendants, provided that the relevant national laws are harmonised to a significant degree by rules of a regional economic integration organisation or by international conventions which are applicable to the disputes in question.

(3) If it is manifest from the facts that one defendant has coordinated the relevant activities or is otherwise most closely connected with the dispute in its entirety, jurisdiction according to paragraph 1 is only conferred on the courts in the State where that defendant is habitually resident. In other cases, jurisdiction is conferred on the courts in the State or States of habitual residence of any of the defendants, unless

(a) the contribution of the defendant who is habitually resident in the State where the court is located is insubstantial in relation to the dispute in its entirety or
(b) the claim against the resident defendant is manifestly inadmissible.

. . .

QUESTION

Consider the questions that followed section 206 of the ALI Principles, above; what would be the responses under article 2:206 of the CLIP Principles?

Article 2:601: Habitual residence

(1) For the purposes of this Part, the habitual residence of a natural person acting in the course of a business activity shall, for actions related to that activity, also be the principal place of business.

(2) For the purposes of this Part, a company or other legal person or association of natural or legal persons shall have its habitual residence in any State

(a) where it has its statutory seat or registered office, or
(b) where it has its central administration, or
(c) where it has its principal place of business.

If the entity lacks a statutory seat or registered office, it may also be sued in the State where it was incorporated or, if no such place exists, under whose law it was formed.

(3) The principal place of business shall be the place from which the main business activities are conducted.

QUESTION

Consider the question under section 201 of the ALI Principles, above; what would be the response under article 2:601 of the CLIP Principles?

Article 2:602: Declaratory actions

Subject to Article 2:401, an action for a declaratory judgment may be based on the same ground of jurisdiction as a corresponding action seeking substantive relief.

QUESTIONS

What would the solution have been in *Penguin* and *Pez Hejduk* under the ALI Principles and the CLIP Principles? What would the ruling have been under *Roche*; *Painer*; and *Solvay* if decided under the ALI Principles and the CLIP Principles?

PROBLEMS

1. An Italian paparazzo photographed the romantic encounters of the French President. In order to prepare his scoop, he left his apartment in Milan and spent six months in Paris tracking the presidential rendezvous. The pictures were published by a French magazine. A Belgian magazine distributed in all European French-speaking countries (Belgium, France, Luxembourg and Switzerland) republished the pictures without any authorization. The publisher of the Belgian magazine is a company registered in Luxembourg with headquarters in Paris. The paparazzo would like to seize a court competent to adjudicate the full territorial extent of the infringement. Which are the options under the ALI Principles? Which are the options under the CLIP Principles?
2. Later, the pictures were integrated in a video game satirizing the presidential romance. Users anywhere in the world can download the video game from a website hosted in Malta. The website is owned by a software programmer living in London. The paparazzo would like to seise a court competent to adjudicate the full territorial extent of the infringement. Which are the options under the ALI Principles? Under the CLIP Principles?

8

Conflict of laws (legislative competence)

Once the competent court has been ascertained, the next question is what law applies to the claim. Under a basic tenet of private international law, the applicable law could be a law other than that of the forum. The way to determine applicable law might be different in Europe and in the U.S. The former often seems abstract and conceptual, while the latter is more concrete and pragmatic. The process of harmonization on an international or a regional basis softens these disparities. For example, while the traditional French choice of law rules for tort claims could lead to opposite outcomes from the American interest analysis, the European choice of law rules (now applicable in France) adopt a hybrid approach.

As to copyright and neighboring rights, choice of law is a highly disputed subject between those favoring a universal approach and those retaining a territorial approach. If the territorial approach presents the advantage of submitting all works to the same level of protection within one country, the universal approach will assure the owner the benefit of the same protection all over the world. Applying the same substantive rule in all countries where the work is exploited (rather than applying the potentially different rules of each country) might be an advantage in a globalized world—at least for issues pertaining to authorship and ownership. Jurisdictions adopting a universalist approach will look to the law of the country of origin to resolve those and other issues. But unless all jurisdictions follow the same approach, discordance and disuniformity will prevail. If the current copyright and neighboring rights treaties do not resolve the question of applicable law, the most efficient way to solve this dispute would be to determine a choice of law approach through an international instrument, binding every member state, or, given the unlikely prospect of such an instrument, through agreement on soft law norms such as the ALI and CLIP proposals. A first question thus requires assessment whether the international Conventions pose any choice of law rules. To the extent that they do not, and therefore leave member states free to determine the law applicable to some or all issues that arise in a dispute, local or regional solutions will have the last word, especially on the tricky issue of ubiquitous infringement.

8.1   International conventions

8.1.1   Berne Convention

Article 5

> **Article 5**
> **Rights Guaranteed**
>
> *1. and 2. Outside the country of origin; . . .*
>
> (1) Authors shall enjoy, in respect of works for which they are protected under this Convention, in countries of the Union other than the country of origin, the rights which their respective laws do now or may hereafter grant to their nationals, as well as the rights specially granted by this Convention.
>
> (2) The enjoyment and the exercise of these rights shall not be subject to any formality; such enjoyment and such exercise shall be independent of the existence of protection in the country of origin of the work. Consequently, apart from the provisions of this Convention, the extent of protection, as well as the means of redress afforded to the author to protect his rights, shall be governed exclusively by the laws of the country where protection is claimed.
>
> . . .

Sam Ricketson and Jane C. Ginsburg, *International Copyright and Neighbouring Rights: The Berne Convention and Beyond* (Oxford 2006) (paras. 20.08–20.14, footnotes omitted)*

Berne Convention Article 5(1) and (2) – A Choice of Law Rule? From its inception, the Berne Convention has combined two different techniques, substantive supranational minimum rules, and national treatment. Under the former approach, the Convention supplies the substantive rule, though member States may enjoy some room for interpretation, and may also provide for greater protection. In that event, or with respect to matters for which the

---

* By permission of Oxford University Press.

Convention does not supply a substantive rule, what law applies? Under the rule of national treatment, as set out in article 5(1), a foreign Berne author is assimilated to a local author, and receives the same rights as the laws of that country would grant a local. . . . This seems to mean that each country of the Union will apply its substantive law to works of foreign Union authors. In other words, the principle of national treatment would supply a choice of law rule directing application of the substantive law of the countries in which the author seeks to enforce her rights. Article 5(2) appears to reinforce this conclusion. Under article 5(2) of the Berne Convention

> the extent of protection, as well as the means of redress afforded to the author to protect his rights, shall be governed exclusively by the laws of the country where protection is claimed.

There is in fact some dispute as to whether this text announces a choice of law rule, or simply a nondiscrimination rule. But the latter characterization begs the question, "non discrimination as to what?" As to the substantive rules governing the claims of local and of foreign authors? Or as to the choice of law rule to determine the law governing local and foreign authors' claims? In the latter event, the "country where protection is claimed" need not apply its own law to a Unionist author, so long as it would apply the same choice of law rule to a local author in the same circumstances. (A similar effect would be achieved were article 5(2) considered a choice of law rule, but one designating the whole law, including the conflicts law, of the country "where protection is claimed.") This approach leads to considerable unpredictability, because its consequences for actual equality of treatment will depend on what the local choice of rule is. Suppose the local choice of law rule directed application of the law of the country where the infringement occurred, and that the infringement occurred in a country other than the forum. In that case, the same law—the law of that other country—would apply to local and to foreign works. But suppose the local choice of law rule selected the law of the country of origin. In that case, local law would determine the infringement of local works, but foreign laws would govern the infringement of foreign works. This, in turn, could lead to different outcomes for domestic and for foreign works. Thus, if the forum applied the same choice of law rule to the infringement of domestic and foreign works, this could result in a denial of substantive national treatment. It seems reasonable to conclude, therefore, that the principle of nondiscrimination calls for the application of the same substantive rules to local and to foreign authors.

But does article 5.2 express not only a principle of nondiscrimination, but also a choice of (substantive) law rule? Certainly the language "shall be governed exclusively by the laws of the country where protection is claimed" looks like a rule of legislative competence, directing application of the law of the territory on which the alleged infringement occurred. But there are at least two problems. First, the text states "country where protection is claimed," rather than "country for which protection is claimed." If this is a choice of law rule, then it looks like a direction to apply the lex fori. As we have seen earlier, however, the forum is not necessarily the place of the infringement. (Although the drafters of article 5(2) may have assumed that the place of litigation and the place of the harm would coincide in practice, and this might have been a reasonable factual assumption at the time the rule was formulated.) Applying the lex fori may result in a disjunction between the law applied to the claim and the law that governs in the place where the infringement occurred; that in turn may mean that the author does not receive the same level of protection as do authors in the country of infringement. This outcome is inconsistent with the general Berne Convention goal of ensuring that authors be protected in as uniform a manner as possible. As a result, many commentators have interpreted article 5(2) to mean "country, or countries, for which protection is claimed." Second, even if article 5(2) announces a choice of law rule, it does not purport to cover all issues of international copyright. Notably, questions of authorship, initial ownership, and transfers of ownership remain unaddressed.

At most, then, article 5(1) and (2) anticipate that the law of the territories on which alleged infringements occur will determine most questions regarding the existence of protection, its scope, and the available remedies. This falls short of a fully territorial approach in two ways. First, as noted above, there are the matters left off the article 5(2) list. Second, at various points, the Convention designates application of a law other than that of the country of protection to determine the existence or scope of protection; this is the case in relation to duration, as well as to the protection of works of applied art and of the droit de suite. These are all variations on the rule of reciprocity, an approach generally spurned by the Convention, ... Nonetheless, these derogations from the rule of national treatment make the law of the work's country of origin applicable to determine the existence or scope of protection in certain—admittedly limited—situations, thus undercutting the primacy of the law of the country of protection.

Inferences to draw from article 14*bis*(2)(a)? Outside article 5(2), there is one instance in which the Berne Convention both addresses questions of ownership and designates the applicable law. Article 14*bis*(2)(a) provides:

> Ownership of copyright in a cinematographic work shall be a matter for legislation in the country where protection is claimed.

Assuming this is not a direction to apply the conflicts law of the country "where" (for which?) protection is claimed, article 14*bis*(2)(a) makes the law of each country of exploitation competent to determine ownership of rights in cinematographic works, subject to a complex set of presumptions of transfers of ownership set out in sub sections (b)–(e). One might question whether the resulting system makes any sense. For present purposes, the question is whether this rule should be understood to reflect a choice of law principle applicable generally to questions of copyright ownership, or indeed to all questions in contention in a copyright dispute. Or should the opposite inference be drawn? If the law of the country of protection was singled out in this instance, that is because it is a special case, and in any other matter of ownership, some other law will apply. Indeed, pushing the negative inference to the extreme, some other law, perhaps that of the country origin, is the residually applicable law, from which articles 5(2) and 14*bis*(2)(a) derogate. It is not necessary to choose between these competing default positions; the point is that the plausibility of either one further underscores the Berne Convention's failure to create a general structure for identifying applicable law.

In the absence of a fully articulated system of treaty-mandated choice of law rules, we turn next to general principles of private international law to consider what might be the laws applicable, first, to the existence and scope of protection, and second to matters of authorship and ownership.

Existence and Scope of Protection: Given article 5(2)'s designation of the law of the country "where" protection is claimed to "govern" the "extent of protection," one might conclude that the Convention at least tells us that the law of the country of protection (lex protectionis) applies to determine whether and to what extent a work is protected. But the matter is more complicated than first appears. We have already discussed the question whether article 5(2)'s use of the term "where" evidences an intent that the substantive law of the forum should apply. . . . It may be reasonable to conclude that the drafters either did not anticipate that the country "where" protection was claimed would not also be the country where the infringement occurred, or assumed that the forum's choice of law rules would lead to the application of the law of the place of infringement. In either event, whether by designating a national substantive law, or a national conflicts rule whose outcome could be predicted, article 5(2) would have led to the ultimate application of a law consistent with the basic notions of territoriality implicit in that article's formulation. But territoriality offers insufficient comfort if the alleged infringement is occurring in many places at once.

QUESTION

In the context of digital media, the alleged infringement may take place pervasively, in the country from which the alleged infringement originated, as well as in the countries to which the infringement was communicated. As a result, a multiplicity of national laws potentially apply. Does the Berne Convention require a strictly territorial approach, applying successively the law of each country of receipt, or will it suffice to apply a single law, for example that of the country of initiation of the infringement, or the country of origin of the work?

Deriving conflicts rules from Berne Convention article 5?

Itar–Tass Russian News Agency v. Russian Kurier, Inc .153 F.3d 82 (2d Cir. 1998)

[In this infringement action brought by the Russian news agency Itar-Tass against a Russian-language newspaper in New York City that allegedly copied the news service's articles, the defendant Russian Kurier disputed the news agency's standing to sue, on the ground that the Russian journalists, and not the news agency, were the owners of the copyrights in the allegedly copied articles. Under U.S. law, if the journalists were the agency's employees, the agency would be initial copyright holder, but defendants asserted that Russian law should determine initial ownership of copyright in the Russian journalists' articles, and that under Russian law, the journalists retained the copyrights. Standing to sue thus turned on who owned the copyrights, a question that in turn required determination of which national copyright law applied to determine ownership: the law of the country of origin, or the law of the country where the alleged infringement occurred.]

Source of conflicts rules. Our analysis of the conflicts issue begins with consideration of the source of law for selecting a conflicts rule. Though [the] Nimmer [copyright treatise] turns directly to the Berne Convention and the U.C.C., we think that step moves too quickly past the Berne Convention Implementation Act of 1988, Pub L. 100–568, 102 Stat. 2853, 17 U.S.C.A. § 101 note. Section 4(a)(3) of the Act amends Title 17 to provide: "No right or interest in a work eligible for protection under this title may be claimed by virtue of ... the provisions of the Berne Convention .... Any rights in a work eligible for protection under this title that derive from this title . . . shall not be expanded or reduced by virtue of . . . the provisions of the Berne Convention." 17 U.S.C. § 104(c).

We start our analysis with the Copyrights Act itself, which contains no provision relevant to the pending case concerning conflicts issues.[10] We therefore fill the interstices of the Act by developing federal common law on the conflicts issue [citation omitted]. In doing so, we are entitled to consider and apply principles of private international law, which are "'part of our law'" [citation omitted].

This provision could be interpreted to be an example of the general conflicts approach we take in this opinion to copyright ownership issues, or an exception to some different approach. See Jane C. Ginsburg, Ownership of Electronic Rights and the Private International Law of Copyright, 22 Colum.-VLA J.L. & Arts 165, 171 (1998). We agree with Prof. Ginsburg and with the amicus, Prof. Patry, that section 104A(b) should not be understood to state an exception to any otherwise applicable conflicts rule. See Ginsburg, id.; Brief for Amicus Curiae at 14–17.

The choice of law applicable to the pending case is not necessarily the same for all issues. See Restatement (Second) of Conflict of Laws § 222 ("The courts have long recognized that they are not bound to decide all issues under the local law of a single state."). We consider first the law applicable to the issue of copyright ownership.

Conflicts rule for issues of ownership. Copyright is a form of property, and the usual rule is that the interests of the parties in property are determined by the law of the state with "the most significant relationship" to the property and the parties. See id. The Restatement recognizes the applicability of this principle to intangibles such as "a literary idea." Id. Since the works at issue were created by Russian nationals and first published in Russia, Russian law is the appropriate source of law to determine issues of ownership of rights. That is the well-reasoned conclusion of the Amicus Curiae, Prof. Patry, and the parties in their supplemental briefs are in agreement on this point. In terms of the United States Copyrights Act and its reference to the Berne Convention, Russia is the "country of origin" of these works, see 17 U.S.C.

---

10 The recently added provision concerning copyright in "restored works," those that are in the public domain because of noncompliance with formalities of United States copyright law, contains an explicit subsection vesting ownership of a restored work "in the author or initial rightholder of the work as determined by the law of the *source country of the work.*" 17 U.S.C. § 104A(b) (emphasis added); see id. § 104A(h)(8) (defining "source country").

§ 101 (definition of "country of origin" of Berne Convention work); Berne Convention, Art. 5(4), although "country of origin" might not always be the appropriate country for purposes of choice of law concerning ownership.[11]

To whatever extent we look to the Berne Convention itself as guidance in the development of federal common law on the conflicts issue, we find nothing to alter our conclusion. The Convention does not purport to settle issues of ownership, with one exception not relevant to this case.[12] See Jane C. Ginsburg, Ownership of Electronic Rights and the Private International Law of Copyright, 22 Colum.-VLA J.L. & Arts 165, 167–68 (1998) (The Berne Convention "provides that the law of the country where protection is claimed defines what rights are protected, the scope of the protection, and the available remedies; the treaty does not supply a choice of law rule for determining ownership.") [footnote concerning article 14bis(2)(a) omitted].

Selection of Russian law to determine copyright ownership is, however, subject to one procedural qualification. Under United States law, an owner (including one determined according to foreign law) may sue for infringement in a United States court only if it meets the standing test of 17 U.S.C. § 501(b), which accords standing only to the legal or beneficial owner of an "exclusive right."

Conflicts rule for infringement issues. On infringement issues, the governing conflicts principle is usually *lex loci delicti*, the doctrine generally applicable to torts [citation omitted.] We have implicitly adopted that approach to infringement claims, applying United States copyright law to a work that was unprotected in its country of origin. See *Hasbro Bradley, Inc. v. Sparkle Toys, Inc.*, 780 F.2d 189, 192–93 (2d Cir. 1985). In the pending case, the place of the tort is plainly the United States. To whatever extent *lex loci delicti* is to be considered only one part of a broader "interest" approach [citation omitted], United States law would still apply to infringement issues, since not only is this country the place of the tort, but also the defendant is a United States corporation.

---

11 In deciding that the law of the country of origin determines the ownership of copyright, we consider only initial ownership, and have no occasion to consider choice of law issues concerning assignments of rights.

12 The Berne Convention expressly provides that "ownership of copyright in a cinematographic work shall be a matter for legislation in the country where protection is claimed." Berne Convention, Art. 14bis(2)(a). With respect to other works, this provision could be understood to have any of three meanings. First, it could carry a negative implication that for other works, ownership is not to be determined by legislation in the country where protection is claimed. Second, it could be thought of as an explicit assertion for films of a general principle already applicable to other works. Third, it could be a specific provision for films that was adopted without an intention to imply anything about other works. In the absence of any indication that either the first or second meanings were intended, we prefer the third understanding.

The division of issues, for conflicts purposes, between ownership and infringement issues will not always be as easily made as the above discussion implies. If the issue is the relatively straightforward one of which of two contending parties owns a copyright, the issue is unquestionably an ownership issue, and the law of the country with the closest relationship to the work will apply to settle the ownership dispute. But in some cases, including the pending one, the issue is not simply who owns the copyright but also what is the nature of the ownership interest. Yet as a court considers the nature of an ownership interest, there is some risk that it will too readily shift the inquiry over to the issue of whether an alleged copy has infringed the asserted copyright. Whether a copy infringes depends in part on the scope of the interest of the copyright owner. Nevertheless, though the issues are related, the nature of a copyright interest is an issue distinct from the issue of whether the copyright has been infringed [citation omitted]. The pending case is one that requires consideration not simply of who owns an interest, but, as to the newspapers, the nature of the interest that is owned.

C-28/04 Tod's SpA and Tod's France SARL v. Heyraud SA ECLI:EU:C:2005:418 [2005]

[For a general presentation see *supra*, Part II, Chapter 4.1.2, pp. 250–54]

32 As is apparent from Article 5(1) of the Berne Convention, the purpose of that convention is not to determine the applicable law on the protection of literary and artistic works, but to establish, as a general rule, a system of national treatment of the rights appertaining to such works.

33 Article 2(7) of that convention contains, for its part, as the Commission rightly observes, a rule of reciprocity under which a country of the Union grants national treatment, that is to say, twofold protection, only if the country of origin of the work also does so.

France, Cour de cassation, N° 11–12508 ECLI:FR:CCASS:2013: C100347 [2013]

The Court of Cassation, first civil chamber, has rendered the following decision:

Whereas, according to the decision appealed-from, Mr X, who became employed in 1978 as a cameraman in the service of the American company ABC News Intercontinental Inc., which exploits an American television channel, was assigned to the Paris bureau as of 1993, then dismissed for economic reasons on October 8, 2004; that he disputed his firing before the Counsel of Prud'hommes [labor relations], demanding various indemnities and back pay; he also claimed a violation of his moral and economic rights under copyright by virtue of the unauthorized exploitation of reports and documentaries of which he claimed to be the author;

. . .

In light of article 5.2 of the Berne Convention of 9 September 1886 for the protection of literary and artistic works;

Whereas, according to this text, the enjoyment and exercise of copyright, which are not subject to any formality, are independent from the existence of protection in the work's country of origin; whereas, as a result, except as otherwise provided by the Convention, the scope of protection as well as the means of enforcement guaranteed to the author to protect his rights are governed exclusively by the law of the country where protection is claimed;

Whereas, in order to dismiss Mr X's copyright claims, the decision below holds that article 5.2 of the Berne Convention governs the content of the protection of the author and the work, but does not supply a rule regarding the ownership of rights, nor their acquisition, nor their transfer, so that, given the silence of this text, it is appropriate to apply the French choice of law rule;

That, in so holding, while the determination of the initial rightholder in a work of authorship is governed by the conflicts rule established by article 5.2 of the Berne Convention, which designates the law of the country where protection is claimed, the court below violated this provision by incorrectly applying it . . .

QUESTIONS

1. Is the French high court's decision consistent with the ECJ's ruling in the *Tod's* decision?
2. Which of the three decisions' interpretation of the Berne Convention seems to you the most convincing?

PROBLEM

An English graphic designer works as on commission from an American company. Working for the company's French branch, he is in charge of the design of the newspapers published by the American company first in the U.S. and the following month in France in a French version. Seeking new clients, the designer posts his works on his own web site without the consent of the publisher. The latter wants to sue the designer. He would like to know what law would apply if he sued in the U.S? If he sued in France? (Assume these courts are competent to adjudicate the copyright infringement action.)

Articles 11bis and 13

Article 11*bis*
Broadcasting and Related Rights

. . .

(2) It shall be a matter for legislation in the countries of the Union to determine the conditions under which the rights mentioned in the preceding paragraph may be exercised, but these conditions shall apply only in the countries where they have been prescribed. They shall not in any circumstances be prejudicial to the moral rights of the author, nor to his right to obtain equitable remuneration which, in the absence of agreement, shall be fixed by competent authority.

Article 13
Possible Limitation of the Right of Recording of Musical Works and Any Words Pertaining Thereto

(1) Each country of the Union may impose for itself reservations and conditions on the exclusive right granted to the author of a musical work and to the author of any words, the recording of which together with the musical work has already been authorized by the latter, to authorize the sound recording of that musical work, together with such words, if any; but all such reservations and conditions shall apply only in the countries which have imposed them and shall not, in any circumstances, be prejudicial to the rights of these authors to obtain equitable remuneration which, in the absence of agreement, shall be fixed by competent authority.

QUESTIONS

1. Why is such a territorial limitation mentioned only for those two exceptions? Does that imply that the other exceptions could have an extraterritorial application? What do these articles suggest from a conflict-of-laws perspective?
2. What about a country submitting satellite broadcasting to the law of emission (uplink)? Is that consistent with the Berne Convention?

8.1.2 Rome Convention

Article 7
Minimum Protection for Performers:

. . .; 2. Relations between Performers and Broadcasting Organizations

(1) If broadcasting was consented to by the performers, it shall be a matter for the domestic law of the Contracting State where protection is claimed to regulate the protection against rebroadcasting, fixation for broadcasting purposes and the reproduction of such fixation for broadcasting purposes.

(2) The terms and conditions governing the use by broadcasting organisations of fixations made for broadcasting purposes shall be determined in accordance with the domestic law of the Contracting State where protection is claimed.

Article 11
Formalities for Phonograms

If, as a condition of protecting the rights of producers of phonograms, or of performers, or both, in relation to phonograms, a Contracting State, under its domestic law, requires compliance with formalities, these shall be considered as fulfilled if all the copies in commerce of the published phonogram or their containers bear a notice consisting of the symbol (P), accompanied by the year date of the first publication, placed in such a manner as to give reasonable notice of claim of protection; and if the copies or their containers do not identify the producer or the licensee of the producer (by carrying his name, trade mark or other appropriate designation), the notice shall also include the name of the owner of the rights of the producer; and, furthermore, if the copies or their containers do not identify the principal performers, the notice shall also include the name of the person who, in the country in which the fixation was effected, owns the rights of such performers.

Article 13
Minimum Rights for Broadcasting Organizations

Broadcasting organisations shall enjoy the right to authorize or prohibit:

(a) the rebroadcasting of their broadcasts;
(b) the fixation of their broadcasts;

(c) the reproduction:
  (i) of fixations, made without their consent, of their broadcasts;
  (ii) of fixations, made in accordance with the provisions of Article 15, of their broadcasts, if the reproduction is made for purposes different from those referred to in those provisions;
(d) the communication to the public of their television broadcasts if such communication is made in places accessible to the public against payment of an entrance fee; it shall be a matter for the domestic law of the State where protection of this right is claimed to determine the conditions under which it may be exercised.

QUESTION

To what extent and in what contexts does the Rome Convention designate the application of the law of the country of origin (first fixation) (*lex originis*), the law of the country for which protection is sought (*lex loci protectionis*), or the law of the forum (*lex fori*)? How does this compare with the Berne Convention?

8.2   National and regional norms

8.2.1   The law applicable to the right

U.S.: A universal approach concerning initial ownership of copyright

Itar-Tass v Russian Kurier

supra pages 655 et seq.

QUESTIONS

How far does one extend the principle that the law of the country with the "most significant relationship" to the work (generally, the source country) determines ownership status? For example, disparities between U.S. copyright law and foreign laws exist not only with respect to the status of employers as owners of copyright, but also regarding joint authorship. Under U.S. law, given the prerequisite intent, the joint authors' contributions may comprise either an inseparable or an interdependent but separable whole. In certain other countries, however, only inseparable contributions form a joint work. Suppose that a foreign work is a dramatico-musical composition, comprising the efforts of a composer and a lyricist. Under most countries' rules of duration of copyright, a joint work's copyright endures until a determined number of years (70 in the E.U. and the U.S.; often 50 elsewhere) from the death of the last surviving author. Assume a musical comedy was created in 1979 in a country which requires inseparable contributions (and considers dramatico-musical works to be separable). The composer died in 1980; the lyricist in 1990. Under the law of the source country (whose copyright term is 70 years *pma*), the copyright in the music will expire in 2050; the copyright in the lyrics in 2060. Under U.S. law, the copyright in the work as a whole will expire in 2060. When will the music fall into the public domain in the U.S.? The answer will depend on whether the U.S. definition or the source country definition of a joint work applies. Does *Itar-Tass* supply an answer to this question?

E.U.

In the E.U., the choice of law rules relating to copyright and neighboring rights have not yet been fully harmonized. As we will see, the Rome II Regulation determines the law applicable to the infringement, but not the law applicable to ownership or other aspects of the IP right. As a result, member states may choose the applicable law, and this choice may effectively accord an extraterritorial scope to the designated law, for example, by applying the law of the country of origin in the country where protection is sought. Nevertheless, the ECJ has implicitly recognized the territorial nature of copyright law in two cases (*Lagardère*; *Pinckney*, below). Among member states, local private international law systems endorse mainly a territorial approach with some major exceptions.

Greek law on Copyright, Official Journal A 25 1993 (Entry into force: 04.03.1993)

Article 67: Applicable Legislation

1. Copyright in a published work shall be governed by the legislation of the State in which the work is first made lawfully accessible to the public. Copyright in an unpublished work shall be governed by the legislation of the State in which the author is a national.

2. Related rights shall be governed by the legislation of the State in which the performance is realized, or in which the sound or visual or sound and visual recording is produced, or in which the radio or television broadcast is transmitted or in which the printed publication is effected.

3. In all cases, the determination of the subject, object, content, duration and limitations of the right shall be governed by the legislation applicable

pursuant to paragraphs (1) and (2), above, with the exception of any exploitation license arrangement. The protection of a right shall be subject to the legislation of the State in which the protection is sought.

4. Paragraphs (1), (2) and (3), above, shall apply except where they run contrary to any international convention ratified by Greece. In the case of States not conjoint with Greece through the ratification of an international convention, paragraphs (1), (2) and (3), above, shall be applicable as regards the protection of copyright or of any particular object of copyright or of any particular related right, provided that the legislation of the relevant state offers adequate copyright protection to works first made accessible to the public in Greece and to related rights stemming from acts effected in Greece.

Italian Law on Private international law
Article 54 (Rights in intangible property)

1. The rights in intangible property shall be governed by the law of the State of use.

C-192/04 Lagardère Active Broadcast, the successor in title to Europe 1 communication SA v. Société pour la perception de la rémunération équitable *(SPRE)* ECLI:EU:C:2005:475 [2005]

[This case concerned the interpretation of two Directives: the Council Directive 93/83/EEC of 27 September 1993 on the coordination of certain rules concerning copyright and rights related to copyright applicable to satellite broadcasting and cable retransmission, and the Council Directive 92/100/EEC of 19 November 1992 on rental right and lending right and on certain rights related to copyright in the field of intellectual property. The issue concerned the payment of an equitable remuneration for the broadcasting of phonograms to the public by satellite and terrestrial repeater stations in France and Germany and more precisely if one or two payments were required. Because the Directive 93/83 did not apply, neither did its exclusive designation of the law of the country of "emission" of the signal. Thus, the Court had to determine where the transmission occurred in order to determine which law(s) applied.]

2   The reference was made in proceedings between Lagardère Active Broadcast, the successor in title to Europe 1 communication SA (hereinafter 'Lagardère' or 'Europe 1'), and Société pour la perception de la rémunération équitable (hereinafter 'SPRE') and Gesellschaft zur Verwertung von

Leistungsschutzrechten mbH (hereinafter 'GVL') concerning the obligation to pay equitable remuneration for the broadcasting of phonograms to the public by satellite and terrestrial repeater stations in France and Germany.

. . .

The main proceedings and the questions referred to the Court of Justice

12   Lagardère is a broadcasting company established in France. Its programmes are created in its Paris studios and are then transmitted to a satellite. The signals return to earth where they are received by repeater stations in French territory, which broadcast the programmes to the public on the frequency modulated (FM) band.

13   Since FM broadcasts do not cover the entire French territory, the satellite also sends signals to a transmitter at Felsberg, in Saarland (Germany), which is technically equipped to broadcast to France on long wave. That broadcasting is carried out by Compagnie européenne de radiodiffusion et de télévision Europe 1 (hereinafter 'CERT'), a subsidiary of Lagardère. The programmes broadcast in the French language can, for technical reasons, also be received in German territory, but only in a limited area. They are not the subject of commercial exploitation in Germany.

14   Lagardère also has a digital audio terrestrial circuit which enables signals from the Paris studios to be sent to the transmitter in Germany in the event of malfunction of the satellite. Before the satellite system was adopted, that terrestrial circuit was the only means of sending signals to that transmitter. However, that circuit is still operational at the present time.

15   Since Lagardère uses for its broadcasts phonograms protected by intellectual property law, in France it pays for the use thereof a royalty accruing to the performers and producers of the phonograms (hereinafter 'the royalty for phonogram use'). That royalty is levied on a collective basis by SPRE. For its part, CERT paid an annual flat-rate royalty in Germany for broadcasting the same phonograms to GVL, a company incorporated under German law which is the counterpart of SPRE.

16   In order to avoid double payment of the royalty for phonogram use, an agreement concluded between Europe 1 and SPRE, which was renewed until 31 December 1993, provided that the amount of the royalty payable by

Europe 1 to performers and producers would be decreased by the amount paid by CERT to GVL.

17   Although with effect from 1 January 1994 there was no longer any agreement authorising Europe 1 to make that deduction, it continued never-theless to do so. Considering that the deduction was unjustified, SPRE com-menced proceedings against Europe 1 before the Tribunal de grande instance (Regional Court) de Paris which upheld its claim that the latter should pay the entire royalty. Lagardère, the successor in title to Europe 1, appealed to the Cour de cassation (Court of Cassation).

. . .

45   By its second question, the national court seeks essentially to ascer-tain whether Article 8(2) of Directive and 92/100 must be interpreted as meaning that, for determination of the equitable remuneration mentioned in that provision, the broadcasting company is entitled unilaterally to deduct from the amount of the royalty for phonogram use payable in the Member State where it is established the amount of the royalty paid or claimed in the Member State in whose territory the terrestrial transmitter broadcasting to the first State is situated.

46   At the outset, it must be emphasized that it is clear from its wording and scheme that Directive 92/100 provides for minimal harmonization regarding rights related to copyright. Thus, it does not purport to detract, in particular, from the principle of the territoriality of those rights, which is recognized in international law and also in the EC Treaty. Those rights are therefore of a territorial nature and, moreover, domestic law can only penalize conduct engaged in within national territory.

C-170/12 *Peter Pinckney v. KDG Mediatech AG* ECLI:EU:C:2013:635 [2013]

See *supra*, Part II, Chapter 7.3.3 at page 623, Question 3.

39   First of all, it is true that copyright, like the rights attaching to a national trade mark, is subject to the principle of territoriality. However, copyrights must be automatically protected, in particular by virtue of Directive 2001/29, in all Member States, so that they may be infringed in each one in accordance with the applicable substantive law.

QUESTIONS

1. To what extent is the Greek position consistent with that expressed by the ECJ? How much freedom remains to member states to design choice of law rules?
2. What, if any, justifications does the Court offer for its application of the principle of territoriality?

8.2.2 The law applicable to infringement

U.S.

Recall that *Itar-Tass, supra,* held that the law applicable to infringement was the *lex loci delicti*, the law of the place of the wrongful act. Thus, if the Russian journalists' articles were copied and reprinted without authorization in Brooklyn, NY, the U.S. Copyright Act would apply to the infringement claim. But what is the place of the wrongful act when the alleged infringement spans more than one country? For example, an infringement may originate in the U.S., but spawn infringing copies around the world. Already true in the case of sales abroad of hard copies made in the U.S., the problem is even more acute on the Internet. U.S. caselaw has elaborated a "root copy" doctrine, which has allowed U.S. courts to award damages for foreign-distributed copies that can be traced back to an infringing U.S. source copy. U.S. courts have applied the "root copy" or "predicate act" approach to justify the application of U.S. copyright law to the ensemble of infringing acts, including those resulting in the receipt of copies abroad. See, e.g., *Tire Engineering and Distribution v. Shandong Linglong Rubber,* 682 F.3d 292 (4th Cir. 2012) (immediately below); *Update Art, Inc. v. Modiin Pub. Ltd.,* 843 F.2d 67, 73 (2d Cir. 1988); *Sheldon v. Metro-Goldwyn Pictures Corp.,* 106 F.2d 45, 52 (2d Cir. 1939). In other words, U.S. courts apply the law of the country of origin of the wrongful act—when that country is the U.S.

Tire Engineering and Distribution v. Shandong Linglong Rubber, 682 F.3d 292 (4th Cir. 2012)

▪ Per Curiam:

Alpha, a domestic producer of mining tires, sued Al Dobowi and Linglong, foreign corporations. Alpha alleged that the defendants conspired to steal its tire blueprints, produce infringing tires, and sell them to entities that had formerly purchased products from Alpha. . . . We affirm the district court's judgment that Al Dobowi and Linglong are liable to Alpha under the Copyright Act . . .

[Al Dobowi obtained the blueprints from a former Alpha employee; copies were sent to Linglong in China to manufacture tires from the blueprints. Linglong was aware that the blueprints had been stolen.]

III.

. . .

A.

Appellants first argue that the Copyright Act has no extraterritorial reach. Because the only claims raised by Alpha involve conduct abroad, Appellants maintain that the Copyright Act affords Alpha no remedy. Alternatively, even if the Copyright Act sometimes reaches foreign conduct that flows from a domestic violation, Appellants urge us to consider that foreign conduct only where, unlike here, the domestic violation is not barred by the Copyright Act's three-year statute of limitations.

We hold that Alpha has presented a cognizable claim under the Copyright Act [for copying the blueprints] and therefore uphold the jury's finding of liability on that count. We adopt the predicate-act doctrine, which posits that a plaintiff may collect damages from foreign violations of the Copyright Act so long as the foreign conduct stems from a domestic infringement. . . .

1.

As a general matter, the Copyright Act is considered to have no extraterritorial reach. *E.g., Nintendo of Am., Inc. v. Aeropower Co.*, 34 F.3d 246, 249 n.5 (4th Cir. 1994). But courts have recognized a fundamental exception: "when the type of infringement permits further reproduction abroad," a plaintiff may collect damages flowing from the foreign conduct. *Update Art, Inc. v. Modiin Pub., Ltd.*, 843 F.2d 67, 73 (2d Cir. 1988).

This predicate-act doctrine traces its roots to a famous Second Circuit opinion penned by Learned Hand. *See Sheldon v. Metro-Goldwyn Pictures Corp.*, 106 F.2d 45, 52 (2d Cir. 1939). The Second Circuit in *Sheldon* was confronted with an undisputed domestic Copyright Act violation. The defendant had converted the plaintiff's motion picture while in the United States and then exhibited the picture abroad. The court was required to decide whether the damages award could include profits made from foreign exhibition of the film. Answering the question in the affirmative, Judge Hand articulated the framework of the predicate-act doctrine:

The Culver Company made the negatives in this country, or had them made here, and shipped them abroad, where the positives were produced and exhibited. The negatives were 'records' from which the work could be 'reproduced,' and it was a tort to make them in this country. The plaintiffs acquired an equitable interest in them as soon as they were made, which attached to any profits from their exploitation, whether in the form of money remitted to the United States, or of increase in the value of shares of foreign companies held by the defendants. . . . [A]s soon as any of the profits so realized took the form of property whose situs was in the United States, our law seized upon them and impressed them with a constructive trust, whatever their form.

Id. Once a plaintiff demonstrates a domestic violation of the Copyright Act, then, it may collect damages from foreign violations that are directly linked to the U.S. infringement.

The Second Circuit has reaffirmed the continuing vitality of the predicate-act doctrine. *Update Art*, 843 F.2d at 73. In *Update Art*, the plaintiff owned the rights to distribute and publish a certain graphic art design. Without authorization from the plaintiff, the defendant published the image in an Israeli newspaper. The court reasoned that "the applicability of American copyright laws over the Israeli newspapers depends on the occurrence of a predicate act in the United States." "If the illegal reproduction of the poster occurred in the United States and then was exported to Israel," the court continued, "the magistrate properly could include damages accruing from the Israeli newspapers." But if the predicate act of reproduction occurred outside of the United States, the district court could award no damages from newspaper circulation in Israel.

More recently, the Ninth Circuit embraced the predicate-act doctrine. *Los Angeles News Serv. v. Reuters TV Int'l.*, 149 F.3d 987, 990–92 (9th Cir. 1998). The court endorsed Second Circuit precedent, which it construed as holding that "[r]ecovery of damages arising from overseas infringing uses was allowed because the predicate act of infringement occurring within the United States enabled further reproduction abroad." To invoke the predicate-act doctrine, according to the Ninth Circuit, damages must flow from "extraterritorial exploitation of an infringing act that occurred in the United States." The court distinguished a previous decision, *Subafilms, Ltd. v. MGM-Pathe Commc'ns Co.*, 24 F.3d 1088 (9th Cir. 1994), as controlling only a narrow class of cases dealing with the Copyright Act's "authorization" provision, in which a plaintiff alleges merely a domestic authorization of infringing conduct that otherwise takes place wholly abroad. Such a case presents concerns not relevant to disputes in which a predicate act of infringement—going beyond mere authorization—occurred in the United States. The Ninth Circuit further noted that the predicate-act doctrine does not abrogate a defendant's right to be free from stale claims.

At least two other circuits have recognized the validity of the predicate-act doctrine, even if they have not had occasion to squarely apply it to the facts before them. *Litecubes, LLC v. N. Light Prods., Inc.*, 523 F.3d 1353, 1371 (Fed. Cir. 2008) (endorsing principle that "courts have generally held that the Copyright Act only does not reach activities 'that take place entirely abroad'" (quoting *Subafilms*, 24 F.3d at 1098)); *Liberty Toy Co. v. Fred Silber Co.*, 149 F.3d 1183 (6th Cir. 1998) (unpublished table decision) ("[I]f all the copying or infringement occurred outside the United States, the Copyright Act would not apply. However, as long as some act of infringement occurred in the United States, the Copyright Act applies."

We join our sister circuits that have adopted the predicate-act doctrine. The doctrine strikes an appropriate balance between competing concerns, pro-tecting aggrieved plaintiffs from savvy defendants while also safeguarding a defendant's freedom from stale claims. Absent the predicate-act doctrine, a defendant could convert a plaintiff's intellectual property in the United States, wait for the Copyright Act's three-year statute of limitations to expire, and then reproduce the property abroad with impunity. Such a result would jeopardize intellectual property rights and subvert Congress's goals as engrafted on to the Copyright Act. But lest the doctrine lead to a windfall for plaintiffs and force a defendant to face liability for stale claims, plaintiffs may collect only those damages "suffered during the statutory period for bringing claims, regardless of where they may have been incurred," *Los Angeles News*, 149 F.3d at 992.

2.

Applying the predicate-act doctrine to this case, we conclude that Alpha has presented a valid claim under the Copyright Act. Accordingly, we sustain the jury's finding of liability on that count.

Distilling applicable case law, we find that a plaintiff is required to show a domestic violation of the Copyright Act and damages flowing from foreign exploitation of that infringing act to successfully invoke the predicate-act doctrine. Alpha has shown both. Appellants concede on appeal that Alpha has established a domestic violation of the Copyright Act. While in the United States, Vance [Alpha's former employee] and Al Dobowi unlawfully converted Alpha's blueprints and reproduced them absent authorization. These acts constitute infringing conduct under the Copyright Act. *See Update Art*, 843 F.2d at 73 (concluding there would be an actionable violation if defendant illegally reproduced image while in the United States). And Alpha has demonstrated damages flowing from extraterritorial exploitation of this infringing conduct. Al Dobowi and Linglong used the converted blueprints to produce mining tires almost identical to those of Alpha. They then sold these tires to former customers of Alpha, causing Alpha substantial damage. *See Sheldon*, 106 F.2d at 52 (finding damages flowing from foreign exploitation of infringing act where defendant converted negatives of motion picture in United States and exhibited the film abroad).

Subafilms, Ltd. v. MGM–Pathé Communications Co.24 F.3d 1088 (9th Cir.) (en banc), cert. denied, 513 U.S. 1001 (1994)

▪ D.W. Nelson, Circuit Judge:

In this case, we consider the "vexing question" of whether a claim for infringement can be brought under the Copyright Act, 17 U.S.C. § 101 et seq. (1988), when the assertedly infringing conduct consists solely of the authorization within the territorial boundaries of the United States of acts that occur entirely abroad. We hold that such allegations do not state a claim for relief under the copyright laws of the United States.

Factual and Procedural Background

In 1966, the musical group The Beatles, through Subafilms, Ltd., entered into a joint venture with the Hearst Corporation to produce the animated motion picture entitled "Yellow Submarine" (the "Picture"). Over the next year, Hearst, acting on behalf of the joint venture (the "Producer"), negotiated an agreement with United Artists Corporation ("UA") to distribute and finance the film. Separate distribution and financing agreements were entered into in May, 1967. Pursuant to these agreements, UA distributed the Picture in theaters beginning in 1968 and later on television.

In the early 1980s, with the advent of the home video market, UA entered into several licensing agreements to distribute a number of its films on videocassette. Although one company expressed interest in the Picture, UA refused to license "Yellow Submarine" because of uncertainty over whether home video rights had been granted by the 1967 agreements. Subsequently, in 1987, UA's successor company, MGM/UA Communications Co. ("MGM/UA"), over the Producer's objections, authorized its subsidiary MGM/UA Home

Video, Inc. to distribute the Picture for the domestic home video market, and, pursuant to an earlier licensing agreement, notified Warner Bros., Inc. ("Warner") that the Picture had been cleared for international videocassette distribution. Warner, through its wholly owned subsidiary, Warner Home Video, Inc., in turn entered into agreements with third parties for distribution of the Picture on videocassette around the world.

In 1988, Subafilms and Hearst ("Appellees") brought suit against MGM/UA, Warner, and their respective subsidiaries (collectively the "Distributors" or "Appellants"), contending that the videocassette distribution of the Picture, both foreign and domestic, constituted copyright infringement and a breach of the 1967 agreements. The case was tried before a retired California Superior Court Judge acting as a special master. The special master found for Appellees on both claims. . . . [T]he district court adopted all of the special master's factual findings and legal conclusions. Appellees were awarded $2,228,000.00 in compensatory damages, split evenly between the foreign and domestic home video distributions. In addition, Appellees received attorneys' fees and a permanent injunction that prohibited the Distributors from engaging in, or authorizing, any home video use of the Picture.

A panel of this circuit, in an unpublished disposition, affirmed the district court's judgment on the ground that both the domestic and foreign distribution of the Picture constituted infringement under the Copyright Act. . . . With respect to the foreign distribution of the Picture, the panel concluded that it was bound by this court's prior decision in *Peter Starr Prod. Co. v. Twin Continental Films, Inc.*, 783 F.2d 1440 (9th Cir. 1986), which it held to stand for the proposition that, although "infringing actions that take place entirely outside the United States are not actionable" [under the Copyright Act, an] "act of infringement within the United States' [properly is] alleged where the illegal *authorization* of international exhibitions t[akes] *place in the United States,*" *Subafilms,* slip op. at 4917–18 (quoting *Peter Starr,* 783 F.2d at 1442, 1443 [emphasis in original] [alterations added]). Because the Distributors had admitted that the initial authorization to distribute the Picture internationally occurred within the United States, the panel affirmed the district court's holding with respect to liability for extraterritorial home video distribution of the Picture.

We granted Appellants' petition for rehearing en banc to consider whether the panel's interpretation of *Peter Starr* conflicted with our subsequent decision in *Lewis Galoob Toys, Inc. v. Nintendo of Am., Inc.,* 964 F.2d 965 (9th Cir. 1992), cert. denied, 113 S. Ct. 1582 (1993), which held that there could be no liability for authorizing a party to engage in an infringing act when the authorized "party's use of the work would not violate the Copyright Act," id. at 970. . .

. . . Because we conclude that there can be no liability under the United States copyright laws for authorizing an act that itself could not constitute infringement of rights secured by those laws, and that wholly extraterritorial acts of infringement are not cognizable under the Copyright Act, we overrule *Peter Starr* insofar as it held that allegations of an authorization within the United States of infringing acts that take place entirely abroad state a claim for infringement under the Act. Accordingly, we vacate the panel's decision in part and return the case to the panel for further proceedings.

Discussion

I. The Mere Authorization of Extraterritorial Acts of Infringement Does Not State a Claim Under the Copyright Act

As the panel in this case correctly concluded, *Peter Starr* held that the authorization within the United States of entirely extraterritorial acts stated a cause of action under the "plain language" of the Copyright Act. *Peter Starr*, 783 F.2d at 1442–43. Observing that the Copyright Act grants a copyright owner *"the exclusive rights to* do and *to authorize"* any of the activities listed in 17 U.S.C. § 106(1)–(5), id. at 1442 [emphasis in original], and that a violation of the "authorization" right constitutes infringement under section 501 of the Act, the *Peter Starr* court reasoned that allegations of an authorization within the United States of extraterritorial conduct that corresponded to the activities listed in section 106 "allege[d] an act of infringement within the United States," id. at 1442–43. Accordingly, the court determined that the district court erred "in concluding that 'Plaintiff allege[d] only infringing acts which took place outside of the United States,'" "and reversed the district court's dismissal for lack of subject matter jurisdiction." Id. at 1443.

The *Peter Starr* court accepted, as does this court, that the acts authorized from within the United States themselves could not have constituted infringement under the Copyright Act because "[i]n general, United States copyright laws do not have extraterritorial effect," and therefore, "infringing actions that take place entirely outside the United States are not actionable." *Peter Starr*, 783 F.2d at 1442 (citing *Robert Stigwood Group, Ltd. v. O'Reilly*, 530 F.2d 1096, 1101 (2d Cir.), cert. denied, 429 U.S. 848 (1976)). The central premise of the *Peter Starr* court, then, was that a party could be held liable as an "infringer" under section 501 of the Act merely for authorizing a third party to engage in acts that, had they been committed within the United States, would have violated the exclusive rights granted to a copyright holder by section 106.

Since *Peter Starr*, however, we have recognized that, when a party authorizes an activity not proscribed by one of the five section 106 clauses, the authorizing party cannot be held liable as an infringer. In *Lewis Galoob*, we rejected the argument that "a party can unlawfully authorize another party to use a copyrighted work even if that party's use of the work would not violate the Copyright Act," *Lewis Galoob*, 964 F.2d at 970, and approved of Professor Nimmer's statement that "'to the extent that an activity does not violate one of th[e] five enumerated rights [found in 17 U.S.C. § 106], authorizing such activity does not constitute copyright infringement,'" id. (quoting 3 David Nimmer & Melville B. Nimmer, Nimmer on Copyright § 12.04[A][3][a], at 12–80 n. 82 (1991)). Similarly, in *Columbia Pictures*, we held that no liability attached under the Copyright Act for providing videodisc players to hotel guests when the use of that equipment did not constitute a "public" performance within the meaning of section 106 of the Act, see *Columbia Pictures*, 866 F.2d at 279–81.

The apparent premise of *Lewis Galoob* was that the addition of the words "to authorize" in the Copyright Act was not meant to create a new form of liability for "authorization" that was divorced completely from the legal consequences of authorized conduct, but was intended to invoke the preexisting doctrine of contributory infringement. See *Lewis Galoob*, 964 F.2d at 970 ("Although infringement by authorization is a form of direct infringement [under the Act], this does not change the proper focus of our inquiry; a party cannot authorize another party to infringe a copyright unless the authorized conduct would itself be unlawful."). We agree.

. . .

Although the *Peter Starr* court recognized that the addition of the authorization right in the 1976 Act "was intended to remove the confusion surrounding contributory. . . . infringement," *Peter Starr*, 783 F.2d at 1443, it did not consider the applicability of an essential attribute of the doctrine: that contributory infringement, even when triggered solely by an "authorization," is a form of third party liability that requires the authorized acts to constitute infringing ones. We believe that the *Peter Starr* court erred in not applying this principle to the authorization of acts that cannot themselves be infringing because they take place entirely abroad. As Professor Nimmer has observed:

Accepting the proposition that a direct infringement is a prerequisite to third party liability, the further question arises whether the direct infringement on which liability is premised must take place within the United States. Given the undisputed axiom that United States copyright law has no extraterritorial application, it would seem to follow necessarily that a primary activity outside the boundaries of the United States, not constituting an infringement cognizable under the Copyright Act, cannot serve as the basis for holding liable under the Copyright Act one who is merely related to that activity within the United States.

3 Nimmer, supra, § 12.04[A][3][b], at 12–86 [footnotes omitted].

Appellees resist the force of this logic, and argue that liability in this case is appropriate because, unlike in *Lewis Galoob* and *Columbia Pictures*, in which the alleged primary infringement consisted of acts that were entirely outside the purview of 17 U.S.C. § 106(1)–(5) (and presumably lawful), the conduct authorized in this case was precisely that prohibited by section 106, and is only uncognizable because it occurred outside the United States. Moreover, they contend that the conduct authorized in this case would have been prohibited under the copyright laws of virtually every nation. See also 1 Goldstein, supra, § 6.1, at 706 n.4 (suggesting that "*Peter Starr's* interpretation of section 106's authorization right would appear to be at least literally correct since the statute nowhere requires that the direct infringement occur within the United States").

. . .

Even assuming arguendo that the acts authorized in this case would have been illegal abroad, we do not believe the distinction offered by Appellees is a relevant one. Because the copyright laws do not apply extraterritorially, each of the rights conferred under the five section 106 categories must be read as extending "no farther than the [United States'] borders." 2 Goldstein, supra, § 16.0, at 675. See, e.g., *Robert Stigwood*, 530 F.2d at 1101 (holding that no damages could be obtained under the Copyright Act for public performances in Canada when preliminary steps were taken within the United States and stating that "[t]he Canadian performances, while they may have been torts in Canada, were not torts here"); see also *Filmvideo Releasing Corp. v. Hastings*, 668 F.2d 91, 93 (2d Cir. 1981) (reversing an order of the district court that required the defendant to surrender prints of a film because the prints could be used to further conduct abroad that was not proscribed by United States copyright laws). In light of our above conclusion that the "authorization" right refers to the doctrine of contributory infringement, which requires that the authorized act itself could violate one of the exclusive rights listed in section 106(1)–(5), we believe that "[i]t is simply not possible to draw a principled distinction" between an act that does not violate a copyright because it is not the type of conduct proscribed by section 106, and one that does not violate section 106 because the illicit act occurs overseas. In both cases, the authorized conduct could not violate the exclusive rights guaranteed by section 106. In both cases, therefore, there can be no liability for "authorizing" such conduct. See also 3 Nimmer, supra, § 12.04[A][3][b], at 12–87 to 12–88.

To hold otherwise would produce the untenable anomaly, inconsistent with the general principles of third party liability, that a party could be held liable as an infringer for violating the "authorization" right when the party that it authorized could not be considered an infringer under the Copyright Act. Put otherwise, we do not think Congress intended to hold a party liable for merely "authorizing" conduct that, had the authorizing party chosen to engage in itself, would have resulted in no liability under the Act. Cf. *Robert Stigwood*, 530 F.2d at 1101.

Appellees rely heavily on the Second Circuit's doctrine that extraterritorial application of the copyright laws is permissible "when the type of infringement permits further reproduction abroad." *Update Art, Inc. v. Modiin Publishing, Ltd.*, 843 F.2d 67, 73 (2d Cir. 1988). Whatever the merits of the Second Circuit's rule, and we express no opinion on its validity in this circuit, it is premised on the theory that the copyright holder may recover damages that stem from a direct infringement of its exclusive rights that occurs within the United States. See *Robert Stigwood*, 530 F.2d at 1101; *Sheldon v. Metro–Goldwyn Pictures Corp.*, 106 F.2d 45, 52 (2d Cir. 1939) (L. Hand, J.) ("The negatives were 'records' from which the work could be 'reproduced,' and it was a tort to make them in this country. The plaintiffs acquired an equitable interest in them as soon as they were made, which attached to any profits from their exploitation. . ."), aff'd, 309 U.S. 390 (1940). . . [9] In these cases, liability is not based on contributory infringement, but on the theory that the infringing use would have been actionable even if the subsequent foreign distribution that stemmed from that use never took place. See, e.g., *Famous Music*, 201 F. Supp. at 569 ("[T]hat a copyright has no extraterritorial effect[ ] does not solve th[e] problem of [whether liability should attach for preparing within the United States tapes that were part of a] manufacture

---

9 Professor Nimmer formulates the doctrine in the following terms: "[I]f and to the extent a part of an 'act' of infringement occurs within the United States, then, although such act is completed in a foreign jurisdiction, those parties who contributed to the act within the United States may be rendered liable under American copyright law." 3 Nimmer, *supra*, § 17.02, at 17–19 [footnotes omitted].

[completed abroad] since plaintiffs seek to hold defendant for what it did *here* rather than what it did abroad." (emphasis in original)). These cases, therefore, simply are inapplicable to a theory of liability based merely on the authorization of noninfringing acts.

Accordingly, accepting that wholly extraterritorial acts of infringement cannot support a claim under the Copyright Act, we believe that the *Peter Starr* court, and thus the panel in this case, erred in concluding that the mere authorization of such acts supports a claim for infringement under the Act.

II.   The Extraterritoriality of the Copyright Act

Appellees additionally contend that, if liability for "authorizing" acts of infringement depends on finding that the authorized acts themselves are cognizable under the Copyright Act, this court should find that the United States copyright laws do extend to extraterritorial acts of infringement when such acts "result in adverse effects within the United States." Appellees buttress this argument with the contention that failure to apply the copyright laws extraterritorially in this case will have a disastrous effect on the American film industry, and that other remedies, such as suits in foreign jurisdictions or the application of foreign copyright laws by American courts, are not realistic alternatives.

We are not persuaded by Appellees' parade of horribles. More fundamentally, however, we are unwilling to overturn over eighty years of consistent jurisprudence on the extraterritorial reach of the copyright laws without further guidance from Congress.

The Supreme Court recently reminded us that "[i]t is a long-standing principle of American law 'that legislation of Congress, unless a contrary intent appears, is meant to apply only within the territorial jurisdiction of the United States.'" *EEOC v. Arabian American Oil Co. (Aramco), 111* S. Ct. 1227, 1230 (1991) (quoting *Foley Bros., Inc. v. Filardo*, 336 U.S. 281, 285 (1949)). Because courts must "assume that Congress legislates against the backdrop of the presumption against extraterritoriality," unless "there is 'the affirmative intention of the Congress clearly expressed'" "congressional enactments must be presumed to be 'primarily concerned with domestic conditions.'" Id. at 1230 (quoting *Foley Bros.*, 336 U.S. at 285 and *Benz v. Compania Naviera Hidalgo, S.A.*, 353 U.S. 138, 147 (1957)).

The "undisputed axiom," 3 Nimmer, supra, § 12.04[A][3][b], at 12–86, that the United States' copyright laws have no application to extraterritorial infringement predates the 1909 Act, see, e.g., *United Dictionary Co. v. G. & C. Merriam Co.*, 208 U.S. 260, 264–66 (1908) (Holmes, J.), and, as discussed above, the principle of territoriality consistently has been reaffirmed, see, e.g., *Capitol Records, Inc. v. Mercury Records Corp.*, 221 F.2d 657, 662 (2d Cir. 1955) (citing *American Code Co. v. Bensinger*, 282 F. 829, 833 (2d Cir. 1922)) ("The copyright laws of one country have no extraterritorial operation, unless otherwise provided." (citing *Ferris v. Frohman*, 223 U.S. 424 (1912)). There is no clear expression of congressional intent in either the 1976 Act or other relevant enactments to alter the preexisting extraterritoriality doctrine. . .

Furthermore, we note that Congress chose in 1976 to expand one specific "extraterritorial" application of the Act by declaring that the unauthorized importation of copyrighted works constitutes infringement even when the copies lawfully were made abroad. See 17 U.S.C.A. § 602(a) (West Supp. 1992). Had Congress been inclined to overturn the preexisting doctrine that infringing acts that take place wholly outside the United States are not actionable under the Copyright Act, it knew how to do so. See *Argentine Republic v. Amerada Hess Shipping Corp.*, 488 U.S. 428, 440 (1989) ("When it desires to do so, Congress knows how to place the high seas within the jurisdictional reach of a statute" (quoted in *Aramco*, 111 S. Ct. at 1235)). Accordingly, the presumption against extraterritoriality, "far from being overcome here, is doubly fortified by the language of [the] statute," *Smith v. United States*, 113 S. Ct. 1178, 1183 (1993) (quoting *United States v. Spelar*, 338 U.S. 217, 222 (1949)), as set against its consistent historical interpretation.

. . . Extraterritorial application of American law would be contrary to the spirit of the Berne Convention, and might offend other member nations by effectively displacing their law in circumstances in which previously it was assumed to govern. Consequently, an extension of extraterritoriality might undermine Congress's objective of achieving "'effective and harmonious' copyright laws among all nations." House Report, supra, at 20. Indeed, it might well send the signal that the United States does not believe that the protection accorded by the laws of other member nations is adequate, which would undermine two other objectives of Congress in joining the convention: "strengthen[ing] the credibility of the U.S. position in trade negotiations with countries where piracy is not uncommon" and "rais[ing] the like[li]hood that other nations will enter the Convention." S. Rep. 352, 100th Cong., 2d Sess. 4–5, reprinted in 1988 U.S.C.C.A.N., 3706, 3709–10.

. . . Accordingly, because an extension of the extraterritorial reach of the Copyright Act by the courts would in all likelihood disrupt the international regime for protecting intellectual property that Congress so recently described as essential to furthering the goal of protecting the works of American authors abroad, . . .

[W]e reaffirm that the United States copyright laws do not reach acts of infringement that take place entirely abroad. It is for Congress, and not the courts, to take the initiative in this field. . . .

Conclusion

We hold that the mere authorization of acts of infringement that are not cognizable under the United States copyright laws because they occur entirely outside of the United States does not state a claim for infringement under the Copyright Act. Peter Starr is overruled insofar as it held to the contrary. . .

NOTES AND QUESTIONS

1. *Subafilms* rules that there can be no liability under U.S. copyright law for "authorizing" an allegedly infringing act that did not take place in the U.S. The decision rests on the assumption that "authorization" is a form of secondary liability, and there can be no secondary liability if there is no primary liability arising out of an act that violates U.S. law. Professors Goldstein and Hugenholtz have disputed this syllogism: "The flaw in this logic is that, for purposes of the territoriality principle, all that matters is that some independently actionable conduct occur inside the territory of the protecting country, and defendant's actions of authorization presumably met this criterion." Paul Goldstein and Bernt Hugenholtz, International Copyright: Principles, Law, and Practice 126–27 (2d ed. 2010). They also criticize the decision on two practical grounds:

   > First, wherever the direct infringements occurred, the acts of authorization in the United States clearly caused economic injury in the United States as measured by lost foreign revenues coming into the country. Second, by immunizing an alleged contributory infringer who orchestrated infringing conduct worldwide and effectively requiring the copyright owner to pursue separate actions against infringers in every other protecting country, the decision eliminated an opportunity for efficient control of international infringement.

   Id. at 127.
2. In rejecting liability under U.S. copyright law for mere acts of "authorization" of copying to be done abroad, the *Subafilms* court specified that it

was not reaching the question of the application of U.S. law to extraterritorial acts when at least one act of copying did occur in the U.S. (compare
Tire Engineering, supra). What practical difference might it make were
foreign laws rather than U.S. law to apply to the foreign-made copies from
the U.S. masters?

3. In *Subafilms*, the disputed "authorizations" for international distribution
of videocassettes of *Yellow Submarine* were at least made under color of
right, since the licensor had financed and initially distributed the film,
pursuant to an agreement with the Beatles. Should it make a difference to
the applicability of U.S. law to extraterritorial exploitation if the "authorizing" party had clearly exceeded the scope of its license from the copyright
owner? What if the "authorizing" party had no prior relationship with the
initial copyright owner? For example, what if defendant, a stranger to the
Beatles, had from its U.S. offices directed the counterfeiting and sale in
Southeast Asia of videocassettes of *Yellow Submarine*?

4. Defendant U.S. company authorizes (without the U.S. copyright owner's
consent) the production of copies of the work abroad for reshipment to
the U.S. by defendant's foreign partner. Does this act of authorization
violate the U.S. copyright law? Or must the U.S. copyright owner wait
until the copies arrive in the U.S.? *See Armstrong v. Virgin Records*, Ltd., 91
F.Supp 2d 628 (2000); *Stewart v. Adidas A.G.*, No. 96 CIV. 6670 (DLC),
1997 U.S. Dist. LEXIS 5578 (S.D.N.Y. April 30, 1997); *Metzke v. May
Department Stores Co.*, 878 F.Supp. 756 (W.D.Pa. 1995).

Digital and other transmissions

The "root copy" (or "predicate act") doctrine is rooted in copies, and the
caselaw involved physical copies. How does that doctrine apply to transmissions from copies originating outside the U.S.?

Shropshire v. Canning, 809 F.Supp.2d 1139 (C.D.Cal. 2011)

[Plaintiff Elmo Shropshire was a co-owner of the musical composition
copyright in the Christmas-holiday season song "Grandma Got Run Over
By A Reindeer." Aubrey Canning, a resident of Canada, uploaded to You
Tube and refused to remove an allegedly infringing video incorporating
the composition. Canning moved to dismiss Shropshire's U.S. infringement action on the ground that the alleged infringing act—uploading the
Grandma video to YouTube—took place in Canada and thus fell outside
the reach of the Copyright Act. The court distinguished the creation of the
alleged infringing work in Canada from its uploading, from Canada, to a
U.S. website:]

Turning to the extraterritorial applicability of the Copyright Act, courts are split on whether the infringing act must occur wholly within the United States or if the infringing act only must not occur wholly outside of the United States. Put differently, the dispute is whether all parts of the infringing act must take place in the United States, or if it is sufficient that some part of the infringing acts take place in the United States. . . .

The Court finds that in this case, the alleged act of direct copyright infringement—uploading a video from Canada to YouTube's servers in California for display within the United States—constitutes an act of infringement that is not "wholly extraterritorial" to the United States. Those cases holding that the Copyright Act requires at least one infringing act to occur entirely within the United States dealt with situations in which the infringing transmission was authorized or sent from within the U.S. but received and accessed abroad. In this case, however, we face the opposite scenario. The allegedly infringing act in this case began in Canada, where Defendant created his Grandma song video. Had Defendant stopped there, there is no doubt that the strict presumption against extraterritoriality would apply and Plaintiff would not have a claim. As noted in the Court's January 11, 2011 Order: "The creation of the video, however, occurred entirely in Canada, and thus cannot constitute copyright infringement under well-settled law."

The problem is that Defendant did not stop at the mere creation of the Grandma song video in Canada, but instead allegedly uploaded it to YouTube's California servers for display in the United States after agreeing to YouTube's Terms of Service agreement. Thus, according to the allegations in the [complaint], Defendant's direct action led to the creation of a copy of the Grandma video on YouTube's servers in California, and to the subsequent viewing of the video by potentially thousands in the United States.

QUESTIONS

Should it matter whether the further communications for which a U.S.-made copy is the source include U.S. recipients? What if the Canadian uploaded the "Grandma" song to a California server that allowed access only by Canadians (or by non-U.S. users)? Is the "predicate act" doctrine more or less persuasive when applied to Internet communications?

Shropshire involved Canadian-originated content transmitted to a U.S. website for further transmission. What if the off-shore defendant is offering to transmit copies or performances from a foreign website (or, in a P2P network, from a foreign user's hard drive)? In *Capitol Records, Inc. v. Bertelsmann AG*, 377 F.Supp.2d 796, 805 (N.D. Cal. 2005) the court described a violation of the § 106(3) distribution right as follows:

> a copyright owner seeking to establish that his or her copyrighted work was distributed in violation of section 106(3) must prove that the accused infringer either (1) actually disseminated one or more copies of the work to members of the public or (2) offered to distribute copies of that work for purposes of further distribution, public performance, or public display.

The first criterion supposes that the "members of the public" are the U.S. public. The point of attachment thus appears to be receipt of the transmission in the U.S. The second criterion may imply U.S. recipients, but it may also extend to actors who, from the U.S., offer to distribute copies, whether or not to U.S. recipients. Which is (are) the relevant point(s) of attachment in the following decisions?

Twentieth Century Fox Film Corp. v. iCrave TV, No 00–121 (W.D. Pa. Jan. 20, 2000).

[iCrave TV, a Toronto-based website, converted into videostreaming format the broadcast signals from Canadian programs, and from U.S. television programming received across the border, and made the programming available via its website. iCrave TV claimed that its capture, conversion, and redistribution of the U.S. programming was lawful under Canadian law concerning secondary transmissions of broadcast performances.

[The producers brought suit in the Western District of Pennsylvania, where iCrave TV's President and its International Sales Manager resided. With respect to the Canadian business entities, the court found general personal jurisdiction over the non-resident defendants on the basis of their continuous and systematic contacts with Pennsylvania. Among the contacts the court identified were: sales of advertising out of a Pittsburgh office, employment of an agent in Pittsburgh to work in that office, and domain name registration for iCraveTV.com in the U.S., with technical and billing contacts listed in Pennsylvania. The court further found that defendants' activities in Pennsylvania were "integrally a part of the activities giving rise to the cause of action asserted." Finally, the court noted that defendants had streamed plaintiffs' programming to U.S. citizens throughout the U.S. overall, and had attempted to sell advertising throughout the U.S. through agents in New York and Pennsylvania.

[On choice of law, the court found sufficient points of attachment with the U.S. to apply the U.S. Copyright Act to defendants' activities. The court found that the alleged infringement occurred in the United States when U.S. citizens "received and viewed defendants' streaming of the copyrighted materials," without plaintiffs' authorization, even though the streaming began in Canada. The receipt of the transmissions in the U.S. constituted public performances under U.S. copyright law. Moreover, the transmissions to the U.S. accounted for a substantial portion of iCrave TV's total business. For example, on January 17, 2000, an iCrave TV employee reported that log books monitoring traffic showed that approximately 45 percent of iCrave TV's traffic was from U.S.-based users; a January 25, 2000 report from a "private ad serving system" counted 1.6 million impressions from U.S. visitors (second only to Canadian visitors); "Real Video" logs of Internet addresses showed "substantial numbers of persons in the U.S. received the streaming of programming." The court ordered iCrave TV to cease retransmitting U.S. television programming. Following initiation of a suit in Canada alleging that iCrave TV's retransmissions were not permitted under Canadian law either, iCrave TV and the producers settled, and iCrave has ceased retransmitting U.S. television programming.]

National Football League v. PrimeTime 24, 211 F.3d 10 (2d Cir. 2000). [This case presented the reverse of the iCraveTV coin. There, the retransmission originated from Canada, but was receivable in the U.S. Here, defendant captured plaintiff's U.S. broadcast signals in the U.S., but sent the retransmitted signals to Canadian households. Primetime 24 asserted that its service of Canadian households fell outside the scope of the U.S. copyright act, because the signals were received in Canada; no "public performance" occurred in the U.S. The Second Circuit disagreed:]

The issue in this case is whether PrimeTime publicly performed or displayed NFL's copyrighted material. PrimeTime argues that capturing or uplinking copyrighted material and transmitting it to a satellite does not constitute a public display or performance of that material. PrimeTime argues that any public performance or display occurs during the downlink from the satellite to the home subscriber in Canada, which is in a foreign country where the Copyright Act does not apply.

In *WGN Continental Broad. Co. v. United Video, Inc.*, 693 F.2d 622, 624–25 (7th Cir. 1982), the Seventh Circuit considered whether an intermediate carrier had publicly performed copyrighted television signals by capturing broadcast signals, altering them and transmitting them to cable television systems. The court determined that "the Copyright Act defines 'perform or display . . . . publicly' broadly enough to encompass indirect transmission to the ultimate public." Consequently, the WGN court concluded that an intermediate carrier is not immune from copyright liability simply because it does not retransmit a copyrighted signal to the public directly but instead routes the signal to cable systems, which then retransmit to the public.

Judge Posner, writing for the court in *WGN*, noted that a contrary result would render the passive carrier exemption in the Act superfluous. The passive carrier exemption provides that a secondary transmission is not copyright infringement if the transmitter has no control over the content or selection of the original signal or over the recipients of the secondary transmission and provides only the wires, cables, or communication channels for the use of others. See 17 U.S.C. § 111(a)(3). In other words, if a copyrighted signal is publicly performed or displayed only when received by viewers, there would be no need for a passive carrier exemption because these passive intermediate carriers "do not transmit directly to the public." . . .

District courts in this Circuit have agreed that a transmission need not be made directly to the public in order for there to be a public performance or display. For example, in *David v. Showtime/The Movie Channel, Inc.*, 697 F.Supp. 752, 759 (S.D.N.Y. 1988), Judge Tenney concluded that "Congress intended the definitions of 'public' and 'performance' to encompass each step in the process by which a protected work wends its way to its audience." Judge Tenney further stated that the definition of transmit "is broad enough to include all conceivable forms and combinations of wired or wireless communications media." . . .

The Court of Appeals for the Ninth Circuit has suggested a different result. When considering whether the Copyright Act preempted state law, that Court stated that copyright infringement does not occur until the signal is received by the viewing public. See *Allarcom Pay Television, Ltd. v. General Instrument Corp.*, 69 F.3d 381, 387 (9th Cir. 1995). This opinion has been subject to some non-judicial criticism, which we need not repeat. See Jane C. Ginsburg, Extraterritoriality and Multiterritoriality in Copyright Infringement, 37 Va. J. Int'l L. 587, 598 (1997); Andreas P. Reindl, Choosing Law in Cyberspace: Copyright Conflicts on Global Networks, 19 Mich. J. Int'l L. 799, 823 n.84 (1998). We accord the decision little weight largely because it contains no analysis of the Copyright Act.

We believe the most logical interpretation of the Copyright Act is to hold that a public performance or display includes "each step in the process by which a protected work wends its way to its audience." Under that analysis, it is clear that PrimeTime's uplink transmission of signals captured in the United States is a step in the process by which NFL's protected work wends its way to a public audience. In short, PrimeTime publicly displayed or performed material in which the NFL owns the copyright. Because PrimeTime did not have authorization to make such a public performance, PrimeTime infringed the NFL's copyright. . .

QUESTION

The combined effect of these two cases is to prohibit under the U.S. Copyright Law any retransmission of a copyrighted program, provided that the retransmission starts in the U.S. or reaches the U.S. Compare the E.U. position on the same issue, immediately following. What would be the outcome if the E.U. had adopted the same position as the U.S.?

E.U.

Edouard Treppoz, Commentary on Regulation No. 864/2007 (Rome II), in Concise International and European IP Law, ed. T. Cottier & P. Veron, Wolters Kluwer 2014*

The Regulation No. 864/2007 (Rome II) is a text of the highest importance for private international law of intellectual property. The aim of this regulation is to determine the law applicable to non-contractual obligations, which includes the infringement of intellectual property rights. Art. 8 of the regulation lays down a specific rule for such infringements.

Three requirements have to be fulfilled in order to apply the Rome II Regulation. The first one is temporal. The question was controversial because of the ambiguity between the articles 31 and 32 of the Rome II Regulation. The issue was solved by the European Court of Justice considering that "Articles 31 and 32 of Regulation (EC) No 864/2007 of the European Parliament and of the Council of 11 July 2007 on the law applicable to non-contractual obligations ('Rome II'), read in conjunction with Article 297 TFEU, must be interpreted as requiring a national court to apply the Regulation only to events giving rise to damage occurring after 11 January 2009 and that the date on which the proceedings seeking compensation for damage were brought or the date on which the applicable law was determined by the court seised have no bearing on determining the scope *ratione temporis* of the Regulation" (ECJ, C-412/10, *Deo Antoine Homawoo*). The second requirement is spatial. Under

---

* Reprinted with permission.

art. 3, the Rome II Regulation possesses a universal application. Following this universal application, the Rome II Regulation is applicable where a judge of a Member State is seized irrespective of whether the law applicable is the law of a Member State. For instance, the Rome II Regulation is applicable as soon as a French judge is seized and even if the American law applies to the infringement. It should be remembered that Denmark is not a Member State of the Rome II Regulation. The last requirement is a substantial requirement. Under art. 1, the Regulation 'shall apply, in situations involving a conflict of laws, to non-contractual obligations in civil and commercial matters'. As it is shown by art. 8, an infringement of intellectual property rights is characterized as a non-contractual obligation in civil and commercial matters justifying the application of Rome II Regulation. A tricky issue could be raised where infringement actions are brought for breach of an IP contract. Two texts could be applicable: the Rome I Regulation for the breach of contract and the Rome II Regulation for the infringement related to this breach of contract. The ECJ adopts such a secessionist approach in a case *Kalfelis* (ECJ, C-189/87) distinguishing between the application of art. 5(1) and (3) of the Regulation No. 44/2001 [arts. 7(1) and (2) Recast]. Nevertheless, it could be argued that art. 2 of the Regulation No. 44/2001 [art. 4 Recast] giving general jurisdiction to the courts of the Member State where the defendant is domiciled for contractual and non-contractual matters might explain this secessionist approach for jurisdiction.* Indeed, the defendant could still choose to use article 2 avoiding the secessionist approach. As to choice of law, if a secessionist approach is adopted, it would not be possible to avoid the application of two different regulations and two different applicable laws, pleading in favor of a contractual approach.

The 2002 Preliminary Draft of Rome II Regulation adopted no specific choice-of-law rule for intellectual property right infringements. The consequence would have been the application of the general choice-of-law rule for non-contractual obligations to intellectual property right infringements. More precisely, the applicable law would have been the law of the country in which the damage arises. Nevertheless, the Preliminary draft carves out exceptions to the general rule in favor of the law of the habitual residence of the person claimed to be liable and the person sustaining damage or more generally in favor of the law of the country manifestly more closely connected with the infringement. Thus, under this Preliminary Draft, French law would have been applicable to the infringement by a French company of an Italian patent held by a French company in Italy. Therefore, the infringement of a national intellectual property right would have been submitted to a different

* See *supra* p. 630 for a decision rendered after the publication of this commentary.

law than the law of the title. Such a solution raised general opposition, mainly because it does not comply with the principle of territoriality requiring the application of the *lex loci protectionis*. While such an argument seems to be overestimated, it justified the enactment of a specific choice-of-law rule for a non-contractual obligation arising from an intellectual property right infringement. The objective was clearly to preserve the *lex loci protectionis* presented as 'a universally acknowledged principle'.

By choosing "the law of the country for which protection is claimed", the Rome II Regulation retains a classical connecting factor for intellectual property right. One could quote art. 110 of the Swiss Federal Act on private international law which is also in favor of the law of the State in respect of which intellectual property protection is sought. Among international conventions, art. 5(2) of the Berne Convention applies the law of the country where protection is claimed. But, this last rule should be read as applying the law of the country for which protection is claimed. The connecting factor seems to be the same under the Berne Convention and the Rome II Regulation and has to be clearly distinguished from the *lex fori*. Let us imagine an infringement in Italy of an Italian patent made by a French company. The owner of the patent could seize the French courts according to art. 2 of Regulation No. 44/2001 [art. 4 Recast]. The French judge will then apply the Italian law being the law for which the protection is claimed. The choice-of-law rule for IP infringements should also be distinguished from the choice of law rule for torts, while both could lead to the same country. First and under the Rome II Regulation, those two choice-of-law rules show some profound differences. The general rule is in favor of the law of the damage, which might be different than the law of the infringement. Moreover, this rule allows some exceptions in favor of the law of the habitual residence of the person claimed to be liable and the person sustaining damage or more generally in favor of the law of the country manifestly more closely connected with the infringement. Those exceptions are not applicable when the non-contractual obligation arises from an intellectual property right infringement. Only the law of the country for which protection is claimed is applicable, whether or not a more appropriate law could be designated. Art. 8 promotes a rigid connecting factor contrary to the general rule enacted at art. 4. Finally, another difference could be mentioned between the *lex loci protectionis* and the *lex loci delicti* as to their scope of application. Generally, the law of the protection is not necessarily limited to the infringement and applied to the right. Article 110 of the Swiss Federal Act on international private law encompasses such a broad scope, leading to the creation of a mosaic of different intellectual property rights, nationally limited. This mosaic system is often linked to the principle of territoriality. It seems then that, broadly speaking, the *lex loci protectionis* might have a larger scope than the *lex loci delicti*. We will see that it is not so obvious under the Rome II Regulation.

The Rome II Regulation applies to non-contractual obligation and more precisely to, as stated by article 8 title, to infringement of intellectual property right. Article 15 of the Rome II Regulation determining the scope of the law applicable clearly limits such a scope to non-contractual issues, excluding to encompass the right infringed. This means that the choice-of-law rule designating by the *lex loci protectionis* covers only issues connected to infringement and not any other issues. A quick comparative study of various domestic private international law systems might illustrate the consequence of such a limited scope. For some countries and under domestic private international law, such as Germany and Italy, the applicable law to intellectual property right is the *lex loci protectionis* whether or not the issue pertains to infringement. This *lex loci protectionis* applies also to the ownership of an intellectual property right, under those systems. The mosaic covers not only the infringement but to every issue concerning intellectual property rights. On the other hand, some countries, like Greece or Portugal, limit the *lex loci protectionis* to infringement of intellectual property right, and most of time copyright, and apply a *lex loci originis* at least for the ownership of copyright. If art. 8 had a general scope beyond infringement including the existence of IP, those secessionist systems would disappear in favor of a wide harmonisation of intellectual property right in Europe based on the application of the *lex loci protectionis*. If art. 8 had a restricted scope, those discrepancies would remain unchanged, excluding a broad harmonisation. The second solution seems, nevertheless, to be the correct one. It is clear that in the case of a non-contractual obligation arising from a damage made to a tangible object, the Rome II Regulation determines the applicable law to the non-contractual obligation. It is also clear that the *lex loci commissi* designated by the Rome Regulation does not apply to the characterization of the tangible object and its ownership. The *lex rei sitae* applies to those issues. The solution should be the same for an intellectual property right, limiting the scope of art. 8 to infringement of intellectual property rights.

In general

> **Regulation (EC) No 864/2007 of the European Parliament and of the Council of 11 July 2007 on the law applicable to non-contractual obligations (Rome II)**
>
> **Recitals**
>
> (26) Regarding infringements of intellectual property rights, the universally acknowledged principle of the *lex loci protectionis* should be

preserved. For the purposes of this Regulation, the term 'intellectual property rights' should be interpreted as meaning, for instance, copyright, related rights, the sui generis right for the protection of databases and industrial property rights.

Article 4 – General rule

1. Unless otherwise provided for in this Regulation, the law applicable to a non-contractual obligation arising out of a tort/delict shall be the law of the country in which the damage occurs irrespective of the country in which the event giving rise to the damage occurred and irrespective of the country or countries in which the indirect consequences of that event occur.

2. However, where the person claimed to be liable and the person sustaining damage both have their habitual residence in the same country at the time when the damage occurs, the law of that country shall apply.

3. Where it is clear from all the circumstances of the case that the tort/delict is manifestly more closely connected with a country other than that indicated in paragraphs 1 or 2, the law of that other country shall apply. A manifestly closer connection with another country might be based in particular on a pre-existing relationship between the parties, such as a contract, that is closely connected with the tort/delict in question.

Article 8 – Infringement of intellectual property rights

1. The law applicable to a non-contractual obligation arising from an infringement of an intellectual property right shall be the law of the country for which protection is claimed.

2. In the case of a non-contractual obligation arising from an infringement of a unitary Community intellectual property right, the law applicable shall, for any question that is not governed by the relevant Community instrument, be the law of the country in which the act of infringement was committed.

3. The law applicable under this Article may not be derogated from by an agreement pursuant to Article 14.

Article 13 – Applicability of Article 8

For the purposes of this Chapter, Article 8 shall apply to non-contractual obligations arising from an infringement of an intellectual property right.

Article 15 – Scope of the law applicable

The law applicable to non-contractual obligations under this Regulation shall govern in particular:

(a) the basis and extent of liability, including the determination of persons who may be held liable for acts performed by them;
(b) the grounds for exemption from liability, any limitation of liability and any division of liability;
(c) the existence, the nature and the assessment of damage or the remedy claimed;
(d) within the limits of powers conferred on the court by its procedural law, the measures which a court may take to prevent or terminate injury or damage or to ensure the provision of compensation;
(e) the question whether a right to claim damages or a remedy may be transferred, including by inheritance;
(f) persons entitled to compensation for damage sustained personally;
(g) liability for the acts of another person;
(h) the manner in which an obligation may be extinguished and rules of prescription and limitation, including rules relating to the commencement, interruption and suspension of a period of prescription or limitation.

Article 16 – Overriding mandatory provisions

Nothing in this Regulation shall restrict the application of the provisions of the law of the forum in a situation where they are mandatory irrespective of the law otherwise applicable to the non-contractual obligation.

Article 27 – Relationship with other provisions of Community law

This Regulation shall not prejudice the application of provisions of Community law which, in relation to particular matters, lay down conflict-of-law rules relating to non-contractual obligations.

Article 28 – Relationship with existing international conventions

1. This Regulation shall not prejudice the application of international conventions to which one or more Member States are parties at the time when this Regulation is adopted and which lay down conflict-of-law rules relating to non-contractual obligations.

2. However, this Regulation shall, as between Member States, take precedence over conventions concluded exclusively between two or more of them in so far as such conventions concern matters governed by this Regulation.

QUESTIONS

1. How do you explain the difference between article 8 and article 4 of the Rome II Regulation?
2. What is the difference between article 8(1)'s designation of the law of the country for which protection is claimed and article 8(2)'s designation of the law of the country in which the act of infringement was committed?
3. Taking into account article 28, when does the Rome II Regulation apply to copyright infringement?

C-5/11 Titus Alexander Jochen Donner ECLI:EU:C:2012:370 [2012]

The dispute in the main proceedings and the question referred for a preliminary ruling

11   Mr Donner, a German national, was, at the time of the facts in the main proceedings, the principal director and shareholder of In.Sp.Em. Srl ('Inspem'), a freight forwarding company established in Bologna (Italy) and essentially conducted his business from his place of residence in Germany.

12   Inspem ensured the transport of goods sold by Dimensione Direct Sales Srl ('Dimensione'), a company also established in Bologna, the head office of which was situated in immediate proximity of that of Inspem. Dimensione used advertisements and supplements in newspapers, direct publicity letters and a German-language internet website to offer replicas of furnishings in the so-called 'Bauhaus' style for sale to customers residing in Germany, without having a licence to market them in Germany. These included replicas of:

* chairs from the Aluminium Group, designed by Charles and Ray Eames, licensed proprietor Vitra Collections AG;
* Wagenfeld lights, designed by Wilhelm Wagenfeld, licensed proprietor Tecnolumen GmbH & Co. KG;
* seating, designed by Le Corbusier, licensed proprietor Cassina SpA;
* the occasional table called the 'Adjustable Table' and 'Tubelight' lamps, designed by Eileen Gray, licensed proprietor Classicon GmbH;
* tubular steel cantilever chairs, designed by Mart Stam, licensed proprietor Thonet GmbH.

13   According to the findings of the Landgericht München II, all of the said items are copyright-protected in Germany as works of applied art. In Italy, however, there was no copyright protection or, alternatively, no enforceable copyright protection as against third parties during the period of relevance, namely from 1 January 2005 to 15 January 2008. Thus the furnishings designed by Eileen Gray did not enjoy copyright protection in Italy in the period between 1 January 2002 and 25 April 2007 as a shorter period of protection applied at that time, which was only renewed as of 26 April 2007. The other furnishings were copyright-protected in Italy during the relevant period but that protection was unenforceable as against third parties under established Italian case-law, at least as against producers who had reproduced or offered the creations for sale and/or marketed them prior to 19 April 2001.

14   The furnishings at issue in the main proceedings, sold by Dimensione, were stored, in their packaging on which the name and address of the purchaser were indicated, in Dimensione's delivery warehouse in Sterzing (Italy). Under the general sales conditions, if customers residing in Germany did not wish to collect the goods they had ordered, or nominate their own freight forwarder, Dimensione recommended that Inspem be instructed. In the cases in the main proceedings the customers instructed Inspem to transport the furnishings that they had purchased. The Inspem drivers collected the items at the warehouse in Sterzing and paid the relevant purchase price to Dimensione. Inspem collected the purchase price and freight charges from the customer on delivery to the person who had placed the order in Germany. Whenever a customer failed to accept or make payment for a delivery of furnishings, the goods were returned to Dimensione, which reimbursed Inspem for the purchase price already advanced and also paid the freight charges.

15   According to the Landgericht München II, Mr Donner thereby committed the criminal offence of aiding and abetting the prohibited commercial exploitation of copyright-protected works, contrary to Paragraphs 106 and 108a of the UrhG and also Paragraph 27 of the Criminal Code.

16   Dimensione was found to have distributed copies of protected works in Germany. Distribution under Paragraph 106 of the UrhG required the transfer of the ownership of the goods sold and as well as a transfer of the power of disposal from the vendor to the purchaser. In the main proceedings, under Italian law the transfer of ownership from vendor to purchaser took place in Italy as a result of the meeting of the minds and the individualisation of the goods at the warehouse in Sterzing. The transfer of the power of disposal over the goods, however, did not take place until the goods were handed

over to the purchaser upon payment of the purchase price in Germany, with the help of Mr Donner. The issue whether the furnishings enjoyed copyright protection in Italy was therefore immaterial. The Landgericht München II found that the restriction on the free movement of goods deriving from national copyright law was justified on grounds of protection of industrial and commercial property.

17   Mr Donner appealed on a point of law (revision) against that judgment to the Bundesgerichtshof. He argues, first, that 'distribution to the public' under Article 4(1) of Directive 2001/29 [Info Soc] and, consequently, under Paragraph 17 of the UrhG, presupposes a transfer of ownership of the goods, which in the main proceedings took place in Italy, the transfer of possession of the goods, that is to say, the actual power of disposal over those goods, not being necessary in that regard. He argues, secondly, that a conviction of him based on any other interpretation would be contrary to the principle of free movement of goods guaranteed under Article 34 TFEU* because it would lead to an unjustified and artificial partitioning of the markets. Lastly and thirdly, he argues that, in any event, the handing-over of the goods in Italy to the carrier, which accepted them on behalf of ascertained customers, gave rise to a change of possession so that, from that point of view as well, the relevant facts occurred in Italy.

18   The Bundesgerichtshof concurs in the interpretation adopted by the Landgericht München II, to the effect that 'distribution to the public' by sale under Article 4(1) of Directive 2001/29 [Info Soc] presupposes that not just ownership but also de facto power of disposal of the copyright-protected reproduction is transferred to a third party. In order to be considered as being distributed to the public, the reproduction of a work has to be transferred from the manufacturer's internal sphere of operation into the public sphere or into the free trade arena. As long as such a reproduction remains within the manufacturer's internal sphere of operation or the same group of companies, it cannot be deemed to have reached the public, since the existence of a business transaction based on genuine external dealings is lacking in such a scenario. This analysis by the Landgericht München II is in line with the settled case-law of the Bundesgerichtshof on the interpretation of Article 4(1) of Directive 2001/29 [Info Soc].

19   On the other hand, the Bundesgerichtshof considers that Articles 34 TFEU and 36 TFEU may preclude upholding Mr Donner's conviction

---

* Editors' Note: Article 34 TFEU provides: Quantitative restrictions on imports and all measures having equivalent effect shall be prohibited between Member States.

should the application of the national criminal law provisions to the facts of the main proceedings be found to give rise to an unjustified restriction on the free movement of goods.

20   In those circumstances the Bundesgerichtshof decided to stay the proceedings before it and to refer the following question to the Court for a preliminary ruling:

> Are Articles 34 and 36 TFEU governing the free movement of goods to be interpreted as precluding the criminal offence of aiding and abetting the prohibited distribution of copyright-protected works resulting from the application of national criminal law where, on a cross-border sale of a work that is copyright protected in Germany,

> • that work is taken to Germany from a Member State of the European Union and de facto power of disposal thereof is transferred in Germany,
> • but the transfer of ownership took place in the other Member State in which copyright protection for the work did not exist or was unenforceable as against third parties?'

The interpretation of Article 4(1) of Directive 2001/29 [Info Soc]

23   Since Directive 2001/29 [Info Soc] serves to implement in the European Union its obligations under, inter alia, the CT [WIPO Copyright Treaty] and, according to settled case-law, European Union legislation must, so far as possible, be interpreted in a manner that is consistent with international law, in particular where its provisions are intended specifically to give effect to an international agreement concluded by the European Union, the notion of 'distribution', contained in Article 4(1) of that directive, must be interpreted in accordance with Article 6(1) of the CT [WIPO Copyright Treaty] (see, to that effect, Case C-456/06 *Peek & Cloppenburg* [2008] ECR I-2731, paragraphs 29 to 32).

24   The notion of 'distribution to the public . . . by sale' in Article 4(1) of Directive 2001/29 [Info Soc] must accordingly, as observed by the Advocate General in points 44 to 46 and 53 of his Opinion, be construed as having the same meaning as the expression 'making available to the public . . . through sale' in Article 6(1) of the CT [WIPO Copyright Treaty].

25   As observed by the Advocate General in point 51 of his Opinion, the content of the notion of 'distribution' under Article 4(1) of Directive

2001/29 [Info Soc], must moreover be given an independent interpretation under European Union law, which cannot be contingent on the legislation applicable to transactions in which a distribution takes place.

26 It must be observed that the distribution to the public is characterised by a series of acts going, at the very least, from the conclusion of a contract of sale to the performance thereof by delivery to a member of the public. Thus, in the context of a cross-border sale, acts giving rise to a 'distribution to the public' under Article 4(1) of Directive 2001/29 [Info Soc] may take place in a number of Member States. In such a context, such a transaction may infringe on the exclusive right to authorise or prohibit any forms of distribution to the public in a number of Member States.

27 A trader in such circumstances bears responsibility for any act carried out by him or on his behalf giving rise to a 'distribution to the public' in a Member State where the goods distributed are protected by copyright. Any such act carried out by a third party may also be attributed to him, where he specifically targeted the public of the State of destination and must have been aware of the actions of that third party.

28 In circumstances such as those at issue in the main proceedings, where the delivery to a member of the public in another Member State is not effected by or on behalf of the trader in question, it is therefore for the national courts to assess, on a case-by-case basis, whether there is evidence supporting a conclusion that that trader, first, did actually target members of the public residing in the Member State where an operation giving rise to a 'distribution to the public' under Article 4(1) of Directive 2001/29 [Info Soc] was carried out and, second, whether he must have been aware of the actions of the third party in question.

29 In the circumstances giving rise to the case in the main proceedings, factors such as the existence of a German-language website, the content and distribution channels of Dimensione's advertising materials and its cooperation with Inspem, as an undertaking making deliveries to Germany, may be taken as constituting evidence of such targeted activity.

30 Accordingly, the answer to the first part of the question referred is that a trader who directs his advertising at members of the public residing in a given Member State and creates or makes available to them a specific delivery system and payment method, or allows a third party to do so, thereby enabling those members of the public to receive delivery of copies of works

protected by copyright in that same Member State, makes, in the Member State where the delivery takes place, a 'distribution to the public' under Article 4(1) of Directive 2001/29 [Info Soc].

QUESTIONS

1. How could you explain the disparities between German law and Italian law concerning the localization of the distribution? Why does it matter? How does the ECJ solve the issue?
2. Under local substantive law, would Donner have been characterized as a direct or indirect infringer? What difference does it make for conflict of laws? Does the Rome II Regulation solve the problem?

Ubiquitous infringements

i. The solution applied to satellite transmissions

Council Directive 93/83/EEC of 27 September 1993 on the coordination of certain rules concerning copyright and rights related to copyright applicable to satellite broadcasting and cable retransmission

Recitals

(7) Whereas the free broadcasting of programmes is further impeded by the current legal uncertainty over whether broadcasting by a satellite whose signals can be received directly affects the rights in the country of transmission only or in all countries of reception together; whereas, since communications satellites and direct satellites are treated alike for copyright purposes, this legal uncertainty now affects almost all programmes broadcast in the Community by satellite;

(14) Whereas the legal uncertainty regarding the rights to be acquired which impedes cross-border satellite broadcasting should be overcome by defining the notion of communication to the public by satellite at a Community level; whereas this definition should at the same time specify where the act of communication takes place; whereas such a definition is necessary to avoid the cumulative application of several national laws to one single act of broadcasting; whereas communication to the public by satellite occurs only when, and in the Member State where, the programme-carrying signals are introduced under the control and responsibility of the broadcasting organization into an uninterrupted

chain of communication leading to the satellite and down towards the earth; whereas normal technical procedures relating to the programme-carrying signals should not be considered as interruptions to the chain of broadcasting;

CHAPTER I DEFINITIONS
Article 1 – Definitions

1. For the purpose of this Directive, 'satellite' means any satellite operating on frequency bands which, under telecommunications law, are reserved for the broadcast of signals for reception by the public or which are reserved for closed, point-to-point communication. In the latter case, however, the circumstances in which individual reception of the signals takes place must be comparable to those which apply in the first case.

2. (a) For the purpose of this Directive, 'communication to the public by satellite' means the act of introducing, under the control and responsibility of the broadcasting organization, the programme-carrying signals intended for reception by the public into an uninterrupted chain of communication leading to the satellite and down towards the earth.

(b) The act of communication to the public by satellite occurs solely in the Member State where, under the control and responsibility of the broadcasting organization, the programme-carrying signals are introduced into an uninterrupted chain of communication leading to the satellite and down towards the earth.

(c) If the programme-carrying signals are encrypted, then there is communication to the public by satellite on condition that the means for decrypting the broadcast are provided to the public by the broadcasting organization or with its consent.

(d) Where an act of communication to the public by satellite occurs in a non-Community State which does not provide the level of protection provided for under Chapter II,

(i) if the programme-carrying signals are transmitted to the satellite from an uplink station situated in a Member State, that act of communication to the public by satellite shall be deemed to have occurred in that Member State and the rights provided for under Chapter II shall be exercisable against the person operating the uplink station; or

(ii) if there is no use of an uplink station situated in a Member State but a broadcasting organization established in a Member State has commissioned the act of communication to the public by satellite, that act shall be deemed to have occurred in the Member State in which the broadcasting organization has its principal establishment in the Community and the rights provided for under Chapter II shall be exercisable against the broadcasting organization.

3. For the purposes of this Directive, 'cable retransmission' means the simultaneous, unaltered and unabridged retransmission by a cable or microwave system for reception by the public of an initial transmission from another Member State, by wire or over the air, including that by satellite, of television or radio programmes intended for reception by the public.

4. For the purposes of this Directive 'collecting society' means any organization which manages or administers copyright or rights related to copyright as its sole purpose or as one of its main purposes.

5. For the purposes of this Directive, the principal director of a cinematographic or audiovisual work shall be considered as its author or one of its authors. Member States may provide for others to be considered as its co-authors.

QUESTIONS

1. To what extent, does the directive lay down a choice-of-law rule? Why is identifying a European source for the act of communication to the public important?
2. Do you think that this solution might be extended to Internet transmissions?
3. Determine the applicable law under the directive for the following examples:
    (a) A German TV channel retransmitting French programs via an uplink satellite station in Belgium.
    (b) An Algerian TV channel retransmitting French programs via an uplink satellite station in Belgium
    (c) An Algerian TV channel retransmitting Turkish programs via an uplink satellite station in Turkey.
    (d) An Italian TV channel retransmitting Turkish programs via an uplink satellite station in Turkey.

ii. The solution applied to the Internet

C-324/09 L'Oréal SA and Others v. eBay International AG ECLI:EU:C:2011:474 [2011]

II – The dispute in the main proceedings and the questions referred for a preliminary ruling

26   L'Oréal is a manufacturer and supplier of perfumes, cosmetics and hair-care products. In the United Kingdom it is the proprietor of a number of national trade marks. It is also the proprietor of Community trade marks.

27   L'Oréal operates a closed selective distribution network, in which authorised distributors are restrained from supplying products to other distributors.

28   eBay operates an electronic marketplace on which are displayed listings of goods offered for sale by persons who have registered for that purpose with eBay and have created a seller's account with it. eBay charges a percentage fee on completed transactions.

29   eBay enables prospective buyers to bid for items offered by sellers. It also allows items to be sold without an auction, and thus for a fixed price, by means of a system known as 'Buy It Now'. Sellers can also set up online shops on eBay sites. An online shop lists all the items offered for sale by one seller at a given time.

. . .

50   By decision of 16 July 2009, which follows on from the judgment of 22 May 2009, the High Court of Justice decided to stay the proceedings and refer the following questions to the Court for a preliminary ruling:

. . .

(7) Where the goods advertised and offered for sale on the website referred to in question 6 above include goods which have not been put on the market within the EEA [European Economic Area] by or with the consent of the trade mark proprietor, is it sufficient for such use to fall within the scope of Article 5(1)(a) of [Trademark Directive 89/104] and Article 9(1)(a) of [Trademark Regulation No 40/94] and outside Article 7(1) of [Directive 89/104] and Article 13(1) of [Regulation No 40/94] that the advertisement or offer for sale is targeted at consumers in the territory covered by the trade mark or must the trade mark proprietor show that the advertisement or offer for sale necessarily entails putting the goods in question on the market within the territory covered by the trade mark?

2. The offer for sale, by means of an online marketplace targeted at consumers in the E.U., of trade-marked goods intended, by the proprietor of the mark, for sale in third States

58   By its seventh question, which it is appropriate to examine first, the referring court asks, in essence, whether, for the proprietor of a trade mark registered in a Member State of the E.U. or of a Community trade mark to be able to prevent, under the rules set out in Article 5 of Directive 89/104 and Article 9 of Regulation No 40/94, the offer for sale, on an online marketplace, of goods bearing that trade mark which have not previously been put on the market in the EEA [European Economic Area] or, in the case of a Community trade mark, in the E.U., it is sufficient that the offer for sale is targeted at consumers located in the territory covered by the trade mark.

59   The rule set out in Article 5 of Directive 89/104 and Article 9 of Regulation No 40/94 confers on the proprietor of a trade mark exclusive rights entitling him to prevent any third party from importing goods bearing that mark, offering the goods, or putting them on the market or stocking them for those purposes, whilst Article 7 of the directive and Article 13 of the regulation have laid down an exception to that rule, providing that the trade mark proprietor's rights are exhausted where the goods have been put on the market in the EEA [European Economic Area] – or, in the case of a Community trade mark, in the E.U. – by the proprietor himself or with his consent (citations omitted).

60   In the situation under consideration in the context of this question, in which the goods have at no time been put on the market within the EEA by the trade mark proprietor or with his consent, the exception set out in Article 7 of Directive 89/104 and Article 13 of Regulation No 40/94 cannot apply. In that regard, the Court has repeatedly held that it is essential that the proprietor of a trade mark registered in a Member State can control the first placing of goods bearing that trade mark on the market in the EEA (Citations omitted).

61   Whilst recognising those principles, eBay submits that the proprietor of a trade mark registered in a Member State or of a Community trade mark cannot properly rely on the exclusive right conferred by that trade mark as long as the goods bearing it and offered for sale on an online marketplace are located in a third State and will not necessarily be forwarded to the territory covered by the trade mark in question. L'Oréal, the United Kingdom Government, the Italian, Polish and Portuguese Governments, and the European Commission contend, however, that the rules of Directive 89/104 and Regulation No 40/94 apply as soon as it is clear that the offer for sale of a trade-marked product located in a third State is targeted at consumers in the territory covered by the trade mark.

62   The latter contention must be accepted. If it were otherwise, operators which use electronic commerce by offering for sale, on an online market place targeted at consumers within the E.U., trade-marked goods located in a third State, which it is possible to view on the screen and to order via that marketplace, would, so far as offers for sale of that type are concerned, have no obligation to comply with the E.U. intellectual property rules. Such a situation would have an impact on the effectiveness (*effet utile*) of those rules.

63   It is sufficient to state in that regard that, under Article 5(3)(b) and (d) of Directive 89/104 and Article 9(2)(b) and (d) of Regulation No 40/94, the use by third parties of signs identical with or similar to trade marks which proprietors of those marks may prevent includes the use of such signs in offers for sale and advertising. As the Advocate General observed at point 127 of his Opinion and as the Commission pointed out in its written observations, the effectiveness of those rules would be undermined if they were not to apply to the use, in an internet offer for sale or advertisement targeted at consumers within the E.U., of a sign identical with or similar to a trade mark registered in the E.U. merely because the third party behind that offer or advertisement is established in a third State, because the server of the internet site used by the third party is located in such a State or because the product that is the subject of the offer or the advertisement is located in a third State.

64   It must, however, be made clear that the mere fact that a website is accessible from the territory covered by the trade mark is not a sufficient basis for concluding that the offers for sale displayed there are targeted at consumers in that territory [citations omitted]. Indeed, if the fact that an online marketplace is accessible from that territory were sufficient for the advertisements displayed there to be within the scope of Directive 89/104 and Regulation No 40/94, websites and advertisements which, although obviously targeted solely at consumers in third States, are nevertheless technically accessible from E.U. territory would wrongly be subject to E.U. law.

65   It therefore falls to the national courts to assess on a case-by-case basis whether there are any relevant factors on the basis of which it may be concluded that an offer for sale, displayed on an online marketplace accessible from the territory covered by the trade mark, is targeted at consumers in that territory. When the offer for sale is accompanied by details of the geographic areas to which the seller is willing to dispatch the product, that type of detail is of particular importance in the said assessment.

66   In the case before the referring court, the website with the address 'www.ebay.co.uk' appears, in the absence of any evidence to the contrary,

to be targeted at consumers in the territory covered by the national and Community trade marks relied on; the offers for sale on that website which form the subject-matter of the main proceedings therefore fall within the scope of the E.U. rules on intellectual property.

67   Accordingly, the answer to the seventh question referred is that where goods located in a third State, which bear a trade mark registered in a Member State of the E.U. or a Community trade mark and have not previously been put on the market in the EEA [European Economic Area] or, in the case of a Community trade mark, in the E.U., (i) are sold by an economic operator through an online marketplace without the consent of the trade mark proprietor to a consumer located in the territory covered by the trade mark or (ii) are offered for sale or advertised on such a marketplace targeted at consumers located in that territory, the trade mark proprietor may prevent that sale, offer for sale or advertising by virtue of the rules set out in Article 5 of Directive 89/104 or in Article 9 of Regulation No 40/94. It is the task of the national courts to assess on a case-by-case basis whether relevant factors exist, on the basis of which it may be concluded that an offer for sale or an advertisement displayed on an online marketplace accessible from the territory covered by the trade mark is targeted at consumers in that territory.

C-173/11 Football Dataco Ltd. And Others v. Sportradar GmbH and Others ECLI:EU:C:2012:642 [2012]

See *supra*, Part III, Chapter 7.3.1 , pp. 615–19.

QUESTIONS

1. Why does the ECJ refuse to adopt the accessibility criterion to localize an IP infringement? How does the Court identify the activity of a website? For tangible distributions? For intangible transmissions? To what extent does the subsequent ruling in the *Pez Hejduk* case affect the analysis?
2. Determine the applicable law(s) for the following examples:
    (a) A free streaming website registered in Fiji (an English-speaking country) and written in English offers streams of mainly U.S. movies in their original versions. Subtitles are proposed in French, German, Spanish and Italian. Local ads are displayed on the basis of the Internet user address.
    (b) An American producer acquired rights in classic black and white U.S. movies. He colorized them and offered them for download everywhere, except in France. The website is equipped with specific software identifying the Internet user's address and blocking any downloads by French users.

(c) A French publisher of children's books exploits a commercial website with a .fr extension. Hardcover books can be ordered on demand. The website is written in French, the currency is in Euros and only French books are sold. After investigation, 90 percent of the orders are for France and 10 percent on specific demand all over the world.

8.2.3 IP contracts

IP contracts raise two different kinds of issues.

The first one concerns the determination of the *lex contractus*, i.e., the law applicable to the contract. The connecting factors are the same as for any international contract. Parties may choose the applicable law and, in the absence of a choice, the applicable law will be the law with the most significant relationship to the contract. While U.S. law and European law seem to converge, some variations exist as to the scope of the freedom of choice and as to the role of the most significant relationship analysis as a starting point (U.S. law) or as an exception (European law).

Once the *lex contractus* is ascertained, a second question concerns its scope—to what issues does the law chosen to govern the contract apply? That law does not in fact determine every matter covered in a contract; some issues will be governed by the *lex loci protectionis*. For example, if a contract governed by U.S. law assigns exploitation rights in a U.S. work for New Zealand, N.Z law, not U.S. law, will determine whether the work is in fact protectable in N.Z. Thus, if the contract assigns rights for the full term of copyright, which in the U.S. is 70 years *pma*, and in N.Z. is 50 years *pma*, the term of protection for the N.Z. rights remains 50 years *pma*; subjecting the contract to U.S. law does not have the effect of adding 20 years to the term of protection in N.Z. Such a *dépeçage* between the *lex contractus* and the *lex loci protectionis* is classical from a conflict of law perspective. Nevertheless, the IP nature of the contracts requires drawing a line between rules which are contractual by nature and rules which are IP by nature. As the questions in this section indicate, drawing such a line is a major issue of characterization: how the question is characterized will determine which law applies. If the matter is considered one of substantive copyright rights, the *lex loci protectionis* will apply; if it is deemed to concern matters of contract, the *lex contractus* will govern.

U.S.

Restatement of the Law (Second) Conflict of Laws 2d

§ 187. LAW OF THE STATE CHOSEN BY THE PARTIES

(1) The law of the state chosen by the parties to govern their contractual rights and duties will be applied if the particular issue is one which the parties could have resolved by an explicit provision in their agreement directed to that issue.

(2) The law of the state chosen by the parties to govern their contractual rights and duties will be applied, even if the particular issue is one which the parties could not have resolved by an explicit provision in their agreement directed to that issue, unless either

(a) the chosen state has no substantial relationship to the parties or the transaction and there is no other reasonable basis for the parties' choice, or

(b) application of the law of the chosen state would be contrary to a fundamental policy of a state which has a materially greater interest than the chosen state in the determination of the particular issue and which, under the rule of s 188, would be the state of the applicable law in the absence of an effective choice of law by the parties.

(3) In the absence of a contrary indication of intention, the reference is to the local law of the state of the chosen law.

§ 188. LAW GOVERNING IN ABSENCE OF EFFECTIVE CHOICE BY THE PARTIES

(1) The rights and duties of the parties with respect to an issue in contract are determined by the local law of the state which, with respect to that issue, has the most significant relationship to the transaction and the parties under the principles stated in s 6*.

---

* s 6. CHOICE OF LAW PRINCIPLES TEXT

(1) A court, subject to constitutional restrictions, will follow a statutory directive of its own state on choice of law.

(2) When there is no such directive, the factors relevant to the choice of the applicable rule of law include

(a) the needs of the interstate and international systems,

(b) the relevant policies of the forum,

(c) the relevant policies of other interested states and the relative interests of those states in the determination of the particular issue,

(d) the protection of justified expectations,

(2) In the absence of an effective choice of law by the parties (see s 187), the contacts to be taken into account in applying the principles of s 6 to determine the law applicable to an issue include:

(a) the place of contracting,
(b) the place of negotiation of the contract,
(c) the place of performance,
(d) the location of the subject matter of the contract, and
(e) the domicile, residence, nationality, place of incorporation and place of business of the parties.

These contacts are to be evaluated according to their relative importance with respect to the particular issue.

(3) If the place of negotiating the contract and the place of performance are in the same state, the local law of this state will usually be applied, except as otherwise provided in ss 189–199 and 203.

Corcovado Music Corp. v. Hollis Music, Inc., 981 F.2d 679 (2d Cir. 1993)

Before: Feinberg, Newman and Cardamone, Circuit Judges.

Feinberg, Circuit Judge:

Plaintiff Corcovado Music Corp. (Corcovado) appeals from a judgment of the United States District Court for the Southern District of New York, Kevin T. Duffy, J., dismissing an action for copyright infringement on the condition that defendants submit to the jurisdiction of the Brazilian courts. For the reasons stated below, we reverse the judgment of the district court and remand.

I. FACTS AND PROCEEDINGS BELOW

In 1958 and 1960, the composer Antonio Carlos Jobim entered into a series of contracts with a Brazilian publisher, Editora Musical Arapua (Arapua), pursuant to which Arapua and its designee obtained United States copyrights for five songs (the Five Songs) composed by Jobim. Soon thereafter, Arapua assigned its copyrights in the Five Songs to Bendig Music Corp.

(d) the protection of justified expectations,
(e) the basic policies underlying the particular field of law,
(f) certainty, predictability and uniformity of result, and
(g) ease in the determination and application of the law to be applied.

(Bendig). Bendig in turn assigned the rights in one of the songs, the bossa nova classic "Desafinado," to Hollis Music, Inc. (Hollis). Songways Service, Inc. (Songways), an affiliate of Hollis, administers the rights in "Desafinado." Bendig, Hollis and Songways are all defendants in this action.

Jobim, apparently believing that he retained United States copyright renewal rights for the Five Songs, assigned those rights in 1987 and 1988 to plaintiff Corcovado. Corcovado's complaint alleges that after the expiration of the original term copyrights, defendants Bendig, Hollis, and Songways continued to receive payments in connection with the Five Songs notwithstanding Jobim's assignment of the renewal rights to Corcovado. Accordingly, the complaint alleges that defendants are infringing the renewal copyrights and seeks relief under the Copyright Act,

Defendants moved to dismiss the complaint on the ground that the 1958 and 1960 contracts in which Jobim had conveyed copyrights to Arapua—negotiated and executed in Brazil and written in Portuguese—required interpretation by a Brazilian court. Defendants claimed that these contracts, which unquestionably conveyed original term copyrights, also conveyed renewal rights. They argued further that Corcovado, as Jobim's contractual successor, was bound by the forum selection clause in the Jobim-Arapua contracts. This clause, defendants contend, required the parties, i.e., Jobim and Arapua, to resolve any disputes in the courts of Brazil. Corcovado responded that it was suing to vindicate its rights under the Copyright Act, not as Jobim's successor under the Jobim-Arapua contracts. Therefore, the Jobim-Arapua contracts and the forum selection clause contained therein were relevant to the cause of action, if at all, only as a defense.

The district court agreed with defendants and granted the motion to dismiss with the following handwritten memorandum endorsement:

> This case is by the initial agreement of the parties [i.e., Jobim and Arapua] to be resolved in the courts of Brazil. It involves citizens of Brazil and the interpretation of a Brazil contract and Brazil law. It is dismissed on condition that defendants submit to the jurisdiction of the Brazilian courts.

This appeal followed.

II. DISCUSSION

. . .

B. OWNER OF RENEWAL RIGHTS

The ownership right at stake in this action is the author's right of renewal found in § 24 of the 1909 Copyright Act, reenacted in § 304 of the 1976 Act, 17 U.S.C. § 304(a).5 The purpose of the right of renewal is to "provide[] authors a second opportunity to obtain remuneration for their works." *Stewart v. Abend*, 495 U.S. 207, 217, 110 S.Ct. 1750, 1758, 109 L.Ed.2d 184 (1990). The Court in *Stewart* described the history of the renewal right and its current status:

> In its debates leading up to the Copyright Act of 1909, Congress elaborated upon the policy underlying a system comprised of an original term and a completely separate renewal term. . . . "It not infrequently happens that an author sells his copyright outright to a publisher for a comparatively small sum." H.R.Rep. No. 2222, 60th Cong., 2d Sess., 14 (1909). The renewal term permits the author, originally in a poor bargaining position, to renegotiate the term of the grant once the value of the work has been tested. "[U]nlike real property and other forms of personal property, [a copyright] is by its very nature incapable of accurate monetary evaluation prior to its exploitation." 2 M. Nimmer & D. Nimmer, Nimmer on Copyright, § 9.02, p. 9–23 (1989). . . . "If the work proves to be a great success and lives beyond the term of twenty-eight years, . . . it should be the exclusive right of the author to take the renewal term, and the law should be framed . . . so that [the author] could not be deprived of that right." H.R.Rep. No. 2222, supra, at 14. With these purposes in mind, Congress enacted the renewal provision of the Copyright Act of 1909, 17 U.S.C. § 24 (1976 ed.).

Id. 495 U.S. at 218, 110 S.Ct. at 1759.

Although *Stewart* tells us what a renewal right is and why it is important to federal copyright law, it does not tell us how an author may convey that right. In the present case, two factors are of primary importance: (1) The Jobim-Arapua contracts did not explicitly convey renewal rights; and (2) the Jobim-Arapua contracts contain no language that is ambiguous enough to permit the inference that they implicitly conveyed renewal rights. Together, these factors compel the conclusion that Jobim did not, as a matter of law, convey renewal rights to Arapua in 1958–60. The reasoning underlying that conclusion follows.

First, there is a strong presumption against the conveyance of renewal rights:

> [I]n the absence of language which expressly grants rights in "renewals of copyright" or "extensions of copyright" the courts are hesitant to

conclude that a transfer of copyright (even if it includes a grant of "all right, title and interest") is intended to include a transfer with respect to the renewal expectancy.

2 Nimmer on Copyright § 9.06[A] at 9–71 to 9–72. The seminal case is *Fred Fisher Music Co. v. M. Witmark & Sons*, 318 U.S. 643, 63 S.Ct. 773, 87 L.Ed. 1055 (1943), in which the Supreme Court held that "an assignment by the author of his 'copyright' in general terms did not include conveyance of his renewal interest." Id., 318 U.S. at 653, 63 S.Ct. at 777. In other words, a contract that conveyed original term copyrights without mentioning future rights did not as a matter of federal copyright law convey renewal rights. . . . The presumption against conveyance of renewal rights serves the congressional purpose of protecting authors' entitlement to receive new rights in the 28th year of the original term. In the present case, Jobim's 1958 and 1960 contracts with Arapua were silent as to renewal rights. Accordingly, under federal copyright law Jobim retained renewal rights to the Five Songs and could validly assign them to Corcovado.

. . .

Citing the English case of *Campbell Connelly & Co., Ltd. v. Noble*, 1 All E.R. 237 (1963),* defendants argue that Brazilian law should apply to the interpretation of the Jobim-Arapua contracts. We disagree. We believe that *Campbell Connelly* is distinguishable on the facts, and, in any event, conclude that its reasoning could not be applied here to preclude the use of United States law. Factors arguing for the application of United States law include the following: United States renewal copyrights reflect a vital policy of United States copyright law; the forum in which the Jobim-Arapua contracts are to be construed is in the United States (for reasons set forth above); and the place of performance of the contracts is also the United States. Under these circumstances, we believe that United States law is applicable. . . .

The judgment of the district court is reversed and the case is remanded to the district court for further proceedings consistent with this opinion.

---

* Editors' note: *Campbell Connelly & Co., Ltd.* v. *Noble* [1963] 1 All E.R. 237 concerned an agreement dated March 2, 1934, made between a composer and a publishing company, that provided "the composer hereby assigns to the publishers the full copyright for all countries for the period of copyright as far as it is assignable by law, together with all rights therein which he now has or may after become entitled to whether now or hereafter known". The agreement was a purely English contract. While, the court held that assignability of renewal rights was a matter of substantive U.S. copyright law, the court ruled that the effectiveness of the contract provision purporting to confer the assignment was a matter of English contract law.

QUESTION

The court considered that the U.S. law should be applicable, regardless of the choice of law clause in favor of Brazilian law. What are the arguments raised by the judge in order to explain such a departure from the contract? Reconsider this case under the Rome I Regulation (immediately below): would the solution have been identical?

E.U.

> **Regulation (EC) No 593/2008 of the European Parliament and of the Council of 17 June 2008 on the law applicable to contractual obligations (Rome I)**
>
> **Article 3 – Freedom of choice**
>
> 1. A contract shall be governed by the law chosen by the parties. The choice shall be made expressly or clearly demonstrated by the terms of the contract or the circumstances of the case. By their choice the parties can select the law applicable to the whole or to part only of the contract.
>
> 2. The parties may at any time agree to subject the contract to a law other than that which previously governed it, whether as a result of an earlier choice made under this Article or of other provisions of this Regulation. Any change in the law to be applied that is made after the conclusion of the contract shall not prejudice its formal validity under Article 11 or adversely affect the rights of third parties.
>
> 3. Where all other elements relevant to the situation at the time of the choice are located in a country other than the country whose law has been chosen, the choice of the parties shall not prejudice the application of provisions of the law of that other country which cannot be derogated from by agreement.
>
> 4. Where all other elements relevant to the situation at the time of the choice are located in one or more Member States, the parties' choice of applicable law other than that of a Member State shall not prejudice the application of provisions of Community law, where appropriate as implemented in the Member State of the forum, which cannot be derogated from by agreement.

5. The existence and validity of the consent of the parties as to the choice of the applicable law shall be determined in accordance with the provisions of Articles 10, 11 and 13.

Article 4 – Applicable law in the absence of choice

1. To the extent that the law applicable to the contract has not been chosen in accordance with Article 3 and without prejudice to Articles 5 to 8, the law governing the contract shall be determined as follows:

(a) a contract for the sale of goods shall be governed by the law of the country where the seller has his habitual residence;

(b) a contract for the provision of services shall be governed by the law of the country where the service provider has his habitual residence;

(c) a contract relating to a right in rem in immovable property or to a tenancy of immovable property shall be governed by the law of the country where the property is situated;

(d) notwithstanding point (c), a tenancy of immovable property concluded for temporary private use for a period of no more than six consecutive months shall be governed by the law of the country where the landlord has his habitual residence, provided that the tenant is a natural person and has his habitual residence in the same country;

(e) a franchise contract shall be governed by the law of the country where the franchisee has his habitual residence;

(f) a distribution contract shall be governed by the law of the country where the distributor has his habitual residence;

(g) a contract for the sale of goods by auction shall be governed by the law of the country where the auction takes place, if such a place can be determined;

(h) a contract concluded within a multilateral system which brings together or facilitates the bringing together of multiple third-party buying and selling interests in financial instruments, as defined by Article 4(1), point (17) of Directive 2004/39/EC, in accordance with non-discretionary rules and governed by a single law, shall be governed by that law.

2. Where the contract is not covered by paragraph 1 or where the elements of the contract would be covered by more than one of points (a) to (h) of paragraph 1, the contract shall be governed by the law of the country where the party required to effect the characteristic performance of the contract has his habitual residence.

3. Where it is clear from all the circumstances of the case that the contract is manifestly more closely connected with a country other than that indicated in paragraphs 1 or 2, the law of that other country shall apply.

4. Where the law applicable cannot be determined pursuant to paragraphs 1 or 2, the contract shall be governed by the law of the country with which it is most closely connected.

Article 9 – Overriding mandatory provisions

1. Overriding mandatory provisions are provisions the respect for which is regarded as crucial by a country for safeguarding its public interests, such as its political, social or economic organisation, to such an extent that they are applicable to any situation falling within their scope, irrespective of the law otherwise applicable to the contract under this Regulation.

2. Nothing in this Regulation shall restrict the application of the overriding mandatory provisions of the law of the forum.

3. Effect may be given to the overriding mandatory provisions of the law of the country where the obligations arising out of the contract have to be or have been performed, in so far as those overriding mandatory provisions render the performance of the contract unlawful. In considering whether to give effect to those provisions, regard shall be had to their nature and purpose and to the consequences of their application or non-application.

Illustration of overriding mandatory rules under French law

[An American movie colorized without the authorization of the co-director was broadcast in France. The heirs of the co-director sued the US producer and the French broadcaster on the ground that the broadcasting of the colorized version violated the plaintiffs' moral rights.]

On 23rd November 1988 the Court of First Instance of Paris (Cour d'appel de Paris, July 6 1989, n° XP060789X, D.1990.152) judged as follows:

Declares the action of Messrs and Mrs HUSTON and Mr Ben MADDOW and the voluntary intervention of T[urner] E[ntertainment]

C[orporation] admissible insofar as they are limited to the television broadcasting of the colorized version of the film entitled "ASPHALT JUNGLE";

Declares the claims of the secondary voluntary intervenors admissible;

Formally takes cognizance of the fact that Societe d'Exploitation de la Cinquieme Chaine has abandoned its plans for broadcasting the colorized version of the film entitled "ASPHALT JUNGLE"; As necessary forbids it from broadcasting this version on television;

Dismisses all other claims; Dismisses the claim of the TEC company.

The Court of Appeal of PARIS, appealed to by the TURNER Company reversed the prior decision by applying US law and thus concluded that the heirs of John HUSTON as well as Ben MADDOW have no moral right to the work filmed in black and white. Finally, the Court refused to apply the public policy exception in order to exclude the application of US law.

States that the author of the film entitled 'ASPHALT JUNGLE' is the TURNER Company and that the heirs of John HUSTON as well as Ben MADDOW have no moral right to this work filmed in black and white;

Notes that the colorized version of the said film is an adaptation, under U.S. law, for which the TURNER Company obtained a registration certificate on 20th June 1988;

States that the principle of colorization is not subject to challenge by the heirs of John HUSTON and by Ben MADDOW, even if they could claim a moral right to the black and white film;

Accordingly, reversing the judgment, Dismisses the claims of the heirs of John HUSTON and Ben MADDOW and judges admissible but unfounded the interventions of the six legal entities supporting their claims;

The French highest civil court declined to apply U.S. law (the law of the work's country of origin), instead perceiving that French law imposed overriding mandatory rules.

France, Cour de cassation, N° 89–19522 89–19725 (Huston) [1991]

In light of article 1 clause 2 of the law n° 64–689 of 8 July 1964, together with article 6 of the [French copyright law] law 11 March 1957;

Whereas, according to the first of these texts, in France no violation may be made to the integrity of a literary or artistic work, whatever may be the State on whose territory this work was first disclosed; that the person who is its author is by the sole fact of its creation vested with moral rights instituted for his benefit by the second of these texts; that these rules are laws of imperative application;

Wheras the consorts X. . . are the heirs of John X [Huston], the co-director of the film The Asphalt Jungle, created in black and white, but which the Turner Company, holding rights from the producer, has made a colorized version; that, invoking their right of respect of the integrity of the work of John [Huston], the consorts X, joined by various juridical entities who also are petitioners, have asked the courts below to prohibit the television company La Cinq from proceeding with the dissemination of this new version; that the court of appeals dismissed their claim on the ground that factual and legal elements prohibited the non application of U.S. law and the sidelining of the contracts concluded between the producer and the directors, contracts which deny the petitioners the status of authors of the film the Asphalt Jungle;

Whereas, in so ruling, the court of appeals violated the referenced texts by refusing their correct application . . .

Regulation (EC) No 593/2008 of the European Parliament and of the Council of 17 June 2008 on the law applicable to contractual obligations (Rome I)

Article 11 – Formal validity

1. A contract concluded between persons who, or whose agents, are in the same country at the time of its conclusion is formally valid if it satisfies the formal requirements of the law which governs it in substance under this Regulation or of the law of the country where it is concluded.

2. A contract concluded between persons who, or whose agents, are in different countries at the time of its conclusion is formally valid if it satisfies the formal requirements of the law which governs it in substance under this Regulation, or of the law of either of the countries where either of the parties or their agent is present at the time of conclusion, or of the law of the country where either of the parties had his habitual residence at that time.

3. A unilateral act intended to have legal effect relating to an existing or contemplated contract is formally valid if it satisfies the formal requirements of the law which governs or would govern the contract in substance under this Regulation, or of the law of the country where the act

was done, or of the law of the country where the person by whom it was done had his habitual residence at that time.

4. Paragraphs 1, 2 and 3 of this Article shall not apply to contracts that fall within the scope of Article 6. The form of such contracts shall be governed by the law of the country where the consumer has his habitual residence.

5. Notwithstanding paragraphs 1 to 4, a contract the subject matter of which is a right in rem in immovable property or a tenancy of immovable property shall be subject to the requirements of form of the law of the country where the property is situated if by that law:

(a) those requirements are imposed irrespective of the country where the contract is concluded and irrespective of the law governing the contract; and
(b) those requirements cannot be derogated from by agreement.

Article 12 – Scope of the law applicable

1. The law applicable to a contract by virtue of this Regulation shall govern in particular:

(a) interpretation;
(b) performance;
(c) within the limits of the powers conferred on the court by its procedural law, the consequences of a total or partial breach of obligations, including the assessment of damages in so far as it is governed by rules of law;
(d) the various ways of extinguishing obligations, and prescription and limitation of actions;
(e) the consequences of nullity of the contract.

2. In relation to the manner of performance and the steps to be taken in the event of defective performance, regard shall be had to the law of the country in which performance takes place.

QUESTIONS

1. To what extent, does the Rome I Regulation authorize the choice of more than one law applicable to the contract? Do you see any advantage for a worldwide license to choose multiple applicable laws?

2. Under article 4, which paragraph applies to an IP contract? What is the characteristic performance for an IP contract?
3. Reconsider the Problem, *supra* pp. 659–60 with the following changes:

> An English graphic designer works as a commissioner for an American company. Working for the French branch, he is in charge of the design of the newspapers published by the American company first in the U.S. and later in France in a French version. He has recently discovered that his latest creations are displayed on the website of the American company in very low resolution and in truncated versions. He would like to claim the protection of his moral rights under French law.

> Consider his chances of success if:
> (a) the contract specifies neither the applicable law nor the forum,
> (b) the contract includes a choice of law clause in favor of U.S. law and a choice of court clause also in favor of the U.S. forum,
> (c) the contract includes a choice of law clause in favor of U.S. law and a choice of court clause in favor of the U.K. courts.

PROBLEMS

1. A Lebanese novelist writing in French met a French publisher at the Frankfurt Book Fair. After a long discussion and on their way back to the airport, they agreed on a publishing contract for the next novel of the Lebanese writer and all his future works. Running out of time and of paper, they recorded on the editor's smartphone their publishing contract specifying that the contract will be governed by the Swiss law.
Back in Beirut, the novelist sent to the publisher his last novel and six previous unpublished novels on which he sought the advice of the publisher. A few days later, the novelist died in a car accident. The publisher decided to publish the first novel first in France and then an Arabic version. He informed the heirs that the publication of the six others novels is planned. They contested the validity of the contract and seized the French court in order to void the contract. The French publisher considered that the contract is valid under the Swiss law, chosen by the parties to govern the contract. What is your analysis?

Swiss Federal Act on Copyright and Related Rights

Article 16 – Assignment of rights

1. Copyright is assignable or may be inherited.
2. The assignment of a right subsisting in the copyright does not include the assignment of other partial rights, unless such was agreed.
3. The assignment of the ownership of a copy of a work does not include the right to exploit the copyright, even in the case of an original work.

French IP Code
Article L131–1

Total transfer of future works shall be null and void.

Article L131–2

The performance, publishing and audiovisual production contracts defined in this Title shall be in writing. The same shall apply to free performance authorizations.

Article L132–4

A clause by which the author undertakes to afford a right of preference to a publisher for the publication of his future works of clearly specified kinds shall be lawful.

Such right shall be limited, for each kind of work, to five new works as from the day of signature of the publishing contract concluded for the first work or to works produced by the author within a period of five years from that same date.

2. Directive 2011/77 extends the term of protection for related rights pertaining to a published phonogram by amending the previous Directive 2006/116. Extending the term of protection, the Directive also provides for its application to preexisting contracts between performers and producers by pronouncing the continuation of those contracts for the new extended term. Such an extension, however, is accompanied by measures in favor of the performer such as entitlements to a percentage of royalties (for non-featured performers) or to a "clean slate" for receiving royalties free of recoupment of the advance (for featured performers) and reversion rights.

Bob is an English performer of country music having assigned his rights for Europe to a U.S. producer. A choice of law clause stipulated that U.S. law would govern the contract. As an English performer, Bob benefits from the additional 20 years of protection under the Directive 2011/77 amending the Directive 2006/116. Does the choice of the U.S. law as the *lex contractus* deprive him of the continuation of the contract and the accompanying measures?

8.3 Soft law

8.3.1 ALI Principles

Chapter 1
In General

§ 301. Territoriality

Except as provided in §§ 302 and 321–323,

(1) The law applicable to determine the existence, validity, duration, attributes, and infringement of intellectual property rights and the remedies for their infringement is:

(a) for registered rights, the law of each State of registration.
(b) for other intellectual property rights, the law of each State for which protection is sought.

(2) The law applicable to a noncontractual obligation arising out of an act of unfair competition is the law of each State in which direct and substantial damage results or is likely to result, irrespective of the State or States in which the act giving rise to the damage occurred.

QUESTIONS

1. Luce is the ghostwriter for a book published under Paul's name. Luce signed a contract with Paul relinquishing attribution rights. The contract does not specify applicable law. The book is distributed in Switzerland and in France. In Switzerland, contracts waiving authorship attribution are permissible; in France, they are not. Luce subsequently brings an action against the publisher demanding that her name appear on the books. Which law applies? Does it matter which court hears the claim?
2. Copyleft.com distributes from Tonga peer-to-peer file-sharing software

to users around the world. Copyleft.com helps users locate files on other users' computers; Copyleft.com does not carry any music or motion-picture content on its own website. Users seeking to copy music or movie files contact the Copyleft.com site to acquire the software and to initiate their searches for other file-sharers. The offering or copying of files from one user's computer to another's infringes the rights of the copied works' copyright holders. What claims could the rightholder have against Copyleft.com and which law(s) applie(s)?

Chapter 2
Title to and Transfer of Rights

§ 313. Initial Title to Other Rights That Do Not Arise Out of Registration

(1) Initial title to other rights that do not arise out of registration is governed by:

(a) If there is one creator, the law of the creator's residence at the time the subject matter was created;
(b) If there is more than one creator:
  (i) the law of one of the creators' residences, as designated by contract between or among the creators;
  (ii) if no contract resolves the issue, the law of the State in which the majority of the creators resided at the time of the creation of the subject matter;
  (iii) if no contract resolves the issue and a majority of the creators did not reside in the same State, the law of the State with the closest connection to the first exploitation of the subject matter; or
(c) If the subject matter was created pursuant to an employment relationship, the law of the State that governs the relationship; or

(2) If the State whose law would govern under subsection (1) does not extend protection to the subject matter, then initial title is governed by the law of the first State in which the subject matter is exploited and the right is recognized.

QUESTION

1. The motion picture "50 Shades of Fuschia" is publicly exhibited for the first time at the annual Film Festival in Berlin. None of the film's creative participants reside in Germany. Moreover, the director, the screenwriter,

and the composer all resided in different States at the time of the work's creation. The issue of the work's initial ownership is raised in litigation. What law or laws apply?

2. Reblanc, a famous painter, resides in France. With the help of Feeney, a sculptor resident in Ireland, he adapted several of his paintings into sculptures, but took sole credit for the three-dimensional versions of his works. Feeney asserts his status as co-author of the sculptures, and demands half the proceeds from Reblanc's exploitation of the sculptures. Were the ALI Principles to govern their dispute, which provision would apply?

Chapter 3
Residual Principles Regarding Choice of Law

§ 321. Law or Laws to Be Applied in Cases of Ubiquitous Infringement

(1) When the alleged infringing activity is ubiquitous and the laws of multiple States are pleaded, the court may choose to apply to the issues of existence, validity, duration, attributes, and infringement of intellectual property rights and remedies for their infringement, the law or laws of the State or States with close connections to the dispute, as evidenced, for example, by:

   (a) where the parties reside;
   (b) where the parties' relationship, if any, is centered;
   (c) the extent of the activities and the investment of the parties; and
   (d) the principal markets toward which the parties directed their activities.

(2) Notwithstanding the State or States designated pursuant to subsection (1), a party may prove that, with respect to particular States covered by the action, the solution provided by any of those States' laws differs from that obtained under the law(s) chosen to apply to the case as a whole. The court shall take into account such differences in determining the scope of liability and remedies.

8.3.2   CLIP Principles

PART 3: APPLICABLE LAW
Section 1: General principles

Article 3:102: Lex protectionis

The law applicable to existence, validity, registration, scope and duration of an intellectual property right and all other matters concerning the right as such is the law of the State for which protection is sought.

QUESTIONS

See questions under Section 301 of the ALI Principles, above pp. 717–18.

Article 3:103: Freedom of choice

Parties may choose the applicable law in the cases specified in Articles 3:501, 3:503, 3:606 and 3:801.

Section 2: Initial ownership

Article 3:201: Initial ownership

(1) Initial ownership including in particular authorship of a copyrighted work and entitlement to intellectual property rights arising out of registration is governed by the law of the State for which protection is sought.

(2) If the situation has a close connection with another State that has a work made for hire provision or deems a transfer or exclusive licence of all economic rights in the work to have taken place by virtue of the parties' contractual relationship, effect may be given to such rules by constructing the parties' relationship under the law applicable according to paragraph 1 as involving a transfer or exclusive licence of all economic rights in the work.

(3) In the framework of a contractual relationship, in particular an employment contract or a research and development contract, the law applicable to the to claim a registered right is determined in accordance with Section 5.

Section 6: Infringement and remedies

Article 3:601: Basic principle

(1) Unless otherwise provided in this Section, the law applicable to the infringement is the law of each State for which protection is sought.

(2) For the purposes of these provisions, 'infringement' includes

(a) the violation of the intellectual property right,. . .

Article 3:602: De minimis rule

(1) A court applying the law or the laws determined by Article 3:601 shall only find for infringement if

(a) the defendant has acted to initiate or further the infringement in the State or the States for which protection is sought, or
(b) the activity by which the right is claimed to be infringed has substantial effect within, or is directed to the State or the States for which protection is sought.

(2) The court may exceptionally derogate from that general rule when reasonable under the circumstances of the case.

. . .

Article 3:604: Secondary infringement

(1) Subject to paragraph 2, the law applicable to liability based upon acts or conduct that induce, contribute to or further an infringement is the same as the law applicable to that infringement.

(2) In case of facilities or services being offered or rendered that are capable of being used for infringing and non-infringing purposes by a multitude of users without intervention of the person offering or rendering the facilities or services in relation to the individual acts resulting in infringement, the law applicable to the liability of that person is the law of the State where the centre of gravity of her/his activities relating to those facilities or services is located.

(3) The law designated by paragraph 2 shall only apply if it provides at least for the following substantive standards:

(a) liability for failure to react in case of actual knowledge of a primary infringement or in case of a manifest infringement and
(b) liability for active inducement.

(4) Paragraph 2 does not apply to claims relating to information on the identity and the activities of primary infringers.

. . .

Article 3:606: Freedom of choice for remedies

(1) In accordance with Article 3:501, the parties to a dispute concerning the infringement of an intellectual property right may agree to submit the remedies claimed for the infringement to the law of their choice by an agreement entered into before or after the dispute has arisen.

(2) If the infringement is closely connected with a pre-existing relationship between the parties, such as a contract, the law governing the pre-existing relationship shall also govern the remedies for the infringement, unless

(a) the parties have expressly excluded the application of the law governing the pre-existing relationship with regard to the remedies for infringement, or
(b) it is clear from all the circumstances of the case that the claim is more closely connected with another State.

Section 7: Limitations and exceptions, waivability

Article 3:701: Limitations and exceptions, waivability

(1) Limitations and exceptions are governed by the law of the State for which protection is sought.

(2) The waivability of limitations of, and exceptions to, an intellectual property right shall be determined by the law of the State for which protection is sought.

QUESTIONS

1. A famous French artist and set designer is employed by a U.S. movie producer to create a mural for the new European branch of the movie studio in Brussels (the contract is governed by U.S. law). Two years later, the new CEO of the studio, who does not appreciate contemporary art, decides to destroy the mural. The artist determines to sue the studio for breach of moral rights. Which law applies to the determination of the initial ownership of the copyright in the mural? Under the ALI Principles? Under the CLIP Principles?

2. Consider the same case but with a French cosmetic company commissioning under French law a U.S. sculptor for its headquarters in Switzerland. Under the ALI Principles? Under the CLIP Principles?
3. Consider the same case but where the sculptor has been helped by a U.K. assistant.
4. A Canadian writer has a long epistolary relationship with a French novelist, a former Nobel Prize winner, who died five years ago. At the end of his life, the Canadian writer decided to share the letters he received from the French writer by scanning them and posting them on his website. The letters could be seen but not downloaded. Surprised by the success of his enterprise, he found a way to monetize it by offering paying downloads of those letters. He used a commercial platform owned by an American company to organize his new stream of commerce. The French heirs of the novelist would like to sue the Canadian writer and the commercial platform for infringement. Which law(s) applie(s) under the ALI Principles? Under the CLIP Principles?

9

Recognition of judgments

9.1 International conventions

Hague Convention on Choice of Court Agreements (2005)
(this Convention is not yet in force)

CHAPTER I – SCOPE AND DEFINITIONS

Article 1 – Scope

(1) This Convention shall apply in international cases to exclusive choice of court agreements concluded in civil or commercial matters.

(2) For the purposes of Chapter II, a case is international unless the parties are resident in the same Contracting State and the relationship of the parties and all other elements relevant to the dispute, regardless of the location of the chosen court, are connected only with that State.

(3) For the purposes of Chapter III, a case is international where recognition or enforcement of a foreign judgment is sought.

Article 2 – Exclusions from scope

. . .

(2) This Convention shall not apply to the following matters –

. . .

    n) the validity of intellectual property rights other than copyright and related rights;
    o) infringement of intellectual property rights other than copyright and related rights, except where infringement proceedings are brought

for breach of a contract between the parties relating to such rights, or could have been brought for breach of that contract;

. . .

CHAPTER II – JURISDICTION

Article 5 – Jurisdiction of the chosen court

(1) The court or courts of a Contracting State designated in an exclusive choice of court agreement shall have jurisdiction to decide a dispute to which the agreement applies, unless the agreement is null and void under the law of that State.

(2) A court that has jurisdiction under paragraph 1 shall not decline to exercise jurisdiction on the ground that the dispute should be decided in a court of another State.

(3) The preceding paragraphs shall not affect rules –

a) on jurisdiction related to subject matter or to the value of the claim;
b) on the internal allocation of jurisdiction among the courts of a Contracting State. However, where the chosen court has discretion as to whether to transfer a case, due consideration should be given to the choice of the parties.

Article 6 – Obligations of a court not chosen

A court of a Contracting State other than that of the chosen court shall suspend or dismiss proceedings to which an exclusive choice of court agreement applies unless –

a) the agreement is null and void under the law of the State of the chosen court;
b) a party lacked the capacity to conclude the agreement under the law of the State of the court seised;
c) giving effect to the agreement would lead to a manifest injustice or would be manifestly contrary to the public policy of the State of the court seised;
d) for exceptional reasons beyond the control of the parties, the agreement cannot reasonably be performed; or
e) the chosen court has decided not to hear the case.

CHAPTER III – RECOGNITION AND ENFORCEMENT

Article 8 – Recognition and enforcement

(1) A judgment given by a court of a Contracting State designated in an exclusive choice of court agreement shall be recognised and enforced in other Contracting States in accordance with this Chapter. Recognition or enforcement may be refused only on the grounds specified in this Convention.

(2) Without prejudice to such review as is necessary for the application of the provisions of this Chapter, there shall be no review of the merits of the judgment given by the court of origin. The court addressed shall be bound by the findings of fact on which the court of origin based its jurisdiction, unless the judgment was given by default.

(3) A judgment shall be recognised only if it has effect in the State of origin, and shall be enforced only if it is enforceable in the State of origin.

(4) Recognition or enforcement may be postponed or refused if the judgment is the subject of review in the State of origin or if the time limit for seeking ordinary review has not expired. A refusal does not prevent a subsequent application for recognition or enforcement of the judgment.

(5) This Article shall also apply to a judgment given by a court of a Contracting State pursuant to a transfer of the case from the chosen court in that Contracting State as permitted by Article 5, paragraph 3. However, where the chosen court had discretion as to whether to transfer the case to another court, recognition or enforcement of the judgment may be refused against a party who objected to the transfer in a timely manner in the State of origin.

Article 9 – Refusal of recognition or enforcement

Recognition or enforcement may be refused if –

a) the agreement was null and void under the law of the State of the chosen court, unless the chosen court has determined that the agreement is valid;
b) a party lacked the capacity to conclude the agreement under the law of the requested State;
c) the document which instituted the proceedings or an equivalent document, including the essential elements of the claim,

i) was not notified to the defendant in sufficient time and in such a way as to enable him to arrange for his defence, unless the defendant entered an appearance and presented his case without contesting notification in the court of origin, provided that the law of the State of origin permitted notification to be contested; or

ii) was notified to the defendant in the requested State in a manner that is incompatible with fundamental principles of the requested State concerning service of documents;

d) the judgment was obtained by fraud in connection with a matter of procedure;

e) recognition or enforcement would be manifestly incompatible with the public policy of the requested State, including situations where the specific proceedings leading to the judgment were incompatible with fundamental principles of procedural fairness of that State;

f) the judgment is inconsistent with a judgment given in the requested State in a dispute between the same parties; or

g) the judgment is inconsistent with an earlier judgment given in another State between the same parties on the same cause of action, provided that the earlier judgment fulfils the conditions necessary for its recognition in the requested State.

Article 10 – Preliminary questions

(1) Where a matter excluded under Article 2, paragraph 2, . . . arose as a preliminary question, the ruling on that question shall not be recognised or enforced under this Convention.

(2) Recognition or enforcement of a judgment may be refused if, and to the extent that, the judgment was based on a ruling on a matter excluded under Article 2, paragraph 2.

(3) However, in the case of a ruling on the validity of an intellectual property right other than copyright or a related right, recognition or enforcement of a judgment may be refused or postponed under the preceding paragraph only where –

a) that ruling is inconsistent with a judgment or a decision of a competent authority on that matter given in the State under the law of which the intellectual property right arose; or

b) proceedings concerning the validity of the intellectual property right are pending in that State.

. . .

Article 11 – Damages

(1) Recognition or enforcement of a judgment may be refused if, and to the extent that, the judgment awards damages, including exemplary or punitive damages, that do not compensate a party for actual loss or harm suffered.

(2) The court addressed shall take into account whether and to what extent the damages awarded by the court of origin serve to cover costs and expenses relating to the proceedings.

QUESTIONS

1. Why does the Convention distinguish among intellectual property rights? What difference does it make?
2. What might be the causes of non-recognition for a copyright contract including a valid choice of court agreement?

PROBLEM

Reconsider the following case (see in the previous chapter): An English graphic designer works as on commission from an American company. Working for the company's French branch, he is in charge of the design of the newspapers published by the American company first in the U.S. and later in France in a French version. The contract includes a choice of law clause designating U.S. law and a choice of court clause designating a U.S. forum. He has recently discovered that his latest creations are displayed on the website of the American company in very low resolution and in truncated versions. He would like to sue the company in France for breach of his moral rights. Before he can initiate the French action, however, his company seizes the U.S. judge designated by the choice of court clause in order to obtain a declaration of non-infringement. The U.S. judge, applying U.S. law, rules that there is no infringement. Suppose that the U.S. and France were both members of the Hague Convention, could the English designer obtain the non-recognition of the U.S. judgment on the ground that the U.S. action circumvents the French action alleging a violation of moral rights?

9.2   National and regional norms

9.2.1   U.S.

Restatement of the Law (Third) Foreign Relations

§ 481 Recognition and Enforcement of Foreign Judgments

1) Except as provided in § 482, a final judgment of a court of a foreign state granting or denying recovery of a sum of money, establishing or confirming the status of a person, or determining interest in property, is conclusive between the parties, and is entitled to recognition in courts in the United States.

2) A judgment entitled to recognition under Subsection (1) may be enforced by any party or its successors or assigns against any other party, its successors or assigns, in accordance with the procedure for enforcement of judgments applicable where enforcement is sought.

§ 482 Grounds for Nonrecognition of Foreign Judgments

(1) A court in the United States may not recognize a judgment of the court of a foreign state if:

(a) the judgment was rendered under a judicial system that does not provide impartial tribunals or procedures compatible with due process of law; or
(b) the court that rendered the judgment did not have jurisdiction over the defendant in accordance with the law of the rendering state and with the rules set forth in § 421.

(2) A court in the United States need not recognize a judgment of the court of a foreign state if:

(a) the court that rendered the judgment did not have jurisdiction of the subject matter of the action;
(b) the defendant did not receive notice of the proceedings in sufficient time to enable him to defend;
(c) the judgment was obtained by fraud;
(d) the cause of action on which the judgment was based, or the

judgment itself, is repugnant to the public policy of the United States or of the State where recognition is sought;

(e) the judgment conflicts with another final judgment that is entitled to recognition; or

(f) the proceeding in the foreign court was contrary to an agreement between the parties to submit the controversy on which the judgment is based to another forum.

QUESTIONS

1. Recall *Lucas Film supra*, Part III, Chapter 7.3.1, pp. 586 et seq. Applying the Restatement, do you find any ground for nonrecognition of the U.K. judgment in the U.S.?

2. A French director brought an action in France against a U.S. company that distributed his first movie in the U.S. with an altered musical soundtrack. Since article 14 of the Civil Code grants jurisdiction to French court on the sole ground that the plaintiff is a French national, the French court was competent under national law to hear the director's moral rights claim. The court awarded judgment to the director, ordering the U.S. company to restore the original soundtrack. The U.S. defendant neither appealed from the decision, nor complied with it in the U.S. The French director sought recognition of the French decision in the U.S. On which of the Restatement grounds might recognition be refused?

SARL Louis Féraud v. Viewfinder 489 F.3d 474 (2d Cir. 2007)

▪ Pooler, Circuit Judge:

Plaintiffs-appellants Sarl Louis Féraud International ("Féraud") and S.A. Pierre Balmain ("Balmain") appeal from the September 29, 2005, order of the United States District Court for the Southern District of New York (Lynch, J.) dismissing plaintiffs' action to enforce two judgments issued by the Tribunal de grande instance de Paris ("the French Judgments") against defendant-appellee Viewfinder, Inc. ("Viewfinder"). Plaintiffs challenge the district court's conclusion that enforcement of the French Judgments would be repugnant to the public policy of New York under N.Y. C.P.L.R. § 5304(b)(4) because it would violate Viewfinder's First Amendment rights. Because the district court did not conduct the full analysis necessary to reach this conclusion, we vacate its order and remand for further proceedings consistent with this opinion.

BACKGROUND

Plaintiffs-appellants Féraud and Balmain are French corporations that design high-fashion clothing and other items for women. Defendant-appellee Viewfinder is a Delaware corporation with a principal place of business in New York. Viewfinder operates a website called "firstView.com," on which it posts photographs of fashion shows held by designers around the world, including photographs of plaintiffs' fashion shows. Donald Ashby, the president of Viewfinder, is a professional fashion photographer. Viewfinder styles itself as an Internet fashion magazine akin to the online version of Vogue. The firstView website contains both photographs of the current season's fashions, which may be viewed only upon subscription and payment of a fee, and photographs of past collections, which are available for free. An annual subscription to firstView costs $ 999. See http://www.firstview.com/subscribe_info.php (last visited June 1, 2007). Users can also view the content for one hour for $ 5.95. See http://www.firstview.com/subscribe.php (last visited June 1, 2007). Viewfinder does not sell clothing or designs.

In January 2001, Féraud and Balmain, along with several other design houses, each filed suit against Viewfinder in the Tribunal de grande instance de Paris seeking money damages from Viewfinder for alleged unauthorized use of their intellectual property and unfair competition. These civil actions stemmed from Viewfinder displaying photographs of the designers' fashion shows, which revealed designs from their upcoming collection, on the firstView.com website. Viewfinder was served in New York in accordance with the terms of the Hague Convention on the Service of Judicial and Extrajudicial Documents in Civil or Commercial Matters. Viewfinder failed to respond to the complaints, however, and therefore, on May 2, 2001, the French court issued default judgment against Viewfinder. The French court found that plaintiffs' "ready-to-wear" and "haute couture" collections from 1996–2001 were available on the firstView.com website. The court further found that Viewfinder's posting of these photographs of plaintiffs' designs was "without the necessary authorization" and thus "constitute[d] counterfeit and violation of royalties pursuant to articles L 716–1 and L 122–4 of the Intellectual [P]roperty Code." The court also found with respect to each of the plaintiffs that Viewfinder had committed "parasitism" under French law because it had "take[n] advantage of plaintiff's reputation and commercial efforts creating confusion between the two companies." The French court ordered Viewfinder to remove the offending photographs, and awarded damages of 500,000 francs for each plaintiff, costs of the action, and a fine ("astreinte") of 50,000 francs a day for each day Viewfinder failed to comply with the judgment.

On October 6, 2003, Viewfinder appealed these judgments to the Cour d'appel de Paris, but subsequently withdrew its appeal without opposition after plaintiffs filed their brief. The French appellate court accordingly dismissed the appeal in February 2004. In December 2004, plaintiffs filed separate complaints in the United States District Court for the Southern District of New York to enforce the French Judgments. Plaintiffs sought enforcement under New York's Uniform Foreign Money Judgment Recognition Act, which provides that, subject to certain exceptions, foreign judgments that are "final, conclusive and enforceable" in the country where rendered are deemed conclusive between the parties and enforceable by U.S. courts. N.Y. C.P.L.R. §§ 5302, 5303. The district court consolidated these actions and also granted plaintiffs' request for an order of attachment. Federal jurisdiction is based on diversity of citizenship.

On January 18, 2005, Viewfinder filed a motion to dismiss or, in the alternative, a motion for summary judgment and a motion to vacate the attachment order. Viewfinder raised a variety of arguments in its motion papers, one of which was found meritorious by the district court. The district court found that enforcing the French Judgments would be repugnant to the public policy of New York because it would violate Viewfinder's First Amendment rights. See *Sarl Louis Féraud Int'l v. Viewfinder Inc.*, 406 F. Supp. 2d 274, 281 (S.D.N.Y. 2005). Specifically, the district court found that the fashion shows at issue were public events and Viewfinder had a First Amendment right to publish the photographs at issue. Id. at 282–83. Thus, as the district court concluded, the "First Amendment simply does not permit plaintiffs to stage public events in which the general public has a considerable interest, and then control the way in which information about those events is disseminated in the mass media." Id. at 285. The district court also stated that to the extent that plaintiffs' designs were protected by copyright, "the copyright law similarly provides, as a matter of First Amendment necessity, a 'fair use' exception for the publication of newsworthy matters." Id. at 284. Based on its conclusion that enforcing the judgment would impinge upon Viewfinder's free speech rights, the district court dismissed the action and vacated the order of attachment. Id. at 285. Plaintiffs filed a timely notice of appeal.

DISCUSSION

The question presented by this appeal is whether the district court properly found that the French Judgments were unenforceable under New York law. In order to address this question, we begin with the language of the relevant state statute: "A foreign country judgment need not be recognized if . . . the cause of action on which the judgment is based is repugnant to the public policy of this state." N.Y. C.P.L.R. § 5304(b)(4) (emphasis added). As the plain language of the statute makes clear, the first step in analyzing whether a judgment is unenforceable under Section 5304(b)(4) is to identify the "cause of action on which the judgment is based." The district court never identified the French statutes that underlie the judgments at issue in this case. Nor does Viewfinder do so in its submission. In fact, Viewfinder contends that "there is simply no way for this Court to know what substantive law was actually applied in France and on what grounds Defendant was found liable." See Br. of Appellee Viewfinder, at 48. We find this argument curious considering that Viewfinder, as the party invoking Section 5304(b), had the burden to prove that the public policy exception applied [citations omitted]. In any event, we cannot agree with Viewfinder's contention that it is impossible to discern the causes of action on which the French Judgments were based. The default judgments issued by the French court explicitly state that Viewfinder's actions violated "articles L 716–1 and L 122–4 of the Intellectual Property Code." Article L 122–4 is in Book I, Title II, Chapter II of the French Intellectual Property Code, which are entitled "Copyright," "Authors' Rights," and "Patrimonial Rights," respectively. See Code de la propriété intellectuelle art. L 122–4 (Fr.), available at http://www.legifrance.gouv.fr. Article L 122–4 provides: "Any complete or partial performance or reproduction made without the consent of the author or of his successors in title or assigns shall be unlawful." Id. This is analogous to the United States Copyright Act, which defines a copyright infringer as one "who violates any of the exclusive rights of the copyright owner," 17 U.S.C. § 501, including the rights of reproduction, performance, and public display. 17 U.S.C. § 106. Under French copyright law, the "creations of the seasonal industries of dress and articles of fashion" are entitled to copyright protection. Code de la propriété intellectuelle art. L 112–2 (Fr.), available at http://www.legifrance.gouv.fr. The French court found that Viewfinder's publication of numerous photographs depicting plaintiffs' design collections violated plaintiffs' copyrights. Furthermore, the French Judgments concluded that Viewfinder's reproduction and publication of plaintiffs' designs were "without the necessary authorization." Thus, it is apparent that the French Judgments were based in part on a finding of copyright infringement.

We cannot second-guess the French court's finding that Viewfinder's actions were "without the necessary authorization." Viewfinder had the opportunity to dispute the factual basis of plaintiffs' claims in the French court, but it chose not to respond to the complaint. As this court has held: "By defaulting [in the foreign adjudication], a defendant ensures that a judgment will be entered against him, and assumes the risk that an irrevocable mistake of law or fact may underlie that judgment" [citations omitted]. Thus, for the purposes of this action, we must accept that Viewfinder's conduct constitutes an unauthorized reproduction or performance of plaintiffs' copyrighted work infringing on plaintiffs' intellectual property rights, and the only question to consider is whether a law that sanctions such conduct is repugnant to the public policy of New York.

The "public policy inquiry rarely results in refusal to enforce a judgment unless it is inherently vicious, wicked or immoral, and shocking to the prevailing moral sense" [citations omitted]. Furthermore, "it is well established that mere divergence from American procedure does not render a foreign judgment unenforceable." . . . [3]

Laws that are antithetical to the First Amendment will create such a situation. Foreign judgments that impinge on First Amendment rights will be found to be "repugnant" to public policy [citations omitted]. The district court in this case reached the conclusion that the French Judgments were unenforceable because they impinged on Viewfinder's First Amendment rights. In doing so, however, it appears not to have conducted the full analysis for us to affirm its decision.

The district court's decision appears to rest on the assumption that if Viewfinder is a news magazine reporting on a public event, then it has an absolute First Amendment defense to any attempt to sanction such conduct. The First Amendment does not provide such categorical protection. Intellectual property laws co-exist with the First Amendment in this country, and the fact that an entity is a news publication engaging in speech activity does not, standing alone, relieve such entities of their obligation to obey intellectual property laws. While an entity's status as a news publication may be highly probative on certain relevant inquiries, such as whether that entity has a fair use defense to copyright infringement, it does not render that entity immune from liability under intellectual property laws. . . . Because the First Amendment does not provide news entities an exemption from

---

3 For this reason, we reject the argument advanced by Viewfinder and amici that holding Viewfinder liable under French copyright laws would be repugnant to public policy because plaintiffs' dress designs are not copyrightable in the United States. While it is true that United States law does not extend copyright protection to dress designs, see *Knitwaves, Inc. v. Lollytogs Ltd.*, 71 F.3d 996, 1002 (2d Cir. 1995) ("[C]lothes are not copyrightable."), Viewfinder presents no argument as to why this distinction would offend the public policy of New York. As the district court found in rejecting this argument below—which Viewfinder has not challenged on appeal—copyright laws are not "matters of strong moral principle" but rather represent "economic legislation based on policy decisions that assign rights based on assessments of what legal rules will produce the greatest economic good for society as a whole." *Viewfinder*, 406 F. Supp. 2d at 281.

compliance with intellectual property laws, the mere fact that Viewfinder may be characterized as a news magazine would not, standing alone, render the French Judgments repugnant to public policy.

Rather, because Section 5304(b) requires courts to examine the cause of action on which the foreign judgment was based, the district court should have analyzed whether the intellectual property regime upon which the French Judgments were based impinged on rights protected by the First Amendment. This is consistent with the two-step analysis courts apply in deciding whether foreign libel judgments are repugnant to public policy: (1) identifying the protections deemed constitutionally mandatory for the defamatory speech at issue, and (2) determining whether the foreign libel laws provide comparable protection. . . . In deciding whether the French Judgments are repugnant to the public policy of New York, the district court should first determine the level of First Amendment protection required by New York public policy when a news entity engages in the unauthorized use of intellectual property at issue here. Then, it should determine whether the French intellectual property regime provides comparable protections.

With regard to the protections provided by the First Amendment for the unauthorized use of copyrighted material, this court has held that absent extraordinary circumstances, "the fair use doctrine encompasses all claims of first amendment in the copyright field" [citations omitted]. Because the fair use doctrine balances the competing interests of the copyright laws and the First Amendment, some analysis of that doctrine is generally needed before a court can conclude that a foreign copyright judgment is repugnant to public policy. . . .

In this case, the district court dispensed with the issue of fair use in a single sentence: "Similarly, even were plaintiffs' designs copyrightable, the copyright law similarly provides, as a matter of First Amendment necessity, a 'fair use' exception for the publication of newsworthy matters." *Viewfinder*, 406 F. Supp. 2d at 284. To the extent the district court believed that Viewfinder's use was necessarily fair use because it was publishing "newsworthy matters," this was erroneous. See, e.g., *Harper & Row*, 471 U.S. at 557 (finding that The Nation's use of verbatim quotes from upcoming Gerald Ford memoir regarding Watergate scandal was not fair use even though material related to matter of public importance) [citations omitted]. Whether the material is newsworthy is but one factor in the fair use analysis.

While both parties urge this court to resolve the issue of fair use, the record before us is insufficient to determine fair use as a matter of law. See

Harper & Row, 471 U.S. at 560 (noting that an appellate court need not remand "[w]here the district court has found facts sufficient to evaluate each of the statutory factors" for fair use). For instance, the record is unclear as to the percentage of plaintiffs' designs that were posted on firstView.com. While the French Judgments do provide some information as to the number of photographs posted by Viewfinder, that information is both incomplete and unclear because it does not indicate what proportion of plaintiffs' designs were revealed by these photographs. Such factual findings are relevant in determining whether Viewfinder's use would constitute "fair use" under United States law. If the publication of photographs of copyrighted material in the same manner as Viewfinder has done in this case would not be fair use under United States law, then the French intellectual property regime sanctioning the same conduct certainly would not be repugnant to public policy. Similarly, if the sole reason that Viewfinder's conduct would be permitted under United States copyright law is that plaintiffs' dress designs are not copyrightable in the United States, the French Judgment would not appear to be repugnant. However, without further development of the record, we cannot reach any conclusions as to whether Viewfinder's conduct would fall within the protection of the fair use doctrine.

The record is similarly unclear as to the manner of protection afforded plaintiffs' fashion shows by French law as well as the protections afforded to alleged infringers generally, and photographers specifically, under French law. The minutes of the French criminal judgment contained in the record suggest that photographers may well enjoy some protection. These minutes indicate that the "Law covers a right to the benefit of the fashion designers that coexists with that of the photographers." Memorandum from Jean-Marc Fedida to Don Ashby, June 17, 2005, at 3. Moreover, Article L 122–5(3) of the French Intellectual Property Code permits unauthorized use of copyrighted material in limited circumstances similar to uses deemed "fair use" under United States law. See Code de la propriété intellectuelle art. L 122–5(3) (Fr.), available at http://www.legifrance.gouv.fr. n7 Whether such protections are sufficiently comparable to that required by the public policy of New York is a question best addressed in the first instance by the district court on a fully-developed record. . . .

QUESTIONS

1. If the district court on remand finds that defendant's photographs would have been "fair use," does it follow that a contrary French judgment violates New York public policy?
2. If the district court on remand finds that the French law exceptions to

copyright protection resemble the U.S. fair use privilege, but are in some instances less expansive than the exemption provided under 17 USC§ 107, does it follow that a French judgment finding the French exceptions inapplicable violates New York public policy?

3. If U.S. copyright law does not have extraterritorial effect, see *Subafilms, supra*, Part III, Chapter 8.2.2, pp. 671 et seq., should First Amendment-inflected U.S. defenses to copyright infringement have extraterritorial effect?

PROBLEM

King, a well-known U.S. rock star, discovers on WeTube a video of a baby dancing to the sound of one of his best-known recordings. The video becomes especially popular in the U.S. and in France. King obtains from a French judge an injunction ordering WeTube.fr and WeTube.com (situated in the U.S.) to block French users' access to the video, on the grounds that the video violates King's exclusive rights in France to authorize the synchronization of his musical composition to the soundtrack of an audiovisual work, and violates his moral rights by trivializing King's artistic expression. WeTube.fr complies with the court's order, but WeTube.com does not. King requests recognition of the French judgment in the U.S. in order to force WeTube.com to respect the French court's take-down order. WeTube.com considers that such an order violates U.S. public policy. Will the U.S. court enforce the French judgment and order WeTube.com to render the video inaccessible to French viewers?

Claim and issue preclusion

Computer Associates v. Altai, 126 F.3d 365 (2d Cir. 1997)

Walker, Circuit Judge:

Defendant-appellant, Altai, Inc. ("Altai"), appeals from the order of the United States District Court for the Eastern District of New York (Dennis R. Hurley, District Judge) denying its motion for an injunction against Computer Associates International, Inc. ("Computer Associates"). The issue on appeal is whether, under a theory of either claim or issue preclusion, a federal court should enjoin Computer Associates from pursuing an action claiming copyright infringement of a computer program in a French forum where Computer Associates has previously brought and lost a United States copyright infringement action based on the same computer program in federal court. Because we agree with the district court that res judicata and collateral estoppel are inapplicable under the circumstances of this case, we affirm.

I. BACKGROUND

A. The United States Action

In August of 1988, Computer Associates brought a copyright infringement and trade secrets misappropriation action in the Eastern District of New York against Altai, alleging that Altai had copied substantial portions of Computer Associates's ADAPTER computer program into Altai's OSCAR 3.4 and OSCAR 3.5 computer programs in violation of Computer Associates's United States copyright (the "United States action"). On August 9, 1991, following a trial, the district court found that Altai's OSCAR 3.4 computer program infringed Computer Associates's copyright, but held that OSCAR 3.5 was not substantially similar to the ADAPTER portion of Computer Associates's SCHEDULER program and therefore did not infringe Computer Associates's copyright. *Computer Assocs. Int'l, Inc. v. Altai, Inc.,* 775 F. Supp. 544, 560–62 (E.D.N.Y. 1991) ("Altai I"). . . .

On December 17, 1992, the Second Circuit affirmed the district court's findings and judgment with regards to Computer Associates's copyright claims . . .

B. The French Action

On January 23, 1990, Computer Associates and L'Agence pour la Protection des Programmes ("L'Agence") secured an ex parte order from the President of the Tribunal de Grande Instance in Bobigny, France, authorizing seizure of computer programs and business records from the offices of Altai's French distributor, la Société FASTER, S.A.R.L. ("FASTER"), and enjoining FASTER from distributing or marketing its products. On February 2, 1990, a raid of FASTER's offices yielded five object code tapes of Altai software that contained OSCAR 3.5 code.

On February 15, 1990, one month before trial commenced in the United States, Computer Associates and L'Agence filed an action in the Tribunal de Commerce in Bobigny, France (the "Commercial Court"), against Altai and FASTER, charging violations of Computer Associates's French copyright (the "French action"). The French action centered on Computer Associates's allegations that Altai's importation and FASTER's distribution of OSCAR 3.5 in France violated Computer Associates's French copyright.

On October 1, 1991, Altai brought to the Commercial Court's attention the district court's holding in Altai I that its OSCAR 3.5 computer program did not violate Computer Associates's United States copyright and of the status of Computer Associates's appeal to the Second Circuit. Trial in the French action was postponed until September 10, 1992.

On September 16, 1992, Altai requested a stay of the French proceeding from the Tribunal de Grande Instance in Paris (the "Tribunal"), pending disposition of Altai's request for an exequatur, which would make the judgment in Altai I enforceable in France and allow Altai to introduce the judgment during the course of the French action in the Commercial Court. On October 22, 1992, the Commercial Court issued a stay. The exequatur was issued by the Tribunal in June 1993.

On May 14, 1994, Computer Associates moved to resume the French proceedings, and on November 25, 1994, trial in the Commercial Court began. On January 20, 1995, the Commercial Court found that Altai's OSCAR 3.5 program did not violate Computer Associates's rights under French copyright law. The Commercial Court specifically rejected Altai's argument that the United States decision in Altai I governed the disposition of the French action. The Commercial Court stated:

> The United States decision was made with reference to United States law which, even if it is close to French law with regard to the protection of literary and artistic works, cannot be completely and immediately identified with French law without an analysis of the facts under French law. Jurisprudence on the matter of software protection is in flux, as the United States decision shows, with each case having to be considered individually . . .

On April 25, 1995, Computer Associates appealed the decision to the Paris Court of Appeals which scheduled briefing for May 13, 1998, and oral argument for June 18, 1998.

C. Motion To Enjoin French Copyright Infringement Action

On November 16, 1994, Altai moved in the Eastern District of New York to enjoin Computer Associates from continuing to litigate the action in France. On February 22, 1995, in light of the January 20, 1995 decision of the Commercial Court in its favor, Altai voluntarily withdrew this motion.

On April 11, 1995, after learning of Computer Associates's plan to appeal the decision of the Commercial Court, Altai reactivated its motion to enjoin Computer Associates from continuing to proceed with its French action. On

June 17, 1996, the district court denied Altai's motion to enjoin Computer Associates from pursuing its French action. *Computer Assocs. Int'l, Inc. v. Altai, Inc.*, 950 F. Supp. 48, 54 (E.D.N.Y. 1996) ("Altai VI"). This appeal followed.

II. DISCUSSION

On appeal, Altai contends: (i) that Computer Associates's United States action for violation of its United States copyright precludes, under the doctrine of res judicata, its French action for violation of its French copyright; (ii) that, alternatively, Computer Associates is collaterally estopped from claiming that OSCAR 3.5 violates its French copyright because, in the United States action, judgment was rendered to the effect that OSCAR 3.5 does not violate Computer Associates's United States copyright; . . .

A. Res Judicata

Altai argues that the doctrine of res judicata bars Computer Associates from litigating its French action because Computer Associates could have raised its French copyright claims during the course of its United States action on its United States copyright claims. We disagree.

Under the doctrine of res judicata, a final judgment on the merits in an action "precludes the par-ties or their privies from relitigating issues that were or could have been raised in that action" [citation omitted].

Simply put, the doctrine of res judicata provides that when a final judgment has been entered on the merits of a case, it is a finality as to the claim or demand in controversy, concluding parties and those in privity with them, not only as to every matter which was offered and received to sustain or defeat the claim or demand, but as to any other admissible matter which might have been offered for that purpose. [citations omitted] Res judicata therefore bars the subsequent litigation of any claims arising from the transaction or series of transactions which was the subject of the prior suit. . . .

The burden is on the party seeking to invoke res judicata to prove that the doctrine bars the second action [citation omitted]. Without a demonstration that the conduct complained of in the French action occurred prior to the initiation of the United States action, res judicata is simply inapplicable. As we have noted previously:

> With respect to the determination of whether a second suit is barred by res judicata, the fact that both suits involved essentially the same course

of wrongful conduct is not decisive; nor is it dispositive that the two proceedings involved the same parties, similar or overlapping facts, and similar legal issues. A first judgment will generally have preclusive effect only where the transaction or connected series of transactions at issue in both suits is the same, that is where the same evidence is needed to support both claims, and where the facts essential to the second were pre-sent in the first.

Interoceanica Corp., 107 F.3d at 91 (quoting *SEC v. First Jersey Sec.*, 101 F.3d 1450, 1463–64 (2d Cir. 1996)).

In this case, Altai has failed to meet its burden of showing that the conduct which forms the basis of the French action – the unauthorized importation into France of Computer Associates's copyrighted work, and the subsequent distribution of the work in that country – occurred prior to August 1988 when the action was filed in New York. Altai simply asserts that the actions giving rise to the French action "took place prior to February 15, 1990, the date [the French action] was filed" and that they "took place well before [Computer Associates's] United States claims went to trial on March 28, 1990." Appellant's Opening Brief at 23, 34. Absent evidence that the French action is based on conduct by Altai and by FASTER that occurred prior to August 1988, res judicata will not bar Computer Associates from pursuing its claims in France.

Altai argues that res judicata bars the French action nonetheless, because Computer Associates could have amended its complaint in the United States action to assert its French copyright claims of which it became aware prior to the beginning of trial in the United States. We disagree.

For the purposes of res judicata, "the scope of litigation is framed by the complaint at the time it is filed" [citation omitted]. The res judicata doctrine does not apply to new rights acquired during the action which might have been, but which were not, litigated [citation omitted]. Although a plaintiff may seek leave to file a supplemental pleading to assert a new claim based on actionable conduct which the defendant engaged in after a lawsuit is commenced [citations omitted]. Altai was under no obligation to amend its complaint in the United States action, and res judicata does not bar litigation of claims arising from transactions which occurred after the United States action was brought.

Even if we were to assume that the French suit arose from transactions identical to those in the United States suit, there is a second reason why Altai may not invoke res judicata to bar the French action: the New York federal district court in the United States action could not have exercised personal jurisdiction over FASTER, a principal party to the French suit. Res judicata will not apply where "the initial forum did not have the power to award the full measure of relief sought in the later litigation" [citation omitted]. Even where a second action arises from some of the same factual circumstances that gave rise to a prior action, res judicata is inapplicable if formal jurisdictional or statutory barriers precluded the plaintiff from asserting its claims in the first action[citations omitted]. Such a "formal barrier," the absence of personal jurisdiction over FASTER, precludes application of res judictata here.

. . .

In conclusion, there are two reasons why res judicata does not prevent Computer Associates from maintaining its action based on French copyright claims in France: (i) the infringing conduct which formed the basis of the French action occurred after the filing of the United States action; and (ii) the New York federal district court lacked personal jurisdiction over FASTER. We therefore affirm the district court.

B. Collateral Estoppel

Altai argues, in the alternative, that Computer Associates is collaterally estopped from claiming that OSCAR 3.5 infringes its French copyright. We disagree.

The doctrine of collateral estoppel

> bars a party from relitigating in a second proceeding an issue of fact or law that was litigated and actually decided in a prior proceeding, if that party had a full and fair opportunity to litigate the issue in the prior proceeding and the decision of the issue was necessary to support a valid and final judgment on the merits.

Metromedia Co. v. Fugazy, 983 F.2d 350, 365 (2d Cir. 1992). For collateral estoppel to apply, the issues in each action must be identical, and issues are not identical when the legal standards governing their resolution are significantly different [citations omitted].

On appeal, Altai asserts that the French standard for copyrightability of computer programs is not "significantly different" from the standard applied in the United States because, as under United States copyright law, French law protects expression and not ideas. Such a superficial comparison begs key questions: What constitutes expression or ideas in the context of computer software, to what extent may expression be copied with impunity when it is necessary to the communication of the idea, how much expression is not original with the plaintiff or is in the public domain? Altai's argument is far from sufficient to show that the two copyright standards in France and the United States are "identical" as required for application of collateral estoppel. The Commercial Court arrived at a similar conclusion, refusing Altai's request to give the decision in the United States action dispositive effect. We, therefore, affirm the district court's decision that collateral estoppel does not bar litigation of the French action.

QUESTIONS

1. Claiming a multi-territorial infringement, Arthur Author sues Peregrine Publisher at its corporate domicile in the U.K., alleging infringements in the U.K., Ireland and Canada. Peregrine also distributed the work in the U.S. and Australia, but Author did not plead the occurrence of infringements in those countries. If Author obtains a final judgment against Peregrine for infringement in the U.K., Ireland and Canada, may Author later sue in the U.S. alleging infringements there?

2. In Question 1, suppose that after obtaining the judgment in the U.K. against Peregrine for infringement in the U.K., Ireland, Canada and the U.S., Author realizes that the U.S. awards statutory damages in excess of the amount of damages actually proved. If Author seeks to bring an action in the U.S. in order to recover additional damages will Peregrine succeed in its objection to the second action?

9.2.2   E.U.: Brussels I Regulation Recast

SECTION 2 Enforcement

Article 39

A judgment given in a Member State which is enforceable in that Member State shall be enforceable in the other Member States without any declaration of enforceability being required.

Article 40

An enforceable judgment shall carry with it by operation of law the power to proceed to any protective measures which exist under the law of the Member State addressed.

Article 41

1. Subject to the provisions of this Section, the procedure for the enforcement of judgments given in another Member State shall be governed by the law of the Member State addressed. A judgment given in a Member State which is enforceable in the Member State addressed shall be enforced there under the same conditions as a judgment given in the Member State addressed.

2. Notwithstanding paragraph 1, the grounds for refusal or of suspension of enforcement under the law of the Member State addressed shall apply in so far as they are not incompatible with the grounds referred to in Article 45.

3. The party seeking the enforcement of a judgment given in another Member State shall not be required to have a postal address in the Member State addressed. Nor shall that party be required to have an authorised representative in the Member State addressed unless such a representative is mandatory irrespective of the nationality or the domicile of the parties.

Article 42

1. For the purposes of enforcement in a Member State of a judgment given in another Member State, the applicant shall provide the competent enforcement authority with:

(a) a copy of the judgment which satisfies the conditions necessary to establish its authenticity; and
(b) the certificate issued pursuant to Article 53, certifying that the judgment is enforceable and containing an extract of the judgment as well as, where appropriate, relevant information on the recoverable costs of the proceedings and the calculation of interest.

2. For the purposes of enforcement in a Member State of a judgment given in another Member State ordering a provisional, including a protective, measure, the applicant shall provide the competent enforcement authority with:

(a) a copy of the judgment which satisfies the conditions necessary to establish its authenticity;
(b) the certificate issued pursuant to Article 53, containing a description of the measure and certifying that:

(i) the court has jurisdiction as to the substance of the matter;

(ii) the judgment is enforceable in the Member State of origin; and

(c) where the measure was ordered without the defendant being summoned to appear, proof of service of the judgment.

3. The competent enforcement authority may, where necessary, require the applicant to provide, in accordance with Article 57, a translation or a transliteration of the contents of the certificate.

4. The competent enforcement authority may require the applicant to provide a translation of the judgment only if it is unable to proceed without such a translation.

Article 43

1. Where enforcement is sought of a judgment given in another Member State, the certificate issued pursuant to Article 53 shall be served on the person against whom the enforcement is sought prior to the first enforcement measure. The certificate shall be accompanied by the judgment, if not already served on that person.

2. Where the person against whom enforcement is sought is domiciled in a Member State other than the Member State of origin, he may request a translation of the judgment in order to contest the enforcement if the judgment is not written in or accompanied by a translation into either of the following languages:

(a) a language which he understands; or

(b) the official language of the Member State in which he is domiciled or, where there are several official languages in that Member State, the official language or one of the official languages of the place where he is domiciled.

Where a translation of the judgment is requested under the first subparagraph, no measures of enforcement may be taken other than protective measures until that translation has been provided to the person against whom enforcement is sought.

This paragraph shall not apply if the judgment has already been served on the person against whom enforcement is sought in one of the languages referred to in the first subparagraph or is accompanied by a translation into one of those languages.

3. This Article shall not apply to the enforcement of a protective measure in a judgment or where the person seeking enforcement proceeds to protective measures in accordance with Article 40.

Article 44

1. In the event of an application for refusal of enforcement of a judgment pursuant to Subsection 2 of Section 3, the court in the Member State addressed may, on the application of the person against whom enforcement is sought:

(a) limit the enforcement proceedings to protective measures;
(b) make enforcement conditional on the provision of such security as it shall determine; or
(c) suspend, either wholly or in part, the enforcement proceedings.

2. The competent authority in the Member State addressed shall, on the application of the person against whom enforcement is sought, suspend the enforcement proceedings where the enforceability of the judgment is suspended in the Member State of origin.

SECTION 3 Refusal of recognition and enforcement
Subsection 1 Refusal of recognition

Article 45

1. On the application of any interested party, the recognition of a judgment shall be refused:

(a) if such recognition is manifestly contrary to public policy (ordre public) in the Member State addressed;
(b) where the judgment was given in default of appearance, if the defendant was not served with the document which instituted the proceedings or with an equivalent document in sufficient time and in such a way as to enable him to arrange for his defence, unless the defendant failed to commence proceedings to challenge the judgment when it was possible for him to do so;
(c) if the judgment is irreconcilable with a judgment given between the same parties in the Member State addressed;
(d) if the judgment is irreconcilable with an earlier judgment given in another Member State or in a third State involving the same cause of action and between the same parties, provided that the earlier

judgment fulfils the conditions necessary for its recognition in the Member State addressed; or

(e) if the judgment conflicts with:

(i) Sections 3, 4 or 5 of Chapter II where the policyholder, the insured, a beneficiary of the insurance contract, the injured party, the consumer or the employee was the defendant; or

(ii) Section 6 of Chapter II.

2. In its examination of the grounds of jurisdiction referred to in point (e) of paragraph 1, the court to which the application was submitted shall be bound by the findings of fact on which the court of origin based its jurisdiction.

3. Without prejudice to point (e) of paragraph 1, the jurisdiction of the court of origin may not be reviewed. The test of public policy referred to in point (a) of paragraph 1 may not be applied to the rules relating to jurisdiction.

4. The application for refusal of recognition shall be made in accordance with the procedures provided for in Subsection 2 and, where appropriate, Section 4.

Subsection 2 Refusal of enforcement

Article 46

On the application of the person against whom enforcement is sought, the enforcement of a judgment shall be refused where one of the grounds referred to in Article 45 is found to exist.

Article 47

1. The application for refusal of enforcement shall be submitted to the court which the Member State concerned has communicated to the Commission pursuant to point (a) of Article 75 as the court to which the application is to be submitted.

2. The procedure for refusal of enforcement shall, in so far as it is not covered by this Regulation, be governed by the law of the Member State addressed.

3. The applicant shall provide the court with a copy of the judgment and, where necessary, a translation or transliteration of it.

The court may dispense with the production of the documents referred to in the first subparagraph if it already possesses them or if it considers it unreasonable to require the applicant to provide them. In the latter case, the court may require the other party to provide those documents.

4. The party seeking the refusal of enforcement of a judgment given in another Member State shall not be required to have a postal address in the Member State addressed. Nor shall that party be required to have an authorised representative in the Member State addressed unless such a representative is mandatory irrespective of the nationality or the domicile of the parties.

Article 48

The court shall decide on the application for refusal of enforcement without delay.

Article 49

1. The decision on the application for refusal of enforcement may be appealed against by either party.

2. The appeal is to be lodged with the court which the Member State concerned has communicated to the Commission pursuant to point (b) of Article 75 as the court with which such an appeal is to be lodged.

Article 50

The decision given on the appeal may only be contested by an appeal where the courts with which any further appeal is to be lodged have been communicated by the Member State concerned to the Commission pursuant to point (c) of Article 75.

Article 51

1. The court to which an application for refusal of enforcement is submitted or the court which hears an appeal lodged under Article 49 or Article 50 may stay the proceedings if an ordinary appeal has been lodged against the judgment in the Member State of origin or if the time for such an appeal has not yet expired. In the latter case, the court may specify the time within which such an appeal is to be lodged.

2. Where the judgment was given in Ireland, Cyprus or the United Kingdom, any form of appeal available in the Member State of origin shall be treated as an ordinary appeal for the purposes of paragraph 1.

QUESTIONS

1. To which decisions does the Brussels Regulation apply? What about a U.S. decision seeking recognition in France? Why and how would the extra-EU origin of the decision influence the intensity of the recognition court's review?

2. Under the Brussels Regulation, the enforcement court may not revisit the basis of the rendering court's jurisdiction, with the exception of article 24, which designates the country of registration as the exclusive forum for claims relating to the validity of registered rights. Because article 24 does not apply to copyright claims, does it follow that an E.U. court may never review the rendering court's jurisdiction? Suppose the rendering court applied a very broad interpretation of article 7.2, conferring general jurisdiction based on the mere accessibility in the forum of any website. Is there any ground on which an E.U. defendant could contest his home court's recognition of the judgment?

3. In *Authors Guild, Inc.* v. *Google Inc.*, 954 F. Supp. 2d 282, 293 (S.D.N.Y. 2013), the court ruled that Google's scanning of millions of books from the University of Michigan library was a fair use. Suppose that Google had contended that its making available of access to its database of scanned books for the purpose of data mining and for the output of "snippets" of the scanned books, was fair use throughout the world because the database was located in the U.S. and all communications emanated from the U.S. Does *National Football League* v. *Prime Time 24*, 211 F.3d 10 (2d Cir. 2000) (*supra*, Part III, Chapter 8.2.2, pp. 683 et seq.), support the application of U.S. copyright law in order to hold Google's book scanning fair use all over the world? Supposing the U.S. court were to enter such a judgment, what would be the effect of such a decision in France, for example? Could an author party to the U.S. claim nonetheless bring an infringement claim in France? On what ground could a French judge refuse to recognize the U.S. decision? To what extent might the substantive minima of the Berne Convention permit the French court to deny recognition (and res judicata effect) to the U.S. judgment?

4. A U.K. company that employed a Greek photographer brought an action in Athens to terminate the employment contract. The photographer brought an incidental question (counterclaim) concerning the ownership of the photographs he shot while in the U.K. company's employ. The photographs were displayed on the website of the U.K. company

without the photographer's authorization. The Greek judge, applying Greek private international law (see *supra*, Part III, Chapter 8.2.1,
pp. 663–64) determined ownership pursuant to Greek law's designation of the law of the country of origin. Because the court deemed the
photographs to be unpublished (on the grounds that mere disclosure
on a website does not effect a work's publication, and that any publication was unauthorized), the court ruled that the country of origin was
the country of the photographer's nationality, Greece. Under that law,
the photographer was the owner of the photographs. Because the photographer was the defendant in the main action for termination of the
employment contract, the court had general jurisdiction under article
4 of the Brussels Regulation (Recast). Now that the Greek court has
declared the photographer to be the owner of the photographs, would a
U.K. court recognize his copyright ownership?

Public policy and recognition

C-38/98 Régie Nationale des Usines Renault SA v. Maxicar SpA and Others ECLI:EU:C:2000:225 [2000]

[The following case concerned the recognition in Italy of a French judgment of infringement. At that time, spare parts of cars were protected
by copyright in France but not in Italy. As a result, the manufacture
of those spare car parts by Maxicar and Formento in Italy could not
infringe any copyright owned by Renault in Italy. Nevertheless, the distribution of those spare parts in France infringed the copyright owned
by Renault in France. As a result of those domestic disparities, a French
judgment found Formero and Maxicar guilty of infringement. An Italian
judgment rejected the infringement claim with respect to Italy. Renault
applied in Italy for a declaration of enforceability of the French judgment
in Italy.]

2   The questions were raised in proceedings between Régie Nationale
des Usines Renault SA (Renault), whose registered office is in France, and
Maxicar SpA (Maxicar), whose registered office is in Italy, and Mr Formento,
who resides in Italy, concerning the enforcement in that Contracting State
of a judgment delivered on 12 January 1990 by the Cour d'Appel (Court of
Appeal), Dijon, France, ordering Maxicar and Mr Formento to pay Renault
damages of FRF 100 000 for loss incurred as a result of activities found to
constitute forgery.

. . .

The main proceedings

11   By judgment of 12 January 1990 the Cour d'Appel, Dijon, found Mr Formento guilty of forgery for having manufactured and marketed body parts for Renault vehicles. It also declared him jointly and severally liable with Maxicar, the company of which he was director, to pay FRF 100 000 by way of damages to Renault, which had applied to join the proceedings as a civil party. The judgment became final after an appeal lodged before the French Cour de Cassation (Court of Cassation) was dismissed on 6 June 1991.

12   On 24 December 1996 Renault applied to the Corte d'Appello di Torino for a declaration of enforceability of that judgment in Italy under Articles 31 and 32 of the Convention.

13   By decision of 25 February 1997, the Corte d'Appello di Torino dismissed the application on the ground that since the decision was given in criminal proceedings, the application ought to have been made within the time-limit laid down in Article 741 of the Italian Code of Criminal Procedure.

14   On 28 March 1997 Renault appealed against that decision to the Corte d'Appello di Torino, in accordance with Article 40 of the Convention, arguing that the Convention applied in civil and commercial matters whatever the nature of the court or tribunal involved. Mr Formento and Maxicar contended that the judgment of the Cour d'Appel, Dijon, could not be declared enforceable in Italy because it was irreconcilable with a decision given in a dispute between the same parties in Italy and was contrary to public policy in economic matters.

15   In those circumstances, the Corte d'Appello di Torino decided to stay proceedings and refer the following questions to the Court of Justice for a preliminary ruling:

. . .

(3) Is, therefore, a judgment handed down by a court of a Member State to be considered contrary to public policy within the meaning of Article 27 of the Brussels Convention [Recast Article 45] if it recognises industrial or intellectual property rights over such component parts which together make up the bodywork of a car, and affords protection to the holder of such purported exclusive rights by preventing third parties trading in another Member State from manufacturing, selling, transporting, importing or exporting in that

Member State such component parts which together make up the bodywork of a car already on the market, or, in any event, by sanctioning such conduct?

16 The third question, which should be examined first because consideration of the first two questions will depend on the reply to that question, seeks an interpretation from the Court of Justice of a provision of the Convention and, more particularly, a ruling on the concept of public policy in the State in which recognition is sought in Article 27, point 1, of the Convention [Recast Article 45 1].

. . .

Substance

24 Maxicar and Mr Formento wish the Court to define the concept of public policy in economic matters. In particular, they wish it to confirm that Community law, and in particular the principle of free movement of goods and freedom of competition, supports the approach taken by Italian law, which, unlike French law, does not recognise the existence of industrial property rights in spare parts for cars, and to declare that that approach is a principle of public policy in economic matters.

25 The French and Netherlands Governments, and the Commission, after noting that the preliminary issue is whether and to what extent the Court of Justice has jurisdiction to rule on the concept of public policy in the State in which recognition is sought used in Article 27, point 1, of the Convention [Recast Article 45 1], argue in favour of a narrow interpretation of the concept, which should only be applied in exceptional instances. An alleged error in interpreting the rules of Community law is not sufficient, they maintain, to justify recourse to the clause on public policy.

26 The first point to note is that Article 27 of the Convention [Recast Article 45] must be interpreted strictly inasmuch as it constitutes an obstacle to the attainment of one of the fundamental objectives of the Convention [citations omitted]. With regard more specifically to the clause on public policy in Article 27, point 1, of the Convention [Recast Article 45 1], the Court has made it clear that it may be relied on only in exceptional cases [citations omitted].

27 The Court has held that it follows that, while the Contracting States remain free in principle, by virtue of the proviso in Article 27, point 1, of the Convention [Recast Article 45 1], to determine according to their own

conception what public policy requires, the limits of that concept are a matter of interpretation of the Convention [citations omitted].

28   Consequently, while it is not for the Court to define the content of the public policy of a Contracting State, it is none the less required to review the limits within which the courts of a Contracting State may have recourse to that concept for the purpose of refusing recognition of a judgment emanating from another Contracting State [citations omitted].

29   It should be noted that by disallowing any review of a foreign judgment as to its substance, Article 29 and the third paragraph of Article 34 of the Convention prohibit the courts of the State in which enforcement is sought from refusing to recognise or enforce that judgment solely on the ground that there is a discrepancy between the legal rule applied by the court of the State of origin and that which would have been applied by the court of the State in which enforcement is sought had it been seised of the dispute. Similarly, the court of the State in which enforcement is sought cannot review the accuracy of the findings of law or fact made by the court of the State of origin [citations omitted].

30   Recourse to the clause on public policy in Article 27, point 1, of the Convention [Recast Article 45(1)] can be envisaged only where recognition or enforcement of the judgment delivered in another Contracting State would be at variance to an unacceptable degree with the legal order of the State in which enforcement is sought inasmuch as it infringes a fundamental principle. In order for the prohibition of any review of the foreign judgment as to its substance to be observed, the infringement would have to constitute a manifest breach of a rule of law regarded as essential in the legal order of the State in which enforcement is sought or of a right recognised as being fundamental within that legal order [citations omitted].

31   In this case, what has led the court of the State in which enforcement was sought to question the compatibility of the foreign judgment with public policy in its own State is the possibility that the court of the State of origin erred in applying certain rules of Community law. The court of the State in which enforcement was sought is in doubt as to the compatibility with the principles of free movement of goods and freedom of competition of recognition by the court of the State of origin of the existence of an intellectual property right in body parts for cars enabling the holder to prohibit traders in another Contracting State from manufacturing, selling, transporting, importing or exporting such body parts in that Contracting State.

32   The fact that the alleged error concerns rules of Community law does not alter the conditions for being able to rely on the clause on public policy. It is for the national court to ensure with equal diligence the protection of rights established in national law and rights conferred by Community law.

33   The court of the State in which enforcement is sought cannot, without undermining the aim of the Convention, refuse recognition of a decision emanating from another Contracting State solely on the ground that it considers that national or Community law was misapplied in that decision. On the contrary, it must be considered whether, in such cases, the system of legal remedies in each Contracting State, together with the preliminary ruling procedure provided for in Article 177 of the Treaty,* affords a sufficient guarantee to individuals.

34   Since an error of law such as that alleged in the main proceedings does not constitute a manifest breach of a rule of law regarded as essential in the legal order of the State in which enforcement is sought, the reply to the third question must be that Article 27, point 1, of the Convention [Recast Article 45(1)] must be interpreted as meaning that a judgment of a court or tribunal of a Contracting State recognising the existence of an intellectual property right in body parts for cars, and conferring on the holder of that right protection by enabling him to prevent third parties trading in another Contracting State from manufacturing, selling, transporting, importing or exporting in that Contracting State such body parts, cannot be considered to be contrary to public policy.

35   Having regard to the reply given to the third question, it is not necessary to reply to the first and second questions.

QUESTIONS

1. To what extent is the definition of public policy a matter or domestic law or of European law after this case? Could a legal disparity between domestic IP laws be contrary to local public policy? To E.U. public policy?
2. Taking into account the process of copyright harmonization, try to figure out what could constitute a violation of public policy in the recognition of a judgment in a copyright case? What about punitive damages?
3. In the *Maxicar* case, the refusal to recognize was based on grounds of public policy. The facts show that an Italian court decided the same issue in a manner directly opposed to the decision of the French court. Would the

---

* Editors' Note: Now Article 267 of the TFUE.

plaintiff have been more successful in resisting recognition and enforce-ment had it pleaded that the French decision was irreconcilable with the Italian judgment? Suppose that the French decision forbade the distribu-tion of the spare car parts in Italy, would the outcome have been different?

Injunctions and provisional measures

Under article 42 and for the purposes of enforcement in a member state of a judgment given in another member state ordering a provisional, including a protective, measure (such as seizure of the goods pending adjudication), the applicant shall provide the competent enforcement authority with the certificate certifying that the court has jurisdiction as to the substance of the matter. Under article 35, "Application may be made to the courts of a Member State for such provisional, including protective, measures as may be available under the law of that Member State, even if the courts of another Member State have jurisdiction as to the substance of the matter." Does this mean that a decision from a court having jurisdiction only on the ground of article 35 ordering provisional measures could not be enforced in any other E.U. countries? What might be the practical consequences as to the scope of the injunction ordered?

C-235/09 DHL Express France SAS, formerly DHL International SA v. Chronopost SA ECLI:EU:C:2011:238 [2011]

The dispute in the main proceedings and the questions referred for a preliminary ruling

20   Chronopost is the proprietor of the French and Community trade marks for the sign 'WEBSHIPPING'. The Community trade mark, applied for in October 2000, was registered on 7 May 2003 in respect of, inter alia, services relating to: logistics and data transmission; telecommunications; transport by road; collecting mail, newspaper and parcels; and express mail management.

21   It is apparent from the documents before the Court that, having noted that one of its principal competitors, DHL International, had used the signs 'WEB SHIPPING', 'Web Shipping' and/or 'Webshipping' in order to des-ignate an express mail management service accessible via the Internet, on 8 September 2004 Chronopost brought an action against that company before the Tribunal de grande instance de Paris (Regional Court, Paris, France) – which heard the case as a Community trade mark court within the meaning of Article 91(1) of [Trademark] Regulation No 40/94 – alleging,

in particular, infringement of the Community trade mark WEBSHIPPING. By its judgment of 15 March 2006, that court found, inter alia, that DHL Express France, successor to DHL International, had infringed Chronopost's French trade mark WEBSHIPPING, although it did not adjudicate upon the infringement of the Community trade mark.

22   The order for reference states that, by a judgment of 9 November 2007, the Cour d'appel de Paris (Court of Appeal, Paris) – acting as a second-instance Community trade mark court on the appeal brought against the judgment of 15 March 2006 by Chronopost – prohibited DHL Express France, subject to a periodic penalty payment in the event of infringement of the prohibition, from continuing to use the signs 'WEBSHIPPING' and 'WEB SHIPPING' in order to designate an express mail management service accessible, inter alia, via the Internet. The Cour d'appel de Paris regarded such use as infringing the French and Community trade mark WEBSHIPPING.

23   The appeal in cassation which DHL Express France had brought against that judgment was dismissed by the order for reference.

24   However, in the course of the same proceedings before the Cour de cassation (Court of Cassation), Chronopost has brought a cross-appeal in which it submits that the judgment of 9 November 2007 infringes Articles 1 and 98 of Regulation No 40/94 in so far as the prohibition against further infringement of the Community trade mark WEBSHIPPING, subject to a periodic penalty payment, issued by the Cour d'appel de Paris does not extend to the entire area of the European Union.

25   According to the Cour de cassation, it follows expressly from the grounds of the judgment of the Cour d'appel de Paris that, although the judgment does not contain any operative words expressly relating to the application to extend the prohibition issued by that court – which is subject to a periodic penalty payment – to the entire area of the European Union, that prohibition subject to a periodic penalty payment must be construed as applying only to French territory.

26   Since it had doubts as to the interpretation, in that context, of Article 98 of Regulation No 40/94, the Cour de cassation decided to stay proceedings and to refer the following questions to the Court of Justice for a preliminary ruling:

'1. Must Article 98 of . . . Regulation [No 40/94] be interpreted as meaning that the prohibition issued by a Community trade mark court has effect as a matter of law throughout the entire area of the [European Union]?

2. If not, is that court entitled to apply specifically that prohibition to the territories of other States in which the acts of infringement are committed or threatened?

3. In either case, are the coercive measures which the court, by application of its national law, has attached to the prohibition issued by it applicable within the territories of the Member States in which that prohibition would have effect?

4. In the contrary case, may that court order such a coercive measure, similar to or different from that which it adopts pursuant to its national law, by application of the national laws of the States in which that prohibition would have effect?'

Consideration of the questions referred

Preliminary observations

27   As is apparent from its heading, Article 98 of Regulation No 40/94 is concerned with sanctions for Community trade-mark infringement.

28   The first sentence of Article 98(1) provides that where a Community trade mark court hearing a case finds that there have been acts of infringement or threatened infringement of a Community trade mark, it is to issue an order prohibiting the defendant from proceeding with such acts. The second sentence of Article 98(1) provides that that court is required to take such measures in accordance with its national law as are aimed at ensuring that that prohibition is complied with.

29   Article 98(2) provides that the Community trade mark court is to apply '[i]n all other respects . . . the law of the Member State [in] which the acts of infringement or threatened infringement were committed, including the private international law'.

30   It follows from the opening words of Article 98(2), read in the light of the heading of Article 98, and from the various language versions of that provision, in particular the German-language ('in Bezug auf alle anderen Fragen'), French-language ('par ailleurs'), Spanish-language ('por otra parte') and Italian-language ('negli altri casi') versions, that Article 98(2) does not relate to the coercive measures referred to in Article 98(1), which are measures to ensure compliance with a prohibition against further infringement.

31   Since the questions referred by the national court for a preliminary ruling concern only the prohibition against further infringement or threatened infringement and the coercive measures to ensure compliance with that prohibition, those questions must therefore be considered to relate to the interpretation of Article 98(1) of Regulation No 40/94.

. . .

52   By its third and fourth questions, which should be examined together, the national court asks, in essence, whether Article 98(1), second sentence, of Regulation No 40/94 must be interpreted as meaning that a coercive measure, such as a periodic penalty payment, ordered by a Community trade mark court by application of its national law, in order to ensure compliance with a prohibition against further infringement or threatened infringement which it has issued, may have effect in Member States to which the territorial scope of such a prohibition extends other than the Member State of that court. If that is not the case, the national court asks whether the Community trade mark court may order such a coercive measure, similar to or different from that which it adopts pursuant to its national law, by application of the national law of the Member State to whose territory the scope of that prohibition extends.

53   In that connection, it must first be recalled that, as regards the law applicable to coercive measures, the Court has already held that the Community trade mark court seised is required to select, from among the measures provided for under the legislation of its own Member State, such measures as are aimed at ensuring that the prohibition that it has issued is complied with [citation omitted].

54   Second, coercive measures ordered by a Community trade mark court pursuant to its Member State's national law can achieve the objective for which they were issued – namely, ensuring that a prohibition is complied with so that the right conferred by a Community trade mark against the risk of infringement is actually protected throughout the area of the European Union [citation omitted] – only if the measures have effect in the same territory as that in which the prohibition order itself has effect.

55   In the main proceedings, the prohibition order issued by the Community trade mark court was coupled with a periodic penalty payment by that court pursuant to its national law. In order that such a coercive measure may have effect in the territory of a Member State other than that of the court which ordered the measure, a court of that other Member State seised in that regard

must, under the provisions of Chapter III of Regulation No 44/2001, recognise and enforce that measure in accordance with the rules and procedures laid down by the national law of that Member State.

56   Where the national law of the Member State in which recognition and enforcement of the decision of a Community trade mark court is sought does not provide for a coercive measure similar to that ordered by the Community trade mark court which issued the prohibition against further infringement or threatened infringement (and coupled that prohibition with such a measure in order to ensure compliance with the prohibition), the court seised of the case in that Member State must, as the Advocate General has observed at point 67 of his Opinion, attain the objective pursued by the measure by having recourse to the relevant provisions of its national law which are such as to ensure that the prohibition originally issued is complied with in an equivalent manner.

57   That obligation to attain the objective pursued by the coercive measure constitutes an extension of the obligation on the Community trade mark courts to take coercive measures when they issue an order prohibiting further infringement or threatened infringement. Without those related obligations, a prohibition of that kind might not be coupled with measures aimed at ensuring that it is complied with, so that it would, to a large extent, have no dissuasive effect [citations omitted].

58   In that connection, it should be recalled that under the principle of sincere cooperation laid down in Article 4(3), second subparagraph, TEU, it is for the Member States' courts to ensure judicial protection of an individual's rights under European Union law [citations omitted]. By virtue of that same provision, the Member States are to take any appropriate measure, general or particular, to ensure fulfilment of the obligations arising out of the Treaties or resulting from the acts of the institutions of the Union. In particular, under Article 3 of Directive 2004/48, Member States are to provide for the measures, procedures and remedies necessary to ensure the enforcement of the intellectual property rights covered by that Directive, including, inter alia, the rights of trade mark proprietors. In accordance with Article 3(2), those measures, procedures and remedies are to be effective, proportionate and dissuasive and are to be applied in such a manner as to avoid the creation of barriers to legitimate trade and to provide for safeguards against their abuse.

59   In the light of the foregoing, the answer to the third and fourth questions is that Article 98(1), second sentence, of Regulation No 40/94 must

be interpreted as meaning that a coercive measure, such as a periodic penalty payment, ordered by a Community trade mark court by application of its national law, in order to ensure compliance with a prohibition against further infringement or threatened infringement which it has issued, has effect in Member States to which the territorial scope of such a prohibition extends other than the Member State of that court, under the conditions laid down in Chapter III of Regulation No 44/2001 with regard to the recognition and enforcement of judgments. Where the national law of one of those other Member States does not contain a coercive measure similar to that ordered by the Community trade mark court, the objective pursued by that measure must be attained by the competent court of that other Member State by having recourse to the relevant provisions of its national law which are such as to ensure that the prohibition is complied with in an equivalent manner.

QUESTIONS

1. The dispute concerned a Community trademark. To what extent does the solution remain operative for copyright protection?
2. Does the solution foster forum shopping? Why?
3. A French film producer discovered on the Internet the trailer for its latest movie. The trailer is mainly available from an Italian platform. The producer decided to litigate in Italy on the basis of article 2 of the Brussels Regulation (defendant's residence). The Italian judge ordered that the trailer be taken down and remain off websites in all the countries of the E.U. The Italian defendant refused to comply with the stay down order. He considered that the Italian decision could not be recognized in France since the French highest civil court had previously refused to order a stay down injunction in a domestic copyright law dispute. Do you think that the website operator's refusal could be justified under the Brussels Regulation? Would it be sufficient to plead the disparity between Italian law and French law? Would it be more useful to plead the inconsistency of the judgment with the balance drawn by the ECJ in the following cases, *SABAM* and *Telekabel Wien* (see below)? Why?

C-360/10 Belgische Vereniging van Auteurs, Componisten en Uitgevers CVBA (SABAM) v. Netlog NV ECLI:EU:C:2012:85 [2012]

53   The answer to the question referred is that Directives 2000/31 (Directive on electronic commerce), 2001/29 (Info. Soc.) and 2004/48 (on the enforcement of intellectual property rights), read together and construed in the light of the requirements stemming from the protection of the applicable fundamental rights, must be interpreted as precluding an injunction made

against a hosting service provider which requires it to install the contested filtering system.

C-314/12 *UPC* **Telekabel Wien GmbH v. Constantin Film Verleih GmbH and Others ECLI:EU:C:2014:192 [2014]**

64 The fundamental rights recognised by E.U. law must be interpreted as not precluding a court injunction prohibiting an internet service provider from allowing its customers access to a website placing protected subject-matter online without the agreement of the rightholders when that injunction does not specify the measures which that access provider must take and when that access provider can avoid incurring coercive penalties for breach of that injunction by showing that it has taken all reasonable measures, provided that (i) the measures taken do not unnecessarily deprive internet users of the possibility of lawfully accessing the information available and (ii) that those measures have the effect of preventing unauthorised access to the protected subject-matter or, at least, of making it difficult to achieve and of seriously discouraging internet users who are using the services of the addressee of that injunction from accessing the subject-matter that has been made available to them in breach of the intellectual property right, that being a matter for the national authorities and courts to establish.

9.3 Soft law

9.3.1 ALI Principles

§ 401. Foreign Judgments to Be Recognized or Enforced

(1) A court in which recognition or enforcement of a foreign judgment is sought shall first ascertain whether the rendering court applied these Principles to the case.

(a) If the rendering court applied the Principles, then the enforcement court shall recognize or enforce the judgment pursuant to these Principles.
(b) If the rendering court did not apply the Principles, then the enforcement court shall determine whether to recognize or enforce the judgment pursuant to its domestic rules on recognition and enforcement of foreign judgments.

(2) In order to be recognized or enforced, a foreign judgment must be final in the rendering State and not stayed by a court in that State.

(3) The preclusive effect given a foreign judgment shall be no greater than the preclusive effect of the judgment in the rendering State.

. . .

§ 402. Default Judgments

In addition to the provisions of § 403, the enforcement court shall not enforce a foreign judgment that has been rendered in default of appearance unless the enforcement court determines that the rendering court's assertion of personal jurisdiction was consistent with the law of the rendering State.

§ 403. Judgments Not to Be Recognized or Enforced

(1) The enforcement court shall not recognize or enforce a judgment if it determines that:

(a) the judgment was rendered under a system that does not provide impartial tribunals or procedures compatible with fundamental principles of fairness;
(b) the judgment was rendered in circumstances that raise substantial and justifiable doubt about the integrity of the rendering court with respect to the judgment in question;
(c) the judgment was rendered without notice reasonably calculated to inform the defendant of the pendency of the proceeding in a timely manner;
(d) the judgment was obtained by fraud that had the effect of depriving the defendant of adequate opportunity to present its case to the rendering court;
(e) recognition or enforcement would be repugnant to the public policy in the State in which enforcement is sought;
(f) the rendering court exercised jurisdiction on the basis of a court-selection clause inconsistent with the safeguards set out in § 202(4);
(g) the rendering court exercised jurisdiction solely on a basis insufficient under § 207; or
(h) the rendering court exercised jurisdiction in violation of the forum's own rules of judicial competence.

(2) The enforcement court need not recognize or enforce a judgment if it determines that:

(a) the rendering court exercised jurisdiction on a basis inconsistent with the norms of §§ 201, 202(1)-(3), 203–206;
(b) the rendering court chose a law inconsistent with the norms of §§ 301–324;

. . .

(3) Except with respect to judgments rendered in default of appearance, the enforcement court, in making any determination listed in subsections (1)(e)–(g) or (2), shall defer to the facts found by the rendering court. In other cases, the court shall make its own determinations of fact and law.

QUESTIONS

1. Recall the *Féraud* decision, *supra*. Had the ALI Principles applied, would the U.S. court have recognized the French judgment?
2. Constance Consumer downloads a motion picture from the website of its producer, Huge Movie Co. The terms and conditions of the download, to which Constance agreed by clicking on the box that said she had read and understood and assented to the conditions, allow Constance to load the movie onto her computer and one other device. The terms and conditions also provide that any infringement action will be litigated in Plutocratia, the country where Huge's headquarters is located, and that country's laws will apply. Assume Constance does not reside in that country. Despite the contract, Constance copies the movie onto an additional three devices. Huge finds out, and initiates an action in Plutocratia. Constance does not appear, and Huge obtains a default judgment. Under the ALI Principles, if Huge seeks to execute the judgment in the country in which Constance resides, will that court recognize and enforce the Plutocratian judgment?

§ 411. Monetary Relief

If a foreign judgment is recognized by the enforcement court under these Principles:

(1) The rendering court's order awarding compensatory damages, including attorney's fees, costs, accounting for profits, and damages intended to compensate the plaintiff without requiring proof of actual damages, shall be enforced; and

(2) The rendering court's order awarding noncompensatory damages, including exemplary or punitive damages, shall be enforced at least to the

extent that similar or comparable damages could have been awarded in the State of the enforcement court. The enforcement court shall take into account whether and to what extent the damages awarded by the rendering court are not punitive but serve to cover costs and expenses relating to the proceedings not otherwise covered by provisions relating to the award of attorney's fees.

§ 412. Injunctions

(1)

(a) Except as provided in subsection (1)(b), if a foreign judgment is recognized by the enforcement court under these Principles, the rendering court's order awarding an injunction as a remedy for intellectual property infringement shall be enforced in accord with the procedures available to the enforcement court.

(b) If injunctive relief would not have been available for the enforcement court's territory had the enforcement court been the rendering court and reached the same decision on the merits, the enforcement court may decline to enjoin or to order the commission of acts within the territory that impact exclusively within the territory. If the court so limits the scope of the injunction, it shall award monetary relief in lieu of the injunction.

(2) The enforcement court may order such other relief as provided in the judgment, including seizure and destruction of infringing articles and the means of their manufacture or reproduction and to order the publication of the judgment.

QUESTIONS

1. Copyright owner receives a judgment in Country A that Defendant committed infringement there, and that the infringement was willful. The court awards the maximum statutory damages for infringements in A, in accordance with its own law. Assume that the statutory damages considerably exceed actual damages. Copyright owner then seeks enforcement of the judgment in Country B, where all of Defendant's assets are located. Will the courts of B enforce the judgment to the full extent of the statutory damage award? What if the court in Country A awarded only actual damages?

2. Wilhelmina Writer, author of the best-selling novel, *Blown Away by the Breeze*, obtains a judgment in Country A ruling that an unauthorized

sequel, *Breezed Off,* infringes her copyright in the novel in Countries A and B, where the defendant publisher has been distributing the sequel. The court enjoins further publication in Countries A and B. When Wilhelmina seeks to enforce the injunction in Country B, the defendant publisher objects on the ground that the injunction is a restraint on free speech, and that a less restrictive remedy should apply. Under the ALI Principles, will the defendant succeed in preventing enforcement of the injunction in Country B?

9.3.2   CLIP Principles

PART 4: RECOGNITION AND ENFORCEMENT
Section 1: General rules

Article 4:101: Definition of judgment

For the purposes of these Principles, judgment means any judgment given by a court or tribunal of any State, irrespective of the name given by that State to the proceedings which gave rise to the judgment or of the name given to the judgment itself, such as decree, order, decision or writ of execution. It also includes provisional, including protective, measures and the determination of costs or expenses by an officer of the court.

Article 4:102: Recognition and enforcement in general

(1) A judgment given by a foreign court shall be recognised and enforced in accordance with this Part of the Principles.

(2) In order to be recognised, a judgment must have in the State of origin the effect whose recognition is sought in the requested State.

(3) The effect of the judgment is determined by the law of the State of origin. Subject to Article 4:601, the court in the State of recognition shall interpret an injunction in respect of its subjective, territorial and substantial scope and take into account any change of circumstances, in particular the defendant limiting her/his activities and the impact of such activities to a particular State or States whose law has not been applied by the rendering court.

(4) In order to be enforceable, a judgment must be enforceable in the State of origin.

(5) Recognition or enforcement may be postponed or refused if an ordinary appeal against the judgment has been lodged in the State of origin or if the time limit for seeking ordinary review has not expired. A refusal does not prevent a subsequent application for recognition or enforcement of the judgment.

(6) If the foreign judgment contains elements which are severable, one or more of them may be separately recognised or enforced.

Article 4:103: *Favor recognitionis* principle

The provisions of Part 4 of the Principles shall not restrict the application of multilateral or bilateral agreements concerning the recognition and enforcement of judgments entered into by the State in which enforcement or recognition is sought nor deprive any interested party of any right she/he may have to avail herself/himself of a judgment in the manner and to the extent allowed by the law or the treaties of that State including the rules of a regional integration organisation if that State is a Member State of the organisation.

Section 2: Verification of jurisdiction

Article 4:201: Jurisdiction of foreign courts

A judgment shall not be recognised or enforced if there is no ground of jurisdiction under Part 2 of the Principles which would have allowed the foreign court to assert its jurisdiction.

Article 4:202: Validity and registration

Recognition and enforcement of a foreign judgment may not be refused on the ground that in the proceedings before the court of origin the validity or registration of an intellectual property right registered in a State other than the State of origin was challenged, provided that the recognition and enforcement produces effects concerning validity or registration only with regard to the dispute between the parties.

Article 4:203: Findings of fact

In its examination of the grounds of jurisdiction according to Article 4:201 to 4:202, the authority of the requested State shall be bound by the findings of fact on which the authority of the State where the judgment was rendered based its jurisdiction.

Article 4:204: Jurisdictional rules protecting consumers or employees

Recognition and enforcement may be refused if the judgment is manifestly incompatible with specific jurisdictional rules protecting consumers or employees in the State of recognition.

Section 3: Provisional, including protective, measures

Article 4:301: Provisional, including protective, measures

(1) Provisional, including protective, measures adopted by a foreign court shall not be recognised and enforced if there is no ground of jurisdiction under Part 2 of these Principles, which would have allowed the foreign court to decide on the merits.

(2) Provisional, including protective, measures adopted without prior hearing of the adverse party and enforceable without prior service of process to that party shall not be recognised or enforced.

Section 4: Public policy

Article 4:401: Public policy in general

A judgment shall not be recognised or enforced if:

(1) such recognition or enforcement would be manifestly incompatible with the public policy of the requested State;

(2) the specific proceedings leading to the judgment were manifestly incompatible with fundamental principles of procedural fairness of the requested State.

Article 4:402: Non-compensatory damages

(1) Recognition and enforcement of a judgment may be refused if, and only to the extent that, the judgment awards damages, including exemplary or punitive damages, that do not compensate a party for actual loss or harm suffered and exceed the amount of damages that could have been awarded by the courts of the State where enforcement is sought.

(2) The requested court shall take into account whether and to what extent the damages awarded by the court of origin serve to cover costs and expenses relating to the proceedings.

Section 5: Other grounds for non-recognition of foreign judgments

Article 4:501: Other grounds for non-recognition of foreign judgments

A judgment shall not be recognised or enforced if:

(1) the document which instituted the proceedings or an equivalent document was not notified to the defendant in sufficient time and in such a way as to enable her/him to arrange for her/his defence, unless the defendant entered an appearance and presented her/his case without contesting notification in the court of origin, provided that the law of the State of origin permitted notification to be contested;

(2) proceedings between the same parties and having the same cause of action are pending before a court of the requested State, provided that those proceedings were the first to be instituted, unless the foreign judgment resulted from a proceeding in a court other than the court first seised in accordance with Articles 2:701 paragraph 1 lit. (a) and paragraph 2 lit. (a);

(3) it is irreconcilable with a judgment given in the requested State between the same parties;

(4) it is irreconcilable with a judgment given in another State between the same parties and having the same cause of action, provided that this judgment fulfils the conditions necessary for its recognition in the requested State and it was given earlier or its recognition has already been declared in the requested State.

Section 6: Exclusion of substantive review

Article 4:601: Exclusion of substantive review

A foreign judgment may not be reviewed as to its substance or merits, without prejudice to the application of the provisions of this Part.

Section 7: Procedure

Article 4:701: General principles

(1) Recognition and enforcement procedures shall not be unnecessarily complicated or costly, or entail unreasonable time-limits or unwarranted delays.

(2) The requested court shall act expeditiously.

Article 4:702: Recognition

(1) A foreign judgment shall be recognised by operation of law and without any special procedure being required. Recognition may be raised as an incidental question and by way of counterclaim, cross-claim or defence.

(2) Without prejudice to paragraph 1, any interested party may request from the competent authorities of a State that they decide on the recognition or non-recognition of a foreign judgment. The procedure shall be governed by the law of the requested State.

(3) Recognition may be refused only for one of the reasons set out in this Part of the Principles.

Article 4:703: Enforcement

(1) The law of the requested State determines the methods by which a foreign judgment is declared enforceable.

(2) The declaration of enforceability may be refused only for one of the reasons set out in this Part of the Principles.

(3) Foreign judgments declared enforceable in the requested State shall be enforced as if they had been taken by the authorities of that State. Enforcement takes place in accordance with the law of the requested State to the extent provided by such law.

Section 8: Settlements

Article 4:801: Settlements

A settlement to which a court has given its authority shall be recognised and declared enforceable in the requested State under the same conditions as judgments, so far as those conditions apply to settlements.

QUESTIONS

1. Recall the *Féraud* decision, *supra*. Had the CLIP Principles applied, would the U.S. court have recognized the French judgment?
2. See Question 1, *supra*, following ALI Principles §§ 401–401. What result under the CLIP Principles?
3. See Question 1, *supra*, following ALI Principles §§ 411 and 412. What result under the CLIP Principles?
4. See Question 2, *supra*, following ALI Principles §§ 411 and 412. Under the CLIP Principles, will the defendant succeed in preventing enforcement of the injunction in Country B?

Appendix: Treaty texts

Berne Convention

Bilingual Version

Articles 1–20, 36–37

Article 1
Establishment of a Union

The countries to which this Convention applies constitute a Union for the protection of the rights of authors in their literary and artistic works.

Article 2
Protected Works:

(1) The expression "literary and artistic works" shall include every production in the literary, scientific and artistic domain, whatever may be the mode or form of its expression, such as books, pamphlets and other writings; lectures, addresses, sermons and other works of the same nature; dramatic or dramatico-musical works; choreographic works and entertainments in dumb show; musical compositions with or without words; cinematographic works to which are assimilated works expressed by a process analogous to cinematography; works of drawing, painting, architecture, sculpture, engraving and lithography; photographic works

Article premier
Constitution d'une Union

Les pays auxquels s'applique la présente Convention sont constitués à l'état d'Union pour la protection des droits des auteurs sur leurs œuvres littéraires et artistiques.

Article 2
Œuvres protégées:

(1) Les termes «œuvres littéraires et artistiques» comprennent toutes les productions du domaine littéraire, scientifique et artistique, quel qu'en soit le mode ou la forme d'expression, telles que: les livres, brochures et autres écrits; les conférences, allocutions, sermons et autres œuvres de même nature; les œuvres dramatiques ou dramatico-musicales; les œuvres chorégraphiques et les pantomimes; les compositions musicales avec ou sans paroles; les œuvres cinématographiques, auxquelles sont assimilées les œuvres exprimées par un procédé analogue à la cinématographie; les œuvres de dessin, de peinture, d'architecture, de sculpture, de gravure, de lithographie; les œuvres

to which are assimilated works expressed by a process analogous to photography; works of applied art; illustrations, maps, plans, sketches and three-dimensional works relative to geography, topography, architecture or science.

(2) It shall, however, be a matter for legislation in the countries of the Union to prescribe that works in general or any specified categories of works shall not be protected unless they have been fixed in some material form.

(3) Translations, adaptations, arrangements of music and other alterations of a literary or artistic work shall be protected as original works without prejudice to the copyright in the original work.

(4) It shall be a matter for legislation in the countries of the Union to determine the protection to be granted to official texts of a legislative, administrative and legal nature, and to official translations of such texts.

(5) Collections of literary or artistic works such as encyclopaedias and anthologies which, by reason of the selection and arrangement of their contents, constitute intellectual creations shall be protected as such, without prejudice to the copyright in each of the works forming part of such collections.

(6) The works mentioned in this Article shall enjoy protection in all

photographiques, auxquelles sont assimilées les œuvres exprimées par un procédé analogue à la photographie; les œuvres des arts appliqués; les illustrations, les cartes géographiques; les plans, croquis et ouvrages plastiques relatifs à la géographie, à la topographie, à l'architecture ou aux sciences.

(2) Est toutefois réservée aux législations des pays de l'Union la faculté de prescrire que les œuvres littéraires et artistiques ou bien l'une ou plusieurs catégories d'entre elles ne sont pas protégées tant qu'elles n'ont pas été fixées sur un support matériel.

(3) Sont protégés comme des œuvres originales, sans préjudice des droits de l'auteur de l'œuvre originale, les traductions, adaptations, arrangements de musique et autres transformations d'une œuvre littéraire ou artistique.

(4) Il est réservé aux législations des pays de l'Union de déterminer la protection à accorder aux textes officiels d'ordre législatif, administratif ou judiciaire, ainsi qu'aux traductions officielles de ces textes.

(5) Les recueils d'œuvres littéraires ou artistiques tels que les encyclopédies et anthologies qui, par le choix ou la disposition des matières, constituent des créations intellectuelles sont protégés comme telles, sans préjudice des droits des auteurs sur chacune des œuvres qui font partie de ces recueils.

(6) Les œuvres mentionnées ci-dessus jouissent de la protection dans

of the Union. This protection shall operate for the benefit of the author and his successors in title.

(7) Subject to the provisions of Article 7(4) of this Convention, it shall be a matter for legislation in the countries of the Union to determine the extent of the application of their laws to works of applied art and industrial designs and models, as well as the conditions under which such works, designs and models shall be protected. Works protected in the country of origin solely as designs and models shall be entitled in another country of the Union only to such special protection as is granted in that country to designs and models; however, if no such special protection is granted in that country, such works shall be protected as artistic works.

(8) The protection of this Convention shall not apply to news of the day or to miscellaneous facts having the character of mere items of press information.

Article 2*bis*
Possible Limitation of Protection of Certain Works:

(1) It shall be a matter for legislation in the countries of the Union to exclude, wholly or in part, from the protection provided by the preceding Article political speeches and speeches delivered in the course of legal proceedings.

(2) It shall also be a matter for legislation in the countries of the Union to determine the conditions under which lectures, addresses

tous les pays de l'Union. Cette protection s'exerce au profit de l'auteur et de ses ayants droit.

(7) Il est réservé aux législations des pays de l'Union de régler le champ d'application des lois concernant les œuvres des arts appliqués et les dessins et modèles industriels, ainsi que les conditions de protection de ces œuvres, dessins et modèles, compte tenu des dispositions de l'article 7.4) de la présente Convention. Pour les œuvres protégées uniquement comme dessins et modèles dans le pays d'origine, il ne peut être réclamé dans un autre pays de l'Union que la protection spéciale accordée dans ce pays aux dessins et modèles; toutefois, si une telle protection spéciale n'est pas accordée dans ce pays, ces œuvres seront protégées comme œuvres artistiques.

(8) La protection de la présente Convention ne s'applique pas aux nouvelles du jour ou aux faits divers qui ont le caractère de simples informations de presse.

Article 2*bis*
Possibilité de limiter la protection de certaines œuvres:

(1) Est réservée aux législations des pays de l'Union la faculté d'exclure partiellement ou totalement de la protection prévue à l'article précédent les discours politiques et les discours prononcés dans les débats judiciaires.

(2) Est réservée également aux législations des pays de l'Union la faculté de statuer sur les conditions dans lesquelles les conférences, allocutions

and other works of the same nature which are delivered in public may be reproduced by the press, broadcast, communicated to the public by wire and made the subject of public communication as envisaged in Article 11bis(1) of this Convention, when such use is justified by the informatory purpose.

(3) Nevertheless, the author shall enjoy the exclusive right of making a collection of his works mentioned in the preceding paragraphs.

Article 3
Criteria of Eligibility for Protection:

(1) The protection of this Convention shall apply to:

(a) authors who are nationals of one of the countries of the Union, for their works, whether published or not;

(b) authors who are not nationals of one of the countries of the Union, for their works first published in one of those countries, or simultaneously in a country outside the Union and in a country of the Union.

(2) Authors who are not nationals of one of the countries of the Union but who have their habitual residence in one of them shall, for the purposes of this Convention, be assimilated to nationals of that country.

(3) The expression "published works" means works published with the consent of their authors, whatever may be the means of manufacture of the copies, provided

et autres œuvres de même nature, prononcées en public, pourront être reproduites par la presse, radiodiffusées, transmises par fil au public et faire l'objet des communications publiques visées à l'article 11bis.1) de la présente Convention, lorsqu'une telle utilisation est justifiée par le but d'information à atteindre.

(3) Toutefois, l'auteur jouit du droit exclusif de réunir en recueil ses œuvres mentionnées aux alinéas précédents.

Article 3
Critères pour la protection:

(1) Sont protégés en vertu de la présente Convention:

(a) les auteurs ressortissant à l'un des pays de l'Union, pour leurs œuvres, publiées ou non;

(b) les auteurs ne ressortissant pas à l'un des pays de l'Union, pour les œuvres qu'ils publient pour la première fois dans l'un de ces pays ou simultanément dans un pays étranger à l'Union et dans un pays de l'Union.

(2) Les auteurs ne ressortissant pas à l'un des pays de l'Union mais ayant leur résidence habituelle dans l'un de ceux-ci sont, pour l'application de la présente Convention, assimilés aux auteurs ressortissant audit pays.

(3) Par «œuvres publiées», il faut entendre les œuvres éditées avec le consentement de leurs auteurs, quel que soit le mode de fabrication des exemplaires, pourvu que la mise à

that the availability of such copies has been such as to satisfy the reasonable requirements of the public, having regard to the nature of the work. The performance of a dramatic, dramatico-musical, cinematographic or musical work, the public recitation of a literary work, the communication by wire or the broadcasting of literary or artistic works, the exhibition of a work of art and the construction of a work of architecture shall not constitute publication.

(4) A work shall be considered as having been published simultaneously in several countries if it has been published in two or more countries within thirty days of its first publication.

Article 4
Criteria of Eligibility for Protection of Cinematographic Works, Works of Architecture and Certain Artistic Works

The protection of this Convention shall apply, even if the conditions of Article 3 are not fulfilled, to:

(a) authors of cinematographic works the maker of which has his headquarters or habitual residence in one of the countries of the Union;

(b) authors of works of architecture erected in a country of the Union or of other artistic works incorporated in a building or other structure located in a country of the Union.

disposition de ces derniers ait été telle qu'elle satisfasse les besoins raisonnables du public, compte tenu de la nature de l'œuvre. Ne constituent pas une publication la représentation d'une œuvre dramatique, dramaticomusicale ou cinématographique, l'exécution d'une œuvre musicale, la récitation publique d'une œuvre littéraire, la transmission ou la radiodiffusion des œuvres littéraires ou artistiques, l'exposition d'une œuvre d'art et la construction d'une œuvre d'architecture.

(4) Est considérée comme publiée simultanément dans plusieurs pays toute œuvre qui a paru dans deux ou plusieurs pays dans les trente jours de sa première publication.

Article 4
Critères pour la protection des œuvres cinématographiques, des œuvres d'architecture et de certaines œuvres des arts graphiques et plastiques

Sont protégés en vertu de la présente Convention, même si les conditions prévues à l'article 3 ne sont pas remplies,

(a) les auteurs des œuvres cinématographiques dont le producteur a son siège ou sa résidence habituelle dans l'un des pays de l'Union;

(b) les auteurs des œuvres d'architecture édifiées dans un pays de l'Union ou des œuvres des arts graphiques et plastiques faisant corps avec un immeuble situé dans un pays de l'Union.

Article 5
Rights Guaranteed:

(1) Authors shall enjoy, in respect of works for which they are protected under this Convention, in countries of the Union other than the country of origin, the rights which their respective laws do now or may hereafter grant to their nationals, as well as the rights specially granted by this Convention.

(2) The enjoyment and the exercise of these rights shall not be subject to any formality; such enjoyment and such exercise shall be independent of the existence of protection in the country of origin of the work. Consequently, apart from the provisions of this Convention, the extent of protection, as well as the means of redress afforded to the author to protect his rights, shall be governed exclusively by the laws of the country where protection is claimed.

(3) Protection in the country of origin is governed by domestic law. However, when the author is not a national of the country of origin of the work for which he is protected under this Convention, he shall enjoy in that country the same rights as national authors.

(4) The country of origin shall be considered to be:

(a) in the case of works first published in a country of the Union, that country; in the case of works published simultaneously in several countries of the Union

Article 5
Droits garantis:

(1) Les auteurs jouissent, en ce qui concerne les œuvres pour lesquelles ils sont protégés en vertu de la présente Convention, dans les pays de l'Union autres que le pays d'origine de l'œuvre, des droits que les lois respectives accordent actuellement ou accorderont par la suite aux nationaux, ainsi que des droits spécialement accordés par la présente Convention.

(2) La jouissance et l'exercice de ces droits ne sont subordonnés à aucune formalité; cette jouissance et cet exercice sont indépendants de l'existence de la protection dans le pays d'origine de l'œuvre. Par suite, en dehors des stipulations de la présente Convention, l'étendue de la protection ainsi que les moyens de recours garantis à l'auteur pour sauvegarder ses droits se règlent exclusivement d'après la législation du pays où la protection est réclamée.

(3) La protection dans le pays d'origine est réglée par la législation nationale. Toutefois, lorsque l'auteur ne ressortit pas au pays d'origine de l'œuvre pour laquelle il est protégé par la présente Convention, il aura, dans ce pays, les mêmes droits que les auteurs nationaux.

(4) Est considéré comme pays d'origine:

(a) pour les œuvres publiées pour la première fois dans l'un des pays de l'Union, ce dernier pays; toutefois, s'il s'agit d'œuvres publiées simultanément dansplusieurs pays de

which grant different terms of protection, the country whose legislation grants the shortest term of protection;

(b) in the case of works published simultaneously in a country outside the Union and in a country of the Union, the latter country;

(c) in the case of unpublished works or of works first published in a country outside the Union, without simultaneous publication in a country of the Union, the country of the Union of which the author is a national, provided that:

(i) when these are cinematographic works the maker of which has his headquarters or his habitual residence in a country of the Union, the country of origin shall be that country, and

(ii) when these are works of architecture erected in a country of the Union or other artistic works incorporated in a building or other structure located in a country of the Union, the country of origin shall be that country.

Article 6
Possible Restriction of Protection in Respect of Certain Works of Nationals of Certain Countries Outside the Union:

(1) Where any country outside the Union fails to protect in an adequate manner the works of authors who are nationals of one of the countries of the Union, the latter country may restrict the protection

l'Union admettant des durées de protection différentes, celui d'entre eux dont la législation accorde la durée de protection la moins longue;

(b) pour les œuvres publiées simultanément dans un pays étranger à l'Union et dans un pays de l'Union, ce dernier pays;

(c) pour les œuvres non publiées ou pour les œuvres publiées pour la première fois dans un pays étranger à l'Union, sans publication simultanée dans un pays de l'Union, le pays de l'Union dont l'auteur est ressortissant; toutefois,

(i) s'il s'agit d'œuvres cinématographiques dont le producteur a son siège ou sa résidence habituelle dans un pays de l'Union, le pays d'origine sera ce dernier pays, et

(ii) s'il s'agit d'œuvres d'architecture édifiées dans un pays de l'Union ou d'œuvres des arts graphiques et plastiques faisant corps avec un immeuble situé dans un pays de l'Union, le pays d'origine sera ce dernier pays.

Article 6
Possibilité de restreindre la protection à l'égard de certaines œuvres des ressortissants de certaines œuvres des ressortissants, de certains pays étrangers à l'Union:

(1) Lorsqu'un pays étranger à l'Union ne protège pas d'une manière suffisante les œuvres des auteurs qui sont ressortissants de l'un des pays de l'Union, ce dernier pays pourra restreindre la protection des œuvres

given to the works of authors who are, at the date of the first publication thereof, nationals of the other country and are not habitually resident in one of the countries of the Union. If the country of first publication avails itself of this right, the other countries of the Union shall not be required to grant to works thus subjected to special treatment a wider protection than that granted to them in the country of first publication.

(2) No restrictions introduced by virtue of the preceding paragraph shall affect the rights which an author may have acquired in respect of a work published in a country of the Union before such restrictions were put into force.

(3) The countries of the Union which restrict the grant of copyright in accordance with this Article shall give notice thereof to the Director General of the World Intellectual Property Organization (hereinafter designated as "the Director General") by a written declaration specifying the countries in regard to which protection is restricted, and the restrictions to which rights of authors who are nationals of those countries are subjected. The Director General shall immediately communicate this declaration to all the countries of the Union.

Article 6bis
Moral Rights:

(1) Independently of the author's economic rights, and even after the transfer of the said rights, the

dont les auteurs sont, au moment de la première publication de ces œuvres, ressortissants de l'autre pays et n'ont pas leur résidence habituelle dans l'un des pays de l'Union. Si le pays de la première publication fait usage de cette faculté, les autres pays de l'Union ne seront pas tenus d'accorder aux œuvres ainsi soumises à un traitement spécial une protection plus large que celle qui leur est accordée dans le pays de la première publication.

(2) Aucune restriction, établie en vertu de l'alinéa précédent, ne devra porter préjudice aux droits qu'un auteur aura acquis sur une œuvre publiée dans un pays de l'Union avant la mise à exécution de cette restriction.

(3) Les pays de l'Union qui, en vertu du présent article, restreindront la protection des droits des auteurs, le notifieront au Directeur général de l'Organisation Mondiale de la Propriété Intellectuelle (ci-après désigné «le Directeur général») par une déclaration écrite, où seront indiqués les pays vis-à-vis desquels la protection est restreinte, de même que les restrictions auxquelles les droits des auteurs ressortissant à ces pays sont soumis. Le Directeur général communiquera aussitôt le fait à tous les pays de l'Union.

Article 6bis
Droits moraux:

(1) Indépendamment des droits patrimoniaux d'auteur, et même après la cession desdits droits, l'auteur

author shall have the right to claim authorship of the work and to object to any distortion, mutilation or other modification of, or other derogatory action in relation to, the said work, which would be prejudicial to his honor or reputation.
(2) The rights granted to the author in accordance with the preceding paragraph shall, after his death, be maintained, at least until the expiry of the economic rights, and shall be exercisable by the persons or institutions authorized by the legislation of the country where protection is claimed. However, those countries whose legislation, at the moment of their ratification of or accession to this Act, does not provide for the protection after the death of the author of all the rights set out in the preceding paragraph may provide that some of these rights may, after his death, cease to be maintained.
(3) The means of redress for safeguarding the rights granted by this Article shall be governed by the legislation of the country where protection is claimed.

Article 7
Term of Protection:

(1) The term of protection granted by this Convention shall be the life of the author and fifty years after his death.
(2) However, in the case of cinematographic works, the countries of the Union may provide that the term of protection shall expire fifty years after the work has been made

conserve le droit de revendiquer la paternité de l'œuvre et de s'opposer à toute déformation, mutilation ou autre modification de cette œuvre ou à toute autre atteinte à la même œuvre, préjudiciables à son honneur ou à sa réputation.
(2) Les droits reconnus à l'auteur en vertu de l'alinéa 1) ci-dessus sont, après sa mort, maintenus au moins jusqu'à l'extinction des droits patrimoniaux et exercés par les personnes ou institutions auxquelles la législation nationale du pays où la protection est réclamée donne qualité. Toutefois, les pays dont la législation, en vigueur au moment de la ratification du présent Acte ou de l'adhésion à celui-ci, ne contient pas de dispositions assurant la protection après la mort de l'auteur de tous les droits reconnus en vertu de l'alinéa 1) ci-dessus ont la faculté de prévoir que certains de ces droits ne sont pas maintenus après la mort de l'auteur.
(3) Les moyens de recours pour sauvegarder les droits reconnus dans le présent article sont réglés par la législation du pays où la protection est réclamée.

Article 7
Durée de la protection:

(1) La durée de la protection accordée par la présente Convention comprend la vie de l'auteur et cinquante ans après sa mort.
(2) Toutefois, pour les œuvres cinématographiques, les pays de l'Union ont la faculté de prévoir que la durée de la protection expire cinquante ans après que l'œuvre aura été rendue

available to the public with the consent of the author, or, failing such an event within fifty years from the making of such a work, fifty years after the making.

(3) In the case of anonymous or pseudonymous works, the term of protection granted by this Convention shall expire fifty years after the work has been lawfully made available to the public. However, when the pseudonym adopted by the author leaves no doubt as to his identity, the term of protection shall be that provided in paragraph (1). If the author of an anonymous or pseudonymous work discloses his identity during the above-mentioned period, the term of protection applicable shall be that provided in paragraph (1). The countries of the Union shall not be required to protect anonymous or pseudonymous works in respect of which it is reasonable to presume that their author has been dead for fifty years.

(4) It shall be a matter for legislation in the countries of the Union to determine the term of protection of photographic works and that of works of applied art in so far as they are protected as artistic works; however, this term shall last at least until the end of a period of twenty-five years from the making of such a work.

accessible au public avec le consentement de l'auteur, ou qu'à défaut d'un tel événement intervenu dans les cinquante ans à compter de la réalisation d'une telle œuvre, la durée de la protection expire cinquante ans après cette réalisation.

(3) Pour les œuvres anonymes ou pseudonymes, la durée de la protection accordée par la présente Convention expire cinquante ans après que l'œuvre a été licitement rendue accessible au public. Toutefois, quand le pseudonyme adopté par l'auteur ne laisse aucun doute sur son identité, la durée de la protection est celle prévue à l'alinéa 1). Si l'auteur d'une œuvre anonyme ou pseudonyme révèle son identité pendant la période ci-dessus indiquée, le délai de protection applicable est celui prévu à l'alinéa 1). Les pays de l'Union ne sont pas tenus de protéger les œuvres anonymes ou pseudonymes pour lesquelles il y a tout lieu de présumer que leur auteur est mort depuis cinquante ans.

(4) Est réservée aux législations des pays de l'Union la faculté de régler la durée de la protection des œuvres photographiques et celle des œuvres des arts appliqués protégées en tant qu'œuvres artistiques; toutefois, cette durée ne pourra être inférieure à une période de ving-cinq ans à compter de la réalisation d'une telle œuvre.

(5) The term of protection subsequent to the death of the author and the terms provided by paragraphs (2), (3) and (4) shall run from the date of death or of the event referred to in those paragraphs, but such terms shall always be deemed to begin on the first of January of the year following the death or such event.

(6) The countries of the Union may grant a term of protection in excess of those provided by the preceding paragraphs.

(7) Those countries of the Union bound by the Rome Act of this Convention which grant, in their national legislation in force at the time of signature of the present Act, shorter terms of protection than those provided for in the preceding paragraphs shall have the right to maintain such terms when ratifying or acceding to the present Act.

(8) In any case, the term shall be governed by the legislation of the country where protection is claimed; however, unless the legislation of that country otherwise provides, the term shall not exceed the term fixed in the country of origin of the work.

Article 7*bis*
Term of Protection for Works of Joint Authorship

The provisions of the preceding Article shall also apply in the case of a work of joint authorship, provided that the terms measured from the death of the author shall be calculated from the death of the last surviving author.

(5) Le délai de protection postérieur à la mort de l'auteur et les délais prévus aux alinéas 2), 3) et 4) cidessus commencent à courir à compter de la mort ou de l'événement visé par ces alinéas, mais la durée de ces délais n'est calculée qu'à partir du premier janvier de l'année qui suit la mort ou ledit événement.

(6) Les pays de l'Union ont la faculté d'accorder une durée de protection supérieure à celles prévues aux alinéas précédents.

(7) Les pays de l'Union liés par l'Acte de Rome de la présente Convention et qui accordent, dans leur législation nationale en vigueur au moment de la signature du présent Acte, des durées inférieures à celles prévues aux alinéas précédents ont la faculté de les maintenir en adhérant au présent Acte ou en le ratifiant.

(8) Dans tous les cas, la durée sera réglée par la loi du pays où la protection sera réclamée; toutefois, à moins que la législation de ce dernier pays n'en décide autrement, elle n'excédera pas la durée fixée dans le pays d'origine de l'œuvre.

Article 7*bis*
Durée de protection des œuvres de collaboration

Les dispositions de l'article précédent sont également applicables lorsque le droit d'auteur appartient en commun aux collaborateurs d'une œuvre, sous réserve que les délais consécutifs à la mort de l'auteur soient calculés à partir de la mort du dernier survivant des collaborateurs.

Article 8
Right of Translation

Authors of literary and artistic works protected by this Convention shall enjoy the exclusive right of making and of authorizing the translation of their works throughout the term of protection of their rights in the original works.

Article 9
Right of Reproduction:

(1) Authors of literary and artistic works protected by this Convention shall have the exclusive right of authorizing the reproduction of these works, in any manner or form.

(2) It shall be a matter for legislation in the countries of the Union to permit the reproduction of such works in certain special cases, provided that such reproduction does not conflict with a normal exploitation of the work and does not unreasonably prejudice the legitimate interests of the author.

(3) Any sound or visual recording shall be considered as a reproduction for the purposes of this Convention.

Article 10
Certain Free Uses of Works:

(1) It shall be permissible to make quotations from a work which has already been lawfully made available to the public, provided that their making is compatible with fair practice, and their extent does not exceed that justified by the

Article 8
Droit de traduction

Les auteurs d'œuvres littéraires et artistiques protégés par la présente Convention jouissent, pendant toute la durée de leurs droits sur l'œuvre originale, du droit exclusif de faire ou d'autoriser la traduction de leurs œuvres.

Article 9
Droit de reproduction:

(1) Les auteurs d'œuvres littéraires et artistiques protégés par la présente Convention jouissent du droit exclusif d'autoriser la reproduction de ces œuvres, de quelque manière et sous quelque forme que ce soit.

(2) Est réservée aux législations des pays de l'Union la faculté de permettre la reproduction desdites œuvres dans certains cas spéciaux, pourvu qu'une telle reproduction ne porte pas atteinte à l'exploitation normale de l'œuvre ni ne cause un préjudice injustifié aux intérêts légitimes de l'auteur.

(3) Tout enregistrement sonore ou visuel est considéré comme une reproduction au sens de la présente Convention.

Article 10
Libre utilisation des œuvres dans certains cas:

(1) Sont licites les citations tirées d'une œuvre, déjà rendue licitement accessible au public, à condition qu'elles soient conformes aux bons usages et dans la mesure justifiée par le but à atteindre, y compris les citations d'articles de journaux et recueils

purpose, including quotations from newspaper articles and periodicals in the form of press summaries.

(2) It shall be a matter for legislation in the countries of the Union, and for special agreements existing or to be concluded between them, to permit the utilization, to the extent justified by the purpose, of literary or artistic works by way of illustration in publications, broadcasts or sound or visual recordings for teaching, provided such utilization is compatible with fair practice.

(3) Where use is made of works in accordance with the preceding paragraphs of this Article, mention shall be made of the source, and of the name of the author if it appears thereon.

Article 10*bis*
Further Possible Free Uses of Works:

(1) It shall be a matter for legislation in the countries of the Union to permit the reproduction by the press, the broadcasting or the communication to the public by wire of articles published in newspapers or periodicals on current economic, political or religious topics, and of broadcast works of the same character, in cases in which the reproduction, broadcasting or such communication thereof is not expressly reserved. Nevertheless, the source must always be clearly indicated; the legal consequences of a breach of this obligation shall be

périodiques sous forme de revues de presse.

(2) Est réservé l'effet de la législation des pays de l'Union et des arrangements particuliers existants ou à conclure entre eux, en ce qui concerne la faculté d'utiliser licitement, dans la mesure justifiée par le but à atteindre, des œuvres littéraires ou artistiques à titre d'illustration de l'enseignement par le moyen de publications, d'émissions de radiodiffusion ou d'enregistrements sonores ou visuels, sous réserve qu'une telle utilisation soit conforme aux bons usages.

(3) Les citations et utilisations visées aux alinéas précédents devront faire mention de la source et du nom de l'auteur, si ce nom figure dans la source.

Article 10*bis*
Autres possibilités de libre utilisation des œuvres:

(1) Est réservée aux législations des pays de l'Union la faculté de permettre la reproduction par la presse, ou la radiodiffusion ou la transmission par fil au public, des articles d'actualité de discussion économique, politique ou religieuse, publiés dans des journaux ou recueils périodiques, ou des œuvres radiodiffusées ayant le même caractère, dans les cas où la reproduction, la radiodiffusion ou ladite transmission n'en est pas expressément réservée. Toutefois, la source doit toujours être clairement indiquée; la sanction de cette obligation est déterminée

determined by the legislation of the country where protection is claimed. (2) It shall also be a matter for legislation in the countries of the Union to determine the conditions under which, for the purpose of reporting current events by means of photography, cinematography, broadcasting or communication to the public by wire, literary or artistic works seen or heard in the course of the event may, to the extent justified by the informatory purpose, be reproduced and made available to the public.

Article 11
Certain Rights in Dramatic and Musical Works:

(1) Authors of dramatic, dramatico-musical and musical works shall enjoy the exclusive right of authorizing:

(i) the public performance of their works, including such public performance by any means or process;

(ii) any communication to the public of the performance of their works.

(2) Authors of dramatic or dramatico-musical works shall enjoy, during the full term of their rights in the original works, the same rights with respect to translations thereof.

Article 11*bis*
Broadcasting and Related Rights:

(1) Authors of literary and artistic works shall enjoy the exclusive right of authorizing:

---

par la législation du pays où la protection est réclamée. (2) Il est également réservé aux législations des pays de l'Union de régler les conditions dans lesquelles, à l'occasion de comptes rendus des événements d'actualité par le moyen de la photographie ou de la cinématographie, ou par voie de radiodiffusion ou de transmission par fil au public, les œuvres littéraires ou artistiques vues ou entendues au cours de l'événement peuvent, dans la mesure justifiée par le but d'information à atteindre, être reproduites et rendues accessibles au public.

Article 11
Certains droits afférents aux œuvres dramatiques et musicales:

(1) Les auteurs d'œuvres dramatiques, dramatico-musicales et musicales jouissent du droit exclusif d'autoriser:

(i) la représentation et l'exécution publiques de leurs œuvres, y compris la représentation et l'exécution publiques par tous moyens ou procédés;

(ii) la transmission publique par tous moyens de la représentation et de l'exécution de leurs œuvres.

(2) Les mêmes droits sont accordés aux auteurs d'œuvres dramatiques ou dramatico-musicales pendant toute la durée de leurs droits sur l'œuvre originale, en ce qui concerne la traduction de leurs œuvres.

Article 11*bis*
Droits de radiodiffusion et droits connexes:

(1) Les auteurs d'œuvres littéraires et artistiques jouissent du droit exclusif d'autoriser:

(i) the broadcasting of their works or the communication thereof to the public by any other means of wireless diffusion of signs, sounds or images;

(ii) any communication to the public by wire or by rebroadcasting of the broadcast of the work, when this communication is made by an organization other than the original one;

(iii) the public communication by loudspeaker or any other analogous instrument transmitting, by signs, sounds or images, the broadcast of the work.

(2) It shall be a matter for legislation in the countries of the Union to determine the conditions under which the rights mentioned in the preceding paragraph may be exercised, but these conditions shall apply only in the countries where they have been prescribed. They shall not in any circumstances be prejudicial to the moral rights of the author, nor to his right to obtain equitable remuneration which, in the absence of agreement, shall be fixed by competent authority.

(3) In the absence of any contrary stipulation, permission granted in accordance with paragraph (1) of this Article shall not imply permission to record, by means of instruments recording sounds or images, the work broadcast. It shall, however, be a matter for legislation in the countries of the Union to determine the regulations

(i) la radiodiffusion de leurs œuvres ou la communication publique de ces œuvres par tout autre moyen servant à diffuser sans fil les signes, les sons ou les images;

(ii) toute communication publique, soit par fil, soit sans fil, de l'œuvre radiodiffusée, lorsque cette communication est faite par un autre organisme que celui d'origine;

(iii) la communication publique, par haut-parleur ou par tout autre instrument analogue transmetteur de signes, de sons ou d'images, de l'œuvre radiodiffusée.

(2) Il appartient aux législations des pays de l'Union de régler les conditions d'exercice des droits visés par l'alinéa 1) ci-dessus, mais ces conditions n'auront qu'un effet strictement limité au pays qui les aurait établies. Elles ne pourront en aucun cas porter atteinte au droit moral de l'auteur, ni au droit qui appartient à l'auteur d'obtenir une rémunération équitable fixée, à défaut d'accord amiable, par l'autorité compétente.

(3) Sauf stipulation contraire, une autorisation accordée conformément à l'alinéa 1) du présent article n'implique pas l'autorisation d'enregistrer, au moyen d'instruments portant fixation des sons ou des images, l'œuvre radiodiffusée. Est toutefois réservé aux législations des pays de l'Union le régime des enregistrements éphémères effectués

for ephemeral recordings made by a broadcasting organization by means of its own facilities and used for its own broadcasts. The preservation of these recordings in official archives may, on the ground of their exceptional documentary character, be authorized by such legislation.

Article 11*ter*
Certain Rights in Literary Works:

(1) Authors of literary works shall enjoy the exclusive right of authorizing:

(i) the public recitation of their works, including such public recitation by any means or process;

(ii) any communication to the public of the recitation of their works.

(2) Authors of literary works shall enjoy, during the full term of their rights in the original works, the same rights with respect to translations thereof.

Article 12
Right of Adaptation, Arrangement and Other Alteration

Authors of literary or artistic works shall enjoy the exclusive right of authorizing adaptations, arrangements and other alterations of their works.

Article 13
Possible Limitation of the Right of Recording of Musical Works and Any Words Pertaining Thereto:

(1) Each country of the Union may impose for itself reservations

par un organisme de radiodiffusion par ses propres moyens et pour ses émissions. Ces législations pourront autoriser la conservation de ces enregistrements dans des archives officielles en raison de leur caractère exceptionnel de documentation.

Article 11*ter*
Certains droits afférents aux œuvres littéraires:

(1) Les auteurs d'œuvres littéraires jouissent du droit exclusif d'autoriser:

(i) la récitation publique de leurs œuvres, y compris la récitation publique par tous moyens ou procédés;

(ii) la transmission publique par tous moyens de la récitation de leurs œuvres.

(2) Les mêmes droits sont accordés aux auteurs d'œuvres littéraires pendant toute la durée de leurs droits sur l'œuvre originale, en ce qui concerne la traduction de leurs œuvres.

Article 12
Droit d'adaptation, d'arrangement et d'autres transformations

Les auteurs d'œuvres littéraires ou artistiques jouissent du droit exclusif d'autoriser les adaptations, arrangements et autres transformations de leurs œuvres.

Article 13
Possibilité de limiter le droit d'enregistrement des œuvres musicales et de toutes paroles qui les accompagnent:

(1) Chaque pays de l'Union peut, pour ce qui le concerne, établir des

and conditions on the exclusive right granted to the author of a musical work and to the author of any words, the recording of which together with the musical work has already been authorized by the latter, to authorize the sound recording of that musical work, together with such words, if any; but all such reservations and conditions shall apply only in the countries which have imposed them and shall not, in any circumstances, be prejudicial to the rights of these authors to obtain equitable remuneration which, in the absence of agreement, shall be fixed by competent authority.

(2) Recordings of musical works made in a country of the Union in accordance with Article 13(3) of the Conventions signed at Rome on June 2, 1928, and at Brussels on June 26, 1948, may be reproduced in that country without the permission of the author of the musical work until a date two years after that country becomes bound by this Act.

(3) Recordings made in accordance with paragraphs (1) and (2) of this Article and imported without permission from the parties concerned into a country where they are treated as infringing recordings shall be liable to seizure.

réserves et conditions relatives au droit exclusif de l'auteur d'une œuvre musicale et de l'auteur des paroles, dont l'enregistrement avec l'œuvre musicale a déjà été autorisé par ce dernier, d'autoriser l'enregistrement sonore de ladite œuvre musicale, avec, le cas échéant, les paroles; mais toutes réserves et conditions de cette nature n'auront qu'un effet strictement limité au pays qui les aurait établies et ne pourront en aucun cas porter atteinte au droit qui appartient à l'auteur d'obtenir une rémunération équitable fixée, à défaut d'accord amiable, par l'autorité compétente.

(2) Les enregistrements d'œuvres musicales qui auront été réalisés dans un pays de l'Union conformément à l'article 13.3) des Conventions signées à Rome le 2 juin 1928 et à Bruxelles le 26 juin 1948 pourront, dans ce pays, faire l'objet de reproductions sans le consentement de l'auteur de l'œuvre musicale jusqu'à l'expiration d'une période de deux années à partir de la date à laquelle ledit pays devient lié par le présent Acte.

(3) Les enregistrements faits en vertu des alinéas 1) et 2) du présent article et importés, sans autorisation des parties intéressées, dans un pays où ils ne seraient pas licites, pourront y être saisis.

Article 14
Cinematographic and Related Rights:

(1) Authors of literary or artistic works shall have the exclusive right of authorizing:

(i) the cinematographic adaptation and reproduction of these works, and the distribution of the works thus adapted or reproduced;

(ii) the public performance and communication to the public by wire of the works thus adapted or reproduced.

(2) The adaptation into any other artistic form of a cinematographic production derived from literary or artistic works shall, without prejudice to the authorization of the author of the cinematographic production, remain subject to the authorization of the authors of the original works.

(3) The provisions of Article 13(1) shall not apply.

Article 14*bis*
Special Provisions Concerning Cinematographic Works:

(1) Without prejudice to the copyright in any work which may have been adapted or reproduced, a cinematographic work shall be protected as an original work. The owner of copyright in a cinematographic work shall enjoy the same rights as the author of an original work, including the rights referred to in the preceding Article.

Article 14
Droits cinématographiques et droits connexes:

(1) Les auteurs d'œuvres littéraires ou artistiques ont le droit exclusif d'autoriser:

(i) l'adaptation et la reproduction cinématographiques de ces œuvres et la mise en circulation des œuvres ainsi adaptées ou reproduites;

(ii) la représentation et l'exécution publiques et la transmission par fil au public des œuvres ainsi adaptées ou reproduites.

(2) L'adaptation sous toute autre forme artistique des réalisations cinématographiques tirées d'œuvres littéraires ou artistiques reste soumise, sans préjudice de l'autorisation de leurs auteurs, à l'autorisation des auteurs des œuvres originales.

(3) Les dispositions de l'article 13.1) ne sont pas applicables.

Article 14*bis*
Dispositions particulières concernant les œuvres cinématographiques:

(1) Sans préjudice des droits de l'auteur de toute œuvre qui pourrait avoir été adaptée ou reproduite, l'œuvre cinématographique est protégée comme une œuvre originale. Le titulaire du droit d'auteur sur l'œuvre cinématographique jouit des mêmes droits que l'auteur d'une œuvre originale, y compris les droits visés à l'article précédent.

(2)

(a) Ownership of copyright in a cinematographic work shall be a matter for legislation in the country where protection is claimed.

(b) However, in the countries of the Union which, by legislation, include among the owners of copyright in a cinematographic work authors who have brought contributions to the making of the work, such authors, if they have undertaken to bring such contributions, may not, in the absence of any contrary or special stipulation, object to the reproduction, distribution, public performance, communication to the public by wire, broadcasting or any other communication to the public, or to the subtitling or dubbing of texts, of the work.

(c) The question whether or not the form of the undertaking referred to above should, for the application of the preceding subparagraph (b), be in a written agreement or a written act of the same effect shall be a matter for the legislation of the country where the maker of the cinematographic work has his headquarters or habitual residence. However, it shall be a matter for the legislation of the country of the Union where protection is claimed to provide that the said undertaking shall be in a written agreement or a written act of the same effect. The countries whose legislation so provides

(2)

(a) La détermination des titulaires du droit d'auteur sur l'œuvre cinématographique est réservée à la législation du pays où la protection est réclamée.

(b) Toutefois, dans les pays de l'Union où la législation reconnaît parmi ces titulaires les auteurs des contributions apportées à la réalisation de l'œuvre cinématographique, ceux-ci, s'ils se sont engagés à apporter de telles contributions, ne pourront, sauf stipulation contraire ou particulière, s'opposer à la reproduction, la mise en circulation, la représentation et l'exécution publiques, la transmission par fil au public, la radiodiffusion, la communication au public, le sous-titrage et le doublage des textes, de l'œuvre cinématographique.

(c) La question de savoir si la forme de l'engagement visé ci-dessus doit, pour l'application du sous-alinéa b) précédent, être ou non un contrat écrit ou un acte écrit équivalent est réglée par la législation du pays de l'Union où le producteur de l'œuvre cinématographique a son siège ou sa résidence habituelle. Est toutefois réservée à la législation du pays de l'Union où la protection est réclamée la faculté de prévoir que cet engagement doit être un contrat écrit ou un acte écrit équivalent. Les pays qui font usage de cette faculté devront le notifier au Directeur général par une déclaration écrite qui sera aussitôt communiquée par

shall notify the Director General by means of a written declaration, which will be immediately communicated by him to all the other countries of the Union.

(d) By "contrary or special stipulation" is meant any restrictive condition which is relevant to the aforesaid undertaking.

(3) Unless the national legislation provides to the contrary, the provisions of paragraph (2)(b) above shall not be applicable to authors of scenarios, dialogues and musical works created for the making of the cinematographic work, or to the principal director thereof. However, those countries of the Union whose legislation does not contain rules providing for the application of the said paragraph (2)(b) to such director shall notify the Director General by means of a written declaration, which will be immediately communicated by him to all the other countries of the Union.

Article 14*ter*
"Droit de suite" in Works of Art and Manuscripts:

(1) The author, or after his death the persons or institutions authorized by national legislation, shall, with respect to original works of art and original manuscripts of writers and composers, enjoy the inalienable right to an interest in any sale of the work subsequent to the first transfer by the author of the work.

(2) The protection provided by the preceding paragraph may be claimed in a country of the Union

ce dernier à tous les autres pays de l'Union.

(d) Par «stipulation contraire ou particulière», il faut entendre toute condition restrictive dont peut être assorti ledit engagement.

(3) À moins que la législation nationale n'en décide autrement, les dispositions de l'alinéa 2)b) ci-dessus ne sont applicables ni aux auteurs des scénarios, des dialogues et des œuvres musicales, créés pour la réalisation de l'œuvre cinématographique, ni au réalisateur principal de celle-ci. Toutefois, les pays de l'Union dont la législation ne contient pas des dispositions prévoyant l'application de l'alinéa 2) b) précité audit réalisateur devront le notifier au Directeur général par une déclaration écrite qui sera aussitôt communiquée par ce dernier à tous les autres pays de l'Union.

Article 14*ter*
«Droit de suite» sur les œuvres d'art et les manuscrits:

(1) En ce qui concerne les œuvres d'art originales et les manuscrits originaux des écrivains et compositeurs, l'auteur — ou, après sa mort, les personnes ou institutions auxquelles la législation nationale donne qualité — jouit d'un droit inaliénable à être intéressé aux opérations de vente dont l'œuvre est l'objet après la première cession opérée par l'auteur.

(2) La protection prévue à l'alinéa ci-dessus n'est exigible dans chaque pays de l'Union que si la législation

only if legislation in the country to which the author belongs so permits, and to the extent permitted by the country where this protection is claimed.

(3) The procedure for collection and the amounts shall be matters for determination by national legislation.

Article 15
Right to Enforce Protected Rights:

(1) In order that the author of a literary or artistic work protected by this Convention shall, in the absence of proof to the contrary, be regarded as such, and consequently be entitled to institute infringement proceedings in the countries of the Union, it shall be sufficient for his name to appear on the work in the usual manner. This paragraph shall be applicable even if this name is a pseudonym, where the pseudonym adopted by the author leaves no doubt as to his identity.

(2) The person or body corporate whose name appears on a cinematographic work in the usual manner shall, in the absence of proof to the contrary, be presumed to be the maker of the said work.

(3) In the case of anonymous and pseudonymous works, other than those referred to in paragraph (1) above, the publisher whose name appears on the work shall, in the absence of proof to the contrary, be deemed to represent the author, and in this capacity he shall be entitled to protect and enforce the author's rights.

nationale de l'auteur admet cette protection et dans la mesure où le permet la législation du pays où cette protection est réclamée.

(3) Les modalités et les taux de la perception sont déterminés par chaque législation nationale.

Article 15
Droit de faire valoir les droits protégés:

(1) Pour que les auteurs des œuvres littéraires et artistiques protégés par la présente Convention soient, sauf preuve contraire, considérés comme tels et admis en conséquence devant les tribunaux des pays de l'Union à exercer des poursuites contre les contrefacteurs, il suffit que le nom soit indiqué sur l'œuvre en la manière usitée. Le présent alinéa est applicable, même si ce nom est un pseudonyme, dès lors que le pseudonyme adopté par l'auteur ne laisse aucun doute sur son identité.

(2) Est présumé producteur de l'œuvre cinématographique, sauf preuve contraire, la personne physique ou morale dont le nom est indiqué sur ladite œuvre en la manière usitée.

(3) Pour les œuvres anonymes et pour les œuvres pseudonymes autres que celles dont il est fait mention à l'alinéa 1) ci-dessus, l'éditeur dont le nom est indiqué sur l'œuvre est, sans autre preuve, réputé représenter l'auteur; en cette qualité, il est fondé à sauvegarder et à faire valoir les droits de celui-ci. La disposition du présent

The provisions of this paragraph shall cease to apply when the author reveals his identity and establishes his claim to authorship of the work.

(4)

(a) In the case of unpublished works where the identity of the author is unknown, but where there is every ground to presume that he is a national of a country of the Union, it shall be a matter for legislation in that country to designate the competent authority which shall represent the author and shall be entitled to protect and enforce his rights in the countries of the Union.

(b) Countries of the Union which make such designation under the terms of this provision shall notify the Director General by means of a written declaration giving full information concerning the authority thus designated. The Director General shall at once communicate this declaration to all other countries of the Union.

Article 16
Infringing Copies:

(1) Infringing copies of a work shall be liable to seizure in any country of the Union where the work enjoys legal protection.

(2) The provisions of the preceding paragraph shall also apply to reproductions coming from a country where the work is not protected, or has ceased to be protected.

(3) The seizure shall take place in accordance with the legislation of each country.

alinéa cesse d'être applicable quand l'auteur a révélé son identité et justifié de sa qualité.

(4)

(a) Pour les œuvres non publiées dont l'identité de l'auteur est inconnue, mais pour lesquelles il y a tout lieu de présumer que cet auteur est ressortissant d'un pays de l'Union, il est réservé à la législation de ce pays la faculté de désigner l'autorité compétente représentant cet auteur et fondée à sauvegarder et à faire valoir les droits de celui-ci dans les pays de l'Union.

(b) Les pays de l'Union qui, en vertu de cette disposition, procéderont à une telle désignation, le notifieront au Directeur général par une déclaration écrite où seront indiqués tous renseignements relatifs à l'autorité ainsi désignée. Le Directeur général communiquera aussitôt cette déclaration à tous les autres pays de l'Union.

Article 16
Œuvres contrefaites:

(1) Toute œuvre contrefaite peut être saisie dans les pays de l'Union où l'œuvre originale a droit à la protection légale.

(2) Les dispositions de l'alinéa précédent sont également applicables aux reproductions provenant d'un pays où l'œuvre n'est pas protégée ou a cessé de l'être.

(3) La saisie a lieu conformément à la législation de chaque pays.

Article 17
Possibility of Control of Circulation, Presentation and Exhibition of Works

The provisions of this Convention cannot in any way affect the right of the Government of each country of the Union to permit, to control, or to prohibit, by legislation or regulation, the circulation, presentation, or exhibition of any work or production in regard to which the competent authority may find it necessary to exercise that right.

Article 18
Works Existing on Convention's Entry Into Force:

(1) This Convention shall apply to all works which, at the moment of its coming into force, have not yet fallen into the public domain in the country of origin through the expiry of the term of protection.

(2) If, however, through the expiry of the term of protection which was previously granted, a work has fallen into the public domain of the country where protection is claimed, that work shall not be protected anew.

(3) The application of this principle shall be subject to any provisions contained in special conventions to that effect existing or to be concluded between countries of the Union. In the absence of such provisions, the respective countries

Article 17
Possibilité de surveiller la circulation, la représentation et l'exposition d'œuvres

Les dispositions de la présente Convention ne peuvent porter préjudice, en quoi que ce soit, au droit qui appartient au Gouvernement de chacun des pays de l'Union de permettre, de surveiller ou d'interdire, par des mesures de législation ou de police intérieure, la circulation, la représentation, l'exposition de tout ouvrage ou production à l'égard desquels l'autorité compétente aurait à exercer ce droit.

Article 18
Œuvres qui existent au moment de l'entrée en vigueur de la Convention:

(1) La présente Convention s'applique à toutes les œuvres qui, au moment de son entrée en vigueur, ne sont pas encore tombées dans le domaine public de leur pays d'origine par l'expiration de la durée de la protection.

(2) Cependant, si une œuvre, par l'expiration de la durée de la protection qui lui était antérieurement reconnue, est tombée dans le domaine public du pays où la protection est réclamée, cette œuvre n'y sera pas protégée à nouveau.

(3) L'application de ce principe aura lieu conformément aux stipulations contenues dans les conventions spéciales existantes ou à conclure à cet effet entre pays de l'Union. À défaut de semblables stipulations, les pays respectifs régleront, chacun pour ce

shall determine, each in so far as it is concerned, the conditions of application of this principle.

(4) The preceding provisions shall also apply in the case of new accessions to the Union and to cases in which protection is extended by the application of Article 7 or by the abandonment of reservations.

Article 19
Protection Greater than Resulting from Convention

The provisions of this Convention shall not preclude the making of a claim to the benefit of any greater protection which may be granted by legislation in a country of the Union.

Article 20
Special Agreements Among Countries of the Union

The Governments of the countries of the Union reserve the right to enter into special agreements among themselves, in so far as such agreements grant to authors more extensive rights than those granted by the Convention, or contain other provisions not contrary to this Convention. The provisions of existing agreements which satisfy these conditions shall remain applicable.

. . .

Article 37
Final Clauses:

(1)

(a) This Act shall be signed in a single copy in the French and English languages and, subject to paragraph (2), shall be deposited with the Director General.

qui le concerne, les modalités relatives à cette application.

(4) Les dispositions qui précèdent s'appliquent également en cas de nouvelles accessions à l'Union et dans le cas où la protection serait étendue par application de l'article 7 ou par abandon de réserves.

Article 19
Protection plus large que celle qui découle de la Convention

Les dispositions de la présente Convention n'empêchent pas de revendiquer l'application de dispositions plus larges qui seraient édictées par la législation d'un pays de l'Union.

Article 20
Arrangements particuliers entre pays de l'Union

Les Gouvernements des pays de l'Union se réservent le droit de prendre entre eux des arrangements particuliers, en tant que ces arrangements conféreraient aux auteurs des droits plus étendus que ceux accordés par la Convention, ou qu'ils renfermeraient d'autres stipulations non contraires à la présente Convention. Les dispositions des arrangements existants qui répondent aux conditions précitées restent applicables.

. . .

Article 37
Clauses finales:

(1)

(a) Le présent Acte est signé en un seul exeplaire dans les langues anglaise et française et, sous réserve de l'alinéa 2), est déposé auprès du Directeur général.

(b) Official texts shall be established by the Director General, after consultation with the interested Governments, in the Arabic, German, Italian, Portuguese and Spanish languages, and such other languages as the Assembly may designate.

(c) In case of differences of opinion on the interpretation of the various texts, the French text shall prevail.

(2) This Act shall remain open for signature until January 31, 1972. Until that date, the copy referred to in paragraph (1)(a) shall be deposited with the Government of the French Republic.

(3) The Director General shall certify and transmit two copies of the signed text of this Act to the Governments of all countries of the Union and, on request, to the Government of any other country.

(4) The Director General shall register this Act with the Secretariat of the United Nations.

(5) The Director General shall notify the Governments of all countries of the Union of signatures, deposits of instruments of ratification or accession and any declarations included in such instruments or made pursuant to Articles 28(1)(c), 30(2)(a) and (b), and 33(2), entry into force of any provisions of this Act, notifications of denunciation, and notifications pursuant to Articles 30(2)(c), 31(1) and (2), 33(3), and 38(1), as well as the Appendix.

(b) Des textes officiels sont établis par le Directeur général, après consultation des Gouvernements intéressés, dans les langues allemande, arabe, espagnole, italienne et portugaise, et dans les autres langues que l'Assemblée pourra indiquer.

(c) En cas de contestation sur l'interprétation des divers textes, le texte français fera foi.

(2) Le présent Acte reste ouvert à la signature jusqu'au 31 janvier 1972. Jusqu'à cette date, l'exemplaire visé à l'alinéa 1)a) sera déposé auprès du Gouvernement de la République française.

(3) Le Directeur général transmet deux copies certifiées conformes du texte signé du présent Acte aux Gouvernements de tous les pays de l'Union et, sur demande, au Gouvernement de tout autre pays.

(4) Le Directeur général fait enregistrer le présent Acte auprès du Secrétariat de l'Organisation des Nations Unies.

(5) Le Directeur général notifie aux Gouvernements de tous les pays de l'Union les signatures, les dépôts d'instruments de ratification ou d'adhésion et de déclarations comprises dans ces instruments ou faites en application des articles 28.1)c), 30.2)a) et b) et 33.2), l'entrée en vigueur de toutes dispositions du présent Acte, les notifications de dénonciation et les notifications faites en application des articles 30.2)c), 31.1) et 2), 33.3) et 38.1), ainsi que les notifications visées dans l'Annexe.

Rome Convention

Articles 1–16
International Convention for the Protection of Performers, Producers of Phonograms and Broadcasting Organizations

Article 1
Safeguard of Copyright Proper

Protection granted under this Convention shall leave intact and shall in no way affect the protection of copyright in literary and artistic works. Consequently, no provision of this Convention may be interpreted as prejudicing such protection.

Article 2
Protection given by the Convention. Definition of National Treatment

1. For the purposes of this Convention, national treatment shall mean the treatment accorded by the domestic law of the Contracting State in which protection is claimed:

(a) to performers who are its nationals, as regards performances taking place, broadcast, or first fixed, on its territory;

(b) to producers of phonograms who are its nationals, as regards phonograms first fixed or first published on its territory;

(c) to broadcasting organisations which have their headquarters on its territory, as regards broadcasts transmitted from transmitters situated on its territory.

2. National treatment shall be subject to the protection specifically guaranteed, and the limitations specifically provided for, in this Convention.

Article 3
Definitions

For the purposes of this Convention:

(a) "performers" means actors, singers, musicians, dancers, and other persons who act, sing, deliver, declaim, play in, or otherwise perform literary or artistic works;

(b) "phonogram" means any exclusively aural fixation of sounds of a performance or of other sounds;

(c) "producer of phonograms" means the person who, or the legal entity which, first fixes the sounds of a performance or other sounds;

(d) "publication" means the offering of copies of a phonogram to the public in reasonable quantity;

(e) "reproduction" means the making of a copy or copies of a fixation;

(f) "broadcasting" means the transmission by wireless means for public reception of sounds or of images and sounds;

(g) "rebroadcasting" means the simultaneous broadcasting by one broadcasting organisation of the broadcast of another broadcasting organisation.

Article 4
Performances Protected

Each Contracting State shall grant national treatment to performers if any of the following conditions is met:

(a) the performance takes place in another Contracting State;

(b) the performance is incorporated in a phonogram which is protected under Article 5 of this Convention;

(c) the performance, not being fixed on a phonogram, is carried by a broadcast which is protected by Article 6 of this Convention.

Article 5
Protected Phonograms

1. Each Contracting State shall grant national treatment to producers of phonograms if any of the following conditions is met:

(a) the producer of the phonogram is a national of another Contracting State (criterion of nationality);

(b) the first fixation of the sound was made in another Contracting State (criterion of fixation);

(c) the phonogram was first published in another Contracting State (criterion of publication).

2. If a phonogram was first published in a non–contracting State but if it was also published, within thirty days of its first publication, in a Contracting State (simultaneous publication), it shall be considered as first published in the Contracting State.

3. By means of a notification deposited with the Secretary–General of the United Nations, any Contracting State may declare that it will not apply the criterion of publication or, alternatively, the criterion of fixation. Such notification may be deposited at the time of ratification, acceptance or accession, or at any time thereafter; in the last case, it shall become effective six months after it has been deposited.

Article 6
Protected Broadcasts

1. Each Contracting State shall grant national treatment to broadcasting organisations if either of the following conditions is met:

(a) the headquarters of the broadcasting organisation is situated in another Contracting State;

(b) the broadcast was transmitted from a transmitter situated in another Contracting State.

2. By means of a notification deposited with the Secretary–General of the United Nations, any Contracting State may declare that it will protect broadcasts only if the headquarters of the broadcasting organisation is situated in another Contracting State and the broadcast was transmitted from a transmitter situated in the same Contracting State. Such notification may be deposited at the time of ratification, acceptance or accession, or at any time thereafter; in the last case, it shall become effective six months after it has been deposited.

Article 7
Minimum Protection for Performers

1. The protection provided for performers by this Convention shall include the possibility of preventing:

(a) the broadcasting and the communication to the public, without their consent, of their performance, except where the performance used in the broadcasting or the public communication is itself already a broadcast performance or is made from a fixation;

(b) the fixation, without their consent, of their unfixed performance;

(c) the reproduction, without their consent, of a fixation of their performance:

(i) if the original fixation itself was made without their consent;

(ii) if the reproduction is made for purposes different from those for which the performers gave their consent;

(iii) if the original fixation was made in accordance with the provisions of Article 15, and the reproduction is made for purposes different from those referred to in those provisions.

2.

(1) If broadcasting was consented to by the performers, it shall be a matter for the domestic law of the Contracting State where protection is claimed to regulate the protection against rebroadcasting, fixation for broadcasting purposes and the reproduction of such fixation for broadcasting purposes.

(2) The terms and conditions governing the use by broadcasting organisations of fixations made for broadcasting purposes shall be determined in accordance with the domestic law of the Contracting State where protection is claimed.

(3) However, the domestic law referred to in sub–paragraphs (1) and (2) of this paragraph shall not operate to deprive performers of the ability to control, by contract, their relations with broadcasting organisations.

Article 8
Performers acting jointly

Any Contracting State may, by its domestic laws and regulations, specify the manner in which performers will be represented in connection with the exercise of their rights if several of them participate in the same performance.

Article 9
Variety and Circus Artists

Any Contracting State may, by its domestic laws and regulations, extend the protection provided for in this Convention to artists who do not perform literary or artistic works.

Article 10
Right of Reproduction for Phonogram Producers

Producers of phonograms shall enjoy the right to authorize or prohibit the direct or indirect reproduction of their phonograms.

Article 11
Formalities for Phonograms

If, as a condition of protecting the rights of producers of phonograms, or of performers, or both, in relation to phonograms, a Contracting State, under its domestic law, requires compliance with formalities, these shall be considered as fulfilled if all the copies in commerce of the published phonogram or their containers bear a notice consisting of the symbol (P), accompanied by the year date of the first publication, placed in such a manner as to give reasonable notice of claim of protection; and if the copies or their containers do not identify the producer or the licensee of the producer (by carrying his name, trade mark or other appropriate designation), the notice shall also include the name of the owner of the rights of the producer; and, furthermore, if the copies or their containers do not identify the principal performers, the notice shall also include the name of the person who, in the country in which the fixation was effected, owns the rights of such performers.

Article 12
Secondary Uses of Phonograms

If a phonogram published for commercial purposes, or a reproduction of such phonogram, is used directly for broadcasting or for any communication to the public, a single equitable remuneration shall be paid by the user to the performers, or to the producers of the phonograms, or to both. Domestic law may, in the absence of agreement between these parties, lay down the conditions as to the sharing of this remuneration.

Article 13
Minimum Rights for Broadcasting Organizations

Broadcasting organisations shall enjoy the right to authorize or prohibit:

(a) the rebroadcasting of their broadcasts;

(b) the fixation of their broadcasts;

(c) the reproduction:

(i) of fixations, made without their consent, of their broadcasts;

(ii) of fixations, made in accordance with the provisions of Article 15, of their broadcasts, if the reproduction is made for purposes different from those referred to in those provisions;

(d) the communication to the public of their television broadcasts if such communication is made in places accessible to the public against payment of an entrance fee; it shall be a matter for the domestic law of the State where protection of this right is claimed to determine the conditions under which it may be exercised.

Article 14
Minimum Duration of Protection

The term of protection to be granted under this Convention shall last at least until the end of a period of twenty years computed from the end of the year in which:

(a) the fixation was made–for phonograms and for performances incorporated therein;

(b) the performance took place–for performances not incorporated in phonograms;

(c) the broadcast took place–for broadcasts.

Article 15
Permitted Exceptions

1. Any Contracting State may, in its domestic laws and regulations, provide for exceptions to the protection guaranteed by this Convention as regards:

(a) private use;

(b) use of short excerpts in connection with the reporting of current events;

(c) ephemeral fixation by a broadcasting organisation by means of its own facilities and for its own broadcasts;

(d) use solely for the purposes of teaching or scientific research.

2. Irrespective of paragraph 1 of this Article, any Contracting State may, in its domestic laws and regulations, provide for the same kinds of limitations with regard to the protection of performers, producers of phonograms and broadcasting organisations, as it provides for, in its domestic laws and regulations, in connection with the protection of copyright in literary and artistic works. However, compulsory licences may be provided for only to the extent to which they are compatible with this Convention.

<h3 style="text-align:center">Article 16</h3>
<h3 style="text-align:center">Reservations</h3>

1. Any State, upon becoming party to this Convention, shall be bound by all the obligations and shall enjoy all the benefits thereof. However, a State may at any time, in a notification deposited with the Secretary–General of the United Nations, declare that:

(a) as regards Article 12:

(i) it will not apply the provisions of that Article;

(ii) it will not apply the provisions of that Article in respect of certain uses;

(iii) as regards phonograms the producer of which is not a national of another Contracting State, it will not apply that Article;

(iv) as regards phonograms the producer of which is a national of another Contracting State, it will limit the protection provided for by that Article to the extent to which, and to the term for which, the latter State grants protection to phonograms first fixed by a national of the State making the declaration; however, the fact that the Contracting State of which the producer is a national does not grant the protection to the same beneficiary or beneficiaries as the State making the declaration shall not be considered as a difference in the extent of the protection;

(b) as regards Article 13, it will not apply item (d) of that Article; if a Contracting State makes such a declaration, the other Contracting States shall not be obliged to grant the right referred to in Article 13, item (d), to broadcasting organisations whose headquarters are in that State.

2. If the notification referred to in paragraph 1 of this Article is made after the date of the deposit of the instrument of ratification, acceptance or accession, the declaration will become effective six months after it has been deposited.

WIPO Copyright Treaty

Articles 1–14

Preamble

The Contracting Parties,

Desiring to develop and maintain the protection of the rights of authors in their literary and artistic works in a manner as effective and uniform as possible,

Recognizing the need to introduce new international rules and clarify the interpretation of certain existing rules in order to provide adequate solutions to the questions raised by new economic, social, cultural and technological developments,

Recognizing the profound impact of the development and convergence of information and communication technologies on the creation and use of literary and artistic works,

Emphasizing the outstanding significance of copyright protection as an incentive for literary and artistic creation,

Recognizing the need to maintain a balance between the rights of authors and the larger public interest, particularly education, research and access to information, as reflected in the Berne Convention,

Have agreed as follows:

Article 1
Relation to the Berne Convention

(1) This Treaty is a special agreement within the meaning of Article 20 of the Berne Convention for the Protection of Literary and Artistic Works, as regards Contracting Parties that are countries of the Union established by that Convention. This Treaty shall not have any connection with treaties other than the Berne Convention, nor shall it prejudice any rights and obligations under any other treaties.

(2) Nothing in this Treaty shall derogate from existing obligations that Contracting Parties have to each other under the Berne Convention for the Protection of Literary and Artistic Works.

(3) Hereinafter, "Berne Convention" shall refer to the Paris Act of July 24,

1971 of the Berne Convention for the Protection of Literary and Artistic Works.

(4) Contracting Parties shall comply with Articles 1 to 21 and the Appendix of the Berne Convention.

Article 2
Scope of Copyright Protection

Copyright protection extends to expressions and not to ideas, procedures, methods of operation or mathematical concepts as such.

Article 3
Application of Articles
2 to 6 of the Berne Convention

Contracting Parties shall apply mutatis mutandis the provisions of Articles 2 to 6 of the Berne Convention in respect of the protection provided for in this Treaty.

Article 4
Computer Programs

Computer programs are protected as literary works within the meaning of Article 2 of the Berne Convention. Such protection applies to computer programs, whatever may be the mode or form of their expression.

Article 5
Compilations of Data (Databases)

Compilations of data or other material, in any form, which by reason of the selection or arrangement of their contents constitute intellectual creations, are protected as such. This protection does not extend to the data or the material itself and is without prejudice to any copyright subsisting in the data or material contained in the compilation.

Article 6
Right of Distribution

(1) Authors of literary and artistic works shall enjoy the exclusive right of authorizing the making available to the public of the original and copies of their works through sale or other transfer of ownership.

(2) Nothing in this Treaty shall affect the freedom of Contracting Parties to determine the conditions, if any, under which the exhaustion of the right in paragraph (1) applies after the first sale or other transfer of ownership of the original or a copy of the work with the authorization of the author.

Article 7

Right of Rental

(1) Authors of

(i) computer programs;

(ii) cinematographic works; and

(iii) works embodied in phonograms, as determined in the national law of Contracting Parties,

shall enjoy the exclusive right of authorizing commercial rental to the public of the originals or copies of their works.

(2) Paragraph (1) shall not apply

(i) in the case of computer programs, where the program itself is not the essential object of the rental; and

(ii) in the case of cinematographic works, unless such commercial rental has led to widespread copying of such works materially impairing the exclusive right of reproduction.

(3) Notwithstanding the provisions of paragraph (1), a Contracting Party that, on April 15, 1994, had and continues to have in force a system of equitable remuneration of authors for the rental of copies of their works embodied in phonograms may maintain that system provided that the commercial rental of works embodied in phonograms is not giving rise to the material impairment of the exclusive right of reproduction of authors.

Article 8

Right of Communication to the Public

Without prejudice to the provisions of Articles 11(1)(ii), 11bis(1)(i) and (ii), 11ter(1)(ii), 14(1)(ii) and 14bis(1) of the Berne Convention, authors of literary and artistic works shall enjoy the exclusive right of authorizing any communication to the public of their works, by wire or wireless means, including the making available to the public of their works in such a way that members of the public may access these works from a place and at a time individually chosen by them.

Article 9

Duration of the Protection of Photographic Works

In respect of photographic works, the Contracting Parties shall not apply the provisions of Article 7(4) of the Berne Convention.

Article 10

Limitations and Exceptions

(1) Contracting Parties may, in their national legislation, provide for limitations of or exceptions to the rights granted to authors of literary and artistic works under this Treaty in certain special cases that do not conflict with

a normal exploitation of the work and do not unreasonably prejudice the legitimate interests of the author.

(2) Contracting Parties shall, when applying the Berne Convention, confine any limitations of or exceptions to rights provided for therein to certain special cases that do not conflict with a normal exploitation of the work and do not unreasonably prejudice the legitimate interests of the author.

Article 11
Obligations concerning Technological Measures

Contracting Parties shall provide adequate legal protection and effective legal remedies against the circumvention of effective technological measures that are used by authors in connection with the exercise of their rights under this Treaty or the Berne Convention and that restrict acts, in respect of their works, which are not authorized by the authors concerned or permitted by law.

Article 12
Obligations concerning Rights Management Information

(1) Contracting Parties shall provide adequate and effective legal remedies against any person knowingly performing any of the following acts knowing, or with respect to civil remedies having reasonable grounds to know, that it will induce, enable, facilitate or conceal an infringement of any right covered by this Treaty or the Berne Convention:

(i) to remove or alter any electronic rights management information without authority;

(ii) to distribute, import for distribution, broadcast or communicate to the public, without authority, works or copies of works knowing that electronic rights management information has been removed or altered without authority.

(2) As used in this Article, "rights management information" means information which identifies the work, the author of the work, the owner of any right in the work, or information about the terms and conditions of use of the work, and any numbers or codes that represent such information, when any of these items of information is attached to a copy of a work or appears in connection with the communication of a work to the public.

Article 13
Application in Time

Contracting Parties shall apply the provisions of Article 18 of the Berne Convention to all protection provided for in this Treaty.

Article 14
Provisions on Enforcement of Rights

(1) Contracting Parties undertake to adopt, in accordance with their legal systems, the measures necessary to ensure the application of this Treaty.

(2) Contracting Parties shall ensure that enforcement procedures are available under their law so as to permit effective action against any act of infringement of rights covered by this Treaty, including expeditious remedies to prevent infringements and remedies which constitute a deterrent to further infringements.

WIPO Performances and Phonograms Treaty

Preamble

The Contracting Parties,

Desiring to develop and maintain the protection of the rights of performers and producers of phonograms in a manner as effective and uniform as possible,

Recognizing the need to introduce new international rules in order to provide adequate solutions to the questions raised by economic, social, cultural and technological developments,

Recognizing the profound impact of the development and convergence of information and communication technologies on the production and use of performances and phonograms,

Recognizing the need to maintain a balance between the rights of performers and producers of phonograms and the larger public interest, particularly education, research and access to information,

Have agreed as follows:

CHAPTER I
General Provisions

Article 1
Relation to Other Conventions

(1) Nothing in this Treaty shall derogate from existing obligations that Contracting Parties have to each other under the International Convention for the Protection of Performers, Producers of Phonograms and Broadcasting Organizations done in Rome, October 26, 1961 (hereinafter the "Rome Convention").

(2) Protection granted under this Treaty shall leave intact and shall in no way affect the protection of copyright in literary and artistic works. Consequently, no provision of this Treaty may be interpreted as prejudicing such protection.

(3) This Treaty shall not have any connection with, nor shall it prejudice any rights and obligations under, any other treaties.

Article 2
Definitions

For the purposes of this Treaty:

(a) "performers" are actors, singers, musicians, dancers, and other persons who act, sing, deliver, declaim, play in, interpret, or otherwise perform literary or artistic works or expressions of folklore;

(b) "phonogram" means the fixation of the sounds of a performance or of other sounds, or of a representation of sounds, other than in the form of a fixation incorporated in a cinematographic or other audiovisual work;

(c) "fixation" means the embodiment of sounds, or of the representations thereof, from which they can be perceived, reproduced or communicated through a device;

(d) "producer of a phonogram" means the person, or the legal entity, who or which takes the initiative and has the responsibility for the first fixation of the sounds of a performance or other sounds, or the representations of sounds;

(e) "publication" of a fixed performance or a phonogram means the offering of copies of the fixed performance or the phonogram to the public, with the consent of the rightholder, and provided that copies are offered to the public in reasonable quantity;

(f) "broadcasting" means the transmission by wireless means for public reception of sounds or of images and sounds or of the representations thereof; such transmission by satellite is also "broadcasting"; transmission of encrypted signals is "broadcasting" where the means for decrypting are provided to the public by the broadcasting organization or with its consent;

(g) "communication to the public" of a performance or a phonogram means the transmission to the public by any medium, otherwise than by broadcasting, of sounds of a performance or the sounds or the representations of sounds fixed in a phonogram. For the purposes of Article 15, "communication to the public" includes making the sounds or representations of sounds fixed in a phonogram audible to the public.

Article 3
Beneficiaries of Protection under this Treaty

(1) Contracting Parties shall accord the protection provided under this Treaty to the performers and producers of phonograms who are nationals of other Contracting Parties.

(2) The nationals of other Contracting Parties shall be understood to be those performers or producers of phonograms who would meet the criteria for eligibility for protection provided under the Rome Convention, were all the Contracting Parties to this Treaty Contracting States of that Convention.

In respect of these criteria of eligibility, Contracting Parties shall apply the relevant definitions in Article 2 of this Treaty.

(3) Any Contracting Party availing itself of the possibilities provided in Article 5(3) of the Rome Convention or, for the purposes of Article 5 of the same Convention, Article 17 thereof shall make a notification as foreseen in those provisions to the Director General of the World Intellectual Property Organization (WIPO).

Article 4
National Treatment

(1) Each Contracting Party shall accord to nationals of other Contracting Parties, as defined in Article 3(2), the treatment it accords to its own nationals with regard to the exclusive rights specifically granted in this Treaty, and to the right to equitable remuneration provided for in Article 15 of this Treaty.

(2) The obligation provided for in paragraph (1) does not apply to the extent that another Contracting Party makes use of the reservations permitted by Article 15(3) of this Treaty.

CHAPTER II
Rights of Performers

Article 5
Moral Rights of Performers

(1) Independently of a performer's economic rights, and even after the transfer of those rights, the performer shall, as regards his live aural performances or performances fixed in phonograms, have the right to claim to be identified as the performer of his performances, except where omission is dictated by the manner of the use of the performance, and to object to any distortion, mutilation or other modification of his performances that would be prejudicial to his reputation.

(2) The rights granted to a performer in accordance with paragraph (1) shall, after his death, be maintained, at least until the expiry of the economic rights, and shall be exercisable by the persons or institutions authorized by the legislation of the Contracting Party where protection is claimed. However, those Contracting Parties whose legislation, at the moment of their ratification of or accession to this Treaty, does not provide for protection after the death of the performer of all rights set out in the preceding paragraph may provide that some of these rights will, after his death, cease to be maintained.

(3) The means of redress for safeguarding the rights granted under this Article shall be governed by the legislation of the Contracting Party where protection is claimed.

Article 6
Economic Rights of Performers in their Unfixed Performances

Performers shall enjoy the exclusive right of authorizing, as regards their performances:

(i) the broadcasting and communication to the public of their unfixed performances except where the performance is already a broadcast performance; and

(ii) the fixation of their unfixed performances.

Article 7
Right of Reproduction

Performers shall enjoy the exclusive right of authorizing the direct or indirect reproduction of their performances fixed in phonograms, in any manner or form.

Article 8
Right of Distribution

(1) Performers shall enjoy the exclusive right of authorizing the making available to the public of the original and copies of their performances fixed in phonograms through sale or other transfer of ownership.

(2) Nothing in this Treaty shall affect the freedom of Contracting Parties to determine the conditions, if any, under which the exhaustion of the right in paragraph (1) applies after the first sale or other transfer of ownership of the original or a copy of the fixed performance with the authorization of the performer.

Article 9
Right of Rental

(1) Performers shall enjoy the exclusive right of authorizing the commercial rental to the public of the original and copies of their performances fixed in phonograms as determined in the national law of Contracting Parties, even after distribution of them by, or pursuant to, authorization by the performer.

(2) Notwithstanding the provisions of paragraph (1), a Contracting Party that, on April 15, 1994, had and continues to have in force a system of equitable remuneration of performers for the rental of copies of their performances fixed in phonograms, may maintain that system provided that the commercial rental of phonograms is not giving rise to the material impairment of the exclusive right of reproduction of performers.

Article 10
Right of Making Available of Fixed Performances

Performers shall enjoy the exclusive right of authorizing the making available to the public of their performances fixed in phonograms, by wire or wireless means, in such a way that members of the public may access them from a place and at a time individually chosen by them.

CHAPTER III
Rights of Producers of Phonograms

Article 11
Right of Reproduction

Producers of phonograms shall enjoy the exclusive right of authorizing the direct or indirect reproduction of their phonograms, in any manner or form.

Article 12
Right of Distribution

(1) Producers of phonograms shall enjoy the exclusive right of authorizing the making available to the public of the original and copies of their phonograms through sale or other transfer of ownership.
(2) Nothing in this Treaty shall affect the freedom of Contracting Parties to determine the conditions, if any, under which the exhaustion of the right in paragraph (1) applies after the first sale or other transfer of ownership of the original or a copy of the phonogram with the authorization of the producer of the phonogram.

Article 13
Right of Rental

(1) Producers of phonograms shall enjoy the exclusive right of authorizing the commercial rental to the public of the original and copies of their phonograms, even after distribution of them, by or pursuant to, authorization by the producer.
(2) Notwithstanding the provisions of paragraph (1), a Contracting Party that, on April 15, 1994, had and continues to have in force a system of equitable remuneration of producers of phonograms for the rental of copies of their phonograms, may maintain that system provided that the commercial rental of phonograms is not giving rise to the material impairment of the exclusive rights of reproduction of producers of phonograms.

Article 14
Right of Making Available of Phonograms

Producers of phonograms shall enjoy the exclusive right of authorizing the making available to the public of their phonograms, by wire or wireless means, in such a way that members of the public may access them from a place and at a time individually chosen by them.

CHAPTER IV
Common Provisions

Article 15
Right to Remuneration for Broadcasting and Communication to the Public

(1) Performers and producers of phonograms shall enjoy the right to a single equitable remuneration for the direct or indirect use of phonograms published for commercial purposes for broadcasting or for any communication to the public.

(2) Contracting Parties may establish in their national legislation that the single equitable remuneration shall be claimed from the user by the performer or by the producer of a phonogram or by both. Contracting Parties may enact national legislation that, in the absence of an agreement between the performer and the producer of a phonogram, sets the terms according to which performers and producers of phonograms shall share the single equitable remuneration.

(3) Any Contracting Party may, in a notification deposited with the Director General of WIPO, declare that it will apply the provisions of paragraph (1) only in respect of certain uses, or that it will limit their application in some other way, or that it will not apply these provisions at all.

(4) For the purposes of this Article, phonograms made available to the public by wire or wireless means in such a way that members of the public may access them from a place and at a time individually chosen by them shall be considered as if they had been published for commercial purposes.

Article 16
Limitations and Exceptions

(1) Contracting Parties may, in their national legislation, provide for the same kinds of limitations or exceptions with regard to the protection of performers and producers of phonograms as they provide for, in their national legislation, in connection with the protection of copyright in literary and artistic works.

(2) Contracting Parties shall confine any limitations of or exceptions to rights provided for in this Treaty to certain special cases which do not conflict with a normal exploitation of the performance or phonogram and do not unreasonably prejudice the legitimate interests of the performer or of the producer of the phonogram.

Article 17
Term of Protection

(1) The term of protection to be granted to performers under this Treaty shall last, at least, until the end of a period of 50 years computed from the end of the year in which the performance was fixed in a phonogram.

(2) The term of protection to be granted to producers of phonograms under this Treaty shall last, at least, until the end of a period of 50 years computed from the end of the year in which the phonogram was published, or failing such publication within 50 years from fixation of the phonogram, 50 years from the end of the year in which the fixation was made.

Article 18
Obligations concerning Technological Measures

Contracting Parties shall provide adequate legal protection and effective legal remedies against the circumvention of effective technological measures that are used by performers or producers of phonograms in connection with the exercise of their rights under this Treaty and that restrict acts, in respect of their performances or phonograms, which are not authorized by the performers or the producers of phonograms concerned or permitted by law.

Article 19
Obligations concerning Rights Management Information

(1) Contracting Parties shall provide adequate and effective legal remedies against any person knowingly performing any of the following acts knowing, or with respect to civil remedies having reasonable grounds to know, that it will induce, enable, facilitate or conceal an infringement of any right covered by this Treaty:

(i) to remove or alter any electronic rights management information without authority;

(ii) to distribute, import for distribution, broadcast, communicate or make available to the public, without authority, performances, copies of fixed performances or phonograms knowing that electronic rights management information has been removed or altered without authority.

(2) As used in this Article, "rights management information" means information which identifies the performer, the performance of the performer, the producer of the phonogram, the phonogram, the owner of any right in the performance or phonogram, or information about the terms and conditions of use of the performance or phonogram, and any numbers or codes that represent such information, when any of these items of information is attached to a copy of a fixed performance or a phonogram or appears in connection with the communication or making available of a fixed performance or a phonogram to the public.

Article 20
Formalities

The enjoyment and exercise of the rights provided for in this Treaty shall not be subject to any formality.

Article 21
Reservations

Subject to the provisions of Article 15(3), no reservations to this Treaty shall be permitted.

Article 22
Application in Time

(1) Contracting Parties shall apply the provisions of Article 18 of the Berne Convention, mutatis mutandis, to the rights of performers and producers of phonograms provided for in this Treaty.

(2) Notwithstanding paragraph (1), a Contracting Party may limit the application of Article 5 of this Treaty to performances which occurred after the entry into force of this Treaty for that Party.

Article 23
Provisions on Enforcement of Rights

(1) Contracting Parties undertake to adopt, in accordance with their legal systems, the measures necessary to ensure the application of this Treaty.

(2) Contracting Parties shall ensure that enforcement procedures are available under their law so as to permit effective action against any act of infringement of rights covered by this Treaty, including expeditious remedies to prevent infringements and remedies which constitute a deterrent to further infringements.

Agreement on Trade-Related aspects of Intellectual Property (TRIPS)

Articles 1–14, 41–45

Preamble

Members,

Desiring to reduce distortions and impediments to international trade, and taking into account the need to promote effective and adequate protection of intellectual property rights, and to ensure that measures and procedures to enforce intellectual property rights do not themselves become barriers to legitimate trade;

Recognizing, to this end, the need for new rules and disciplines concerning:

(a) the applicability of the basic principles of GATT 1994 and of relevant international intellectual property agreements or conventions;

(b) the provision of adequate standards and principles concerning the availability, scope and use of trade-related intellectual property rights;

(c) the provision of effective and appropriate means for the enforcement of trade-related intellectual property rights, taking into account differences in national legal systems;

(d) the provision of effective and expeditious procedures for the multilateral prevention and settlement of disputes between governments; and

(e) transitional arrangements aiming at the fullest participation in the results of the negotiations;

Recognizing the need for a multilateral framework of principles, rules and disciplines dealing with international trade in counterfeit goods;

Recognizing that intellectual property rights are private rights;

Recognizing the underlying public policy objectives of national systems for the protection of intellectual property, including developmental and technological objectives;

Recognizing also the special needs of the least-developed country Members in respect of maximum flexibility in the domestic implementation of laws and regulations in order to enable them to create a sound and viable technological base;

Emphasizing the importance of reducing tensions by reaching strengthened commitments to resolve disputes on trade-related intellectual property issues through multilateral procedures;

Desiring to establish a mutually supportive relationship between the WTO and the World Intellectual Property Organization (referred to in this Agreement as "WIPO") as well as other relevant international organizations;

Hereby agree as follows:

PART I
GENERAL PROVISIONS AND BASIC PRINCIPLES

Article 1
Nature and Scope of Obligations

1. Members shall give effect to the provisions of this Agreement. Members may, but shall not be obliged to, implement in their law more extensive protection than is required by this Agreement, provided that such protection does not contravene the provisions of this Agreement. Members shall be free to determine the appropriate method of implementing the provisions of this Agreement within their own legal system and practice.

2. For the purposes of this Agreement, the term "intellectual property" refers to all categories of intellectual property that are the subject of Sections 1 through 7 of Part II.

3. Members shall accord the treatment provided for in this Agreement to the nationals of other Members.[1] In respect of the relevant intellectual property right, the nationals of other Members shall be understood as those natural or legal persons that would meet the criteria for eligibility for protection provided for in the Paris Convention (1967), the Berne Convention (1971), the Rome Convention and the Treaty on Intellectual Property in Respect of Integrated Circuits, were all Members of the WTO members of those conventions.[2] Any Member availing itself of the possibilities provided in paragraph 3 of Article 5 or paragraph 2 of Article 6 of the Rome Convention shall

---

1 When "nationals" are referred to in this Agreement, they shall be deemed, in the case of a separate customs territory Member of the WTO, to mean persons, natural or legal, who are domiciled or who have a real and effective industrial or commercial establishment in that customs territory.

2 In this Agreement, "Paris Convention" refers to the Paris Convention for the Protection of Industrial Property; "Paris Convention (1967)" refers to the Stockholm Act of this Convention of 14 July 1967. "Berne Convention" refers to the Berne Convention for the Protection of Literary and Artistic Works; "Berne Convention (1971)" refers to the Paris Act of this Convention of 24 July 1971. "Rome Convention" refers to the International Convention for the Protection of Performers, Producers of Phonograms and Broadcasting Organizations, adopted at Rome on 26 October 1961. "Treaty on Intellectual Property in Respect of Integrated Circuits" (IPIC Treaty) refers to the Treaty on Intellectual Property in Respect of Integrated Circuits, adopted at Washington on 26 May 1989. "WTO Agreement" refers to the Agreement Establishing the WTO.

make a notification as foreseen in those provisions to the Council for Trade-Related Aspects of Intellectual Property Rights (the "Council for TRIPS").

Article 2
Intellectual Property Conventions

1. In respect of Parts II, III and IV of this Agreement, Members shall comply with Articles 1 through 12, and Article 19, of the Paris Convention (1967).
2. Nothing in Parts I to IV of this Agreement shall derogate from existing obligations that Members may have to each other under the Paris Convention, the Berne Convention, the Rome Convention and the Treaty on Intellectual Property in Respect of Integrated Circuits.

Article 3
National Treatment

1. Each Member shall accord to the nationals of other Members treatment no less favourable than that it accords to its own nationals with regard to the protection[3] of intellectual property, subject to the exceptions already provided in, respectively, the Paris Convention (1967), the Berne Convention (1971), the Rome Convention or the Treaty on Intellectual Property in Respect of Integrated Circuits. In respect of performers, producers of phonograms and broadcasting organizations, this obligation only applies in respect of the rights provided under this Agreement. Any Member availing itself of the possibilities provided in Article 6 of the Berne Convention (1971) or paragraph 1(b) of Article 16 of the Rome Convention shall make a notification as foreseen in those provisions to the Council for TRIPS.
2. Members may avail themselves of the exceptions permitted under paragraph 1 in relation to judicial and administrative procedures, including the designation of an address for service or the appointment of an agent within the jurisdiction of a Member, only where such exceptions are necessary to secure compliance with laws and regulations which are not inconsistent with the provisions of this Agreement and where such practices are not applied in a manner which would constitute a disguised restriction on trade.

Article 4
Most-Favoured-Nation Treatment

With regard to the protection of intellectual property, any advantage, favour, privilege or immunity granted by a Member to the nationals of any other

---

3 For the purposes of Articles 3 and 4, "protection" shall include matters affecting the availability, acquisition, scope, maintenance and enforcement of intellectual property rights as well as those matters affecting the use of intellectual property rights specifically addressed in this Agreement.

country shall be accorded immediately and unconditionally to the nationals of all other Members. Exempted from this obligation are any advantage, favour, privilege or immunity accorded by a Member:

(a) deriving from international agreements on judicial assistance or law enforcement of a general nature and not particularly confined to the protection of intellectual property;

(b) granted in accordance with the provisions of the Berne Convention (1971) or the Rome Convention authorizing that the treatment accorded be a function not of national treatment but of the treatment accorded in another country;

(c) in respect of the rights of performers, producers of phonograms and broadcasting organizations not provided under this Agreement;

(d) deriving from international agreements related to the protection of intellectual property which entered into force prior to the entry into force of the WTO Agreement, provided that such agreements are notified to the Council for TRIPS and do not constitute an arbitrary or unjustifiable discrimination against nationals of other Members.

Article 5
Multilateral Agreements on Acquisition or Maintenance of Protection

The obligations under Articles 3 and 4 do not apply to procedures provided in multilateral agreements concluded under the auspices of WIPO relating to the acquisition or maintenance of intellectual property rights.

Article 6
Exhaustion

For the purposes of dispute settlement under this Agreement, subject to the provisions of Articles 3 and 4 nothing in this Agreement shall be used to address the issue of the exhaustion of intellectual property rights.

Article 7
Objectives

The protection and enforcement of intellectual property rights should contribute to the promotion of technological innovation and to the transfer and dissemination of technology, to the mutual advantage of producers and users of technological knowledge and in a manner conducive to social and economic welfare, and to a balance of rights and obligations.

Article 8
Principles

1. Members may, in formulating or amending their laws and regulations, adopt measures necessary to protect public health and nutrition, and to

promote the public interest in sectors of vital importance to their socio-economic and technological development, provided that such measures are consistent with the provisions of this Agreement.

2. Appropriate measures, provided that they are consistent with the provisions of this Agreement, may be needed to prevent the abuse of intellectual property rights by right holders or the resort to practices which unreasonably restrain trade or adversely affect the international transfer of technology.

PART II
STANDARDS CONCERNING THE AVAILABILITY, SCOPE AND USE OF INTELLECTUAL PROPERTY RIGHTS
SECTION 1: COPYRIGHT AND RELATED RIGHTS

Article 9
Relation to the Berne Convention

1. Members shall comply with Articles 1 through 21 of the Berne Convention (1971) and the Appendix thereto. However, Members shall not have rights or obligations under this Agreement in respect of the rights conferred under Article 6*bis* of that Convention or of the rights derived therefrom.

2. Copyright protection shall extend to expressions and not to ideas, procedures, methods of operation or mathematical concepts as such.

Article 10
Computer Programs and Compilations of Data

1. Computer programs, whether in source or object code, shall be protected as literary works under the Berne Convention (1971).

2. Compilations of data or other material, whether in machine readable or other form, which by reason of the selection or arrangement of their contents constitute intellectual creations shall be protected as such. Such protection, which shall not extend to the data or material itself, shall be without prejudice to any copyright subsisting in the data or material itself.

Article 11
Rental Rights

In respect of at least computer programs and cinematographic works, a Member shall provide authors and their successors in title the right to authorize or to prohibit the commercial rental to the public of originals or copies of their copyright works. A Member shall be excepted from this obligation in respect of cinematographic works unless such rental has led to widespread copying of such works which is materially impairing the exclusive right of reproduction conferred in that Member on authors and their successors in title. In respect of computer programs, this obligation does not apply to rentals where the program itself is not the essential object of the rental.

Article 12
Term of Protection

Whenever the term of protection of a work, other than a photographic work or a work of applied art, is calculated on a basis other than the life of a natural person, such term shall be no less than 50 years from the end of the calendar year of authorized publication, or, failing such authorized publication within 50 years from the making of the work, 50 years from the end of the calendar year of making.

Article 13
Limitations and Exceptions

Members shall confine limitations or exceptions to exclusive rights to certain special cases which do not conflict with a normal exploitation of the work and do not unreasonably prejudice the legitimate interests of the right holder.

Article 14
Protection of Performers, Producers of Phonograms (Sound Recordings) and Broadcasting Organizations

1. In respect of a fixation of their performance on a phonogram, performers shall have the possibility of preventing the following acts when undertaken without their authorization: the fixation of their unfixed performance and the reproduction of such fixation. Performers shall also have the possibility of preventing the following acts when undertaken without their authorization: the broadcasting by wireless means and the communication to the public of their live performance.

2. Producers of phonograms shall enjoy the right to authorize or prohibit the direct or indirect reproduction of their phonograms.

3. Broadcasting organizations shall have the right to prohibit the following acts when undertaken without their authorization: the fixation, the reproduction of fixations, and the rebroadcasting by wireless means of broadcasts, as well as the communication to the public of television broadcasts of the same. Where Members do not grant such rights to broadcasting organizations, they shall provide owners of copyright in the subject matter of broadcasts with the possibility of preventing the above acts, subject to the provisions of the Berne Convention (1971).

4. The provisions of Article 11 in respect of computer programs shall apply *mutatis mutandis* to producers of phonograms and any other right holders in phonograms as determined in a Member's law. If on 15 April 1994 a

Member has in force a system of equitable remuneration of right holders in respect of the rental of phonograms, it may maintain such system provided that the commercial rental of phonograms is not giving rise to the material impairment of the exclusive rights of reproduction of right holders.

5. The term of the protection available under this Agreement to performers and producers of phonograms shall last at least until the end of a period of 50 years computed from the end of the calendar year in which the fixation was made or the performance took place. The term of protection granted pursuant to paragraph 3 shall last for at least 20 years from the end of the calendar year in which the broadcast took place.

6. Any Member may, in relation to the rights conferred under paragraphs 1, 2 and 3, provide for conditions, limitations, exceptions and reservations to the extent permitted by the Rome Convention. However, the provisions of Article 18 of the Berne Convention (1971) shall also apply, *mutatis mutandis*, to the rights of performers and producers of phonograms in phonograms.

PART III
ENFORCEMENT OF INTELLECTUAL PROPERTY RIGHTS
SECTION 1: GENERAL OBLIGATIONS

Article 41

1. Members shall ensure that enforcement procedures as specified in this Part are available under their law so as to permit effective action against any act of infringement of intellectual property rights covered by this Agreement, including expeditious remedies to prevent infringements and remedies which constitute a deterrent to further infringements. These procedures shall be applied in such a manner as to avoid the creation of barriers to legitimate trade and to provide for safeguards against their abuse.

2. Procedures concerning the enforcement of intellectual property rights shall be fair and equitable. They shall not be unnecessarily complicated or costly, or entail unreasonable time-limits or unwarranted delays.

3. Decisions on the merits of a case shall preferably be in writing and reasoned. They shall be made available at least to the parties to the proceeding without undue delay. Decisions on the merits of a case shall be based only on evidence in respect of which parties were offered the opportunity to be heard.

4. Parties to a proceeding shall have an opportunity for review by a judicial authority of final administrative decisions and, subject to jurisdictional provisions in a Member's law concerning the importance of a case, of at least the legal aspects of initial judicial decisions on the merits of a case. However, there shall be no obligation to provide an opportunity for review of acquittals in criminal cases.

5. It is understood that this Part does not create any obligation to put in place a judicial system for the enforcement of intellectual property rights distinct from that for the enforcement of law in general, nor does it affect the capacity of Members to enforce their law in general. Nothing in this Part creates any obligation with respect to the distribution of resources as between enforcement of intellectual property rights and the enforcement of law in general.

SECTION 2: CIVIL AND ADMINISTRATIVE PROCEDURES AND REMEDIES

Article 42
Fair and Equitable Procedures

Members shall make available to right holders[72] civil judicial procedures concerning the enforcement of any intellectual property right covered by this Agreement. Defendants shall have the right to written notice which is timely and contains sufficient detail, including the basis of the claims. Parties shall be allowed to be represented by independent legal counsel, and procedures shall not impose overly burdensome requirements concerning mandatory personal appearances. All parties to such procedures shall be duly entitled to substantiate their claims and to present all relevant evidence. The procedure shall provide a means to identify and protect confidential information, unless this would be contrary to existing constitutional requirements.

Article 43
Evidence

1. The judicial authorities shall have the authority, where a party has presented reasonably available evidence sufficient to support its claims and has specified evidence relevant to substantiation of its claims which lies in the control of the opposing party, to order that this evidence be produced by the opposing party, subject in appropriate cases to conditions which ensure the protection of confidential information.

2. In cases in which a party to a proceeding voluntarily and without good reason refuses access to, or otherwise does not provide necessary information within a reasonable period, or significantly impedes a procedure relating to an enforcement action, a Member may accord judicial authorities the authority to make preliminary and final determinations, affirmative or negative, on the basis of the information presented to them, including the com-

---

72 For the purpose of this Part, the term "right holder" includes federations and associations having legal standing to assert such rights.

plaint or the allegation presented by the party adversely affected by the denial of access to information, subject to providing the parties an opportunity to be heard on the allegations or evidence.

Article 44
Injunctions

1. The judicial authorities shall have the authority to order a party to desist from an infringement, *inter alia* to prevent the entry into the channels of commerce in their jurisdiction of imported goods that involve the infringement of an intellectual property right, immediately after customs clearance of such goods. Members are not obliged to accord such authority in respect of protected subject matter acquired or ordered by a person prior to knowing or having reasonable grounds to know that dealing in such subject matter would entail the infringement of an intellectual property right.

2. Notwithstanding the other provisions of this Part and provided that the provisions of Part II specifically addressing use by governments, or by third parties authorized by a government, without the authorization of the right holder are complied with, Members may limit the remedies available against such use to payment of remuneration in accordance with subparagraph (h) of Article 31. In other cases, the remedies under this Part shall apply or, where these remedies are inconsistent with a Member's law, declaratory judgments and adequate compensation shall be available.

Article 45
Damages

1. The judicial authorities shall have the authority to order the infringer to pay the right holder damages adequate to compensate for the injury the right holder has suffered because of an infringement of that person's intellectual property right by an infringer who knowingly, or with reasonable grounds to know, engaged in infringing activity.

2. The judicial authorities shall also have the authority to order the infringer to pay the right holder expenses, which may include appropriate attorney's fees. In appropriate cases, Members may authorize the judicial authorities to order recovery of profits and/or payment of pre-established damages even where the infringer did not knowingly, or with reasonable grounds to know, engage in infringing activity.

Index